The Complete Private Pilot

Eleventh Edition
Bob Gardner

Aviation Supplies & Academics, Inc.
Newcastle, Washington

The Complete Private Pilot, Eleventh Edition
by Bob Gardner

Aviation Supplies & Academics, Inc.
7005 132nd Place SE
Newcastle, Washington 98059-3153

Visit the ASA website often, as any updates due to FAA
regulatory and procedural changes will be posted there:
www.asa2fly.com

Printed in the United States of America

2016 2015 2014 2013   9 8 7 6 5 4 3 2

ASA-PPT-11
ISBN 1-56027-781-5
     978-1-56027-781-1

Original illustration: Dick Bringloe and Don Szymanski
Photo credits: cover photos, front and back are © Cirrus
Aircraft, used by permission; p.vi, Jim Fagiolo; p.1-7,
courtesy NASA; p.1-8, Robert Gardner; p.1-14, courtesy
General Aviation News & Flyer; p.1-15, Robert Gardner;
p.1-23, NASA; pp.2-14 and 3-1, Robert Gardner; p.3-4,
courtesy Safe Flight; pp.3-5 and 3-10, Sigma-Tek Aircraft
Instruments; p.3-8, courtesy American Avionics; p.5-7, Robert
Gardner; p.5-10, NASA; p.7-23, courtesy 3-M StormScope
Weather Mapping System; p.9-9, Robert Gardner; p.10-2,
Henry Geijsbeek; pp.10-9 and 10-12, courtesy NARCO;
p.11-2, courtesy Garmin; p.11-8, NARCO; pp.11-23,
11-24, and 11-26, courtesy Washington State Aeronautics
Commission; pp.D-1 and D-2, courtesy Garmin and Avidyne;
p.D-2 courtesy Chelton Flight Systems.

Library of Congress Cataloging-in-Publication data:

Gardner, Robert E.
    The complete private pilot / Robert E. Gardner.
        p.   cm.
    Includes index.
    1. Private flying. I. Title
TL 721.4.G34 1994   94-5805
629.132'5217 — dc20   CIP

03

Contents

Continued

Foreword

A new aviation book—one that plows new ground, one that develops material never before considered—is pretty hard to come by. And until there are some radical changes in the types of aircraft we fly and the techniques necessary to fly them, the situation is quite likely to stay that way.

But there are always better, if not "new," ways to communicate aviation information...that's what Bob Gardner has accomplished with *The Complete Private Pilot*.

A writer embarking on the task of creating a fundamental aviation text is faced with a formidable challenge; if prospective pilots are to reap the benefits of his work, the writing must be at once very readable and very comprehensive.

The Complete Private Pilot does both of those in spades, as Bob Gardner reaches into his own aeronautical experience and brings to the reader a clear exposition of the knowledge required by the budding private pilot.

It's not all here—you'll continue learning (we hope!) long after your initial study of regulations, weather, navigation, and so on—but this book is a great way to get started.

Your author has met the challenge well. *The Complete Private Pilot* is indeed readable, comprehensive, and perhaps more important than those, it's a book which will lead you to a greater understanding of flying's fundamentals.

I've always contended that a smart pilot is a safe pilot...you are to be commended for your choice of *The Complete Private Pilot* as a bedrock book in your aviation library.

Richard Taylor

About the Author

Robert Gardner has long been an admired member of the aviation community. He began his flying career in Alaska in 1960 while in the U.S. Coast Guard. By 1966, Bob accomplished his Private land and sea, Commercial, instrument, Instructor, CFII and MEL. Over the next 16 years he was an instructor, charter pilot, designated examiner, freight dog and Director of ASA Ground Schools.

Currently, Bob holds an Airline Transport Pilot Certificate with single- and multi-engine land ratings; a CFI certificate with instrument and multi-engine ratings, and a Ground Instructor's Certificate with advanced and instrument ratings. In addition, Bob is a Gold Seal Flight Instructor and has been instructing since 1968; he has been recognized as a Flight Instructor of the Year in Washington State. To top off this impressive list of accomplishments, Bob is also a well-known author, journalist and airshow lecturer.

Books by Bob Gardner

The Complete Private Pilot

The Complete Advanced Pilot

The Complete Multi-Engine Pilot

Say Again, Please—
Guide to Radio Communications

Getting Started
Introduction to the Eleventh Edition

by Bob Gardner

So you want to be a pilot! You've come to the right place. If you haven't already done so, go to **www.beapilot.com** or **www.learntofly.com** for background and then visit your local airport for an introductory ride. Since the first edition of this book was published in 1985, computer use is widespread. Students and certificated pilots who do not own computers have access through schools, libraries, and community centers. I will use web addresses throughout this book. *Note:* When I suggest using a search box on a web page, I will put the suggested search term in quotation marks for clarity; do not use quotation marks when entering the search term.

You will want to get an up-to-date copy of Part 61 of the Federal Aviation Regulations (FARs), which fully details the regulatory requirements for obtaining a pilot certificate. Or go to **www.faa.gov** and click on "Regulations and Procedures." This website will save you a lot of money. The following is a summary of the adventure on which you are embarking:

First, there is the Part 61/Part 141 quandary. Are there flight schools of which the FAA does not approve? Are they safe? Understandable confusion. Flight schools that operate under Part 141 of the FARs are strictly regulated by the Federal Aviation Administration (FAA or Feds), their flight and ground school courses must be FAA-approved, among many, many other requirements. Students who learn better in a structured climate will choose a Part 141 school. Instructors at a Part 61 school should operate from a syllabus, just as in a Part 141 school, but they are not required to do so. Ground school is not required at a Part 61 school. If your life and work schedule do not fit into a relatively strict training regime, Part 61 is for you. Safety? The airplanes and instructors at both types of school must meet the same standards.

Then there is the sport pilot/recreational pilot/private pilot question. If you just want to experience the joy of flight, boring holes in the sky and going to pancake breakfasts at small airports, working toward the recreational pilot certificate will require less flight time (and money) but your privileges will be somewhat restricted. Some of the restrictions can be removed by an instructor's endorsement in your logbook, others cannot. Still, getting a sport or recreational pilot certificate is a good first step toward the unrestricted private pilot certificate. Rest assured, your flight instructor wants you to know as much as possible and, if your ultimate goal is the private pilot certificate, will strongly urge you to start working on it right away.

Recreational Pilot Certificate

A minimum of 30 hours of flight time is required (a minimum of 3 solo and 15 with an instructor—the balance divided between dual instruction and solo practice). During your training you will learn to take off, maneuver, and land under a variety of conditions, how to navigate by pilotage (finger-on-the-map method), and dead-reckoning using map, compass, and watch. You will learn how to communicate with ground stations when communication is optional, but will be prohibited from entering airspace where communication is required (this restriction can be lifted by your instructor by a logbook endorsement after additional training). You will not receive any training in night flight, and in fact will not be allowed to fly at night, and you will not receive any training in electronic navigation or aircraft control by reference to instruments. As a recreational pilot, cross-country flights will be limited to less than 50 nautical miles from the departure airport; this is another restriction that can be removed after you have received additional training to private pilot standards. You and your instructor will take at least one two-hour cross-country flight; no solo cross-country flights are required. Finally, your instructor will devote three hours of flight instruction to prepare you for the practical test with a designated pilot examiner (DPE).

With your recreational pilot certificate in your pocket you will be able to take one passenger at a time for a flight during daylight hours in an airplane with no more than four seats, powered by an engine of 180 horsepower or less with fixed landing gear. As stated above, without additional training you will not be able to fly more than 50 miles from the departure airport or fly into airspace where radio communication is required. But you will be carrying that passenger while your private-pilot-in-training counterpart is still accumulating cross-country hours, unable to carry passengers at all.

Private Pilot Certificate

A minimum of 40 hours of flight time is required (10 solo and a minimum of 20 with an instructor); the national average is closer to 70 hours because of the additional training required to assimilate all of the complexities that have developed since the 40 hour figure was set decades ago. You will learn to take off, maneuver, and land just as the recreational pilot does; "stick and rudder" skills are not dependent on the type of certificate you hold. You will learn electronic navigation in addition to pilotage, you will learn to communicate with air traffic controllers both enroute and at tower-controlled airports, and you will learn how a pilot sees the difference between night and day. Your instructor will also give you three hours of instruction on how to control the airplane solely by reference to the flight instruments (without reference to the outside world) in case you inadvertently fly into poor visibility conditions. *Note:* This training is to be used to escape from those conditions—it does not make you an instrument pilot.

You will log at least three hours of training to fly cross-country (which for purposes of certification is any flight with a landing at an airport more than 50 nautical miles from the departure airport), including one night flight of at least 100 nautical miles in preparation for your solo cross-country flight time. (Pilots learning to fly in Alaska, where the sun doesn't set for months at a time, have special regulatory provisions for night flight).

After your instructor endorses your student pilot certificate for solo cross-country, you will log at least five hours of cross-country flying including one trip of 150 nautical miles. Finally, your instructor will devote three hours of training in preparation for the practical test.

With your Private Pilot, Airplane, Single-Engine Land (or Sea) certificate in your pocket, you will be able to carry passengers day and night in good weather in a single-engine airplane. The certificate itself is good forever—but you must have a current medical certificate and take a proficiency check from a flight instructor every other year (if you achieve a new rating or certificate, this requirement is waived).

Both the Recreational Pilot and Private Pilot certificates require a Third-Class Medical Certificate (which is also your student pilot certificate, renewable every 24 or 60 months, depending on your age on the date of the physical exam) issued by an FAA-designated medical examiner before you can fly solo…if you have any medical condition that might affect your flying, get the medical examination before proceeding with your training. Waivers are available for just about any physical problems; you will meet wheelchair pilots, deaf pilots, and pilots with only one eye in the pilot population.

For each certificate, you will be required to pass a knowledge examination administered by an authorized testing center; pilots training under Part 61 are not required to attend a formal ground school, but doing so really helps you to get ready for the exam. Go to www.faa.gov and click on Education and Research to see a selection of sample test questions. Sorry…no answers are provided. But there is a thriving industry eager to help; ASA's Test Prep Series is the best of the lot, but there are DVD courses, online courses…using a search engine will be like rubbing the genie's lamp.

The regulations do require that you have logged ground training—this is not the same thing as ground school, and many instructors miss this distinction. Ground training is best accomplished one-on-one with your instructor; Part 61 outlines the subjects that must be covered. Again, the ground training must be logged. Expect to pay your instructor for ground instruction time, by the way—it's only fair that they be compensated for their time and knowledge whether it is in the air or in the classroom. "Free instruction is worth what you pay for it" is a facile phrase that in itself is unfair to instructors who will bite the bullet and let you get away without paying.

When you have completed the minimum flight hour requirements and your instructor feels that you are ready (his or her certificate is on the line, too), you will take a practical test from a DPE. There are no mysteries to the flight test; the examiner must follow the Practical Test Standards. Get a copy of the PTS early in your training, and be sure that your instructor does not omit anything. Go to www.faa.gov and click on "Education and Training."

You can enjoy the privileges of the recreational or private pilot certificates for as long as you can meet the physical exam requirements, or you can keep going for the following certificates and ratings (of course, recreational pilots must advance to private pilot status before adding ratings).

Instrument Rating

Smart Visual Flight Rules (VFR) pilots stay on the ground when the clouds are low and the visibility is poor (or they make the six o'clock news), and they begin to work toward their instrument rating as soon as possible. The training makes you a better pilot, even if you never fly in the clouds, but those who use the rating know the joy of breaking through a low cloud layer into a sunlit sky while their VFR comrades stay in the coffee shop. The rating requires a minimum of 40 hours of actual or simulated instrument time (Part 61; 35 for Part 141), of which 15 hours must be dual instruction from a flight instructor with an instrument rating on his or her instructor certificate. A CFII, in other words. The other 25 hours can be flown with a safety pilot, but that is a discussion for another book such as *The Complete Advanced Pilot.*

Commercial Pilot Certificate

Before you can begin to get paid for flying instead of paying for it, you must have a commercial pilot certificate. You must have logged at least 250 hours of flight time (190 for Part 141), of which 100 hours must be pilot-in-command (PIC) time and 50 must be cross-country as PIC. Unless you already have an instrument rating when you get your commercial certificate, your fly-for-pay activities will be severely curtailed. Again, read my advanced pilot book when the time comes.

To fly for hire you must hold a Second Class Medical Certificate (renewable annually). As was the case with the private pilot certificate, the Part 61 ground training is done one-on-one over a cup of coffee with your instructor. Alternatives for ground school to pass the knowledge exam are the same as for the private.

What kind of jobs can a pilot who holds a commercial pilot certificate get? Pipeline patrol, glider towing, traffic reporter, fire bomber, fire patrol, banner towing, pilot for an organization that owns its own aircraft—those are only a few of the options. What can't he or she do? Carry passengers for hire except under the most restrictive conditions, of which participation in a drug-testing program is only one. Sightseeing flights must take off and land at the same airport without any other stops; they can't go more than 25 miles from the departure airport—good for scenic rides and that is about all. Becoming a charter pilot involves getting qualified under Parts 119 and 135 of the FARs and working for an air taxi company.

Multi-Engine Rating

If you think that two engines are better than one, there is no minimum flight time or knowledge exam requirement for the multiengine rating. Just demonstrate proficiency in a twin to a DPE via a practical test. People typically spend 10 to 20 hours learning to fly a twin—mostly dealing with emergencies—and preparing for the checkride. The expense of maintaining proficiency will drive your decision on getting this rating.

Flight Instructor Certificate (CFI)

If you enjoy sharing what you have learned, maybe teaching others to fly is for you. There is no minimum flight time requirement, but you must have a commercial pilot certificate with an instrument rating and pass two knowledge exams—one on the Fundamentals of Instruction and one that covers everything a private or commercial pilot should know plus a few extra mind-benders just to see if you have been paying attention.

If your only goal is to log flight hours toward that airline job, please do not become an instructor—your primary goal should be to graduate motivated, proficient students. If getting your CFI means just getting your ticket punched, and you can't wait to move up, you will be unfair to your students. Unmotivated instructors disillusion hundreds of potential pilots every year. There are lots of ways to log hours without taking a student's money under false pretenses.

The other side of the coin is that being a flight instructor is a truly fulfilling career—I know. There are many, many dedicated instructors who could move up to the airlines but are having too much fun giving flight instruction. And have you checked on what a newbie first officer is taking home these days?

Airline Transport Pilot

This is the pinnacle, the top of the heap. Very few of the pilots that you have referred to as "commercial pilots" all of your life have only a commercial pilot certificate in their pockets. The airlines can afford to be choosy, and an ATP certificate is only one of their requirements. If the front seat of an airliner is in your future, get a four-year college degree and log at least 1,200 hours of flight time—flying turbine-powered airplanes preferred. You must also be 23 years old.

Sport Pilot

No, I didn't forget the Sport Pilot certificate. This certificate allows you to fly light sport aircraft (LSA) just for fun (you cannot fly out of a tower-controlled airport without further training, you may not carry more than one passenger, nor can you fly at night). Your driver's license is your medical certificate. Whether or not the hours you log as a sport pilot count toward private pilot eligibility depends on the instructor. Time logged with a sport pilot flight instructor does not count, while time logged with a full-fledged CFI does. Check the ASA website for updates on this (see the note about online book Updates on Page ii, in the front pages of this book). Sport pilot training takes two paths when the level flight cruising speed (V_H) of the plane exceeds 87 knots; students flying the faster planes must receive training in control of the airplane by reference to the flight instruments in the event that they encounter visibility of less than three miles. Also, some sport pilot privileges are grandfathered in for those applicants with prior light plane experience. In this book I am going to assume no prior experience. Passing a knowledge test and a practical (flight) test are required for all pilot certificates.

The stick-and-rudder skills you learn in Sport Pilot training will serve you well if you decide to move

up and it's the least expensive and quickest path to a pilot certificate with half the required experience requirements. ASA publishes "Be a Sport Pilot," which explains everything you need to know.

A personal note: When I was a student pilot all I knew was what my instructor told me and what I read in FAA texts. I did not know what students across the field were learning, and I certainly did not know what students in other cities and states were learning or what uncertainties they were encountering. There were few opportunities to compare notes. Today, using the internet, students can do their own research on virtually anything, and they can have discussions with students in other states and even other countries. Many areas of confusion have been uncovered when students have gone online and asked the world at large for help. Take advantage of this wonderful opportunity.

Other Ratings

There are many other flying possibilities: you can add categories, such as rotorcraft or lighter-than-air, to your pilot certificates. You will read about "type ratings," as in "category, class, and type if required," and think that a Cessna 150 is a different type than a Bonanza, but that is not true *at the present time*. Everything you have read thus far relates to regulations and practices in 2011, and right now you need a type rating only if you want to act as PIC of an airplane that is jet-powered or weighs more than 12,500 pounds. For those aircraft, you will take a "type rating ride" with an examiner, and will have that rating added to your pilot certificate. In some countries, however, the civil aeronautics authorities *do* consider a Cessna 150 to be a different type than a Bonanza, a Seneca to be a different type than a Baron, and so forth, because to those authorities the differences between the aircraft are significant.

The regulations for pilot certification that I have cited are based on what we now understand is outdated technology. They prepare a student to pass a test, instead of introducing realistic scenarios, and emphasize maneuvers instead of decision making and risk management. Also, there is insufficient emphasis on new flight technologies such as GPS and multifunction devices. In the old days, a pilot or instructor could move from one type (current definition) of aircraft to another and expect the controls and electronics to be functionally the same. No more. An instructor who speaks Garmin 1000 fluently will have no idea how to use the Avidyne PFD without advance study and practice. Manufacturers of these advanced airframes and avionics have taken the lead by developing their own training systems; there are on-line simulators for many of these devices.

Advances in avionics and aircraft manufacturing have outstripped the FAA's ability to keep pace, and the FAA readily admits that this is the case. That is why FITS is important now, and why it will become more important in the future.

FAA and Industry Training Standards (FITS)

As I write this, pilots are learning to fly ab initio (latin for "right from the beginning") in sleek, composite-construction airplanes that have autopilots, single-knob, computerized engine controls, and "glass cockpits" consisting of digital displays of flight instrumentation, weather, terrain, moving-map navigation information, engine operating parameters, and on and on. These "Technically Advanced Aircraft (TAA)" are so different from those we have instructed in for the past several decades that the old regulations no longer meet our goal of preparing pilots to fly safely in a complex airspace structure at speeds only dreamed of in the past.

You might be one of those pilots. Or, after being trained in a 1940s technology aircraft, you might buy or join a club that uses TAA. One way or the other, you are going to be affected, so let's see what FITS, a new FAA/Industry plan will do.

The program will integrate the following:

- Aeronautical Decision Making (Lesson 5)
- Situational Awareness
- Single Pilot Resource Management (Lesson 12)
- Risk Management
- Task Management
- Controlled Flight Into Terrain Awareness (CFIT)

See www.faa.gov/education_research/training/fits/ to see how FITS will work.

Note that FITS applies to technically advanced aircraft only. If you are training in a "legacy" airplane, nothing changes.

After I have covered the individual nuts and bolts of what you need to know under today's standards, I will put it all together at the end in Lesson 12.

What Will This Book Do For You?

Your mind is like a computer's memory bank. When you have a new experience or sensation, your mind compares it to earlier experiences and sensations and either modifies what was stored or adds the new data to the memory bank. Each flight will add new experiences and soon your mind will say "That's not new—I've done that before!"...and flying high above the mountains or gliding quietly onto a grass strip will quickly become a part of you. This book is intended to build your aviation knowledge the same way.

Like all instructors, I talk a lot, and I might repeat myself on occasion. I learned long ago that presenting the same material in different ways can be the key to understanding. If you think I am going over the same ground more than once, it is to meet an instructional goal.

Several of the lessons refer to aeronautical charts, and an excerpt from the Seattle sectional chart is provided inside the back cover of this book—you'll be using this chart excerpt for many interactive exercises throughout the text. Aviation has a language all its own, and you want to speak it fluently, so we have provided a glossary. It includes the Pilot/Controller Glossary, compiled from the *Aeronautical Information Manual,* for understanding the terms used in the Air Traffic Control System. Always look there first when you hear something new.

Each lesson contains review questions so that you can test your understanding of the material contained in that lesson—but you can go to www.faa.gov to read many more questions you might be asked on your knowledge exam or, as I mentioned earlier, you could purchase a separate book such as ASA's *Private Pilot Test Prep* that is written specifically to prepare you for this test.

But First, a Word from Your Instructor...

Lesson 4 contains a laundry list of publications that you will need as your training progresses. It would be nice if I could teach you everything you have to know to operate safely and legally in the National Airspace System on a one-to-one basis. Unfortunately, this is impossible, because I do not know everything. No one does. I can ensure that you know the basics, and I will encourage you to add to your knowledge with self-study. As you read through the publications you will, I hope, come across areas that are unclear or that I haven't mentioned. Ask me about them. We will be using a building-block method of instruction, and it is possible that your question will be covered in future flight or ground training sessions...but ask anyway.

As you read Part 61 of the Federal Aviation Regulations, specifically 61.81 through 61.85, you will note that the responsibility for ensuring that all required areas are covered is yours. Those sections are addressed to student pilots, not to instructors. (If your instructor is using a syllabus, as is recommended, this should be a slam dunk...but it is still your job to look at the requirements and ask your instructor "Why haven't we done this yet?" if a subject has not been covered.) Read the regulations—all of them—and know what is required of you both before and after your checkride. When the examiner asks you a question or tells you to perform a maneuver, you don't want to say "My instructor never told me/taught me that..."

During your training, you might fly with another instructor; some schools require it. I'm very much in favor of having your progress monitored by someone else. When flying with another instructor, however, you may run into the procedure versus technique problem: Procedures are contained in manufacturer's manuals and handbooks, while techniques are pretty much a matter of individual taste. For example, the pilot's operating handbook might have "Carburetor Heat – On" in the pre-landing checklist; this is a procedure. Different instructors might disagree on just where in the pattern the carburetor heat should be applied...that is technique.

If an instructor wants you to divert from a recommended procedure, ask him or her where the changed procedure is documented; the manufacturer is always right. If an instructor wants you to add flaps at a different point in the pattern than I have taught you to do, or tells you to reduce power at a different place or a different amount than I have taught you to do, that is technique...follow his or her instruction, note the result, and file it away for future reference. No instructor knows it all, and the more insights you develop, the better. Don't get into the "...but Bob told me to..." discussion.

If the airplane you train in is equipped with state-of-the-art navigation equipment, you may need training in its use beyond that which I can give you. Manufacturers provide online training materials and in some cases put on training seminars. The FAA also supplies a lot of information on the website www.faasafety.gov. I encourage you to take advantage of these sources.

You are my customer (or a customer of the flight school), and I am here to provide a service. If you are not satisfied with the way I teach, go to the chief flight instructor and ask to try another instructor or instructors. Our common goal is to make you a safe pilot.

Good luck!

Lesson 1 Basic Aerodynamics

In this book we are going to assume that your training airplane is all-metal (although airplanes that are partially or completely made of composites are increasingly available), has one engine, a fixed-pitch propeller, and a non-retractable landing gear. A stroll along the ramp of your hometown airport will show you there are many variables, however, and you may want to compare features on other airplanes with the one you fly. Here are some things to look for:

Fuselage Construction

The fuselage (or cabin, in most modern airplanes) is the basic structure to which the wings and empennage (*see* Figure 1-1 on the next page) are attached. Most of the small airplanes you will see during your flight training are unpressurized (Lesson 2)—you can tell by the square windows and non-airtight doors. Airplanes that are pressurized for passenger comfort at high altitudes have round or oval windows and tight-fitting doors.

The fuselage of almost every airplane you see will be of aluminum construction with internal strengthening members. A close look will show that on some models more attention has been paid to reducing drag caused by rivet heads and other protrusions. Looking at non-metal airplanes will take you to both the past and the future. Fabric-covered airplanes with

tubing structures (wood-framed airplanes are really classics!) are lovingly restored and flown by proud owners. No less proud are the pilots of modern composite aircraft, formed of plastic reinforced with glass fibers, carbon fibers, or similar materials which offer great strength and minimal drag. Most light sport aircraft (LSA) and technically advanced aircraft (TAA) are made of composites. Technically advanced aircraft, by definition, have an IFR-approved Global Positioning System navigator with a moving-map display, and an integrated autopilot. Most go beyond this to replace the traditional "six-pack" of analog instruments (*see* Lesson 3) with digital instruments, leading to the term "glass cockpit."

It is altogether possible that you might take your initial training in a composite airplane, but right now they are outnumbered by aluminum planes and that is what I will emphasize.

Wings

The "main spar" within the wing is the structural member that supports the load. Airfoil-shaped ribs are attached to the main spar and the metal or fabric skin is attached to the ribs to give the wing its shape, and it is that airfoil shape that makes the wing capable of developing enough lift to support the airplane in flight. The wings of composite aircraft are

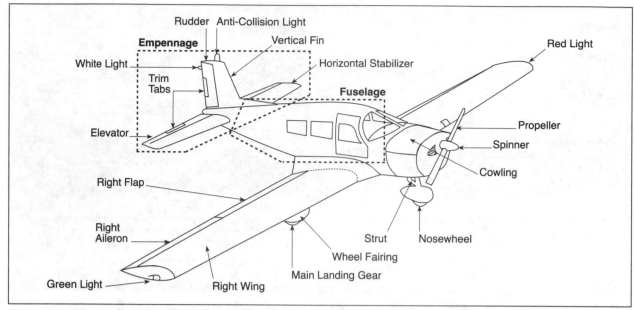

Figure 1-1

formed with molds and have no internal ribs. They do have a main spar, of course.

Almost all modern airplanes have a single wing, mounted either above or below the fuselage. Most, but not all, high wing airplanes have supporting struts. Low wing and strutless high wing airplanes are cantilevered: the internal structure is designed to support the load so there are no struts.

Wing fuel tanks are either "wet wings" with the wing structure serving as the fuel container, or there are rubber bladders contained within the wing.

Empennage

The horizontal stabilizer, the rudder, the vertical fin, the elevator, or any combination thereof is called the airplane's empennage or "tail feathers." These surfaces allow the pilot to change the airplane's attitude in relation to the horizon by moving the nose up and down (using the yoke or control stick) or left and right (using the rudder pedals) as seen by the pilot. There may be a fixed horizontal stabilizer with a movable elevator, or the whole horizontal assembly may be movable (called a stabilator).

Flight Controls

See Figure 1-2: Fore-and-aft movement of the control wheel or stick is transmitted by pushrods or cables and pulleys to these control surfaces, and left-right movement is controlled by the rudder, which is mounted at the rear of the vertical fin. The pilot depresses the rudder pedal in the desired direction of nose movement and a cable system moves the control surface. You will see V-tails, T-tails, and straight tails, and maybe a home-built airplane with no horizontal surfaces mounted on the tail.

Ailerons

You won't find many airplanes that do not have ailerons, which are movable control surfaces at the outer trailing edge of the wings. Ailerons are used to bank the airplane. A control wheel or stick at the pilot station is moved in the direction of bank desired (left or right). The ailerons are deflected through a system of cables, pulleys, and bellcranks or pushrods. When no control force is exerted, the ailerons are held flush with the wing surface by the airstream.

Flaps

The hinged portions of the trailing edges of the wings near the fuselage are called flaps, and are normally used to steepen the glide angle without increasing airspeed. As you walk along the ramp you will see many different types of flaps, some that simply hinge down and others that extend down and backward. Older airplanes may not have any flaps at all.

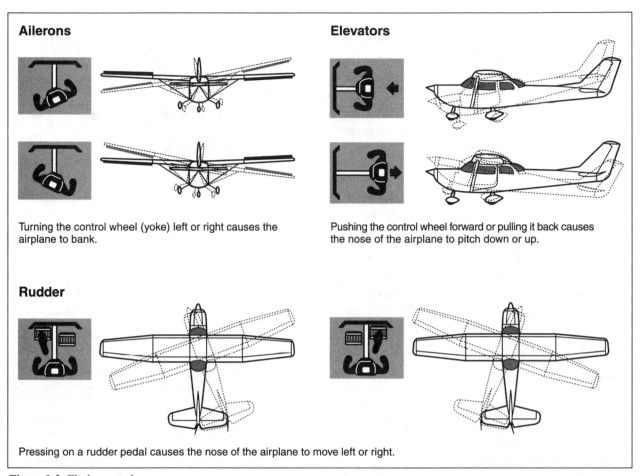

Ailerons

Turning the control wheel (yoke) left or right causes the airplane to bank.

Elevators

Pushing the control wheel forward or pulling it back causes the nose of the airplane to pitch down or up.

Rudder

Pressing on a rudder pedal causes the nose of the airplane to move left or right.

Figure 1-2. Flight controls

Landing Gear

The two main landing wheels and their supporting structure are designed to withstand landing loads and support the airplane on the ground. A third, smaller wheel mounted either forward (tricycle) or aft (conventional) is for ground steering control only. Nosewheels are usually close to or a part of the engine mount and are definitely not designed to absorb landing loads. (Your instructor will devote a lot of training time to making sure that you do not land on the nose wheel!)

The shiny cylinders on nose wheels and some main landing gear are called struts (the Katana's nose-wheel uses replaceable rubber "doughnuts"). They absorb the bumpiness of runways and taxiways. The shiny kind are filled with air and oil, just like your car's shock absorbers. When a strut is "flat" there is no cushioning effect and vibrations are transmitted to the entire airframe. You will see some airplanes which use a spring steel assembly on the main landing gear instead of a strut.

Wheel pants, or fairings, may or may not be present. They reduce aerodynamic drag and add a knot or two to airspeed. Your airplane may have either non-retractable (straight leg) or retractable landing gear. Landing gear that retract into the wing or fuselage add considerably to cruise speed.

Almost all airplanes use disc brakes on the main landing gear, and you can see the discs if there are no wheel pants. Checking brake condition is considerably easier to do on airplanes than it is on cars. The nose wheel is usually not steerable with the rudder pedals and swivels freely, so steering is accomplished by tapping the brake lightly on the side toward the turn.

Propeller

The propellers you see may be either fixed or variable in pitch, or blade angle. You will probably see some amphibians (airplanes that can land on either land or water) with pusher-type propellers, but most are mounted up front and pull the airplane through the air. The conical spinner is not only decorative but serves to direct air into the cooling air intakes.

Engine

Modern airplanes have four- or six-cylinder flat opposed engines: when you open the cowling you will see that the cylinders are on opposite sides of the engine, and that the flat profile allows maximum aerodynamic streamlining of the cowling. As you walk along the ramp you may see an older airplane with a radial engine, its cylinders arranged in a "star" pattern. Most light sport aircraft use water-cooled Rotax engines.

Lights

The lighting system on a modern airplane consists of position lights on the wing tips (red on the left, green on the right) and a white light on the tail, an anticollision light system which may be either red or white (or both) and one or more landing lights. Many airplanes also have bright flashing strobe lights to increases the chances of being seen during both day and night flights.

Light Sport Aircraft

When your pilot certificate says "PRIVATE PILOT Airplane—Single Engine—Land" you are free to fly any single-engine airplane, subject to the requirement for tailwheel, high performance, and complex airplanes. When it says SPORT PILOT, however, you are limited to those weighing less than 1,320 pounds with no more than two seats, fixed landing gear, and a cruise speed of no more than 120 knots.

Introduction to the Cockpit

This is a typical instrument panel layout. Airplane manufacturers have their own ideas about where engine instruments should be located, but the locations of the six flight instruments on the left side of the panel are standardized among manufacturers. (*See* Figure 1-3.)

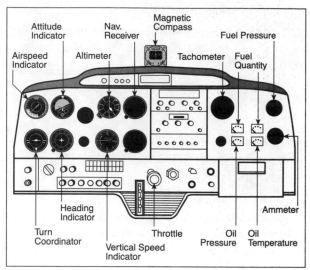

Figure 1-3. Typical "six-pack" of traditional non-digital instruments

If you are training in a Technically Advanced Aircraft ("TAA" in FAA-speak), all of these "steam gauges" will exist on a flat-screen digital display, similar to the G1000 illustrated on Page D-1 in the color section (Appendix D).

Aerodynamics

The subject of aerodynamics deals with forces acting on bodies in motion through the air; in fact "aerodyne" means an aircraft deriving lift from its motion through the air. To oversimplify, an airplane flies because the pilot causes it to accelerate down the runway until its wings develop a lifting force greater than its weight, and it lands because the pilot causes the lifting force to be less than its weight. In flight, the pilot controls the magnitude and direction of lift through use of the flight controls.

To make the airplane go where you want it to go and do what you want it to do, you must use the flight controls as tools and, like any artisan, you have to know what your tools are capable of and how they are used to accomplish the four fundamentals of flight... straight-and-level, turns, climbs, and descents.

As a pilot you will be working with the forces of lift, drag, thrust, and weight. Of these, lift is the force that allows you to move in three dimensions. While it is true that *anything* can be made to "fly" if enough power is applied, an airplane features **airfoils**—shapes specifically designed to develop lift. The amount of lift generated by an airfoil is a function of the area of the lifting surface, the density of the air, the velocity of the airflow over the lifting surface, and the coefficient of lift. This is how these elements are related:

$$\text{Lift} = \text{Coefficient of Lift} \times \text{Area} \times \text{Velocity}^2 \times \text{Density}/2$$

Coefficient of Lift

Don't be intimidated by the words "coefficient of lift"—they apply to physical relationships that are easy to visualize. Before investigating just what coefficient of lift means, or how the other factors affect lift development, you should understand how an airfoil develops lift. Figure 1-4 shows a fluid (illustrated as ping-pong balls) moving through a tube with a restriction in it. If 1,000 units of fluid enter one end of the tube each second, and 1,000 units leave the tube each second, and there is not enough room at the restriction for 1,000 units of fluid to pass, something clearly has to change at the restriction. That "something" is velocity—fewer units must travel at a higher velocity if 1,000 units per second are going to pass the restriction.

As the fluid moves through the tube, its total energy consists of forward movement (**kinetic energy**) and the static force it exerts against the walls of the tube. At the restriction, the energy of forward movement increases, and since total energy can neither increase nor decrease within the system, the static pressure has to decrease. A scientist named Daniel Bernoulli discovered this effect: when a fluid is accelerated the pressure it exerts is reduced. Bernoulli's Theorem accounts for most of the lift developed by an airfoil. You might think of an airfoil as a device designed to accelerate airflow and change its direction.

For an online animation of Bernoulli's Principle, go to http://home.earthlink.net/~mmc1919/. Be sure to scroll down to read the discussion of airfoils.

If you are having difficulty relating tubes and fluids to airplane wings, the airfoil in Figure 1-5 represents the bottom half of Bernoulli's restricted tube, and the length of the arrows indicates the energy imparted to air molecules as they travel over it. They move most rapidly over the curved surface, which is the area of least pressure.

A second contributor to total lift is Newton's Third Law: for every action there is an equal and opposite reaction. As the airfoil moves through the air it pushes the air downward and, in accordance with Newton's Law, the air exerts an equal upward force. Because of differences in wing design and operating conditions, it is impossible to say what percentage of total lift can be attributed to Bernoulli or to Newton at any time. In Figure 1-6, the dashed lines represent lift due to pressure difference and the solid lines indicate lift due to Newton's Law.

Don't get into any arguments about what creates lift—Bernoulli and Newton share the credit, with Newton holding a slight edge. The bottom line is that there must be a net positive pressure difference between the top and bottom of the lifting surface.

Part of the explanation of coefficient of lift has to do with the curvature, or **camber**, of the upper surface of the wing and angle of incidence. A large curve, or camber, means greater acceleration of the air over the upper surface. Oncoming free air is drawn upward toward the low pressure area on top of the

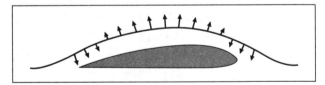

Figure 1-5. Bernoulli airfoil

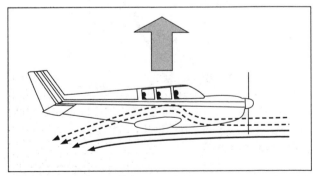

Figure 1-6. Sources of lift

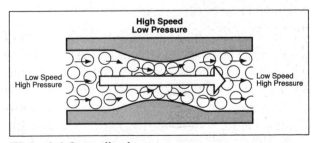

Figure 1-4. Bernoulli tube

wing, accelerates over the curvature, and flows off the trailing edge creating **downwash**. Most general aviation airplanes change camber and increase lift by moving the trailing edge up or down with control surfaces called ailerons and flaps. Changing lift development by changing wing camber is largely the province of the designer, and is only partially under the control of the pilot. **Angle of incidence**, *which is defined as the angle at which the wing is fastened to the fuselage*, is set by the designer at 1° to 3° in relation to the longitudinal axis and is beyond the control of the pilot.

Wing design is one element of the coefficient of lift, and the other is **angle of attack**—over which the pilot has direct control. An imaginary line drawn from the leading edge of the wing to the trailing edge is called the chord line, and *the angle between the chord line and the relative wind is called the angle of attack* (Figure 1-7). If relative wind is an unfamiliar term, consider this: you are sitting in a convertible at a stop light with the wind blowing on the left side of your face; the wind that you feel is the true wind. When the light changes, and the car accelerates, the wind strikes you directly in the face—that is the relative wind, caused by motion.

In flight, *the relative wind is parallel and opposite to the flight path*. Figure 1-8 shows this relationship in level flight, climbing, and descending. To the wing of a military jet climbing almost vertically, the relative wind is coming straight down, while to the wing of an aerobatic airplane completing a loop, the relative wind is coming straight up. More importantly, when a pilot attempts to maintain altitude by using angle of attack alone, without adding power, the relative wind strikes the bottom of the wing as shown in

Figure 1-9. This is called mushing flight, and if the pilot does not lower the nose to decrease the angle of attack, an aerodynamic **stall** is imminent.

Lift developed by pressure difference (Bernoulli lift) depends on a smooth flow of air over the upper surface of the wing. As angle of attack is increased (Figure 1-10), the air being drawn over the top surface of the wing begins to tear away from the wing surface at the trailing edge, causing loss of lift. At high angles of attack the airflow near the trailing edge of the wing even reverses and begins to flow forward! Aerodynamicists devote considerable time and effort to designing wings that maintain a layer of smoothly flowing air over the maximum area of wing surface. It doesn't take much in the way of

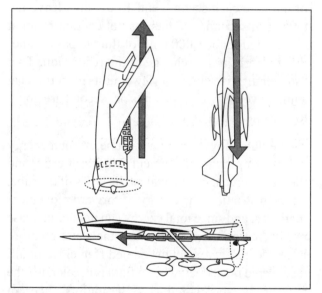

Figure 1-8. *Relative wind is opposite to flight path*

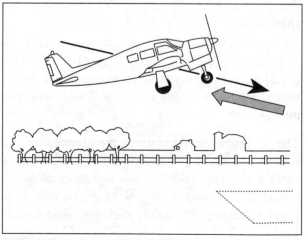

Figure 1-9. *Mushing flight*

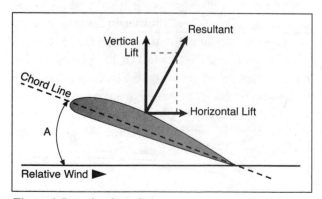

Figure 1-7. *Angle of attack*

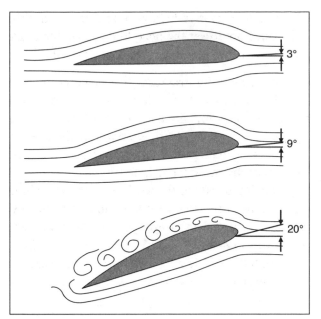

Figure 1-10. *Increasing angle of attack to the stall point*

Figure 1-11. *NASA photo: 17° angle of attack*

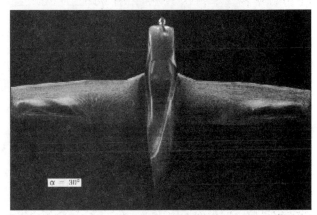

Figure 1-12. *NASA photo: 30° angle of attack*

contamination by ice, frost, or dead bugs to have an impact on lift development.

A simple explanation of the aerodynamic stall is that the angle of attack can be increased until the oncoming air is unable to make the sharp turn necessary to follow the wing's surface, and begins to separate from it at the trailing edge. The separation point moves forward on the wing as the angle of attack is increased. The designer controls the progression of this process by twisting the wing slightly from the wing roots to the tips so that the inner sections of the wing lose lift first, and the outer sections (where the ailerons are located), continue to develop lift until the wing is fully stalled.

The NASA photographs (Figures 1-11 and 1-12) show how increasing the angle of attack causes the area of disturbed airflow to expand until total loss of lift occurs. With an angle of attack of 17°, there is still smooth airflow at the outer ends of the wings, while the inner sections are covered with disturbed airflow.

The airflow in the vicinity of the ailerons on this experimental airfoil remains attached to the wing surface and the "pilot" of this wind-tunnel model would retain some roll control. The same wing at an angle of attack of 30° is fully stalled, with no smooth airflow remaining on the wing surface. Notice that air flowing through the gap between the aileron and the wing provides a small area of smooth airflow over the aileron itself. A normal (unmodified) wing stalls at an angle of attack of 18°–20°.

To ensure that the wing root stalls first, some manufacturers install "stall strips" on the leading edge of the wing near the root. Some airplanes have slots in the leading edge near the wing tip which direct high pressure air from beneath the wing to the upper surface and ailerons, and thus retain controllability at high angles of attack (Figure 1-13 on the next page). Short takeoff and landing (STOL) airplanes usually have some type of device on the leading edge of the wing which extends only at high angles of attack and which channels airflow in the same manner as the fixed slot in the illustration. Large jet aircraft also use leading edge lift devices.

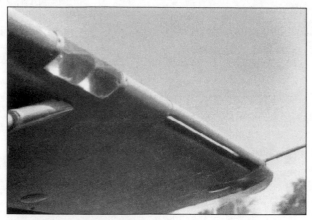
Figure 1-13. Leading edge slots

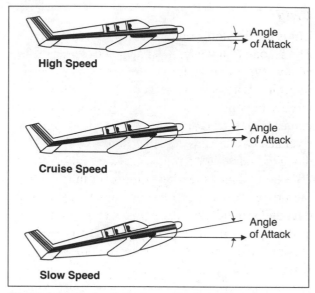
Figure 1-14. Angle of attack vs. attitude and speed

Figure 1-10 also shows that the lift developed by the wing increases as angle of attack increases, until the angle of attack reaches a critical value (usually 18°–20°) beyond which the air no longer flows smoothly over the wing surface and the wing stalls. The *only* way to stall the wing is to exceed the critical angle of attack. In training, most of your stall practice will be at slow speeds, with the nose of the airplane above the horizon, but you must realize that *the wing can be stalled at any airspeed and in any attitude*. The lift developed by the wing must support the weight of the airplane, and the pilot controls lift by varying the angle of attack. If the weight being supported by the wing is increased, either by overloading the airplane or by adding "G" (gravity) forces while maneuvering, the angle of attack must be increased to provide the necessary lift. There is always the danger of exceeding the critical angle of attack and stalling the wing.

Velocity

Velocity of airflow over the lifting surface plays a major role in lift development. The effect of airspeed is dramatically evident because lift varies as the square of the airspeed: double the airspeed and the lift quadruples; cut the airspeed in half and the lift drops to 25% of the former value. Your control of lift through airspeed will play a major role in your ability to fly efficiently—flying "by the numbers" ensures that you always have the proper angle of attack for the condition of flight (Figure 1-14).

Area

The pilot has very little control over the area of the lifting surface except when the flaps are designed to add area. The wing area of a jet airliner increases considerably as it approaches the runway, as its flaps are extended downward and backward. A wing with a large surface area is desirable at low speeds but would add unacceptable amounts of drag due to skin friction at high speeds.

Air Density

Changes in air density affect the creation of lift because it takes molecules of air flowing over the lifting surface to create lift, and as you encounter higher density altitudes there are fewer air molecules. High altitude means less lift, unless angle of attack or airspeed or both are increased. Water vapor in the air (high relative humidity) means that fewer air molecules are available for lift generation (it takes air, not water, to create lift), so high moisture content also means less lift. Air density decreased by either high altitude or high moisture content will also decrease propeller efficiency (the propeller is an airfoil), and will decrease the power output of the engine which needs air, not moisture, to burn fuel efficiently. It isn't necessary to climb to high altitudes to encounter reductions in air density because air (a gas) expands when heated. At sea level on a hot day in July there will be fewer air molecules available to develop lift.

Drag

Lift is the first tool you will learn to control and use. The second tool you must understand is drag. There are two types of drag for you to be concerned about: **parasite drag** and **induced drag**. Parasite drag is largely beyond the control of the pilot because it comes from such things as struts, fixed landing gear, rivet heads, antennas, and the friction of air passing along the skin of the airplane. Engine cooling drag is 20% of total parasite drag—those air inlets behind the propeller channel a tremendous volume of air over and around the engine. Parasite drag increases as the square of the speed: double the airspeed and the drag quadruples. That is what limits top speed—when all of the available horsepower is being used to overcome drag, you can't go any faster. Figure 1-15 shows how parasite and induced drag vary with airspeed and how each contributes to total drag.

Induced drag is the inevitable result of lift development. Remember how Bernoulli's and Newton's effects in combination provide high pressure on the bottom of the wing and low pressure on the top? These forces are resolved at the wing tip as the high pressure air corkscrews up and around the wing tip toward the low pressure area. This meeting of high and low pressure air, with the rotational velocity imparted to the air, creates induced drag (Figure 1-16).

At large angles of attack with great pressure differences, induced drag is a considerable force; however, as airspeed increases and angle of attack is reduced, induced drag becomes less of a factor. Every time you change the angle of attack, you change the induced drag. Induced drag varies inversely as the square of the airspeed. You will see many modern airplanes with winglets, devices which reduce induced drag by controlling the mixing of high and low pressure air at the tip of a lifting surface. Anything that reduces total drag adds to efficiency. Most recent design advances have been accomplished through drag reduction programs, because increasing performance through the addition of sheer horsepower has reached a practical limit.

Some airplanes can be equipped with spoilers, pilot-controlled flat plates that extend perpendicular to the top of the wing and destroy a large portion of the wing's lift. These after-market modifications allow the pilot to lose altitude rapidly without changing airspeed or thrust.

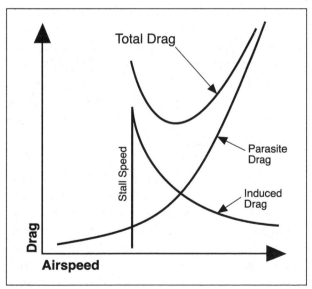

Figure 1-15. Drag and speed graph

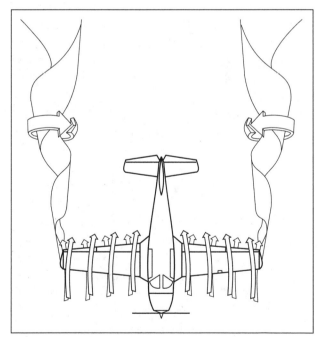

Figure 1-16. Wing-tip vortices create induced drag

Thrust

Besides lift and drag, your third tool will be the thrust developed by the propeller as it is rotated by the engine and pulls the airplane through the air. Remember, the propeller is an airfoil, and all of the relationships of velocity, air density, and angle of attack apply. During the takeoff roll, thrust is at its maximum, and total drag is at a minimum. This imbalance of forces allows the airplane to accelerate. As airflow over the wing increases, lift begins to develop, and when the recommended takeoff speed has been attained the pilot helps the process by increasing the angle of attack. The airplane then becomes airborne (accelerates upward) as lift exceeds weight. The contribution of parasite drag, which increases with speed, will cause total drag to equal total thrust, and as airspeed stabilizes lift will

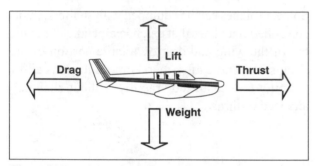

Figure 1-17. *Relationship of forces acting on an airplane*

equal weight. *In any steady state flight condition, whether climbing, descending, or flying straight and level, the forces of lift and weight are equal and the forces of thrust and drag are equal.*

Adding thrust will cause the airplane to accelerate (just as reducing power will cause it to decelerate) until the thrust/drag relationship has equalized and the airplane is stable at a new airspeed. You control the airplane's flight path by adjusting its attitude in relation to the horizon, and by changing thrust with the throttle. Attitude plus power equals performance.

Region of Reversed Command

If you haven't heard the terms "hanging on the prop" or "behind the power curve" yet, you will hear them from your instructor when you start working on short-field takeoffs and landings. Induced drag is greatest at high angles of attack, and it is possible for you to fly at such an extreme angle of attack that it takes all of the available power just to equal induced drag and maintain altitude! Figure 1-18 shows seven airplanes, with the airspeed and power being used by each. Airplane 4 is operating at the speed and power setting for best endurance—using the least power to maintain altitude with an airspeed of 66 miles per hour. The airplanes to the right of airplane 4 are operating normally: with increased power each airplane

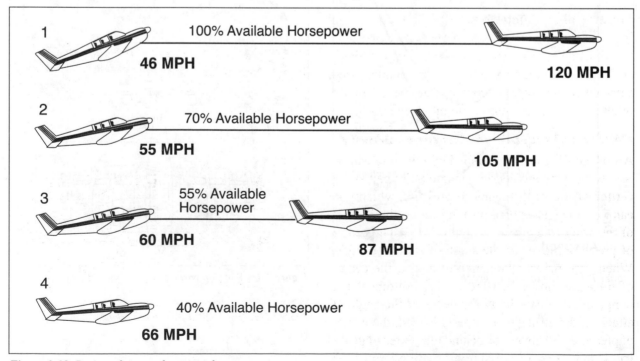

Figure 1-18. *Region of reversed command*

achieves a higher airspeed. Look above airplane 4, however. Airplane 3 is using 15% more horsepower than airplane 4 but is going slower! Look at airplane 2—using almost twice as much power as airplane 4 to fly 10 knots slower. Finally, look at poor airplane 1. That is "hanging on the prop!" Airplane 1 is using every available ounce of power to maintain altitude while flying at only 46 miles per hour. Check each horsepower line and note that reducing the angle of attack (and thus reducing induced drag) at any power setting results in a speed increase.

Airplanes 1, 2, and 3 are all operating in the **region of reversed command** (behind the power curve), where it takes more power to fly more slowly. That's just the reverse of the normal power and airspeed relationship, and that's where the "region of reversed command" got its name.

You can tell by looking at the illustration that the pilots of airplanes 1, 2, and 3 probably can't see over the noses of their airplanes, and that is a good warning that speed is dangerously slow. (Additionally, the airspeed indicator is least accurate at high angles of attack!) If the pilot of an airplane operating in the region of reversed command reduces power or suddenly retracts the flaps, the only means of regaining the lost lift is to lower the nose, and there may not be enough altitude available for that.

You, the pilot, control both lift *and* drag. If you increase drag by operating at a high angle of attack you must add thrust (power) to overcome that drag, and you only have so much power available. Keep some power in reserve—don't operate at high angles of attack which put you behind the power curve.

Center of Pressure vs. Center of Gravity

All of the lift forces developed by the wing can be said to be concentrated in a single point called the **center of lift**, or the center of pressure, which you can visualize as a force pushing up on the bottom of the wing (the arrow in Figure 1-19). The center of pressure moves as the angle of attack changes. When you increase the angle of attack, the center of pressure moves forward on the bottom of the wing, and it moves aft as you decrease the angle of attack. If the airplane is properly loaded, the center of pressure will always be behind the **center of gravity**. If the center of pressure moves forward of the

center of gravity, the nose of the airplane will pitch uncontrollably upward. With the center of pressure aft of the center of gravity, the tendency is for the airplane to be nose heavy. The designer counteracts this by having the horizontal stabilizer at a negative angle of attack, which creates a downward pressure at the tail (Figure 1-20). Lesson 8 discusses airplane loading in more detail.

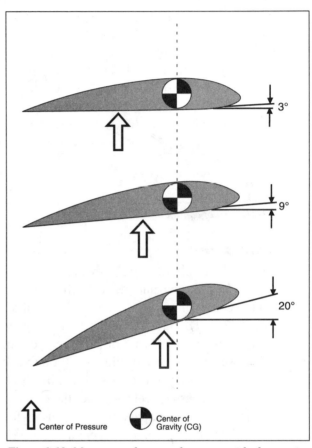

Figure 1-19. *Movement of center of pressure with changes in angle of attack*

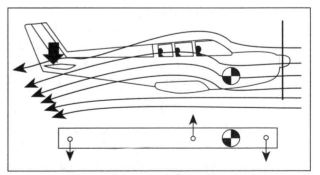

Figure 1-20. *How downforce on tail creates balance*

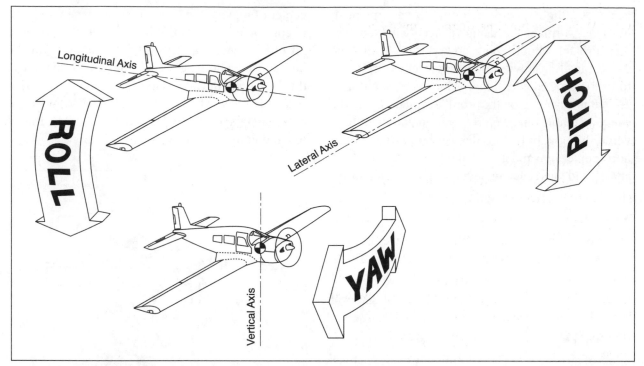

Figure 1-21. *Axes of control around center of gravity*

Axes of Control

You control the airplane around three axes of rotation: lateral, longitudinal and vertical. All three pass through the center of gravity (note the CG symbols in Figure 1-21). The lateral axis of your airplane extends from wing tip to wing tip, and you control the pitch (nose up-nose down) attitude of the airplane by use of the elevator control. As you apply back pressure to the control wheel (or yoke) the elevator deflects upward and the air passing over it pushes the tail down. Note that control movement using a stick is exactly the same as when using a control wheel.

You have effectively increased the camber or curvature of the horizontal stabilizer/elevator, and have developed a downward force. In the cockpit, you see this as the nose rising in relation to the horizon. Relaxing the back pressure, or exerting forward pressure, will lower the nose by reducing the downward force.

The throttle also contributes to control around the lateral axis: as you add throttle, the increased air flow from the propeller will push the tail down as it passes over the elevator ("blowing the tail down"). A power reduction will result in less downward pressure on the elevator, and the nose will move below the hori-

zon (Figure 1-22). This is a built-in safety factor, insuring that the angle of attack will be reduced and the airplane will maintain flying speed if power is suddenly reduced.

You control the airplane around the longitudinal or roll axis (which extends from nose to tail) with the ailerons, and the resultant movement is called "banking." Deflecting an aileron downward increases both the angle of attack and the camber of that portion of

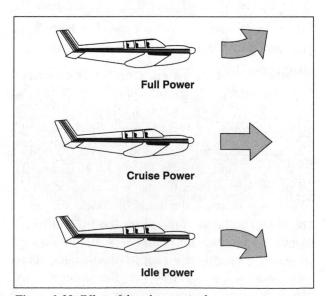

Figure 1-22. *Effect of throttle on attitude*

the wing, and the resulting increased lift raises the wing. At the same time, the aileron on the other wing is being deflected upward, decreasing both angle of attack and camber and reducing the lift of that wing. One wing rises, the other lowers, and the airplane banks (Figure 1-23).

When you deflect one aileron down into the windstream, the other aileron "hides" behind the curvature of the wing. The wing on the side of the down aileron is dragged backward, which slows the turn. The slowing effect of the down aileron is called adverse aileron drag, and is overcome by the rudder. Designers have overcome this imbalance in some cases by equalizing the drag caused by both ailerons.

The rudder controls the airplane around the vertical, or yaw, axis. You use the rudder to offset any force which attempts to move the nose of the airplane from side to side (such as adverse aileron drag). The rudder is a movable surface attached to the rear of the vertical fin which changes the camber and angle of attack and varies the lift force being exerted on either side of the tail surfaces. Because of the long lever arm between the cockpit and the tail surfaces, a very small rudder movement is seen as a large nose movement.

In Figure 1-24, a large yawing force to the right caused by a crosswind on takeoff or landing is offset by a small force applied to the rudder. Some airplanes are called "short coupled" because the tail is so close to the cockpit that very large rudder inputs are required for directional control, especially at low speeds.

The vertical fin itself is a fixed surface very slightly offset from the longitudinal axis to counteract the discharge air from the propeller. This airflow corkscrews around the fuselage and impinges on the vertical fin, imparting a yaw to the left and a roll to the right. This correction is valid for only one airspeed and power setting, and the designer provides either a ground-adjustable rudder trim tab or a cockpit rudder trim control to correct for changing conditions.

The rudder is the most misunderstood and misused flight control, and many pilots create work for themselves by relying on the ailerons to perform actions

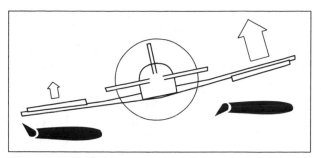

Figure 1-23. Ailerons are used for roll control

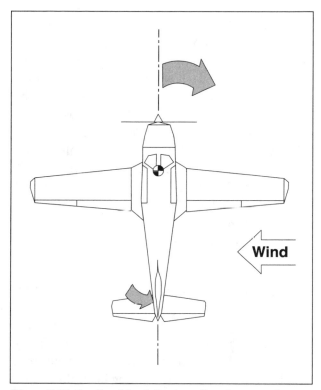

Figure 1-24. Small rudder deflection offsets large yawing tendency

the rudder is better suited for. Take your hands off of the yoke and steer/keep the wings level with rudder; try it, you'll like it.

Control Effects and Stability

The three axes of control pass through the center of gravity. How the designer has related the centers of lift or pressure to the center of gravity affects the stability of the airplane. An inherently stable air-plane requires little effort to control, but is slow to react to maneuvering forces; as stability is decreased, it will react more quickly but require constant attention. Aerobatic airplanes and airliners represent the extremes of stability.

Your airplane is designed to be stable around the yaw (vertical) axis by placing the tail surfaces away from the center of gravity. If you are in straight and level flight and depress the right rudder pedal, the nose will swing to the right, but will return very quickly to the original position when pressure is released. This is called "streamlining"—if no pressure is exerted on a control surface it will align itself with the airstream. (Do this experiment without passengers on board; it's unsettling for those in the back seat!)

Stability around the longitudinal axis is provided by dihedral, the upward slant of the wings from their roots to the wing tips (Figure 1-25). If the airplane is disturbed from straight-and-level flight by a wing being lowered, the descending wing will be at a greater angle of attack than the rising wing. The resulting increase in lift on the lowered wing will result in the wings leveling themselves. This built-in leveling effect makes small bank angles more difficult to sustain than larger bank angles. Almost all airplanes have good short-term lateral stability but poor long-term lateral stability: in the absence of an autopilot, don't expect hands-off, wings-level flight for long periods of time.

Stability around the lateral (pitch) axis is determined by the relationship between the center of gravity and the position of the center of lift, which moves as the downward force on the horizontal stabilizer changes (Figure 1-26). If you disturb the airplane from straight-and-level flight by pulling back slightly on the control yoke and then releasing it, the airplane will climb briefly until airflow over the horizontal stabilizer diminishes, and then the reduced download on the stabilizer will allow the nose to drop below the horizon. The airspeed will then increase (momentarily) and the increasing download on the horizontal stabilizer created by the added airflow will raise the nose above the horizon. These oscillations will gradually diminish in amplitude until the airplane regains level flight.

The designer provides this stability when establishing the permissible limits of center of gravity movement. For every pitch attitude there is a power setting that creates just enough download on the horizontal stabilizer for the airplane to maintain level flight; an increase in power will cause the nose to pitch up, the speed to decrease, and the airplane to climb, and

a reduction in power will have the opposite effect. Airplanes with the horizontal stabilizer mounted high on the vertical fin (T-tails) get little or no control effect from power changes because the control surface is above the propeller's discharge air (propwash). T-tailed airplanes (and all jets) must derive pitch control force solely from the relative wind.

An aerodynamic surface from the early days of flight is reappearing on modern aircraft. A canard (Figure 1-27) is a lifting surface mounted forward of the

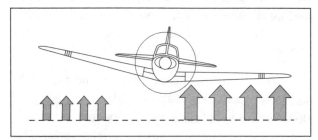

Figure 1-25. *Effect of dihedral*

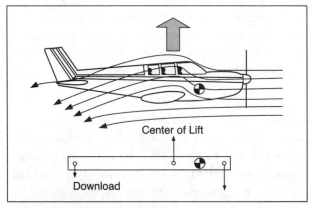

Figure 1-26. *Longitudinal stability*

Figure 1-27. *Canard*

center of gravity which looks like a small wing. It has a slightly greater angle of attack than the main wing and thus will stall before the main wing. The lift developed by the canard is forward of the center of gravity, eliminating the need for a horizontal stabilizer. With the drag of the horizontal stabilizer and any elevator deflection eliminated, canards are faster and more fuel efficient than conventional airplanes.

Trimming Control Surfaces

Control surfaces are provided with trim tabs (Figure 1-28) so that the pilot can maintain a desired control position without exerting constant pressure.

Most trimming surfaces move in the opposite direction from desired control movement: if you want the elevator to be deflected upward the trim tab is deflected downward, and it exerts a force to hold the elevator in the desired position.

As you move into more complicated, higher-powered airplanes, you will find that trim controls for all three axes are available in the cockpit. At the basic trainer level, some trim tabs are literally metal tabs to be adjusted on the ground and then test flown to assess the effect of the change. Airplanes with movable tail surfaces rotate the whole horizontal stabilizer/rudder assembly in reaction to trim wheel movement, and airplanes with stabilators (a movable stabilizer/elevator) move the stabilator with trim force. Three forms of elevator trim control are pictured (Figure 1-29): a horizontal stabilizer with elevator and elevator trim tab, a movable horizontal stabilizer, and (on Mooneys) an entire tail surface which moves with trim input. V-tailed airplanes use ruddervators which, as their name implies, are combination control surfaces.

Trim tabs are used *only* to relieve control pressures, and are not to be used by themselves to change the airplane's attitude. When the airspeed and altitude are at the desired values, any remaining control pressures should be trimmed off. When the airplane is stabilized in level flight, it is flying at its "trim speed." See Lesson 8 for a further discussion of trim speed.

Electric trim is both a blessing and a curse; it is a blessing because you can trim without moving your hands off the yoke, but it is also a curse because, like

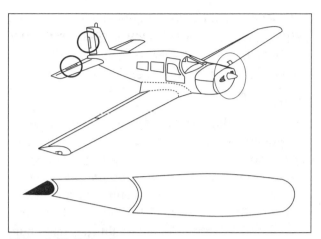

Figure 1-28. Trim tabs

Figure 1-29. Three forms of elevator trim control

any electrical device, it can malfunction. When you are flying an airplane with electric trim, be sure that you know how it can be shut off quickly if it decides to take control of the airplane.

Flaps

Flaps are auxiliary control surfaces; that is, you do not use flaps to control the airplane around the three axes of control. *Flaps allow the pilot to descend at a steep angle without increasing airspeed*, which becomes very important during approaches to land (Figures 1-30 and 1-31). *Flaps are not speed brakes* — in fact, the designer establishes maximum speeds for flap deflection to avoid structural overloads. Because flaps increase both the camber of the wing and the angle of attack by lowering the trailing edge, they allow the same amount of lift to be developed at a lower airspeed. You will experiment with this in training by maintaining altitude while extending flaps and gradually slowing the airplane.

Typically, the first increments of flap extension add more lift than drag, and so some airplanes use a take-off flap setting of 10°–20°. Retracting the flaps when you do not have sufficient airspeed to support the airplane in the no-flaps configuration will cause loss of altitude—do not retract the flaps until you have sufficient airspeed. As you near full flap extension you get more drag than lift and these are the approach settings. Flap extension changes the location of the center of pressure on the wing and causes a pitch change. You should find out whether extending the flaps will cause your airplane to pitch nose up or nose down, and be ready to maintain a constant attitude as you apply flaps.

There are several types of flaps in general use (Figure 1-32). Plain flaps are hinged portions of the trailing edge of the wing: deflecting them increases wing camber and thereby increases lift. Fowler Flaps extend downward and also back, adding to wing area as well as camber. Split flaps extend downward from the trailing edge, while the upper wing surface is undisturbed. Designers also add high lift devices to the leading edge of the wing to channel high pressure air over the upper wing surface. These leading edge flaps are also referred to as slats, and you will see them on modern airline jets as well as short-takeoff-and-landing (STOL) airplanes.

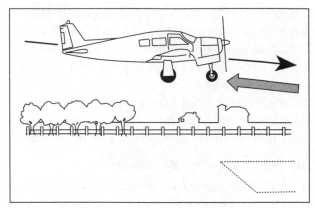

Figure 1-30. Landing approach without flaps

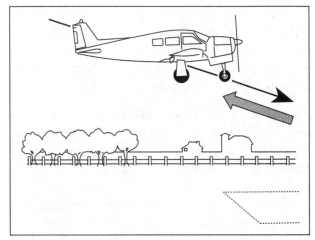

Figure 1-31. Use of flaps allows a steeper descent angle

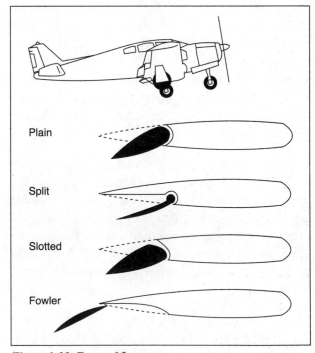

Figure 1-32. Types of flaps

Flaps can be extended electrically, hydraulically, or manually, and some leading edge devices are extended by decreasing aerodynamic pressure. Another means of increasing descent rate without increasing airspeed is the use of spoilers. Spoilers are vertical "fences" that may be extended from the top surface of the wing to disrupt airflow, killing lift. Spoilers have been used as flight controls on gliders for many years, and are now being used on powered airplanes.

Because the extension of flaps affects the angle of attack (by moving the chord line), or changes the wing area, flap use lowers the stall speed—with a greater angle of attack (or more area), less air has to flow over the wing to develop the same amount of lift. Figure 1-33 is a typical table of stall speed vs. flap extension related to bank angle. When referring to similar tables, you should be aware that airspeed indicator accuracy suffers at high angles of attack (low airspeeds).

Gross Weight	Angle of Bank			
2750 Lbs	Level	30°	45°	60°
Power	**Gear and Flaps Up**			
On	MPH 62	67	74	88
	KTS 54	58	64	76
Off	MPH 75	81	89	106
	KTS 65	70	77	92
	Gear and Flaps Down			
On	MPH 54	58	64	76
	KTS 47	50	56	66
Off	MPH 66	71	78	93
	KTS 57	62	68	81

Figure 1-33. *Stall speed table*

Torque

Torque is really the result of four factors, although the end effect is the same: a tendency to yaw to the left in airplanes with propellers and engines that rotate clockwise as seen from the pilot's seat (Figure 1-34). One major factor is discharge air from the propeller corkscrewing around the fuselage as it moves aft, and striking the left side of the vertical tail surfaces. During the takeoff roll, the force it exerts to move the tail to the right is seen by the pilot as a movement of the nose to the left.

Another factor is Newton's law of equal and opposite reactions: as the engine and propeller rotate clockwise, a counterclockwise force is transmitted through the engine mounts to the airframe. The designer may increase the angle of incidence of the left wing to offset this force, or mount the engine offset from the centerline to minimize the torque reaction.

A third major contributor is called **P-factor**, because the culprit is the propeller. As the blade on the right side of the propeller disc descends, it is exerting a force on the air (downwash effect, because the propeller is an airfoil), while the blade on the left side of the disc is at a low angle of attack and is exerting little or no force. The descending blade is also moving at a higher speed relative to the air than is the ascending blade, and this increased velocity creates more lift on the right side of the propeller disc, pulling the nose of the airplane to the left. The NASA wind-tunnel photographs (Figures 1-11 and 1-12) of disturbed airflow also dramatically illustrate P-factor and the corkscrew flow of discharge air from the propeller at high angles of attack.

The last factor contributing to left-turning tendency is **gyroscopic precession**, and this is especially noticeable in airplanes with conventional land-

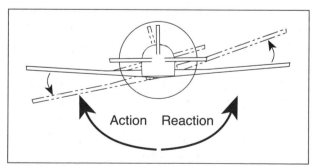

Figure 1-34. *Action/reaction*

ing gear (taildraggers). The propeller is a rotating mass, just like a solid disc of metal, and if a force is applied to a rotating mass it will act as though the force had been applied 90° in the direction of rotation (Figure 1-35). When the pilot of a taildragger lifts the tail during the takeoff run, the forward tilting of the propeller disc exerts a force at the right rear of the propeller disc which adds to the left-turning tendency. The illustration (Figure 1-35) shows the raising of the tail creating a left-turning force.

As you begin the takeoff roll, power is at a maximum and airflow over the control surfaces (with the exception of propeller discharge air) is at a minimum. Discharge air and P-factor will combine to turn the airplane to the left unless you provide offsetting rudder pressure to keep the plane moving straight down the runway. As you rotate the airplane to climb attitude, P-factor increases because the angle of attack of the blade descending on the right side of the propeller disc has increased, and you must continue to apply right rudder. A high power-low airspeed situation will always call for right rudder pressure. A common error is an attempt to offset torque effects by banking to the right rather than by using right rudder.

While you're leveling off at cruise altitude, the forces of discharge air and P-factor still exist, but they are diminished because of reduced power. Here, the airplane designer provides a corrective force: the left wing is rigged so that it develops slightly more lift at cruise speed than the right wing, offsetting the left-turning tendency. The vertical fin is also slightly offset, so that at cruise speeds the push of discharge air on the left side of the tail surfaces is corrected for.

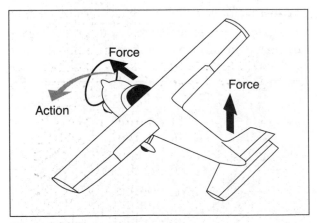

Figure 1-35. Gyroscopic precession

These corrections are exactly effective at only one airspeed: go faster or slower and aileron or rudder trim will be required.

Dynamics of the Turn

The lift developed by an airfoil acts perpendicular to the relative wind, and in level flight that force is vertical with no horizontal component. If you roll into a 90° bank, all of the lifting force will act horizontally, and with no vertical lift the airplane cannot maintain altitude (Figure 1-36). (The military demonstration teams do it but they have a tremendous power-to-weight ratio, and jet fighter fuselages are designed to provide some lift.)

In normal flying, you will not bank more than about 55° (60° of bank requires a parachute when flying with more than one person in the airplane), and as you bank the wings you will be varying the relationship between the **vertical** and **horizontal components of lift**. It is the horizontal component of lift that causes the airplane to turn. When a portion of the total lift developed by the wing acts horizontally, the remaining vertical component will be inadequate to support the weight of the airplane, and additional lift must be supplied by increasing the angle of attack, or the airspeed, or both to avoid loss of altitude. Increasing the angle of attack increases induced drag (remember that induced drag is the price you pay for lift), and unless that drag is offset with thrust, you must inevitably lose airspeed in a level turn.

As you bank more and more steeply, and increase the angle of attack to maintain altitude (without adding power), you will soon reach the critical angle of attack and the wing will stall. Figure 1-37 shows the relationship between the bank angle in degrees and the percentage increase in stall speed. Note that in a 60° bank the stall speed will increase by 40%, from 60 knots to 84 knots, for example.

Load factor is the ratio between the weight that the wing is being required to support and the weight of the airplane. If an airplane which weighs 2,000 pounds is banked 60°, the horizontal component of lift is 2,000 pounds and the vertical lift required to maintain altitude is also 2,000 pounds: the wing is supporting 4,000 pounds and the load factor is 2.0. As Figures 1-36 and 1-38 show, the horizontal component of lift is equal to apparent centrifugal force

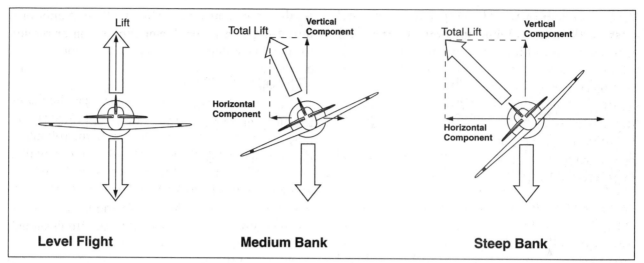

Figure 1-36. *Forces during normal coordinated turns*

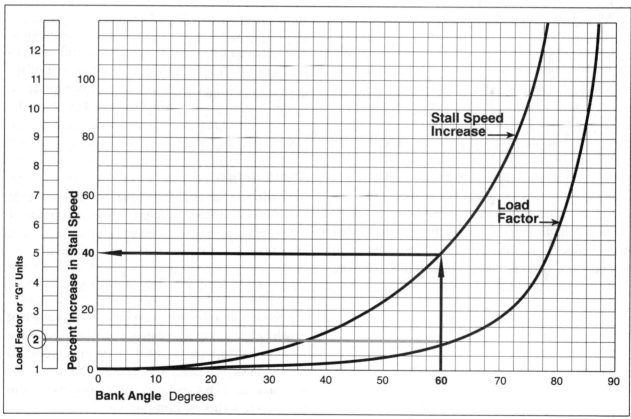

Figure 1-37. *Increase in stall speed and load factor*

and the vertical component is equal to weight, and as the bank steepens the resultant load and the lift required to support it increase dramatically.

From what has been said so far, you would assume that the rudder plays no part in turning an airplane, since it is the horizontal component of lift that supplies the turning force. This is true to the extent that no rudder pressure is required to sustain the turn itself, but rudder pressure *is* required to roll into and out of the turn because of adverse aileron drag, and may be required to overcome "torque" forces.

The rudder controls the airplane around the yaw (or vertical) axis. As an aileron is deflected downward to initiate a bank, that down aileron creates drag which opposes the turn. Rudder pressure is required to overcome this adverse aileron drag. The amount of rudder pressure required depends on the degree of aileron deflection. When the desired bank has been established, and the ailerons are neutralized, there is no aileron drag and therefore no rudder pressure is required to offset it. Rolling back to wings level flight requires aileron deflection, and rudder must be applied to offset the resulting drag. The slip and skid, or ball, instrument reflects your skill in providing just enough rudder pressure (coordinating aileron and rudder): if you use too much rudder you will force the ball to the outside of the turn, resulting in a skid. If you use too little rudder pressure the ball will fall to the inside of the turn and the airplane will be in a slip. (*See* Lesson 3, Pages 3–7 and 3–8, for more about this instrument.)

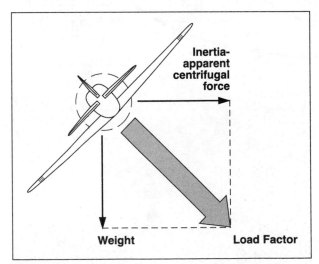

Figure 1-38. *Two forces cause load factor during turns*

As discussed earlier, airplanes with propellers that turn clockwise as seen from the pilot's seat tend to turn left unless design features or pilot action counteract that tendency. Therefore, when you are established in a turn to the left, little rudder pressure is required. It may take slight rudder pressure to hold your airplane in a right turn, however, since these forces act to roll it back to level flight. Again, the ball tells the tale.

One of the stock production numbers at an ice skating show has a line of skaters pivoting around a center, with the central skaters marking time and the outer skaters racing madly to keep up. When you bank your airplane's wings steeply, you re-create this situation aerodynamically: the inside, or lower wing is moving quite slowly, while the top, or outside wing has to cover a greater distance in exactly the same time and so must travel considerably faster. This results in more lift being developed by the outside wing, and the plane develops an overbanking tendency which may require opposite aileron to avoid a too-steep bank. Pilots who combine rudder to maintain a turn with opposite aileron to avoid overbanking risk a cross-control stall.

Coordination

You will hear the word "coordination" frequently as you learn how to use the flight controls. Its meaning is "to balance the use of aileron and rudder so as to keep the ball in the center," and it would make you think that cross-controlling (right aileron with left rudder, for example) is a recipe for disaster.

There are two occasions on which cross-controlling is called for: a side slip to offset a crosswind, and a forward slip to lose airspeed and altitude when too high and fast on a landing approach. Your instructor will teach you how to perform both of these useful maneuvers without stalling.

Ground Reference Maneuvers

This discussion of turns has not yet taken into account the effects of wind. Whenever you fly, your airplane is surrounded by an air mass that is moving over the ground (dead calm conditions at altitude are rare). You travel with the air mass, whether you like it or not. If you want to follow a specific ground track, you must learn to correct for wind drift.

Very early in your training, shortly after you have been introduced to turns and are competent at performing level turns, your instructor will move on to ground reference maneuvers: the rectangular course, S-turns, and turns around a point. Each of these maneuvers is directly applicable to operating in the airport traffic pattern (Lesson 5).

You must first learn to crab into a wind blowing from the side of your airplane and causing it to move sideways as well as forward. This is unacceptable in a traffic pattern, where everyone tries to follow the same track over the ground. Exact precision is impossible, of course, so you will see airplanes flying parallel paths, but their direction over the ground will be the same. Figure 1-39 illustrates the rectangular course. An airplane located between positions 1 and 2 would be crabbed (pointed) to the right just enough to offset the drift down the page due to the wind. Between positions 3 and 4, its nose would be pointed to the left for the same reason. Flying directly into the wind, from position 4 toward position 1, no wind correction is required…but the airplane's speed over the ground is reduced; flying with a direct tailwind, from 2 to 3, increases the ground speed but requires no wind correction.

Whenever you turn the airplane from one heading to another you must consider how many degrees of turn are required and how much time the turn will take. For example, when turning from position 1 to fly across the page you will turn fewer than 90 degrees because the airplane will be pointing to the right at the completion of the turn. The slow ground speed caused by the headwind, however, means a shallower-than-normal bank, allowing more time for the turn. Turning from position 2 to fly down the page, the increased ground speed calls for a steeper bank because you have a greater number of degrees to turn in a shorter time. Rectangular courses can be flown using any straight road or powerline as an imaginary runway.

S-turns add to your mastery of wind correction at relatively low altitude. You must fly a series of consecutive semicircles along a road or powerline that is 90° to the wind. Figure 1-40 illustrates. The semicircles must be symmetrical and the wings must be level each time you cross the reference line. Once again, you must "play" the bank to accomplish the maneuver. From position 1 to position 2, the tailwind requires a steep bank angle to avoid being drifted too far away from the reference line; as the turn continues the bank angle is gradually reduced, until the wings are level at point 3. The second semicircle begins with a shallow but increasing bank angle, with the steepest bank when the airplane is flying downwind approaching position 6. The tricky part is rolling from a steep left bank to a steep right bank at position 6, with the wings level just as you cross the reference line. Thumb rule: The bank angle is always directly proportional to the ground speed.

Like S-turns, flying "turns around a point" will increase your mastery of wind correction while dividing your attention between aircraft control and ground reference. Pick a prominent landmark (remember to stay away from persons or property) and fly a constant-radius turn around that point at about 600 feet above the ground. Again, the steepest bank is required when you are flying directly downwind and the shallowest bank is required when you are flying directly into the wind.

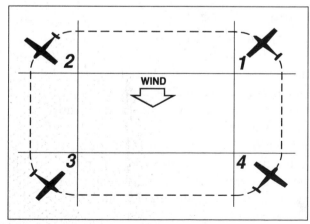

Figure 1-39. *Rectangular Course*

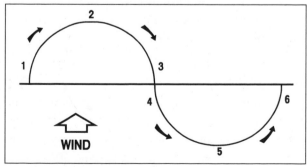

Figure 1-40. *Turn Diagram*

Stalls and Spins

Increasing the angle of attack until the air no longer flows smoothly over the wing surface will result in an aerodynamic stall as discussed earlier, and the designer's placement of the center of lift and the center of gravity make the stall self-correcting *if both wings stall simultaneously*. If one wing stalls before the other, the stalled wing will drop, the airplane will yaw toward the stalled wing, and the nose of the airplane will drop below the horizon; if you don't stop the yaw with opposite rudder (not aileron!) and decrease the angle of attack by moving the control yoke forward, a spin will result. *An airplane must be stalled before it will spin.* In a well-developed spin, the lower or inside wing is fully stalled while the higher or outside wing is less stalled—the indicated airspeed in a spin will be quite low. Because a spin must be preceded by a stall, your flight instruction will emphasize stall recognition and recovery. Most airplanes are not approved for intentional spins, and before you or your instructor attempt an intentional spin you should check the Approved Flight Manual or Pilot's Operating Handbook (all airplanes manufactured since the early 1970s have AFMs, not POHs). Most flight manuals include instructions on how to recover from an inadvertent spin, and you should become familiar with these instructions.

During primary training you will learn to recognize and recover from power-on and power-off stalls (formerly called departure and approach stalls); in spite of the fact that the Practical Test Standard allows banks of up to 20° when approaching a stalled condition, almost all instructors teach stalls as wings-level maneuvers. My take on this is that most instructors are reluctant to set up a condition that might lead to a spin because most instructors are uncomfortable with spins. An hour of dual instruction in an airplane certificated for intentional spins with a qualified instructor will erase any doubt about your ability to handle an inadvertent spin.

Look back at Figure 1-37. Note that any bank increases both the load on the wing and the stall speed. Your first priority when a stall is imminent is "unloading the wing" by simultaneously rolling the wings level and briskly applying forward pressure to the yoke. Pushing the yoke forward when close to the ground is counter-intuitive, but it must be done.

Figure 1-41 shows a test airplane on which NASA has installed experimental flow control devices on the outboard sections of the wings to improve spin recovery characteristics. This airplane has a pilot's emergency escape door and a drag parachute.

Glide Ratio

If you are ever faced with an emergency landing because the engine stops, the airplane's ability to glide will suddenly become your top priority. An airplane's glide ratio is the number of feet forward that it will glide for each foot of altitude lost. If an airplane with a ten-to-one glide ratio is one mile above sea level, it will be able to glide (in no-wind conditions) ten miles before reaching the surface. Gliding with the wind, of course, increases the range, while gliding into the wind reduces it.

Section 3 of your Pilot's Operating Handbook should list the best glide speed at maximum gross weight. Some manufacturers publish glide speeds for different weights. You probably won't be at max gross when you need to glide to safety (unless you have a problem immediately after takeoff with a full load), so you should know that the best glide speed varies directly with weight. That is, if the airplane is lighter than gross, the best glide speed is lower than the published speed. Just how much lower depends on the weight decrease, but in an emergency you're not going to be fooling with formulas. For most trainers, to get the speed much more than ten knots below the published figure, you and your instructor would have to jump out.

Energy Management

Energy cannot be destroyed; you can change it into different forms, but you can't destroy it. When you push the throttle in at the beginning of the takeoff roll, you are converting the energy contained in the fuel into kinetic energy—the energy of movement. Its value is the product of mass (aircraft weight, for our purpose) times the square of the airspeed. As your airplane lifts off, the energy from the burning fuel is also transformed into potential energy—the energy of position (altitude, for pilots). When you

Figure 1-41. *Experimental spin recovery flow control devices (black cuffs)*

are in flight—climbing, descending, or cruising, you are working with combined kinetic and potential energy. If you leave the throttle untouched and pull back on the yoke, the resulting zoom will add to potential energy but the airplane will lose airspeed (kinetic energy). Push the nose over into a dive and the loss of altitude means less potential energy while the increased airspeed boosts kinetic energy. Push in on the throttle and the added energy will cause the airplane to climb (potential), unless you hold forward pressure on the elevator to maintain altitude, in which case the added energy will increase airspeed (kinetic).

As a pilot, you are a manager of energy. Manage it properly, and you will get the result you desire. When you add drag, either by use of the control surfaces, the flaps, or extending the landing gear, the airflow around the airplane is disturbed by its passage—and that is another conversion of energy.

This balancing act becomes most important when landing. You need enough kinetic energy to keep the airspeed at the recommended value, but no more than that, and you want the potential energy to decrease until the wheels touch the runway surface. As you descend toward the runway, your airspeed (and thus kinetic energy) should be constant. When you level off (round out, flare…instructors use different terms), the airplane stops descending momentarily. Kinetic energy decreases while drag remains unchanged, causing further settling, but you offset this with a slight increase in back pressure. Potential energy (height above the surface) decreases, as does kinetic energy due to the drag caused by the increased angle of attack. Add enough back pressure to keep the airplane from settling, but not enough to convert your kinetic energy back into potential energy by ballooning, and the total energy will soon consist only of the forward motion as the airplane rolls to a stop (if you use the brakes, you will convert kinetic energy to heat).

Use this knowledge to salvage bad landings…if you level off too high, and start bleeding off kinetic energy, lower the nose enough to convert some potential energy into kinetic energy, or correct by burning more fuel. One way or the other, you need more energy. It is far better to level off too high than to fail to level off at all. Can't get it down in the first one-third of the runway? Add a whole bunch of energy by pushing the throttle all the way in and going around for another try.

If you have too much airspeed when leveling off…a common error…the airplane will float until its kinetic energy has been decreased by total drag; no amount of wishing will change the laws of physics. When the wheels touch down, all you have to work with is brake friction and the friction of the tires on the runway surface. Going around for another approach is a much better solution.

"Give me your best speed on final, 737 on final behind you." Now you have to forget everything I have said about reducing energy on final. What to do? Keep your speed up, as requested, extending no more than one notch (10°) of flaps until on very short final. Then pull the throttle to idle, hold back pressure until the airspeed falls into the white arc, extend full flaps and pitch for normal touchdown speed. A brief forward slip can dump airspeed in a hurry.

Summary

You won't find a better source of information on aerodynamics than the FAA's *Airplane Flying Handbook* (FAA-H-8083-3). You'll find it at pilot supply and book stores (and it is also reprinted by ASA).

Lesson 1
Aerodynamics Review Questions

1. When are the four aerodynamic forces that act on an airplane in equilibrium?

   A— When the aircraft is at rest on the ground.
   B— When the aircraft is accelerating.
   C— During unaccelerated flight.

2. The purpose of the rudder on an airplane is to

   A— control the yaw.
   B— control the overbanking tendency.
   C— maintain a crab angle to correct drift.

3. The term angle of attack is defined as the

   A— angle between the wing chord line and the relative wind.
   B— angle between the airplane's climb angle and the horizon.
   C— angle formed by the longitudinal axis of the airplane and the chord line of the wing.

4. As altitude increases, the indicated airspeed at which a given airplane stalls in a particular configuration will

   A— decrease as the true airspeed increases.
   B— decrease as the true airspeed decreases.
   C— remain the same regardless of altitude.

5. What causes an airplane (except a T-tail) to pitch nosedown when power is reduced and the controls are not adjusted?

   A— The CG shifts forward when thrust and drag are reduced.
   B— The downwash on the elevators from the propeller slipstream is reduced and elevator effectiveness is reduced.
   C— When thrust is reduced to less than weight, lift is also reduced and the wings can no longer support the weight.

6. What effect does an increased load factor have on an airplane during an approach to a stall?

   A— The airplane will stall at a higher airspeed.
   B— The airplane will have a tendency to spin.
   C— The airplane will have a tendency to yaw and roll as the stall is encountered.

7. What determines the longitudinal stability of an airplane?

   A— The location of the CG with respect to the center of lift.
   B— The effectiveness of the horizontal stabilizer, rudder, and rudder trim tab.
   C— The relationship of thrust and lift to weight and drag.

8. The left-turning tendency of an airplane caused by P-factor is the result of the

   A— clockwise rotation of the engine and the propeller turning the airplane counterclockwise.
   B— propeller blade descending on the right, producing more thrust than the ascending blade on the left.
   C— gyroscopic forces applied to the rotating propeller blades acting 90° in advance of the point the force was applied.

9. What is the purpose of wing flaps?

   A— To enable the pilot to make steeper approaches to a landing without increasing airspeed.
   B— To relieve the pilot of maintaining continuous pressure on the controls.
   C— To decrease wing area to vary the lift.

10. In what flight condition is torque effect the greatest in a single-engine airplane?

    A— Low airspeed, high power, high angle of attack.

    B— Low airspeed, low power, low angle of attack.

    C— High airspeed, high power, high angle of attack.

11. What makes an airplane turn?

    A— Vertical component of lift.
    B— Horizontal component of lift.
    C— Centrifugal force.

12. As you maneuver an airplane you should realize that it can be stalled

    A— only when the nose is high and the speed is low.

    B— only when the airspeed decreases to the published stalling speed.

    C— at any airspeed and in any attitude.

13. To counteract the effect of torque in a conventional single engine propeller-driven airplane, a pilot would normally add

    A— left rudder pressure during the takeoff roll and while climbing with full power.

    B— right rudder pressure when entering a glide from level cruising flight.

    C— right rudder pressure during the takeoff roll and while climbing with full power.

14. To generate the same amount of lift as altitude is increased, an airplane must be flown at

    A— the same true airspeed regardless of angle of attack.

    B— a lower true airspeed and a greater angle of attack.

    C— a higher true airspeed for any given angle of attack.

15. During a spin to the left, which wing(s) are stalled?

    A— Both wings are stalled.
    B— Neither wing is stalled.
    C— Only the left wing is stalled.

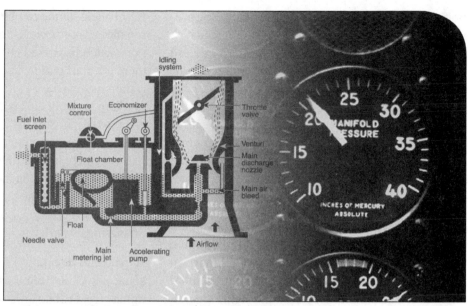

Lesson 2 Aircraft Systems

You don't have to be a mechanic to be a safe pilot, but a knowledge of how your engine works and what the engine instruments are telling you will make it easier to give your engine tender loving care and get long, reliable service from it.

There are many similarities between an automobile engine and an airplane engine. Both are **internal combustion engines**, both use spark plugs, and both use some type of fuel metering system related to throttle position. Many advances in modern automotive engines such as turbocharging and fuel injection are based on earlier aviation applications. *Note: Diesel engines, which do not use spark plugs, are moving into general aviation. They will be discussed later.*

An aircraft engine is a four-cycle engine: Figure 2-1 on the next page illustrates the four cycles (some homebuilt aircraft use two-cycle engines). The fuel-air mixture is drawn into the cylinder as the piston moves downward on the intake stroke; as the piston moves upward with the valves closed, the mixture is compressed during the compression stroke. The burning of the fuel-air mixture after ignition drives the piston downward during the power stroke, and as the piston rises again with the exhaust valve open the exhaust stroke ends the four stroke cycle. Because

your aircraft engine has four or more cylinders, each igniting at a different time, there is always one piston on a power stroke, and the process is continuous.

The valves do not open and close as neatly as Figure 2-1 implies—at times both the intake and exhaust valves are open to improve efficient movement of the fuel-air charge into the cylinder and removal of exhaust products from the cylinder. Their movement is controlled by the camshaft through pushrods, and valve timing is critical to performance. A worn cam, a weak valve spring—anything that affects valve movement affects power output.

Ignition

Your gas-powered airplane engine uses a **magneto** as the source of ignition. Magneto may not be a familiar term to you, but your gas lawnmower, chain saw, or outboard motor all use magnetos. A magneto is a self-contained source of electrical impulses, using the physical motion of a coil and a fixed magnetic field to develop ignition voltage. To start the engine, you provide that physical motion by pulling a cord on your lawnmower, chain saw, or outboard. The starter motor does the job in the airplane, rotating the engine until the magneto-developed spark ignites the mixture. You have probably seen older airplanes without electrical systems (and newer airplanes with starter problems) being started manually—rotating the propeller by hand ("propping") causes the magneto to generate a voltage which goes to the spark plug to ignite the fuel/air mixture. Hand-propping an airplane is a hazardous undertaking which requires an experienced and knowledgeable person both in the cockpit and at the propeller. Once an airplane engine is started, the magnetos provide continuous ignition on their own—the airplane's electrical system and the starter motor have done their jobs. The master switch plays no further role in engine operation.

Each cylinder in your airplane engine has two spark plugs, each fired by a different magneto (*see* Figure 2-2). This has two advantages: better combustion efficiency, and safety. The engine will run on either magneto if one should develop a problem. *Magnetos are totally independent of the aircraft electrical system.*

When you turn the ignition off, with a key or with switches, you are connecting the electrical output of the magneto to the metal block of the engine where it is shorted to electrical ground and cannot fire the spark plugs. This "shorting out" is done through a wire called a P-lead, and if a P-lead is broken its associated magneto can fire the spark plugs even with the ignition in the OFF position. For this reason, you should treat all propellers with respect—moving the propeller might cause a magneto to start the engine unexpectedly if a P-lead has broken. During the pre-

flight check of the airplane and its systems you will run the engine on each magneto separately. The ignition switch is marked OFF-LEFT-RIGHT-BOTH, if there is a start button, and OFF-L-R-BOTH-START if there is not (the START position is spring-loaded to return to the BOTH position when finger pressure is removed). In the OFF position, the P-leads of both magnetos are grounded; in the LEFT position, the right magneto is grounded and you are checking the operation of the left magneto. In the RIGHT position, then, the P-lead of the left magneto is grounded, and in the BOTH position, both magnetos are capable of delivering a spark.

As you cut the ignition sources in half you will lose some power, reflected as a drop in revolutions per minute (rpm). If no drop occurs when one magneto is shut off, that magneto probably has a broken P-lead, and the flight should be delayed until a mechanic checks it. Some authorities recommend checking for a broken P-lead just before shutting the engine down after a flight, by turning the ignition switch to its "OFF" position momentarily while at idle power; if the engine continues to run, there is probably a broken P-lead.

You should check your engine's magnetos each time you are in the runup area preparing for takeoff. Magnetos can develop faults that are not readily detectable in cruising flight but which might rob the engine of the power required for takeoff.

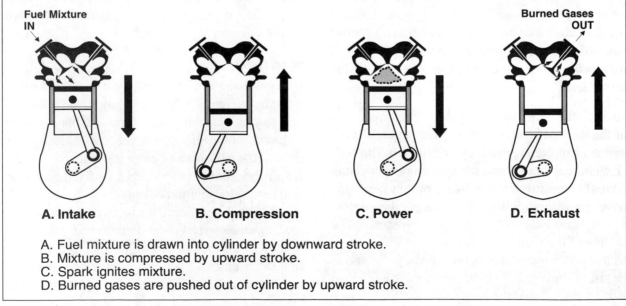

A. Fuel mixture is drawn into cylinder by downward stroke.
B. Mixture is compressed by upward stroke.
C. Spark ignites mixture.
D. Burned gases are pushed out of cylinder by upward stroke.

Figure 2-1. Four strokes of an aircraft engine

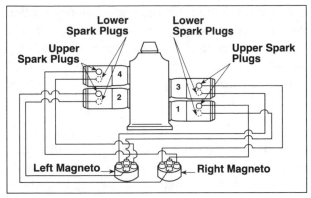

Figure 2-2. Spark plugs and magnetos

The Katana A-1's Rotax engine uses two electronic ignition systems similar to those used in automobiles. They are powered by an engine-driven generator (independent of the alternator that provides electrical power to the airplane's systems). The Katana C-1 uses a 125-HP fuel-injected Continental engine.

After-market electronic ignition systems that replace magnetos are available for Lycoming engines. With this type of ignition, shutting off the master switch *does* stop the engine.

Induction Systems

An airplane engine is a big air pump, taking in air through the induction system, mixing it with fuel, burning it, then pumping it overboard through the exhaust system. You will become familiar with two types of induction systems: **carburetor** and **fuel injection.** Figure 2-3 shows a float-type carburetor similar to those in most light airplane installations.

Carburetor-type induction systems are generally less expensive than fuel injection, and are easier to adjust. However, they do not deliver an equal fuel/air mixture to each cylinder, and are prone to induction system icing.

Almost all aircraft carburetors are "updraft" carbs; air is drawn in at the bottom and flows upward. Excess fuel caused by improper starting technique flows downward into the bottom of the cowling or onto the ground.

As air flows upward through a restriction called the venturi, its speed increases and pressure drops (remember Bernoulli's Theorem?). The air in the float chamber is vented to the outside, so the difference between outside air and the reduced pressure

in the venturi forces fuel out of the float chamber, through the main discharge nozzle, and into the airstream. The amount of airflow through the carburetor is governed by the position of the throttle valve—you control that directly from the cockpit. The amount of fuel metered into the mixture is governed by the mixture control, and you control that in the cockpit as well. When you "step on the gas" in your automobile, or add power in your airplane, you are really controlling airflow directly and fuel flow indirectly. You actually increase power by stepping on the air, not the gas.

As the fuel and air mixture expands in the carburetor throat, it drops in temperature by 40° to 60°, due to both expansion of the air and evaporation of the fuel. If there is any moisture in the intake air, this sudden drop in temperature may cause the moisture to freeze on the carburetor walls and throttle valve, restricting airflow and reducing power just as surely as if you had retarded the throttle. Power loss due to carburetor ice is a possibility any time the outside air temperature is between 20°F and 70°F, with high rela-tive humidity or visible moisture in the air. *Warning:* Your engine can develop carburetor ice on a nice clear day in July, if the relative humidity is high enough! Prove this to yourself by taking a can of soda outside on such a day…beads of water will form on the surface of the can. Where does the water come from, through the side of the can? Of course not—it condenses out of the air.

To counter this threat, the manufacturer provides a carburetor heat control which takes heated air from

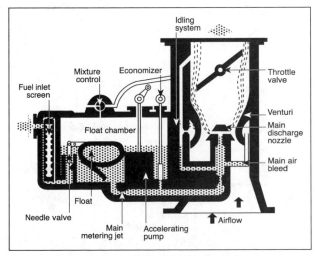

Figure 2-3. Float-type carburetor

a muff around the exhaust and directs it into the carburetor to melt the ice. Because the air gets its heat from the exhaust, carburetor heat must be used before the engine loses so much power that the heat from the exhaust is inadequate to do the job. This should be no problem if you keep an eye on your engine power instruments when operating in conditions where carburetor ice is possible.

As ice forms on the throttle valve and in the carburetor throat the reduction in power will be reflected in a reduction in rpm (with a fixed-pitch propeller). Application of FULL carburetor heat will result in a momentary further loss of rpm; then, as the ice melts and makes its way through the engine in the form of water, the rpms will rise again. (Expect a moment or two of engine roughness!) The initial reduction in power experienced when the carburetor heat is applied is due to hot air being less dense than cold air—this reduction in intake air density makes the fuel/air mixture ratio richer. As you can see in Figure 2-4, the carburetor heat control selects either cold, filtered air or hot, unfiltered air.

Carburetor heat should be either full ON, which causes a slight power loss, or full OFF while you watch for symptoms of icing. Applying full carburetor heat continuously cannot hurt the engine, and most of the rpms lost when heat is applied can be regained by leaning the mixture. A slight loss of power is better than the complete power loss that can result from carburetor icing. Partial heat is only used when you have additional instrumentation intended specifically for the detection of carburetor ice. The National Transportation Safety Board recommends that full carburetor heat be used whenever power is reduced below that required for cruise (as does

Lycoming). Figure 2-5 illustrates the temperature and relative humidity relationships leading to potential carburetor ice. Note that warm summer days afford plenty of opportunity for carb icing, and few pilots recognize the danger when the sky is clear and the temperature is high.

The Rotax 912 used in the Katana A-1 has two carburetors that self-adjust for altitude so that there is no need for a mixture control. It does, however, have a choke to enrich the mixture for starting. Its carburetor heat control operates conventionally.

The Primer

Nothing about engine operation is more subject to "old wive's tales" and "my instructor told me..." stories than starting the engine. The boilerplate warning is, of course, to follow the procedure in the manufacturer's operating handbook, but in many cases that information is sketchy, such as "prime with one to three strokes of manual priming pump."

First, though, let's get past the idea of pumping the throttle. The carburetors of most engines rated at

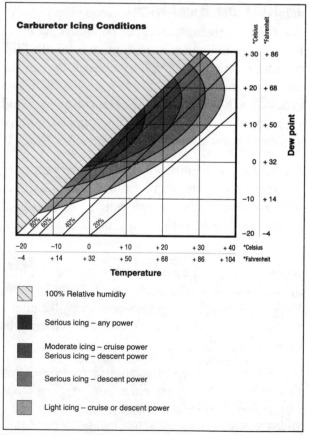

Figure 2-5. Carburetor icing conditions

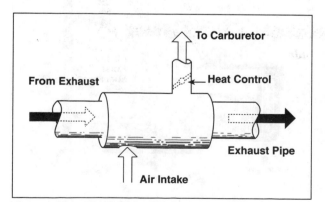

Figure 2-4. Carburetor heat muff

more than 115 horsepower have accelerator pumps, which give an extra shot of fuel into the carburetor throat if the throttle is moved briskly. The design function of an accelerator pump is to increase the normal fuel output during acceleration for takeoff. Check the "Ignition and Starting" data contained in Section 7 of your operating manual to determine whether or not your engine has an accelerator pump.

Remember what I said about improper starting dumping raw fuel into the cowling or onto the ground? The primer (that round silver knob over on the left side of the panel) delivers fuel to the intake ports of the cylinders, where it can't leak out but is available to be mixed with air in the cylinders to create a combustible mixture.

Crack the throttle about one-half inch, then unlock the primer by turning the knob until the little protrusions clear the slots; as you pull out on the plunger, you are creating suction that draws fuel into the primer body. When the plunger barrel is completely full (you will hear it in most cases), press the plunger in as quickly as you can…you are creating a spray of fuel into the intake manifold. Use the recommended number of strokes, then push the knob in and lock it. Tug on it to be sure that it is locked, because air will leak past an unlocked primer and make the engine run rough. Engage the starter.

In extremely cold weather, an old bush pilot trick is to have the plunger pulled out and the barrel filled as the engine is cranked…as it begins to fire, pushing the plunger in feeds fuel where it is needed most. But check to be sure that the knob is in and locked after the engine is running.

Fuel Injection

A fuel-injected induction system delivers an equal fuel/air mixture to each cylinder and requires careful adjustment. Because there is no carburetor, there can be no carburetor ice. Fuel injection systems are installed in more powerful airplanes, and virtually all **turbocharged** engines. The Katana C-1's Continental engine uses fuel injection, as does the Liberty XL-2. This is unusual for trainers, but gives students no trouble at all. Fuel injection systems cannot develop carburetor ice, but induction system icing is not impossible. The intake air passes through a filter, and if that filter is clogged by wet snow or ice, the air supply to the engine will be reduced and a power loss will result. (*See* Figure 2-6.)

The primary power instrument in a fuel-injected engine installation is the **manifold pressure gauge.** Induction system icing will show up as a reduction in manifold pressure, and if you suspect that a loss of power is due to icing, there will always be some form

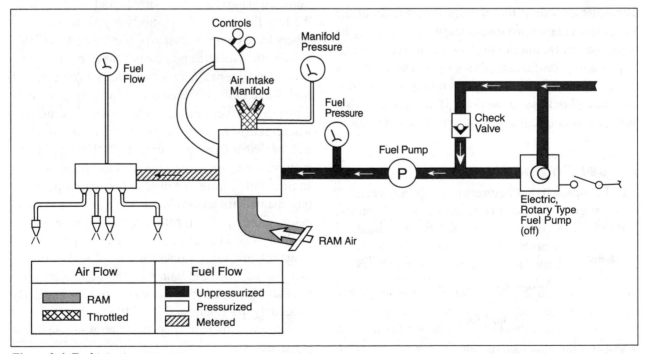

Figure 2-6. Fuel injection system

of alternate air source so that the engine can breathe. When a controllable pitch (or constant speed) propeller is installed, the reduction in manifold pressure will be the only indication of induction system icing because the rpm will be held constant by a governor. Both the Katana A-1 and C-1 have constant-speed propellers, and their engine instrumentation includes a manifold pressure gauge.

A manifold pressure gauge acts like a barometer, measuring the pressure in the intake manifold downstream (on the engine side) of the throttle butterfly. (This is identified in Figure 2-3 as the **throttle valve**, and serves the same function in a fuel injection system—control of the amount of air entering the induction system.) At power settings near idle, when the descending pistons are trying to pull air past the closed throttle butterfly, the manifold pressure is low. As you open the throttle to increase power, the pressure measured in the intake manifold increases as airflow increases. Without turbocharging, manifold pressure will approach but never equal the outside air pressure (unless you shut the engine down, something I don't recommend unless all three wheels are on the ground).

Fuel injected engines have a reputation of being hard to start when hot. This problem, when it exists, is usually caused by vapor lock, the result of fuel boiling into vapor in the fuel lines. When you shut down the engine at the completion of a flight the flow of cooling air no longer exists, and the engine must simply radiate its heat to its surroundings. It is inevitable that the fuel lines absorb some of this heat. The manufacturer's approved flight manual will include a "hot start" procedure. If this doesn't work you may simply have to wait until the fuel cools to a liquid state.

Diesel Engines

Two European manufacturers have already certified diesel engines for use in U.S.-certificated airframes, and American manufacturers can't be far behind. As a student, you probably won't fly behind a diesel, but as a certificated pilot you might own or rent one.

Why diesel? Our domestic petroleum industry has been trying to get out of the aviation gasoline business for decades; diesel fuel is easier for them to make and the market is larger. JetA is not the same as automotive diesel (you can't use automotive diesel in aircraft diesels); the market is the military and the airlines, not highway users. Your local FBO may not even have a JetA tank unless they do a lot of corporate jet/turboprop business.

In the middle of 2011, the price differential is not that much different—JetA is slightly less expensive than 100LL. Aircraft diesels burn fewer gallons per hour, though, bringing overall costs down and extending range.

The certificated engines are turbocharged and liquid-cooled, and they have single-control power management—no mixture control, no carb heat, no propeller control. They maintain sea-level takeoff power to 10,000 feet MSL without the loss of power we experience with gas engines. They use glow plugs for starting, so there is no need for special hot start/cold start procedures. One significant drawback for those pilots who like to run a tank dry before switching is a diesel's reluctance to air-start at cruising altitude; they like the denser air at lower altitudes for air-starts.

You can expect significant changes in the Pilot Operating Handbooks for those airplanes certificated with diesel engines.

Fuel Systems

Some airplanes have very simple fuel systems, with the fuel flowing to the engine by gravity feed, and others have complex systems of main and auxiliary tanks with associated pumps and switches. You must understand your airplane's fuel system to be sure that fuel is available to the engine from startup to shutdown. Every year pilots make forced landings (or worse) due to fuel starvation, only to learn that fuel was available from another tank. Follow the manufacturer's starting instructions to the letter. A cold engine will require priming, either with a plunger-type manual primer, an electric fuel pump, or in some cases, pumping the throttle. Avoid overpriming—you may flood the engine or create a fire hazard. If your manufacturer's operating handbook requires that you take off and land with the fuel selector on the main tanks, or cautions you to use the auxiliary tanks only in straight-and-level flight, observe those restrictions—there may be interruptions in fuel flow if you don't.

High-wing airplanes use gravity to feed fuel to the engine; low-wing airplanes use engine-driven fuel pumps to pull fuel up to the engine. The fuel system for low-wing airplanes includes an electric fuel pumps both to establish fuel pressure for starting and to take over if the engine-driven pump fails. Some high-wing airplanes have electric fuel pumps with two- or three-position switches designed to deliver fuel to the intake system under low or high pressure depending on the situation. Study and understand the use of these switches before you fly an airplane with such a system—the high-pressure position is *usually* intended for use only in case of engine-driven pump failure, and selecting high pressure can flood and/or cause an operating engine to shut down. Installations are sufficiently different that this text will make no attempt to discuss details.

All fuel tanks must be vented to the atmosphere. As fuel flows to the engine, air must replace it in the tank; if the vent is clogged, the resulting vacuum will result in engine stoppage at best, fuel tank collapse at worst. The location of the vent is usually obvious, but can occasionally be found on the fuel filler cap.

Note: Do not use automobile fuel in an engine for which no Supplemental Type Certificate has been issued, and always be sure that the airplane and fuel truck are both grounded to avoid a spark from the discharge of static electricity. For the same reason, never fuel an airplane from a plastic container—use a metal container that is grounded to the airplane.

Mixture Control

An airplane engine needs a mixture of approximately 15 parts of air for each part of fuel. If there is more air than 15:1 the mixture is called "lean," and when the ratio falls below 15:1 it is a "rich" mixture. There is a mixture control on your automobile carburetor or fuel injection system which is adjusted during tune-ups or when you move to the mountains from the flatlands (if you have electronic fuel injection a computer accomplishes this task). Airplanes make altitude changes of that magnitude in a matter of minutes, and you can't pull off the road to adjust the mixture, so the manufacturer provides a mixture control in the cockpit. Your engine needs additional cooling while supplying the power demands of takeoff and initial climb, and that additional cooling is provided by burning extra fuel or using a full rich

mixture. Some carburetors have an enrichment valve that provides extra fuel for cooling when the throttle is full forward (a good argument against reducing power while climbing). Pumping the throttle will cause raw fuel to drip from the carburetor into the bottom of the cowl and drip all over the nosewheel, causing a potential fire condition. But check your manual…engines with certain carburetors require that your pump the throttle.

The mixture is purposely set slightly rich for ease in starting. Remembering that the correct ratio of fuel to air must exist before ignition can be sustained, and that the throttle controls the air supply, if the engine is reluctant to start it is good practice to *slowly* advance the throttle. Sooner or later, the fuel-air ratio will be "just right" and the engine will fire. Shoving the throttle forward simply makes the mixture too lean to burn.

In most cases, spark plug fouling is caused by a mixture that is overly rich; this is especially true during ground operations. Don't be reluctant to lean the mixture while taxiing—you can't possibly hurt the engine by leaning at such a low power setting—but be sure to return it to full rich as you roll out onto the active runway. In fact, leaning aggressively will help in another way: if you forget to move the mixture control to full rich for a sea-level takeoff, the mixture will be too lean to burn when you apply power for takeoff, and the engine will let you know about it in a hurry. Anyway, your manufacturer's checklist almost certainly includes "Mixture—RICH" in its "Before Takeoff" section. However, full rich is not needed when the density altitude is high—that's when you want to do a full-power runup and lean for best power. Some pilots, when taking off from a high-altitude airport, begin the takeoff roll with the mixture full rich and slowly retard the control until they can hear and feel the engine delivering the best power for takeoff. The seat of your pants will tell you when the mixture is right.

As the airplane climbs into air of diminishing density, the volume of air passing through the carburetor does not decrease but its weight does, and that upsets the 15:1 ratio toward the rich side: weight of fuel is unchanged, weight of air is decreased. Most manufacturer's operating handbooks require that the mixture control be full rich during climbs—

check your handbook. When you arrive at cruise altitude, lean the mixture as recommended by the manufacturer. If you fail to lean at cruise altitude you are wasting fuel and are not operating the engine efficiently. Retarding the mixture control until the tachometer reaches a peak will do the trick in the absence of instrumentation for precise mixture adjustment. (See the section below on "Mixture Instrumentation.") As noted before (Page 2–4), the Katana A-1's carburetors automatically adjust for changes in altitude.

As you descend from cruise altitude, the reverse situation occurs: the mixture control has been leaned back to reduce the amount of fuel entering the mixture, and as the airplane descends into air of increasing density, the ratio swings to the lean side, with too much air for the amount of fuel. The recommended procedure is to enrich the mixture during the descent—but if you forget, the situation will be called to your attention by roughness as the engine tries to run on too little fuel. You will probably make several small mixture adjustments during the descent prior to going to full rich as a part of the pre-landing checklist. The best way to lean the mixture is to keep it at the leanest setting compatible with safe operating temperatures; too hot is better than too cold. You can't get the mixture too lean without the engine letting you know that it is unhappy. One thing is certain—pushing the red knob full-forward when starting a descent does nothing positive for the engine.

Any time air of reduced density is introduced into the induction system, you can expect the symptoms of a too-rich mixture. If you are flying at 9,500 feet with the mixture properly leaned and add carburetor heat "just in case," the hot, less dense air will enrich the mixture and may cause rough running until the carburetor heat control is returned to the cold position. If you are operating at a high-altitude airport, the thin air may cause roughness during idle operation and taxiing, and the addition of carburetor heat during runup will make the roughness worse. Under those conditions, lean the mixture for the highest rpm during a *full-power* runup and leave it in that position for takeoff.

Because the mixture control is used to shut the engine down on the ground, pilots are occasionally reluctant to lean the mixture for fear of killing the engine in flight. Eliminate this fear by leaning aggressively during a flight lesson. Just pull the red knob back until the engine complains, and then push it forward until the engine runs smoothly again.

Mixture Instrumentation

Your airplane may be equipped with an **exhaust gas temperature gauge** (EGT) for precise mixture adjustment. These instruments read the highest temperature when the mixture is "just right": too much air or too much fuel, and the exhaust temperature drops. There are also mixture settings to be used for best power and for best economy. Each engine manufacturer has guidelines on how the EGT instrument should be used, so before you use the EGT for mixture adjustment, familiarize yourself with the manufacturer's recommendations.

Airplanes with fuel injection systems will have a fuel flow gauge calibrated in gallons per hour or pounds per hour, and the performance tables will tell you the correct fuel flow for climb and cruise power at different altitudes. Although these instruments are calibrated as flow meters, they actually measure fuel pressure, and a restriction in the fuel metering system may cause an incorrect high fuel flow indication. Solid state transducers are becoming available which actually measure fuel flow very accurately. For a few dollars more you can get an instrument that tells fuel flow, fuel remaining, how much fuel will remain when you reach your destination (based on GPS, of course) and other nuggets of information.

Fuel Grade and Contamination

An airplane engine is designed to operate most efficiently on one grade of fuel. There are three grades of aviation fuel in use today: Grade 80, which contains a pink dye and is increasingly hard to find, Grade 100LL, which is colored blue, and grade 100, which is colored green. The latter two differ only in lead content. Where the correct fuel for your engine is not available, it is permissible to use a higher grade temporarily; only take on board enough fuel to get you to the nearest airport with the correct fuel. If your engine specifications call for Grade 80, you can use a higher grade but check the engine manufacturer's website to see if special procedures have been issued. Believe me, if your engine is old enough to require Grade 80, the information in the Owner's Manual/

Flight Manual is almost certainly out of date. *Never use a fuel of a lower grade than that specified for your engine. Non-aviation diesel fuel is dyed a deep red; 80-octane users should look for a pink tint. If in doubt, drop some suspect fuel on a piece of paper. Aviation gasoline evaporates quickly, leaving a dye stain; Kerosene, diesel, or jet fuel will spread out and feel greasy to the touch.*

If the wrong grade of aviation gasoline has been pumped into your tanks (or, even worse, jet fuel), it will take only a few minutes of operation for destructive forces to be generated. It is always good practice to supervise the fueling of your airplane; make sure that both your airplane and the fuel truck are connected to an electrical ground to avoid static discharge.

Note: Many airplane engines have received Supplemental Type Certificates (STCs) authorizing the use of automotive fuel. Make no assumptions: do not use automobile gas unless you are sure it is approved for your engine. Do not use any fuel containing ethanol; it attacks fuel system components. You will hear hangar-flying stories from pilots who have used autogas with ethanol for years without any problems. Ethanol attacks different materials in different ways...don't bet your engine's life on someone else's experience.

FAA tests indicate that engines using automobile fuel are more prone to induction system icing.

In addition to being sure that the fuel being pumped into your tanks is the correct grade, you must also guard against fuel contamination. The most common contaminant is water: airplane engines refuse to burn water, and your engine will let you know there is water in the fuel by running rough or stopping entirely. A common source of water in the tank is condensation. If you leave the fuel tanks less than full overnight, the cooling temperatures will cause moisture that is present in the air in the tanks to condense on the cold walls of the tank and sink to the bottom because water is heavier than gasoline.

One of your preflight duties is to drain fuel samples from low points in the fuel system; if any water shows up in the sample, continue to drain until no further contamination is apparent. The fuel pickup for the engine is at the low point in the tank, and water should show up there first, but it is possible for water to pool in the tank and not move toward the low point until the airplane moves. If the airplane has been parked in one place for an extended period, rock the wings vigorously and drain the sumps again after giving any trapped water time to move toward the low point of the fuel system. If the airplane has been parked on a slope, water may collect in the tank on the downhill side—drain the sumps with the airplane on a level surface.

You can practically eliminate condensation by being sure that the airplane's tanks are full at the end of each day's flying. While you are checking for water in the fuel, look for dirt or any other foreign matter which might cause a problem in the carburetor or fuel injectors. The fuel passes through many filters by the time it reaches your tanks from the refinery, and the odds of having a contaminant pumped into your tanks are low, but a moment's inattention during the fueling process can lead to disaster. All states have "sump and dump" laws, prohibiting the dumping of fuel on the ground or ramp, so you will have to find an environmentally safe place to dump the fuel you have drained from the sumps.

Any discussion of fuel contamination must address the question of running a tank dry. Never run a tank dry. The primary consideration, especially true with fuel injection, is introducing air into the fuel tank. A secondary consideration, especially true with fuel injection, is introducing air into the fuel lines when the tank runs dry. Fuel injected engines may be difficult to re-start even when you have switched to a full tank. Both electric and engine-driven fuel pumps work best with fluid, not with air, and it may take a few moments before the pumps are re-primed to deliver fuel to the engine. *Do not run a fuel tank dry.*

The Federal Aviation Regulations require that your fuel gauge be accurate at only one reading—empty. Any other reading should be viewed with suspicion. Never trust a fuel gauge—unless it is reading empty, of course. Always check the fuel level visually or with a dip stick. (*See* Lesson 11 for fuel planning.)

Detonation and Preignition

When driving your automobile, any unusual noise usually gets your attention. If you notice a pinging or knocking sound when adding power, you know that you may have to make a shop visit to have the timing checked. In flight, you can't hear the engine pinging, and must be sure to avoid conditions which might lead to **detonation**. Detonation occurs when the fuel/air mixture explodes instead of burning evenly. This develops stresses that can destroy the engine in a very short time. Factors which lead to detonation are fuel of too low a grade, high operating temperature, or a mixture which is too lean. To avoid detonation, you must use the specified fuel grade (or a higher grade), avoid operation with too lean a mixture, and keep a watchful eye on engine temperatures. You cannot cause detonation by leaning while taxiing.

Preignition occurs when a "hot spot" within the cylinder causes the fuel/air mixture to ignite prematurely, and is usually caused by deposits on the spark plugs or valves. It usually has the same causes as detonation, and can be prevented in the same way. Your reaction, when detonation or preignition are suspected, must be directed toward cooling the engine. A richer mixture, a lower power setting, or a higher airspeed will help cool the engine and reduce any tendency toward detonation.

Oil

Oil performs two functions in an airplane engine—lubrication and cooling. The lubrication function is obvious, but just as important is its function of carrying heat away from the engine block on its way through the oil cooler and back to the oil sump. When you check the oil level during your preflight inspection, you are ensuring that there is sufficient oil to provide the cooling function—the minimum oil level stated in the Pilot's Operating Handbook is just enough to handle lubrication. If the manual calls for six quarts and you put six quarts in, one of those quarts will probably be blown overboard when the oil heats up in flight—so operating a bit short of full is not a bad idea. A good rule-of-thumb is about ⅔ of capacity: Five or six quarts in an 8-quart engine and 8 quarts in a 12-quart engine. It never hurts to have a quart of oil in the baggage compartment just in case.

If you are not careful to ensure that the oil filler cap is firmly in place after checking the oil level, you might find oil all over the engine (and maybe the windshield). If the cap is the screw-on kind, using too much muscle when securing it might make it impossible for the next person to check the oil without a pipe wrench—just make it tight enough to compress the O-ring.

Engine Instrumentation

An airplane *must* have at least an oil temperature gauge and an oil pressure gauge, but may have additional instruments to give you a better picture of what is going on inside the cowling. A major consideration is avoiding overheating, and the engine manufacturer uses several methods to accomplish this. Almost all aircraft engines are air-cooled; an increasing number of liquid-cooled engines are showing up in the general aviation fleet. During preflight, you will see the cooling fins on the cylinders and may have to check the level of coolant. The excess fuel in a rich mixture is used as a cooling agent during takeoff and climb, while oil serves as a coolant at all times. The oil which circulates through and around the engine as a lubricant picks up heat as it travels. It passes through an oil cooler, where the heat is given up to the air, and the oil is cooled for another trip around. The oil temperature gauge will reflect how well the oil is able to perform this cooling task. If you have allowed the oil level to fall below recommended levels, the amount available may not be enough to do the job adequately, and high oil temperature will result. Oil temperature at or near the red line should be a cause for concern, but so should low oil temperature. The oil temperature gauge (which usually gets its information from a relatively cool location in the system) should read between 180° and 200° for most engines; at cooler temperatures, any moisture in the oil will not be boiled away.

Just how long it takes for the oil pressure gauge to register a reading depends to a great extent on where the oil-pressure gauge pickup is and engine temperature before a start is attempted. Your engine suffers greater wear during starts than during any other phase of operation, because if the airplane has been idle for any length of time most of the oil will have drained down into the sump and the top end of the engine (especially where the cam follower rests against the cam lobe...this is the area that gets the greatest wear during starts) will be essentially without lubrication for several seconds while the oil makes its way up. After the engine starts, keep the rpm as low as practicable while the engine heats up enough for the oil temperature gauge to show an indication.

Be alert to "morning sickness." That's when the engine runs rough momentarily and then smooths out during the first start of the day. Instead of heaving a sigh of relief, you should head for the maintenance hangar. If the engine has one or more sticky valves or valve lifters, it will run rough until the oil warms up a little. Left untreated, this could lead to a valve sticking open or a bent valve stem.

The oil pressure gauge is an indication of how well the oil is lubricating the engine. High oil temperature *and* low oil pressure would indicate a *major* problem and usually calls for a landing at the nearest airport. The **cylinder head temperature** (CHT) **gauge**, when installed, is an excellent indicator of potentially damaging overheating. When the CHT (Figure 2-7) starts rising toward the red line, enriching the mixture, reducing power, increasing airspeed, or opening the cowl flaps (if installed) will all contribute to temperature reduction. Excessively high temperatures will cause power loss, detonation, increased oil consumption, and possible internal engine damage.

If your airplane has a constant speed propeller, read your engine's limitations in Section 2 of the Approved Flight Manual. See where it says (in most cases), "maximum power for continuous operation"? Then why reduce power to climb? Doing so doesn't help the engine, and may cause overheating. In any event, keep an eye on the cylinder head temperatures.

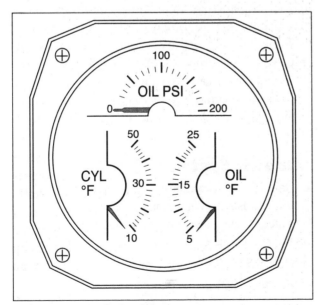

Figure 2-7. Cylinder head temperature gauge

A number of engine analyzers are available on the aftermarket, and they pay for themselves through fuel efficiency and early warning of engine problems.

Electrical System

The airplane's electrical system consists of a battery and a generator or alternator with associated voltage regulators, current limiters or other protective devices. The primary function of the battery is to provide power to the starter motor—after the engine starts, the magnetos provide ignition, and the generator or alternator takes on the task of powering the radios, instruments, lights, electrical landing gear or flaps, and recharging the battery. Individual circuits are protected by circuit breakers or fuses. Unlike fuses, circuit breakers can be reset rather than be replaced after an overload. The FAA cautions against resetting circuit breakers in flight because of the danger of fire. If you find a popped circuit breaker during preflight checks, don't simply reset it; something caused it to pop and you don't want to find out what it was when you are airborne.

Note that the magnetos are not part of the airplane's electrical system; if you lose your alternator and the battery drains down to nothing, the engine will still keep running. You will, of course, lose all lighting, means of navigation/communication (an argument in favor of backup handheld devices), and the electric fuel pump if you have one.

Most modern airplanes use alternators rather than generators. Early electrical systems used generators (first wind-driven, then geared to the engine). They were large and heavy in relation to their output; a generator creates voltage by rotating an armature in a magnetic field developed by current flowing through field coils. This would be a chicken-and-egg thing if it were not for residual magnetism in the field winding frame—it gets things started when the engine (and armature) are rotated by the starter. After that, a voltage regulator controls the current flow through the field windings and thus the output. The electrical output of an engine-driven generator is a function of engine speed, and generators became unable to handle the electrical demands of modern airplanes at taxiing and idle speeds. Airplane manufacturers switched to alternators because alternators are smaller and lighter for a given output and because the output voltage of an alternator is not dependent on engine speed. In combination with a voltage regulator, an alternator can provide a constant output voltage from idle rpm to full throttle.

Like a generator, however, an alternator requires current flow through its field windings in order to produce electricity. This current must come from the battery to the field windings through the solenoid (that's the click you hear when you turn on the master switch). If the airplane battery is totally discharged, the solenoid will not close (no click), therefore no current is available for the alternator field coils and the alternator is inoperative. If an external power source is available, use it, but follow the manufacturer's recommended procedure to the letter. Hand-propping will get the airplane back in the air, but the battery will not be recharged by the alternator. A new or recharged battery is the only answer. Alternator failure (which can be as simple as a broken or slipping drive belt) means that the battery must supply all required power until it is completely discharged, which may occur in a disconcertingly short time. Most airplanes with alternators have split electrical master switches (Figure 2-8) which allow the pilot to disconnect the alternator field coils from the battery after all non-essential electrical loads have been reduced. This will extend battery life for a few precious minutes.

You will find an **ammeter** on your instrument panel with a zero center and + and - indications, or a **loadmeter** which reads from zero to some value such as

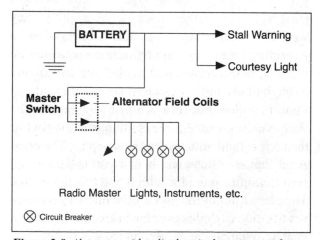

Figure 2-8. Alternator with split electrical master switches

75 amperes and reflects the actual electrical load on the alternator. With the zero center ammeter, a reading on the minus side indicates that the alternator is not providing enough electricity to recharge the battery. With a loadmeter, a reading of zero indicates that there is no alternator output. During the preflight runup, turn on the landing light or pilot heat momentarily to see if the ammeter reflects a change in the electrical load. If system failure is indicated or suspected in flight, turn off unnecessary electrical equipment to reduce the load on the battery. A clue: almost all fuel gauges are electric, and if both fuel gauges begin to sink toward empty you may be out of electricity instead of gas.

On the ground, when you turn on the airplane's master switch, listen for the click of the solenoid being operated by battery current, and for the electric gyro instruments to begin spinning. The absence of these audible clues means a dead battery. Learn what your airplane has for an electrical supply and what the normal and abnormal indications are. You may find that a re-set function (or a second voltage regulator) has been provided so that you can overcome momentary electrical failure. In any case, an electrical failure will not affect engine operation.

If your airplane has a split master switch, leaving the "ALT" side off during engine start will reduce the load on the battery. Don't forget to turn it *on* after the engine starts.

If your airplane has an avionics master switch, be sure that it is OFF during engine starts and is turned ON only after the engine is running smoothly, and after you have turned the ALT side of a split master switch ON. In airplanes without avionics master switches, all electronic devices should be turned OFF to avoid damage due to voltage fluctuations during starts.

Vacuum System

Certain flight instruments are powered by vacuum, just as windshield wipers on older cars were vacuum operated (Figure 2-9). The vacuum pump is mounted on the rear of the engine, together with other engine driven accessories such as fuel pumps and magnetos.

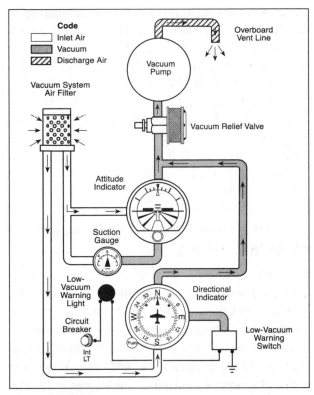

Figure 2-9. *Vacuum system*

There is a vacuum indicator on the instrument panel so that you can keep tabs on the health of the vacuum system. Vacuum pump drive shafts are designed to shear (like an outboard motor shear pin) if internal mechanical failure occurs.

Fixed-Pitch Propellers

A fixed-pitch propeller is a compromise between performance and speed. A propeller with a very flat blade angle (pitch) is called a climb prop. It takes very small bites of the air as it pulls itself and the airplane forward. The engine is able to develop takeoff power very quickly—you will notice in the specifications for your airplane a statement such as "150 horsepower at 2700 rpm"—and you will get good takeoff performance. When that flat-pitch propeller which revved up to 2,700 rpm very rapidly at sea level gets to 10,000 feet, however, taking small bites of thin air won't give you much cruise airspeed. If high speed at cruise altitude is what you want, you need a propeller with a greater blade angle, which will take bigger bites of the thin air and improve cruise speed. When taking off and climbing with a cruise propeller, however, you will be amazed at how much runway you will leave behind before that

propeller—now taking big bites of dense air—gets up to 2,700 rpm. You have sacrificed takeoff and climb performance for cruise speed. Any fixed-pitch propeller is, therefore, a performance compromise.

Controllable-Pitch (Constant-Speed) Propellers

The solution is a propeller that has a flat pitch (high rpm) for takeoff, and a coarse pitch (low rpm) for cruise: a **controllable-pitch propeller** or constant-speed propeller. These two names are used almost interchangeably. Although a controllable-pitch propeller was at one time a ground-adjustable propeller, today's installations use a governor to change blade angle and thus maintain constant rpm.

You will have two power instruments with a constant-speed propeller installation: the **tachometer**, and a **manifold pressure gauge** which is now your primary power instrument (Figure 2-10 on the next page). The manifold pressure gauge reacts directly to throttle movement. For takeoff, the propeller control (linked to the governor to control rpm) is set full forward for high rpm. After the engine/propeller team have done their work and gotten you into the air in a hurry, leave the throttle alone (for best cooling) and pull the prop control back 100–200 rpm to decrease noise complaints from airport neighbors. This goes against the accepted wisdom (to reduce power use the throttle first, then the prop control, but this reduces noise, not power). During the climb, because barometric pressure decreases 1 inch per 1,000 feet of altitude, you must adjust the throttle setting to maintain climb power.

At cruise altitude, set cruise power according to the manufacturer's cruise chart for that altitude; a good thumb rule is the lowest rpm setting that allows smooth engine operation without vibration, and a manifold pressure (throttle) setting that meets your requirements for either speed or economy. The commonly accepted wisdom is that you should avoid high manifold pressure with low RPMs...but that is exactly how Lindbergh taught pilots to manage power for long flights over the Pacific during World War II. There is a test question for which the commonly accepted wisdom is the correct answer, but there are many situations to which it does not apply.

Figure 2-10. *Tachometer and manifold pressure gauge*

As you retard the prop control at altitude, the governor will increase the blade angle to take bigger bites of the air (low rpm): the characteristics of a cruise prop. Once you have set the propeller control to the desired rpm, the governor will change blade angle as required to maintain that rpm. If you have to add power to climb, or to increase airspeed, always advance the propeller control before the throttle; this will ensure that dangerously high pressures are not developed in the cylinders. Most pre-landing checklists include a reminder to move the propeller control to the high rpm position, to position it properly in case of an aborted landing. Before blindly following this procedure, however, use a little common sense. Is there an airplane at the hold line waiting for take-off? Is there a child with a bicycle or a loose animal near the runway? In that kind of situation, it is wise to prepare for a go-around. If there is no potential conflict, leave the mixture and prop controls alone until the wheels are on the runway. If you do push

the prop control full forward, you have completed the first half of the "increase power" procedure.

Noise is another consideration. When you move the propeller controller forward to its high rpm position while carrying enough power to bring the governor into play, people on the ground will hear an annoying brr-a-a-a-p-p-p—I know you have heard it, too. That's the kind of thing that leads to airport closures. Either push the prop forward while at a fairly high altitude above the ground or hold off until the manifold pressure is less than 15 inches.

Full Authority Digital Engine Controls (FADEC)

Coming soon to an airplane near you: single-knob control over throttle, propeller, and mixture. This one-control-does-all system is already being installed on some new production airplanes, such as the Liberty XL-2, and some entrepreneur will surely get permission to retrofit older airplanes. When that day comes, you won't have to worry about mixture control or whether to advance the throttle or prop control first…the magic of microprocessors will do the worrying for you. This is part of a movement toward optimized engine operation, in which pilot technique has been replaced by technology.

Turbocharging

We have discussed how the decrease in air density with altitude causes the manifold pressure to drop, requiring more throttle to maintain climb power. A turbocharger (Figure 2-11) allows sea level manifold pressure to be maintained to much higher altitudes by compressing air and packing it into the intake manifold. A turbine wheel is spun by exhaust gas, and a compressor on the same shaft compresses outside air and directs it into the induction system.

A "waste gate" controls the amount of exhaust that passes over the turbine. When no turbocharging is needed or desired, the waste gate is fully open and the exhaust gases bypass the turbine.

As manifold pressure drops off, and "boosting" is required, the waste gate is adjusted so that more of the exhaust gases pass through the turbine. When the waste gate is fully closed, all of the exhaust passes through the turbine before being discharged to the atmosphere, and further climb will cause manifold pressure to decrease. When full boost from the turbocharger is being used, and further climb will result in reduced power, the engine has reached its critical altitude.

Some turbocharger installations require that you control the manifold pressure manually, while others use automatic controllers. Where manual control is provided, the pilot must be sure that the waste gate is fully open prior to takeoff, except at high altitude airports where additional power may be required. Applying the full exhaust force to the turbine at a low altitude airport by having the waste gate closed will cause destructive pressures (overboosting). Automatic controllers adjust the waste gate position in accordance with power demands, and the possibility of overboosting is eliminated. Many turbocharger installations have a fixed orifice through which a minimum amount of exhaust gas always passes, bypassing the waste gate. This limits the maximum available power but reduces the possibility of overboosting.

Turbocharging allows you to get above most of the weather, but it has its drawbacks. The discharge air from the compressor to the induction system is very hot, and hot air is less dense than cool air. This raises the possibility of having to run an overly rich mixture to keep temperatures down. Many turbocharger installations include an intercooler, a heat exchanger which cools the air coming from the compressor before it enters the intake manifold.

Pilots of turbocharged airplanes must be very temperature conscious, keeping in mind that high temperatures can lead to preignition or detonation. They must also guard against sudden power reductions which will shock-cool the red-hot turbocharger. Turbocharger installations may have additional engine instrumentation, such as a **compressor discharge temperature gauge** (CDT), so that the pilot can get maximum utilization from the turbocharger without developing damaging internal engine temperatures.

It is critically important for you to allow at least five minutes at idle before shutting down a turbocharged

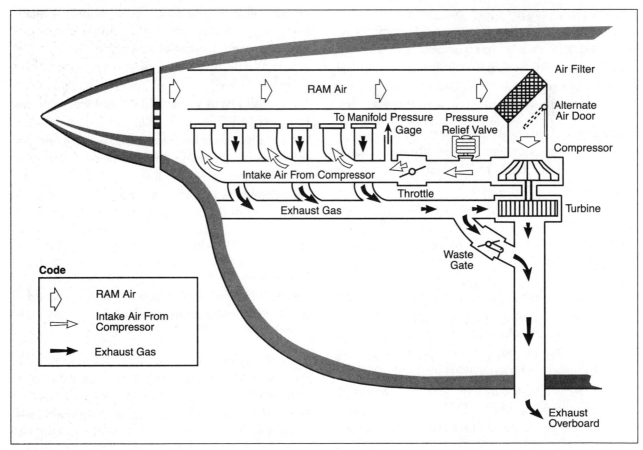

Figure 2-11. Turbocharging system

engine. As long as the engine is running, oil is being circulated through the turbo's bearings to carry away the intense heat developed as it spins at over 60,000 rpm. If you starve those bearings of circulating oil, the thin film of oil remaining will turn to carbon ("coke") and create major problems in the future as it breaks into small pieces and clogs up the plumbing. A quick shot of power to position the airplane for parking restarts the five-minute clock.

Pressurization

A turbocharged airplane can take a pilot to altitudes where there is insufficient oxygen to sustain life, and a supplemental oxygen supply is mandatory to take full advantage of turbocharging unless the airplane is pressurized. Pressurization allows the pilot and passengers to enjoy near-sea level pressure in the cabin at flight altitudes above 10,000 feet, and cabin pressures in the order of 8,000 feet at altitudes up to 40,000 feet.

A pressurized airplane is very tightly sealed, and is much stronger structurally than an unpressurized airplane. As you walk around the ramp, you can identify pressurized airplanes by their rounded windows and doors. The pressurization system takes compressed air (called "bleed air") from the turbocharger and, in effect, "inflates" the cabin to maintain a comfortable cabin pressure for passengers. Bleed air is also used for cabin heating and deicing functions on jet aircraft.

Every pressurized airplane has a maximum allowable differential between the pressure in the cabin and the outside atmosphere. This maximum is based on structural considerations, because it is possible to have too much cabin pressure (*see* Figure 2-12). A pressurization controller operates an "outflow valve," which allows air to leak out of the cabin at a controlled rate to maintain a pressure differential well below the maximum allowable. The outflow valve is backed up by a safety valve that will release pressure before the maximum differential is reached. Air constantly leaks out of the cabin of a pressurized airplane through the outflow valve, and only a large opening (such as a failed window) would lower the cabin pressure enough to require that the occupants use an emergency oxygen system.

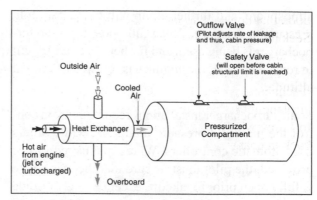

Figure 2-12. *Pressurization system*

The operation of the pressurization system varies with different types and models of airplanes, and you should study the operation of any system thoroughly before using it. One of your major concerns should be that the pressurization system activate and deactivate without discomfort for yourself and your passengers. Pressurization "bumps," when the occupants feel sudden pressure changes in their ears, are usually caused by incorrect use of the pressurization controls.

Autopilots

You may buy, rent, or get checked out in an airplane with some type of autopilot (A/P), and it is important that you have a full understanding of the autopilot system. An autopilot simply gets roll, pitch, yaw, information from the flight instruments and moves the controls just as you would if you were in control. The most basic system is a wing leveler, which does nothing more than keep the wings level while you unfold maps or eat your lunch. The next step up in sophistication adds "heading hold," which allows you to command a turn to a heading and then holds that heading with the wings level.

For a few more dollars you get VOR tracking capability, which takes a signal from the VOR receiver/ indicator and steers the airplane along a radial (*see* Lesson 10 for an explanation of VOR). You don't need any more than this as a non-instrument rated pilot.

If you are going to fly an autopilot-equipped airplane, insist on a thorough explanation and demonstration of all of its capabilities. There may be a pre-takeoff check of the autopilot in the Pilot Operating Handbook that does not appear on the airplane checklist. Seek it out and perform that check. Be sure that you are familiar with all available methods of disconnecting the autopilot—if there is an electrical or mechanical problem and the A/P decides to put the airplane into a dive or roll upside down, you need to know which switches to throw to put yourself back in charge.

Some instructors will tell you to just ignore the autopilot if one is installed. Don't accept that. You should know how to operate every item of equipment in the airplane, even if you don't intend to use it. The examiner may require an applicant to demonstrate autopilot use.

Rotax Engines

Many homebuilt and production airplanes use Rotax engines. Unlike the Lycomings and Continentals used in most trainers, Rotaxes differ in that they get air-cooling from fins on the cylinders but their engine blocks are liquid-cooled. This adds a "check the fluid level" to the preflight checklists. Also, many Rotax models have a choke instead of a mixture control; you use the choke for starting while the mixture is adjusted automatically. They use dual electronic ignition systems for redundancy and improved combustion; the ignition key is used to shut off the engine since there is no mixture control.

Rotax makes both four- and two-cycle engines. The smaller two-cycle engines are used in some light sport aircraft and powered parachutes. A two-cycle engine fires on every stroke, resulting in the high-pitched whine we usually associate with leaf blowers and chain saws. You know that you have to mix fuel and oil for those types of engines, and that is equally true for two-cycle aircraft engines. The high revolutions of the engine are reduced to more reasonable propeller speeds through gear reduction boxes; this requires a soft touch on the throttle to avoid over-revving the reduction gearing. Fuel enters two-cycle engines through an intake port and intake valve, and the exhaust leaves through an exhaust port.

The Rotax 912's cylinder heads are water-cooled, so you will check the radiator in your airplane just as you check the radiator in your car. It has a choke, used in starting, instead of a mixture control—mixture is adjusted automatically—so you use the ignition key to shut the engine off. (Takes me back to my 1940 Ford.) The Rotax has dual electronic ignition. Those are the major differences.

Lesson 2
Aircraft Systems Review Questions

1. What action can a pilot take to aid in cooling an engine that is overheating during a climb?

   A— Lean the mixture to best power condition.
   B— Increase rpm and reduce climb speed.
   C— Reduce rate of climb and increase airspeed.

2. A precaution for the operation of an engine equipped with a constant-speed propeller is to

   A— avoid high RPM settings with high manifold pressure.
   B— avoid high manifold pressure settings with low RPM.
   C— always use a rich mixture with high RPM settings.

3. Filling the fuel tanks after the last flight of the day is considered a good operating procedure because this will

   A— force any existing water to the top of the tank away from the fuel lines to the engine.
   B— prevent expansion of the fuel by eliminating airspace in the tanks.
   C— prevent moisture condensation by eliminating airspace in the tanks.

4. Which condition is most favorable to the development of carburetor icing?

   A— Any temperature below freezing and a relative humidity of less than 50 percent.
   B— Temperature between 32 and 50°F and low humidity.
   C— Temperature between 20 and 70°F and high humidity.

5. The uncontrolled firing of the fuel/air charge in advance of normal spark ignition is known as

   A— combustion.
   B— preignition.
   C— detonation.

6. If the engine oil temperature and cylinder head temperature gauges have exceeded their normal operating range, the pilot may have been

   A— operating with the mixture set too rich.
   B— using fuel that has a higher-than-specified fuel rating.
   C— operating with too much power and with the mixture set too lean.

7. If an engine continues to run after the ignition switch is turned to the OFF position, the probable cause may be

   A— the mixture is too lean and this causes the engine to diesel.
   B— a broken magneto ground wire.
   C— fouled spark plugs.

8. Detonation occurs in a reciprocating aircraft engine when

   A— hot spots in the combustion chamber ignite the fuel/air mixture in advance of normal ignition.
   B— there is too rich a fuel/air mixture.
   C— the unburned charge in the cylinders explodes instead of burning evenly.

9. An abnormally high engine oil temperature indication may be caused by

   A— the oil level being too low.
   B— operating with a too high viscosity oil.
   C— operating with an excessively rich mixture.

10. What type fuel can be substituted for an aircraft if the recommended octane is not available?

A — The next higher octane aviation gas.
B — The next lower octane aviation gas.
C — Unleaded automotive gas of the same octane rating.

11. In an aircraft equipped with a constant-speed propeller and a normally aspirated engine, which procedure would be used to avoid placing undue stress on the engine components?

A — When power is being increased or decreased, the rpm should be adjusted before the manifold pressure.
B — When power is being decreased, reduce the rpm before reducing the manifold pressure.
C — When power is being increased, increase the rpm before increasing the manifold pressure.

12. The main purpose of the mixture control is to

A — adjust the fuel flow to obtain the proper air/fuel ratio.
B — increase the oxygen supplied to the engine.
C — decrease the oxygen supplied to the engine.

13. Which statement is true regarding the effect of the application of carburetor heat?

A — It reduces the density of air entering the carburetor, thus enriching the fuel/air mixture.
B — It reduces the density of air entering the carburetor, thus leaning the fuel/air mixture.
C — It reduces the volume of air entering the carburetor, thus enriching the fuel/air mixture.

14. What will occur if no leaning is made with the mixture control as the flight altitude increases?

A — The volume of air entering the carburetor remains constant and the amount of fuel decreases.
B — The volume of air entering the carburetor decreases and the amount of fuel decreases.
C — The density of air entering the carburetor decreases and the amount of fuel remains constant.

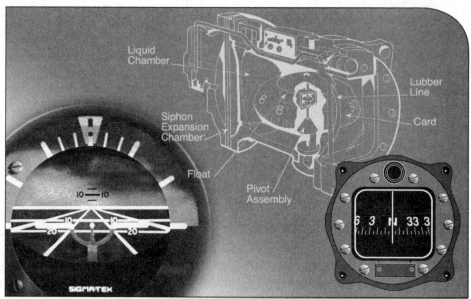

Lesson 3 Flight Instruments

This Lesson will cover the operation of so-called "steam gauges," the analog instruments that have been installed in general aviation cockpits for decades. The instrument questions on your Knowledge Exam will use illustrations of these instruments and will probably continue to do so for the next ten years.

The airplane you train in may very well have a "glass cockpit," with instruments displayed digitally on a CRT or LCD screen.* However, the various inputs to these instruments and how instrument indications are affected by atmospheric conditions and aircraft maneuvering has not changed.

It will be impossible for me to describe or explain specifics of these glass cockpits. As of this writing, the major glass cockpit manufacturers are Garmin, Avidyne, and Chelton. Each has its advantages and disadvantages. What is standard equipment with one box might require an external sensor with another. The airframe manufacturers have specified which avionics they want in their new airplanes, and that is what you will get. For older airplanes with six-pack round instruments there are several upgrades to glass available.

*(For example, see the G1000 illustration at the beginning of the color section at the back of the book. Note that the airspeed and altitude are displayed on vertical tapes beside the attitude indicator.)

No matter which equipment is installed in the airplane you fly, it will have a learning curve and box-specific training.

Pitot-Static Instruments

The **pitot-static system** consists of a pitot (pressure-sensing) tube, a static (zero pressure) source and related plumbing and filters. The pitot-static instruments are the **airspeed indicator**, the **altimeter**, and the **vertical speed indicator** (Figure 3-1);

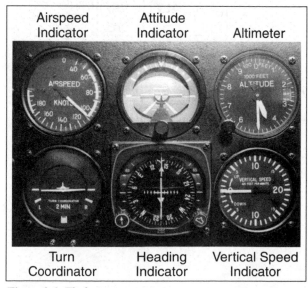

Figure 3-1. Flight instruments

they measure changes in air pressure caused by the airplane's vertical and horizontal movements in the atmosphere (Figure 3-2).

The airspeed indicator requires input from both the pitot (pressure) and static (unchanging) sources (Figure 3-3 below). Air from the static port fills the airspeed instrument case, while air from the pitot tube is led to a diaphragm. As airspeed changes, the pressure exerted on the diaphragm also changes and the movement of the diaphragm in response to these changes is transmitted to the indicator needle. The designer tries to locate the pitot tube so that it registers pressure in free air and is not affected by local airflow around the supporting structure. The airspeed indicator is the only instrument which uses air pressure from the pitot tube.

The static port is located where the airplane's motion through the air will create no pressure at all: on the side of the fuselage or on the back of the pitot tube. The airspeed indicator is calibrated to read the difference in pressure between impact air and still air—

both inputs are required. If either the pitot tube or the static port is blocked, the system will be useless, much like trying to get electricity from only one side of an electrical outlet.

Blockage of the static system would disable the airspeed indicator, the altimeter, and the vertical speed indicator.

At the start of the takeoff roll, there is no difference in pressure between the pitot and static inputs, and the airspeed indicator reads zero. As the airplane accelerates, the pressure in the pitot tube increases and that pressure is transmitted to the airspeed indicator needle. The designer cannot completely isolate the pitot and static inputs from the effects of airflow around the wing or fuselage, so an airspeed correction table is provided (Figure 3-4). The needle on the airspeed indicator reads **indicated airspeed** (IAS); when corrected for installation or position error, it becomes **calibrated airspeed** (CAS). Note in Figure 3-4 that the greatest difference between indicated and calibrated airspeed occurs at low speeds which require high angles of attack, and that as the angle of attack is reduced and speed increases, the difference between IAS and CAS becomes negligible. The colored arcs on the airspeed indicator are usually based on calibrated airspeed; other operating speeds may be based on indicated airspeed. Check the operator's handbook to be sure.

It takes a pressure of about 34 pounds per square foot on the pitot side of the airspeed indicator's diaphragm to make the airspeed needle register 100 knots at sea level. As the airplane climbs to altitude, the air becomes less dense. The airplane will have to move much faster through the less dense air at altitude in order to develop a pressure of 34 psf in the pitot tube, so the **true airspeed** will be faster

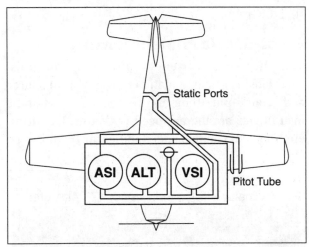

Figure 3-2. Pitot-static system

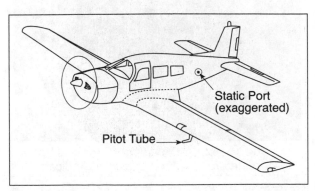

Figure 3-3. Pitot-static sources

Flaps Up												
KIAS	50	60	70	80	90	100	110	120	130	140	150	160
KCAS	55	63	71	80	89	99	108	118	128	138	147	157
Flaps 10°												
KIAS	40	50	60	70	80	90	100	110	120	130	---	---
KCAS	50	54	62	71	81	91	100	110	120	130	---	---
Flaps 30°												
KIAS	40	50	60	70	80	90	100	---	---	---	---	---
KCAS	47	54	62	71	81	90	101	---	---	---	---	---

Figure 3-4. Airspeed correction table

than 100 knots when the airspeed indicator shows 100 knots. Your flight computer will allow you to make accurate calculations of *true* airspeed using IAS, pressure altitude, and temperature, but a good rule of thumb is that *true airspeed increases by 2% per 1,000 feet of altitude*. At sea level under standard conditions, indicated and true airspeed will be equal; at 10,000 feet MSL, an indicated 100 knots means a true airspeed of 120 knots. Your airplane may have an airspeed indicator similar to Figure 3-5, which allows you to enter pressure altitude and temperature and read true airspeed directly. A "glass cockpit" airspeed indicator may have true airspeed displayed at the bottom of the vertical tape.

You will use true airspeed in flight planning, but most airspeeds that you will use in actual flight are indicated airspeeds. You will always use the same indicated airspeeds when landing, regardless of altitude. For example, if you are taking your flight training at a sea level airport and find that 70 knots indicated is the correct final approach speed, you will use 70 knots indicated airspeed on final when you fly to an airport at 5,000 feet above sea level. Your true airspeed will be 77 knots (2% times 5 = 10%, 1.1 times 70 = 77). Because the airplane approaching the airport at 5,000 feet is moving faster through the air in order to have an indicated airspeed of 70 knots, its ground speed will be higher and landing roll will be longer. A pilot who adds a few knots "just in case" while on final approach at a high altitude airport may have difficulty getting stopped on the available

runway. Flying at the manufacturer's recommended airspeed will have predictable results.

Your takeoff speeds will be affected by altitude; the section on airspeeds not marked on the airspeed indicator on Page 3–4 discusses these changes.

Airspeed Indicator Markings

The airspeed indicator has colored arcs to alert you to limiting airspeeds, and you should be aware of their significance (Figure 3-6). Most markings are based on calibrated airspeed. Check your airplane's Approved Flight Manual.

White Arc

The low-speed end indicates the power-off stall speed in the landing configuration (V_{S0}), and the high-speed end indicates the maximum allowable speed with flaps fully extended (V_{FE}).

Green Arc

The low-speed end indicates the power-off stall speed in a specified configuration, usually gear and flaps up (V_{S1}), and the high-speed end indicates maximum structural cruising speed (V_{NO}) which should be exceeded only in smooth air.

Yellow Arc

The caution range: pilots should avoid operating at airspeeds in the caution range except when in smooth air.

Red Line

This is the never-exceed speed (V_{NE}). Destructive aerodynamic forces may result from flight at or above the red line.

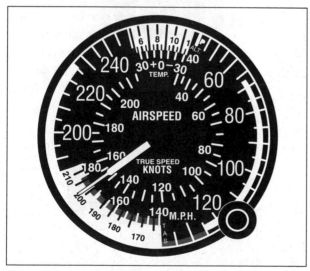

Figure 3-5. Airspeed indicator

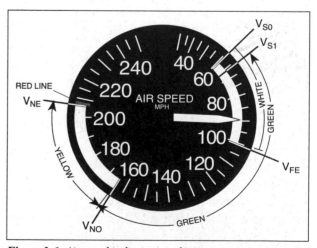

Figure 3-6. Airspeed indicator markings

Speeds Not Marked on the Airspeed Indicator

Every airplane has a design maneuvering speed (V_A), which is the optimum speed in turbulence at maximum gross weight. *Maneuvering speed is reduced as weight is reduced.* Flight at maneuvering speed ensures that the airplane will stall before damaging aerodynamic loads are imposed on the wing structure.

Best angle-of-climb speed (V_X) is that speed which gives the most altitude in a given distance. You should fly at V_X to clear obstructions and *only* to clear obstructions. Because flight at V_X requires a steep pitch attitude, engine cooling airflow and visibility are reduced. Climb at V_X only as long as necessary to clear the obstruction, then accelerate to V_Y. These speeds are for operation at maximum gross weight, and may be reduced by one-half of any weight decrease. That is, if the aircraft weighs 5 percent less than gross, V_X and V_Y can be reduced by 2½ percent.

Best rate-of-climb speed (V_Y) will produce the greatest gain in altitude in a given time, better visibility over the nose, and better engine cooling. If getting to altitude quickly is your goal, use V_Y.

V_X and V_Y are affected by density altitude as well as weight. Your aircraft operating manual's performance section will show you how the optimum indicated airspeed for best rate of climb *decreases* as density altitude increases. Most operating handbooks do not show how best angle of climb is affected—the optimum indicated airspeed for best angle of climb *increases* as density altitude increases. Of course, if you find yourself faced with an obstacle clearance problem at a high density altitude, the best plan might be to wait until the wind picks up or the sun goes down. Do not make a list of V-speeds taken from the operating manual and use that list at all weights and density altitudes; you will cheat yourself out of performance at best, and endanger your flight at worst. You can recover some lost performance by leaning the mixture as you climb.

Glass cockpit airspeed indicators usually have rotation speed, V_X, V_Y, and best glide speed displayed next to the tape; in some cases, these "bug" speeds are pre-set by the pilot while in others the bugs change dynamically based on instrumentally-derived density altitude.

The manufacturer may designate other speeds, which you will find in the Pilot's Operating Handbook and possibly placarded on the instrument panel. Landing gear extension and retraction speeds, and speeds for partial flap extension will be found in the operating handbook and not on the airspeed indicator.

Angle of Attack Indicators

The airspeed indicator can be considered a form of angle of attack indicator, since indicated airspeed is dependent on angle of attack in addition to power setting. Several manufacturers provide actual angle of attack indicators, however, which are calibrated to measure the actual angle between the chord line and the relative wind and provide you with angle of attack information by some form of "safe-unsafe" instrument reading (Figure 3-7). One such instrument compares air pressure changes both vertically and horizontally and measures sink rate. In every case, you need only keep the instrument's needle in the "safe" area and no interpretation is required.

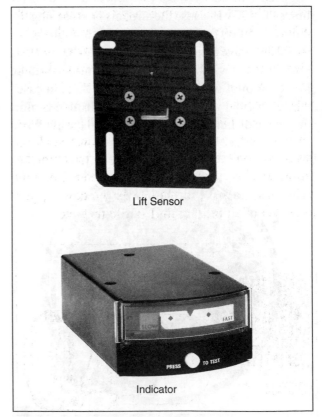

Lift Sensor

Indicator

Figure 3-7. Angle of attack indicator

Altimeter

Aircraft altimeters are aneroid (dry) barometers calibrated to read in feet above sea level. The altimeter gets its input from the static port, which is unaffected by the airplane's movement through the air. An aneroid barometer contains several sealed wafers with a partial internal vacuum, so as the airplane moves vertically and the outside pressure changes, the wafers expand and contract much like an accordion. This expansion and contraction is transmitted through a linkage to the altimeter needles (Figure 3-8).

Barometers provide a means of weighing the earth's atmosphere at a specific location. At a flight service station or National Weather Service office, an actual mercury barometer may be used, and on a standard day the weight of the atmosphere will support a column of mercury (Hg) 29.92 inches high at sea level. Inches of mercury are the units of measure for barometric pressure and altimeter settings. The equivalent metric measure is 1013.2 millibars; since our weather is transmitted internationally, the Weather Service uses both inches and millibars in its reports.

Up to 18,000 feet, altitude is measured above sea level, and sea level pressure may vary from 28.50" to 30.50" Hg (these are extremes). Your altimeter has an adjustment knob and an altimeter setting window (Figure 3-8), so that you can enter the sea level barometric pressure (altimeter setting) at your location as received from a nearby flight service station or air traffic control facility. The altimeter will, when properly set, read altitude above mean sea level (MSL). As you increase the numbers in the altimeter setting window, the hands on the altimeter also show an increase: each .01 increase in the window is equal to 10 feet of altitude, each .1 is 100 feet, etc.

Above 18,000 feet (and after you get your instrument rating, since all operations above that altitude must be under instrument flight rules), you will set the window to 29.92" Hg and you will be reading your altitude above the **standard datum plane**. By international agreement, a standard day at sea level is defined as having a barometric pressure of 29.92 (with the temperature 15°C or 59°F), and by setting your altimeter to 29.92 it will read altitude above that standard level. Below 18,000 feet, having the correct altimeter setting will keep you out of the trees, while above 18,000 feet (where there are no trees or mountains), the common altimeter setting of 29.92 provides altitude separation for IFR flights. There are several altitude terms with which you should be-come familiar:

Indicated altitude is simply what the hands on the altimeter point to. The long hand reads hundreds of feet (the calibrations are 20 feet), the next largest hand reads thousands of feet, and the third indicator reads in tens of thousands. The three-needle altimeter is easily misread, and many new airplanes are being equipped with a drum-pointer altimeter which has only one needle and a counter (Figure 3-9).

Figure 3-9. *Drum-pointer altimeter*

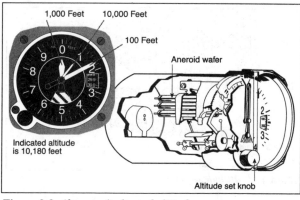

Figure 3-8. *Altimeter/indicated altitudes*

Refer to Figure 3-10.

Altimeter A's smallest (10,000 feet) needle is just past one, the second largest (1,000 feet) needle is between zero and one, and the largest (100 feet) needle is on the five:

One 10,000
+ No.................................... 0
+.............................. ___500___
                                    10,500

Use the same method to read altimeter B—your answer should be 9,500 feet.

Absolute altitude is your actual height above the surface as read by a radar altimeter. The Chelton Flight Systems "Highway in the Sky" includes a readout of height above the surface in its digital display; that's the "2320" in the illustration on Page D-2.

Pressure altitude is what the hands of the altimeter indicate when the altimeter setting window is set to 29.92" Hg. You will use pressure altitude in com-putations of density altitude, true airspeed and true altitude.

Density altitude is a critically important altitude; however, you can't read it on your altimeter but must calculate it, using pressure altitude and temperature. Density altitude is performance altitude—the air-plane and engine perform as though they are at a different altitude than their true altitude. All perfor-mance charts are based on density altitude, and this book will deal with it in detail in Lesson 8.

True altitude is your height above sea level. When you set your altimeter setting window to the local altimeter setting, the altimeter should read field elevation (above sea level). If it doesn't, record the instrument error. Differences of over 75 feet indicate that the instrument needs overhaul or replacement. (Before you take any drastic steps, be sure that your airplane is not simply located at a point below the published field elevation.) The illustration in Figure 3-11 shows an airplane with its altitude above the ground (absolute altitude), above sea level (true alti-tude), and above the standard datum plane of 29.92" Hg (pressure altitude).

Any obstruction to the static port or static lines will make the altimeter unusable, so some aircraft have alternate static sources vented inside the cockpit. When using the alternate static source, there will be slight errors in the altimeter and airspeed indications. The pressure inside the cockpit is lower than the outside pressure—with the alternate static source selected, the altimeter will read slightly high, the airspeed indicator will read high, and the vertical speed indicator will read correctly after momentarily indicating a climb.

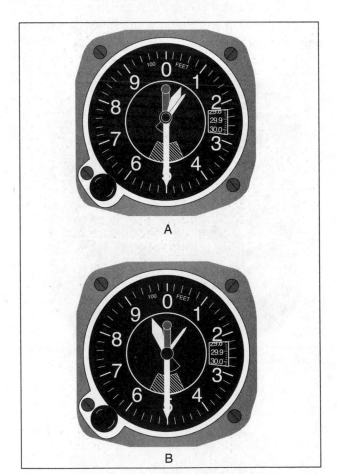

Figure 3-10. *Three-needle instrument indicators*

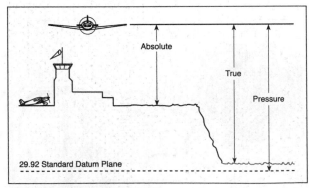

Figure 3-11. *Altitude definitions*

Effects of Temperature and Pressure on Altimeters

When you fly into an area of lower barometric pressure (while maintaining a constant altimeter setting) your true altitude will be lower than your indicated altitude, and that can be dangerous. Avoid this by frequently checking with ground stations to keep the altimeter set to an altimeter setting received from a station within 100 miles. If you fly into an area of colder temperatures, where air density is increased, indicated altitude will again be higher than true altitude.

"From High to Low, Look Out Below" applies to both pressure and temperature. You have no means of adjusting for temperature changes, so remember that pressure levels rise on warm days and descend on cold days, and if you are flying a constant pressure level (altimeter setting), you may be dangerously low on a cold day.

Encoding Altimeter

An encoding altimeter automatically reports pressure altitude to the radar scopes of air traffic controllers, and is required equipment in most controlled airspace (to be discussed in later lessons). As a pilot, you have no control over an encoder and cannot adjust it—you can't even turn it on and off.

Vertical Speed Indicator

The vertical speed indicator (Figure 3-12) is a static-pressure instrument which reflects rate of climb or descent by detecting rate of change in air pressure. Its internal construction is similar to that of the altimeter, but the aneroid wafer in the vertical speed indicator has a very small leak which allows its internal pressure to stabilize when altitude is not changing. During changes, there is a pressure differential between the air in the wafer and the air surrounding it, and the instrument indicates the change in this differential as climb or descent rate in feet per minute. The needle will lag actual changes in altitude until the rate of change stabilizes. However, if your instrument is marked "IVSI", this lag has been eliminated and it is an Instantaneous Vertical Speed Indicator. The VSI is not a required instrument for either VFR or IFR flight, but you won't find many airplanes without one. If the static port is clogged or frozen the VSI will be unusable—select the alternate static source if one is available.

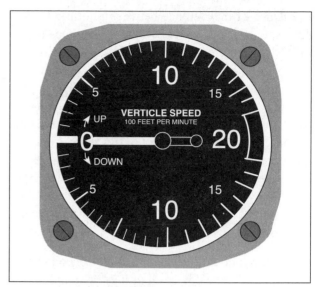

Figure 3-12. *Vertical speed indicator*

Gyroscopic Instruments

The attitude indicator, the turn indicator, and the directional gyro or heading indicator operate on the principle of gyroscopic rigidity in space. A spinning body, such as a bicycle wheel, will maintain its position in space as long as a rotational force is applied—riding your bike "no hands" is an example of this. Precession, or turning, occurs when any external force is applied to the spinning body, which will react as though the force has been applied at a point 90° away in the direction of rotation. If you lean your bicycle to the right, the turning force is as though pressure has been applied to the left front of the wheel—90° in the direction of rotation. Actually turning the wheel to the right may cause the bicycle to topple over to the right, again the result of gyroscopic precession.

For the foreseeable future, questions about the gyroscopic instruments on your knowledge exam will be based on mechanical gyros—those that have an actual metal disk being driven by either air passing over vanes or an electric motor—because the test-writers have not yet caught up with technology. The bicycle example is easy to visualize and demonstrate in the classroom.

Gyroscopic "instruments" in this modern age are displayed on a screen, and their inputs come from solid-state devices that deal in forms of mass that it is hard to get our brains around. The most accurate (and expensive) of these is the laser-ring gyro that makes use of interference between multiple lasers; less expensive but least accurate are devices using MEMs (micro-electro-mechanical). A MEM might be as simple as a vibrating crystal...try to visualize the mass being detected in that situation. The whole package, consisting of MEM gyroscopes, accelerometers, and magnetometers, is called an Attitude and Heading Reference System (AHRS). An Air Data Computer can be added, providing airspeed, outside air temperature, actual winds aloft, etc. There is a reason why this book does not contain an illustration of a solid-state gyro: It is just another circuit board with components mounted on it.

The errors inherent in mechanical gyroscopes still exist in solid-state devices, but they are small, constantly monitored internally, and easily corrected without any action on the pilot's part. If the system detects an anomaly it simply blacks out the display screen or displays a big red X.

Turn and Slip Indicator

Your airplane may have either a turn needle or a turn coordinator, but in either case a ball instrument will be included. Both the turn needle and the turn coordinator (Figure 3-13) indicate the rate of turn of the aircraft: when the turn needle is deflected one needle-width, or when the turn coordinator's airplane wing is on the index, the airplane is turning at the rate of 3° per second, and a complete circle will take 2 minutes. The turn and slip indicator shows rotation around the yaw axis (the ball), and around the roll axis (the miniature airplane or the needle).

Unlike the turn needle, the turn coordinator is designed so that it reflects *roll* rate as well as turn rate. Neither instrument indicates bank angle. Bank angle, turn rate, and airspeed are interrelated, as shown in Figure 3-14. For a given bank angle, the rate of turn increases as the airspeed decreases. Consider a light trainer and a jet, both banked 20°: the trainer would complete a 360° turn in a much shorter time than the jet and with a much smaller radius. If both airplanes maintained a 3° per second turn rate, they would both complete the circle at the same time—but the jet would be at an extreme bank angle. The bank angle for a 3° per second turn is approximately 15 percent of the true airspeed, so the trainer at 80 knots would bank 12°, while the jet at 400 knots would have to bank 60°.

The ball indicates the *quality* of the turn, with respect to rudder-aileron coordination. The force that causes an airplane to turn is the horizontal component of lift (*see* Figure 1-36 on Page 1–19), which is opposed by centrifugal force. If the rate of turn is too great for the angle of bank, centrifugal force is greater than the horizontal component of lift, and the ball rolls toward the outside of the turn. This is termed a "skidding" turn, and either a steeper bank angle (increasing horizontal component) or less rudder pressure on the inside of the turn (reduced centrifugal force) will return the ball to the center. The reverse situation has the ball falling to the inside of the turn in a "slip," caused by too little centrifugal force and too much horizontal component.

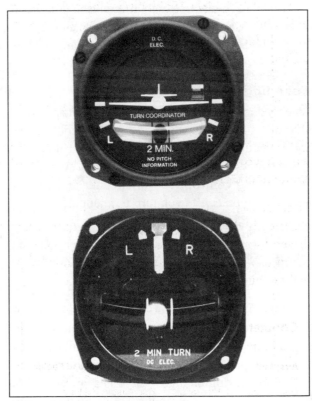

Figure 3-13. Turn and slip indicator

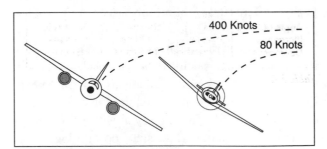

Figure 3-14. Rate and radius of turn vs. speed

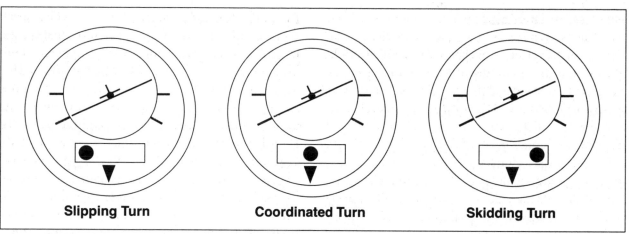

Figure 3-15. *Interpreting the ball instrument*

Less bank angle or more inside rudder will return the ball to the center when slipping (Figure 3-15). A rule of thumb is to *"step on the ball"*—apply pressure to the rudder pedal on the side of the instrument that the ball is on.

Table 3-1 illustrates how various elements of a turn are affected if either bank angle or airspeed is kept constant. For example, with a constant bank angle, an increase in airspeed will decrease the rate of turn while increasing the turn radius; the load factor would not be affected.

Turn needles or turn coordinators are almost always electrically driven, but you may find a turn needle driven by vacuum from an engine-driven vacuum pump or a **venturi**. Be sure that you know what makes your turn indicator operate.

Constant Bank

If... Airspeed	Then... Rate	Radius	Load Factor
Increases	Decreases	Increases	Same
Decreases	Increases	Decreases	Same

Constant Airspeed

If... Angle of Bank	Then... Rate	Radius	Load Factor
Increases	Increases	Decreases	Increases
Decreases	Decreases	Increases	Decreases

Table 3-1

In most trainer-type airplanes, the gyro instruments (attitude and heading indicator) are vacuum operated. An engine-driven vacuum pump draws air into the instrument case and as the air passes over turbine wheels it imparts a rotational force (*see* Figure 2-9 on Page 2–13). When the gyroscope rotors are up to speed they become fixed in the plane of rotation, and the airplane moves around them. The instrument presentations are so designed that the pilot has an accurate representation of airplane attitude and heading. Not all gyro installations are entirely vacuum operated—you may find that your heading indicator is electric and the attitude indicator is vacuum, or both may be electrically operated. The service life of a vacuum pump averages about 600 hours; be wary of a pump that has been in use for a longer period. Check the power source for each instrument in your airplane so that you can better deal with failures.

Note: The turn instrument can be replaced by a second, separately-powered attitude indicator. FAA *Advisory Circular 91.75* has details.

Where is the ball? Glass cockpit displays do not have the familiar ball, but combine it with the triangular turn index at the top of the heading indicator in the form of a line parallel to the base of the triangle; if the line slides away from the triangle, indicating lack of coordination, just "step on it" with rudder pressure to move it to its proper location.

Attitude Indicator

The gyroscope and its linkage cause the horizon disc (Figure 3-16) to move in both pitch and roll behind the miniature airplane. If you compare the movement of the horizon line in the attitude indicator with the movement of the natural horizon, you will see that the instrument instantly and accurately reflects changes in the pitch and roll attitude of the airplane. It is this instantaneous representation that makes the attitude indicator the most valuable instrument on the panel when reference to the natural horizon is lost. The bank angle markings at the top of the instrument are 10°, 20°, 30°, 45° (the dot), 60° and 90°. For control of pitch attitude—nose up or nose down—keeping the miniature airplane's wings near the horizon line is the thing to do if you are caught unexpectedly in poor visibility, or while flying at night with a poorly defined horizon.

As part of your flight training, your instructor will have you control the airplane solely by reference to the flight instruments, and you will be expected to demonstrate your ability to maneuver the airplane by instruments on your private pilot checkride. (This does not count as instrument instruction).

When you can't see the horizon and must maintain the airplane's attitude by instruments, don't bank any more than ten degrees (the first reference mark at the top of the attitude indicator).

Heading Indicator

You shouldn't always trust your heading indicator (directional gyro—*see* Figure 3-17) to tell you which way you are heading. The heading indicator is not a very smart instrument—it only repeats the heading that has been set into it. For that reason, it has an adjustment knob, and must be set to correspond to the magnetic compass (or to the runway heading) before it can be used for navigation. (Here again it must be noted that glass cockpit heading indicator displays do not need to be reset by the pilot.)

If you fail to set the heading indicator properly before takeoff, and do not notice that it disagrees with the **magnetic compass**, you can be many miles off course in a very short time.

Because the gyro's rotor spins at a velocity of about 18,000 rpm, its bearings must have a minimum of friction. As the bearings wear, or as dirt and contaminants (such as tobacco tar) collect at these critical points, the gyro will begin to slowly precess (drift) away from the heading you have set. You should check the heading indicator against the magnetic compass at least every 15 minutes, and more often if the instrument is showing signs of age such as grinding noises or rapid precession. Reset the heading indicator to the magnetic compass only when the airplane is in straight-and-level, unaccelerated flight. The magnetic compass develops errors during banks,

Figure 3-16. Attitude indicator

Figure 3-17. Heading indicator

climbs, and descents, and you do not want to set these errors into your heading indicator. Of course, if you're flying behind glass instruments the AHRS eliminates the need to reset the heading indicator.

Magnetic Compass

The only instrument in your airplane that does not depend on some source of external power is the magnetic compass (Figure 3-18). All of your navigational procedures are based on magnetic information. Unfortunately, the magnetic compass is subject to more errors than any other instrument.

The magnetic compass consists of a card floating in a liquid, pivoted on a needle point, and having affixed to it small permanent magnets that align themselves (and therefore the card) with the earth's magnetic field. The card is marked so that you see your magnetic heading on the compass when the magnets are being attracted to the magnetic North Pole. The magnetic compass is subject to several errors: **oscillation error**, and **northerly turning error**, and **acceleration error**. Because of the single point suspension, the compass card swings in even the slightest turbulence, and you must average its swings to approximate a constant heading. If your compass does *not* swing when the air gets rough, check to be sure that the fluid hasn't leaked out!

Northerly turning error is caused by the fact that the lines of force of the earth's magnetic field are parallel to the earth's surface at the Equator, but bend downward toward the surface as latitude increases, and are essentially vertical at the magnetic poles. This force, which pulls the ends of the compass magnets downward, is called "magnetic dip": When the airplane banks and the compass card tilts, the compass magnets, affected by dip, introduce a compass error. When you turn from a generally northerly heading, the compass will momentarily turn in the opposite direction, slow to a stop, and then follow the progress of the turn—but *lagging* the actual heading change. The amount of lag diminishes as the heading approaches east or west. Conversely, when you turn from a southerly heading the compass jumps out ahead of the turn, and *leads* the heading change, with the amount of lead again diminishing as east or west is approached. The amount of lead or lag which is attributable to northerly turning error is approximately equal to the airplane's latitude.

Acceleration error is evident on headings of east or west. If the airplane is accelerated, without changing heading, the compass will indicate a turn to the north, while deceleration on an east or west heading will cause the compass to indicate a turn to the south.

Use this memory aid: **A N D S**—*Accelerate North, Decelerate South. See* Figure 3-19.

It is because of northerly turning error and acceleration error that you must set the heading indicator to agree with the magnetic compass *only* in straight and level, unaccelerated flight.

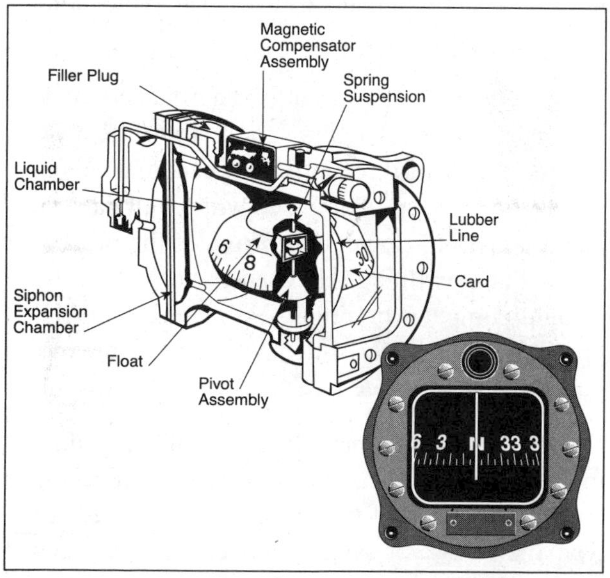

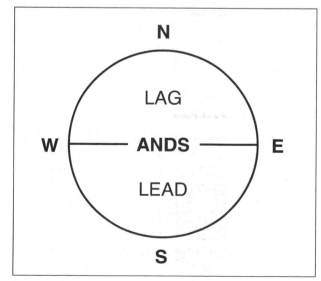

Figure 3-18. *Magnetic compass*

Figure 3-19. *Compass errors*

Magnetic deviation is an error which affects the accuracy of the magnetic compass but is caused by external forces. The magnetic influence of ferrous (steel) engine parts and electrical wiring cause deviation; Lesson 9 discusses the effect of deviation on navigation.

If you must rely solely on your magnetic compass for navigation, the most effective way to change heading is the timed turn. Note the magnetic compass heading, determine how many degrees you want to turn, and turn at 3° per second (using the index on the turn coordinator or turn needle) for the appropriate number of seconds. If you complete the turn within 5° or 10° of your target heading you are within acceptable limits.

Vertical Card Magnetic Compass

You may come across an airplane with a vertical card magnetic compass. These relatively new devices contain no liquid, and have little or no oscillation error. Acceleration error and northerly turning error are present but are quickly damped by internal electrical currents. They are considerably more expensive (but easier to use) than liquid-filled compasses.

Slaved Gyro Systems

If your airplane has a horizontal situation indicator (HSI) as a heading indicator, it may derive its directional information from a remote magnetic compass (or flux detector) mounted in the tail or wingtip, away from electrical influences. The weak electrical signals from the remote magnetic flux detector are amplified before being transmitted to the heading indicator, which then rotates or "slaves" into agreement with the directional information from the remote source. The system includes compensating devices to minimize or eliminate any deviation error. The exact location of the amplifier and compensating devices varies between manufacturers, and the location of the magnetic flux detector is determined by the installer. Figure 3-20 illustrates a possible installation with optional flux detector locations.

In most installations, a "slaving switch" is provided so that you can rapidly adjust the heading indicator card to agree with the liquid-filled magnetic compass during the preflight checks, and in some installations you can select "free gyro" and adjust the heading indicator just as you do with simpler systems.

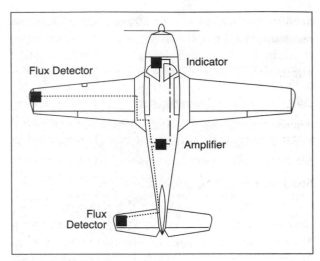

Figure 3-20. *Slaved gyro system*

Glass Cockpit

Throughout this Lesson I have referred to glass cockpits together with their analog counterparts to give you a basis for comparison or transition. These displays are much better than the instruments we have been using for decades, but they require study and understanding, and you will save money if you learn as much about their use as possible before you get into the airplane. Every manufacturer provides training materials, and the pilot supply industry has made videos and DVDs available.

A typical installation consists of two panels—a primary flight display (PFD) and a multifunction display (MFD); see the PFD/MFD illustration on appendix Page D-1. If one display panel fails, the information is automatically switched to the remaining panel.

Input data comes from a "digital air data computer" and can be manipulated to supply all of the normal outputs plus wind direction and speed, true airspeed, density altitude, etc. Combined with an air data computer, an AHRS (Page 3–8) provides the pilot with just about everything that used to be derived from a flight computer or simply estimated. The AHRS provides attitude information, while the air data computer provides airspeed, vertical speed, and altitude.

Despite the whiz-bang attraction of glass instruments, they still depend on external inputs. Airspeed, altitude, and vertical speed still need input from the pitot-static system, and it should be checked as required by the regulations. Some devices will need to be checked by the manufacturer, but your mechanic will have the details on that.

There are many add-on devices that can be connected to the multifunction display to provide engine analysis, fuel use and status, terrain and obstructions, inflight weather, etc. Just as in buying an automobile, some features are standard and some are optional at extra cost.

Multifunction Devices

By definition, multifunction devices perform (or have optional inputs that perform) tasks including navigation, engine parameter monitoring, traffic monitoring, and weather uplink. These tasks are all discussed in other Lessons; therefore, this is the only place appropriate to provide an overview. The appendix Page D-1 photo shows a primary flight display on the left and a multifunction device on the right.

A multifunction device can take inputs from many sources: a global positioning system receiver for navigation, a traffic alerting system for monitoring traffic, a lightning detector for storm avoidance, a fuel monitoring system, an engine parameters monitoring system, ground-based weather radar uplink, and many more. Their only limitations are panel space and cost. I just want you to know that the analog gauges (known to pilots as "steam gauges") in your basic trainer will most likely be replaced by digital displays as you get checked out in more sophisticated aircraft, and that tasks that seem almost overwhelming to a student are magically solved by microprocessors and dollars. However, never lose sight of the fact that electronic devices can and do fail, and that you need to maintain your ability to operate the airplane without their help.

Lesson 3
Flight Instruments Review Questions

1. The turn coordinator provides an indication of

   A— the movement of the airplane about the yaw and roll axes.

   B— the angle of bank to but not exceeding 30°.

   C— attitude of the airplane with reference to the longitudinal axis.

2. To receive accurate indications during flight from a heading indicator the instrument must be

   A— set prior to flight on a known heading.

   B— adequately powered so that it seeks the proper direction.

   C— periodically realigned with the magnetic compass as the gyro precesses.

3. In the Northern Hemisphere, a magnetic compass will normally indicate a turn toward the north if

   A— a left turn is entered from a west heading.

   B— an aircraft is decelerated while on an east or west heading.

   C— an aircraft is accelerated while on an east or west heading.

4. Deviation in a magnetic compass is caused by

   A— the difference in the location between true north and magnetic north.

   B— magnetic ore deposits in the Earth distorting the lines of magnetic force.

   C— magnetic fields within the airplane distorting the lines of magnetic force.

5. In the Northern Hemisphere, a magnetic compass will normally indicate initially a turn toward the east if

   A— an aircraft is accelerated while on a north heading.

   B— a right turn is entered from a north heading.

   C— a left turn is entered from a north heading.

6. How do variations in temperature affect the altimeter?

   A— Pressure levels are raised on warm days and the indicated altitude is lower than true altitude.

   B— Higher temperatures expand the pressure levels and the indicated altitude is higher than true altitude.

   C— Lower temperatures lower the pressure levels and the indicated altitude is lower than true altitude.

7. If it is necessary to set the altimeter from 29.15 to 29.85, what change is made on the indicated altitude?

   A— 70-foot increase.

   B— 700-foot increase.

   C— 700-foot decrease.

8. The pitot system provides impact pressure for only the

   A— airspeed indicator, altimeter, and vertical speed indicator.

   B— altimeter and vertical speed indicator.

   C— airspeed indicator.

9. Which V-speed represents maneuvering speed?

   A— V_A.

   B— V_{LO}.

   C— V_{NE}.

10. Refer to Figure 3-6 on Page 3–3. Which of the color-coded markings on the airspeed indicator identifies the never-exceed speed?

    A— Upper limit of the white arc.

    B— Upper limit of the green arc.

    C— The red radial line.

11. Refer to Figure 3-6 on Page 3–3. Which of the color-coded markings identifies the power-off stalling speed with wing flaps and landing gear in the landing position?

A— Upper limit of the white arc.
B— Lower limit of the green arc.
C— Lower limit of the white arc.

12. Refer to Figure Q3-1. How should a pilot determine the direction of bank from an attitude indicator such as the one illustrated?

A— By the direction of deflection of the banking scale (A).
B— By the direction of deflection of the horizon bar (B).
C— By the relationship of the miniature airplane (C) to the deflected horizon bar (B).

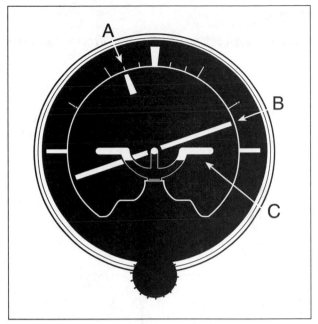

Figure Q3-1. *Attitude indicator*

Lesson 4 Regulations

Government Regulations and Other Procedures Publications

As you progress with your pilot training, your instructor will give you what will seem to be a never-ending series of instructions, procedures, methods, restrictions and advisories, and you will wonder how you will be able to remember it all. You don't have to. The Government Printing Office (GPO) distributes hundreds of publications on aviation subjects and you should become familiar with what is available. All government publications are available from the Government Printing Office in Washington, D.C. and GPO bookstores in major cities, but you will find that your local pilot supply store carries many of them. Private publishers have reprints which are more convenient to use and considerably less expensive than the government publication (but no less official). The ASA editions of the Federal Aviation Regulations and *Aeronautical Information Manual* are excellent examples. The FAA publications are also available in electronic form on CD-ROM (such as ASA's Flight Library Series), which has the additional benefit of the search function (so you can search any single or multiple documents for a specific word or topic).

Many of these publications are available online for pilots with access to the worldwide web on the inter-net. The web addresses in this book are only suggestions — there are many sources. You can find almost any FAA publication by going to www.faa.gov and typing the name of the desired publication into the search window.

Aeronautical Information Manual: Basic Flight Information and ATC Procedures (AIM)

I have provided the full title of this publication because many pilots miss the part about ATC procedures and look elsewhere for information included in its pages. It contains information on a host of aviation subjects. This list of chapter headings will give you some idea of the extent of coverage:

1. Navigation Aids
2. Aeronautical Lighting and Other Airport Visual Aids
3. Airspace
4. Air Traffic Control
5. Air Traffic Procedures
6. Emergency Procedures
7. Safety of Flight
8. Medical Facts for Pilots
9. Aeronautical Charts and Related Publications
10. Helicopter Operations

Section 3. AIRPORT OPERATIONS

4-3-1. GENERAL

Increased traffic congestion, aircraft in climb and descent attitudes, and pilot preoccupation with cockpit duties are some factors that increase the hazardous accident potential near the airport. The situation is further compounded when the weather is marginal– that is, just meeting VFR requirements. Pilots must be particularly alert when operating in the vicinity of an airport. This section defines some rules, practices, and procedures that pilots should be familiar with and adhere to for safe airport operations.

4-3-2. AIRPORTS WITH AN OPERATING CONTROL TOWER

a. When operating at an airport where traffic control is being exercised by a control tower, pilots are required to maintain two-way radio contact with the tower while operating within the Class B, Class C, and Class D surface area unless the tower authorizes otherwise. Initial callup should be made about 15 miles from the airport. Unless there is a good reason to leave the tower frequency before exiting the Class B, Class C, and Class D surface areas, it is a good operating practice to remain on the tower frequency for the purpose of receiving traffic information. In the interest of reducing tower frequency congestion, pilots are reminded that it is not necessary to request permission to leave the tower frequency once outside of Class B, Class C, and Class D surface areas. Not all airports with an operating control tower will have Class D airspace. These airports do not have weather reporting which is a requirement for surface based controlled airspace, previously known as a control zone. The controlled airspace over these airports will normally begin at 700 feet or 1,200 feet above ground level and can be determined from the visual aeronautical charts. Pilots are expected to use good operating practices and communicate with the control tower as described in this section.

b. When necessary, the tower controller will issue clearances or other information for aircraft to generally follow the desired flight path (traffic patterns) when flying in Class B, Class C, and Class D surface areas and the proper taxi routes when operating on the ground. If not otherwise authorized or directed by the tower, pilots of fixed-wing aircraft approaching to land must circle the airport to the left. Pilots approaching to land in a helicopter must avoid the flow of fixed-wing traffic.

However, in all instances, an appropriate clearance must be received from the tower before landing.

Components of a Traffic Pattern

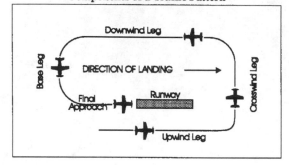

FIG 4-3-1

NOTE–
THIS DIAGRAM IS INTENDED ONLY TO ILLUSTRATE TERMINOLOGY USED IN IDENTIFYING VARIOUS COMPONENTS OF A TRAFFIC PATTERN. IT SHOULD NOT BE USED AS A REFERENCE OR GUIDE ON HOW TO ENTER A TRAFFIC PATTERN.

c. The following terminology for the various components of a traffic pattern has been adopted as standard for use by control towers and pilots (See FIG 4-3-1):

1. *Upwind leg:* A flight path parallel to the landing runway in the direction of landing.

2. *Crosswind leg:* A flight path at right angles to the landing runway off its takeoff end.

3. *Downwind leg:* A flight path parallel to the landing runway in the opposite direction of landing.

4. *Base leg:* A flight path at right angles to the landing runway off its approach end and extending from the downwind leg to the intersection of the extended runway centerline.

5. *Final approach:* A flight path in the direction of landing along the extended runway centerline from the base leg to the runway.

d. Many towers are equipped with a tower radar display. The radar uses are intended to enhance the effectiveness and efficiency of the local control, or tower, position. They are not intended to provide radar services or benefits to pilots except as they may accrue through a more efficient tower operation. The four basic uses are:

1. *To determine an aircraft's exact location:* This is accomplished by radar identifying the VFR aircraft through any of the techniques available to a radar

Figure 4-1. Example from a page of the AIM

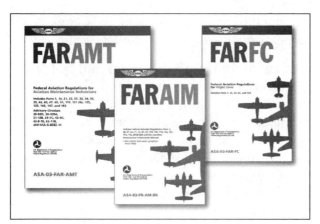

Figure 4-2. Federal Aviation Regulations in ASA's FAR/AIM series.

Figure 4-1 is an example of the type of detailed information on procedures available in the *Aeronautical Information Manual*. The AIM also includes a Pilot/Controller Glossary, so that you will know exactly what the controller means when instructions are given (controllers have an identical glossary in the Air Traffic Control Handbook). The AIM is updated every two years, with changes every six months, and is available by subscription from the Government Printing Office. You will also find it for sale by ASA, combined with the Federal Aviation Regulations, at your pilot supply store. ASA provides a free online Update (www.asa2fly.com*) to keep pilots current on changes in regulations and procedures.

Every new edition of the AIM contains a list of changes since the previous edition, and there are always many. Be very suspicious of information from a copy of the AIM that is more than a year old, unless it contains at least one change. The AIM may be viewed online at www2.faa.gov/atpubs/aim/index.htm.

Federal Aviation Regulations

The FAA expects you to be familiar with all of the Federal Aviation Regulations which apply to your flight operations, but as you read through the regulations you should be able to distinguish between those that are nice to know but do not affect your day-to-day flying (carriage of candidates in Federal elections, for example), and those which you simply *must* know (basic visual flight rules or right-of-way rules). This lesson will discuss those regulations

which require explanation or illustration for full understanding, but all 199 Parts of the regulations apply to you. Before you say "I can't find it in the regs," be sure that you have checked all sources. Note also that the regulations list things that you cannot do—if something is not prohibited by a regulation, it is permitted. A searchable version of all of the regulations can be found on the FAA's website.**

Part 61 Certification: Pilots and Flight Instructors

In August 2009, the FAA issued sweeping changes to Part 61. If you are using an older reference you may be confused. Go to www.faa.gov and click on Regulations and Policies to get the most recent information.

14 CFR 61.3 Requirements for certificates, ratings, authorizations. If you are going to act as pilot-in-command or as a required flight crewmember you must have in your possession your pilot certificate and medical certificate. These must be accompanied by a picture ID such as a driver's license. You must present these documents for inspection upon request by an official of the FAA, the NTSB, or any law enforcement officer. You are not surrendering your documents, just presenting them for inspection; surrender is a formal process, with lots of paperwork.

14 CFR 61.5 Certificates and ratings. There are seven pilot certificates: student, sport pilot, recreational, private, commercial, airline transport pilot, and flight instructor.

Student Pilot: Limited to solo or dual (instructional) flights only.

Sport pilot: See limitations in 14 CFR 61.315 (*see* Pages 4–9 through 4–12).

Recreational Pilot: Can carry only one passenger. Must receive additional instruction and endorsements to fly beyond 50 NM of the airport at which the pilot has received flight and ground instruction. Limited to a single engine of less than 180 hp and fixed landing gear. Cannot fly where radio communication is required. Cannot fly at night or internationally. Some of these restrictions can be removed with additional training and logbook endorsements.

---

* From the home page, go to Customer Service, then "Updates and Patches."

** http://www.faa.gov/regulations_policies

Private Pilot: May carry passengers or cargo, day or night, as long as no charge is made. Is permitted to share expenses with passengers. May fly in conjunction with employment if flying is only incidental to the employment.

Commercial Pilot: May fly for compensation or hire. Must also meet requirements of Part 135 to fly as air taxi pilot.

Airline Transport Pilot: May fly as pilot-in-command on an airline flight or on a multiengine scheduled commuter flight.

A certificated flight instructor can give both flight and ground instruction under the conditions stated in 61.193 and 61.195. A flight instructor certificate must be renewed every 24 calendar months.

Your certificate will carry a category and class rating such as Airplane: Single Engine Land (Figure 4-3). You cannot carry passengers unless you hold the appropriate category and class ratings, and an instrument rating is required for instrument flight rules (IFR) whether you are carrying passengers or not. You can begin training for the instrument rating as soon as you receive your private pilot certificate; there is no minimum flight time requirement. Figure 4-3 shows the categories and the applicable class ratings.

14 CFR 61.15 Offenses involving alcohol or drugs. If you are convicted on a drug charge, or for driving while impaired by alcohol or drugs, you must report the circumstances of the conviction to the FAA Civil Aviation Security Division (not your local FSDO)

Category	Class	Example or Type
Airplane	Single-engine land Multi-engine land Single-engine sea Multi-engine sea	B-727
Rotorcraft	Helicopter Gyroplane	S-61
Lighter-Than-Air	Airship Free balloon	—
Glider	—	—
Powered-lift	—	(tilt rotor)

Figure 4-3. Categories and class ratings

within 60 days. Failure to comply is grounds for suspension/revocation of your pilot certificate.

14 CFR 61.19 Duration of pilot and instructor certificates. Student pilot certificates expire when the underlying Third Class Medical Certificate expires…24 or 60 calendar months depending on age. Flight instructor certificates expire after 24 calendar months. All other pilot certificates have no expiration date and are kept active by having a current and valid medical certificate and a current flight review.

14 CFR 61.23 Medical certificates: Requirement and duration. The type of medical certificate you hold determines the privileges you can exercise according to the pilot certificate you hold. Figure 4-4 lists the classes of medical certificates, their durations, and the privileges authorized during the valid period. Medical certificates expire at the end of the *calendar* month; for example, a physical taken on the 15th of the month will expire at the *end* of the 6th, 12th, 24th, or 36th month, depending on the class of physical and age of the applicant.

You must have a medical certificate (which doubles as a student pilot certificate) before you can solo. If you have the slightest doubt about your ability to pass a third-class physical exam (see Part 67), take your physical exam early in your training…it is painful to put in several hours of training, to fall in love with flying, and then find out that you do not qualify for a medical certificate.

Holders of Sport Pilot certificates flying light sport airplanes can use their valid driver's license as their medical certificate.

14 CFR 61.31 Type rating requirements, additional training and authorization requirements. Type ratings are required for airplanes weighing over 12,500 pounds or those powered by turbojets. A commercial pilot cannot operate an aircraft for compensation or hire without holding an appropriate category and class rating for that aircraft. No person may operate an airplane with more than 200 horsepower ("high performance"), or one that has retractable landing gear, flaps, and a controllable propeller ("complex aircraft"), without having received flight instruction in that type of airplane, with a logbook endorsement to that effect made by the instructor. To

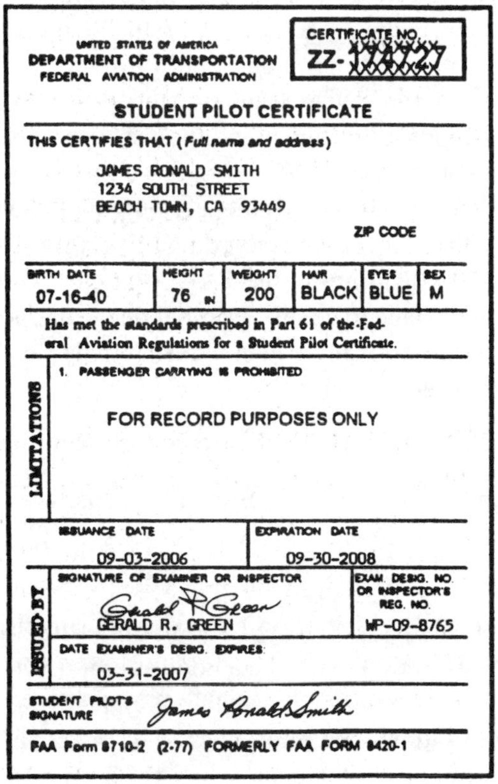

STUDENT PILOT CERTIFICATE

UNITED STATES OF AMERICA
DEPARTMENT OF TRANSPORTATION
FEDERAL AVIATION ADMINISTRATION

CERTIFICATE NO.
ZZ-XXXXXXX

THIS CERTIFIES THAT (*Full name and address*)

JAMES RONALD SMITH
1234 SOUTH STREET
BEACH TOWN, CA 93449

ZIP CODE

BIRTH DATE	HEIGHT	WEIGHT	HAIR	EYES	SEX
07-16-40	76 IN	200	BLACK	BLUE	M

Has met the standards prescribed in Part 61 of the Federal Aviation Regulations for a Student Pilot Certificate.

LIMITATIONS

1. PASSENGER CARRYING IS PROHIBITED

FOR RECORD PURPOSES ONLY

ISSUANCE DATE	EXPIRATION DATE
09-03-2006	09-30-2008

SIGNATURE OF EXAMINER OR INSPECTOR	EXAM. DESIG. NO. OR INSPECTOR'S REG. NO.
Gerald R. Green GERALD R. GREEN	WP-09-8765

DATE EXAMINER'S DESIG. EXPIRES:
03-31-2007

STUDENT PILOT'S SIGNATURE: *James Ronald Smith*

FAA Form 8710-2 (2-77) FORMERLY FAA FORM 8420-1

To Exercise Privileges	Valid Months
Third Class Medical Certificate	
Private Pilot	
Under age 40*	60 months
Over age 40*	24 months
*on date of examination.	
Second Class Medical Certificate	
Commercial Pilot	12
Private Pilot	
Under age 40	24
Over age 40	60
First Class Medical Certificate	
Airline Transport Pilot	
Under age 40	12
Over age 40	6
Commercial Pilot	12
Private Pilot	60

To exercise the privileges of their pilot certificates, ATPs must get new medicals every 6 months, commercial pilots every 12 months, and private pilots every 24 months.

Medical certificates expire the last day of the 6th, 12th, or 24th month after they are issued, depending on the class of certificate.

Figure 4-4. Medical Certificates; sport pilots need only a valid driver's license.

act as pilot-in-command of a tailwheel airplane, you need a logbook endorsement from an instructor who has given you instruction in a tailwheel airplane. To act as PIC of an airplane with a service ceiling or maximum operating altitude of 25,000 feet (whichever is lower), you need both ground and flight training in high altitude operations.

This regulation provides for the use of night vision goggles, but only by pilots who have been trained in their use and whose logbooks have been endorsed to reflect this training. Pilots with military training in their use are grandfathered in by documenting their training.

14 CFR 61.51 Pilot logbooks. As a student pilot, you can log solo and dual instruction time; solo time is pilot-in-command time. As soon as you pass your private pilot checkride, every minute you spend at the controls of an airplane for which you are rated (airplane, single-engine, land, in most cases) is loggable as PIC regardless of weather conditions or who is sitting in the other seat. It is legal for a private pilot in training for the commercial certificate or instrument rating to log PIC time while his or her instructor is also logging PIC time if the category and class requirements are met.

If there is any possibility that you might want to upgrade a Sport Pilot certificate to a Private Pilot certificate, first make sure that the instructor who administered your sport pilot dual instruction is not limited to sport pilot instruction. Instructors now come in two flavors: Subpart H, which is the "old fashioned" certificate permitting instruction in anything the CFI is rated for, and Subpart K, which governs light sport instructors. Make sure that all logbook entries go into detail about which regulation governs the instruction being logged. Your instructor should know this, but it is in your best interest to get involved in making sure that the entry is logged correctly. For example, "Ground reference maneuvers: rectangular course, constant radius turns. Meets 61.89 and 61.311 standards, Joe Blow 12345678 CFI(H)." Note that all *solo* flight time logged in a light sport aircraft counts toward the private pilot requirements.

As a private pilot, you can log as second-in-command time only that flight time when you act as SIC of an airplane requiring more than one pilot or when operating under regulations that require more than one pilot. The required three hours of flight training under the hood do not constitute instrument training and should not be logged as such. As a student pilot you must carry your logbook on all solo cross-country flights as evidence of the required instructor clearances and endorsements.

The FAA does not get involved in the publication of logbooks, and as you shop around you will see different column headings in different styles of logbook…you can even buy logbooks with no column headings and make up your own. You are only *required* to make logbook entries for two purposes: to substantiate the experience requirements for a new certificate or rating, and to prove currency. Those who say "I have 10,000 hours and no longer keep a log" will have trouble proving that they have made the required takeoffs and landings under 61.57. In the event of an accident, insurance companies look for logged hours...so it is wise to keep an accurate log of all flying time.

Your logbook is yours…it does not belong to your instructor or your flight school. You can write in it whatever you choose to write. However, you do want to make sure that the contents of each flight lesson are accurately described, and the entry signed by your instructor. Pilots frequently ask, "Can I legally log ____?" and the answer is, "Log whatever you want to log." I feel that each logbook entry should use more than one line, and describe the weather and anything interesting that happened during the flight. When you get old and grey, "Slips, steep turns, take-offs and landings" won't bring back any memories.

Acting as pilot-in-command and logging PIC time are two different things. The pilot with responsibility for the safety of flight *acts* as PIC under Part 1 of the regulations, but need not ever touch the controls. As a certificated private or commercial pilot you can log as PIC all of the time during which you are the sole manipulator of the controls of an airplane for which you are rated. "High performance" and "complex" are endorsements, not ratings, and are irrelevant in this context. Make a photocopy of your logbook regularly, just in case it gets lost or stolen. Be sure that all endorsements are included.

To avoid future confusion, assign a column in your logbook to cross-country time, if the logbook printer has not already provided one. In this column, list only those trips with a landing more than 50 NM from the original departure point; those are the flights that will count toward qualifying for another certificate or rating and, for convenience, should not be mixed in with other flights. According to a recent (December 2009) ruling by the FAA, you can reposition your airplane to a new "original departure point" if necessary to make a planned trip legal—but don't log the repositioning flight as cross-country. To help in your search, a good source is www.airnav.com. Click on "Airports," then on "Where do you want to search?" Insert the identifier of the departure airport, then scroll down to 75 NM to get a list of all airports within that radius.

Pilots like to save money, and sharing a training trip with a buddy seems like a good solution. However, some methods have drawbacks…to qualify as cross-country time, one pilot must be at the controls for the entire trip; if Joe and Mary fly from A to B and back with Joe flying one way and Mary flying the other, neither pilot can log the time.

14 CFR 61.53 Operations during medical deficiency. If you have contracted an illness, have been injured, or for any reason could not pass a physical examination on a given day, your medical is not valid. For example, if you had a mild heart attack but your medical certificate will not expire for six months, you are still grounded as of the date of the heart attack. You can't say "My medical is good for six more months, I'll report it then."

14 CFR 61.55 Second-in-Command Qualifications. After you have achieved your private pilot certificate, situations will arise in which you will be legally able to log second-in-command (SIC) time. One example is when you serve as safety pilot for another pilot who is wearing a view-limiting device in visual flight conditions (if the flight is under instrument flight rules, no matter what the meteorological conditions are, you would have to hold an instrument rating). In this situation you become a required crewmember. My recommendation is that you ignore this provision of the regulations because the time logged as SIC has no value whatsoever... you can't even log it as cross-country.

14 CFR 61.56 Flight review. To act as pilot-in-command you must have satisfactorily accomplished a flight review within the past 24 calendar months. You can take the review with any instructor, FAA operations inspector, or U.S. Armed Forces check pilot. The flight review must include at least one hour of ground instruction including a review of Part 91 and one hour of flight time performing maneuvers of the instructor/check pilot's choice. If you participate in a pilot proficiency award program such as the FAA's Wings Program, satisfactory completion is a substitute for a flight review. If you take a checkride for a new certificate or rating, that flight also constitutes a flight review—make sure that the examiner endorses your logbook accordingly.

You can take the review in any aircraft for which you are rated. That is, if you hold certificates for airplanes, gliders, and hot air balloons a flight review in any of those aircraft meets the requirements of the regulation.

Note that you cannot fly solo unless you have a current flight review.

14 CFR 61.57 Recent flight experience: Pilot-in-command. You may not carry passengers unless you have current experience, and that means 3 takeoffs and landings within the preceding 90 days in an aircraft of the same category and class as that in which you plan to carry passengers. You may fly solo to make those three takeoffs and landings, of course. If you are going to carry passengers in a tailwheel airplane, your 3 takeoffs and landings must have been in a taildragger, and to a full stop—no touch-and-goes permitted. Touch-and-goes are approved for tricycle gear airplanes. To carry passengers at night you must, within the preceding 90 days, have made 3 takeoffs and landings to a full stop *in an aircraft of the same category and class* during the period from one hour after sunset to one hour before sunrise. The Part 1 definition of "night" is that period between the end of evening civil twilight and the beginning of morning civil twilight. If you really want them, you can find twilight times at www.usno.navy.mil/USNO/astronomical-applications. That means that if you are current at night in single-engine landplanes, for instance, your night currency does not extend to multi-engine landplanes, and you must do the 3 full-stop landings at night before carrying passengers in a twin at night. You must be sole manipulator of the controls when regaining currency—you cannot carry passengers, but you could do your night landings with a pilot who is current acting as pilot-in-command.

A current pilot is one who meets the requirement for 3 takeoffs and landings within 90 days, and who also has accomplished a satisfactory flight review within 24 months.

14 CFR 61.60 Change of address. If you change your permanent mailing address and do not advise the FAA within 30 days you cannot exercise the privileges of your pilot certificate. Just as soon as you have notified them you are back in the air again. You will not receive a corrected certificate.

14 CFR 61.63 Additional aircraft ratings. If you want to add a category or class rating to your certificate (rotorcraft might be a new category, multiengine land a new class rating), you must take a checkride, but no knowledge exam is required if you already hold a rating in powered aircraft in a different category. You must present a logbook record that you have received instruction and are competent in the category or class for which the addition is sought. "Complex aircraft" and "high performance aircraft" are instructor endorsements, not aircraft ratings.

14 CFR 61.65 Instrument rating requirements. You can begin training for the instrument rating as soon as you receive your private pilot certificate; but before you take the instrument rating practical test you must have logged 50 hours of cross-country time as a private pilot. You will probably want to stretch your new wings and do some exploring anyway.

14 CFR 61.87 Solo flight requirements for student pilots. This regulation provides an extensive list of procedures and maneuvers at which you must demonstrate acceptable proficiency before your instructor can sign you off for solo. Your logbook should be endorsed to show that you have received training in each item listed. It also requires that your instructor administer and grade a written examination on the appropriate portions of Parts 61 and 91 before you can solo.

To a student pilot, solo cross-country means a one-way flight of more than 50 NM culminating in a landing; you can make solo flights to airports within 25 NM of your home airport with an instructor's endorsement in your logbook. Those short flights do not count toward the cross-country time required before your checkride, but they get you out of home airspace and introduce some situations that will be new to you. To count toward the total cross-country hours for the private pilot certificate, a solo flight must land at a point more than 50 straight-line nautical miles from the departure airport. This need not be a 50-plus mile leg between points A and B, but could be a 25-mile flight between A and B followed by a 30 mile flight between B and C, assuming that C is more than 50 NM from A, measured in a straight line. The "long" cross-country requires a flight of at least 150 NM total distance with landings at a minimum of three points, with one nonstop segment of at least 50 NM. The recreational pilot certificate requires two hours of instruction in cross-country flight; there is no solo cross-country requirement for the recreational pilot certificate. An instructor can lift the 50-mile limitation on recreational pilots with additional training and a logbook endorsement.

Reading Part 61.87 will give you an excellent insight into how your initial training will be conducted and what you must learn, regardless of which certificate you are working toward.

14 CFR 61.89 General limitations; Solo cross-country flight requirements, student pilot. Student pilots may not carry passengers, act as pilot-in-command on an international flight, fly for compensation or hire, or fly in furtherance of a business. A student pilot must have his or her solo endorsement renewed every 90 days by a flight instructor, and must be specifically signed off for each cross-country flight with very narrowly limited exceptions.

Student pilots are not permitted to fly solo when the visibility is less than 3 miles in daylight and 5 miles at night. Also, student pilots must be in visual contact with the ground at all times; flight above a cloud layer is prohibited.

A student is a student is a student. You are not a private pilot student or a recreational pilot student, you are a student pilot. Restrictions placed on hold-ers of recreational pilot certificates do not apply to students working toward that certificate under the supervision of an instructor.

14 CFR 61.93(e)(12). This obscure regulation tells students working toward their Sport Pilot certificate in airplanes with cruise speeds greater than 87 knots that they must receive instruction in control of the airplane solely by reference to the flight instruments during their two hours of cross-country training.

14 CFR 61.95 Operations in Class B airspace and at airports located within Class B airspace. This regulation says that a student pilot must receive both flight and ground instruction regarding operations in specific Class B airspace and to or from an airport lying within its surface area. Your instructor must endorse your logbook accordingly and renew the endorsement every 90 days until you receive your private pilot certificate. If you plan a cross-country trip that will take you into another Class B airspace, you can't go until you and your instructor have gone through the same procedure for that location.

14 CFR 61.101 Recreational pilot privileges and limitations. The aeronautical knowledge and flight proficiency requirements for the recreational and private pilot certificates are virtually identical. However, because recreational pilots do not receive training in night flight, flight by reference to instruments, and radio navigation, their privileges are limited: No night flight; no flight above 10,000' MSL or 2,000' above the terrain, whichever is higher; no more than one passenger; 180 hp maximum engine power; airplane no larger than four-place; no flights exceeding 50 NM from the departure airport; no flights into airspace where radio communication is required (the last two restrictions can be removed by additional instruction and a logbook endorsement). A recreational pilot with less than 400 hours logged who has not acted as pilot-in-command within the past 180 days needs additional training and an instructor's endorsement before acting as PIC.

14 CFR 61.105, 61.107, 61.109 Aeronautical knowledge, experience and flight proficiency. Part 61 enumerates the aeronautical knowledge areas required to apply for the private pilot certificate—exactly what the student needs to glean from ground training or a home study course. It also specifies the kind of flight training, and how much of it (in hours), the student must receive from an authorized instructor before applying.

14 CFR 61.113 Private pilot privileges and limitations; pilot-in-command. Private pilots may not accept compensation for flying; they are allowed to share the direct operating expenses of the flight with their passengers (fuel, oil, rental charges). Beware — your insurance might not cover a flight for which a charge is made. Private pilots are allowed to fly in connection with their employment if they are not being paid solely for their piloting activities. For instance, you can fly some clients over some property they are considering as a part of your duties in real estate, but you cannot be asked by your employer to transport customers on flights unrelated to real estate if your employer reimburses you. You, as a private pilot, may carry paying passengers on a flight for a charitable organization if the passengers have contributed to the organization. Approved charities are very narrowly defined by the IRS; the airplane must meet commercial maintenance requirements (Part 135), you must have logged 500 hours of flight time, and you must meet drug testing program requirements. You may demonstrate airplanes as an airplane salesperson after you have logged 200 hours of flight time as pilot-in-command.

The question of sharing expenses has resulted in some legal decisions. If you are flying somewhere and want to take someone along to share expenses but would go anyway if no passenger could be found, that is acceptable. If the only reason you are taking a trip is that someone will share expenses with you, that is considered compensation. If you rent airplanes to take your friends on trips just to build time, trips that you would not take without their financial contribution, you are flirting with a violation of this regulation.

The FAA calls this principle "Commonality of Purpose." You and your passengers must have a common purpose in making the flight; if you would not have made the flight for your own purposes, its legality is questionable.

14 CFR 61.307 Testing. You must pass a knowledge examination and a practical test administered by a sport pilot examiner to qualify as a sport pilot. From that point on, all upgrades (except to the Private Pilot certificate) are accomplished by instructor endorsement. *See* Table 4-1 (on the next three pages) for details.

14 CFR 61.313 Aeronautical experience. For the Sport Pilot certificate you must have logged a minimum of 20 hours of flight time including at least 15 hours from an authorized instructor and 5 hours of solo flight. This must include two hours of training for cross-country flights, ten takeoffs and landings to a full stop at an airport with an operating control tower, and three hours of flight training in preparation for the practical test. The solo hours must include one cross-country flight of at least 75 nautical miles total distance with full stop landings at a minimum of two points, and one segment consisting of a straight-line segment of at least 25 nautical miles. Again, *see* Table 4-1 for details.

14 CFR 61.315 Sport Pilot privileges and limitations; pilot-in-command. Sport pilots are limited to flying airplanes certificated as light sport aircraft: Single engine, no more than two seats, 120 knots maximum cruise speed, 1,320 maximum gross weight, daytime only, with at least three miles visibility while maintaining visual contact with the ground. Maximum authorized altitude is 10,000 feet MSL or 2,000 feet AGL, whichever is higher. Sport Pilot certificates do not list category or type…all you need is an instructor's endorsement that you have received ground and flight training in order to operate another category or class of light sport aircraft (Table 4-1 has details).

14 CFR 61.325 Radio communications. To operate a light sport aircraft in Class B, C, or D airspace you must receive and log ground and flight training in the use of radios, navigation systems, and radar services. You must perform three takeoffs and landings to a full stop at an airport with an operating control tower. You must observe all flight rules in Part 91.

14 CFR 61.327 Operating aircraft with a cruise speed greater than 87 knots. You must receive and log ground and flight training in the operation of aircraft with a cruise speed greater than 87 knots, with a qualified instructor's endorsement.

If you hold	And you hold	Then you may operate	And
(1) A medical certificate,	(i) A sport pilot certificate,	(A) Any light-sport aircraft for which you hold the endorsements required for its category and class,	(1) You must hold any other endorsements required by this subpart, and comply with the limitations in §61.315.
	(ii) At least a recreational pilot certificate with a category and class rating,	(A) Any light-sport aircraft in that category and class,	(1) You do not have to hold any of the endorsements required by this subpart, nor do you have to comply with the limitations in §61.315.
	(iii) At least a recreational pilot certificate but not a rating for the category and class of light-sport aircraft you operate,	(A) That light-sport aircraft, only if you hold the endorsements required in §61.321 for its category and class,	(1) You must comply with the limitations in §61.315, except §61.315 (c)(14) and, if a private pilot or higher, §61.315(c)(7).
(2) Only a U.S. driver's license,	(i) A sport pilot certificate,	(A) Any light-sport aircraft for which you hold the endorsements required for its category and class,	(1) You must hold any other endorsements required by this subpart, and comply with the limitations in §61.315.
	(ii) At least a recreational pilot certificate with a category and class rating,	(A) Any light-sport aircraft in that category and class,	(1) You do not have to hold any of the endorsements required by this subpart, but you must comply with the limitations in §61.315.
	(iii) At least a recreational pilot certificate but not a rating for the category and class of light-sport aircraft you operate,	(A) That light-sport aircraft, only if you hold the endorsements required in §61.321 for its category and class,	(1) You must comply with the limitations in §61.315, except §61.315(c)(14) and, if a private pilot or higher, §61.315(c)(7).
(3) Neither a medical certificate nor a U.S. driver's license,	(i) A sport pilot certificate,	(A) Any light-sport glider or balloon for which you hold the endorsements required for its category and class,	(1) You must hold any other endorsements required by this subpart, and comply with the limitations in §61.315.
	(ii) At least a private pilot certificate with a category and class rating for glider or balloon,	(A) Any light-sport glider or balloon in that category and class,	(1) You do not have to hold any of the endorsements required by this subpart, nor do you have to comply with the limitations in §61.315.
	(iii) At least a private pilot certificate but not a rating for glider or balloon,	(A) Any light-sport glider or balloon, only if you hold the endorsements required in §61.321 for its category and class,	(1) You must comply with the limitations in §61.315, except §61.315(c)(14) and, if a private pilot or higher, §61.315(c)(7).

Table 4-1(a). Sport pilot requirements from 14 CFR §61.303

If you are applying for a sport pilot certificate with...	Then you must log at least...	Which must include at least...
(a) Airplane category and single-engine land or sea class privileges,	(1) 20 hours of flight time, including at least 15 hours of flight training from an authorized instructor in a single-engine airplane and at least 5 hours of solo flight training in the areas of operation listed in §61.311,	(i) 2 hours of cross-country flight training, (ii) 10 takeoffs and landings to a full stop (with each landing involving a flight in the traffic pattern) at an airport; (iii) One solo cross-country flight of at least 75 nautical miles total distance, with a full-stop landing at a minimum of two points and one segment of the flight consisting of a straight-line distance of at least 25 nautical miles between the takeoff and landing locations, and (iv) 2 hours of flight training with an authorized instructor on those areas of operation specified in §61.311 in preparation for the practical test within the preceding 2 calendar months from the month of the test.
(b) Glider category privileges, and you have not logged at least 20 hours of flight time in a heavier-than-air aircraft,	(1) 10 hours of flight time in a glider, including 10 flights in a glider receiving flight training from an authorized instructor and at least 2 hours of solo flight training in the areas of operation listed in §61.311,	(i) Five solo launches and landings, and (ii) at least 3 training flights with an authorized instructor on those areas of operation specified in §61.311 in preparation for the practical test within the preceding 2 calendar months from the month of the test.
(c) Glider category privileges, and you have logged 20 hours flight time in a heavier-than-air aircraft,	(1) 3 hours of flight time in a glider, including five flights in a glider while receiving flight training from an authorized instructor and at least 1 hour of solo flight training in the areas of operation listed in §61.311,	(i) Three solo launches and landings, and (ii) at least 3 training flights with an authorized instructor on those areas of operation specified in §61.311 in preparation for the practical test within the preceding 2 calendar months from the month of the test.
(d) Rotorcraft category and gyroplane class privileges,	(1) 20 hours of flight time, including 15 hours of flight training from an authorized instructor in a gyroplane and at least 5 hours of solo flight training in the areas of operation listed in §61.311,	(i) 2 hours of cross-country flight training, (ii) 10 takeoffs and landings to a full stop (with each landing involving a flight in the traffic pattern) at an airport, (iii) One solo cross-country flight of at least 50 nautical miles total distance, with a full-stop landing at a minimum of two points, and one segment of the flight consisting of a straight-line distance of at least 25 nautical miles between the takeoff and landing locations, and (iv) 2 hours of flight training with an authorized instructor on those areas of operation specified in §61.311 in preparation for the practical test within the preceding 2 calendar months from the month of the test.

Table 4-1(b). *Sport pilot limitations from 14 CFR §61.313 (continued on following page)*

If you are applying for a sport pilot certificate with…	Then you must log at least…	Which must include at least…
(e) Lighter-than-air category and airship class privileges,	(1) 20 hours of flight time, including 15 hours of flight training from an authorized instructor in an airship and at least 3 hours performing the duties of pilot in command in an airship with an authorized instructor in the areas of operation listed in §61.311,	(i) 2 hours of cross-country flight training, (ii) Three takeoffs and landings to a full stop (with each landing involving a flight in the traffic pattern) at an airport, (iii) One cross-country flight of at least 25 nautical miles between the takeoff and landing locations, and (iv) 2 hours of flight training with an authorized instructor on those areas of operation specified in §61.311 in preparation for the practical test within the preceding 2 calendar months from the month of the test.
(f) Lighter-than-air category and balloon class privileges,	(1) 7 hours of flight time in a balloon, including three flights with an authorized instructor and one flight performing the duties of pilot in command in a balloon with an authorized instructor in the areas of operation listed in §61.311,	(i) 2 hours of cross-country flight training and (ii) 1 hour of flight training with an authorized instructor on those areas of operation specified in §61.311 in preparation for the practical test within the preceding 2 calendar months from the month of the test.
(g) Powered parachute category land or sea class privileges,	(1) 12 hours of flight time in a powered parachute, including 10 hours of flight training from an authorized instructor in a powered parachute, and at least 2 hours of solo flight training in the areas of operation listed in §61.311,	(i) 1 hour of cross-country flight training, (ii) 20 takeoffs and landings to a full stop in a powered parachute with each landing involving flight in the traffic pattern at an airport; (iii) 10 solo takeoffs and landings to a full stop (with each landing involving a flight in the traffic pattern) at an airport, (iv) One solo flight with a landing at a different airport and one segment of the flight consisting of a straight-line distance of at least 10 nautical miles between takeoff and landing locations, and (v) 1 hour of flight training with an authorized instructor on those areas of operation specified in §61.311 in preparation for the practical test within the preceding 2 calendar months from the month of the test.
(h) Weight-shift-control aircraft category land or sea class privileges,	(1) 20 hours of flight time, including 15 hours of flight training from an authorized instructor in a weight-shift-control aircraft and at least 5 hours of solo flight training in the areas of operation listed in §61.311,	(i) 2 hours of cross-country flight training; (ii) 10 takeoffs and landings to a full stop (with each landing involving a flight in the traffic pattern) at an airport, (iii) One solo cross-country flight of at least 50 nautical miles total distance, with a full-stop landing at a minimum of two points, and one segment of the flight consisting of a straight-line distance of at least 25 nautical miles between takeoff and landing locations, and (iv) 2 hours of flight training with an authorized instructor on those areas of operation specified in §61.311 in preparation for the practical test within the preceding 2 calendar months from the month of the test.

Table 4-1(b). Sport pilot limitations from 14 CFR §61.313 (continued from previous page)

14 CFR 91.3 Responsibility and authority, pilot-in-command. You, as the pilot-in-command, are the final authority as to the operation of your aircraft. In an emergency, you can take any action required to meet the emergency, even though that action might violate the regulations. If, however, you do deviate from the rules in an emergency, you may be *requested* to send a written report to the FAA. This regulation is your authority to tell a controlling agency that you cannot follow a directive because in your estimation to do so would be unsafe. The magic words are "unable," when you are instructed to do something that you deem unsafe, such as flying into a cloud, and "emergency." Do not hesitate to declare an emergency if you are lost, disoriented, low on fuel, etc. Don't worry about paperwork or repercussions because there will probably be none. Accident statistics tell us that some pilots would rather die than admit that they are in over their heads.

14 CFR 91.7 You, as pilot-in-command, are responsible for the airplane's airworthiness. At a minimum, that means a careful, thorough preflight inspection; you can't go wrong by following the manufacturer's checklist. The owner or operator bears responsibility for maintaining the aircraft in an airworthy condition, and for ensuring that all Airworthiness Directives are complied with. It is still your responsibility to check the aircraft and engine logs and assure yourself that the owner or operator has performed that duty.

14 CFR 91.9 Every certificated airplane must have an Approved Flight Manual, and you must observe any limitations in that flight manual and its supplements. Limitations posted as placards or panel markings must also be observed. This applies equally to airplanes certificated in the Experimental and Light Aircraft categories.

14 CFR 91.13 Careless or reckless operation. This is a catch-all regulation. If you have any type of accident or incident, the assumption is that you must have been either careless or reckless. Your responsibility is to leave nothing to chance: use written checklists rather than rely on memory. As pilot-in-command, do not let anyone interfere with your control of the airplane (see the regulations regarding alcohol and drugs, below).

14 CFR 91.15 Dropping objects. You may not drop or allow to be dropped from your aircraft any object that creates a hazard to persons or property. If reasonable precautions to avoid injury or damage are taken, dropping objects is authorized. Make sure that your proposed drop does not violate any state or local laws…strewing the ashes of a decedent is unlawful in many jurisdictions.

14 CFR 91.17 Alcohol or drugs. You cannot act as a crewmember of a civil aircraft within 8 hours of consuming alcoholic beverages. This is the "bottle to throttle" rule. Also, you may not allow a passenger under the influence of alcohol or drugs on your aircraft unless that person is under the care of medical personnel. Also, when you accept your pilot certificate you agree to submit to a breathalyzer or blood test at the request of any law officer or FAA official if you operate or attempt to operate an aircraft. If your blood alcohol content exceeds .04 percent you may face certificate action. (Note the reporting requirements of 61.15.)

14 CFR 91.21 Portable electronic devices. Some portable electronic devices interfere with the airplane's radio navigation systems, and may not be used on air carrier airplanes or when operating IFR. You, as pilot-in-command, should ensure that any such device in use in your airplane will not affect the operation of your radios. The Federal Communication Commission (FCC), not the FAA, prohibits the use of cellular telephones from an airplane in flight.

14 CFR 91.103 Preflight action. Before beginning any flight, you are required to familiarize yourself with *all* information concerning the flight. You can't say, "I didn't know." The information must always include runway lengths at airports you intend to use, and the takeoff and landing performance figures for your airplane under the conditions to be expected. For flights not in the vicinity of an airport (cross-country flights), you must also have an alternative plan of action in mind if your planned flight cannot be completed, know the fuel requirements for the flight, and get weather reports *and forecasts* for the time of flight. Technology now affords pilots the ability to see actual conditions en route or at a destination using webcams, and a low-tech phone call to an operator at a destination can avoid unpleasant surprises ("The electricity is out and we can't pump gas.")

14 CFR 91.105 Flight crewmembers at stations. During takeoff and landing, each required crewmember must be at his or her station with seatbelt and shoulder harness fastened (if shoulder harnesses are provided). The shoulder harness can be temporarily unfastened if you can show that you cannot perform required duties—tune radios or operate controls—with it fastened.

14 CFR 91.107 Use of safety belts. You and your passengers must have seatbelts fastened before you begin to taxi, and it is your responsibility to ensure that they are fastened and that passengers have been briefed on how to fasten and unfasten their seatbelts.

14 CFR 91.111 Operating near other aircraft. Formation flying looks easy, but it isn't. This regulation prohibits formation flight except by prior arrangement, and forbids formation flight if passengers are carried for hire. Let the pros do air-to-air photography.

14 CFR 91.113 Right-of-way rules. The right-of-way rules are first broken down on the basis of maneuverability, except that an aircraft in distress, regardless of category, has the right of way over all other aircraft (Figure 4-5). Balloons, being least maneuverable, have the right of way over any other category. An aircraft towing another aircraft has priority over all other engine-driven aircraft. Gliders have the right of way over airships, airplanes, and rotorcraft. Airships have the right of way over airplanes and rotorcraft. When two aircraft of the same category converge, the one on the right has the right of way. Refer to Figure 4-6 and 91.113 for these situations: the pilot seeing a red light and an anticollision light must pass behind the other airplane (lower left), while the pilot who sees a green light and an anticollision light maintains course (lower right). In an overtaking situation, the white position light and the anticollision light are visible, and the overtaking airplane must give way to the right while the overtaken airplane maintains course (upper left). When you see both a red and a green light, you are head-on, and both pilots must change course to the

right (upper right). A provision of this regulation that causes problems, usually at non-tower airports, is this: when two aircraft are approaching an airport to land, the lower of the two has the right of way—but it may not take advantage of this rule by cutting in front of the other aircraft.

If your airplane is equipped with traffic alert and collision avoidance software that provides avoidance advisories, you can deviate from an ATC clearance—but inform the controller as soon as you can.

Pilots of amphibians or floatplanes must be familiar with and observe the rules of the road for vessels when operating on water.

14 CFR 91.117 Aircraft speed. There is no speed limit above 10,000 feet MSL. That is why the visibility and cloud clearance requirements are more stringent above that altitude. Below 10,000 feet MSL, the *general* speed limit is 250 knots. When flying on a jet you will experience what seems like a period of "coasting" as you approach the destination airport—your pilot is holding altitude and reducing speed to 250 knots before descending through 10,000 feet. That 250-knot speed limit extends to the ground in Class B airspace. When you fly beneath the horizontal limits of Class B airspace or in a VFR corridor through Class B airspace your speed is limited to 200 knots—very few student pilots have trouble complying! Within 4 NM of the primary airport of Class C or D airspace, all airplanes are limited to 200 knots.

14 CFR 91.119 Minimum safe altitudes, general. Figure 4-7 illustrates minimum safe altitudes. *Except when necessary for takeoff or landing,* you must always fly high enough to be able to make a safe emergency landing without hazard to persons or property on the ground. Over a congested area, you must fly 1,000 feet above the highest obstacle within 2,000 feet horizontally. *Question:* If you are only 1,000 feet above the highest obstacle over downtown Houston or Chicago, for example, can you make a safe emergency landing? Probably not. Roads and freeways look like great emergency landing strips until you get too low to change your mind; they should be your very last resort. Considerably more altitude would be better. Over other than congested areas, you must stay at least 500 feet above the surface, except that over sparsely settled areas and over

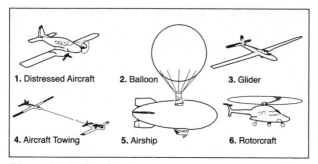

Figure 4-5. *Right-of-way priority*

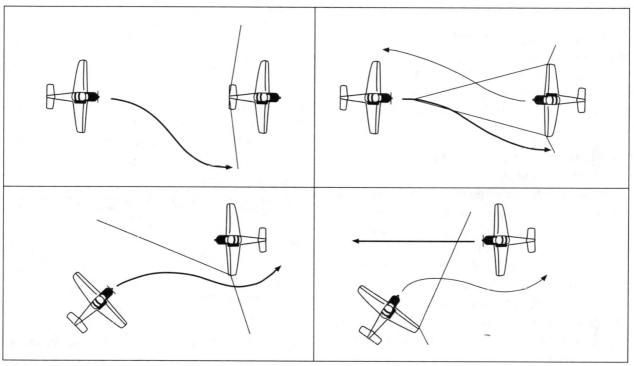

Figure 4-6. *Rules of the road*

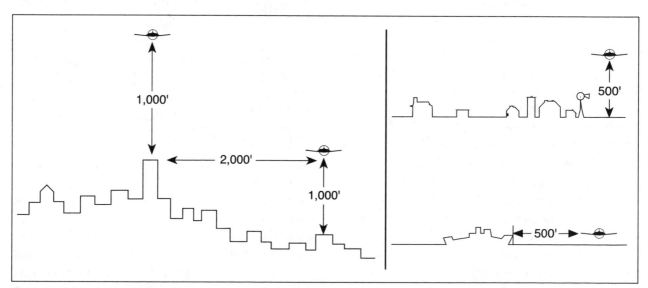

Figure 4-7. *Minimum safe altitudes*

water you must stay at least 500 feet horizontally from any person, vessel, vehicle, or structure on the surface. This means boats, barns, swimmers, etc.

14 CFR 91.121 Altimeter settings. If you can receive an altimeter setting by radio (or by visiting the flight service station) you must adjust your altimeter setting window accordingly. If you are en route, you must update the altimeter setting by calling a FSS within 100 miles along your route of flight (every time you contact Air Traffic Control or a flight service station you will be given an altimeter setting).

If you are on the ground, and no altimeter setting information is available, you should set your altimeter to read field elevation, and then get a correction as soon as you are able to contact a flight service station by radio. Above 18,000 feet MSL, all altimeters must be set to 29.92" Hg.

14 CFR 91.123 Compliance with Air Traffic Control clearances and instructions. An air traffic controller can only provide you with vectors and traffic information in controlled airspace—when you enter Class G (uncontrolled) airspace you are on your own. When you receive an instruction from an air traffic controller you must comply *except* when, in your opinion, to do so would be unsafe. Just tell the controller that you can't comply (due to weather, for example)—again, the magic word is "unable." You can always exercise your pilot's emergency authority. *If you are given priority* over other aircraft, even if no emergency is involved, you *may* be requested to make a written report within 48 hours to the Chief of the ATC facility that gave you the priority.

14 CFR 91.125 ATC light signals. Light signals are used by tower controllers when you have no radio or when your radio has failed (Figure 4-8). The wisest course, in the event of radio failure, is to land at an uncontrolled airport and make arrangements with the tower controllers by telephone. If this option is not available, you are allowed to join the controlled airport's traffic pattern (after determining the direction of traffic flow) and your actions will be directed with light signals.

Color and Type of Signal	On the Ground	In Flight
STEADY GREEN	Cleared for takeoff	Cleared to land
FLASHING GREEN	Cleared to taxi	Return for landing (to be followed by steady green at proper time)
STEADY RED	Stop	Give way to other aircraft and continue circling
FLASHING RED	Taxi clear of landing area (runway) in use	Airport unsafe — do not land
FLASHING WHITE	Return to starting point on airport	
ALTERNATING RED & GREEN	General Warning Signal — Exercise Extreme Caution	

Figure 4-8. Light signals

14 CFR 91.135 Class A Airspace. As a VFR-rated private pilot you may not climb above 18,000 feet MSL without an instrument rating and an instrument clearance.

14 CFR 91.145 Management of aircraft operations in the vicinity of aerial demonstrations and major sporting events. This regulation is the basis for Temporary Flight Restriction areas such as the Super Bowl, the President's ranch, a Blue Angels demonstration, etc. Your only salvation is to check Notices to Airmen just before takeoff and frequently thereafter.

14 CFR 91.151 Fuel requirements for flight in VFR conditions. You must carry enough fuel to reach your destination plus 30 minutes reserve for day VFR and 45 minutes for night VFR. Fuel consumption should be based on normal cruise speed, not on best economy or best endurance speed. It should be apparent that if everyone followed this rule, there would be no fuel exhaustion incidents. Don't be the exception to this rule. To be sure, always plan to land with one hour's fuel in the tanks. Subtract one hour's fuel burn from the fuel on board when planning your flight.

14 CFR 91.153 VFR flight plan; information required. Figure 4-9 (flight plan form) includes all of the information called for by this section. You should list as your destination airport the last airport at which you intend to land (you can include en route airports in block 11). Block 12 should reflect total fuel on board. VFR flight plans, although not mandatory, aid in search-and rescue efforts if you do not complete your planned flight. If you do not file a flight plan, be sure that someone is aware of your plans and will call authorities if you do not complete your flight on time. If you have a VFR GPS on board, note that fact in Block 11.

US DEPARTMENT OF TRANSPORTATION FEDERAL AVIATION ADMINISTRATION **FLIGHT PLAN**	(FAA USE ONLY) ☐ PILOT BRIEFING ☐ STOPOVER	☐ VNR	TIME STARTED	SPECIALIST INITIALS

1 TYPE	2 AIRCRAFT IDENTIFICATION	3 AIRCRAFT TYPE/ SPECIAL EQUIPMENT	4 TRUE AIRSPEED	5 DEPARTURE POINT	6 DEPARTURE TIME		7 CRUISING ALTITUDE
VFR IFR DVFR					PROPOSED (Z)	ACTUAL (Z)	

8 ROUTE OF FLIGHT

9 DESTINATION (Name of airport and city)	10 EST TIME ENROUTE		11 REMARKS
	HOURS	MINUTES	

12 FUEL ON BOARD		13 ALTERNATE AIRPORT(S)	14 PILOT'S NAME, ADDRESS & TELEPHONE NUMBER & AIRCRAFT HOME BASE	15 NUMBER ABOARD
HOURS	MINUTES		17 DESTINATION CONTACT/TELEPHONE (OPTIONAL)	

16 COLOR OF AIRCRAFT	CIVIL AIRCRAFT PILOTS. FAR Part 91 requires you file an IFR flight plan to operate under instrument flight rules in controlled airspace. Failure to file could result in a civil penalty not to exceed $1,000 for each violation (Section 901 of the Federal Aviation Act of 1958, as amended). Filing of a VFR flight plan is recommended as a good operating practice. See also Part 99 for requirements concerning DVFR flight plans.

FAA Form 7233-1 (8-82)   CLOSE VFR FLIGHT PLAN WITH _____ FSS ON ARRIVAL

Figure 4-9. Flight plan form

14 CFR 91.155 Basic VFR weather minimums. VFR visibility and cloud clearance requirements will be discussed further in Lesson 9. Table 4-2 lists these minimums in detail. Three miles visibility is not very much; go up with your instrument-rated instructor on a scuzzy day and see for yourself. When flying toward the sun, even five miles visibility is not enough. A conservative low-time VFR pilot wants a 2,000-foot ceiling and five miles visibility.

14 CFR 91.159 VFR cruising altitudes or flight levels. This is called the hemispherical rule. It is based on magnetic *course*, not magnetic heading, and applicable only when you are more than 3,000 feet above the ground (Figure 4-10).

14 CFR 91.203 Civil aircraft: Certifications required. You must have your aircraft registration certificate and the airplane's *Certificate of Airworthiness* (Figure 4-11) on board at all times; weight and balance data and the FAA Approved Flight Manual must also be carried, although markings and placards can be substituted for the Flight Manual if the airplane did not require such a manual when it was certificated (pre-1973 in most cases). *Airplane and engine logs are not required to be on board the airplane.* Remember:

A Certificate of **A**irworthiness.

R **R**adio station license.*

R **R**egistration.

O **O**perating limitations (flight manual).

W **W**eight and balance data.

The Certificate of Airworthiness must be displayed where it can be seen easily by passengers and crew.

14 CFR 91.207 Emergency locator transmitter. Your airplane must have an emergency locator transmitter (ELT); there is an exemption for short-range training flights, but almost all trainers have ELTs anyway. It is important that you know where the battery is located, and how the device can be removed from the aircraft if necessary. The battery must be replaced when the transmitter has been used more than one cumulative hour (during tests), or when it has reached 50 percent of its useful life. The expi-

* The FCC has eliminated the radio station license requirement; however, a station license will still be needed for international flights.

Airspace	Flight Visibility	Distance from Clouds
Class A	Not Applicable	Not Applicable
Class B	3 statute miles	Clear of clouds
Class C	3 statute miles	500 feet below 1,000 feet above 2,000 feet horizontal
Class D	3 statute miles	500 feet below 1,000 feet above 2,000 feet horizontal
Class E Less than 10,000 feet MSL	3 statute miles	500 feet below 1,000 feet above 2,000 feet horizontal
At or above 10,000 feet MSL	5 statute miles	1,000 feet below 1,000 feet above 1 statute mile horizontal
Class G 1,200 feet or less above the surface (regardless of MSL altitude) Day, except as provided in § 91.155(b)	1 statute mile	Clear of clouds
Night, except as provided in § 91.155(b)	3 statute miles	500 feet below 1,000 feet above 2,000 feet horizontal
More than 1,200 feet above the surface but less than 10,000 feet MSL Day	1 statute mile	500 feet below 1,000 feet above 2,000 feet horizontal
Night	3 statute miles	500 feet below 1,000 feet above 2,000 feet horizontal
More than 1,200 feet above the surface and at or above 10,000 feet MSL	5 statute miles	1,000 feet below 1,000 feet above 1 statute mile horizontal

Table 4-2. Weather minimums

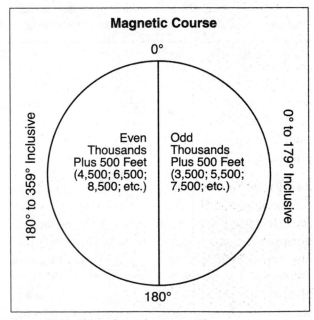

Figure 4-10. Hemispherical cruising rule

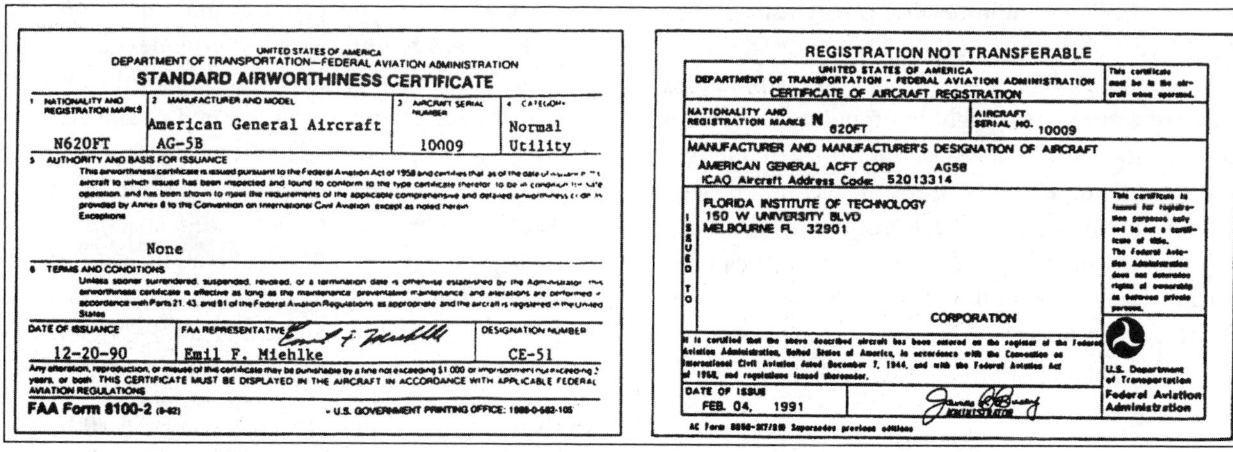

UNITED STATES OF AMERICA
DEPARTMENT OF TRANSPORTATION—FEDERAL AVIATION ADMINISTRATION
STANDARD AIRWORTHINESS CERTIFICATE

1 NATIONALITY AND REGISTRATION MARKS	2 MANUFACTURER AND MODEL	3 AIRCRAFT SERIAL NUMBER	4 CATEGORY
N620FT	American General Aircraft AG-5B	10009	Normal Utility

5 AUTHORITY AND BASIS FOR ISSUANCE

Exceptions

None

6 TERMS AND CONDITIONS

DATE OF ISSUANCE	FAA REPRESENTATIVE	DESIGNATION NUMBER
12-20-90	Emil F. Miehlke	CE-51

THIS CERTIFICATE MUST BE DISPLAYED IN THE AIRCRAFT IN ACCORDANCE WITH APPLICABLE FEDERAL AVIATION REGULATIONS

FAA Form 8100-2

REGISTRATION NOT TRANSFERABLE

UNITED STATES OF AMERICA
DEPARTMENT OF TRANSPORTATION - FEDERAL AVIATION ADMINISTRATION
CERTIFICATE OF AIRCRAFT REGISTRATION

NATIONALITY AND REGISTRATION MARKS	AIRCRAFT SERIAL NO.
N 620FT	10009

MANUFACTURER AND MANUFACTURER'S DESIGNATION OF AIRCRAFT

AMERICAN GENERAL ACFT CORP AG5B

ICAO Aircraft Address Code: 52013314

ISSUED TO

FLORIDA INSTITUTE OF TECHNOLOGY
150 W UNIVERSITY BLVD
MELBOURNE FL 32901

CORPORATION

DATE OF ISSUE FEB. 04, 1991

U.S. Department of Transportation Federal Aviation Administration

Figure 4-11. Certificate of registration and airworthiness certificate

ration date must be marked on the exterior of the transmitter.

14 CFR 91.209 Aircraft lights. During the period from sunset to sunrise (there are special rules for Alaska), you must turn on your position lights: a red light on the left wing tip, green light on the right wing tip, and a white light on the tail. Position lights allow a pilot who sees your lights at night to determine your direction of movement. You must also have a flashing anti-collision light system, either red or white. Many airplanes have both red rotating beacons and white strobe lights—if either system fails, the remaining system meets the requirements of the regulation. The anti-collision system cannot take the place of the position lights, however.

It is a good idea (although not a regulation) to leave the rotating beacon switch ON at all times; it may keep you from walking away from the airplane with the master switch left on to drain the battery. It is another good but nonregulatory idea to keep your landing light(s) on when below 10,000' MSL to enhance the visibility of your airplane.

14 CFR 91.211 Supplemental oxygen. If your flight will be above 12,500 feet MSL for more than 30 minutes, then you, the pilot, must use supplemental oxygen (either a portable tank or a fixed installation) for any time over 30 minutes. If the flight will be above 14,000 feet MSL, you must use oxygen at all times. At altitudes above 15,000 feet you must provide oxygen for your passengers. Be sure they know how to use it before you leave the ground and NO SMOKING.

14 CFR 91.213 Inoperative instruments and equipment. Every airplane has a list of equipment required to be operable by its type certificate; it might be in the Operating Handbook (Section 6, preceded by an R) or in another form provided by the manufacturer, but there is one and you should be able to find and discuss it with the examiner. For multiengine airplanes, the MEL is provided by the local Flight Standards District Office. It may be possible to tag an inoperative article of equipment as defective or unusable or even to have it removed if permitted by the MEL. You and your instructor should go over this before you go for your practical test.

14 CFR 91.215 ATC transponder and altitude reporting equipment and use. You must have a transponder with altitude encoding (Mode C) capability to enter Class B or C airspace. You also need Mode C to fly above 10,000 feet MSL, to operate within the horizontal boundaries of Class C airspace and above its ceiling up to 10,000 feet MSL, and to operate between the surface and 10,000 feet MSL within 30 miles of the primary airport in Class B airspace (see the magenta 30-mile circle on the Seattle chart excerpt).

14 CFR 91.303 Aerobatic flight. Aerobatics are prohibited over a congested area, over an open air assemblage of persons (air shows get waivers of this regulation), within the lateral boundaries of Class B, C, or D airspace or Class E airspace when designated for an airport, below 1,500 feet AGL, or when flight visibility is less than 3 statute miles.

14 CFR 91.307 Parachutes and parachuting. Parachutes must be worn by all occupants of an aircraft if certain maneuvers are to be performed, unless the maneuvers are being taught in preparation for a certificate or rating. The FAA defines these maneuvers as any bank angle that exceeds 60°, or any nose-up or nose- down attitude that exceeds 30° relative to the horizon. Flight training maneuvers for the private pilot and commercial pilot certificates do not include any of these maneuvers. Any parachute used must have been packed within the preceding 120 days by a rated parachute rigger.

14 CFR 91.313 Restricted Category Civil Aircraft; operating limitations. Restricted category aircraft include cropdusters and banner towing airplanes, and they are not to be operated over congested or densely populated areas.

14 CFR 91.319 Aircraft having experimental certificates; operating limitations. You cannot fly an airplane with an *experimental* certificate (such as a homebuilt airplane) over a densely populated area or on a congested airway.

14 CFR 91.403 General [maintenance]. The owner or operator of an aircraft is primarily responsible for maintaining that aircraft in an airworthy condition. If it's your airplane, of course, that's you. If you are a renter, the responsibility lies with the fixed base operator or flight school as "operator." The responsibility for determining that the aircraft is in condition for safe flight is yours as pilot-in-command—that's why you do a preflight check. If you fly an airplane after its annual inspection has expired, the violation belongs to you, not the owner or mechanic. Learn to read and check aircraft logs. A thorough preflight should include a review of the maintenance records. This will not make you popular with the flight school or fixed-base operator, but remember that the liability is yours as pilot-in-command.

14 CFR 91.407 Operation after maintenance, preventive maintenance, rebuilding or alteration. This section requires a test flight by a *private pilot* or better before passengers can be carried on an airplane that has had maintenance or repair that affected the flight characteristics. Never fly an airplane that is just out of the shop at night or in bad weather. If something is wrong, find out about it under good conditions.

14 CFR 91.409 Inspections. Annual maintenance inspections are required for all airplanes not on an approved progressive maintenance program. An annual inspection expires at the end of the twelfth month following the inspection. 100-hour inspections are required on all airplanes operated for hire, and the FAA interprets 100 hours very strictly. If you want to rent an airplane that received its last inspection when the tachometer read 1259.6 and it now reads 1360.0, don't get in the airplane—it is unairworthy until the inspection has been accomplished.

An annual inspection may substitute for a 100-hour inspection. After a required inspection has been completed, the airplane is "returned to service" by an appropriate logbook entry by the inspector. *The aircraft's Certificate of Airworthiness never expires as long as the required inspections have been made.* An aircraft is "out of license" if an inspection is overdue, and it is the responsibility of the owner or operator to be sure that all required inspections have been performed. As stated above, however, it is the responsibility of the pilot-in-command to ensure that the airplane is airworthy—and that means checking that all required inspections have been made and logged, and the airplane "returned to service."

Remarkably, pilots have purchased airplanes that haven't flown for years, loaded them with passengers, and crashed on the first takeoff. Airplanes that have been idle for more than 60 days should be treated with suspicion.

Whether it has been a required inspection or necessary maintenance, the first flight out of the shop is always a test flight—no passengers, no night, no IFR. This is common sense, not regulation. Even the wrench-handling involved in a simple oil change can cause unrelated damage.

Airworthiness Directives are FAA mandated repairs or inspections, and the aircraft and engine logs should show that all required ADs have been performed. It is the responsibility of the pilot-in-command to insure the airworthiness of the aircraft, and this is usually interpreted to mean that you should make a thorough preflight inspection. As a renter pilot, however, you should also check the aircraft and engine logs.

This section does not contain all of the regulations, only those which are critical to private pilot operations. There are many more regulations in Parts 61 and 91 than are covered in this book, and we recommend that you get a copy of ASA's combination FAR/AIM book.

The Aviation Safety Reporting System

The FAA has designated the National Aeronautics and Space Administration (NASA) to administer the Aviation Safety Reporting System (ASRS). Several times in this text you have been warned that a violation of a Federal Aviation Regulation might result in a penalty and/or loss of your pilot certificate. Under ASRS, if you suspect (or know darn well) that you have inadvertently violated a regulation, you can fill out an ASRS form (ask your instructor, a tower controller, or FSS specialist for a copy of this form) with the circumstances of the incident, send it in to NASA at Moffet Field, CA within 10 days (the address is on the form), and the FAA will not be able to take action against you. The error has to be inadvertent, and you can only use this "Get out of jail free" card to avoid certificate action once every five years, but it gets you off the hook. Some pilots say that they file one after every flight, and I'm not sure they're joking.

The ASRS folks publish CALLBACK, a review of reports submitted by pilots and controllers; you can read them at http://asrs.arc.nasa.gov/main.htm.

Accident Reporting

National Transportation Safety Board Regulations, Part 830: These regulations govern accidents and accident reporting. They are not Federal Aviation Administration regulations, but need discussion as they lay out the rules for accident and incident reporting that pilots need to know.

The first thing you should know about Part 830 is the difference between an accident and an incident. An accident is an occurrence during which any person suffers death or serious injury, or one in which the aircraft receives substantial damage. There are fine points on just what constitutes serious injury, of course. The NTSB definition is hospitalization for more than 48 hours commencing within 7 days of the injury. An incident is an occurrence, other than an accident, which affects the safety of operations.

The following *incidents* require that the NTSB be notified:

1. Flight control malfunction or failure.
2. Inability of a required flight crewmember to perform flight duties as a result of injury or illness.
3. Failure of structural components of a turbine engine, *excluding* compressor and turbine blades and vanes.
4. In-flight fire.
5. Aircraft collide in flight.
6. Failure of Electronic Flight Information System and/or primary flight display.
7. Collision avoidance system warnings received while operating under instrument flight rules.
8. Propeller failure resulting from anything other than a ground strike.

The NTSB must also be notified when an aircraft is overdue and is believed to have been involved in an accident.

The following types of damage are exempt from being defined as "substantial damage":

Engine failure, damage limited to an engine, bent fairings or cowling, dented skin, small puncture holes in the skin or fabric, ground damage to rotor or propeller blades, damage to landing gear, wheels, tires, flaps, engine accessories, brakes, or wing tips.

In practical terms, this means that a gear-up landing in which no one was seriously injured is not a reportable accident. A fire while taxiing is not a reportable accident. Running into a structure or another airplane on the ground is not reportable. Failure of flaps to extend (or failure of one flap to extend) is not reportable, because flaps are not flight controls.

When a reportable accident does occur, the NTSB is to be notified immediately (this is usually, but not always, done by the FAA). If a written report is required, it must be submitted within 10 days. Also, don't let anyone touch or move the airplane until the NTSB arrives at the scene, except to protect the wreckage from further damage or to protect the public from injury.

Memory Aid: Notify immediately, report within 10 days.

Part 43
Preventive Maintenance

The FAA provides for a limited amount of owner-operator-performed preventive maintenance. 14 CFR Part 43 is the governing regulation, and this is what you can do:

1. Removal, installation, and repair of landing gear tires.

2. Servicing landing gear shock struts by adding oil, air, or both.

3. Servicing landing gear wheel bearings.

4. Lubrication not requiring disassembly, other than removal of nonstructural items such as coverplates, cowlings, and fairings.

5. Making simple fabric patches not requiring rib stitching or the removal of structural parts or control surfaces.

6. Replenishing hydraulic fluid in the hydraulic reservoir.

7. Making small, simple repairs to fairings, non-structural cover plates, cowlings, and small patches and reinforcements, but not changing the contour so as to interfere with proper airflow.

8. Replacing safety belts.

9. Replacing seats or belt parts with replacement parts approved for the aircraft, not involving disassembly of any primary structure or operating system.

10. Troubleshooting and repairing broken circuits on landing light wiring circuits.

11. Replacing bulbs, reflectors, and lenses of position and landing lights.

12. Replacing wheels and skis where no weight and balance computation is involved.

13. Replacing or cleaning spark plugs and setting spark plug gap clearance.

14. Replacing any hose connection except hydraulic connections.

15. Cleaning fuel and oil strainers.

16. Replacing batteries and checking fluid level and specific gravity.

You can perform other preventive maintenance activities under the supervision of a certificated mechanic if you hold a private or commercial pilot certificate. 14 CFR 91.417 says that you should keep a record of your preventive maintenance activities (the aircraft and engine logs would seem like a good place).

Airworthiness Directives

When the FAA determines that there is a problem with a specific aircraft or engine model or an operating procedure, it issues an Airworthiness Directive (AD)—it is unlikely that you will ever see an AD in your everyday flying activities. Compliance with ADs is mandatory, and responsibility for carrying out the provisions of an AD is placed on the owner or operator. Many ADs require inspections on a scheduled basis ("Every 50 hours"), or allow time for compliance ("Within the next 100 flight hours…"), so you can fly an airplane on which an AD has been issued if the AD makes provision for continued flight.

Minimum Equipment Lists

As mentioned under FAR 91.213, the FAA does not want you to fly an aircraft that has something important inoperative or missing without some kind of warning—after takeoff is a bad time to learn about such things. Twins have an MEL; most singles do not. The example usually given to drive home the importance/silliness of this regulation is the cigarette lighter; if it is listed under Required Equipment in the Approved Flight Manual, it must be present and working. Very few FAA inspectors would go to such an extreme looking for violations, but that is what the regulation calls for.

You determine the equipment required for your airplane by first considering the type of operation you are about to embark on. Day or night? VFR or IFR? Look in 91.205 for the basics; 91.207, 91.209, and 91.215 add the ELT, lights, and a transponder. Then look at the parts list in the AFM; in most cases, required items will have an "R" after the item number.

Now you or a mechanic must decide if the inoperative gizmo is essential to the safety of flight. If it is not, it must be removed or deactivated, and a placard warning of its status placed on the empty hole. At the next inspection, a mechanic must repair, replace, or inspect the item to return it to service, or authorize its continued placarded state and make an airframe logbook entry to that effect.

Airport/Facility Directory

Before setting off on a cross-country flight, you are required to become familiar with all available information regarding the flight, and the Airport/Facility Directory (A/FD) is your source of information on the destination airport and any others along the route you may decide to visit. Aeronautical charts show the elevation, runway length, and limited radio frequency information for an airport, but only in the Airport/Facility Directory will you learn that the runway is gravel, 75 feet wide, with trees on the west, and that it slopes upward to the north. The legend for individual airport listings is provided in Appendix C of this text. You will also find pertinent excerpts in Lesson 11. In addition to the individual airport listings, the A/FD contains:

- Special notices in regard to airports listed
- FSS and National Weather Service telephone numbers
- Frequencies of Air Route Traffic Control Centers
- FAA General Aviation District Office telephone numbers
- VOR receiver check points
- Parachute jumping areas
- Aeronautical Chart Bulletin (contains information about obstacles and hazards that have been noted since the last chart was printed and which will be included in the next printing)
- Location of Enroute Flight Advisory Stations (Flight Watch)
- Airport diagrams for all public airports; detailed airport diagrams for large airports; airport diagrams are also available at www.naco.faa.gov
- VFR GPS waypoints

The Airport/Facility Directory is published in seven volumes depending on geographic location and is revised every 56 days.

An online version is available by going to www.naco.faa.gov and clicking on "Free Digital Products" in the left column. The resulting page offers a number of valuable AeroNav products in addition to the A/FD. The A/FD and its online counterpart are the only *official* sources of airport information; do not rely on commercial publications.

Appendix C reprints the A/FD Legend. Read it thoroughly. An amazing number of "Where does it say…?" or "where can I find out?" questions can be answered by reading the Legend. The ability to interpret the airport listings is only part of what you need to know.

Much of the information contained in the A/FD (but not the Aeronautical Chart Bulletin) can be found at www.airnav.com, www.landings.com, www.runwayfinder.com or, for members only, www.aopa.org.

Advisory Circulars

The Federal Aviation Regulations are brief and concise, written by and for lawyers, not pilots. There are many situations where a regulation or a procedure needs to be explained in detail so that the flying public can understand exactly what is required. This is the function of Advisory Circulars. ACs are non-regulatory in nature, serving only to explain the actual regulation or provide additional useful information to aid in compliance; however, the government expects every pilot to be aware of information published only in Advisory Circulars! Unfortunately, many pilots are unaware of their existence. Advisory Circulars are available online at the www.faa.gov home page, in the right-hand column.

Advisory Circulars are numbered to correspond with the regulations—here are two examples: 14 CFR Part 61 deals with airman and flight instructor certification, while Advisory Circular 61-65 explains flight instructor duties and responsibilities; 14 CFR Part 91 is General Operating Rules, and Advisory Circular 91-13 deals with cold-weather operations of aircraft. Most pilots are only aware of those Advisory Circulars which are published in book form, such as *Aviation Weather* (AC 00-6A) or the *Airplane Flying Handbook* (FAA-H-8083-3), but you should investigate whether the FAA publishes an AC on any subject you may be curious about. You can order Advisory Circulars (most are free, but some are for sale) from the Superintendent of Documents at the Government Printing Office in Washington, D.C., or order ASA's CD-ROM Flight Library which includes all the ACs. ACs can be found online at www.faa.gov; they are accessed from the home page.

Notices to Airmen

Information that might affect the safety of a flight, such as a runway closure, Temporary Flight Restriction (TFR), NAVAID outage, lighting system change, etc., is available from your flight service station briefer.

Your briefer has access to NOTAMs. So do you, at https://pilotweb.nas.faa.gov/distribution/atcscc.html. If you get an error message, click on "I accept the risk." This is a browser problem; the FAA site is secure. If you use one of the computer flight planning programs, such as DUAT, DUATS, or the AOPA flight planner, you will also receive current NOTAMs.

NOTAM (L) no longer exists. Information formerly included in L NOTAMs is now included in NOTAM (D). If you want to know about VOR outages, runway closures, lighting system outages, men and equipment on the runway, etc., look or ask for D NOTAMs. For long cross-country trips it is sometimes valuable to call one of the operators at the destination airport for last-minute information like "the gas pump is broken!"

To make it easier for pilots to scan through a list of NOTAMs for information specific to their flight, the FAA uses "key words" in the first line of text. See Figure 4-12.

Checking for Temporary Flight Restrictions (TFRs) is absolutely essential; they are published as Flight Data Center (FDC) NOTAMs. TFRs are usually designated to protect public figures. Making this check will avoid having a couple of F-16s escort you to the nearest airport.

Every 28 days the FAA releases the *Notices to Airmen* publication that contains all current NOTAM (D)s and FDC NOTAMs, except for Temporary Flight Restrictions. When a NOTAM is published here (or in the A/FD) it no longer shows up on the briefer's screen; if you don't *ask* the briefer for any published NOTAMs that will affect your flight, you will never find out about them. You can get this publication online at www.faa.gov/NTAP.

Aviation Media

All pilots are expected to stay abreast of changes in regulations and procedures, but advancing technology is teaching new ways of navigating and of solving some of the mysteries of weather, and pilots cannot expect today's methods to apply forever. The aviation press is the best source of information on the changing world of flight, and we recommend that you read aviation newspapers and magazines. The FAA's *Aviation Safety Bulletin,* published six times a year, is available from the FAA home page, and you will find a wealth of information on the Air Safety Foundation website, www.asf.org.

The "hangar flying" that used to offer pilots and instructors an opportunity to ask questions and exchange ideas is now accomplished via computer. On the internet, there are a number of aviation websites such as www.aopa.org, www.eaa.org, www.pilotsofamerica.com, and www.studentpilot.com. Many well-known aviation authors have their own websites (but I don't), and using a search engine will always help you find what you need. The FAA offers excellent online resources for their publications, education and training materials. These will be important bookmarks for your favorite browser:

www.faa.gov

www.faasafety.gov

http://www.gpo.gov/fdsys/

The "D" NOTAM

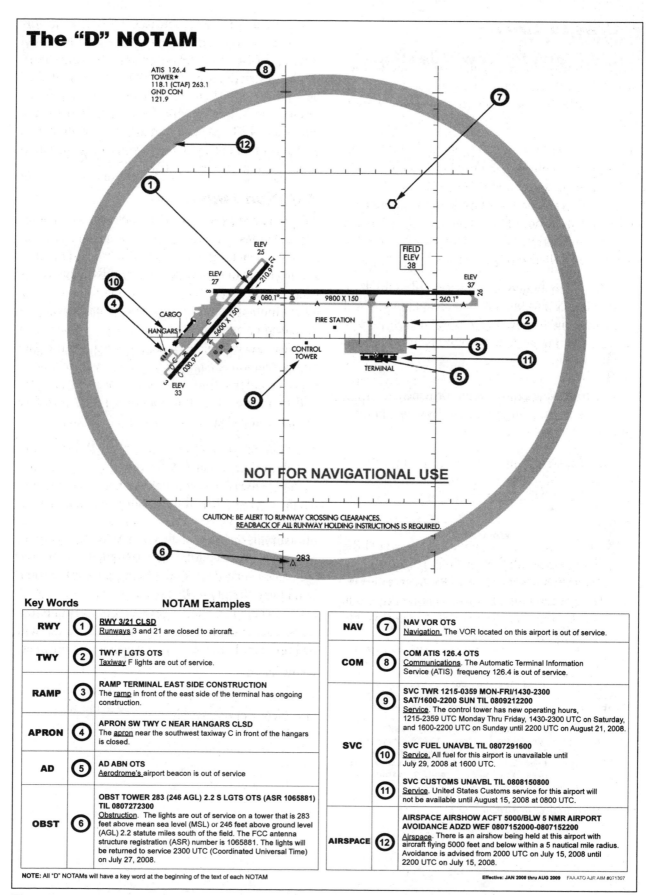

NOT FOR NAVIGATIONAL USE

CAUTION: BE ALERT TO RUNWAY CROSSING CLEARANCES.
READBACK OF ALL RUNWAY HOLDING INSTRUCTIONS IS REQUIRED.

Key Words   NOTAM Examples

Key Word		NOTAM Example
RWY	(1)	**RWY 3/21 CLSD** Runways 3 and 21 are closed to aircraft.
TWY	(2)	**TWY F LGTS OTS** Taxiway F lights are out of service.
RAMP	(3)	**RAMP TERMINAL EAST SIDE CONSTRUCTION** The ramp in front of the east side of the terminal has ongoing construction.
APRON	(4)	**APRON SW TWY C NEAR HANGARS CLSD** The apron near the southwest taxiway C in front of the hangars is closed.
AD	(5)	**AD ABN OTS** Aerodrome's airport beacon is out of service
OBST	(6)	**OBST TOWER 283 (246 AGL) 2.2 S LGTS OTS (ASR 1065881) TIL 0807272300** Obstruction. The lights are out of service on a tower that is 283 feet above mean sea level (MSL) or 246 feet above ground level (AGL) 2.2 statute miles south of the field. The FCC antenna structure registration (ASR) number is 1065881. The lights will be returned to service 2300 UTC (Coordinated Universal Time) on July 27, 2008.

Key Word		NOTAM Example
NAV	(7)	**NAV VOR OTS** Navigation. The VOR located on this airport is out of service.
COM	(8)	**COM ATIS 126.4 OTS** Communications. The Automatic Terminal Information Service (ATIS) frequency 126.4 is out of service.
SVC	(9)	**SVC TWR 1215-0359 MON-FRI/1430-2300 SAT/1600-2200 SUN TIL 0809212200** Service. The control tower has new operating hours, 1215-2359 UTC Monday Thru Friday, 1430-2300 UTC on Saturday, and 1600-2200 UTC on Sunday until 2200 UTC on August 21, 2008.
	(10)	**SVC FUEL UNAVBL TIL 0807291600** Service. All fuel for this airport is unavailable until July 29, 2008 at 1600 UTC.
	(11)	**SVC CUSTOMS UNAVBL TIL 0808150800** Service. United States Customs service for this airport will not be available until August 15, 2008 at 0800 UTC.
AIRSPACE	(12)	**AIRSPACE AIRSHOW ACFT 5000/BLW 5 NMR AIRPORT AVOIDANCE ADZD WEF 0807152000-0807152200** Airspace. There is an airshow being held at this airport with aircraft flying 5000 feet and below within a 5 nautical mile radius. Avoidance is advised from 2000 UTC on July 15, 2008 until 2200 UTC on July 15, 2008.

NOTE: All "D" NOTAMs will have a key word at the beginning of the text of each NOTAM

Effective: JAN 2008 thru AUG 2009   FAA ATO AJR AIM #071307

Figure 4-12. Example of FAA NOTAM "key words"

Lesson 4
Regulations Review Questions

Refer to Notices to Airmen (Figure Q4-1) for questions 1 and 2.

1. What is the status of the runway lights for a landing at New Smyrna Beach Muni 1 on Rwy 15 after 2400?

    A— For runway lights, key the transmitter the proper number of times on 122.8 MHz.

    B— The lights on this runway are not operated at night.

    C— The runway lights operate from dusk to dawn.

2. The traffic pattern for light airplanes and gyroplanes at Ft. Lauderdale-Hollywood International Airport is changed to

    A— 800 feet.

    B— 1,000 feet.

    C— 1,300 feet.

```
                    FLORIDA

FT LAUDERDALE EXECUTIVE ARPT:    TPA 800 ft.
TPA for jets 1300 ft. 4 box VASI cmsnd
left side Rwy 26. 2 Box VASI cmsnd left
side Rwy 13.  (3/81)
FT LAUDERDALE-HOLLYWOOD INTL ARPT:   TPA 1000
ft.  Thr Rwy 27L dsplcd 401 ft.  Thr Rwy
09L dsplcd 609 ft.  Thr Rwy 27R dsplcd 599
ft. (3/81)
FT MYERS PAGE FIELD ARPT:     Unicom Freq
123.05. (3/81)
MIAMI INTL ARPT: Wide Body & DC-8 acft lndg
Rwy 09L & desiring to taxi west on Twy M
are advised to use Twys M-8, M-9, M-10, M-11
or the end. Twys are numbered W to E.
(3/81) RVR Rwy 27L OTS UFN. (3/81)
NEW SMYRNA BEACH MUNI ARPT: Rwy 15/33 Rwy
lgts oper dusk-dawn. Rwy 11/29 Rwy lgts
oper dusk-2400.  For VASI and Rwy 11/29
Rwy lgts after 2400 key 122.8 3 times for
low,  5 times for med,  and 7 times for
high. (1/81)
```

Figure Q4-1. *Notices to Airmen*

3. FAA Advisory Circulars (some free, others at cost) are available to all pilots and are obtained by

    A— distribution from the nearest FAA district office.

    B— ordering those desired.

    C— subscribing to the Federal Register.

4. Information concerning parachute jumping sites maybe found in the

    A— Graphic Notices and Supplemental Data.

    B— Airport/Facility Directory.

    C— NOTAMs.

5. Between publication dates for sectional charts, information as to changes can be found in

    A— Airport/Facility Directory.

    B— NOTAM(D)s.

    C— Aeronautical Information Manual.

6. What is the general direction of movement of the other aircraft during a night flight if you observe a steady red light and a flashing red light ahead and at the same altitude?

    A— The other aircraft is crossing to the left.

    B— The other aircraft is crossing to the right.

    C— The other aircraft is approaching head-on.

7. If an aircraft is involved in an accident which resulted in substantial damage to the aircraft, the nearest NTSB field office should be notified

    A— immediately.

    B— within 7 days.

    C— within 10 days.

8. Of the following incidents, which would require an immediate notification to the nearest NTSB field office?

   A — An in-flight generator/alternator failure.
   B — An in-flight fire.
   C — Ground damage to the propeller blades.

9. A private pilot acting as pilot-in-command, or in any other capacity as a required pilot flight crewmember, must have in their personal possession while aboard the aircraft

   A — a current logbook endorsement to show that a flight review has been satisfactorily accomplished.
   B — the current and appropriate pilot and medical certificates.
   C — the pilot logbook to show recent experience requirements to serve as pilot-in-command have been met.

10. What is the duration, if any, of a private pilot certificate?

   A — It expires 24 months after issuance.
   B — As long as the flight review and the medical certificate are current.
   C — Indefinite.

11. A third-class medical certificate was issued on May 3, this year, to a pilot less than 40 years of age. To exercise the privileges of a private pilot certificate, the medical certificate will be valid through

   A — May 31, 1 year later.
   B — May 31, 5 years later.
   C — May 3, 2 years later.

12. To act as pilot-in-command of an airplane that has more than 200 hp, a person is required to do which of the following?

   A — Make three solo takeoffs and landings in such an airplane.
   B — Receive flight instruction and an endorsement in an airplane that has more than 200 hp.
   C — Hold a 200 hp class rating.

13. To act as pilot-in-command of an airplane with passengers aboard, the pilot must have made at least three takeoffs and landings in an aircraft in the same category and class within the preceding

   A — 120 days.
   B — 90 days.
   C — 12 months.

14. If recency of experience requirements for night flight have not been met and official sunset is 1830, the latest time passengers may be carried is

   A — 1829.
   B — 1859.
   C — 1929.

15. To meet the recent flight experience requirements for acting as pilot-in-command carrying passengers at night, a pilot must have made, within the preceding 90 days and at night, at least

   A — three takeoffs and landings to a full stop in the same category and class of aircraft to be used.
   B — three takeoffs and landings in the same category and class of aircraft to be used.
   C — three takeoffs and landings to a full stop in the same category but not necessarily in the same class of aircraft to be used.

16. In regard to privileges and limitations, a private pilot may

   A — not pay less than the pro rata share of the operating expenses of a flight with passengers provided the expenses involve only fuel, oil, airport expenditures, or rental fees.
   B — act as pilot-in-command of an aircraft carrying a passenger for compensation if the flight is in connection with a business or employment.
   C — not be paid in any manner for the operating expenses of a flight.

17. What preflight action is required for every flight?

   A — Check weather reports and forecasts.
   B — Determine runway length at airports of intended use.
   C — Determine alternatives if the flight cannot be completed.

18. In addition to other preflight actions for a VFR flight away from the vicinity of the departure airport, regulations require the pilot-in-command to

A — file a flight plan.
B — check each fuel tank visually to ensure that it is full.
C — determine runway lengths at airports of intended use and the airplane's takeoff and landing distance data.

19. Under what condition may a person act as pilot-in-command of an aircraft after consuming alcohol which may affect that person's faculties?

A — Passengers may not be carried.
B — A waiver must be obtained.
C — Only after the expiration of 8 hours.

20. What is the fuel requirement for flight under VFR at night?

A — Enough to complete the flight at normal cruising flight with adverse wind conditions.
B — Enough to fly to the first point of intended landing and to fly after that for 30 minutes at normal cruising speed.
C — Enough to fly to the first point of intended landing and to fly after that for 45 minutes at normal cruising speed.

21. Where, in the 48 contiguous United States and District of Columbia, is a radar beacon transponder equipped with a Mode C required?

A — In Class D airspace.
B — In Class B airspace and in controlled airspace above 10,000 feet MSL.
C — In Class B airspace.

22. An aircraft had a 100-hour inspection when the tachometer read 1259.6. When is the next 100-hour inspection due?

A — 1269.6 hours
B — 1309.6 hours
C — 1359.6 hours

23. A 100-hour inspection was due at 3302.5 hours on the tachometer but was actually done at 3309.5 hours. When is the next 100-hour inspection due?

A — 3409.5 hours
B — 3402.5 hours
C — 3809.5 hours

24. Which operation would be described as preventive maintenance?

A — Removing and installing glider wings.
B — Repair of landing gear brace struts.
C — Refinishing decorative coating of fuselage.

25. Preventive maintenance has been performed on an aircraft. What paperwork is required?

A — A full, detailed description of the work done must be entered in the airframe logbook.
B — The date the work was completed and the name of the person who did the works must be entered in the pilot's logbook.
C — The signature, certificate number, and kind of certificate held by the person approving the work and a description of the work must be entered in the aircraft maintenance records.

26. You plan a night flight in uncontrolled airspace, intending to stay about 1,000 feet above the terrain. What cloud clearance and visibility restrictions must you observe? You do not have an instrument rating.

A — One mile visibility and clear of clouds.
B — Three miles visibility, 500 feet below, 1,000 feet above, and 2,000 feet horizontally from all clouds.
C — One mile visibility, 500 feet below, 1,000 feet above, and 2,000 feet horizontally from all clouds.

27. Would the answer to question 21 be different if you planned to fly more than 1,200 feet above the ground in Class G (uncontrolled) airspace?

Procedures and Airport Operations

Lesson **5**

The Five P's

The preceding lessons have provided the basics—the airframe, aerodynamics, the engine, and the instrumentation. Now we are going to put this information to use. As we do, we will place each element in one of the 5 P's as defined by the FAA's single-pilot resource management (SRM) program:

- Plan
- Plane
- Pilot
- Passengers
- Programming

The Plan

Does your planned flight take you into or near any restricted airspace? Class B? Military Operations Area? Have you checked with Flight Service for any last-minute Temporary Flight Restrictions? Lesson 9 will help. Will the altitude you have selected provide comfortable clearance over terrain? How about cloud cover-can you fly over the clouds, or can you fly beneath them and still have safe terrain clearance? Can you take off and clear any obstacles by a comfortable margin? Is the enroute weather getting better or worse? Will your passengers have a comfortable ride? Lessons 6 and 7 will help. Do you have all necessary charts and publications close at hand,

not in the back seat? Lessons 4 and 9 will tell you what you need. Do you have enough fuel on board to complete your planned flight plus reserves? Chapters 8 and 9 will help with the calculations.

The Plane

Is the airplane suited to the mission, able to carry the planned load, take off with a comfortable margin, and provide a lively climb rate with something in reserve (Lesson 8)? Does the weight and balance of the planned load fall within the plane's performance envelope (Lesson 8)? Is the plane's inspection status current? Any unresolved squawks? Any Minimum Equipment List issues (Lesson 4)?

The Pilot

Could you pass a physical examination today for the class of medical you hold? Extra eyeglasses on hand, if you are required to have them? Have you taken any medications whose effects might be magnified by altitude? Anything stressful going on in your life? Can you close your mind to outside influences and concentrate on a safe, comfortable flight? Surely, you haven't had any alcoholic drinks in the past 8 hours. No drugs whatsoever? Are you fatigued, or have you had restful sleep? Are you taking off with an empty stomach? A cup of coffee and a doughnut won't hack it. If you plan to fly at altitudes where supplemental oxygen is required, do you have enough for everyone on board for the period of time at those altitudes? Masks or cannulae for everyone?

The Passengers

Are your passengers pilots, non-pilots, or a mix? Are the non-pilots nervous? Have they flown with you before? Are they all in good health (no colds)? Do they understand how to clear their ears? Will they be helpful or distracting? Do they understand silent cockpit? Is the trip urgent for them, or optional? Do they understand that you might land short of your destination, be delayed, or even turn back? If it is a business trip, will that put pressure on you to perform beyond your abilities and proficiency?

The Programming

This "P" is more important to pilots who fly under Instrument Flight Rules than it is to those who fly visually. The programming of onboard navigation equipment (Lesson 9) is less important to VFR pilots because they can change altitude or course at any time. However, now is the time for you to master the nuances of the equipment you have on board, so that by the time you begin training for the instrument rating you will not be fumbling with knobs and switches.

The Airport

At any airport, you will have to be able to identify the runway in use, taxi safely, be aware of wake turbulence hazards, deal with the line crew, know who (if anyone) controls your actions, interpret lights and markings, etc. This lesson will discuss general airport operations, differentiate between tower and non-tower airports, and provide guidance on what you should expect.

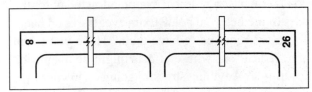

Figure 5-1. *Runway numbering*

As your flying experience expands to include more airports, you will find some features that they all have in common. For instance, all runways are numbered according to their direction in relation to magnetic north, to the closest 10°. A runway laid out 078° from magnetic north would be numbered 8: rounded off to 080° and the zeros dropped. The opposite end of the runway would be numbered 26, the reciprocal (Figure 5-1). Some large airports have parallel runways which are identified as left, right, or center: runway 27R, runway 6L, etc. Be sure to set your heading indicator to agree with the runway number before takeoff.

You will normally take off and land into the wind; the wind indicator tells the direction the wind is blowing from. Every airport should have some form of wind indicator or landing direction indicator. Figure 5-2 shows several types of landing direction indicators: the tetrahedron, the windsock, and the wind tee. All of the indicators in the illustration indicate a wind from the west. Sport pilots must be especially sensitive to wind direction and velocity and the presence of gusts, because light sport aircraft must be flown all the way to the ground, unlike planes weighing more than 1,320 pounds that can "punch through" gusts.

At some airports, the tetrahedron or wind tee may be tied down to show the favored runway and will not accurately reflect wind conditions. Always observe what other pilots in the pattern are doing and con-

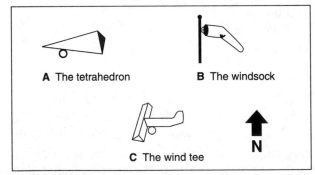

Figure 5-2. *Wind indicators*

form with the pattern in use; if there are no other airplanes in the pattern it is your choice. Figures 5-3 and 5-4 show landing strip indicators and landing pattern indicators—the landing strip indicators parallel the runways and the landing pattern indicators show the direction traffic flows to and from the runways. Your pattern should conform with the traffic flow indicated for the runway in use. *See* Figure 5-4.

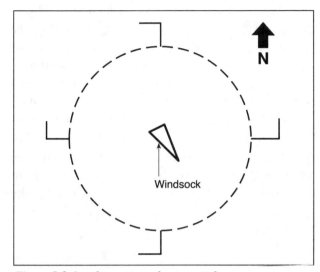

Figure 5-3. *Landing strip and pattern indicators*

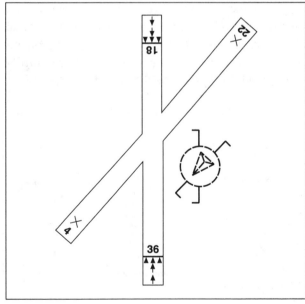

Figure 5-4. *Pattern markings*

Although the standard traffic pattern uses a left-hand pattern, frequently terrain or the presence of a congested area dictate the use of a right-hand pattern. Figure 5-5 shows pattern indicators which keep traffic from overflying the area northwest of the water tank. Where there are no pattern indicators, the regulations require that all turns in the pattern be made to the left. When you fly over an unfamiliar airport and do not see a pattern indicator, you are safe in assuming a left-hand pattern. If an airport requires a right-hand pattern for any runway, the data block on the sectional chart will have a notation such as "RP 11 16," indicating that runways 11 and 16 have right-hand patterns (*see* Page 5-4). If the notation includes an asterisk: *RP 12, the right-hand pattern is in effect only during certain hours—check the A/FD for details.

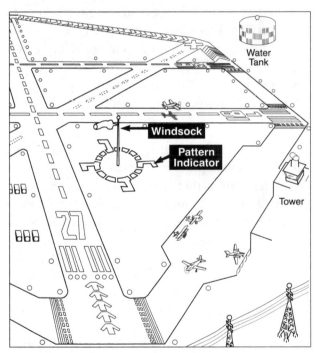

Figure 5-5. *Traffic pattern indicators*

Figure 5-6 shows the FAA *recommended* standard left-hand traffic pattern with arrival and departure procedures (note the recommended—not required—45° entry to the downwind leg…but understand that almost everyone uses this entry). If the airport has an *FAA required* traffic pattern, you must use that pattern (few airports have such patterns—14 CFR Part 93 lists them). Don't let courthouse lawyers tell you that the right turn onto the downwind leg shown at position 1 in Figure 5-6 is a violation of the left turn rule—you are not "in the pattern" until you have completed that turn. You should always be at pattern altitude when on the 45; never descend into the pattern.

Not illustrated but frequently used is the downwind departure. In the illustration, airplane #'s 5 and 6 are departing in the direction of takeoff…but what if their destination is in the opposite direction? Then they perform (or ask the tower for) a downwind departure. To avoid conflict with airplanes entering the pattern on the 45, pilots performing downwind departures should climb as indicated by plane #5 until well above pattern altitude before turning downwind.

It is an unfortunate fact of life that not all pilots observe recommended procedures. You must be alert to the possibility that another pilot is entering the pattern from a different direction, or straight in—instrument students almost always make straight-in

approaches. The instrument runway might not be the one in use by VFR pilots. Listen carefully to the position reports by other pilots, and expect the unexpected.

Adjacent to every airport symbol on an aeronautical chart is an airport data block with the airport name and identifier, its elevation above sea level, the length of the longest runway in hundreds of feet, an "RP" to identify runways with right-hand patterns, an **Ⓡ** if radar is available, a **Ⓒ** indicating the Common Traffic Advisory Frequency (CTAF), the AWOS/ASOS frequency if available, the Automated Terminal Information Service (ATIS) frequency for most tower-controlled airports, and information on runway lighting. All of the information can be deciphered by use of the sectional chart legend, but you should be able to get the essential information at a glance. A few pre-flight moments devoted to researching the Airport/Facility Directory for the destination and any enroute airports will be time well spent.

For example, look at the data block for Seattle-Tacoma International Airport on the sectional chart excerpt at the back of the book. The airport is 433 feet above sea level, the longest runway is 11,900 feet long, and runway lighting is available from sunset to sunrise. Radio frequencies for the control tower, Automatic Terminal Information Service, and Aeronautical Advisory Service (UNICOM) are also listed.

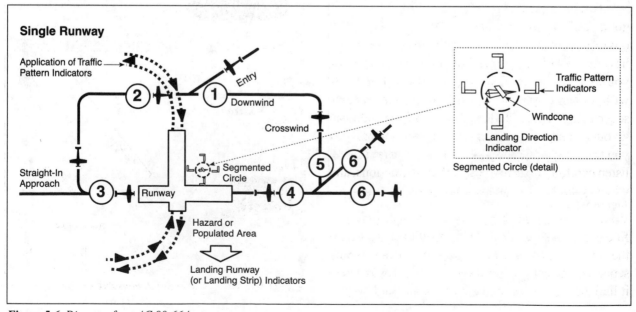

Figure 5-6. Diagram from AC 90-66A

On the sectional chart you will notice many airports without runway symbols: these airports have unpaved runways or paved runways less than 1,500 feet in length. Airport symbols with little protrusions around their edges indicate that services (usually fuel) are available. You will also find airports with no radio service and airports without lighting. You should never be surprised by what you find at the end of a flight—you should know all about your destination airport before you take off. Charts and the *Airport/Facility Directory* are the government's means of providing airport information; there are also several private publishers of booklets with VFR airport information.

Airports can be divided into two categories: those with control towers and those without. On the sectional chart excerpt, you will see that airport symbols printed in blue are those airports with towers and those printed in magenta have no towers. When the tower is not in operation, the airports with blue symbols are to be treated as non-tower airports. Part-time towers are indicated by an asterisk next to the control tower frequency. Check the data blocks for the Tacoma Narrows and Olympia airports ((**J**) and (**F**) on the sectional chart excerpt) as examples of part-time towers. The *Airport/Facility Directory* also contains information on hours of operation.

You should always have a runway diagram, if one is available. Computer users can find diagrams for most large airports (which are the most confusing) by searching online for "airport diagrams." Two good sources are www.aopa.org/airports and www.ourairports.com. These aerial photographs will not have the detail of a printed diagram but will allow you to get a sense of the airport layout. For pilots without computer access, pilot supply stores carry several flight guides that include runway and taxiway layouts. Treat your ground operations as seriously as you treat flight planning—pre-plan your taxi route, listen carefully to ground controller instructions, and when in doubt, stop and ask for assistance.

Where runway markings are provided, you will find centerline marking, a threshold marking where the landing surface begins, and a "hold line" which separates the active runway from the taxiway (treat it like the lane separation on a two-lane highway—

if the two solid lines are closest to you, do not let any portion of your airplane project past them; the solid lines are always on the taxiway side, and the broken lines are always on the runway side). Runways used for instrument approaches have additional markings. If there are obstacles in the approach path, the threshold may be displaced; arrows will lead to the displaced threshold. Note that in the illustration (Figure 5-7) the threshold of runway 27 has been displaced because of the power lines. Any paved area which appears to be usable, but which is not usable for normal operations, is marked with yellow chevrons. Such areas may be used as overruns at the end of a runway. In Figure 5-7, the taxiway beyond the threshold of runway 18R is marked as unusable.

On taxiways, a double yellow line separates movement areas from non-movement areas. The taxiway itself is a movement area, and the ground controller directs your movements; non-movement areas (usually called "the ramp") include tiedowns, hangars, fuel islands, etc. Although it is good practice to let the ground controller know what you are doing and where you are going, you are not required to do so because those areas do not belong to the ground controller. Ramp markings in non-movement areas are white lines.

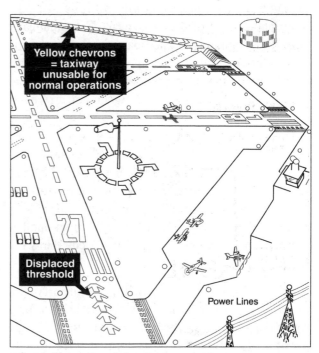

Figure 5-7. *Displaced threshold; unusable taxiway*

A runway is closed when a yellow X is placed at its center. If there are multiple runways, a runway with an X at each end is closed, and an X at the center of the runway complex indicates that the whole airport is closed. You can take off or land using a closed runway—the FAA would consider a resulting accident or incident as careless or negligent operation, and the airport owner might have recourse under civil law. At a controlled airport, the controller will let you do anything you want to do on a closed or inactive runway after advising that you are doing so at your own risk. The FAA does not close runways, they are closed by local authorities.

For night operations, taxiways are marked with **omnidirectional** blue lights and the active runway is marked with omnidirectional white lights. Green lights mark the threshold, and red lights alert you to the end of the landing surface—these are directional lights, showing green in one direction and red in the other. Hazards, such as the water tank in Figure 5-5, are marked with red lights.

At many airports the lighting is controlled by the pilot, who transmits on a specified frequency (usually the CTAF) and keys the microphone briefly to turn on the lights. At most airports with pilot-controlled lighting, the pilot can control the intensity of the lighting by varying the number of "clicks" on the microphone button. The lights turn off automatically after fifteen minutes. On aeronautical charts, airports with pilot-controlled lighting are indicated by *L; details on the frequency and keying code are found in the A/FD. If the lights are on when you arrive it is a good operating practice to click your microphone button seven times, just in case it has been almost fifteen minutes since the lights were activated—you don't want the lights to go out when you are on short final. At some airports, the operation of the rotating beacon is pilot-controlled; you won't see its welcoming beam until you transmit the correct number of clicks on the correct frequency. Check the A/FD before the sun goes down.

Rotating beacons are installed at all airports with towers and at many non-tower airports, and as they rotate the pilot sees a white flash followed by a single green flash. Military airports are identified at night by two white flashes between each green flash. When the rotating beacon is lighted in the daytime, it means

that the weather is below the minimums required for visual flight. You should check the actual weather and not rely on the light, however, since many rotating beacons are turned on by timers or photoelectric cells.

Online Sources for Airport Information

Computer users can learn more than they need to know about any public airport by searching databases maintained by www.avweb.com, www.landings.com, www.airnav.com and www.aopa.org among many others.

VASI

Visual Approach Slope Indicators (VASI) are installed at both tower-controlled and non-tower airports, and provide a visual means for the pilot to maintain a constant glide angle (usually 3 degrees) on final approach. Information on the type of VASI and the glide path angle can be found in the A/FD listing for the desired airport. A VASI installation defines the approach slope by providing light boxes adjacent to the runway—each box contains a light source and filters so arranged that when the pilot is on the desired glide path the box closest to the threshold (downwind) will show a white light, and the box furthest from the threshold (upwind) will show a red light. To the pilot on the correct glide path this appears as red over white: "red over white is right." Two white lights indicate a position too high on the glide path: "white over white, you're high as a kite." If a pilot is below the desired glide path both light boxes will show a red light: "red over red—you're dead" (a little morbid, but it rhymes and conveys a strong warning). Where a VASI is provided, you are required to use it by flying on or above the visual glide path until descent is required for landing. Figure 5-8 shows 2- and 3-bar VASI.

The eyes of the pilot of a long-bodied jet are about 50 feet above the surface when the landing gear touches

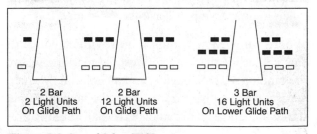

Figure 5-8. 2- and 3-bar VASI

down, so three sets of VASI boxes are provided on runways where such jets operate. The two sets of boxes closest to the threshold define the glide path for light aircraft and the two furthest define the glide path for jets.

The FAA is installing the Precision Approach Path Indicator (PAPI) shown in Figure 5-9 at many airports because it gives a more accurate indication of off-glidepath flight than a VASI installation. The FAA has designated the PAPI as the standard visual approach aid for new installations.

The FAA has approved use of other types of visual approach aids, such as a single-source amber-green-red indicator. This VASI shows a green light when you are on the glide path, an amber light when you are high, and a red light when you are dangerously low. Other approved lighting systems include a single line of lights which show red or white depending on your position on the glide path.

Providing the pilot with accurate descent path information is so important that some small airports have a visual aid consisting of painted boards installed beside the runway 50-100 feet apart. The pilot aligns the boards visually to stay on the glide path. This is called a "POMOLA," for Poor Man's Optical Landing Aid (Figure 5-10).

Taxiing

Strong gusty winds can make taxiing a chore, and mishandling the controls might result in loss of control. You must understand how to use the controls so that the wind cannot get beneath the wing or tail surfaces and cause you to drag a wing tip or have the propeller strike the ground. This is especially true of light sport aircraft, which are more responsive to the vagaries of the wind than standard category aircraft.

When the wind is coming from a direction in front of the airplane, from wing tip to wing tip, hold the ailerons as though you are banking into the wind.

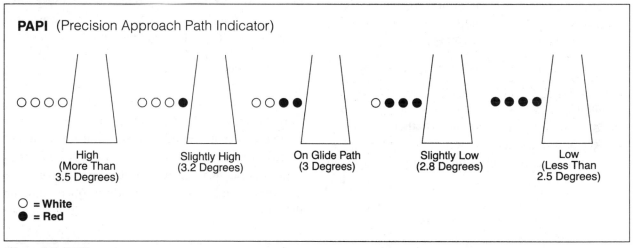

Figure 5-9. PAPI

Figure 5-10. POMOLA

The up-aileron on the windward side will depress the wing as the wind strikes it—the down-aileron on the opposite wing will create enough lift to oppose any overturning tendency. The elevator should be in a neutral position unless you are flying a taildragger, in which case full back elevator control will pin the tailwheel to the ground for steering control.

A quartering tailwind is most hazardous for a tricycle gear airplane, because a gust can lift the wing and tail and upset the airplane. To counter this tendency, when the wind is coming from any direction behind the airplane, the ailerons should be held away from the wind, and the elevator held in neutral or slightly forward (well forward in a taildragger). The down-aileron will now be on the windward side, and the wind from behind the wing will hold it down. Figure 5-11 illustrates this technique.

At tower-controlled airports, a solid double yellow line separates "movement areas," where permission from the ground controller is required, from non-movement areas where the ground controller has no authority. This would include moving between rows of hangars, taxiing to the fueling area, etc.

Look ahead to Figure 5-18. If you were on the parking ramp and runway 36R was being used for takeoffs and landings at this towered airport, your instructions will be to stop at every hold line, whether the runway is active or not, and ask for permission to cross. The closed runway has no hold lines, but you must stop and ask anyway. This has always been a good idea; now it is a requirement placed on controllers. So if your controller fails to tell you to stop before crossing a runway, stop anyway and call for clarification.

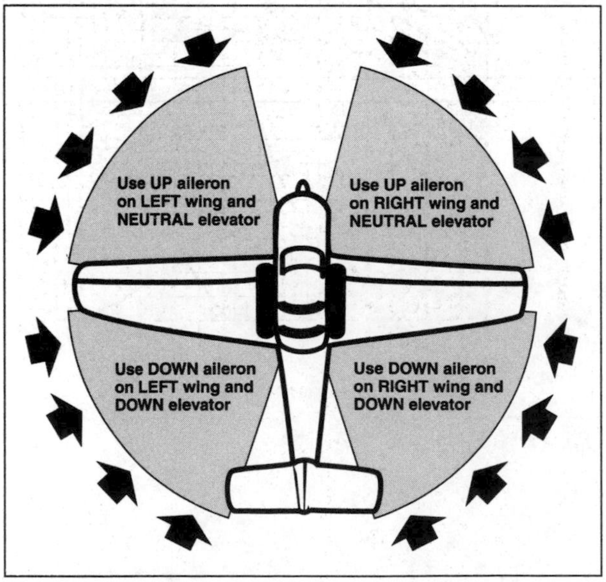

Crosswind Operations

Although airport designers try to align runways with the prevailing winds, there is always the possibility that the wind may not be blowing directly down the runway you intend to use. The manufacturer of your airplane has designated a maximum crosswind component for your airplane, and you will find it either placarded in the cockpit or in the Pilot's Operating Handbook. It is called "maximum *demonstrated* crosswind component" if the factory test pilot demonstrated that the airplane was controllable with a crosswind component at the published figure. You offset the crosswind component by using ailerons to control sideways drift and rudder to keep the longitudinal axis (and the airplane's direction of motion) aligned with the runway. When the crosswind component exceeds the published maximum, these aerodynamic controls may not be able to overcome the sideways drift and the tendency of the airplane to yaw or weathercock into the wind. You will "run out of rudder." *See* Figure 5-12.

Many pilots have trouble with crosswind operations because they are reluctant to use full control deflections. You should be ready to use full rudder or full aileron when required. A crosswind takeoff roll should begin with full aileron toward the crosswind, and a crosswind landing roll should end the same way.

Figure 5-11. *Taxiing diagram*

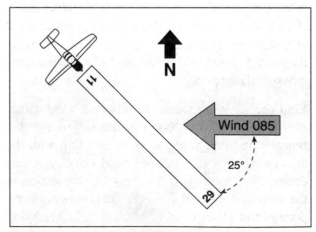

Figure 5-12. *Crosswind component*

The difference between airplanes with conventional landing gear ("taildraggers") and those with tricycle landing gear becomes most obvious in crosswind takeoffs and landings. The center of gravity of a taildragger is behind the landing gear, and if a swerve begins (due to a crosswind or misuse of the rudders and/or brakes), the airplane will want to "swap ends." Quick and proper use of the rudders and/or brakes will stop this tendency. Taildragger pilots are justly proud of their abilities, and will tell you that a landing in a taildragger is not complete until the airplane is safely tied down.

The center of gravity of a tricycle gear airplane is forward of the landing gear, and upon landing the tendency is for the airplane to continue moving in the direction that it was moving at touchdown. It is your job as the pilot to be sure that at the moment of touchdown the airplane's motion is straight down the runway and the longitudinal axis of the airplane is also aligned with the runway. If the airplane is pointed across the runway at touchdown, that is the direction it will go until you get on the rudders and straighten it out. If it is drifting sideways at touchdown due to inadequate crosswind correction, the landing gear will be subjected to side loads it was not designed to handle.

There are several techniques for crosswind takeoffs and landings and they all have one common thread: *the airplane must be pointing and moving parallel to the runway heading at liftoff or touchdown.* Some tricycle-gear airplanes have free-swiveling nose gear which aligns itself with the direction of travel as soon as it touches the runway, while on other airplanes the nose gear reacts to rudder input. If your trainer is one of the latter, any rudder input at touchdown may result in a swerve. The crosswind diagram (Figure 5-13) is one method of determining crosswind component.

Find the angle between the reported wind direction and the runway heading, and follow the line representing that angle to its intersection with the arc representing the reported wind velocity. A line drawn downward from the point of intersection to the bottom scale will give you the crosswind component, and a horizontal line will give the headwind component:

Example 1

See Figure 5-13 (from Pilot's Operating Handbook).

Wind speed...20 knots
Angle between wind direction
    and flight path..50°
Headwind Component ....13 knots
Crosswind Component............................15 knots

Example 2

Reported wind................................270 at 20 knots
Runway in use.. runway 30
Wind angle ....30°
Headwind Component ....17 knots
Crosswind Component............................10 knots

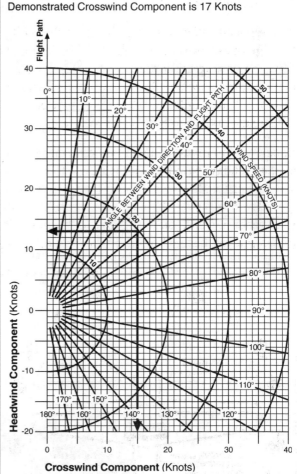

Figure 5-13. *Crosswind diagram*

If you don't have a diagram available, use these rules of thumb to compute crosswind component; for wind angles of less than 20 degrees, ignore the crosswind component; for wind angles of 20-40 degrees multiply the reported wind velocity by .5, for angles of 40-60 degrees multiply by .7, and for angles of 60 degrees or more, consider the full wind velocity to be the crosswind component.

Wake Turbulence

An important consideration for pilots at any airport is the avoidance of wake turbulence. Every airplane leaves behind it two twin tornadoes corkscrewing aft from the wing tips. As the high pressure air below the wing tries to travel around the wing tip to the low pressure area on the top surface and the airplane moves forward, the circulation is clockwise from the left wing tip and counterclockwise from the right wing tip as seen from behind. In the NASA photograph (Figure 5-14), the airplane has flown between two smoke generators and the vortices are clearly seen. Because these wing-tip vortices are a product of lift development, they are strongest and most hazardous behind airplanes that are heavy, slow, and with landing gear and flaps retracted: a takeoff situation. Second most hazardous is the heavy slow airplane in the landing configuration.

Any lifting surface creates tip vortices. How severely they affect an airplane that encounters them depends on the relative weights and wingspans. A very light airplane encountering a vortex from a heavy jet may be thrown out of control, while a medium jet in the same position might experience only momentary turbulence. Research has shown that the wing-tip vortices descend 900 to 1,000 feet behind the generating airplane and then slowly dissipate. Crossing behind a heavy airplane and encountering both vortices can create destructive forces. An airplane with a wingspan smaller than the vortex can be rolled at a rate faster than its pilot can control (Figure 5-15).

When preparing to take off, if a heavy airplane is landing you should note the point at which it touched down — *vortices are only generated when the wings are developing lift.* Vortices can upset light airplanes waiting at the hold line…be careful. You should plan your takeoff roll so that you lift off beyond the point at which the airplane ahead touched down. If you are preparing to take off and a heavy airplane has just departed, you should wait at least 3 minutes for its wake turbulence to dissipate (at airports with control towers the tower controller will probably delay your takeoff clearance). You can avoid its wake turbulence by lifting off at a point on the runway before its liftoff point and then climbing to windward above the heavy airplane's flight path. (Light airplanes can climb more steeply than a jet's flight path for a short distance.) You should be aware that wake vortices drift downwind; wait a few moments longer if you suspect they will drift into your path.

If you are landing behind an airplane that is generating hazardous wing-tip vortices, note its touchdown point and overfly its landing roll so that you land beyond its touchdown point (Figure 5-16). Heavy jets use up a lot more runway than you need. When landing after a heavy jet has just taken off, land on the runway numbers. Its vortices do not begin until it rotates for takeoff and begins generating lift.

Figure 5-14. *Wing-tip vortices*

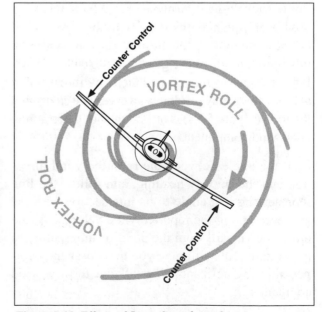

Figure 5-15. *Effects of flying through wind vortices*

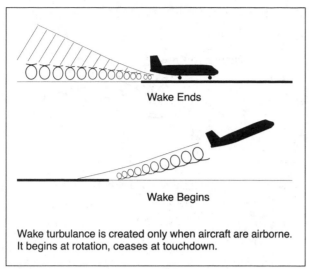

Wake Ends

Wake Begins

Wake turbulance is created only when aircraft are airborne. It begins at rotation, ceases at touchdown.

Figure 5-16. When to watch for wake turbulence

UNICOM Frequencies			
122.700	122.725	122.800	
122.975	123.00	123.050	123.075

Table 5-1. UNICOM

Operating at an airport with crossing runways requires special care. Avoid being airborne when crossing a runway where a heavy airplane has just taken off or landed, and land short of the intersection if possible. *Remember that the heavy airplane creates vortices only when creating lift.*

Line Signals

An aspect of airport operations which is the same at all airports is the set of standardized hand and arm signals used by line personnel to direct ground operations. Figure 5-17 is self explanatory. When no line personnel are available to guide you, it is usually more prudent to shut down the airplane and push it into a parking space than to attempt to gauge clearances visually. Miscalculations are sure to be expensive.

Operations at Non-Tower Airports

Unless you learn to fly at a tower-controlled airport and never venture far from the comforting sound of a controller's voice, you will spend most of your time flying at non-tower airports. There are approximately 13,589 airports and only 688 had towers in 2008 (the latest year for which statistics are available).

A few non-tower airports have on-field flight service stations, a larger number have UNICOM (*see* Table 5-1), and many have no radio facility at all. Your airplane does not have to be radio-equipped to operate at these airports. Remember, even a tower-controlled airport becomes Class E or G airspace when the controller goes home; the Airspace listing in the A/FD will tell you which applies at a given airport. Also, the sectional chart will have a note saying "See NOTAMS/Directory for D/E (or D/G) effective hours". (*See* Lesson 9 for airspace class descriptions.) Figure 5-18 shows a control tower and traffic pattern indicators around the windsock. When the tower is closed at night, only one of the parallel runways will be lighted and the traffic pattern indicators will dictate traffic flow. If the wind direction changes during the night, the lighted runway may not be aligned with the wind; check the windsock.

Fixed-base operators at both towered and non-towered airports can have private frequencies for use in calling for fuel or parking; you will not find them listed in the A/FD or on charts, but they can be found using airnav.com, Flight Guide, or by checking with the operator by phone before departure.

If a tower-controlled airport is the equivalent of an intersection with a traffic light, an uncontrolled airport is the equivalent of a four-way stop—don't move until you have looked in all directions for conflicting traffic, then proceed cautiously.

In preparing to depart a non-tower airport, it is your responsibility to be sure that VFR conditions exist and are expected to continue or improve during your flight. You must also check the wind direction and velocity and the runway in use, and taxi safely to the runway area. If you have a runway diagram with the taxi route illustrated, be sure that you understand how and where to taxi before you begin to move. Follow your progress on the diagram. Remember that there is no such thing as "taxi into position and hold" or an active runway at a nontowered airport; when making announcements, always include a runway number.

Because the FAA has consolidated the FSS system and contracted it out to private industry, we no longer have the luxury of on-field flight service stations. However, FSS briefers can access information from

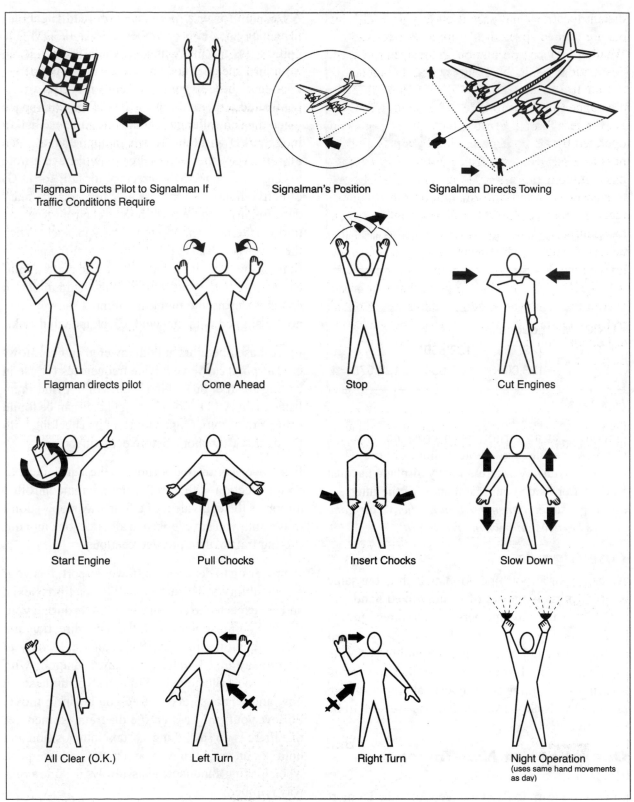

Flagman Directs Pilot to Signalman If
Traffic Conditions Require

Signalman's Position

Signalman Directs Towing

Flagman directs pilot

Come Ahead

Stop

Cut Engines

Start Engine

Pull Chocks

Insert Chocks

Slow Down

All Clear (O.K.)

Left Turn

Right Turn

Night Operation
(uses same hand movements
as day)

Figure 5-17. Hand signals

distant locations and pass it on to you. FSS briefers are trained specialists, with access to National Weather Service information on local, en route, and destination weather conditions. FSS personnel are not air traffic controllers—they cannot give you clearance to taxi or to take off or land. UNICOM is even less formal, because the radio station is not operated by the government but by a private business as a service to the flying public. The operator has many other duties, and may not always be able to answer your call. Information on runway in use received from a UNICOM is advisory only. At a non-tower airport *you* decide which runway to use—but be ready to defend your decision if you decide not to go with the flow! If you are unable to communicate with UNICOM, the AIM suggests that you broadcast in the blind (no specific addressee: "Podunk traffic, Chieftain 4125 GOLF departing runway 16 at Podunk") on the Common Traffic Advisory Frequency for that airport.

You will occasionally find runways at non-tower airports marked off with a large X at each end or in the center. An X-ed off *runway* is closed, and an X in the center of an airport indicates that the *airport* is closed. Some runways have displaced thresholds usually because of obstructions in the approach path, and you must land beyond the displaced threshold markings. You can taxi on or begin your takeoff run from that area of the runway between the end of the paved surface and the displaced threshold, unless chevron markings indicate it is unusable. Figure 5-18 includes a closed runway, an unusable taxiway, displaced thresholds, and parallel runways.

When approaching a non-tower airport to land, you should begin planning your pattern entry about 10 miles out. Every airport has a CTAF, even though there may be no radio facility on the airport. Where there is a UNICOM, listen briefly to learn which runway other pilots are using so that you can plan your entry.

Because no clearance is required to enter the traffic pattern and land at a non-tower airport, it is not required that you maintain continuous radio contact with the ground station. The AIM does recommend that you announce your position and intentions when 10 miles out and when on downwind, base, and final so that other pilots in the area can coordinate their

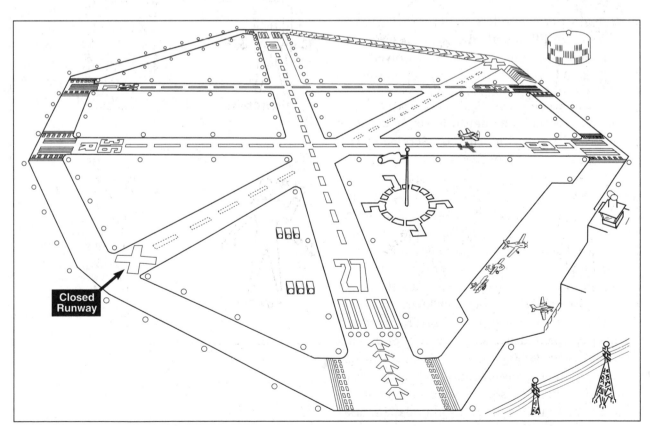

Figure 5-18. *Airport runway and taxiway markings*

movements with yours. Also, because the CTAF may be shared by several airports, your transmissions should include the name of the airport at which you intend to land. "Podunk Traffic, Duke 2345X on left downwind for runway 23, Podunk." Keep your transmissions brief and to the point so that others may use the frequency and remember that there may be "no-radio" airplanes in the pattern. Do not use the blind call "Any traffic in the area please advise"—the AIM says that this phrase should not be used under any conditions.

Operations at Airports with Control Towers

A controlled airport is one with an operating control tower. Control towers are commissioned at airports because the volume of traffic demands a high degree of coordination, so when you operate into or depart from such an airport you should expect your movements to be controlled by the tower. You can ask the **tower controller** for a runway other than the active, and if safety and traffic permits, you might get it. With that exception, there is no opportunity for a pilot to make his or her own decision on where to taxi or which runway to use.

Note that tower controllers do not provide separation between VFR aircraft in Class D airspace; that responsibility belongs to the pilots involved, who must "see and avoid." Never rely on a controller to keep you out of a potential collision.

At many airports with control towers there is an Automatic Terminal Information Service (ATIS) which continuously broadcasts non-control information on existing weather conditions, runway in use, and applicable Notices to Airmen. Non-control means that the ATIS gives you the information necessary to plan your arrival, but you still to communicate with the tower or approach control to operate in Class C or D airspace and you must have a clearance from approach control to operate in Class B airspace (Lesson 9). Your first action, whether arriving or departing, should be to monitor the ATIS broadcast. Each ATIS tape is identified with a letter of the phonetic alphabet (*see* Page 11–12). When contacting ground control, the tower controller, or an approach control facility, you should state in your initial contact that you have the ATIS information: "Bay

Approach, Comanche 587 Sierra, 10 miles southeast with DELTA." Federal Aviation Regulation Part 91 requires that you establish communications with an air traffic control tower before entering Class B, C or D airspace, but if your radio fails in flight (or if you have no radio and have made prior arrangements with the tower) you can still enter the pattern and receive clearance to land through light gun signals (Table 5-2).

Note: There are a few control towers in Class G airspace (Lake City, FL, for example—*see* color page D-8). At these airports, there is no dashed line denoting Class D airspace, only magenta tint denoting Class E beginning at 700 feet AGL. Class G cloud clearance and visibility requirements are in effect, and you still have to communicate with the tower for landing/takeoff clearance.

Some towers are equipped with BRITE (visible in daylight) radar display, to aid controllers. If you are disoriented at an unfamiliar airport, or because the visibility is restricted by haze or smoke, these towers can suggest headings for you to fly to get into the airport traffic pattern. There is no publication listing towers with radar displays.

At a tower controlled airport you may be directed to make a "low approach," or "go around at pattern altitude." Either way, the controller has a conflict of some kind on the ground, and letting you land would complicate matters. See the Pilot/Controller Glossary for details.

Color and Type of Signal	On the Ground	In Flight
STEADY GREEN	Cleared for takeoff	Cleared to land
FLASHING GREEN	Cleared to taxi	Return for landing (to be followed by steady green at proper time)
STEADY RED	Stop	Give way to other aircraft and continue circling
FLASHING RED	Taxi clear of landing area (runway) in use	Airport unsafe — do not land
FLASHING WHITE	Return to starting point on airport	
ALTERNATING RED & GREEN	General Warning Signal — Exercise Extreme Caution	

Table 5-2. *Light gun signals*

Ground Operations

When taxi instructions are received from the **ground controller**, they will be specific; you will be directed to hold short of any active, inactive, or closed runways en route to your departure runway. When in doubt, make no assumptions—stop and ask for clarification. Do not cross any runway without authorization that is crystal clear. So that there is no misunderstanding, you are required to read back to the controller all "hold short" instructions.

Make it a point to have available in the cockpit an airport diagram for any airport you intend to use (or might divert to in an emergency), and study it before you need it. Airport diagrams for large airports are included in the A/FD, from www.naco.faa.gov, and from many online sources.* When given taxi instructions, follow the taxi route with your finger on the diagram and do not hesitate to call the ground controller for help. Ask for "progressive taxi" and you will get turn-by-turn directions.

At night, the tower controller will not direct you to taxi onto the runway into takeoff position to hold awaiting takeoff clearance, and will not clear you for takeoff from an intersection, if the intersection is not clearly visible from the tower cab. At any time of day, if the tower clears you into position on the runway, you will be advised of any inbound traffic with clearance to land on that runway; and you can expect to be released before that traffic becomes a problem. The ground controller's area of responsibility ends at the yellow hold lines, and the tower controller "owns" the runway and the Class D airspace associated with the airport. After landing, remain on the tower controller's frequency until you are told to contact ground control.

"Line up and Wait"

Controllers will instruct you to "line up and wait," which has replaced the "position and hold" instruction, in order to conform with international standards. This instruction will be issued when an airplane further down the runway has not yet cleared or while waiting for another conflict to be resolved, and should be issued when you report ready for takeoff. Be nervous when you have your back to traffic landing on the same runway, and question the controller

if the delay is more than 15 seconds or so (unless it is a wake turbulence precaution, in which case the arriving traffic will be advised of your status). Neither "line up and wait" nor "position and hold" are appropriate at uncontrolled airports.

"Cleared for Immediate Takeoff or Hold Short"

The appropriate response to this transmission is "I'll wait." Never let yourself be rushed into anything in an airplane. This instruction is usually given when an airplane is on final approach, and in the controller's opinion there is time for you to depart before that airplane's arrival. What if the controller is wrong? What if your engine coughs when you apply takeoff power? What if??

"Land and Hold Short" Operations (LAHSO)

When a tower-controlled airport has intersecting runways and the visibility is three miles or more, the tower controller might ask you to land and hold short of the intersecting runway. Imagine that you are turning final for runway 9 at an airport that has a runway 16-34 crossing runway 9-27, 3,000 feet from the threshold. The wind is out of the east at 10 knots, right on the nose for you. There is a 747 five miles out on final for runway 34—the 10-knot crosswind is not a problem for the big jet. The controller tells you "Cleared to land runway 9; hold short of runway 34." Can you get your airplane down and stopped before the intersection? If there is the slightest doubt, say "Unable," because if you overestimate your ability you might meet the 747 at the intersection, and you know who will win that contest. Never hesitate to reject a "land and hold short" clearance—it might cost you a few extra minutes of maneuvering until the intersecting runway is clear, but the consequences of being overconfident are terrible to contemplate. Student pilots must not accept LAHSO clearances.

Where LAHSO operations are a possibility, the Available Landing Distance (ALD) between the approach threshold and the intersection can be found in the A/FD listed under "Special Notices," not under the airport listing. Unfortunately, few pilots refer to the Special Notices on a regular basis. Fortunately, the ALD will also be included in the ATIS broadcast.

* http://www.faa.gov/airports/runway_safety/diagrams

"Cleared to Land"

Does a landing clearance mean that you own the runway? Should you initiate a go-around if there is another airplane on the runway? The answers are "no," and a qualified "no." When a tower controller applies runway separation between small airplanes, there need be only 3,000 feet between a landing aircraft and one still on the runway but approaching an intersection. When larger airplanes are involved, the controller must provide greater separation. Just don't be surprised if you are cleared to land while another airplane is still on the runway. (This also means that you can be cleared for takeoff while another airplane is 3,000 feet down the runway.)

A controller can clear you to land, and clear an airplane that is on the runway for takeoff, as long as he or she estimates that the departing airplane will be 3,000 feet down the runway when you cross the threshold—after all, the departure is accelerating and you are (or will be) decelerating. Best thing to do in this situation is to follow instructions and land. Still, you are the pilot in command—if the situation looks dicey, tell the controller "Unable," and go around. Slide off to the side of the runway so that you can keep the departing airplane in sight, and expect to justify your action to the controller on request.

Operations at Class C Airports

Hundreds of tower-controlled airports are protected by Class C airspace and more are being designated every year. Use current charts and check for NOTAMs What you need to know in the context of operations at airports with control towers is that the controller at the radar facility that governs the airspace surrounding the airport serves as a sort of perimeter guard for the tower controller. You can't enter Class C airspace (shown on sectional charts with a solid magenta line) until you have established two-way communication with that controller, who is usually called "Podunk Approach Control."

The controller wants to know who you are, where you are, and your intentions. "Spokane Approach Control, Cessna 4836G is 15 miles northeast, landing at Felts Field." If the controller says to remain clear of the Class C airspace, you must do just that. The regulations do not require that you receive a clearance, just that communications be established, but if the airspace is busy the effect is the same—you

can't enter until the controller says you can. The approach controller will sequence you for landing and then hand you off to the tower controller. Keep a sharper-than-usual lookout, because if the area weren't congested there would be no need to designate it as Class C airspace.

Operations at Class D Airports

Because it is always associated with an operating control tower, Class D airspace imposes a communication requirement on all pilots desiring to land, take off, or just pass through. It also imposes a weather restriction.

Note: There are a few airports that have towers but no associated Class D airports. I have previously pointed out Lake City, Florida as an example (*see* LCQ on Page D-8).

As a VFR pilot you cannot fly through Class C, D or E airspace unless the flight visibility is at least 3 statute miles and you can stay 500 feet below, 1,000 feet above, and 2,000 feet horizontally from any cloud. You can't take off or land under basic visual flight rules if the reported ceiling is less than 1,000 feet above the ground, or the *ground* visibility is less than 3 statute miles.

When the weather observer reports that the ground visibility is less than 3 miles or the ceiling is less than 1,000 feet, you cannot land in or take off from Class D airspace under basic VFR (when you are inbound, this sounds like "the weather at Podunk is below basic VFR; what are your intentions?" Don't say "I want to come in and land"). You must ask for and receive a Special VFR clearance; you can't even do that if the ground visibility is less than 1 mile and you can't remain clear of clouds. Furthermore, unless you hold an instrument rating you cannot operate under SVFR at night. At some airports (*see* the Class B discussion) you can't get SVFR at all.

A Special VFR clearance authorizes you to take off and operate within the Class B, C, D, or E airspace if the ground visibility is at least 1 statute mile and you can remain clear of all clouds, and to enter the airspace and land if the flight visibility is at least 1 statute mile and you can stay clear of clouds. *Note:* If ground visibility is not reported by an official source, you can use flight visibility (the distance you can see from the cockpit in takeoff position) for SVFR takeoff minimums. Special VFR is useful when bad weather is localized and you know that you will be in good visual conditions once you leave the immediate area of the airport. This authorization can be a trap if you will be dodging clouds, buildings, and antennas after you cross the boundary of the Class B, C, D, or E airspace.

It is possible to operate in Class D airspace without a radio. If your airplane simply doesn't have a radio, the best thing to do is call the tower on the telephone and tell the controller the type and color of your airplane, your estimated time of arrival, and the direction from which you will be coming. Expect a light gun signal. If your radio fails in flight, a landing at a non-tower airport and a phone call is still the best solution; but if that is impossible just fly to the tower airport, observe the direction of flight in the pattern, and join the pattern while wiggling your wings furiously and/or flipping your landing light on and off. Once again, expect light gun signals.

When the tower controller goes home, most Class D airspace becomes Class E airspace (Class G if there is no weather observer; check the A/FD). The communication requirement goes away but the visibility and cloud clearance requirements stay. Of course, there is no one to report ground visibility when this happens and it is your responsibility to ensure that the flight visibility is at least three statute miles.

Operations at Class E Airports

There are airports with the same weather restrictions as Class D but no control tower; at those airports, controlled airspace (Class E) extends down to the airport surface. They are shown with a dashed magenta line on sectional charts (an example from the sectional chart foldout is Bremerton National (**D**)). You can still get a Special VFR authorization to take off or land, but you must get it through a flight service station. The FSS must check with air traffic controllers to be sure that no instrument approaches or departures are taking place before issuing a clearance to you.

When an airport has either Class B, C, D, or E airspace, the lighting of the rotating beacon during daylight hours is intended to indicate that the weather is below basic VFR minimums (1,000-foot ceiling and three statute miles visibility). In many cases these beacons are controlled by automatic devices and your decision on whether or not basic VFR minimums exist should not depend on the beacon alone.

Landing Fees

An increasing number of airports, both tower-controlled and uncontrolled, are charging landing fees. Sometimes the fee is collected by fixed-base operators, sometimes it is the airport operator. One thing for sure…they've got your airplane's tail number and someone is going to pay. In most cases, buying fuel will get you off the hook, but the smart thing to do is to check the A/FD and call ahead to be sure.

"I'm a Stranger Here, Myself…"

Surely the most daunting task for a new pilot is going to a strange airport—"Who do I call?" "Where do I park?" "Do I need tiedowns?" "How will I get into town?" You can eliminate all doubt by calling a fixed-base operator at your proposed destination. It might cost a buck or two, but the assurance that being armed with information provides is worth it. Phone numbers are available in many places; www.airnav.com is one, www.aopa.org/airports is another. A listing saying that a restaurant or motel is "adjacent to the airport" might mean a very long walk, so call to be sure.

Part 139 Airports

Part 139 airports are those served by the airlines and commuters. When you are planning your flight, check the A/FD to see if your destination or an en route stop is a Part 139 airport (but it will say ARFF, not Part 139). There are about 700 of them, so the chances are pretty good that you will encounter one or more in your travels. Computer users can find airport diagrams for Part 139 airports at www.naco.faa.gov; AOPA members can get them on the organization's website.

The FAA has instituted a program of signage at Part 139 airports to make them consistent with one another, and to make it easier for pilots to take the correct taxiway to the runway or other point on the airport. There are six kinds of signs; examples of these are included in the full-color Appendix on Page D-11.

Mandatory Instruction Signs have white letters on a red background; they denote entrances to runways or areas where aircraft are prohibited. Figure

A (on Page D-11) is a runway/hold position sign and would be placed where a taxiway intersects runway 15-33. Figure C would be placed at a more complex intersection where two runways cross.

You should be aware of two special mandatory instruction signs: First, a red sign with ILS in white (Figure D) indicates an area on a taxiway where airplanes can interfere with the ILS signal, and when you see that sign you will also see a special hold line that looks like railroad tracks.

The second important sign has, for example, a white 15-APCH on a red background (Figure E). This indicates that the approach path for runway 15 crosses the taxiway and that you should hold there until authorized to cross by the ground controller. It's another way of saying "DANGER—LOW FLYING AIRCRAFT." This sign does not mean that you are at the approach end of runway 15—that location is indicated by a simple white-on-red 15 (Figure B would be at the takeoff end of runway 33). A white-on-red sign is always significant; if you have any doubts about its meaning, stop and ask.

Figure F is the "no entry" sign—the area beyond the sign is forbidden territory for taxiing.

Location Signs have yellow inscriptions on a black background, with a yellow border. They tell you on which runway or taxiway you are located. You would see a sign like Figure G if you were turning from an intersection onto a runway where the proximity of another runway might be confusing. A taxiway location sign would have a letter instead of a number.

Direction Signs have black inscriptions on a yellow background (no border), and they are normally located on the left prior to an intersection. They are used to tell pilots which way to taxi to get to a runway or to another taxiway, and are called, "outbound destination signs." You would see Figure I where the taxi route leads to two runways, and Figure J where two different taxi routes exist. When the controller says "Turn right at taxiway Alfa," look for a sign like Figure H.

Destination Signs also have black inscriptions on a yellow background, and they tell you which way to taxi to get to the runway, the ramp, the terminal, the military area, etc.

Information Signs also have black inscriptions on a yellow background; they are installed by the airport operator and include things like noise abatement procedures, density altitude reminders, radio frequencies, etc.

Runway Distance Remaining Signs have white numerals on a black background and are spaced 1,000 feet apart. Figure K tells you that the runway remaining is 3,000 feet.

Memory aid: If the sign has a yellow border it tells you the designation of the taxiway or runway on which you are located. If the controller told you to hold short of runway 15 and you see Figure G, you're in real trouble.

At airports equipped for low-visibility takeoffs and landings, these signs and markings are backed up by lights and additional signage.

Stop Bar Lights are installed at intersections where a centerline-lighted taxiway meets an active runway where low-visibility takeoffs are in progress. They are red until the controller clears the aircraft onto the runway, at which time green lead-on lights illuminate the path to the takeoff position.

Runway Guard Lights are flashing yellow lights that denote the presence of an active runway and identify the location of the hold line.

Taxiway Centerline Lighting consists of green in-pavement lights to guide ground traffic at night and during low-visibility operations.

Clearance Bar Lights are yellow in-pavement lights denoting holding positions. They are co-located with...

Geographic Position Markings, so-called "pink spots" with an identifying letter or number. They can also be used for reporting one's position on the airport.

Taxiway Centerline Marking is a solid yellow line, outlined with black for emphasis on light colored pavement.

Pattern Work

Whether an airport has a tower or not, expect the unexpected. Other pilots will misinterpret tower instructions, use creative pattern entries unimagined by any instructor, and fail to use perfectly good radios simply because they are not required to use them at uncontrolled airports. They will land and/or take off downwind or opposite to the traffic flow.

When at the hold line or, where there is none, turn toward the final approach course before crossing the hold line and take one last look to be sure that someone isn't turning base-to-final or on final approach; it only takes a few seconds.

At airports with one runway and no taxiways, you may have to back-taxi to the departure end of the runway, rolling toward landing traffic. The problems are obvious. Make a blind transmission telling others what you are doing, and keep your eyes open.

Refer back to the discussion of energy management in Lesson 1. When landing, your goal should be to touch down at the minimum speed consistent with safety. Your target airspeed at 50 feet above runway elevation on short final should be the speed given in the landing distance chart in Section 5 (Performance) of your AFM. It will be higher than the airspeed you calculate by using the bottom of the white arc. Call this your reference speed, V_{REF}. Now work backwards to establish pattern speeds: Add five knots to get the target speed on final, add another five knots for the target speed on base leg, another five for speed on downwind, and a final five knots for pattern entry speed. For a 1980 Cessna 152, with a V_{REF} of 54 knots, you would enter the pattern at 74 knots, slow to 69 on downwind, bleed off airspeed to 64 on base, and aim at maintaining 60 (round number) on final until you are on short final. This assumes full flaps for a normal landing. You know from practicing power-off stalls that the airplane will not stall at 54 knots. If you can see the touchdown point over the nose, you are not going to stall. Conversely, if the nose of the airplane obscures the touchdown point you should be doing something about it—lower the nose, add flaps, whatever.

Try the "dirty spot" method of landing—find a deceased bug or other spot on the windshield in front of your eyes (or use a grease pencil). When you turn final, adjust the pitch attitude to align the dirty spot with the place on the runway where you want to touch down. Keep it there with subtle pressures on the yoke, adjusting speed with the throttle (this is what electronic flight management systems do—change pitch to follow the glide path while moving the throttles to maintain a set airspeed). Of course, you will touch down nosewheel-first on the desired spot if you fail to flare.

If you ever have to land with a tailwind due to an emergency, expect the faster ground speed to result in a longer ground roll, and forget about landing "on the numbers."

Flying at Night

Your private pilot flight training will include three hours of dual at night, including a 100-mile cross-country flight. The ground references you used to determine what kind of airspace you are in will be invisible, as will the terrain. Stars can merge with ground lighting, making it difficult to maintain level flight without reference to the flight instruments, and you will not be able to see those clouds you are supposed to avoid. Still, night flight can be magical. Pay attention to the maximum elevation figures (MEF) on your sectional chart and be sure to add an extra 1,000 feet to those altitudes. Don't fly at night if low clouds are forecast. Learn to use visual landing aids, and never descend to less than 50 feet above published airport elevation unless you can see the runway surface clearly.

If you are using radar flight following (Lesson 11), the controller has an "Enroute Minimum Safe Altitude" function that provides an alert if you are approaching terrain. You must request this service, however, it is not automatic for VFR flights. "See and avoid" only works if you can see what you want to avoid; always ask for the altitude alert when flying VFR at night.

Note: Sport pilots are not permitted to fly at night; this restriction cannot be lifted with an instructor's endorsement.

Visibility: Ground vs. Flight

In discussing the regulations for flight in various kinds of airspace the terms "flight visibility" and "ground visibility" were used without comment. If you are departing an airport where ground visibility is reported by an observer, you are governed by that report. If you are landing at an airport where ground visibility is reported and you determine that the flight visibility meets the legal requirements of the airspace, your decision governs. Of course, if the tower is calling the ground visibility one mile and you decide that the flight visibility is three miles you can go ahead and land—but expect to be quizzed by the FAA. If you are operating at an airport where visibility is not reported, the decision is yours—if you say that the visibility is three miles no one can argue with you. However, newspaper reports of the accident will say "witnesses told investigators that the visibility was less than one-half mile when the airplane disappeared."

Sermon: The reputation of general aviation pilots goes right down the tube when someone who absolutely has to get home or to a destination crashes and kills a few people. You want to become a general aviation pilot or you wouldn't be reading this—please remember this: no job, no trip, no birthday, no wedding, nothing is important enough to kill yourself for. Do not push the limits of your ability, and don't overestimate what those limits are.

Inflight Emergencies

The most common emergency is low fuel state, and as I have mentioned elsewhere, that is the most unforgivable error a pilot can make...so let's go on to other kinds of emergencies.

When a non-instrument rated pilot flies into instrument meteorological conditions, is that an emergency? It is to the pilot! We all know that following the basic rules of visual flight with regard to cloud clearance and flight visibility makes flight into poor visibility impossible...but pilots do it every year and give us all a black eye. During your flight training you will learn to control the airplane using only the flight instruments; this is not intended to make you an instrument pilot in three hours (even honest-to-goodness instrument students devote more time than that to basic airplane control), but to give you tools that will allow you to turn, descend, or whatever it takes to get back to visual conditions.

Research has shown that an untrained pilot, deprived of visual references, will enter a spiral dive in a frighteningly short time. Cessna Pilot Information Manuals contain a method of coping with loss of visual references that can be applied to pretty much any airplane and can be summarized as follows:

- Apply full carburetor heat; make the mixture full rich.
- Keep wings level using the rudders and turn instrument; do not touch the yoke for either pitch or roll control.
- Reduce the power to that required for a 500–800 foot-per-minute rate of descent (typically 1,700 rpm in a general light single-engine aircraft).
- Extend full flaps; trim for 70–80 knots indicated airspeed.
- Keep hands off of the control wheel.
- Make corrections using rudder only.

If a turn is necessary, use just enough rudder pressure to cause the turn instrument to indicate 1/3 of a standard rate turn; you won't turn very rapidly, but you won't overbank into a spiral, either. Keep your hands off of the yoke. With a free hand, select 7700 on your transponder; if you have time and presence of mind, transmit a MAYDAY on 121.5 Mhz.

Is having a door pop open an emergency? Trying to close a door in flight has caused far too many accidents. When a door pops open, the rush of air is deafening, and anything light (such as charts) departs through the opening. Other than that, the airplane flies perfectly well. Why not just land at the nearest airport (usually the one you just left), and close the door in a reasoned manner? No need to rush around the pattern or perform any shortcuts, just fly the pattern and land. If there is too much noise for radio communication, exercise your pilot-in-command authority and do without; at towered airports, watch for lights from the tower.

Can't get the "landing gear down" light after gear extension? Don't panic...check the position of the instrument panel lighting switch; in most cases, turning on the panel lights dims the gear lights.

Renting

Whether you learn to fly at a busy tower-controlled airport or at a sleepy country strip, after you get your license you will probably become a renter-pilot or join a flying club. You will be bound by the club's regulations and insurance requirements, so I will not address clubs in this text. As a renter, however, you have to be on your toes.

Most fixed-base operators (FBOs) will want to see your pilot certificate, current medical certificate, and evidence that you are current (*see* Lesson 4). Their insurance will almost certainly require a checkout flight with one of their instructors, no matter how much time you have logged or how sophisticated the airplanes you normally fly, so budget some time and money for this. After all, they are giving you access to an airplane that is almost certainly more expensive than a luxury automobile. If the FBO does not have a list of renter's restrictions, be sure to ask what you should do if there is a mechanical or weather problem and if there are any insurance restrictions on where you can land. Buying a renter's insurance policy is an excellent idea — you will find that the FBO's insurance only covers its losses, and its insurer might look to you to make up those losses.

Be a responsible renter. Turn off the master switch. Take the food wrappers, empty water bottles, and other loose material with you when you leave the plane. Tie it down safely. Turn off the master switch. If the FBO has a refueling policy, follow it. Turn the master switch off. Make sure that no switches are left ON that should not be in that position for engine start. Put the master switch in the OFF position. Set the transponder to 1200. If you even suspect that you have damaged the airplane (landed with brakes applied?), bite the bullet and write it up. Did I mention the master switch?

"Pilot-in-command" carries a lot of responsibility. Check the aircraft logbooks to assure yourself that all required inspections have been accomplished and that there are no deferred maintenance items. If you have a problem, the regulations put the onus on the PIC, not the FBO.

Human Factors

Lesson 2 discussed how to determine the health of the engine, and Lesson 8 will discuss airplane performance under different conditions. The remainder of this lesson will discuss the human element: how the performance of the pilot is affected by health and environmental factors, and the decision-making process.

Medical Factors for Pilots

Many physical conditions which have minimal effect on the body's performance at ground level can have severe consequences "at altitude," which includes the upper limit operating levels of even small, single-engine airplanes. You should be aware of these conditions so that you can avoid problems with your own physical state during flight, and help your passengers have a safe and comfortable experience.

If you have a question in your mind as to how a prescription or over-the-counter drug or even illness symptoms, check with an Aviation Medical Examiner, not your family doctor, to be sure. Plain vanilla doctors might be unaware of the effects of medications at high altitudes. Prescription analgesics and histamines, the very things that we reach for when we have problems, are the most likely to cause problems.

Figure 5-19. Self-grounding is required when a pilot is feeling ill.

Drugs and Alcohol

The effects of drugs and alcohol on performance are intensified by altitude, and pilots are prohibited from flying within 8 hours of ingesting *any* alcoholic beverage and from flying while under the influence of any drug or medication. Even over-the-counter medications as seemingly innocuous as cough suppressants can affect judgment, memory, and alertness at altitude; pilots should check with an Aviation Medical Examiner for advice if in doubt about any medication. Pilots are required to ground themselves if they have any medical condition which affects their abilities as flight crewmembers.

Hypoxia

Our bodies are acclimated to life on the ground where the atmosphere contains approximately 21 percent oxygen, and they require that same *amount* of oxygen in order to operate efficiently at altitude, where the atmosphere is thinner. A small pressure differential is required in your lungs to allow oxygen to be transferred to your bloodstream. As you climb to altitudes where pressure is reduced, the exchange of oxygen is inhibited, and the symptoms of **hypoxia** (oxygen sickness) begin to occur unless *supplemental* oxygen is used. These symptoms usually do not affect healthy, non-smoking pilots at altitudes below 12,000 feet in the daytime; however, deterioration in night vision can occur as low as 5,000 feet.

The body has no built-in alarm system to warn of hypoxia! Symptoms of hypoxia include impaired judgment, memory, alertness, coordination, and the loss of ability to make calculations, and are followed by headache and drowsiness. The most insidious symptom is a state of euphoria or well-being: "I feel great! I just can't seem to figure out this VOR." (Figure 5-21.) A device that clips onto a fingertip to display the oxygen saturation level of your blood is available from aviation supply sources. They are not cheap, but if they prevent an error caused by the onset of hypoxia they will pay for themselves.

The agent in the blood which absorbs oxygen is called **hemoglobin**, and the ability of the hemoglobin to utilize oxygen can be reduced by carbon monoxide from smoking or exhaust fumes. Heavy smokers may experience the symptoms of hypoxia at much lower altitudes than non-smokers.

You can experience the symptoms of hypoxia under controlled conditions in an altitude chamber at a military facility. The local office of the Federal Aviation Administration has details on how to apply for this valuable physiology training. You may say "it can't happen to me," but when you find that you can't write your name or add a column of figures when deprived of oxygen in an altitude chamber, you will be convinced of the value of supplemental oxygen. The regulations governing use of oxygen are discussed in Lesson 4.

Hyperventilation

Rapid breathing under stress can reduce the amount of carbon dioxide in the lungs, leading to light-headedness, drowsiness, tingling in the fingers, and eventual unconsciousness. The body requires a certain level of carbon dioxide in order to trigger the breathing reflex.

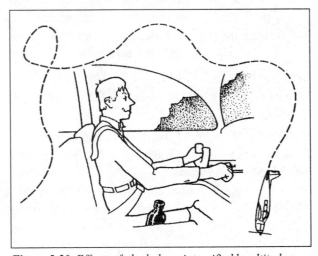

Figure 5-20. *Effects of alcohol are intensified by altitude.*

Figure 5-21. *Euphoria is a symptom of hypoxia.*

Flight situations which seem quite normal to a pilot may create stress in passengers, and hyperventilation is usually a passenger problem. A conscious slowing of the breathing rate will relieve symptoms of hyperventilation, and breathing into cupped hands or a paper bag to increase intake of carbon dioxide will also help. It is usually difficult to get children to control their breathing rate, and the cupped hands or bag method is most effective with them.

It is possible to experience the symptoms of hypoxia and hyperventilation simultaneously. (If you are above 14,000 feet without oxygen you will surely be under stress!) If oxygen *is* available it should be set to deliver full flow immediately. As is the case in many other precarious flight situations, the best prevention is not getting into the situation in the first place.

Carbon Monoxide Poisoning

Even small amounts of carbon monoxide in the lungs inhibit the ability of the blood's hemoglobin to use oxygen efficiently, and the most common source of carbon monoxide in flight is the airplane's heater system. Carbon monoxide is tasteless and odorless, and the smell of exhaust gas cannot be relied on to warn of its presence. Chemical detectors which darken in the presence of carbon monoxide are available at pilot supply stores. If the smell of exhaust *is* noticed, of course, the heater should be shut off, all air vents opened, and a landing made at the nearest airport. If carbon monoxide does get into your bloodstream, it may take several days to dissipate — you can't get the heater fixed and take off again the same day without the possibility of experiencing hypoxia.

Toxic Fumes

Don't fly immediately after using acetone or any other solvent or cleaner that leaves fumes in or around the airplane. This should be common sense, but is sometimes overlooked in the rush to take off.

Flying and Diving

Many pilots enjoy both flying and scuba diving, and if you are in this group you should be aware that the two do not mix. Diving immediately after landing should cause no problems. Flying immediately after diving will cause problems, because the nitrogen forced into your joints while underwater may cause the "bends" in flight due to the reduced pressure at altitude. An extra day on the beach will probably eliminate that possibility.

Ear Problems

The changing pressures of flight can cause painful ear problems if the pilot or passenger is unable to equalize the pressure in the middle ear. When the airplane is climbing, air trapped in the middle ear expands and exits through the Eustachian tubes into the mouth, causing no problems. During descent, however, the pilot or passenger must attempt to equalize the pressure in the middle ear by yawning, swallowing, or tensing the throat muscles. Chewing gum can help. Holding the nose and "blowing gently" with the head held back can open the Eustachian tubes this is called the "valsalva" maneuver. *Caution:* don't ever "valsalva" when you have a head cold, as serious sinus infection may result.

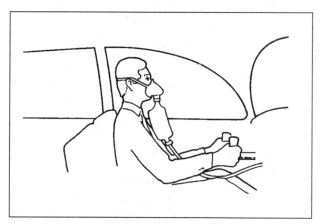

Figure 5-22. *Supplementary oxygen is recommended at altitudes above 10,000 feet MSL.*

Figure 5-23. *Hyperventilation causes dizziness and may lead to loss of consciousness.*

If a passenger is experiencing ear blockage during descent, it may be necessary to climb until the pain is relieved, and then descend at a reduced rate. Because the potential for ear problems is always present when flying, pilots should not fly with any upper respiratory infection, such as a cold or sore throat. Be very wary of accepting passenger's assurances that, although they have a cold, they will not be bothered by flying. Remember, the problem becomes apparent on the way *down*, after it is too late to avoid it!

Vertigo

There are several illusions in flight which can lead to vertigo, which is best described as a disagreement between what your eyes and your body report to your brain. Almost everyone has had the experience of sitting in an automobile when an adjacent automobile begins to move slowly—the natural reaction is to step on your brakes, because for an instant your brain isn't sure which vehicle is moving. That is one form of vertigo, or **spatial disorientation**.

There are many situations which can lead to spatial disorientation in flight, but the most common is loss of visual reference to the horizon. Non-instrument rated pilots, or pilots who have not learned to use the flight instruments when visual reference is lost, react to bodily sensations and may lose control of the airplane. It is not possible to "fly by the seat of your pants."

Your middle ear contains three tubes filled with liquid, and the inner surfaces of these tubes are lined with thousands of tiny hairs which sense movement of the liquid. It is the messages that these tiny hairs send to your brain that provide your sense of bal-

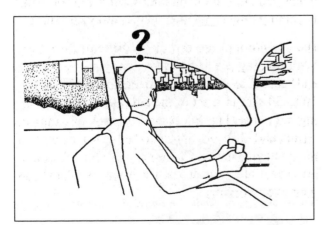

Figure 5-24. Disorientation results when the senses disagree.

ance. When a turn begins, your brain gets the correct message, but if the maneuver is protracted the liquid stops moving, and the information to the brain is that the turn has stopped. If you then actually stop the turn, the liquid begins to flow the other way, and your middle ear tells your brain that the turn has reversed! During your training for the private pilot certificate, you will be taught how to use the flight instruments to keep the airplane under control while returning to visual conditions.

The most valuable of the five senses in flight is vision: believe the instruments, and avoid head movement.

Another source of illusion and the potential for vertigo is flight on a clear, starlit night with scattered lights on the ground. With no horizon to separate the lights on the ground from the stars, it is possible to become disoriented and lose control of the airplane. Again, training in the use of the flight instruments will keep you right side up.

Visual Illusions

As a VFR pilot, you will rely on your eyes to keep you out of trouble—but under certain conditions your eyes can lie. Here are a few subtle traps to watch out for:

Somotographic illusion: This one usually bites at night, with few visual references. The rapid acceleration of takeoff can create the illusion of being in a nose-up attitude; if you react with forward stick pressure, you can dive into the ground. Watch the altimeter and VSI to verify that you are climbing.

False horizon: As a private pilot, you can fly on top of a cloud deck ("VFR over-the-top"). If you maintain what you think is a wings-level attitude by reference to a sloping cloud deck, the airplane will turn and you will be correcting continually. Use the attitude indicator and heading indicator to maintain level flight when on top.

Autokinesis: Another night-time trap. If you stare at a fixed light, it will appear to move...might even lead you to believe it is a star. Solution? Don't stare at a fixed light.

Runway width illusion: If the landing runway is narrower than the runway you have become accustomed to, you will think that you are higher than you really are and you might land short or not flare in time; if it is wider than you are used to, you might level out too high or overshoot the runway.

Runway slope illusion: The A/FD contains information about runway slope, and you should refer to it when visiting an unfamiliar airport. If the runway slopes upward, away from your approach path, you might land short and/or hard. If the runway slopes downward, away from you, judging the flare will be difficult and you might level off too high.

Featureless terrain illusion: This one gets you when approaching over water or desert, with no structures or vegetation to help with depth perception. You will think that you are too high and your approach path will be lower than normal. Refer to your altimeter.

Atmospheric illusions: Rain on the windshield will make you think you are higher, and haze will make you think you are further from the runway than you really are.

Ground lighting illusions: Pilots have mistaken lights on roads and on trains (and even fairgrounds) for runway lights. Check the A/FD to see what kind of approach lighting is installed, and check the sectional to see what nearby non-aviation activity might be confusing.

Dehydration

In these days when virtually everyone seems to be carrying a bottle of water, it hardly seems necessary to warn pilots about the hazards of dehydration. The old advice about drinking six 8-ounce glasses of water a day has been discredited, but no one denies that dehydration can cause disorientation and problems with speech. Make sure that you have plenty of liquids available, and provide for your passengers as well.

Night Vision and Scanning

Your eyes will adapt to dim light conditions, but only after a considerable period of time. It takes at least 30 minutes in total darkness for complete dark adaptation, and that adaptation can be lost by a few seconds exposure to a bright light. The use of red lights for cockpit lighting at night causes difficulty in reading aeronautical charts, and dim white lighting is standard. Pilot supply shops sell flashlights with switchable filters or colored LEDs; green light seems to be the best. You should make every effort to become dark adapted, however, because other airplanes can only be detected at night by their lights and you want to detect them as far away as possible.

When landing at night, do not fly any differently than you do in daytime VFR conditions; visual illusions at night can lead you to dive for the runway or level off too high. Check your flight instruments to ensure that your attitude and airspeed are within normal limits.

Scanning the sky for other aircraft is just as important as maintaining control of your airplane, and deserves equal attention. You should not limit your scan to those areas ahead of the airplane at your altitude, but should scan systematically from over your left shoulder to as far to the right as you can see, looking both below and above your altitude. A constant sweep of the eyes will not be effective, because your eyes need time to focus on objects, so momentarily stopping for at least a second will enhance your ability to detect other airplanes. At night, because of the way your eyes work, you will see only those objects which are slightly out of your direct line of sight, and your scan will have to be slower and more deliberate.

If another airplane remains on the same relative bearing, the danger of collision exists. Keeping the right-of-way rules in mind, maneuver your aircraft so that the intruder either moves forward or back in your field of vision. (This is a helpful rule to remember when you are driving on the freeway and someone is coming down a ramp to merge into your lane.)

Hazy conditions are especially difficult for pilots. With nothing specific to focus on, your eyes relax and "coast," seeking a comfortable focusing distance 10 to 30 feet in front of the aircraft. You are looking but not seeing. Because of the lack of contrast, terrain and obstacles appear to be further away than their actual distance. Choose any distant object that presents itself, even the top of a distant cloud, to keep your eyes working.

Sun-blindness

Flying directly toward a rising or setting sun can effectively blind you to other traffic. Even a moment spent looking toward the sun can shrink your pupils to the size of BBs and it takes a while for them to recover. Use some form of opaque film on the windshield, or better yet forget about miles and gallons-per-hour and tack toward your destination just as a sailor tacks. Turn 30 or 45 degrees so that the sun is no longer straight ahead; after a few minutes turn so that the sun hits the other side of the airplane. You'll give up efficiency but gain safety.

Decision-Making and Judgment

Over 80 percent of aviation accidents can be attributed to some form of pilot error; it might be a poor decision under stress, or it might be the exercise of poor judgment. FAA psychologists have identified five subject areas for decision making, five risk elements, and five hazardous attitudes. Learning about these will be part of your pilot training.

The five decision-making subject areas are:

Pilot—Your state of health, level of fatigue, competency.

Aircraft—Any question about its airworthiness.

Environment—Weather, traffic, runway length and condition, etc.

Operation—The go/no-go decision.

Situation—Know what is going on around you.

The five risk elements follow the same pattern:

Pilot—Physical stress (too hot, too cold, too noisy, lack of oxygen); physiological stress (lack of sleep, missed meals); psychological stress (sick child, marital problems, work problems)

Aircraft—Radios OK? Fuel quantity sufficient?

Environment—Density altitude, day/night, deteriorating weather.

Operation—Pressure to keep a schedule.

Situation—"Get-home-itis" (*see* next section)

The five hazardous attitudes should be easy to identify:

Anti-authority—"Nobody is going to tell me what to do!" *Antidote:* Follow the rules.

Impulsivity—"Don't just sit there, do something even if it's wrong!" *Antidote:* Not so fast, think first.

Invulnerability—"Accidents happen to the other guy; I'm too good a pilot to make a dumb mistake." *Antidote:* It could happen to me.

Macho (or macha)—"I can do it in spite of _____ " *Antidote:* Taking chances is foolish.

Resignation—"What's the use of trying, there's nothing I can do." *Antidote:* I am not helpless.

FAA Advisory Circular 60-22 contains example situations and grading sheets so that you can test yourself on decision-making, risk elements, and hazardous attitudes.

The DECIDE Model

Aeronautical Decision Making lays the groundwork for rational actions in flight. Even if you display none of the hazardous attitudes listed above, there are many points in every flight where a decision is called for and you should have a mental template to use—this is the DECIDE model:

Detect the fact that a change has occurred (or is needed).

Estimate the need to react to the change (hardly anything in aviation requires immediate action).

Choose a desirable outcome for your decision.

Identify actions to take in order to achieve the desirable outcome.

Do. Take the necessary action.

Evaluate the effect of your action on the needed change.

Most preventable aviation accidents are caused by human error. Mechanical malfunctions are rare, and structural failure is almost always the result of flying into severe weather…a very human error. Accident investigators look for and identify an "error chain," in which one bad decision leads to another—break just one link in the chain and the accident would not have happened.

Scud-running (attempting flight beneath a low cloud layer in order to maintain visual contact with the ground) can result in a number of bad things: hitting a structure; flying into zero-visibility conditions; controlled flight into terrain are a few. Deciding that scud-running is hazardous at best and waiting for better conditions breaks the error chain.

Peer pressure "I've got to get the boss back in time for the meeting" or self-induced pressure "I have to get home for my daughter's birthday" can lead to unpleasant outcomes. Just say no. Attempting to show colleagues that you have "the right stuff" instead of admitting that you have personal limitations can lead to disaster.

Get-Home-Itis

The leading medical cause of airplane accidents and fatalities is a disease called "get-home-itis." Symptoms include a tendency to overestimate one's abilities and to underestimate the problems associated with fatigue, poor visibility caused by nightfall, inclement weather, or a combination of both. Making it to a family celebration, getting back to work on time, or a simple failure to accept the fact that the laws of physics apply to everyone, no matter how many flight hours or pilot certificates they hold or what their net worth is—these are all contributing factors. There is no cure for get-home-itis; however, the realization that nothing is important enough to risk life and limb for will keep you from catching this disease.

You can save yourself from this kind of stress by establishing an unbreakable Code of Conduct for yourself: "I will not go unless enroute weather is no worse than a 3,000 foot ceiling and five miles visibility." "I will not go if winds aloft are forecast to be 50 knots or stronger over the mountains." "I will tell my passengers that we might not arrive at the scheduled time, or even at the scheduled destination airport, and we might not return when we expect to. They might have to drive, fly commercially, or take the train to complete the trip as planned." Have alternatives in mind before you get into the airplane, and be sure that your passengers are aware of them.

Refresher Training

Man was not meant to fly. That is, the human organism was designed to operate in two dimensions on the surface of the earth. Soaring into the air or plumbing the depths of the seas requires training and mechanical devices to overcome the shortcomings of the human body. Even when the adaptive devices are present, if the training has been forgotten the body is in mortal danger.

Flight training is a process of substituting trained reactions for normal reactions. For example, for a non-pilot the normal reaction to the nose-down pitching motion of a stall is to pull back on the yoke or stick as hard as possible and hold it there until the airplane hits the ground. The trained reaction, as you know (or will learn) is to reduce the angle of attack by relaxing stick pressure or even applying positive forward pressure. All pilots know that it is counter-intuitive to push the nose down when you are close to the ground, but if that is what it takes to reduce the angle of attack, then it must be done.

Whether you enjoy stall practice or just resign yourself to it, your instructor will have you go through the recovery process over and over from different starting scenarios. To some, this means "teaching the test." In reality, according to physiologists, this repetition creates pathways in the brain that shortcut normal reactions, direct the muscles to react properly, and deliver what are called psychomotor responses.

These pathways lose their effectiveness unless they are refreshed with practice, and when that happens normal reactions take their place. You regress to the same state you were in before you learned to fly— pulling back on the stick to keep the airplane up in the air. Don't think that your instructor's constant emphasis on refresher training or the FAA's Wings program and flight review are just jump-through-hoops requirements. They are the absolute *minimum* necessary to keep those lifesaving neural pathways open. If you have to be forced to do an occasional stall recovery, night landing, or engine-out procedure, you are placing yourself and your passengers at risk.

Discipline

We have all heard the jokes about the passengers who became upset when the pilot referred to a checklist or manual...their assumption was that a good pilot knows everything without having to look it up. We know better. Using a checklist not only gets brownie points from the examiner but it is the sign of a disciplined and competent pilot. Don't rely on your short- or long-term memory...use your checklist.

The FAA mandates a silent cockpit for airliners when descending through 10,000 feet. Any conversation after that must relate to the impending approach and landing. For many light plane pilots, just getting up to 10,000 feet is an adventure, but when coming back down they should be concentrating on flying, not talking. Don't feel that you are insulting your passengers by asking that they refrain from asking you questions during the approach and landing...tell them it is an FAA regulation. Just don't mention that it is in Part 121, not Part 91.

My last admonition about discipline has to do with who is flying the airplane when there are two pilots at the control positions, especially when one is an instructor. Accidents have happened when both pilots tried to fly at the same time and also when each pilot thought that the other one was in control. Eliminate all doubt and use a proven three-step procedure—

Pilot transferring control:
"You have the flight controls."

Pilot taking over control:
"I have the flight controls."

Pilot transferring control:
"You have the flight controls."

I'll be the first to admit that this exchange will be a little rushed when the airplane is close to stalling 50 feet above the runway.

Lesson 5
Procedures and Airport Operations Review Questions

1. An air traffic control clearance provides

   A — priority over all other traffic.
   B — adequate separation from all traffic.
   C — authorization to proceed under specified traffic conditions in controlled airspace.

2. A flashing green air traffic control signal directed to an aircraft on the surface is a signal that the pilot

   A — is cleared to taxi.
   B — should exercise extreme caution.
   C — should taxi clear of the runway in use.

3. Which is the correct traffic pattern departure to use at an airport without a control tower?

   A — Depart in any direction consistent with safety, after crossing the airport boundary.
   B — Make all turns to the left.
   C — Comply with any FAA traffic pattern established for the airport.

4. If instructed by ground control to taxi to runway 9, the pilot may proceed

   A — via taxiways and across runways to, but not onto, runway 9.
   B — to the next intersecting runway where further clearance is required.
   C — via any route at the pilot's discretion onto runway 9 and hold until cleared for takeoff.

5. Prior to entering an airport advisory area, a pilot

   A — must obtain a clearance from air traffic control.
   B — should monitor ATIS for weather and traffic advisories.
   C — should contact the local FSS for airport and traffic advisories.

6. The numbers 9 and 27 on a runway indicate that the runway is oriented approximately

   A — 090° and 270° magnetic.
   B — 090° and 270° true.
   C — 009° and 027° magnetic.

7. An airport's rotating beacon operated during the daylight hours indicates

   A — that there are obstructions on the airport.
   B — that weather in the Class B, C, D, E airspace is below basic VFR weather minimums.
   C — the airport is temporarily closed.

8. Airport taxiways are identified at night by

   A — alternating red and green edge lights.
   B — white directional edge lights.
   C — blue omnidirectional edge lights.

9. A below-glideslope indication from a tri-color VASI is

   A — a pink light signal.
   B — an amber light signal.
   C — a red light signal.

10. How is a runway recognized as being closed?

   A— Red lights are placed at the approach end of the runway.

   B— Yellow chevrons are painted on the runway beyond the threshold.

   C— X is displayed on the runway.

11. According to the diagram in Figure Q5-1,

   A— takeoffs and landings are permissible at position C since this is a short takeoff and landing runway.

   B— Runway 30 is equipped at position E with emergency arresting gear to provide a means of stopping military aircraft.

   C— takeoffs may be started at position A on runway 12, and the landing portion of this runway begins at position B.

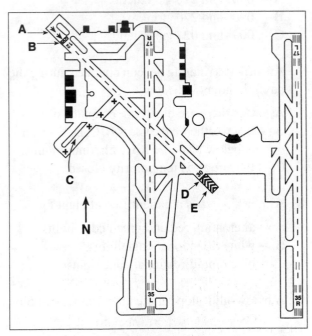

Figure Q5-1. *Airport diagram*

12. That portion of the runway identified by the letter A in Figure Q5-1

   A— may be used for taxiing but should not be used for takeoffs or landings.

   B— may be used for taxiing or takeoffs but not for landings.

   C— may not be used except in an emergency.

13. What is the crosswind component for landing on runway 18 if the tower reports the wind as 220° at 30 knots? *See* Figure 5-13 on Page 5–9.

   A—19 knots

   B—23 knots.

   C—30 knots.

14. How should the controls be held while taxiing a tricycle-gear equipped airplane into a left quartering headwind?

   A— Left aileron up, neutral elevator.

   B— Left aileron down, neutral elevator.

   C— Left aileron up, down elevator.

15. Of the following conditions, which is the most critical when taxiing a nosewheel-equipped high-wing airplane?

   A— Direct crosswind.

   B— Quartering tailwind.

   C— Quartering headwind.

16. Wing-tip vortices, the dangerous turbulence that might be encountered behind a large aircraft, are created only when that aircraft is

   A— operating at high airspeeds.

   B— heavily loaded.

   C— developing lift.

17. Wing-tip vortices created by large aircraft tend to

A — sink below the aircraft generating the turbulence.

B — rise into the takeoff pattern.

C — rise into the takeoff or landing path of a crossing runway.

18. The segmented circle shown in Figure Q5-2 indicates that the airport traffic is

A — left-hand for Rwy 17 and right-hand for Rwy 35.

B — right-hand for Rwy 9 and left-hand for Rwy 27.

C — left-hand for Rwy 35 and right-hand for Rwy 17.

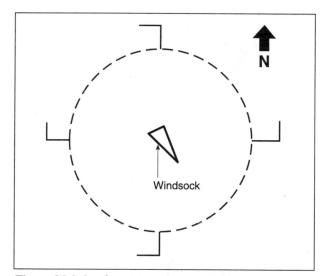

Figure Q5-2. *Landing strip and pattern indicators*

19. When approaching to land on a runway served by a VASI, the pilot shall

A — intercept and remain on the glideslope until touchdown only if the aircraft is operating on an instrument flight plan.

B — maintain an altitude at or above the glideslope.

C — remain on the glideslope and land between the light bars.

20. You are on final approach to a runway equipped with a Precision Approach Path Indicator (PAPI), and see three white lights and one red light. You are

A — low on the glide path.

B — slightly high on the glide path.

C — slightly low on the glide path.

21. A state of temporary confusion resulting from misleading information being sent to the brain by various sensory organs is defined as

A — spatial disorientation.

B — hyperventilation.

C — hypoxia.

22. To preclude the effects of hypoxia, you should

A — avoid flying above 10,000 feet MSL for prolonged periods without breathing supplemental oxygen.

B — rely on your body's built-in alarm system to warn when you are not getting enough oxygen.

C — avoid hyperventilation which is caused by rapid heavy breathing and results in excessive carbon dioxide in the bloodstream.

23. Hypoxia is caused by

A — nitrogen bubbles forming in the blood at high altitudes.

B — trapped gasses in the body.

C — reduced atmospheric pressure.

24. What is the most effective way to use the eyes during night flight?

A — Look only at far away, dim lights.

B — Scan slowly to permit off center viewing.

C — Concentrate directly on each object for a few seconds.

25. The danger of spatial disorientation during flight in poor visual conditions may be reduced by

　A— shifting the eyes quickly between the exterior visual field and the instrument panel.

　B— having faith in the instruments rather than taking a chance on the sensory organs.

　C— leaning the body in the opposite direction of the motion of the aircraft.

26. What effect does haze have on the ability to see traffic or terrain features during flight?

　A— Haze causes the eyes to focus at infinity.

　B— Contrasting colors become less distinct making objects easier to see.

　C— All traffic or terrain features appear to be farther away than their actual distance.

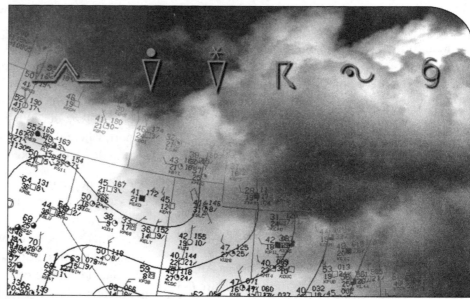

6 Lesson **Weather**

As a pilot limited to flight under Visual Flight Rules, your primary interest in weather and weather changes should be "How will this weather affect visibility for departure, en route, and at my destination?" Your second area of concern will be clouds, because you must maintain separation from clouds at all times. You need to know whether clouds might form where none now exist or if scattered clouds might merge into an impenetrable overcast. You will want to avoid thunderstorms and other severe weather for safety reasons. Flying is fun, but fighting the weather is not. Every pilot should be a student of the weather, and as the hours in your flight log accumulate you should develop a "weather sense" to keep the fun in flying.

The primary source of all weather changes is the sun. It heats the surface of the earth at varying rates, depending not only on cloud cover and the angle at which the sun's rays strike the earth but on the type of surface being heated. For instance, land changes temperature far more rapidly than water, deserts and barren areas change temperature more rapidly than forested areas, and cloud cover affects the rate at which any surface gains and loses heat. Heated air, being less dense than cool air, rises and creates low pressure areas. When the rising air has cooled, it descends and creates areas of high pressure. Air heated at the Equator rises, cools, and moves toward

the North and South Poles. Meteorologists have identified three loops of rising and descending air, as illustrated, with a net flow toward the poles at high altitude (Figure 6-1). The relatively weak cell over the mid-latitudes (including the United States) flows south-to-north. The moisture content of an air mass depends on its temperature and affects its density, and it is these variations in pressure, density, temperature, and moisture content that define air masses

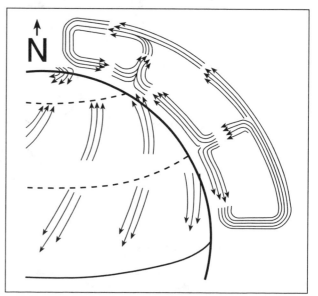

Figure 6-1. *Three-cell circulation pattern and prevailing winds*

and weather systems. The earth of course, rotates beneath these weather systems and their effects are felt many miles distant from where the sun's heat began the process. If the earth did not rotate, air descending from the Poles would flow directly south to the Equator, to be heated again to repeat the cycle.

Because of the earth's rotation, a phenomenon known as the **Coriolis force** deflects the moving air, so that in the latitudes of the United States the prevailing upper level winds are westerly.

Air rising in a low pressure area draws air from outside the low into the center, and the general circulation pattern is counterclockwise (see Figure 6-2, and the full-color surface analysis chart on Appendix page D-4). Find the station models (Figure 6-3) around the highs and lows on the surface analysis

chart to see how actual winds follow this rule. An extreme example of this is the tornado or cyclone which, as it rotates, draws air, houses, trees, and other debris into its center and up, depositing them many miles away. As you can imagine, this incoming air contains moisture, and rising moisture means clouds, poor visibility, etc. When you are at your departure airport, where is that wind coming from? A lake? A snowfield? Land soaked with rain?

Air descending in a high pressure system circulates clockwise, and as the air reaches the surface it travels away from the center. Descending air warms and dries...that's good news when you are flying under visual flight rules. Pilots on long cross-country trips can take advantage of these circulation patterns to get favorable winds (Figure 6-4).

On a surface weather analysis chart, you can see high and low pressure areas. These are defined by meteorologists who take barometric pressure readings at airports and National Weather Service offices across the country, and plot their findings on a chart. By connecting the points of equal pressure (called **isobars**) they define pressure patterns. Where the isobars are tightly packed, pressure is changing rapidly, and strong winds should be expected. Isobars which are widely spaced indicate less force to drive the wind. As the air from high pressure areas rushes to fill in the low pressure areas, you would expect

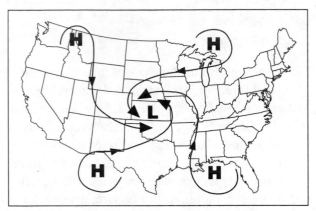

Figure 6-2. Circulation around pressure centers

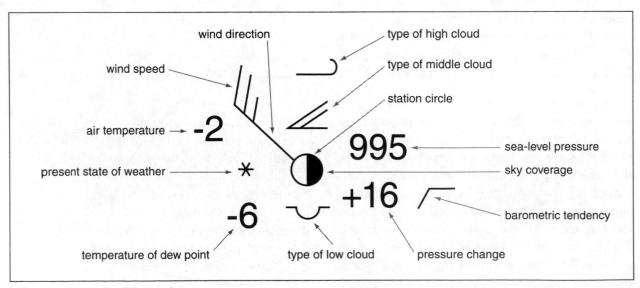

Figure 6-3. Station model example

the wind to blow downhill; that is, directly outward from the center of a high to the center of a low.

Black-and-white weather charts are difficult to find online, but still exist in FAA knowledge examination booklets. Get real-life weather at http://adds. aviationweather.noaa.gov/ (ADDS webpage).

The air tries to do exactly that, and the driving force is called the **pressure gradient** force. This force, combined with Coriolis force, deflects the wind so that the direction of air motion actually crosses the isobars at an angle (Figure 6-5). This figure describes how air moves from high pressure toward low pressure—you might call a high pressure area a "pile of air," and a low pressure area a "hole in the air" that the high pressure air seeks to fill. If the earth did not rotate, the general circulation of air shown in Figure 6-1 would be from south to north over the United States, and it would be at 90° to the gradient wind. However, the earth does rotate, and that rotation causes the wind to veer to the right. The

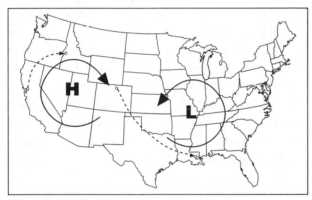

Figure 6-4. *Taking advantage of pressure systems*

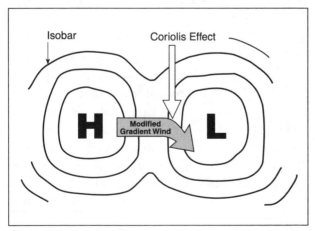

Figure 6-5. *Coriolis effect*

prevailing winds over the United States are from the west and weather systems tend to move across the country from west to east.

On the surface analysis chart you will see wind arrows that do not seem to agree with any rule, because of the effects of local conditions or surface friction. Mountain ranges, passes, valleys—all have local influence on the direction of air movement up to about 2,000 feet above ground level.

Using the ADDS webpage, you get more detail. On the winds page there you can select an altitude.

As a general rule, winds above 2,000 feet AGL come from a direction several degrees clockwise from the surface wind: with a surface wind of 180°, the wind at 2,000 feet AGL might be from 220° and the wind at 4,000 feet AGL from 240°.

To understand and anticipate weather changes, you must be aware of pressure systems and their movement. To know what might happen with cloud formations and obstructions to visibility you must consider the moisture content of the air. All air contains moisture in the form of water vapor; *the amount of water a given volume of air can hold is dependent on the temperature of the air.* As a volume of air is heated, the amount of moisture it can hold in invisible form increases: a temperature increase of 20°F (11°C) doubles the air's capacity to hold moisture. Conversely, cooling the air reduces the amount of water vapor that can be hidden from sight. When the air contains 100% of the moisture it can hold invisibly, the moisture becomes visible in the form of clouds, fog, or precipitation. The moisture condenses into droplets which can be seen, and which restrict your ability to see.

Moisture can be added to the atmosphere through evaporation or sublimation. Evaporation can be from a body of water, a field of snow, or from rainfall; sublimation occurs when water changes state from solid to vapor without a liquid phase. In your future, when you are instrument rated and pick up a trace of ice in a cloud, you will see it slowly disappear even though the outside temperature is below freezing... this is an example of sublimation.

The temperature at which the air becomes saturated and can contain no more moisture, without that moisture getting you wet, is called the **dew point**. You have heard the television weather person report "The temperature is 65°, the dew point is 48°"—under those conditions, if the air suddenly cools 17° it will be saturated, and any further cooling or addition of moisture to the air will result in fog or rain. What the weather reporter calls **relative humidity** is simply how close the air is to being saturated. The illustration (Figure 6-6) uses a cup of liquid (representing the atmosphere) at different temperatures to show how the percentage of moisture content increases from 50% to 100%. A good example of high relative humidity is a hot July day when the air is full of moisture but there isn't a cloud in the sky. You feel uncomfortable because perspiration on your body cannot evaporate into air already full of moisture.

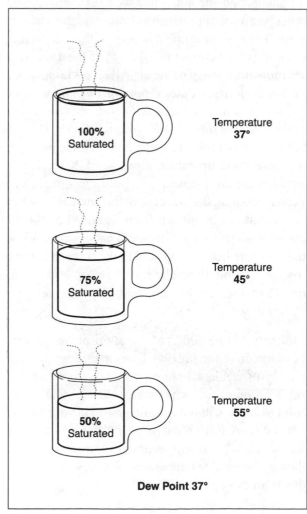

Figure 6-6. *Temperature vs. saturation*

Take a cold can out of a soft drink dispenser on a clear July day and watch beads of water form on its sides. Where do you think that water comes from?

The measure of relative humidity is the spread between temperature and dew point. If that spread is reported to be less than 5°F, you should investigate further to determine the potential for a reduction in visibility. Is the sun rising, or setting? The answer can help you predict the temperature trend and whether the temperature/dew point spread will increase or decrease. Is the wind blowing from over water or from over land? Moisture can be added to the air by evaporation from rain or bodies of water. Moisture being added to the air can tip the balance toward saturation. If your investigation shows the potential for a decrease in the difference between temperature and dew point for any reason, you must consider the possibility that you will not be able to complete the trip under visual conditions.

Knowledge of the temperature/dew point relationship is valuable in estimating the height of cloud bases. When rising air currents are evidenced by the formation of cumulus clouds, the air is cooling at the rate of approximately 4.4°F per 1,000 feet. For example, if the temperature at the surface is 78°F and the dew point is 62°F, the difference is 16° ÷ 4.4 x 1,000 = 3,600 feet above the surface. This is where you would expect cloud bases to be, under the conditions stated. For height of cloud bases above sea level, you must add the elevation of the station at which the observations were made.

Fronts

A weather front exists where air masses with different properties meet. The terms "warm" and "cold" are relative: 30°F air is warmer than 10°F air, but that "warm" air doesn't call for bathing suits. Cold air is more dense than warm air, so where two dissimilar masses meet, the cold air stays near the surface. Figure 6-7 shows a cold front: cold air advancing from west to east and displacing warm air. Because the cold air is dense and relatively heavy, it moves rapidly across the surface, pushing the warm air up. Notice that in both cases the warm air is forced aloft and the cold air stays at the surface. When air is lifted, stuff happens. Just how bad that "stuff" might be is determined by the moisture content of the warm air and where that moisture is coming from.

Friction slows the cold air movement at the surface, so that the front is quite vertical in cross-section and the band of frontal weather is narrow. Cold fronts can move as fast as 30 knots. Your awareness of this rapid movement, together with facts you already know about temperature and dew point will allow you to make the following generalizations about **cold front weather**.

Visibility: Good behind the front. Warm air and pollutants rise rapidly because warm air is less dense than cold air.

Flight conditions: Bumpy as thermal currents rise.

Precipitation: Showery in the frontal area as the warm air is forced aloft and its moisture condenses. The ability of the air to hold moisture decreases as the air cools, and as the moisture contained in each column of rising air condenses into water droplets, showers result.

Cloud type: Cumulus, due to air being raised rapidly to the condensation level. Cumulus clouds are a sign of unstable air; the rising air columns are warmer than the surrounding air and continue to rise under their own power.

Icing possibility: Clear ice. Cumulus clouds develop large water droplets which freeze into clear sheets of ice when they strike an airplane.

A warm front exists when a warm air mass overtakes a slow-moving cold air mass; the lighter warm air cannot displace the heavier cold air, and the warm air is forced to rise as it moves forward (Figure 6-8). This slow upward movement combined with the slow forward movement characteristic of warm fronts allows the warm air to cool slowly. As it reaches the condensation level, stratiform clouds develop. While cold frontal conditions exist over a very short distance, warm fronts slope upward for many miles, and warm frontal weather may be extensive.

You may encounter warm front clouds 50 to 100 miles from where the front is depicted on the surface analysis chart. The following are the characteristics of **warm frontal weather**:

Visibility: Poor; pollutants trapped by warm air aloft. Air warmed at the surface can only rise until it reaches air at its own temperature.

Flight conditions: Smooth, no thermal activity.

Precipitation: Drizzle or continuous rain as moist air is slowly raised to the condensation level.

Cloud type: Stratus or layered, the result of slow cooling.

Icing possibility: Rime ice; small water droplets freeze instantly upon contact with an airplane and form a rough, milky coating.

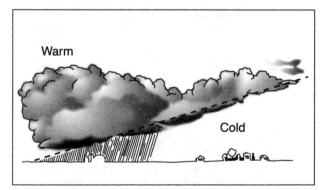

Figure 6-8. *Cross-section of a typical warm front*

Figure 6-7. *Cross-section of a typical cold front*

Occasionally, a fast-moving cold front will overtake a warm front (Figure 6-9) and lift the warm air away from the surface. This is called an *occlusion*, and occluded frontal weather contains the worst features of both warm and cold fronts: turbulent flying conditions, showers and/or continuous precipitation, poor visibility in precipitation, and broad geographic extent of frontal weather conditions.

Air masses can maintain their warm/cold identity and yet not exert any displacement force. When this happens, the front becomes stationary, and the associated weather covers a large geographic area. In your planning, what you see is probably what you will get during the flight.

When you look at a weather map which shows frontal positions, cold fronts will be marked in blue, warm fronts in red, occluded fronts will be purple, and stationary fronts will alternate red and blue. You can identify fronts on black-and-white charts because the cold front symbols look like icicles and warm front symbols appear as blisters (Figure 6-10). Visualize the lifting process, and you will be on your way to being your own weather forecaster.

In flight, when you fly through a front you will notice a change in outside air temperature and wind direction; you will change heading to the right in order to stay on course.

Occluded fronts show both icicles and blisters on the same side of the front in the direction of movement, and stationary fronts show the symbols on opposite sides of the frontal line, indicating opposing forces.

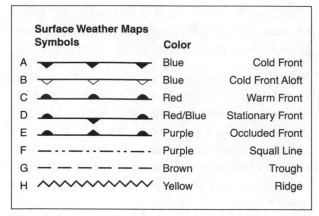

Surface Weather Maps Symbols

	Symbol	Color	
A	▼▼▼	Blue	Cold Front
B	▽▽▽	Blue	Cold Front Aloft
C	◠◠◠	Red	Warm Front
D	◠▼◠	Red/Blue	Stationary Front
E	▲◠▲	Purple	Occluded Front
F	— · — ·· — ·	Purple	Squall Line
G	— — — —	Brown	Trough
H	∿∿∿∿	Yellow	Ridge

Figure 6-10. Surface analysis chart symbols

Stability

You need a general understanding of air mass stability in order to anticipate weather changes which might affect your flight. The amount of moisture in the air influences the rate at which the air cools with increasing altitude. The **standard "lapse rate,"** or rate at which cooling takes place, is 2°C per 1,000 feet of altitude. An air mass that cools more rapidly than 2° per 1,000 feet is considered unstable. Any situation that has cool or cold air overlying warm air is a potentially unstable situation, because the warm air, being lighter, will rise and cool more slowly than the surrounding air. The column of rising air then has the impetus to continue to rise; this is the basis upon which thunderstorms develop.

An air mass with warm air overlying cold air is stable, because the heavy cold air cannot rise to displace the lighter warm air. *When the temperature rises abruptly with altitude, a* **temperature inversion** *exists*—this condition is marked by poor visibility because warm, polluted air cannot rise above the inversion level. This is the familiar smog or haze layer, and it usually takes the passage of a major system to clean it out. The possibility of turbulence always exists at the top of an inversion layer.

Cloud Families

What you have learned about air movement and the relationship of temperature to moisture content leads right into the study of cloud formation, and by "reading" the clouds you will be able to anticipate the effects of weather changes on your flight.

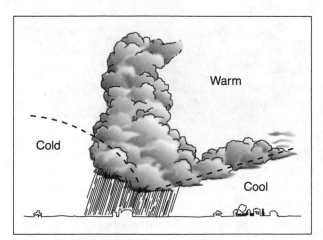

Figure 6-9. Occluded fronts

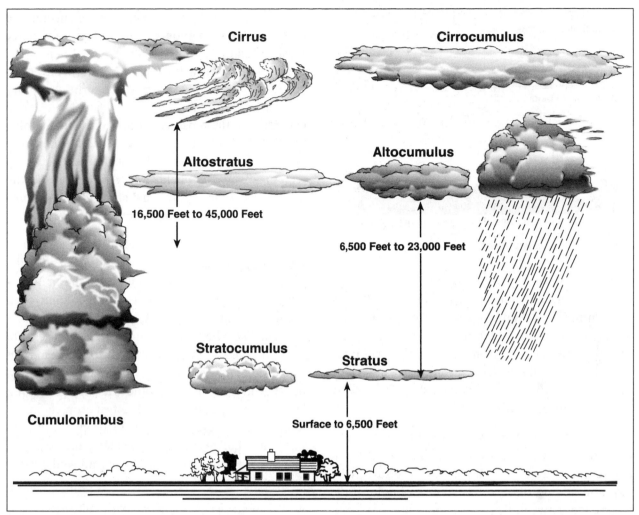

Figure 6-11. *Typical cloud formations*

Meteorologists divide clouds into four families: high clouds, middle clouds, low clouds, and clouds with extensive vertical development. The latter group signals the presence of strong columns of rising air (called convective air currents) which at the very least mean a rough ride, and may herald the onset of precipitation or a developing thunderstorm (Figure 6-11).

When a ground station reports a dewpoint in excess of 50°F, it is a sign of strong convective currents. If you find yourself flying toward that station in silky smooth air, with increasing groundspeed, your airplane is entrained in a mass of air being drawn rapidly toward the core of a thunderstorm. Check that station's weather carefully, and land short of your goal if necessary.

Nice fluffy-looking clouds marking the tops of columns of rising air are called **cumulus** clouds, because they are in a building or accumulating stage as the air rises to the condensation level—you can expect a bumpy ride beneath them and a smooth ride above (Figure 6-12 on the next page). **Stratocumulus** clouds are in the low family, altocumulus in the middle altitudes, and cirrocumulus is the word for fluffy clouds at high altitudes. Cumulus clouds are a sign of instability in the air mass because stable air has no tendency to move vertically.

Stratus or layered clouds indicate a stable air mass; they have little vertical development—fog is defined as a stratus cloud at the surface. A stratus cloud deck may make the day dark and gloomy, but the smooth ride will make up for it. **Altostratus** clouds are found in the mid-altitudes and cirrostratus are very high

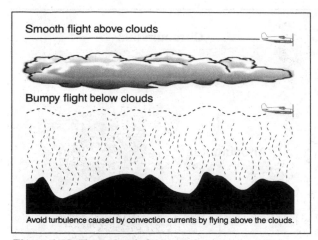

Smooth flight above clouds

Bumpy flight below clouds

Avoid turbulence caused by convection currents by flying above the clouds.

Figure 6-12. *Thermal turbulence*

thin layers of ice crystals. Cloud names can be combinations: stratocumulus is a good example. Clouds with "nimbo" or "nimbus" in their names indicate the presence of precipitation. **"Virga"** is the name for moisture that falls from a cloud but evaporates before reaching the surface. It is a visible indication of a downdraft and possible wind shear. Do not fly beneath or through virga.

You can calculate the approximate altitude of a cloud base above ground level by dividing the Fahrenheit temperature-dewpoint spread at the surface by 4.4, and adding three zeroes. For example, if the difference between the temperature and dewpoint is 9°F, the cloud bases are at 9 ÷ 4.4 = 2.05 — or approximately 2,000 feet AGL. To convert that figure to "above mean sea level" you must add the field elevation of the reporting station.

Thunderstorms

Thunderstorms deserve special treatment, and they even have a special cloud name: **cumulonimbus**, abbreviated as CB or CU. When you hear pilots on the radio talking about "towering cues to the northwest" or "several CBs to the east" they aren't talking about pool halls or CB radio but about clouds indicating threatening weather. Three items must be present for thunderstorm development: sufficient water vapor, an unstable lapse rate, and a lifting force. With all three present, it takes very little to begin the process: the sun heating a parking lot or a plowed field, wind blowing up a mountain slope — these are typical of the things that can start a column of rising air.

Storms begun by the sun heating the surface are called air mass thunderstorms. They are usually localized and you can fly around them. When warm, moist air moves up a mountain and a storm develops, it is called an orographic thunderstorm. A rapidly moving cold front forcing warm unstable air to rise can result in the most hazardous of thunderstorms, the **squall line thunderstorm**. It is not unusual, especially in the midwest, for squall lines to develop well in advance of a cold front. As you can see, the only variable is the force that starts the lifting process — after that, the storm grows on its own.

Figure 6-13 shows the life cycle of a thunderstorm, beginning with the cumulus or building stage as the warm moist air rises. The instability of the air allows this process to feed on itself as the air column, even though cooling with altitude, is warmer than the surrounding air. The moisture in the air condenses into water droplets, adding more heat to the rising air. The droplets do not fall out of the cloud initially, but are carried to higher altitudes as they grow even larger through collision with other droplets in the turbulent air. These growing water droplets can even freeze into hail at the top of the cloud and be blown downwind to create a hazard to aircraft well outside the cloud mass.

A thunderstorm has reached maturity when the water droplets are big enough to overcome the upward air currents and precipitation reaches the ground (Figure 6-14). The falling rain creates downdrafts in opposition to the updrafts which began the whole process. This updraft/downdraft combination within a short distance makes penetrating a thunderstorm hazardous to the structural integrity of *any* size aircraft.

The downdrafts soon overpower the updrafts and the storm cell dissipates into heavy rain. The process just described is continuous as long as the conditions of warm, moist air, instability, and lifting force are present and as far as the pilot is concerned, the birth and death of individual cells is not apparent. The rapid vertical movement of air up and down in close proximity develops electrical charges, and lightning from cloud to cloud or from cloud to ground is a part of all thunderstorm activity.

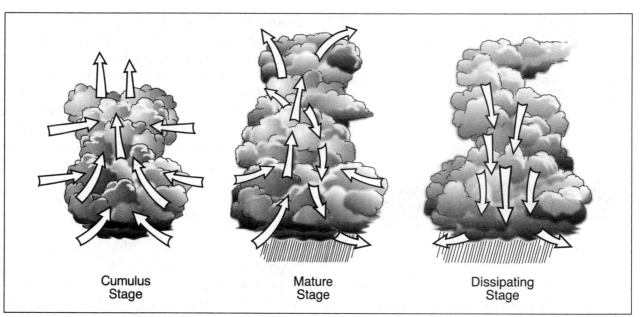

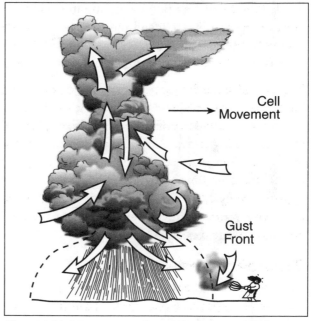

Figure 6-13. *Life cycle of a thunderstorm*

The external appearance of cumulus clouds should never be used as an indicator of what might be found inside. Gleaming white, puffy, clouds with all the outward menace of a pile of marshmallows might contain destructive forces, while a threatening grey-black area might contain only heavy rain and a few bumps. As a VFR pilot you must not fly into *any* cloud, but a knowledge of thunderstorms may save you from encountering hail in clear air downwind from a cumulonimbus cloud or from being punished by turbulence as you fly through conflicting air currents beneath one. Severe turbulence should be expected up to 20 miles from a severe thunderstorm, and up to 10 miles from lesser storms. Thunderstorm clouds may be embedded in a continuous layer of other clouds, creating an unseen hazard for the pilot attempting to fly visually in marginal conditions. Pilots may also experience gusty winds and turbulence near the surface many miles around the actual location of a thunderstorm cell as the downdrafts strike the ground and move outward (Figure 6-14).

Weather associated with thunderstorms is more severe on the side toward which the storm is moving; you'll see a dark column extending to the ground with occasional shafts of lightning. Surface winds will be gusting. Approached from the back, a thunderstorm can be misleading—you don't realize what you have flown into until it is almost too late. You may see some scuddy clouds at middle altitudes, then

Figure 6-14. *Mature stage of a steady-state thunderstorm cell*

low clouds as you get closer. In other words, if you see lowering clouds and decreasing visibility, don't go any farther.

"**Microbursts**" have recently been identified as small shafts of descending air associated with thunderstorms. Because of their small diameter, microbursts are not easily detected by weather instruments, making it even more important that pilots stay away from areas where thunderstorms are existing or forecast.

Wind Shear

Wind shear is defined as a change in direction or speed of air movement, either horizontal or vertical, that takes place within a short distance. It can occur at any level in the atmosphere. It can be the result of mechanical forces such as turbulence around buildings adjacent to the runway, or may be encountered when flying into the wind on the lee (downwind) side of a mountain ridge (Figures 6-15 and 6-16). Wind shear is most frequently related to a weather phenomena such as thunderstorms. A rapid wind shift from a headwind to a tailwind can cause an unexpected loss of altitude and airspeed, and, if a storm cell is within 15 miles of the airport you should delay your takeoff to avoid such a shift.

You are already aware of the vertical shear forces present when an aircraft enters a mature thunderstorm and encounters updrafts and downdrafts in rapid succession—a pilot attempting to fight these forces could quickly exceed the load limit on the aircraft structure. The pilot's only recourse is to keep the wings level, maintain attitude (not altitude), and

go along for the ride until clear of the cell. Other types of wind shear encounters will require that you keep the aircraft under control but should not endanger its safety. An example is flying through a front: the wind always shifts as you fly through a front, and this is a form of wind shear. If you are departing an airport which is under the influence of a temperature inversion, with little or no air movement near the surface, you may be surprised by wind shear turbulence as you climb through the inversion layer if the winds 2,000 to 4,000 feet above the surface are at least 25 knots. This is an example of low-level wind shear.

The gust front associated with thunderstorm-generated downdrafts can create wind shear hazards 15 to 25 miles from the storm itself, and unless its presence is revealed by blowing dust, there will be no warning. Winds aloft blowing at 50 knots or more can create severe turbulence downwind from mountain ranges (Figure 6-17).

If there is sufficient moisture in the air for cloud formation, a lens-shaped cloud will form which remains stationary in relation to the ground. This "standing lenticular" (called an "altocumulus standing lenticular" or ACSL) is a signpost warning of turbulence (Figure 6-18). Note the rotor cloud; destructive tur-

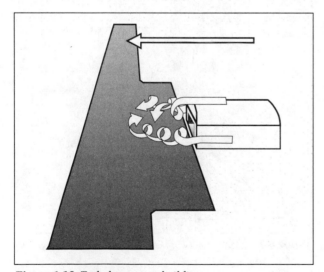

Figure 6-15. *Turbulence near buildings*

Figure 6-16. *Turbulence near mountains*

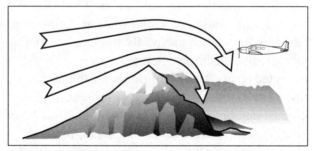

Figure 6-17. *Turbulence near mountains*

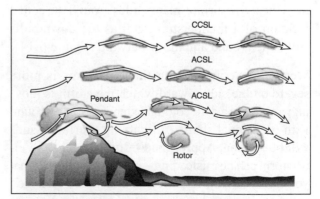

Figure 6-18. *Standing lenticular wave pattern*

bulence can be present in and beneath rotor clouds. In your flight planning, be sure to check into the possibility of thunderstorm activity on or near your route and of strong winds aloft. If you will be flying in mountainous terrain, wind shear and turbulence are uncomfortable at best.

Fog

Fog is probably the most deceptive hazard to safe flight that a VFR pilot has to consider in flight planning. Fog can form or dissipate virtually instantaneously, and it can form under conditions that appear to be ideal for flight. Still, with your knowledge of the movement of air masses and of the temperature/dew point relationship, you can guard against unpleasant surprises.

Radiation fog catches many pilots off guard. Calm winds and clear skies would seem to be the answers to a pilot's prayers, but when these conditions occur and the temperature/dew point spread is small, radiation fog is a good possibility. The clear skies allow the land to radiate heat, cooling the air near the surface to the dew point and causing fog to form (Figure 6-19). This is a night or early morning phenomenon, and a few hours of sunlight will raise the air temperature above the dew point, "burning off" the fog. From cruise altitude, a thin ground fog layer (ground fog is a type of radiation fog) may seem fairly harmless to a pilot who can see runways and buildings as though through a veil.

On a landing approach, however, what looked thin from altitude obscures everything because the pilot is now looking at the fog layer horizontally. When

Figure 6-19. Radiation (ground) fog

ground fog is predicted (or any time the T/DP spread is less than 3°F), include a fog-free alternate airport in your planning.

Advection fog results when moist air moves, and to anticipate it you must consider where the moist air is coming from and what it is moving toward. Typically, the moist air is moving from over water to over colder land; the moist air condenses into fog when cooled by the land (Figure 6-20). The process can be reversed when warm moist air from land moves over cold water.

Your key for planning purposes is knowing the wind direction, surface temperatures, and dew points, and whether the wind is coming from over land or water. What is the relative humidity at a reporting station upwind from you? Because advection fog is created by moving air, wind will not blow it away, and it will not burn off as readily as radiation fog; advection fog can be persistent and can form at any time.

Upslope fog's name gives away its origin. As moist, stable air is moved toward higher terrain, it cools to its dew point and condenses as fog. While flying you will see it first in valleys, filling them and obscuring as much of the high ground as the moisture content of the air allows and lasting as long as the upward force exists. Contrast this with the upward movement of moist *unstable* air which can lead to thunderstorm formation.

We don't stop flying just because it's raining, but what starts out as a simple rainy day flight can end up quite differently. When rain falls into cool, almost saturated air, the moisture it adds can result in what is called precipitation-induced fog, and can lower visibilities well below the minimums required for flight. Occluded fronts, warm fronts, slow-moving cold fronts and stationary fronts all have the ingredients necessary for the onset of precipitation-induced fog. When any of these conditions are forecast for your time or route of flight (or if you encounter precipitation), you must consider the possibility of reduced visibility due to fog.

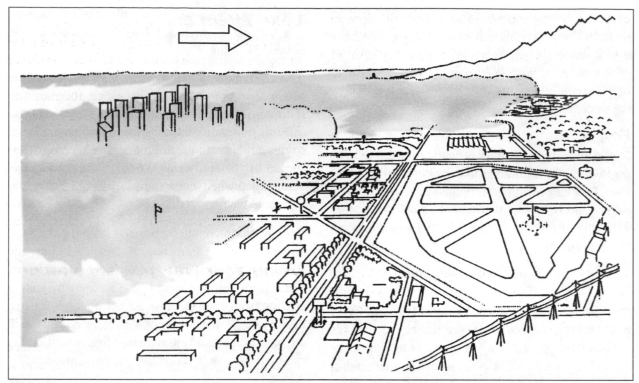

Figure 6-20. *Advection fog*

Condensation Nuclei

In industrial areas, or anywhere that pollutants might be found in the air, fog will form more readily and dissipate more slowly. When the water vapor has something to condense on, such as a pollutant particle, fog will be more persistent than when such nuclei are not present.

Structural Icing and Frost

Structural icing and frost adversely affect airplane performance. For an airplane without deicing equipment, an encounter with inflight airframe icing is viewed as an emergency—to be avoided at all costs. As a VFR pilot (if you are following the rules), the only way you can encounter hazardous structural icing is to fly into an area of freezing rain. It takes both visible moisture and temperatures below freezing to produce ice on your airplane, and while you can comfortably fly in the rain and will enjoy flying in crisp, clear, cold air, you never want to mix the two. Freezing rain will coat your entire airplane (not just the leading edges of the wings and tail surfaces) with ice almost instantaneously, resulting in an immediate, unplanned descent.

The presence of ice pellets at the surface indicates that there is freezing rain at a higher altitude and you definitely should not be flying. The bright side of freezing rain is that conditions conducive to it are readily forecast.

Frost presents more of a hazard to the VFR pilot than does freezing rain, because frost looks so harmless. When the surface temperature is below freezing, and the relative humidity is high, frost will form all over your airplane in a process called sublimation: the direct change from water vapor to solid form. Frost does not fall on your airplane, it forms on it. Frost does not weigh much, and it does not change the basic aerodynamic shape of the lifting surfaces; it does, however, create so much drag that it may be impossible to develop enough airspeed to become airborne. Airplanes that do manage to get airborne with a coat of frost find that stall speed has increased dramatically and/or they cannot climb.

Although it is time-consuming and delays your flight, all frost must be removed from the airplane before flight is attempted. The National Transportation Safety Board says that there is no substitute for using your hands to check for frost...don't trust your eyes. Do not attempt to remove frost (or snow, or ice) with water, either hot or cold. It can run back into control hinges, balanced control surfaces, or gear retraction mechanisms and freeze after take-off. Use a deicing fluid diluted as recommended by the manufacturer.

Frost can also be an inflight hazard if the surface temperature of the airplane is below freezing and you fly into moist air. A layer of frost can form all over the airplane, including the windshield, and turn you into an unprepared, unsuspecting instrument pilot. The only answer is the defroster and/or a descent into warmer air.

Taxiing through puddles on a very cold day can also lead to complications. If you are flying a retract-able gear airplane, cycle the gear once or twice after takeoff to be sure that water doesn't freeze the mechanism.

Cold Weather Operations

In addition to the hazards of icing, you must con-sider the effects of cold weather and precipitation while your airplane is tied down. Remember back in Lesson 2, when getting oil to the top end of the engine (camshaft, valve lifters) was discussed? Cold weather makes this situation worse. When outside temperatures are 20°F or colder, the engine must be pre-heated unless the airplane has been hangared. There are a number of pre-heating systems available. Heating the oil at the bottom of the engine is a good first start, but in the interest of long engine life the whole engine block should be preheated. Check the breather tubes…they may be plugged with ice caused by condensation of crankcase vapors. Don't forget the cabin—those gyro-powered instruments don't like low temperatures any more than engines do.

Wings are designed to support the weight of the airplane...they are not designed to support weight on their upper surfaces. Even if you do not plan to fly in snowy weather, be sure to clean snow accu-mulations off of the wing. Snow looks light and fluffy, but it isn't.

Lake Effect Snow

If you plan to fly downwind of a large body of water during the winter (think the Great Lakes), you should be aware of lake effect snow. Water temperature is warm, compared to the overlying air, meaning that the air over the water surface picks up moisture. When the windspeed increases up to seven knots or more it begins to pick up that moisture and carry it over the colder land downwind of the lake. This means snow and much reduced visibility. The result-ing clouds are layered; tops pretty much depend on wind strength. Be alert to the possibility of lake effect snow.

Using Your Weather Knowledge

The greatest hazard you face as a pilot limited to flight under Visual Flight Rules is loss of visual con-tact with the terrain and the resulting potential for becoming disoriented. Statistics show that a loss or a reduction in visibility is the most common factor in general aviation accidents. Armed with the informa-tion in this chapter and a little common sense, you can avoid this hazard.

Obstructions to vision are related to moisture in the air. That moisture might take the form of a cloud, a rain shower, snow, or fog. Look at the big picture:

Is the wind coming from over a body of water toward rising terrain? (It doesn't have to be a lake or ocean. Rain-soaked ground can provide plenty of moisture.) Are you flying toward an area where the air mass is cooler? Is the temperature-dew point spread decreas-ing? Will the air in your vicinity be cooled enough by the approach of nightfall that any moisture it contains will condense into clouds?

If the natural horizon becomes obscured, consider a 180-degree turn toward safety. Don't assume that the horizon is where the base of the clouds meets the mountains, and reverse your vertical speed if climb-ing or descending—that can be a trap. Don't fly on top of a scattered cloud layer unless you are prepared to reverse course when they begin to thicken beneath you. Never fly on top of a broken or overcast layer. Always fly toward improving weather.

Attempting visual flight into weather conditions that require an instrument rating is the leading cause of accidents for non-instrument rated pilots with less than 400 hours of flight experience. If your flight will only be completed safely if the tailwind forecast holds up, or if the scattered thunderstorms don't occur on your flight path, or any similar "if," don't go.

When looking at a marginal weather situation and contemplating whether or not to go and take a look, remember the old pilot's motto: It is better to be on the ground wishing you were flying than to be up in the air wishing you were on the ground.

Learning More About Weather

The more you know about the physics of weather, the better off you will be as a pilot. The FAA's tried-and-true Advisory Circular 00-6A *Aviation Weather* is the source of all weather questions on the knowledge examinations, but there are dozens of other places for you to look and learn. *Aviation Weather Services,* Advisory Circular 00-45, is your reference to all weather reports and weather charts and will be more fully explored in Chapter 7. Some of the full-color screen shots in Appendix D come from that source and are only a small sample. Be aware that you can go to www.faa.gov and read or download all of the government publications mentioned in this book. Excellent weather videos are available at www.aopa.org/asf/online_courses/.

Lesson 6
Weather Review Questions

1. The conditions necessary for the formation of cumulonimbus clouds are a lifting action and

   A — unstable air containing an excess of condensation nuclei.
   B — unstable, moist air.
   C — either stable or unstable air.

2. The wind at 5,000 feet AGL is southwesterly while the surface wind is southerly. This difference in direction is primarily due to

   A — stronger pressure gradient at higher altitudes.
   B — friction between the wind and the surface.
   C — stronger Coriolis force at the surface.

3. Clouds, fog, or dew will always form when

   A — water vapor condenses.
   B — water vapor is present.
   C — relative humidity reaches 100 percent.

4. Steady precipitation preceding a front is an indication of

   A — stratiform clouds with moderate turbulence.
   B — cumuliform clouds with little or no turbulence.
   C — stratiform clouds with little or no turbulence.

5. How does frost affect the lifting surfaces of an airplane on takeoff?

   A — Frost may prevent the airplane from becoming airborne at normal takeoff speed.
   B — Frost will change the camber of the wing, increasing lift during takeoff.
   C — Frost may cause the airplane to become airborne with a lower angle of attack at a lower indicated airspeed.

6. What types of fog depend upon wind in order to exist?

   A — Radiation fog and ice fog.
   B — Steam fog and ground fog.
   C — Advection fog and upslope fog.

7. What conditions are necessary for the formation of thunderstorms?

   A — High humidity, lifting force, and unstable conditions.
   B — High humidity, high temperature, and cumulus clouds.
   C — Lifting force, moist air, and extensive cloud cover.

8. If there is thunderstorm activity in the vicinity of an airport at which you plan to land, which hazardous atmospheric phenomenon might be expected on the landing approach?

   A — Precipitation static.
   B — Wind-shear turbulence.
   C — Steady rain.

9. An almond or lens-shaped cloud which appears stationary, but which may contain winds of 50 knots or more, is referred to as

   A — an inactive frontal cloud.
   B — a funnel cloud.
   C — a lenticular cloud.

10. Every physical process of weather is accompanied by, or is the result of, a

    A — movement of air.
    B — pressure differential.
    C — heat exchange.

11. What causes variations in altimeter settings between weather reporting points?

   A — Unequal heating of the Earth's surface.
   B — Variation of terrain elevation.
   C — Coriolis force.

12. What are the standard pressure and temperature values for sea level?

   A — 15°C and 29.92" Hg.
   B — 59°C and 1013.2 millibars.
   C — 59°F and 29.92 millibars.

13. Upon encountering severe turbulence, which flight condition should the pilot attempt to maintain?

   A — Constant altitude and airspeed.
   B — Constant angle of attack.
   C — Level flight attitude.

14. In which situation is advection fog most likely to form?

   A — A warm, moist air mass on the windward side of mountains.
   B — An air mass moving inland from the coast in winter.
   C — A light breeze blowing colder air out to sea.

Answers:
1-B, 2-B, 3-A, 4-C, 5-A, 6-C, 7-A, 8-B, 9-C, 10-C, 11-A, 12-A, 13-C, 14-B.

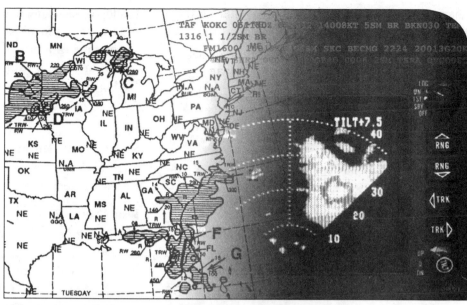

Lesson 7 Weather Services

The Go/No Go Decision

Lesson 6 acquainted you with the physics of weather. Now you have to locate those areas of high and low pressure, frontal boundaries, and sources of moisture to see how they will affect your flight. Lesson 4 taught you the Federal Aviation Regulations regarding visual flight rules and flight in visual meteorological conditions and prepared you to answer knowledge test questions on these regulations. The National Weather Service (NWS) has a different take on things—a far more conservative approach—and I recommend that you fly using these definitions, not the ones in Part 91. To the NWS, VFR means a ceiling higher than 3,000 feet AGL and visibility greater than five miles; MVFR (marginal VFR) means a ceiling of 1,000 to 3,000 feet AGL and/or visibility three to five miles; IFR means a ceiling of 500 feet AGL to below 1,000 feet AGL; and LIFR (Low IFR) means ceiling below 500 feet and/or visibility less than one mile. You will see these definitions used when Java METARs are discussed and illustrated on Pages 7–5 and D-3.

Believe me, even though 14 CFR §91.155 says that you can legally fly in Class E airspace under visual flight rules with only three miles visibility, that's not very much when you are covering a mile and a half or more every minute; if you are flying toward the sun the situation is even worse. Don't even think about the "one mile visibility and clear of clouds" provision in Class G airspace...those cell towers and windmills seem to appear out of nowhere. My advice is "no go" if the weather sources we are now going to investigate show anything worse than VFR using the NWS definition.

Sources of Weather Information

Your first choice when looking for weather reports and forecasts should be the Aviation Digital Data Service (ADDS) webpage (http://aviationweather.gov/ADDS/). In the left column, click on "Standard Briefing" and you will access a bewildering variety of graphic and textual products. To learn how to interpret the reports and forecasts, refer to *Aviation Weather Services*, FAA Advisory Circular 00-45 (or, "AWS"). Ideally, you should have a copy of the AWS in your library, but it is available for reading or download at the FAA website (www.faa.gov). The advantage of the online publication over the book is that the online version includes changes and updates; the disadvantages are that it is a huge file and it is not searchable. Still, it is the only place where you can find explanations for all of the online weather charts and graphics. In this lesson, I will just scratch the surface of what is available to you at the click of a mouse.

The FAA makes the Direct User Access Terminal Service available free to civil pilots and authorized users. There are two providers:

DTC DUAT   1-800-245-3828   www.duat.com

CSC DUATS   1-800-767-9989   www.duats.com

Both provide official weather reports and forecasts in text and graphic form, and both make it possible to file a flight plan with Flight Service. There are minor differences between services and I can't recommend one over the other. However, neither has the complete coverage of NWS products that the ADDS webpage provides.

If you prefer to get your weather from a live human being, a telephone briefing by an FSS specialist who refers to the weather data to help you plan your flight; however, you must know the right questions to ask in this situation. Calling **1-800-WX-BRIEF** will connect you to the Automated Flight Service Station system. To learn how to make the most of your contact, go to www.afss.com, click on News and Feedback and then Pilot Tips.

Three types of **preflight briefings** are available: standard, abbreviated, and outlook. If you have not collected any weather information before calling the FSS, ask for the standard briefing—then you can be sure that nothing will be left out. Ask for an abbreviated briefing if you want to update an earlier briefing

or add to information you have already received from another source. In this situation, tell the briefer where you got the original information so that he or she can fill in any gaps. It is possible to get an in-flight briefing, but doing so ties up the radio frequency and is not good manners.

Request an outlook briefing when your proposed departure time will be more than six hours after the briefing, then back it up with a standard briefing closer to takeoff time.

Weather URLs

Members of the Aircraft Owners and Pilots Association have access to dozens of weather products at www.aopa.org; members of the Experimental Aircraft Association (EAA) get access to Aeroplanner as a membership benefit. Internet users with worldwide web browsers will find links to dozens of weather products, both textual and graphic, to be readily available (*see* Table 7-1). There are a myriad of aviation weather sites on the web; just search for "aviation weather" and you will be inundated. The URLs listed are just a sample. The ADDS webpage is invaluable for flight planning, and its java tools tab includes a Flight Planning Application that you can download to your computer. One caution: Pages marked "Experimental Display" are not to be relied on when making a go/no-go decision, although they will give you the big picture. You are supposed to rely on primary sources such as METAR, TAF, etc. when making planning decisions. Finally, *Aviation Weather Services* (AC 00-45) includes several pages of weather URLs.

URL	Name
adds.aviationweather.noaa.gov	Aviation Weather Center ADDS Page
www.faa.gov/asos/asos.htm	ASOS Information
www.accuweather.com	AccuWeather Website
www.weather.unisys.com	Unisys Weather
www.wunderground.com	Weather Underground
www.spc.noaa.gov	Storm Prediction Center
www.uswx.com/us/wx	United States Weather Pages
www.weathermeister.com	general weather information
weather.aero/tools/weatherproducts/metars	Experimental ADDS page

Table 7-1. *Weather URLs*

They tell us that one picture is worth a thousand words, so search the web for weather cams and road cams—in many areas you will be able to see the weather enroute and at your destination in real time. Check the forecasts carefully, because what you see on your monitor will surely change before your ETA.

If you don't have a computer, the flight service station briefers (and the Flight Watch specialists) have satellite pictures of cloud cover available to supplement the printed weather data. NWS meteorologists are stationed at FAA radar facilities to evaluate weather radar information and make it available to pilots on a current basis. Your local TV weather broadcaster is an excellent source of weather information, and will probably also have satellite pictures available.

In-Flight Sources

You can also listen to the Hazardous Inflight Weather Advisory Service (HIWAS) on selected radio navigational aids (VORs and NDBs) for weather updates. Check your chart legend or the A/FD to identify navaids that broadcast weather information—a blue circle with a reversed "T" in the upper right-hand corner of the frequency box on sectionals for TWEBs (Transcribed Weather Broadcasts, available only in Alaska), or a reversed "H" in the same location for HIWAS. In flight, the Enroute Flight Advisory Service (EFAS), or Flight Watch, can be contacted on 122.0 MHz between 0600 and 2200 local time for direct contact with a weather briefer. If you have a radio in your airplane you will always have access to up-to-date weather information and must not rely solely on a pre-takeoff briefing. You will find locations of EFAS stations on the inside back cover or the A/FD, or if you know which air traffic control center's airspace you are in, use that name: "Chicago Flight Watch..."

The National Oceanic and Atmospheric Administration (NOAA) broadcasts weather continuously on UHF frequencies in the 162 MHz range. These frequencies cannot be tuned by your aircraft radio. Radios designed specifically for receiving these broadcasts are available at electronics stores.

Overview

Weather information can be divided into two categories: observations, and forecasts. An observation is a snapshot of weather conditions at a stated time; its utility degrades over time. Some observations can be as much as an hour old when you first see them. Examples of observations are:

METARs (Aviation Routine Weather Reports): These answer the question "What's going on at my departure airport, my destination, and at enroute airports?" and will be discussed in detail.

Satellite Images: Literally, snapshots of cloud cover. Can be augmented with LIFR/IFR/MVFR/VFR symbology.

Pilot Reports: Eyewitness news from the cockpit. Used by the NWS to fine-tune their forecast models. Their utility suffers because the wide range of aircraft types and pilot experience makes them subjective. The NWS actively solicits pilot reports and you should make at least one during each flight.

Automated Weather Observations (AWOS/ASOS)

NEXRAD/Doppler Radar: Not to be taken at face value; can be misleading. I'll explain later in this lesson.

Let's take them in order.

METAR

Every reporting weather station issues an hourly observation called an aviation routine weather report, or METAR, which includes cloud cover and visibility, wind direction and velocity, altimeter setting, and remarks. If you see SPECI instead of METAR, that means something important has changed since the hourly METAR was issued...and it is usually a change for the worse. Figure 7-1 contains the key to interpreting METARs. *Note:* This key will not be available to you for your FAA Knowledge Exam, so learn to read and understand the information without the key.

Click on the METAR/TAF tab on the ADDS webpage, and insert the 4-letter identifier of the airport you are interested in; you will have your choice of

Key to Aerodrome Forecast (TAF) and Aviation Routine Weather Report (METAR) — *Front*

TAF KPIT 091730Z 0918/1024 15005KT 5SM HZ FEW020 WS010/31022KT
FM01930 30015G25KT 3SM SHRA OVC015
TEMPO 0920/0922 1/2SM +TSRA OVC008CB
FM100100 27008KT 5SM SHRA BKN020 OVC040
PROB30 1004/1007 1SM -RA BR
FM101015 18005KT 6SM -SHRA OVC020
BECMG 1013/1015 P6SM NSW SKC

Note: Users are cautioned to confirm *DATE* and *TIME* of the TAF. For example FM100000 is 0000Z on the **10th**. Do not confuse with *1000Z!*

METAR KPIT 091955Z COR 22015G25KT 3/4SM R28L/2600FT TSRA OVC010CB
18/16 A2992 RMK SLP045 T01820159

Forecast	Explanation	Report
TAF	Message type: TAF: routine or TAF AMD: amended forecast; METAR: hourly; SPECI: special or TESTM: noncommissioned ASOS report	METAR
KPIT	ICAO location indicator	KPIT
091730Z	Issuance time: ALL times in UTC "Z", 2-digit date, 4-digit time	091955Z
0918/1024	Valid period: Either 24 hours or 30 hours. The first two digits of EACH four-digit number indicate the date of the valid period, the final two digits indicate the time (valid from 18Z to 24Z on the 10th). In U.S. METAR: CORrected ob; or AUTOmated ob for automated report with no human intervention; omitted when observer logs on.	COR
15005KT	Wind: 3-digit true-north direction, nearest 10 degrees (or VaRiaBle); next 2–3 digits for speed and unit, KT (KMH or MPS); as needed, Gust and maximum speed; 00000KT for calm; for METAR, if direction varies 60 degrees or more, Variability appended, e.g., 180V260	22015G25KT
5SM	Prevailing visibility: In U.S., Statute Miles and fractions; above 6 miles in TAF Plus6SM. (Or, 4-digit minimum visibility in meters and as required, lowest value with direction.)	3/4SM
	Runway Visual Range: R: 2-digit runway designator Left, Center, or Right as needed; "/" Minus or Plus in U.S., 4-digit value, FeeT in U.S. (usually meters elsewhere); 4-digit value Variability, 4-digit value (and tendency Down, Up, or No change)	R28L/2600FT
HZ	Significant present, forecast and recent weather: See table (Fig 7-1-22)	TSRA
FEW020	Cloud amount, height and type: SKy Clear 0/8, FEW >0/8-2/8, SCaTtered 3/8-4/8, BroKeN 5/8-7/8, OVerCast 8/8; 3-digit height in hundreds of feet; Towering CUmulus or CumulonimBus in METAR; in TAF, only CB. Vertical Visibility for obscured sky and height "VV004". More than 1 layer may be reported or forecast. In automated METAR reports only, CLeaR for "clear below 12,000 feet."	OVC010CB
18/16	Temperature: Degrees Celsius; first 2 digits, dewpoint temperature; Minus for below zero, e.g., M06	18/16
A2992	Altimeter setting: Indicator and 4 digits; in U.S., A: inches and hundredths; (Q: hectoPascals, e.g., Q1013)	A2992
WS010/ 31022KT	In U.S. TAF, nonconvective low-level (≤2,000 feet) Wind Shear; 3-digit height (hundreds of feet); "/"; 3-digit wind direction and 2–3 digit wind speed above the indicated height, and unit, KT	

Key to Aerodrome Forecast (TAF) and Aviation Routine Weather Report (METAR) — *Back*

Forecast	Explanation	Report
	In METAR, BeMarK indicator and remarks. For example: Sea-Level Pressure in hectoPascals and tenths, as shown: 1004.5 hPa; Temp/dewpoint in tenths °C, as shown: temp. 18.2°C, dewpoint 15.9°C	RMK SLP045 T01820159
FM091930	FroM: Changes are expected at: 2-digit date, 2-digit hour, and 2-digit minute beginning time; indicates significant change. Each FM starts on a new line, indented 5 spaces	
TEMPO 0920/0922	TEMPOrary: Changes expected for <1 hour and in total, < half of the period between the 2-digit date and 2-digit hour beginning, and 2-digit date and 2-digit hour ending time	
PROB30 1004/1007	PRObability and 2-digit percent (30 or 40): Probable condition in the period between the 2-digit date and 2-digit hour beginning time, and the 2-digit date and 2-digit hour ending time	
BECMG 1013/1015	BECoMinG: Change expected in the period between the 2-digit date and 2-digit hour beginning time, and the 2-digit date and 2-digit hour ending time	

Table of Significant Present, Forecast and Recent Weather — Grouped in categories and used in the order listed below; or as needed in TAF, No Significant Weather

QUALIFIERS

Intensity or Proximity

"-" = Light   No sign = Moderate   "+" = Heavy

"VC" = Vicinity, but not at aerodrome. In the U.S. METAR, 5 to 10 SM from the point of observation. In the U.S. TAF, 5 to 10 SM from the center of the runway complex. Elsewhere, within 8000m.

Descriptor

BC Patches	BL Blowing	DR Drifting	FZ Freezing
MI Shallow	PR Partial	SH Showers	TS Thunderstorm

WEATHER PHENOMENA

Precipitation

DZ Drizzle	GR Hail	GS Small hail or snow pellets
IC Ice crystals	PL Ice pellets	RA Rain	SG Snow grains
SN Snow	UP Unknown precipitation in automated observations	

Obscuration

BR Mist (≥5/8SM)	DU Widespread dust	FG Fog (<5/8SM)	FU Smoke
HZ Haze	PY Spray	SA Sand	VA Volcanic ash

Other

DS Dust storm	FC Funnel cloud	+FC Tornado or waterspout
PO Well-developed dust or sand whirls	SQ Squall	SS Sandstorm

- Explanations in parentheses "( )" indicate different worldwide practices.
- Ceiling is not specified; defined as the lowest broken or overcast layer, or the vertical visibility.
- NWS TAFs exclude BECMG groups and temperature forecasts, NWS TAFs do not use PROB in the first 9 hours of a TAF; NWS METARs exclude trend forecasts. U.S. Military TAFs include Turbulence and Icing groups.

August 2009

Figure 7-1. TAF/METAR weather report code keys

the "raw data" METAR or the plain language version. For a more general view, go to the left side of the ADDS page and click on Java Tools; drill down to METARs. The result will be a display of the entire continent. Hover your cursor over an airport symbol and the current METAR will be displayed; note at the bottom that you can select the information you want to see. (*See* a full-color example on Page D-3 in Appendix D.)

Learning to read METARs is a basic pilot skill. The general format is: Station identifier, date-time group, wind, visibility, weather (obstructions to visibility), sky condition, temperature and dewpoint, altimeter setting, and remarks.

Figure 7-2 displays some hourly METARs for several stations: Omaha, NE (KOMA); Pittsburgh, PA (KPIT); Dallas-Fort Worth, TX (KDFW); and Chicago, IL (KORD). It should be apparent that you will never see a report with observations from such widely scattered sites, but each example contains something of interest.

Each report begins with METAR (or SPECI, for a special report), followed by K and the airport's three-letter identifier. Reports from Alaska begin with PA, while reports from Hawaiian stations begin with PH. The six-digit date-time group is the time of observation in Coordinated Universal Time, also known as Zulu time or Greenwich Mean Time. All four examples are for the 23rd day of the month. If the report is from an automatic observing station such as AWOS or ASOS, "AUTO" will follow the date-time group.

The first group after the date-time group is for wind; the direction relative to true north is given in three digits, and the velocity is given in two digits. At Omaha, the wind at the time of observation was from 130 degrees at 10 knots, at Pittsburgh it was from 240 degrees at 10 knots, and at Dallas-Fort Worth it was from 060 at 6 knots. At Chicago-O'Hare, however, the wind was gusty, blowing from 020 at 29 knots with gusts to 49 knots. You probably would stay away from O'Hare anyway, but this wind gives you an additional excuse.

A calm wind is reported as 00000KT, and a variable wind as VRB. If the wind direction is varying 60 degrees or more at a speed greater than 6 knots, that will be shown as 180V260.

The wind group (which is easily identified by KT for knots), is followed by the visibility group—it always ends in SM for statute miles. Omaha and Pittsburgh look pretty good for VFR, but the reports for KDFW and KORD wave a red flag at VFR pilots. Down in Texas, the visibility is only one-quarter mile, while in the Windy City the visibility is 1½ miles (when the visibility element contains whole numbers and fractions, they are separated by a space).

If there is any restriction to visibility, the next group tells you what is causing it. At Pittsburgh, there are SHowers in the ViCinity (within ten miles). SHVC seems backward to me, but that's the way it is. *Aviation Weather Services* contains a reference list of abbreviations. At Dallas-Fort Worth, the visibility on runway 17L (R17L) is less than 1,000 feet (M for minus; if it was over 1,000 feet, it would be P1000—the P stands for plus). The restriction to visibility at DFW is fog (FG) and drizzle (DZ). As a VFR pilot, you don't really care about the details—you're not going there anyway. There is something tricky about low visibility readings, though; FG is used only when the visibility is between zero and ⅝ of a mile. From ⅝ to six miles, BR (from the French BRume, "mist") is used.

At O'Hare, things are really nasty: a thunderstorm (TS), rain (RA), and hail (GR). The METAR format is used internationally, and GRaupel is German for hail. The report uses "+" to indicate "heavy" and "−" to indicate "light." This applies only to the

```
METAR KOMA 232151Z 13010KT 12SM SCT030TCU SCT080
SCT250 34/20 A2982 RMK TCU SW-W SLP101

METAR KPIT 232250Z 24010KT 10SM VCSH SCT030 BKN 100
29/26 A2986 RMK SCT V BKN SLP 121

METAR KDFW 232050Z 06006KT 1/4SM R17LM1000FT FG-DZ
VV003 06/06 A2969 RMK DZB28 SLP058

SPECI KORD 230452Z 020452Z 02029G49KT 1 1/2SM TSRAGR
OVC005CB 22/17 A2982 RMK LTGICCG
GRB12 TS OHD MOV NE GR 3/4 SLP059
```

Figure 7-2. METARs

first type of precipitation listed; therefore +RASNSH means heavy rain showers, not heavy snow showers.

A nice addition to weather observations is an indication of what is going on in the vicinity (VC, 5 to 10 miles). VCRA means that it is raining in the vicinity, but not at the airport. If the prevailing visibility noted by the official observer differs from the tower visibility, the lower of the two readings is included in the body of the METAR, and the other is placed in "Remarks."

To operate legally under VFR, you must know what the reported ceiling is, and the next data group gives you that information. Now you know the wind and visibility and the question becomes "What is the cloud cover?" The observer divides the sky into eight sections, or octas. FEW is used if the clouds cover less than ¼ of the sky. SCT still means scattered clouds covering ⅝ to ½ of the sky, while BKN still means a broken layer covering ⅝ to ⅞ of the sky. OVC still means an unbroken overcast layer. "Sky clear," (SKC) has replaced "clear" (CLR).

There is no such thing as a "thin" layer any more, and the METAR will not tell you the official ceiling: FEW and SCT do not constitute a ceiling, while BKN and OVC are ceiling reports.

The height of each cloud layer is given in hundreds of feet, but with three digits. Omaha, where the wind and visibility are fairly benign, reports a scattered layer at 3,000 feet and Towering Cumulus—not a good sign. The inclusion of TCU in the body of the report means that the towering cumulus is within 10 miles of the station. Omaha also has a scattered layer at 8,000 feet and another scattered layer at 25,000 feet. Pittsburgh reports a scattered layer at 3,000 feet and a broken layer at 10,000 feet. Dallas-Fort Worth (a quarter of a mile in fog and drizzle, remember) is reporting VV003, meaning that the observer estimated the vertical visibility into the cloud layer to be 300 feet; VV000 means essentially that the vertical visibility is zero. You won't be surprised to learn that O'Hare is reporting an overcast at 500 feet with cumulonimbus clouds (CB).

Right after the cloud cover comes the temperature and dew point—in Celsius. (Before you complain, remember that the Europeans wanted us to use meters instead of feet for both visibility and cloud height.) If either the temperature or the dew point is below zero degrees Celsius, the letter M for minus will be used. At OMA, the temperature-dew point spread is 14 degrees; at PIT the spread is only three degrees, which makes you wonder how long that ten-mile visibility will last. At DFW, the temperature and dew point are equal, so the air is saturated with moisture. That explains the fog and drizzle. ORD has a five-degree spread, getting close to saturation.

A quick way to convert Celsius to Fahrenheit is to double the Celsius figure and add 32. The result will not be exact, but the error will be on the conservative side—the actual Fahrenheit temperature will not be as hot as the calculated temperature. This won't work very well at Celsius temperatures below freezing, but when it is that cold, you won't be worrying about loss of performance due to density altitude problems.

The altimeter setting is always given in four digits preceded by "A." Nothing hard about that. Jumping ahead a bit, SLP is always in "Remarks"; it means Sea Level Pressure.

Remarks (RMK) expands on the body of the report. At Omaha, the towering cumulus is reported to be southwest through west; the wind is out of the southeast, so it is possible that they are moving away. But maybe not. Check further. At Pittsburgh, the scattered layer at 3,000 feet is variable to broken. If you are flying at 6,500 feet and it turns into a broken layer at 3,000 feet, will you be able get down while staying the legal minimum distance from clouds? At DFW, the drizzle began at 28 minutes past the hour and was obviously still present when the observation was made. At O'Hare there is a light show in progress: lightning in clouds and cloud-to-ground, the hail began at 12 minutes past the hour, the thunderstorm is overhead (OHD) but moving northeast. The hailstones are ¾-inch in diameter. What a great day to be somewhere else!

A full discussion of the criteria used in these reports and a full list of abbreviations can be found in *Aviation Weather Services* (AC 00-45), or Chapter 7 of the *Aeronautical Information Manual*.

An important part of your flight planning is to look at or ask for the most recent METAR for your destination airport and several enroute reporting stations, so that you can see whether the weather is good enough for VFR operations at your destination. Check those reports against the TAF, (explanation later), to see if the forecast is holding up. You should also be sure that you can make an enroute stop if you need to. Check the METAR for the previous hour (if available) to see if there are trends you can detect. Is the spread between temperature and dew point increasing or decreasing? Is the barometric pressure rising or falling? (Check the altimeter setting.) Are the cloud layers rising or lowering? Wind picking up? Shifting? Which runway will probably be in use at the destination when you get there? Any Notices to Airmen? Remember, you are required to inform yourself about anything that could affect the safety of your flight.

Satellite Images

While you are still in the "can I get there from here… and back?" stage of planning, the ADDS webpage gives you another easy reference to reported weather. On the ADDS page, click the Satellite tab and select either the Western U.S. or Eastern U.S. with overlay of color-coded LIFR, IFR, MVFR, and VFR station models. You will be able to see the cloud cover at the time the image was taken and get an overview of the reported cloud cover at each station…you obviously want to stay away from any station symbol colored red or pink and look for more information when the color is blue (marginal VFR). *See* Figure 7-3, and a full-color example on Page D-7 in the Appendix.

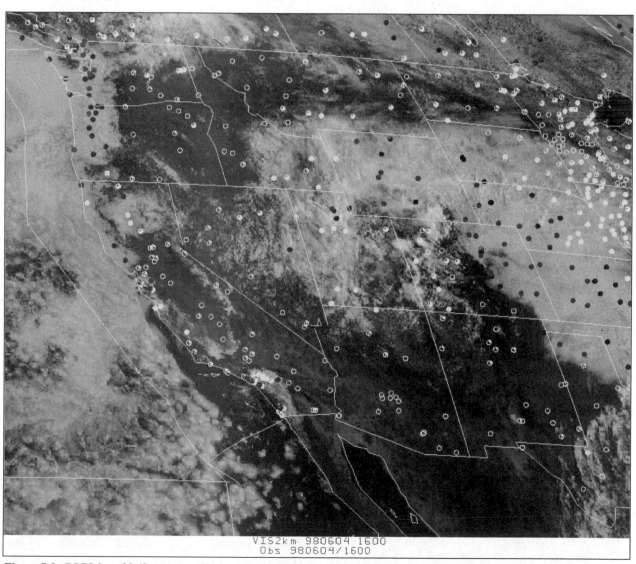

Figure 7-3. *GOES 9 visible/fog image with sky cover and aviation flight condition symbols.*

Pilot Reports

The best resource available to the weather briefers is an observation made by a pilot in flight—a pilot report, or PIREP. There is no better way for the National Weather Service to fill in the gaps between reporting stations than by PIREPs, and they solicit your cooperation.

Forecasters rely on pilot reports to verify the accuracy of their forecasts; they need to know where forecast conditions do not exist just as much as they need reports of the weather conditions you encounter. The only way for a forecaster, who called for a broken layer at 5,000 feet, to know that the forecast is not accurate, is for some conscientious pilot to call a flight service station and report that the layer doesn't exist (or that it appears to be at 10,000 feet). That PIREP ends up at the Aviation Weather Center in Kansas City, which passes it on to other interested parties, including researchers.

There is no space on the PIREP form for precipitation, so the AWC requests that pilots include the type of precipitation they encounter (if any) in the Remarks section. If the forecast calls for snow and you encounter rain, that fact is important to the AWC.

Figure 7-4 is a PIREP form, available in pads from your local FSS. You don't need a form to make a report, however. Just call Flight Watch on 122.0 or contact a flight service station on its published frequency (you can't go wrong by using 122.2). If you have the form available it will help you organize your report, but if not, the briefer knows what questions to ask.

A PIREP shows up on the computer screen or teletype at the flight service station looking like this:

UA/ OV OKC-TUL / TM 1800 / FL120 / TP BE90 / SK 012 BKN 055 / 072 OVC O89 / WX CLR ABOVE / TA-09 / WV 090021 / TB MDT 055-072 / IC LGT-MDT CLR 072-089

The pilot of this BE90 reported en route from Oklahoma City to Tulsa at 1800 UTC while at 12,000 feet. Two layers of clouds had been encountered, a broken layer with its base at 1,200 feet and its top at 5,500 feet, and a second, overcast layer beginning at 7,200 feet and extending to 8,900 feet, with clear skies above.

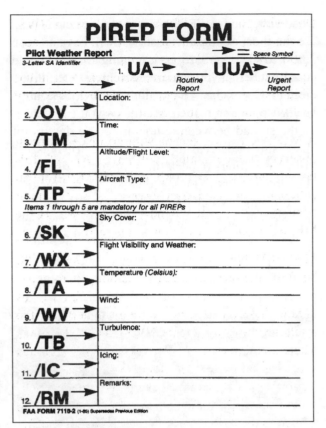

Figure 7-4. PIREP form

The temperature at 12,000 feet was -9°C, and the wind was reported to be from 090 degrees at 21 knots. Moderate turbulence was being experienced between 5,500 feet and 7,200 feet, and light to moderate clear icing was encountered while climbing between 7,200 feet and 8,900 feet.

If you had checked the weather for a trip along that route and had been told that the tops were forecast to be at 18,000 feet, you would be grateful to the anonymous BE90 pilot. On the other hand, if you had planned a VFR flight at 6,500 feet you would be making other arrangements.

Automated Weather Reporting Stations

Advances in sensor technology have made it possible for automated weather reporting stations to replace human observers in many locations. Some of these observations are incorporated in METARs, others are available by phone or radio, still others show up at the flight service station for use by the briefer. The Automated Weather Observing Station (AWOS), designed by the FAA, and the Automated Surface

Observing Station (ASOS), designed by the NWS, are the most common. The NWS will have almost 2,000 ASOS installations in operation across the country when their program is complete. You'll find a blue circle with a reversed "A" in the frequency box when an automatic sensor is used.

A METAR from a sensor with no nearby human observer (unaugmented) will have "AUTO" following the date-time group. If the METAR from an automated site is fed to an observer for modification or augmentation, you will never know it because the METAR from that station won't give you a clue.

The ASOS has many advantages over the AWOS, but both measure cloud cover, visibility, barometric pressure, precipitation and wind. The difference lies in how these measurements are made and how the results are transmitted to the NWS. At those locations where a computerized voice transmits the readings over aviation radio frequencies, the necessary information will be on sectional charts. Where the ASOS can be contacted by telephone, the number will be printed in the A/FD. Go to www.faa.gov/air_traffic/weather/asos/, click on the states you will be flying over, and you will get a list of all frequencies and phone numbers.

The measurements sent to the NWS by these automatic stations help the meteorologists develop the "big picture" on how weather systems are forming and moving. While ceilings and visibility measurements from an ASOS are accepted by the FAA as a legal basis for making pilot decisions, if the data from a specific station goes against the local trend you want to think long and hard before accepting it at face value.

For example, if the area forecast (*see* Page 7–13) calls for ceilings below 1,000 feet AGL with visibilities less than 3 miles and the ASOS at your destination says that the weather is clear and the visibility is greater than ten miles, you should investigate what other reporting stations in the vicinity have to say; the ASOS might be looking straight up through a hole in the cloud cover or checking visibility in the only direction not affected by a fog bank. Similarly, if the weather in the area is supposed to be VFR and the automated station reports instrument meteorological conditions you should look for a reason.

The ASOS is much better at avoiding this kind of problem than is the AWOS.

During the development of the ASOS its measurements were compared with those made by human observers and the correlation was quite close. As a pilot, you must remember that a weather observer spends only a few minutes each hour looking at the weather and spends the rest of the time on the telephone or radio and doing paperwork; the ASOS takes measurements constantly and transmits them to the NWS where they are integrated by computer with other reports from other facilities. This provides a better picture of a changing weather situation than hourly observations.

You should realize that what you hear from an ASOS is not a snapshot of the weather at an instant in time; through the magic of microprocessors, the measurements made by the sensors over a short period of time are averaged for broadcast. Listen to an ASOS several times as you approach its location to pick up trends.

Figure 7-5 shows how some automatic observations show up on the FSS teletype. KPWT is completely automated, as indicated by "AUTO" in the body of the report. The Remark "A01" means that the sensor does not have a precipitation discriminator that can tell the difference between liquid and freezing precipitation. KOLM does not have the word AUTO because at the time of this observation there was an NWS observer present; still, there is an ASOS there and it does have a precipitation discriminator (A02). Note that wind direction is relative to true north.

The AWOS/ASOS keys in Figure 7-6 on the next page are still valid; you just won't see very many purely automated reports as METARs become more common.

```
METAR KKLS 122055Z AUTO 19006KT 10SM BKN026 17/12
A982 RMK A01

METAR KPWT 122056Z AUTO 18007G15KT 110V200 10SM
SCT028 19/08 A2981 RMK A01

METAR KOLM 121956Z 20006KT 10SM OVC025 17/11 A2981
RMK A02 SLP095

METAR KYKM 121956Z 04004KT 10SM CLR 29/11 A2964 RMK
A02 SLP028
```

Figure 7-5. *OLM and YKM have towers, KLS and PWT do not.*

KEY TO AWOS (AUTOMATED WEATHER OBSERVING SYSTEM) OBSERVATIONS

LOCATION IDENTIFIER TYPE OF REPORT TIME OF REPORT STATION TYPE	SKY CONDITION AND CEILING BELOW 12,000'	VISIBILITY	TEMPERATURE / DEW POINT / WIND DIRECTION, SPEED AND CHARACTER / ALTIMETER SETTING /	REMARKS: AUTOMATED REMARKS GENERATED AUTOMATICALLY IF CONDITIONS EXIST. AUGMENTED REMARKS ADDED IF CONDITIONS EXIST AND CERTIFIED WEATHER OBSERVER IS ATTENDING THE SYSTEM
HTM SA 1755 AWOS	M20 OVC	1V	36/34/2015G25/990/	P010/VSBY 1/2V2 WND 17V23/WEA: R — F

LOCATION IDENTIFIER: 3 or 4 alphanumeric characters (usually the airport identifier).

TYPE OF REPORT: SA = Scheduled record (routine) observation. All observations identified as SA. Most are transmitted at 20-minute intervals (approximately 15, 35 and 55 minutes past each hour).

TIME OF REPORT: Coordinated Universal Time (UTC or Z) using 24-hour clock.

STATION TYPE: AWOS = Automated Weather Observing System site. **Note:** In the future, some systems will use "AO" designators.

SKY CONDITION AND CEILING: Sky condition contractions are for each layer in ascending order. Numbers preceding contractions are base heights in hundreds of feet above ground level (AGL).

CLR BLO 120 = No clouds below 12,000 ft.
SCT = Scattered: 0.1 to 0.5 sky cover.
BKN = Broken: 0.6 to 0.9 sky cover.
OVC = Overcast: More than 0.9 sky cover.
X = Obscured sky —X = Partially obscured
A letter preceding the height of a base identifies a ceiling layer and indicates how ceiling height was determined.
M = Measured   **W** = Indefinite

VISIBILITY: Reported in statute miles and fractions. Visibility greater than 10 not reported. V= variable: see Automated Remarks.

TEMPERATURE AND DEW POINT: Reported in degrees Fahrenheit.

WIND DIRECTION, SPEED & CHARACTER: Direction in tens of degrees from true north, except voice broadcast is in degrees magnetic. Speed in knots. **0000** = calm. **G** = gusts. See Automated Remarks for variable direction.

ALTIMETER SETTING: Hundredths of inches of mercury. Shown as last 3 digits only without decimal point (e.g., 30.05 inches = 005).

PRESENT WEATHER/OBSTRUCTIONS TO VISION: Reported only when observer is available. See Augmented Remarks. In the future, some systems will report precipitation, fog, and haze in the body of the observation.

AUTOMATED REMARKS: Precipitation accumulation reported in hundredth of inches (e.g., P110 = 1.10 inches; P010 = 0.10 inch). **WND V** = variable wind direction. **VSBY V** = variable visibility. **DENSITY ALTITUDE** is included in the voice broadcast when more than 1000 feet above airport elevation.

MISSING DATA: Reported as "M".

AUGMENTED REMARKS: "WEA:" indicates manual observer data. Remarks include operationally significant weather conditions within a five mile radius of the airport (e.g., thunderstorms, precipitation, obstructions to vision when visibility is 3 miles or less, fog banks). Standard weather observation contractions are used.

DECODED REPORT: Hometown Municipal Airport, observation at 1755 UTC, AWOS report. Measured ceiling 2000 feet overcast. Visibility 1 mile variable. Temperature 36 degrees (F), dew point 34 degrees (F), wind from 200 degrees true at 15 knots gusting to 25 knots, altimeter setting 29.90 inches. Precipitation accumulation during past hour 0.10 inch. Visibility variable between 1/2 and 2 miles. Wind direction variable from 170 degrees to 230 degrees true. Observer reports light rain (R—) and fog (F).

NOTE: Refer to the *Airman's Information Manual* for more information. Refer to the *Airport/Facility Directory*, aeronautical charts, and related publications for broadcast, telephone and location data. Check *Notices to Airmen* for AWOS system status.

KEY TO ASOS (AUTOMATED SURFACE OBSERVING SYSTEM) WEATHER OBSERVATIONS

LOCATION IDENTIFIER TYPE OF REPORT TIME OF REPORT STATION TYPE	SKY CONDITION AND CEILING BELOW 12,000'	VISIBILITY, WEATHER, AND OBSTRUCTIONS TO VISION	SEA-LEVEL PRESSURE / TEMPERATURE / DEW POINT / WIND DIRECTION, SPEED AND CHARACTER / ALTIMETER SETTING /	REMARKS AUTOMATED REMARKS GENERATED AUTOMATICALLY IF CONDITIONS EXIST. AUGMENTED REMARKS ADDED IF CONDITIONS EXIST AND CERTIFIED WEATHER OBSERVER IS ATTENDING THE SYSTEM	STATUS REMARKS SYSTEM GENERATED
HTM RS 1755 AO2A	M19V OVC	1R — F	125/36/34/2116G24/990/	R29LVR10V50 CIG 16V22 TWR VSBY 2 PK WND 2032/1732 PRESFR	ZRNO $

LOCATION IDENTIFIER: 3 or 4 alphanumeric characters (usually airport identifier).

TYPE OF REPORT:
SA = Scheduled record (hourly) observation.
SP = Special observation indicating a significant change in one or more of the observed elements.
RS = SA that also qualifies as an SP.
USP = Urgent special observation to report tornado.

TIME OF REPORT: Coordinated Universal Time (UTC or Z) using 24-hr clock.

STATION TYPE:
AO2 = Unattended (no observer) ASOS.
AO2A = Attended (observer present) ASOS.

SKY CONDITION AND CEILING BELOW 12,000' AGL: Sky condition contractions are for each layer in ascending order. Numbers preceding contractions are base height in hundreds of feet above ground level (AGL).
CLR BLO 120 = Less than 0.1 sky cover below 12,000'
SCT = Scattered: 0.1 to 0.5 sky cover.
BKN = Broken: 0.6 to 0.9 sky cover.
OVC = Overcast: More than 0.9 sky cover.
A letter preceding the height of a base identifies a ceiling layer and indicates how ceiling height was determined.
M = Measured   **W** = Indefinite
E = Estimated   **X** = Obscured sky
The letter V is added immediately following the height of a base to indicate a variable ceiling: see Remarks.

VISIBILITY:
Reported in statute miles and fractions from <1/4 through 10+. V = variable: see Remarks.

PRESENT WEATHER:
TORNADO (when augmented).
T = Thunder (when augmented): see Status Remarks.
R = Liquid precipitation that does not freeze (e.g., rain).
P — = Light precipitation in unknown form.
ZR = Liquid precipitation that freezes on impact (e.g., freezing rain): see Status Remarks.
A = Hail (when augmented).
S = Frozen precipitation other than hail (e.g., snow).
+ = Heavy.   No sign = Moderate.   — = Light.

OBSTRUCTIONS TO VISION:
Reported only when visibility is less than 7 statute miles.
F = Fog   **H** = Haze
VOLCANIC ASH (when augmented).

SEA-LEVEL PRESSURE:
Tenths of Hectopascals (millibars). Shown as last 3 digits only without decimal point (e.g., 950 = 995.0).

TEMPERATURE AND DEW POINT:
Degrees Fahrenheit.

WIND DIRECTION, SPEED AND CHARACTER:
Direction in tens of degrees from **true** north. Voice broadcast in degrees from **magnetic**. Speed in knots. **0000** = calm. **E** = estimated. **G** = gusts. **Q** = squalls. Variable wind, peak wind, wind shift: see Remarks.

ALTIMETER SETTING:
Hundredths of inches of mercury. Shown as last 3 digits only without decimal point (e.g., 005 = 30.05 inches).

MISSING DATA: Reported as **M**.

DENSITY ALTITUDE: Included on voice broadcast only when 1000 or more feet above airport elevation.

REMARKS: Can Include:
RVR (Runway Visual Range), **VOLCANIC ASH**, **VIRGA**, **TWR VSBY** (Tower visibility), **SFC VSBY** (Surface visibility), **VSBY V** (Variable visibility), **CIG V** (Variable ceiling), **WSHFT** (Windshift), **PK WND** (Peak wind), **WND V** (Variable wind direction), **PCPN** (Precipitation amount), **PRESRR** (Pressure rising rapidly), **PRESFR** (Pressure falling rapidly), **PRJMP** (Pressure jump), **B** (Time weather began), **E** (Time weather ended).

STATUS REMARKS:
PWINO = Present weather information not available.
ZRNO = Freezing rain information not available.
TNO = Thunderstorm information not available.
$ = Maintenance check indicator.

DECODED REPORT: Hometown Municipal Airport, record special observation at 1755 UTC. ASOS with observer. Measured ceiling 1900 feet variable, overcast. Visibility 1 mile, light rain, fog. Sea-level pressure 1012.5 hectopascals, temperature 36°F, dew point 34°F, wind from 210° true at 16 knots gusting to 24 knots, altimeter 29.90 inches. Runway 29L visual range 1000 variable to 5000 feet. Ceiling 1600 variable to 2200 feet, tower visibility 2 miles, peak wind 200° true at 32 knots at 1732 UTC, pressure falling rapidly. Freezing rain information not available, maintenance check indicator.

NOTE: Refer to *ASOS Guide for Pilots* and the *Airman's Information Manual* for more information. Refer to the *Airport/Facility Directory*, aeronautical charts, and related publications for broadcast, telephone and location data. Check *Notices to Airmen* for ASOS system status.

Figure 7-6. AWOS/ ASOS code keys

Radar Summary Chart

This chart is based on observations; it is not a forecast. Radar will show only precipitation, not clouds or fog. The radar summary chart (Figure 7-7 and the full-color example on Page D-7) shows the location of radar echoes from precipitation, and the direction and speed of movement of lines of cells and individual cells. This is the only weather chart that shows this information. The tops of precipitation as measured by radar are shown, as are any severe weather watch areas. The legend to decipher the chart is contained on the chart itself. You can safely assume that turbulence will be associated with areas of heavy precipitation, and plan to avoid flight near those areas.

Remember, weather radar does not indicate the presence of clouds or fog, only precipitation. Never rely on ground-based radar to steer you through an area of thunderstorms (more on this in the next section), and rely on airborne weather radar for storm avoidance only if you are trained in its interpretation.

Figure 7-7 is another of those black-and-white charts being phased out by the NWS. If you want

to look at one, go to http://aviationweather.gov/data/iffdp/2080.gif. Get the color image by going to the ADDS webpage and clicking on the Radar tab; select "Latest image w/tops derived from radar coded message."

Surface Analysis Chart

The NWS issues surface analysis charts eight times daily (every three hours). These charts reflect the observations of sky cover, visibility, surface wind direction and velocity, temperature, dewpoint, weather (obstructions to visibility), sea level pressure, and pressure trend. (See a full-color example on Appendix Page D-4.) Using this information, meteorologists can locate high and low pressure systems, fronts, and pressure gradients, giving the user a big-picture view of the nation's weather at the time of the observations as shown in the lower left corner of the chart. Note how widely spaced the isobars (lines of constant barometric pressure) are over the southwestern states and consequently how light the surface winds are, compared to the more closely packed isobars between the low pressure area over Nebraska and the Great Lakes states.

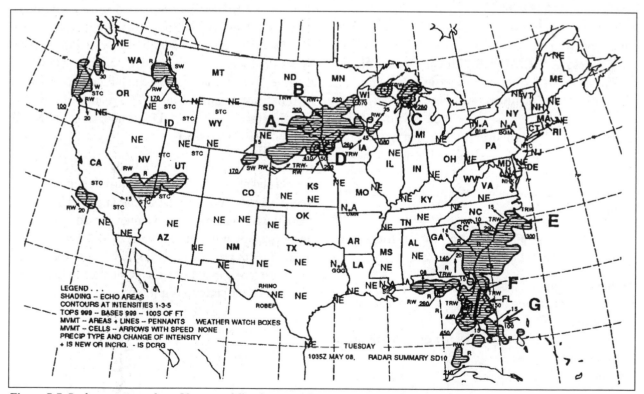

Figure 7-7. Radar summary chart (Note: see full-color example on Page D-7 at bottom.)

Unless you are flying a corporate jet, you are probably not as interested in a surface analysis for the entire country as you are for a specific area. Type "surface analysis" into the ADDS webpage search box and your first hit will be "HPC North American Surface Analysis"; on that page, go down to "Click here to view a list of HPS Surface Analysis Products." From the resulting list, choose your area of interest. Lots of interesting pages on that site.

By going to the ADDS page and typing "surface analysis + loop" into the search box, you will find a wide selection of surface charts that can be looped to show the movement of weather systems/fronts over a period of hours or days. You want to be alert to the movement of low pressure areas and fronts... anything that would cause lifting.

Forecasts

If your planned trip is four to seven days in the future, go to the ADDS webpage and click on "Days 3-7 CONUS" and in the resulting table click on "HPC's Day 4-7 Gridded Forecast." If your departure date is sooner than that, click on Short Range; I prefer the full-color forecast charts over the black-and-white.

SIGMETs and AIRMETs

If there is any chance of bad weather along your route, you want to learn about it early in the planning process. A SIGMET (Significant Meteorological Information) contains warnings applicable to all aircraft, even airliners, and deserve your close attention. A SIGMET warning area covers at least 3,000 square miles; however, the weather event forecast might occur in only a small portion of this total area. Your problem is that you don't know where that portion might be, and neither does the National Weather Service.

A SIGMET is issued when one of the following occurs or is forecast to occur:

- Severe icing not associated with thunderstorms.
- Severe or extreme turbulence not associated with thunderstorms.
- Dust storms or sandstorms lowering visibilities to below 3 miles.
- Volcanic ash.

An AIRMET (Airmen's Meteorological Information) contains information about IFR, strong surface winds, mountain obscuration, turbulence, icing, and freezing levels. An airline pilot will take note of an AIRMET but will probably not cancel because of the forecast conditions. "Little airplane" pilots will take heed. There are three AIRMETs, and they are referred to individually in the Area Forecast (next).

1. AIRMET TANGO forecasts areas where moderate turbulence might be expected, where sustained surface winds of 30 knots or more are expected, or when non-convective low-level wind shear is forecast.

2. AIRMET SIERRA describes IFR conditions or extended mountain obscuration.

3. AIRMET ZULU describes moderate icing and provides freezing level heights.

You will find color-coded warning areas by going to the ADDS page and clicking on AIRMET/SIGMET, CONUS in the left column. You can choose "Graphical AIRMET," select the hazard(s) you want displayed, loop the graphics, pin down geographic areas, and get the text (if needed) from this page.

Convective SIGMETs are issued in the continental United States when tornadoes, lines of thunderstorms, embedded thunderstorms, or hail more than ¾" in diameter are forecast. Convective SIGMETs are issued at 55 minutes past the hour and alerts will be broadcast on all FSS and ATC frequencies except 121.5 Mhz. (See the ADDS convective SIGMET example on Page D-6.)

If you are really into understanding weather and are concerned about predictions of turbulence and convective action, go to www.spc.noaa.gov. This page, from the Storm Prediction Center, has so many tabs and drop-down menu alternatives that I will make no attempt to provide an example in the color pages. Suffice it to say that there is a plethora of information if you take the time to dig it out.

Aviation Area Forecast (FA)

The Area Forecast is your only direct source of information on expected turbulence, icing, and heights of cloud tops. It contains a synopsis of the weather to help you evaluate the potential for change. Do not ignore the synopsis…it will tell you in words what is going on and what to expect. Watch for words like "unstable," "low pressure," and "front." It also includes forecasts of potentially hazardous weather as "flight precautions." Area forecasts are issued three times daily and are amended as required. The "Significant Clouds and Weather" portion is valid for 12 hours and contains an additional 6-hour outlook.

An area forecast covers several states and coastal waters; do not expect an area forecast to be as specific as a "terminal area forecast," to be discussed later.

You will use the area forecast to fill in the gaps between reporting stations. Learning to decipher the abbreviations used in area forecasts is a study in itself—the flight service station briefer will help you with them. *Aviation Weather Services* (AC 00-45) contains a list of commonly used abbreviations.

Because the area covered by an area forecast is so extensive, cloud heights are almost always given in feet above sea level, and you must be aware of terrain heights along your route to evaluate the effect of forecast clouds on your flight. Where "ceiling" (abbreviated as CIG) is used in an area forecast, the cloud height given is above ground level.

"Thunderstorms imply possible severe or greater turbulence, severe icing, and low level wind shear." This warning, near the top of the area forecast in Figure 7-8 (on the next page), applies to Idaho, Montana, Wyoming, Nevada, Utah, Colorado, Arizona, and New Mexico. You are also warned to check AIRMET SIERRA for mountain obscuration and IFR conditions. Note that an AIRMET warns of icing outside of thunderstorms, so if icing is possible you have two warnings: Severe icing is implied by "thunderstorm" and an icing AIRMET extends the hazardous area.

Look at the synopsis first, and recall what you learned about how the weather machine works in Lesson 6. If there is a low-pressure area over the southwestern states, the counterclockwise flow will bring air up from the south. This is confirmed by the statement "Southerly winds aloft ahead of low...". Then you are told that the air mass is moist with clouds and precipitation across much of the region. You know that warm air can hold more moisture than colder air, and air coming from the south will be warm.

The weather doesn't look very good in any of the Rocky Mountain states, with the exception of northern and central Idaho and all of Montana. As you look at the forecast for each of the states, note how high the tops are forecast to be—35,000 feet in southern Idaho to 45,000 feet in New Mexico—and you will probably be unable to see them because of the cloud layers at 10–12,000 feet. If you inadvertently fly under a towering thunderstorm, you can expect a rough ride as you go from rising air to descending air—sometimes in a matter of seconds.

Reading AIRMET SIERRA (Figure 7-8A) requires a knowledge of three-letter VOR identifiers and a really large map (or a computer—the ADDS AIRMET/SIGMET page illustrates the boundaries graphically; *see* Page D-6).

AIRMET TANGO (Figure 7-8B) uses the same VOR-identifier method to outline areas forecast to have moderate turbulence. The ADDS page also defines this area graphically. If you have been checking the Storm Prediction Center webpage (www.spc.noaa.gov) in the days leading up to a trip there should be no surprises in AIRMET TANGO.

The forecast freezing level and areas where moderate icing is possible are contained in AIRMET ZULU. It looks as though the freezing level is forecast to be as low as 8,000 feet over portions of the area.

As a VFR pilot you will not be flying into any clouds, so the only kinds of icing you might be exposed to are freezing rain and freezing drizzle. Neither phenomenon is forecast in this AIRMET, and if you stay beneath the clouds you will be OK. If you fly in mountainous areas such as those covered by the area forecast, though, it is all too easy to get disoriented or fly into a blind canyon in an attempt to stay out of the clouds. Make your decision to reverse course well in advance of crunch time.

Salt Lake City Area Forecast
26 May 1996 - 02:36:59 UTC

```
ZCZC MKCFA5W   ALL OO FAUS6 KSLC 260245
SLCC FA 260245
SYNOPSIS AND VFR CLDS/WX
SYNOPSIS VALID UNTIL 262100
CLDS/WX VALID UNTIL 261500...OTLK VALID 261500-262100
ID MT WY NV UT CO AZ NM


SEE AIRMET SIERRA FOR IFR CONDS AND MTN OBSCN.
TSTMS IMPLY SVR OR GTR TURBC SVR ICG LLWS AND IFR CONDS.
NON MSL HGTS DENOTED BY AGL OR CIG.

.

SYNOPSIS...03Z UPR LOW OVR SWRN U.S. CNTRD VCNTY EED WILL MOV NEWD TO CNTRL
CO BY 21Z AS UPR RDG BLDS ACRS CA/NV. SLY WINDS ALF AHD OF LOW BCMG NLY TO
NELY TO W OF LOW. AMS MOIST WITH CLDS/PCPN ACRS MUCH OF RGN. ...CUNDY...

.

ID
NRN ID...100-120 SCT-BKN 150. OTLK...VFR.
CNTRL MTNS...GENLY CLR OR SCT CI...TIL 06Z OVR SERN PTNS AREA 120
SCT-BKN 150 WITH ISOLD RW-. OTLK...VFR.
SWRN ID...120 SCT-BKN 150 WITH ISOLD RW-. ARND 06Z BCMG 120 SCT.
OTLK...VFR.
SERN ID...80-100 SCT-BKN 120 BKN LYRD 200. WDLY SCT RW-/ISOLD TRW- DMSHG TO
ISOLD RW- ARND 06Z. AFT 12Z BCMG 120 SCT-BKN 150.
CB TOPS TO 350. OTLK...VFR.

.

MT
WEST OF DVD...120 SCT. OTLK...VFR.
SWRN MTNS...80-100 SCT-BKN 120 BKN LYRD 200. WDLY SCT RW-. AFT 12Z BCMG 120
SCT-BKN 150. OTLK...VFR.
RMNDR MT...NRN PTNS AREA CIG 50 BKN-SCT 120 BKN 150 WITH ISOLD RW-...SRN PTNS
CIG 20 BKN-SCT 80 OVC LYRD 200 WITH OCNL VSBYS 3-5R-F. OTLK...MVFR CIG RW
SRN PTNS AREA...VFR NRN PTNS.

.

WY
80 BKN-SCT 100-120 BKN LYRD 200. OCNL VSBYS 3-5R-F. TIL 06Z ISOLD TRW-. CB
TOPS TO 350. OTLK...MVFR CIG R F.
ERN PLAINS...CIG 10-20 BKN-OVC LYRD 200. OCNL VSBYS 3-5R-F. TIL 06Z ISOLD
TRW-. CB TOPS TO 350. OTLK...MVFR CIG R F.

.

NV
NWRN NV...120 SCT...VFR.
RMNDR NRN AND CNTRL NV...90-100 SCT-BKN 120 BKN LYRD 200. WDLY SCT RW-/ISOLD
TRW- DMSHG TO ISOLD RW- BY 06Z. AFT 12Z BCMG 120 SCT-BKN 150. CB TOPS TO
350. OTLK...VFR.
SRN NV...80-100 SCT-BKN LYRD 200. WDLY SCT RW-/ISOLD TRW- DMSHG TO ISOLD
RW- BY 06Z. CB TOPS TO 350. OTLK...VFR.

.

UT
NRN UT...90-100 SCT-BKN 120 BKN LYRD 200. WDLY SCT RW-/TRW- DMSHG TO WDLY
SCT RW- BY 06Z. CB TOPS TO 400. OTLK...VFR.
SRN UT...80-100 SCT-BKN LYRD 200. WDLY SCT RW-/TRW- DMSHG TO ISOLD RW- BY
06Z. CB TOPS TO 350. OTLK...VFR.

.

CO
MTNS AND WEST...100-120 SCT-BKN 140 BKN LYRD 200. WDLY SCT RW-/TRW- DMSHG
TO WDLY SCT RW- BY 06Z. CB TOPS TO 400. OTLK...VFR.
ERN PLAINS...CIG 10-20 BKN-OVC LYRD 200. OCNL VSBYS 3-5R-F. OVR EXTRM ERN
CO WDLY SCT TRW DMSHG TO ISOLD TRW BY 06Z...OVR RMNDR AREA ISOLD TRW-. CB
TOPS TO 400. OTLK...MVFR CIG R F.

.

AZ
NRN AZ...80-100 SCT-BKN 120 BKN LYRD 200. WDLY SCT RW-/ISOLD TRW- DMSHG TO
ISOLD RW- BY 06Z. CB TOPS TO 350. OTLK...VFR.
SWRN AZ...120 SCT-BKN 160. TIL 06Z ISOLD RW-/TRW-. CB TOPS TO 400. OTLK...VFR.
SERN AZ...120-140 SCT. OTLK...VFR.

.

NM
MTNS AND WEST...NRN PTNS AREA 90-100 SCT-BKN LYRD 200 WITH ISOLD RW-/TRW-
DMSHG TO ISOLD RW- BY 06Z...SRN PTNS 120-140 SCT. CB TOPS TO 400. OTLK...VFR.
NERN PLAINS...AGL 20-30 SCT-BKN LYRD 200. OVR ERN PTNS AREA WDLY SCT RW-/TRW-
DMSHG TO ISOLD RW- BY 06Z. 06-08Z BCMG CIG 10-20 BKN-SCT 90. CB TOPS TO
450. OTLK...MVFR CIG BCMG VFR BY 18Z.
SERN PLAINS...AGL 50 SCT 120 SCT. TIL 06Z OVR ERN PTNS AREA WDLY SCT RW/TRW.
CB TOPS TO 450. OTLK...VFR.

....

NNNN
```

A

Salt Lake City Airmet Sierra – IFR and Mountain Obscuration
26 May 1996 - 01:40:20 UTC

```
ZCZC MKCWA5S   ALL OO WAUSONE KSLC 260145
SLCS WA 260145
AIRMET SIERRA FOR IFR AND MTN OBSCN VALID UNTIL
260800


AIRMET IFR...MT WY CO NM
FROM 90SW DIK TO BFF TO GLD TO DHT TO TCC TO
LVS TO 30W DEN TO RKS TO BZN TO 90SW DIK
OCNL CIGS BLO 10 VSBYS BLO 3F. CONDS OVR ERN
WY/ERN CO DVLPG OVR RMNDR AREA BY 06-08Z...CONTG
THRU 14Z.


AIRMET MTN OBSCN...ID MT WY NV UT CO AZ NM CA
FROM GTF TO GCC TO PUB TO LVS TO SJN TO PSP TO
BFL TO MOD TO GTF
MTNS OCNLY OBSCD IN CLDS/PCPN. CONDS CONTG BYD
08Z THRU 14Z.

....

NNNN
```

B

Salt Lake City Airmet Tango – Turbulence, Low Level Wind Shear and Strong Surface Winds
26 May 1996 - 01:40:31 UTC

```
ZCZC MKCWA5T   ALL OO WAUSONE KSLC 260145
SLCT WA 260145
AIRMET TANGO FOR TURBC VALID UNTIL 260800


AIRMET TURBC...NV CA
FROM LKV TO EED TO YUM TO SAN TO 40W SBA TO FOT
TO 70W MFR TO LKV
OCNL MDT TURBC BLO 120. CONDS CONTG BYD 08Z THRU
14Z.


AIRMET TURBC...CO AZ NM
FROM CHE TO AKO TO 40W MAF TO 60S TUS TO YUM TO
EED TO FMN TO CHE
OCNL MDT TURBC BLO 180. CONDS ENDG AZ 08Z...CONTG
NM/CO BYD 08Z ENDG 14Z.


AIRMET TURBC...ID MT WY NV UT CO AZ NM OR CA
FROM YXH TO GGW TO AKO TO TCC TO TCS TO SBA TO
SAC TO YXC TO YXH
OCNL MDT TURBC BTWN 180 AND 390. CONDS CONTG BYD
08Z THRU 14Z.

....

NNNN
```

C

Salt Lake City Airmet Zulu – Icing and Freezing Levels
26 May 1996 - 01:40:40 UTC

```
ZCZC MKCWA5Z   ALL OO WAUSONE KSLC 260145
SLCZ WA 260145
AIRMET ZULU FOR ICG AND FRZLVL VALID UNTIL 260800

.

AIRMET ICG...ID WY NV UT CO AZ NM CA
FROM 80NW RAP TO BFF TO GLD TO 50W LBL TO LVS
TO SJN TO YUM TO 50E BFL TO TPH TO BOI TO COD
TO 80NW RAP
OCNL MDT RIME/MXD ICGIC ABV FRZLVL 200. FRZLVL
80-110 WRN AND NRN PTNS AREA SLPG 120-140 SERN
PTNS. CONDS CONTG BYD 08Z THRU 14Z.

.

FRZLVL...80-120 N AND W OF DMN-GUC-GLD LN SLPG
130-140 SERN PTNS FA AREA.

....

NNNN
```

Figure 7-8. Area forecast examples

Recent research indicates that freezing drizzle is even more hazardous than freezing rain, and the Aviation Weather Center is now including forecasts for freezing rain (ZR) and freezing drizzle (FZ) in AIRMETs when those conditions are anticipated. Look for ZR and/or ZL, or ask your briefer — those two are killers.

Winds Aloft Forecast (FB)
(Formerly "FD.")

These forecasts (Figure 7-9; *see also* the color illustrations on Pages D-5 and D-10) are issued twice daily and include a "valid time." Heights are above sea level, and no forecast is available within 1,500 feet of the reporting station's elevation. Wind direction and velocity are read just as they are in an hourly sequence, except that no gusts are forecast. The last two digits are forecast temperature in degrees Centigrade. Above 24,000 feet, all temperatures are negative, so no + or – signs are used. The color illustration on page D-5 shows circulation patterns better than the text product. Altitude can be selected, and there is a separate page for temperatures.

The raw data for these forecasts comes from twice-daily balloon ascensions from over 100 sites across the country combined with other sources. Because the information comes from widely scattered sites, and can be as much as eleven hours old, do not expect pinpoint accuracy. A good rule (which I do not use in Lesson 11) is to assume that a headwind will be twice as strong as forecast and that a tailwind will be only one-half as strong as forecast.

Wind direction is in relation to true north, and velocity is forecast in knots. Look for rapid changes in wind direction or velocity with altitude as a warning of turbulence. The winds aloft forecast will be the first thing you check in choosing a cruising altitude for favorable winds. The code for calm is 0000, and for "light and variable" it is 9900. When wind velocities are forecast to exceed 100 knots, the weather service still codes the direction, velocity, and temperature using six digits. This is accomplished by adding 50 to the wind direction, and subtracting 100 from the wind velocity. 731624 means wind from 230° (23 + 50 = 73) at 116 knots, temperature -24° above 24,000 feet.

Accuracy is greatest if you fly over one of the reporting points at one of the forecast altitudes exactly at the valid time of the forecast; cross it earlier or later, or farther away from the source, and accuracy suffers.

A major weakness of the FB is the 3,000-foot gap between altitudes and the lack of any relative humidity or dewpoint information. At best, it forces you to interpolate between values; at worst, it glosses over changes that might occur at intermediate altitudes. However, it is the forecast product used in knowledge exams and for that limited purpose you must live with it.

```
        FBUS SWBC 011644
DATA BASED ON 011200Z

  VALID 0220000Z     FOR USE 2100-0600Z.   TEMPS NEG ABV 24000
```

FT	3000	6000	9000	12000	18000	24000	30000	34000	39000
ABI		2512+14	2519+09	2426-02	2438-14	2345-26	234840	234546	254152
ABQ			3115+02	3125-04	2934-18	2944-31	285240	285145	295151
AMA		3013	3120+03	2823-03	2536-16	2447-30	245642	255447	265351
ATL	1510	1811+13	1909+08	2107+02	2708-12	2710-24	271339	271648	252057
BNA	1920	2220+13	2220+08	2319+02	2421-12	2426-24	243240	243449	243659
BRO	1811	1917+17	2015+11	2214+05	2517-09	2626-21	273937	274845	276155
DAL	2115	2322+15	2325+09	2328+02	2335-13	2342-25	234940	244946	254754

Figure 7-9. Winds aloft forecast (see full-color version on Page D-5)

Skew-T Charts

If you want a little more detail when investigating winds and temperatures aloft, go to "http://rucsound-ings.noaa.gov". Scroll down and click on OP40 as the initial data source, check "Latest" for the start time, make the hours 3.0, put in the 3-letter ID of the airport(s) of interest; separate the IDs with commas. No alphanumerics like S67...just 3 letters; then, click on the "java-based plots" button. With three hours selected as the time you can get charts from as many as six sources. You will get what are called skew-T charts such as the one for Walla Walla, Washington (ALW) shown in the full-color Appendix (*see* Page D-5). The gray buttons along the bottom are labeled with the airport identifier and valid time of the forecast.

Altitudes are the vertical axis (logarithmic, with lines closer together at the bottom), temperatures are the left-to-right slanted (skewed) lines leading from the x-axis across the bottom. The red line is temperature, the blue line is dew point...and you can see right away that they get pretty close together between 15,000 and 20,000 feet. Everything to the right of the zero degree (Centigrade) line is above freezing, everything to its left is below freezing. No chance of clouds or ice below 10,000, is there? Along the right margin you will find wind arrows, and on this day the wind was very light and consistently out of the west. This would be a good place to see at which altitude wind shifts occur.

One of my complaints about the FB forecast was the 3,000-foot altitude gap between forecast values. In the skew-T chart, with the desired airport and valid time selected, hit the gray "Get text" button. You will get a pop-up, *continuous* readout of wind direction, velocity, and temperature-dewpoint spread (*see* Figure 7-10, for illustration only—this one is not related to the ALW skew-T example on Page D-5). No interpolation needed, and you can select airports along your route of flight instead of the regional coverage of the FB. Additional information from the text at the top of Figure 7-10: CAPE is a measure of stability...you want it to be below 1,000. Lifted Index (LI) is another measure of stability; for LI, you want it to be a positive number and the larger the better.

```
ALW(F3) 2000 20May10
Op40 3h Forecast, valid 20-May-2010 20:00:00
 (8.9nm/42° from ALW)

CAPE = 76.0 J/Kg, CIn = 0.0 J/Kg, PW = 9.0 Kg/m^2
TT = 56.0 KI = 22.0 LI = 1.0 SI = 2.0 SW = 210.0
LCL = 840.0 LFC = 780.0 EL = 642.0


P_alt    mb     t/td    w_dir/w_spd Time
 (ft)           (°C)       (kts)    (UTC)


 1982    949   10.9/0.600  252°/011  2000
 2044    947    9.8/0.100  251°/012  2000
 2175    943    9.3/-0.40  251°/013  2000
 2369    936    8.7/-1.00  251°/013  2000
 2628    927    7.9/-1.50  251°/014  2000
 2687    925    7.7/-1.60  251°/014  2000
 2894    918    7.1/-1.90  251°/014  2000
 3156    909    6.3/-2.30  251°/015  2000
 3422    900    5.5/-2.70  253°/016  2000
 3691    891    4.6/-3.10  260°/021  2000
 3963    882    3.8/-3.50  260°/021  2000
 4236    873    3.0/-3.90  261°/020  2000
 4508    864    2.2/-4.30  261°/019  2000
 4783    855    1.3/-4.60  260°/019  2000
 4941    850    0.8/-4.90  260°/019  2000
 5062    846    0.5/-5.10  260°/019  2000
 8871    730  -10.1/-14.5  241°/016  2000
 9921    700  -11.9/-15.4  239°/019  2000
11060    669  -13.9/-16.4  236°/023  2000
14829    574  -22.3/-27.8  228°/027  2000
17497    513  -28.5/-33.0  233°/031  2000
18074    500  -29.9/-34.2  234°/032  2000
20279    455  -35.2/-38.6  239°/036  2000
21614    429  -37.6/-40.9  246°/042  2000
22979    404  -40.1/-44.1  250°/044  2000
23173    400  -40.3/-45.3  251°/045  2000
23720    390  -40.7/-48.7  253°/046  2000
```

Figure 7-10. *Skew-T winds, result of using "Get text" function*

Because you are not limited to the approximately 200 stations on which the FB is based, using the skew-T lets you fill in the gaps. To avoid confusion, do not try to mix-and-match the skew-T charts with the FB—the altitudes are not directly comparable.

Terminal Aerodrome Forecast (TAF)

Terminal Aerodrome Forecasts, or TAFs, are prepared four times daily: 0000Z, 0600Z, 1200Z, and 1800Z, for selected reporting stations. TAFs predict conditions for a 5-mile area surrounding the airport. Note that limited area! Many pilots think that they cover more area. Each forecast (with the exception of special forecasts) is valid for 24 hours. Figure 7-11 contains a sample TAF.

```
TAF KOKC 051130Z 051212 14008KT 5SM BR BKN030 TEMPO
1316 1 1/2SM BR
      FM1600 16010KT P6SM SKC BECMG 2224 20013G20KT
      4SM SHRA OVC020 PROB40 0006 2SM TSRA OVC008CB
      BECMG 0608 21015KT P6SM NSW SCT040
```

Figure 7-11. TAF

Those stations that prepare TAFs issue their first report of the day only after two METAR observations have been made. This means that you could be well on your way before a TAF for your destination airport is available.

TAFs use the same abbreviations as METARs, with a few additions based on the fact that they are forecasts, not observation reports (*see* the TAF code key in Figure 7-1).

The station identifier and date-time group are interpreted the same as METARs. The six-digit group following the date-time group is the valid period for the forecast, which is routinely 24 hours. Thus 051212 means that the forecast is valid from 1200Z on the 5th to 1200Z on the 6th, while 110024 means that the forecast is valid from 0000Z on the 11th to 0000Z on the 12th. In this situation, the end of the period is read as 2400Z. An amended forecast, identified up front as TAF AMD, is necessarily valid for less than 24 hours. If you see 010524 on an amended forecast, you know that the TAF is valid from 0500Z on the 1st (the time that the amendment is issued) until 2400Z on the 2nd day of the month.

The format for the body of the forecast is wind-visibility-weather-sky condition-optional data, followed by forecasts for specific time slots when applicable.

Wind is read exactly the same as a METAR: 18010KT means that the wind is forecast to be from 180 degrees true at 10 knots, while 35012G20KT tells you that the wind is forecast to be from 350 degrees true at 12 knots, gusting to 20 knots. Calm is coded as 0000KT and variable winds are forecast as VRB.

Visibility is read using the same qualifiers and contractions used in METAR reports. When the visibility is expected to be better than six statute miles, however, it will be coded as P6SM (the P stands for plus).

Expected weather phenomena that affect visibility are coded the same as METAR; when the forecast visibility is P6SM, there will be no weather group.

Sky condition uses the same format as METAR; CB is the only cloud type used in TAF forecasts.

"Optional data" is a wind shear forecast for the first 2,000 feet of the atmosphere over the station. WS010/18040KT means that a wind shear at 1,000 feet above the ground is expected, with the wind from 180 degrees at 40 knots. Compare this with the surface wind forecast to see how the shear will affect your flight.

PROB30 is used when the probability of thunderstorms or other events occurring is 30 percent; however, it will not be used in the first 9 hours of the TAF effective period. If the forecaster feels that the chance of something bad happening is less than 50 percent during the first 9 hours, either TEMPO or FM will be used (*see* below). PROB30 will be followed by a four-digit group giving the beginning and ending hours of the period during which the change is expected. Assume that the body of the forecast called for "4SM SHRA OVC020." You would expect to have four miles visibility in rain showers with a 2,000-foot overcast during the valid period of the forecast. However, if you saw PROB30 2102 1/2SM +TSRA, you would know that there is about a 30 percent chance that sometime between 2100Z and 0200Z, the visibility will drop to one-half statute mile in a heavy thunderstorm with rain. Not a sure thing, and the timing might be off, but you have been alerted to the possibility.

Change indicators are FM (from), and TEMPO (temporarily).

FM is used when a rapid change, usually occurring in less than one hour, in prevailing conditions is expected. If the valid period of a TAF is 051212 and you see "FM1600 16010KT P6SM SKC," you will know that the forecaster anticipates that at 1600Z the wind will become 160 at 10 knots, the visibility will increase to over six statute miles, and the sky will be clear. A FM group will always mark the beginning of a new line in a TAF, and will include all of the required elements—wind, visibility, weather, and sky condition. A FM group is more definitive and precise and is therefore more useful to pilots.*

TEMPO is used when a change is expected to last less than an hour, and only the changed elements are included. A forecast will include a TEMPO only when the chances of the change occurring are greater than 50 percent. Any unchanged elements are carried forward. SCT030 TEMPO 1923 BKN030 is a forecast for a 3,000-foot scattered layer with the ceiling occasionally worsening to a 3,000-foot broken layer between 1900Z and 2300Z. The forecast wind and visibility aren't expected to change, because they are not mentioned in the TEMPO group. This might be a suitable forecast for a flight from A to B, but what about the return flight a couple of hours later?

NSW in the TEMPO groups means "no significant weather."

This is how you would interpret the TAF in Figure 7-11: It is the TAF for Oklahoma City issued at 1130Z on the fifth day of the month, and valid from 1200Z until 1200Z on the sixth day.

The wind at the beginning of the time period is forecast to be from 140 degrees at 8 knots, and the visibility is forecast to be 5 statute miles in mist. Sky cover is forecast to be a broken layer at 3,000 feet. Temporarily, between 1300Z and 1600Z, the visibility is expected to drop to 1½ statute miles in mist. From 1600Z, expect the wind to be from 160 at 10 knots, visibility greater than 6 statute miles with sky clear, becoming (between 2200Z and 2400Z) wind from 200 at 13 gusting to 20 knots with visibility 4 statute miles in rain showers and an overcast layer at 2,000 feet. There is a 40 to 60 percent chance that between 0000Z and 0600Z the visibility will drop to 2 statute miles in a thunderstorm and rain, with an overcast layer at 800 feet with cumulonimbus clouds becoming, between 0600Z and 0800Z, wind from 210 at 15 knots, visibility better than 6 statute miles, and no significant weather with a scattered layer at 4,000 feet.

Don't try to absorb it all at once; break it down into time periods. What will be happening at the beginning of the period? What change will occur at 1300Z? What should you expect after 1600Z?

* Your FAA Knowledge Exam may include a question using BECMG (becoming). This term is no longer in use by the weather service.

How about 2200Z? Midnight? After all, you should be able to estimate your time of arrival within an hour, shouldn't you? Find the time slot that fits your ETA and then check the time periods on either side—because predicting the weather is an art, not a science.

Weather Depiction Chart

Figure 7-12 in black and white (and the color version of the satellite image shown on Page D-7) give you a quick picture of where IFR and VFR weather was located at the valid time given on the chart. This is not forecast information but allows you to determine general weather conditions on which to base flight planning decisions. The legend is on the chart.

Note that the black-and-white chart version is difficult to find online, and is used only on the FAA Knowledge Exam. Go to the ADDS webpage, click on "Aviation Links," then on "Standard Brief," then scroll down to NWS FAX Products (this also applies to radar summary charts). Color graphic display of this information is available on the ADDS page.

The numbers below the station symbols represent the lowest cloud layer in hundreds of feet where no ceiling exists (25,000 feet in Arkansas and Alabama, for example), and the ceiling in hundreds of feet where a ceiling is present (200 feet to 300 feet at the Oregon-California border). The numbers and symbols to the left of the station report visibility and the type of obstruction to visibility, if any (fog, in east Texas). Just as in a terminal aerodrome forecast visibilities are not given if they are more than 6 miles. Also shown on the weather depiction chart is the location of any frontal activity, using the same symbols as the surface analysis map.

Convective Forecast

You know that rising air means some degree of turbulence, increasing moisture content, and the possibility of thunderstorms. You can get a "big picture" of forecast convective activity by going to the ADDS page, and clicking on Convection, Convective Outlook in the left column. Areas to the right of an arrow have convective potential (Figure 7-13). You can see that the Pacific Northwest and the states between the Great Lakes and the Gulf warrant further investigation.

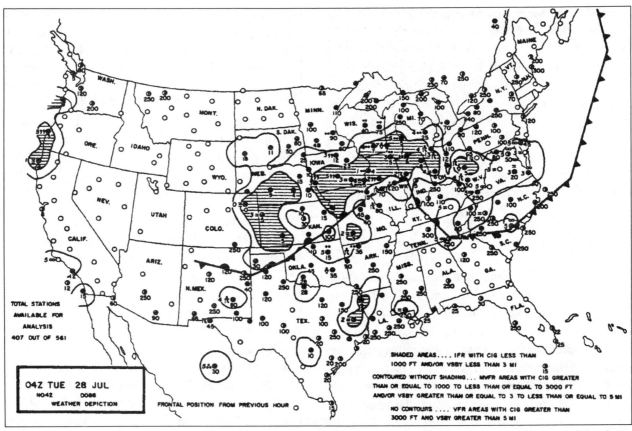

Figure 7-12 Weather depiction chart (Note: This is the old version of this type of chart; see Appendix Page D-7 for a full-color example of what is currently used.)

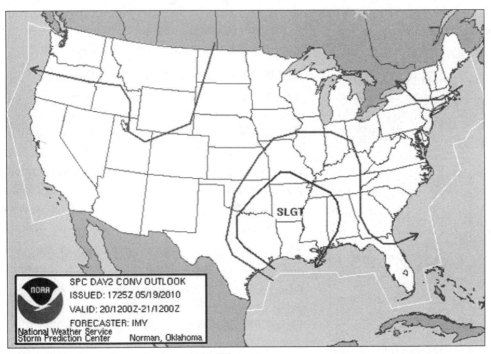

Figure 7-13. Convective outlook: no SIGMETs... yet

Low-Level Significant Weather Prognostic Charts

This panel of four charts (Figure 7-14) is available in color on the ADDS website (Appendix Page D-8). The legend in Table 2 applies to both. Prognostic charts are an important planning tool for all pilots. Using the forecast freezing level positions and cloud cover, instrument pilots can see where icing conditions might exist. VFR pilots can avoid turbulence and marginal ceilings and visibilities. The color prognostic charts can be accessed on the ADDS webpage by clicking on Prognostics in the left column; you will get a table allowing you to select various valid times.

The "low level" means that the data is for those altitudes between the surface and 24,000 feet MSL. "Prognostic" means that this is forecast information, not data based on actual observations, as is the case with the radar summary chart, the weather depiction chart, and the surface analysis map. The two panels on the left are a 12-hour forecast and the two right hand panels are a 24-hour forecast: the valid times are given on the charts. The top panels show the predicted position of the freezing level both at the surface (dotted line) and at altitude (identified by dashed lines), areas of forecast turbulence ("witches' hats"), and areas of IFR and MVFR weather. The bottom panels show predicted frontal positions, location of pressure systems, and type and extent of expected precipitation. The significant weather prognostic charts give you a larger view of tomorrow's weather than does the area forecast.

Weather in the Cockpit

It will probably be awhile before you fly an airplane equipped with airborne weather radar. The airlines have it, the turboprops have it, many general aviation twins have it, and a few single engine airplanes have approved installations.

What you might have in your cockpit is a multi-function display that shows NWS NEXRAD radar returns. Understand that this is not real-time weather. No one gets real-time weather. That is because, unlike the radar displays we see in movies and on television, a Doppler radar antenna is tilted upward at the end of each sweep (beginning at .5 degrees above the horizontal); the maximum tilt depends on whether the operator has chosen "clear air" or "precipitation" mode. There can be a delay of as much as eleven minutes between the time the radar antenna begins its first sweep and the time the information shows up on your display. Use the display to note the direction of movement of yellow and red returns (pretty much "moderate to severe"), and fly well upwind of them so that they do not drift into your flight path. Cockpit weather displays are used for avoidance strategies, not for tactical penetration.

In-Flight Weather Detection Devices

As a VFR pilot you cannot fly into the clouds, but sometimes hazardous weather exists in or above a cloud mass that you are flying beneath. It is also possible to inadvertently encounter hazardous weather at night when it cannot be seen in order to be avoided. You can equip your airplane with devices to ensure that you are able to stay well clear of hazardous weather, day or night.

Airborne weather radar transmits pulses of radio frequency energy that reflect from precipitation. The reflected energy is amplified in the radar receiver and displayed on a cathode ray tube in the cockpit, providing information on the bearing and distance of the precipitation from the airplane. Both monochrome and color displays offer means of determining the relative strength of the reflected energy and there-

Symbol	Meaning	Symbol	Meaning
⌃	Moderate Turbulence	▽	Rain Shower
⌃⌃	Severe Turbulence	⁂	Snow Shower
Ψ	Moderate Icing	℞	Thunderstorm
Ψ	Severe Icing	∿	Freezing Rain
●	Rain	໑	Tropical Storm
✳	Snow	໑	Hurricane (typhoon)
໑	Drizzle		

Table 7-2. Some standard weather symbols

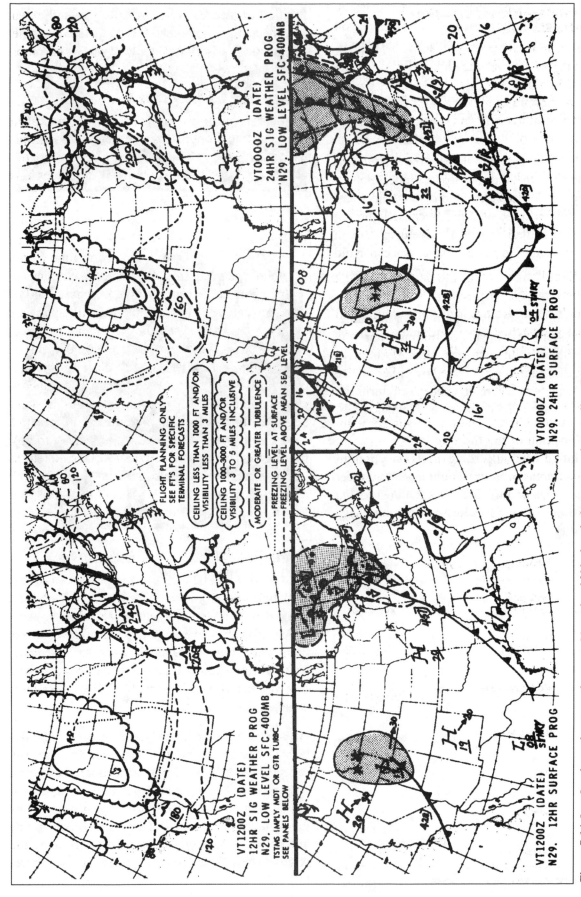

Figure 7-14. *Low-Level significant weather prog (Note: the old black and white version that is still on FAA exams is now obsolete; see the new "prognostic chart" version in color on Appendix Page D-8.)*

fore the intensity of the precipitation. Because heavy precipitation implies the presence of turbulence, you should use the radar information to stay well clear of any radar echoes. Because the return from a nearby heavy precipitation return may mask the existence of other echoes further away from your airplane, the interpretation of radar echoes requires training in the proper use of the equipment (Figure 7-15).

Weather detection systems such as the 3M Storm-scope (Figure 7-16) and the Strike Finder include passive receivers that detect and display electrical activity instead of precipitation. Because lightning is a part of every thunderstorm, these displays can show you where the storms are so that you can avoid them, but give such echoes a wide berth because the displays do not reflect reality.

You should not consider weather radar or a weather detection system as a means of finding your way through a line of thunderstorms, since destructive turbulence that cannot be detected by either device may exist in an area where no echoes or returns are visible. Use these devices as weather avoidance aids.

Datalink

Multifunction devices affording pilots the opportunity to see weather maps and Doppler weather radar returns are now available. Some Global Positioning System (GPS, discussed in Lesson 10) units have this capability.

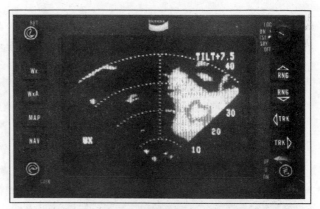

Figure 7-15. Airborne weather radar

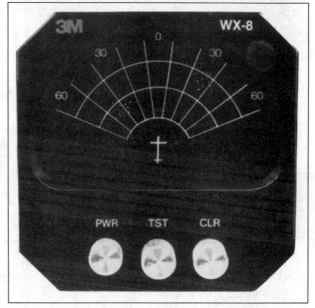

Figure 7-16. Stormscope weather mapping system

Lesson 7
Weather Services Review Questions

1. Radar weather reports are of special interest to pilots because they indicate

   A — large areas of low ceilings and fog.

   B — location of precipitation along with type, intensity, and cell movement of precipitation.

   C — location of broken to overcast clouds.

2. Ceiling is defined as the height above the Earth's surface of the

   A — lowest reported obscuration and the highest layer of clouds reported as overcast.

   B — lowest layer of clouds or obscuring phenomenon reported as broken or overcast.

   C — lowest layer of clouds reported as scattered or broken.

3. From which primary source should information be obtained regarding expected weather at your destination and estimated time of arrival?

   A — Low Level Prog Chart.

   B — Weather Depiction Chart.

   C — Terminal Aerodrome Forecast.

4. The base and tops of the overcast layer reported by a pilot in this PIREP are

   UA / OV ICT / TM 1230 / FL140 /TP M2OK / SK020 BKN 045 / O76 OVC 092 / TA-10 / WV210035 / TB LGT / IC LGT

   A — 2,000 feet MSL and 4,500 feet MSL.

   B — 7,600 feet AGL and 9,200 feet AGL.

   C — 7,600 feet MSL and 9,200 feet MSL.

```
METAR KINK 121845Z 11012G18KT 15SM SKC 25/17 A3000
METAR KBOI 121854Z 13004KT 30SM SCT150 17/6 A3015
METAR KLAX 121852Z 25004KT 6SM BR SCT007 SCT250 16/15
A2991
SPECI KMDW 121856Z 32005KT 1 1/2SM RA OVC007 17/16
A2980 RMK RAB35
SPECI KJFK 121853Z 18004KT 1/2SM FG R04/2200 OVC005
20/18 A3006
```

Figure Q7-1. METAR

For review questions 5 through 9, refer to Figure Q7-1.

5. Which of the reporting stations have VFR weather?

   A — All.

   B — KINK, KBOI, and KJFK.

   C — KINK, KBOI, and KLAX.

6. The wind direction and velocity at KJFK is from

   A — 180° true at 4 knots.

   B — 180° magnetic at 4 knots.

   C — 040° true at 18 knots.

7. What are the wind conditions at Wink, Texas (KINK)?

   A — Calm.

   B — 110° at 12 knots, gusts 18 knots.

   C — 111° at 2 knots, gusts 18 knots.

8. The remarks section for KMDW has RAB35 listed. This entry means

   A — blowing mist has reduced the visibility to 1½ SM.

   B — rain began at 1835Z.

   C — the barometer has risen .35" Hg.

9. What are the current conditions depicted for Chicago Midway Airport (KMDW)?

   A— Sky 700 feet overcast, visibility 1½ SM, rain.

   B— Sky 7,000 feet overcast, visibility 1½ SM, heavy rain.

   C— Sky 700 feet overcast, visibility 11, occasionally 2 SM, with rain.

```
TAF KMEM 121720Z 121818 20012KT 5SM HZ BKN030 PROB40
2022 1SM TSRA OVC008CB
     FM2200 33015G20KT P6SM BKN015 OVC025 PROB40 2202
     3SM SHRA
     FM0200 35012KT OVC008 PROB40 0205 2SM -RASN
     BECMG 0608 02008KT NSW BKN012 BECMG 1012 00000KT
     3SM BR SKC TEMPO 1214 1/2SM FG
     FM1600 VRB04KT P6SM NSW SKC=

KOKC 051130Z 051212 14008KT 5SM BR BKN030 TEMPO 1316
1 1/2SM BR
     FM1600 16010KT P6SM NSW SKC BECMG 2224 20013G20KT
     4SM SHRA OVC020 PROB40 0006 2SM TSRA OVC008CB
     BECMG 0608 21015KT P6SM NSW SCT040=
```

Figure Q7-2. TAF

For review questions 10 through 16, refer to Figure Q7-2.

10. What is the valid time for the TAF for KMEM?

    A— 1200Z to 1200Z.

    B— 1200Z to 1800Z.

    C— 1800Z to 1800Z.

11. In the TAF for KMEM, what does "SHRA" stand for?

    A— Rain showers.

    B— shift in wind direction is expected.

    C— A significant change in precipitation is possible.

12. Between 1000Z and 1200Z, the visibility at KMEM is forecast to be

    A— ½ statute mile.

    B— 3 statute miles.

    C— 6 statute miles.

13. What is the forecast wind for KMEM from 1600Z until the end of the forecast?

    A— No significant wind.

    B— 020° at 8 knots.

    C— Variable in direction at 4 knots.

14. In the TAF from KOKC, the "FM (FROM) Group" is

    A— forecast for the hours from 1600Z to 2200Z with the wind from 160° at 10 knots.

    B— forecast for the hours from 1600Z to 2200Z with the wind from 160° at 10 knots, becoming 220° at 13 knots with gusts to 20 knots.

    C— forecast for the hours from 1600Z to 2200Z with the wind from 160° at 10 knots, becoming 210° at 15 knots.

15. In the TAF from KOKC, the clear sky becomes

    A— overcast at 2,000 feet during the forecast period between 2200Z and 2400Z.

    B— overcast at 200 feet with a 40% probability of becoming overcast at 600 feet during the forecast period between 2200Z and 2400Z.

    C— overcast at 200 feet with the probability of becoming overcast at 400 feet during the forecast period between 2200Z and 2400Z.

16. During the time period from 0600Z to 0800Z, what significant weather is forecast for KOKC?

    A— Wind – 210° at 15 knots.

    B— Visibility – possibly 6 statute miles with scattered clouds at 4,000 feet.

    C— No significant weather is forecast for this time period.

Lesson 8 Aircraft Performance

Weight and Balance

It would be nice to have an airplane in which we could fill all of the seats and all of the baggage area, fuel up to capacity, and take off safely without worrying about loading, but that is seldom (if ever) possible. The manufacturer dictates a maximum gross weight figure based on several factors including structural strength of the landing gear, power loading (weight per horsepower), wing loading (weight per square foot of wing area), strength of the wing structure, etc. *Overloading an airplane can have serious consequences! See* Figure 8-1 — this pilot almost ran out of runway!

Airplanes are assigned to categories depending on the amount of weight the wing structure can sustain, and those categories dictate how the airplane can be used. The requirements are based on "Gs" — one G is 1 x the force of gravity (or the weight of the airplane). A *normal category* airplane can have a load of 3.8 Gs imposed on its wing, a *utility category* airplane is stressed for 4.4 Gs, and an airplane in the *aerobatic category* is designed to withstand a load of 6.0 Gs. Aerobatic airplanes usually have G meters installed to record how many Gs the airplane experienced during an aerobatic maneuver, (some sadder but wiser pilots have said that a G meter gives you information you really don't want to know!). Many airplanes are certificated in both the normal and utility categories, but in the utility category are more limited in gross weight, in weight distribution, or in authorized maneuvers.

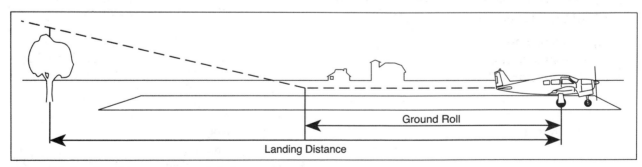

Figure 8-1. *Landing distances over an obstacle*

If you overload an airplane, the wing will have to be flown at a greater than normal angle of attack to develop enough lift to support the extra weight—this increases the stall speed, decreases the cruise speed, and limits the angle you can bank before reaching the critical angle of attack. Carrying more than the design maximum weight also means longer takeoff runs. If you combine overweight with a soft runway surface or a high density altitude, you are asking for trouble—*it takes a lot of power to overcome the rolling resistance of overloaded tires.*

Loads applied to the wing during maneuvering can overstress the airplane's structure. Figure 8-2 shows the relationship between bank angle and load factor while maintaining attitude. You can see that for a normal category airplane 3.8 G will be reached at about a 75° bank angle, and for an airplane certificated in the utility category, a bank of about 77° will bring the load factor to 4.4 Gs. If the wing is designed for a wings-level load of 2,000 pounds and you load the airplane to 2,500 pounds, in a 60° bank you will be adding an additional 1,000 pounds to the load on the wing.

A one-time overload may not cause problems, but repeatedly overstressing components may cause them to fail many flight hours later, while performing normal maneuvers.

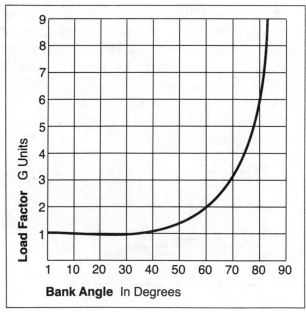

Figure 8-2. *Load factor chart*

V-Speeds and the G-Force Envelope

The graph of velocity versus G-forces in Figure 8-3 tells you, among other things, how the green and yellow arcs on the airspeed indicator are determined. The envelope that begins with a zero load factor is called the maneuvering envelope; the envelope beginning at +1 G is the gust envelope. The arc curving upward from zero load factor to point C is the stall line (maximum lift capability). A normal stall places a load of one G on the wing, so the stall speed is at point A. Speeds above point A on the arc are accelerated stall speeds. Point C, where the accelerated stall arc meets the 3.8 G limit load, represents maneuvering speed.

You know that an airplane certified in the Normal category is built to handle a maximum positive load of 3.8 Gs and a negative load of 1.5 Gs; note that in Figure 8-3, any force greater than those limits is labeled "Structural Damage." The lines labeled plus or minus 15 and 30 feet per second (fps) represent gust factors; you can see that at speeds lower than Point B, an encounter with a 30 fps gust will result in a stall, not structural damage, while hitting the same gust at a higher airspeed will result in forces approaching the load limit. The designer must consider gusts of up to 50 fps when designing the airplane.

The normal operating range, or green arc, extends from the normal stall line A – J to the maximum structural cruise line D – G. You can see that the G-forces imposed by gusts increase as airspeed increases toward line D – G.

The yellow arc, or caution range, exists between line D – G, where a gust of over 30 fps meets the limit load line and the E – F line. This is experimentally determined by a factory test pilot by diving the airplane until control surface flutter is experienced.

Some airplanes are additionally limited to a "zero fuel" weight, which usually shows up as a placard saying "All weight in excess of 3,500 pounds must be in the form of fuel" or a similar statement. The designer establishes this limitation to insure that not all of the weight is concentrated in the fuselage, where an overload can exert a damaging bending force on the wing structure.

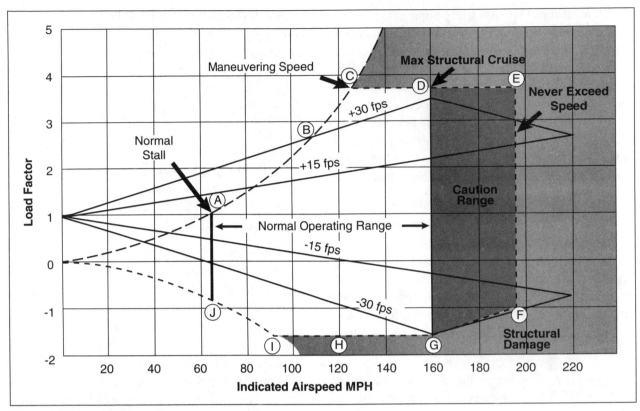

Figure 8-3. *Maneuvering envelope*

Center of gravity (CG) location relates directly to longitudinal stability. You will recall from Lesson 1 that the airplane is maneuvered around three axes which pass through the center of gravity, and that all lift forces are concentrated at the center of pressure on the wing. The designer knows how the center of pressure will move as angle of attack changes, and limits the allowable movement of the center of gravity so that a properly loaded airplane will always be controllable.

Figure 8-4 shows how airflow over the horizontal stabilizer creates a downward pressure (download) which offsets the nose-down tendency caused by the center of pressure being aft of the center of gravity. As angle of attack is increased, the center of pressure moves forward; at the same time, airflow over the horizontal stabilizer is diminishing, reducing the downward pressure.

At the critical angle of attack, the center of pressure is so close to the center of gravity, and the elevator has so little downward pressure, that the nose pitches down and the airplane reduces the angle of attack. This natural tendency to reduce the angle of attack

and avoid stalling is a built-in safety factor available *only* when the airplane is loaded within design limits. (*See* Figure 1-19 on Page 1–11.)

If the airplane is loaded so that the center of gravity is forward of the designed forward limit, a greater than normal downward pressure on the horizontal stabilizer will be required, and the up-elevator necessary to balance the weight up front will add drag. The wing will have to be flown at a greater angle of

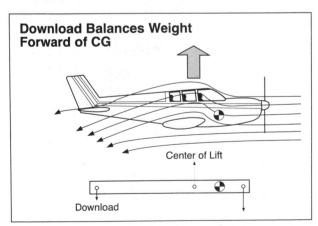

Figure 8-4. *Longitudinal stability; total weight includes the download.*

attack to develop enough lift to support the weight of the airplane *and* the download on the tail, which will slow the airplane and increase the stall speed. During the landing flare, the elevator may not have enough travel available to prevent landing on the nosewheel, especially if power has been reduced and airflow over the tail surfaces diminished. On a takeoff attempt with a forward center of gravity, additional speed (and runway) will be required before the heavy nose can be rotated to climb attitude. *See* Figure 8-5.

Loading the airplane so that the center of gravity is at the aft limit has *some* advantages: less download on the horizontal stabilizer is required, so there is less drag and the airplane can fly at a smaller angle of attack. These factors pay off in cruise speed and fuel economy. Load the airplane so that the CG falls outside of the design limits, however, and you have a tiger by the tail. *See* Figure 8-6.

Stall speed will be lower, but if a stall does occur recovery will be difficult, if not impossible. In cruise flight, the elevator control forces will be so

light that you might inadvertently overstress the airplane, and during the landing flare you may have difficulty maintaining the proper attitude.

It is worthwhile to compute weight and center of gravity location for several typical loadings: for example, full fuel and a single pilot; full fuel, a 170 pound pilot and three 170 pound passengers; or half filled tanks, two persons on board and maximum authorized baggage. These calculations will provide benchmarks so that an unusual loading situation will be recognized, and a weight and balance calculated for that special situation.

Another effect of loading an airplane so that the center of gravity falls outside the aft limits of the envelope relates to rudder authority. You know that the rudder rotates the airplane around the vertical (yaw) axis, and that the vertical axis passes through the center of gravity. Let's design an imaginary airplane with the rudder 12 feet from the center of gravity location with the airplane properly loaded. On a day with gusty crosswind it might take full rudder deflection to keep the airplane pointing straight down the runway during the takeoff roll. Now, let's reload that airplane so that the center of gravity moves aft 12 inches, so that the distance from the rudder to the CG is only 11 feet. With the lever arm reduced by 1 foot, full rudder pressure may not be adequate to handle the crosswind! You will hear some airplanes referred to as "short coupled"—this means that the distance from the CG to the rudder is short even when the airplane is properly loaded, and it takes quick and assertive rudder use to maintain control on takeoff.

Improper (or unbalanced) distribution of weight outside of the fuselage can also have undesirable effects. In a typical single-engine airplane, if one wing tank is full and the other is empty, you will need aileron pressure to hold the wings level. The aileron drag will cause a yaw which must be overcome with rudder. The total effect is a reduction in speed and in fuel economy.

Twin-engine airplanes with baggage compartments in the wings offer ample opportunity for misloading and creating lateral imbalance.

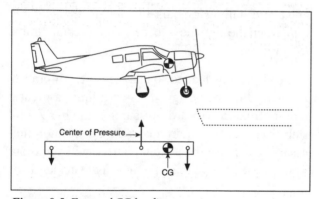

Figure 8-5. *Forward CG loading*

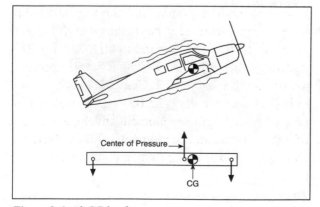

Figure 8-6. *Aft CG loading*

Weight and Balance Calculations

One document which must be in the airplane at all times is the manufacturer's data required to compute the weight and center of gravity location under different loading conditions. You will find this information in the Approved Flight Manual (not the Owner's Handbook) for older airplanes, and in the Pilot's Operating Handbook for newer airplanes. The airplane's empty weight and center of gravity position have been furnished by the manufacturer and serve as a starting point. If equipment has been added or removed since the airplane was built, an FAA Form 337 will have been prepared by the mechanic who performed the work. This updates the empty weight and center of gravity location and that form will be with the weight and balance data (also check the airframe maintenance log). Do not, under any circumstances, use the sample weight-and-balance data from the Approved Flight Manual; it doesn't apply to the specific airplane you are going to fly, and it is an easy way to fail an oral exam.

The empty weight of the airplane includes unusable fuel and optional equipment; full oil *may* be included—check the data for your airplane. Gasoline weighs 6 pounds per gallon and oil weighs 7.5 pounds per *gallon*, not per quart (there are 4 quarts to a gallon). Typically engine oil capacity is given in quarts—a common mistake is to include the weight of the oil at 7.5 pounds per quart and really mess up the calculations!

The balance portion of the weight and balance problem introduces two new terms: **arm** and **moment**. The easiest way to visualize these terms is to go back to your childhood teeter-totter. Assume that it was 12 feet long, pivoted in the center, and that you weighed 50 pounds. When you sat on one end of the teeter-totter the arm (distance from the pivot point to your seat) was 6 feet, making the moment (your weight times the arm) 300 foot-pounds. A 50-pound friend sitting on the other end of the board an equal distance from the center would balance the teeter-totter. Without a 50-pound friend, though, to have any fun at all you needed a 100 pound playmate on the other end of the board 3 feet from the pivot

point, or maybe a 75 pound friend 4 feet from the pivot point. To balance, in other words, there had to be a moment of 300 foot-pounds on each side of the pivot. The airplane manufacturer provides data on distance (arm) from a datum point which you can multiply times the weight of fuel, baggage, or passengers to derive the moment. The manufacturer may provide moments for various weights without requiring the intermediate step of providing the distance (arm). You may have to interpolate between given weights if your passengers, baggage, or fuel load do not exactly match the tabulated values.

Figure 8-7 (next page) shows a graphic method of presenting the weight and balance information and determining the position of the center of gravity, and Figures 8-8 and 8-9 show a tabular method. To avoid large, confusing numbers, moments are presented as moment/1,000 (the Katana weight-and-balance presentation is identical, except that the reduction of 1,000 is not used). With the tabular method, the CG position is determined by dividing the total moments by the total weight. As weights are shifted around within the airplane by moving baggage from forward compartments to aft compartments, by moving passengers, or even by extending and retracting the landing gear, the center of gravity follows the weight—if the weight moves aft so does the CG.

Use Figure 8-7: Calculate the CG and determine the plotted position on the CG moment envelope chart.

	Weight	Mom/1,000
Empty weight	1,350	51.5
Pilot and front passenger	380	—
Fuel 48 gal	288	—
Oil 8 qts	15	-0.2

From the loading graph, find the moment/1,000 for pilot and front seat passenger weight of 380 pounds: 14.0. Find the moment/1,000 for 288 pounds of fuel: 13.8. Total weight = 2,033 pounds, total moment/1,000 = 79.1. Center of gravity = total moment ÷ total weight = 79,100 ÷ 2,033 = 38.9. Plot on the center of gravity moment envelope a weight of 2,033 pounds and a moment/1,000 of 79.1; the *plotted point falls in the normal category area.*

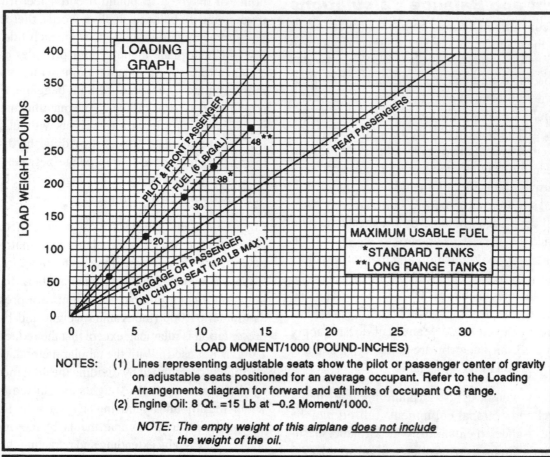

NOTES: (1) Lines representing adjustable seats show the pilot or passenger center of gravity on adjustable seats positioned for an average occupant. Refer to the Loading Arrangements diagram for forward and aft limits of occupant CG range.

(2) Engine Oil: 8 Qt. =15 Lb at –0.2 Moment/1000.

NOTE: *The empty weight of this airplane does not include the weight of the oil.*

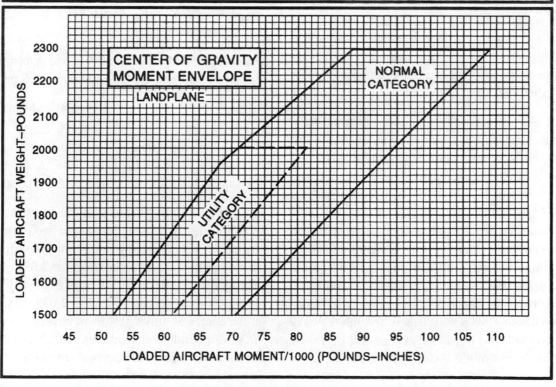

Figure 8-7. Loading graph

Upon landing, the front passenger (180 pounds) departs the airplane. A rear passenger (204 pounds) moves to the front passenger position. What effect does this have on the CG if the airplane weighed 2,690 pounds and the moment/100 was 2,260 just prior to the passenger transfer?

Use Figures 8-7 and 8-8: Compute the CG before the passenger movement:

CG = total moment ÷ total weight
    = 226,000 ÷ 2,690
    = 84.01"

Front passenger departs:	2,690	226,000 = 84.01"
	−180 lbs	−15,300
	2,510	210,700 total moment

Compute the moment for the 204-pound passenger in both rear and front seats:

204 x 121 = 24,684 moment before moving
204 x 85 = − 17,340 moment after moving
             7,344 reduction

210,700 − 7,344 after passenger moves forward
  = 203,356 moment

CG = total moment ÷ total weight
203,356 ÷ 2,510 = 81.02 or 3" forward

Remember, the CG moved with the weight!

Weight and balance are important flight planning considerations, but they are far from being the only ones; you need to consider density altitude, runway surface and slope, fuel burn...well, let's just lump all of the subjects under the heading:

Performance

According to the Federal Aviation Regulations (*see* Lesson 4), one of the five items that must be carried in the airplane is its Approved Flight Manual (AFM), your source for operating limitations and performance data. An AFM is specific to a given airplane, with the airplane's tail number stamped on the first page; manufacturer's revisions and updates are entered on the revisions page. Never switch AFMs between airplanes. On the other hand, a Pilot's Operating Handbook (POH) contains generic information pertaining to that make and model—don't confuse the two. I must point out that older airplanes did not come with AFMs but with a POH and "approved manual material."

Note: The operating and performance data contained in an Approved Flight Manual is provided by the manufacturer and has not been specifically or formally approved by the FAA; only the limitations have been checked. Use the performance charts conservatively and do not depend on their accuracy when making planning decisions. Data in the manual is developed by highly experienced factory test pilots flying brand new airplanes with new engines, and using instrumentation not available to subsequent users. When flying an older airplane you would be wise to add 50% to all takeoff distances and to figure fuel burn will be well in excess of the book figure.

Airplanes are manufactured and fly all over the world, and pilots everywhere rely on consistent performance in accordance with their airplane's Operating Handbook. Would you expect an airplane manufacturer to provide a different handbook to a Peruvian mountain pilot than is provided to a miner in Death Valley?

Obviously, the operating conditions vary widely in altitude and temperature. It is not necessary to have different manuals, and the reason lies in the term "**International Standard Atmosphere (ISA).**" At airplane manufacturing sites, engineering test flights go on in rain and sunshine, in summer and winter. All of the airspeeds, rates of climb, fuel burns, and takeoff and landing distances determined by test pilots are reduced to what they would be on a standard day at sea level.

By internationally accepted standards, a standard day has a barometric pressure of 29.92" Hg and a temperature of 15°C (59°F), and the standard atmospheric temperature lapse rate (decrease in temperature with increasing altitude) is assumed to be 2°C per 1,000 feet of altitude above sea level—the International Standard Atmosphere.

Occupants

Front Seats ARM 85		Rear Seats ARM 121	
Weight	Moment 100	Weight	Moment 100
120	102	120	145
130	110	130	157
140	119	140	169
150	128	150	182
160	136	160	194
170	144	170	206
180	153	180	218
190	162	190	230
200	170	200	242

Baggage or 5th Seat Occupant ARM 140

Weight	Moment 100
10	14
20	28
30	42
40	56
50	70
60	84
70	98
80	112
90	126
100	140
110	154
120	168
130	182
140	196
150	210
160	224
170	238
180	252
190	266
200	280
210	294
220	308
230	322
240	336
250	350
260	364
270	378

Usable Fuel

Main Wing Tanks ARM 75

Gallons	Weight	Moment 100
5	30	22
10	60	45
15	90	68
20	120	90
25	150	112
30	180	135
35	210	158
40	240	180
44	264	198

Auxiliary Wing Tanks ARM 94

Gallons	Weight	Moment 100
5	30	28
10	60	56
15	90	85
19	114	107

*Oil

Quarts	Weight	Moment 100
10	19	5

*Included in Basic Empty Weight

Empty Weight – 2,015

MOM/100 – 1,554

Moment Limits vs Weight

Moment limits are based on the following weight and center of gravity limit data (landing gear down).

Weight Condition	Forward CG Limit	AFT CG Limit
2950 lbs (takeoff or landing)	82.1	84.7
2525 lbs	77.5	85.7
2475 lbs or less	77.0	85.7

Figure 8-8. Tabular method

Weight	Minimum Moment 100	Maximum Moment 100		Weight	Minimum Moment 100	Maximum Moment 100
2100	1617	1800		2600	2037	2224
2110	1625	1808		2610	2048	2232
2120	1632	1817		2620	2058	2239
2130	1640	1825		2630	2069	2247
2140	1648	1834		2640	2080	2255
2150	1656	1843		2650	2090	2263
2160	1663	1851		2660	2101	2271
2170	1671	1860		2670	2112	2279
2180	1679	1868		2680	2123	2287
2190	1686	1877		2690	2133	2295
2200	1694	1885		2700	2144	2303
2210	1702	1894		2710	2155	2311
2220	1709	1903		2720	2166	2319
2230	1717	1911		2730	2177	2326
2240	1725	1920		2740	2188	2334
2250	1733	1928		2750	2199	2342
2260	1740	1937		2760	2210	2350
2270	1748	1945		2770	2221	2358
2280	1756	1954		2780	2232	2366
2290	1763	1963		2790	2243	2374
2300	1771	1971				
2310	1779	1980		2800	2254	2381
2320	1786	1988		2810	2265	2389
2330	1794	1997		2820	2276	2397
2340	1802	2005		2830	2287	2405
2350	1810	2014		2840	2298	2413
2360	1817	2023		2850	2309	2421
2370	1825	2031		2860	2320	2428
2380	1833	2040		2870	2332	2436
2390	1840	2048		2880	2343	2444
				2890	2354	2452
2400	1848	2057		2900	2365	2460
2410	1856	2065		2910	2377	2468
2420	1863	2074		2920	2388	2475
2430	1871	2083		2930	2399	2483
2440	1879	2091		2940	2411	2491
2450	1887	2100		2950	2422	2499
2460	1894	2108				
2470	1902	2117				
2480	1911	2125				
2490	1921	2134				
2500	1932	2143				
2510	1942	2151				
2520	1953	2160				
2530	1963	2168				
2540	1974	2176				
2550	1984	2184				
2560	1995	2192				
2570	2005	2200				
2580	2016	2208				
2590	2026	2216				

Figure 8-9. *Moment limits vs. weight*

Engineers take the information from the test flights, reduce it to its equivalent under standard conditions, and furnish the pilot with charts and graphs to predict airplane performance under widely varying pressure and temperature conditions.

Density Altitude

The basis for predicting performance is density altitude—pressure altitude corrected for non-standard temperature. Your responsibilities as a pilot will include calculating the effect that existing or forecast weather conditions will have on your takeoff and climb performance from a departure airport. You must also consider the true airspeed and fuel consumption rate at your chosen cruise altitude, and compare the predicted landing distance to the amount of runway available at the destination airport (also to any enroute airports you might have to use in an emergency). You will have to compute the den-

sity altitude for the different airports, consult your airplane's performance charts, and get the numbers for the expected conditions. (*See* Page D-9 for an example of the full-color version available at the ADDS website under "Winds/Temps.")

In the discussion of the factors that produce lift, you learned the density of the air has a direct effect on the amount of lift developed at a given airspeed or angle of attack, and you learned that high altitude, high temperature, and high humidity, separately or in combination, have the worst effect on performance. All of the charts, tables, computers, etc., that will be used in the calculation of density altitude performance take into account only pressure altitude and temperature; no provision is made for the effects of humidity on performance (Figure 8-10). A conservative approach is to add 1,000 feet to any density altitude you arrive at by use of pressure altitude and

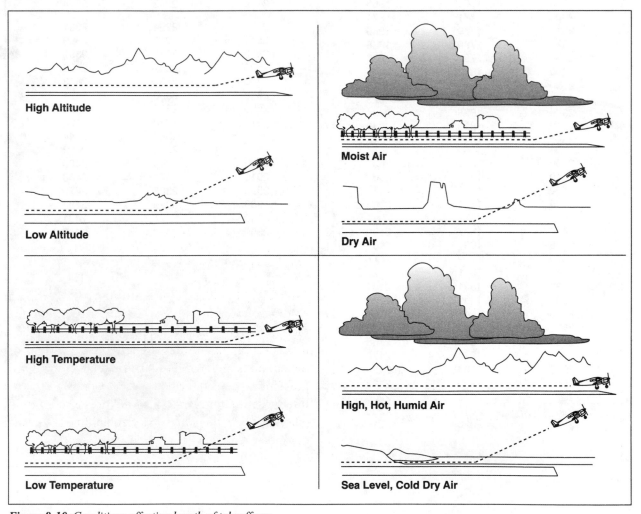

High Altitude

Low Altitude

High Temperature

Low Temperature

Moist Air

Dry Air

High, Hot, Humid Air

Sea Level, Cold Dry Air

Figure 8-10. Conditions affecting length of takeoff run

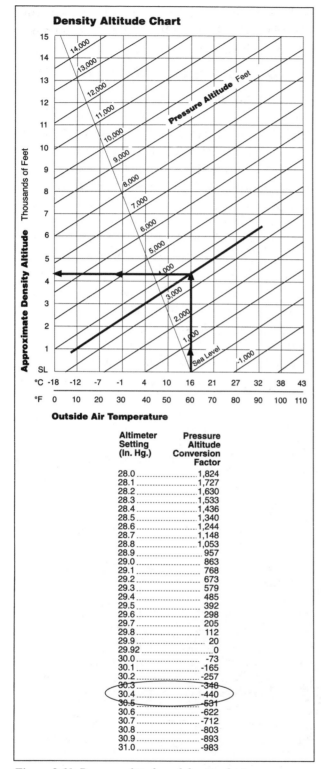

Figure 8-11. *Pressure altitude and density chart*

temperature, then calculate the performance figures based on that altitude.

The quickest way to determine pressure altitude when you are in the airplane is to note the setting in the **Kollsman window** (the little window you use for entering altimeter setting), then set it to 29.92; the altimeter will indicate pressure altitude. (Return the altimeter setting to its previous setting before you forget it!) If you are determining density altitude for a distant airport, and you received its temperature and altimeter setting from the hourly weather sequence reports, determine the difference between 29.92 and the reported altimeter setting and apply the difference to the field elevation:

Altimeter setting

$$
\begin{array}{r}
30.20 \\
-\,29.92 \\
\hline
.28 \\
=\ 280\ \text{feet}
\end{array}
$$

Field elevation

$$
\begin{array}{r}
2{,}348 \\
-\ 280 \\
\hline
2{,}068\ \ \text{Pressure altitude}
\end{array}
$$

(1.00" = 1,000', .1" = 100', .01" = 10')

To be sure that you apply the pressure difference correctly, ask yourself which way the altimeter needles will move as the altimeter setting is changed from 30.20 to 29.92. In the example, they will move counterclockwise, and the pressure difference must be subtracted from the field elevation to derive pressure altitude at that airport.

Figure 8-11 will be found in your Private FAA Knowledge Exam and provides pressure difference factors for you to apply: determine the pressure altitude by applying the pressure difference factor from the columns on the right to the field elevation. Find the temperature on the bottom scale, draw a vertical line from the temperature to the pressure altitude (slanting) line, then draw a horizontal line to the left margin to read density altitude.

Another method is to use the slide rule side of your flight computer by setting the pressure altitude (29.92 reading of the altimeter) in the window opposite the temperature and read density altitude at the index. You can use the reading of your airplane's outside air temperature (OAT) gauge without correction.

Pressure altitude, density altitude, and true altitude are all equal at sea level on a standard day, a condition which does not often occur. Pressure altitude is equal to density altitude only when the temperature is standard for that pressure altitude. If the air mass is warmer than standard, density altitude will be higher than pressure altitude; if the air mass is colder than standard, density altitude will be lower than pressure altitude. You will read performance figures for turbo-props and jets given as "ISA + 10°" or "ISA - 5°." These figures show performance at temperatures differing from the International Standard Atmosphere.

Because true altitude is the actual altitude above mean sea level, when you are on the ground your altimeter should read the published airport elevation when you set the altimeter to the current local altimeter setting.

Takeoff and Climb Performance

In reading and using the information about takeoff and landing performance charts, you must understand that for airplanes having maximum takeoff weights of less than 6,000 pounds, the information provided comes from the manufacturer's test pilots and is not in any way guaranteed by the FAA to be accurate.

Figure 8-12 is a takeoff performance chart. Note the line marked "ISA" which represents the standard temperature for each altitude shown. Also note how an increase in either temperature, pressure altitude, or weight will adversely affect takeoff distance, shown at the right-hand edge, with the shortest distance at the bottom, increasing toward the top. In the left-hand panel, combining altitude and temperature, the lines slope upward; any increase in either altitude or

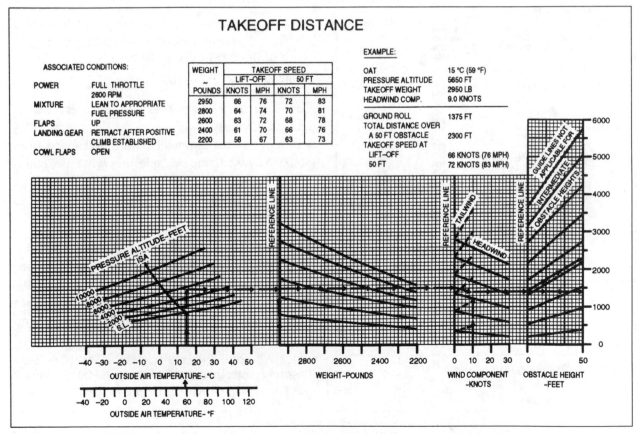

Figure 8-12. *Takeoff distance*

temperature increases takeoff distance. In the center panel, the heaviest weights are at the left, decreasing toward the right; any decrease in weight decreases takeoff distance. Finally, in the wind panel, you can see how headwinds shorten the takeoff run while tailwinds increase it. Of all of these elements, only one is yours to control: weight. You can't change the altitude or the temperature (unless you wait until the sun goes down) and you can't control the wind. All you can do, if you calculate that the runway is not long enough, is offload passengers or baggage. How about ferrying part of your passenger load to a lower, cooler airport and returning to pick up the rest?

Follow the example problem in Figure 8-12 through to see how the takeoff distance was derived. Now, try this one:

OAT .... Standard
Pressure altitude .... 4,000 feet
Takeoff weight ....2,800 lbs
Headwind component ....Calm

Refer to Figure 8-12. Determine total distance required for takeoff to clear a 50-foot obstacle.

The outside air temperature is given as standard for a pressure altitude of 4,000 feet, so follow the International Standard Altitude (ISA) line up to the curve for 4,000 feet. Draw a horizontal line from that point of intersection to the first reference line. From that point, draw a line that parallels the weight curves as accurately as possible until you reach a point directly above the 2,800-pound mark. Again, draw a horizontal line from that point of intersection to the next reference line.

The wind is calm, so continue horizontally to the third reference line. (If there is any wind, you would draw a line following the wind curves just as you did with the weight curves.) The problem wants you to clear a 50-foot obstacle, so from the point at which your horizontal line meets the third reference line follow the obstacle height curves up until you reach the distance line, and read 1,750 feet.

In real life you will need about 2,500 feet of runway under these conditions—never expect your airplane to perform as well as predicted by the performance charts.

Figure 8-13 is another table used to predict takeoff performance. Again, look at how increases in weight, altitude, and temperature affect takeoff distance. It may be necessary to interpolate one or more of the values given. Be conservative; if your answer falls between two values, select the longer

Takeoff Distance from Hard Surface Runway with Flaps Up

Gross Weight Pounds	IAS At 50 feet	Head Wind Knots	At Sea Level & 59°F		At 2500 FT & 50°F		At 5000 FT & 41°F		At 7500 FT & 32°F	
			Ground Run	Total to Clear 50 FT OBS	Ground Run	Total to Clear 50 FT OBS	Ground Run	Total to Clear 50 FT OBS	Ground Run	Total to Clear 50 FT OBS
2,300	68	0	865	1525	1040	1910	1255	2480	1565	3855
		10	615	1170	750	1485	920	1955	1160	3110
		20	405	850	505	1100	630	1480	810	2425
2,000	63	0	630	1095	755	1325	905	1625	1120	2155
		10	435	820	530	1005	645	1250	810	1685
		20	275	580	340	720	425	910	595	1255
1,700	58	0	435	780	520	920	625	1095	765	1370
		10	290	570	355	680	430	820	535	1040
		20	175	385	215	470	270	575	345	745

Notes 1. Increase distance 10% for each 25°F above standard temperature for particular altitude.
2. For operation on a dry, grass runway, increase distances (both "Ground Run" and "Total to Clear 50 Foot Obstacle") by 7% of the "Total to Clear 50 Foot Obstacle" figure.

Figure 8-13. Takeoff data

takeoff distance. Read the notes and be sure that you are duplicating the conditions under which the engineers arrived at the figures, remembering that factory pilots used a new airplane in top condition. Add a "fudge factor" for the effects of time on the airframe and engine.

Gross weight ....1,700 lbs
OAT..66°F
Pressure altitude .... 5,000 feet
Headwind component ....20 knots

Distance to clear a 50-foot obstacle?

The correct answer is 633 feet. The standard temperature at 5,000 feet is 41°, and the notes at the bottom tell you to add 10% for each 25° above standard. With a 20-knot headwind, a 1,700-pound airplane taking off from an airport at 5,000 feet at standard temperature will require 575 feet to clear a 50-foot obstacle, so the warmer temperature increases the takeoff distance.

The manufacturer's takeoff performance tables or the operating procedures section of the approved flight manual will contain a recommended takeoff speed. This speed must be attained before you rotate the airplane to climb attitude—you can't force the airplane to lift off or climb at a slower speed. A good rule to follow is this: you should have accelerated to 75% of takeoff speed in the first half of the available runway. If the airplane has not reached that speed by the midway point you should stop, taxi back, and do some performance calculations. If the airspeed stops increasing, abort.

Your takeoff roll will *always* be longer than the distance you have calculated—be conservative. You may be unable to climb out of ground effect—one-half wingspan above the runway. If you have a heavy load, a short runway, or a high density altitude, it might be wiser to ferry your passengers one or two at a time to an airport that is lower, cooler, or has longer runways.

You can buy a takeoff performance calculator that takes all of these factors into account at any pilot supply shop and eliminate the need for interpolation.

Climb Performance

Figure 8-14 is used to predict rate-of-climb and fuel used during climb. Note how climb performance drops off with altitude (climb performance depends on power in excess of that required for level flight at a constant airspeed, and that decreases as you climb), how indicated airspeed for maximum rate-of-climb decreases with altitude (review this before takeoff), and how much fuel is used during climb.

Pressure altitude ....Sea level
Temperature ....89°F
Gross weight ....2,000 lbs
Indicated airspeed .... 79 MPH

Maximum Rate-of-Climb Data

Gross Weight Pounds	At Sea Level & 59°F			At 5,000 FT & 41°F			At 10,000 FT & 23°F			At 15,000 FT & 5°F		
	IAS MPH	Rate of Climb FT/MIN	GAL of Fuel Used	IAS MPH	Rate of Climb FT/MIN	From S.L. Fuel Used	IAS MPH	Rate of Climb FT/MIN	From S.L. Fuel Used	IAS MPH	Rate of Climb FT/MIN	From S.L. Fuel Used
2300	82	645	1.0	81	435	2.6	79	230	4.8	78	22	11.5
2000	79	840	1.0	79	610	2.2	76	380	3.6	75	155	6.3
1700	77	1085	1.0	76	825	1.9	73	570	2.9	72	315	4.4

Notes   1. Flaps up, full throttle, mixture leaned for smooth operation above 3,000 feet.
2. Fuel used includes warm-up and takeoff allowance.
3. For hot weather, decrease rate-of-climb 20 feet/minute for each 10°F above standard day temperature for particular altitude.

Figure 8-14. Maximum rate-of-climb data

The table indicates that a 2,000-pound airplane taking off from sea level will climb at 840 feet per minute if the temperature is standard (59°F). However, the temperature is 89° and the notes tell you to decrease the rate of climb 20 fpm for every 10° above standard. That brings the climb rate down to 780 fpm, so after five minutes the altimeter should read 3,900 feet (but it won't, because as you make slight left and right turns to clear for traffic the climb rate will suffer).

Climb Gradient

Climb gradient is a performance parameter that is seldom provided in an airplane's operating manual, but one which becomes of paramount importance when you are taking off from a runway that is at a high density altitude—because the outside temperature is hot, the air is humid, or the runway itself is high above sea level. Remember, density altitude is how high the airplane thinks it is, not how high you think you are.

Many pilots learn, to their dismay, that the density altitude problem does not go away when the wheels leave the surface. Sure, high density altitude will make for a longer-than-normal ground roll before takeoff speed is reached, because the less-dense air makes the engine and prop less efficient and because the wings need something to bite on in order to create lift. The after-liftoff climb, however, will be at a rate much lower than that promised by the performance charts, and there will probably be moments of negative climb rate, where the airplane sinks in spite of your best efforts.

Let's revisit that takeoff in a 2,000-pound airplane from sea level with the reported temperature at 89°F—you can be sure that the temperature on a concrete or asphalt runway will be higher. We calculated the climb rate to be 780 feet per minute at an indicated airspeed of 79 knots. Let's call it 80 for ease of calculation. That's 1.33 miles per minute (nautical or statute, whatever your airspeed indicator is calibrated in), or 586 feet per mile. At sea level.

Now let's take the same airplane to an airport located 2,000 feet above sea level, surrounded by hills 1,000 feet higher than field elevation, but two miles away.

Using the standard temperature for 2,000 feet MSL (about 51°F), the climb rate would be 748 fpm (trust me on the interpolation). Bump the temperature the same 30 degrees above standard, up to 81°F, and apply the same decrease in climb rate of 20 feet for every 10 degrees above standard. Now the climb rate is down to 688 fpm or 517 feet per mile. Still think you will clear those thousand-foot mountains by a comfortable margin after climbing for two miles, ignoring the possibility of sinkers or performance loss due to maneuvering? What if the mountains are downwind, and you must approach them with a tailwind? Your climb gradient will be cut in half if your ground speed is doubled. When considering a takeoff under high density altitude conditions, think about the climb gradient as well as the takeoff roll, and consider climbing directly above the departure airport instead of heading out on course.

Best Angle-of-Climb and Best Rate-of-Climb Speeds

Figure 8-15 plots the relationship between airspeed and climb rate in feet per minute for a typical light airplane. A line from the origin of the graph is tangent to the curve at the best angle of climb speed and the apex of the curve is the best rate-of-climb speed.

The best angle-of-climb speed (V_X) is safely above the stall and slightly slower than the best rate of climb speed (V_Y). You will use V_X for clearing obstacles after takeoff and then accelerate to V_Y as soon as the obstacles are cleared. Don't use V_X unless it is absolutely necessary. Both forward visibility and engine cooling are adversely affected by the nose-high attitude at the best angle-of-climb speed (Figures 8-16 and 8-17).

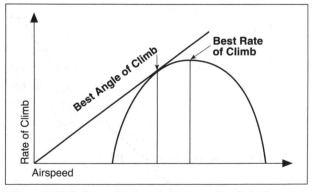

Figure 8-15. *Relationship between airspeed and climb rate*

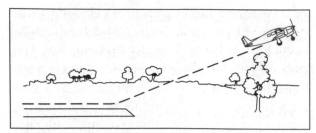

Figure 8-16. Best angle-of-climb speed

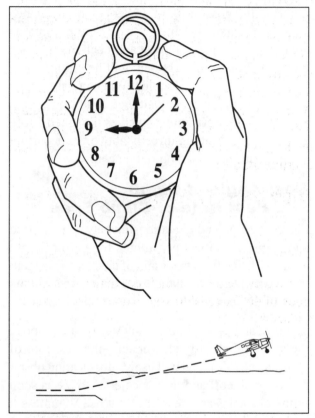

Figure 8-17. Best rate-of-climb speed

The manufacturer's V_X and V_Y speeds are determined at sea level and at maximum gross weight. With increasing elevation (density altitude), V_X increases and V_Y decreases; the altitude at which they become equal is the airplane's absolute ceiling. When taking off from airports with density altitudes above sea level, using the "book" numbers will result in reduced performance; use a slower than published V_Y for best climb performance, and a faster than published V_X to clear obstacles. Do some pre-calculations for various weights and density altitudes to avoid the trap of always using "book" figures...

or buy a performance calculator. When "best" performance is required, calculating climb speed is as important as calculating takeoff distance.

It has nothing to do with design climb speeds, but it is a fact that you will gain more altitude per unit of distance when climbing into the wind than when climbing downwind. You are climbing x number of feet per minute and spending more minutes while climbing into the wind. If you climb at 60 knots into a 60-knot wind you will go straight up!

The Impossible Turn

This is a good point at which to discuss the "impossible turn;" that is, the attempt to turn back to the departure runway in case of an engine failure or other critical situation. If you are really, really good, and really, really lucky, and you do everything just right, you can *almost* make it from a height of 500 feet above the runway if you bank 45° and maintain the slowest possible airspeed (stall warning on continuously). If you are a normal human being and have normal reaction time, you should not attempt to turn back unless you are 1,000 feet above the runway. Remember, you will need to turn more than 180° if you are going to land on the runway surface. It is far better to land straight ahead or, if you absolutely must turn, to turn no more than 90°. *Note:* If a door pops open after takeoff, it is not an emergency, although the noise level will increase dramatically and frighten your passengers. Just make a normal pattern and land to shut the door. Do not attempt to shut the door in flight.

In practicing power-on stall recoveries for your checkride, your instructor will have you lower the nose to or slightly below the horizon and fly out of the stall. This assumes that the engine is operating. In real life, *if you lose the engine* while climbing at V_X or V_Y you will have to go against your natural reluctance to aim the airplane at the ground and lower the nose significantly in order to regain the energy needed in order to flare for the inevitable landing. Think dive. Practice this with your instructor until pushing the stick forward becomes second nature.

Cruise Performance

Figure 8-18 is a cruise chart for a typical single-engine airplane with a controllable-pitch propeller.

This is the 65% power chart for this airplane; its approved flight manual will contain similar charts for 55% and possibly 45%. True airspeed and fuel consumption figures are given for standard atmospheric conditions, and also for temperatures much colder and warmer than standard. You must check the winds and temperatures aloft forecast (*see* Lesson 7) to *estimate* time en route and fuel burn. *Note:* These performance figures have not been checked and approved by the FAA—do not bet your life on their accuracy.

What is the expected fuel consumption for a 1,000-nautical mile flight under the following conditions?

Pressure altitude .... 8,000 feet
Temperature .... 22°C
Manifold pressure .... 20.8" Hg
Wind .... Calm

Find the line for a pressure altitude of 8,000 feet; move horizontally to the block headed "ISA +20°C." Under Manifold Pressure, find 20.8. The adjacent fuel flow and TAS figures are 11.5 GPH and 164 knots, respectively. Using your flight computer, how long will it take to fly 1,000 miles at 164 knots in no-wind conditions? Should take about 6.1 hours,

and if the engine gulps 11.5 gallons each hour it will consume 70.1 gallons during the flight. Realistically, I would use at least 12 GPH for fuel burn and 160 knots for this calculation—but that doesn't work for written exams.

If the manufacturer of your airplane provides a maximum rate-of-climb chart your figures can be further refined. Remember that for a VFR flight in the daytime you must have enough fuel on board to fly to your point of first intended landing, plus 30 minutes at cruise speed (45 minutes reserve at night). In planning your flight, don't look for the altitude and power setting that will give maximum speed if the fuel consumption will force a fuel stop en route. A slower speed that makes the fuel stop unnecessary will pay off in the long run because of the time lost on the ground and the fuel burned in climbing back to cruise altitude.

High Density Altitude Operations

As temperature, humidity, and/or altitude increase, the numbers you used under standard, sea level conditions change radically. Here are some examples:

Turn radius increases. Your radius of turn with a bank angle of 45° is equal to your *true* airspeed squared divided by 11.2 (a constant). But you fly by *indicated* airspeed, right? At a constant indicated airspeed, your turn radius (and turn diameter, which is what

Cruise Power Settings 65% Maximum Continuous Power (or Full Throttle) 2,800 lbs

Pressure Altitude Feet	ISA -20°C (-36°F)						Standard Day (ISA)						ISA +20°C (+36°F)					
	IOAT °F °C	Engine Speed RPM	Manifold Pressure IN HG	Fuel Flow Per Engine PSI GPH	TAS KTS MPH		IOAT °F °C	Engine Speed RPM	Manifold Pressure IN HG	Fuel Flow Per Engine PSI GPH	TAS KTS MPH		IOAT °F °C	Engine Speed RPM	Manifold Pressure IN HG	Fuel Flow Per Engine PSI GPH	TAS KTS MPH	
Sea Level	27 -3	2450	20.7	6.6 11.5	147 169		63 17	2450	21.2	6.6 11.5	150 173		99 37	2450	21.8	6.6 11.5	153 176	
2000	19 -7	2450	20.4	6.6 11.5	149 171		55 13	2450	21.0	6.6 11.5	153 176		91 33	2450	21.5	6.6 11.5	156 180	
4000	12 -11	2450	20.1	6.6 11.5	152 175		48 9	2450	20.7	6.6 11.5	156 180		84 29	2450	21.3	6.6 11.5	159 183	
6000	5 -5	2450	19.8	6.6 11.5	155 178		41 5	2450	20.4	6.6 11.5	158 182		79 26	2450	21.0	6.6 11.5	161 185	
8000	-2 -9	2450	19.5	6.6 11.5	157 181		36 2	2450	20.2	6.6 11.5	161 185		72 22	2450	20.8	6.6 11.5	164 189	
10,000	-8 -22	2450	19.2	6.6 11.5	160 184		28 -2	2450	19.9	6.6 11.5	163 188		64 18	2450	20.3	6.5 11.4	166 191	
12,000	-15 -26	2450	18.8	6.4 11.3	162 186		21 -8	2450	18.8	6.1 10.9	163 188		57 14	2450	18.8	5.9 10.6	163 188	
14,000	-22 -30	2450	17.4	5.8 10.5	159 183		14 -10	2450	17.4	5.6 10.1	160 184		50 10	2450	17.4	5.4 9.8	160 184	
16,000	-29 -34	2450	16.1	5.3 9.7	156 180		7 -14	2450	16.1	5.1 9.4	156 180		43 6	2450	16.1	4.9 9.1	155 178	

Notes   1. Full throttle manifold pressure settings are approximate.   2. Shaded area represents operation with full throttle.

Figure 8-18. Cruise chart

counts in a canyon or in the pattern) will be about 30% greater at a density altitude of 8,000 feet than it is at sea level. A smaller bank angle will increase the radius/diameter.

Induced drag/power required increases. You know that back pressure is required to make a level turn; that causes induced drag to increase. The amount of power required to overcome a drag increase is the *cube* of the drag increase. A 15° bank increases drag 7%, a 30° bank increases drag 33%, a 45° bank doubles the induced drag. You do the math—without turbocharging, your throttle will be full forward at a density altitude above 7,000 feet or so. Where are you going to get the power to overcome the increased drag?

You use the same indicated airspeed on final at Denver that you would use at a sea level airport, but your true airspeed is 10% higher (2% per 1,000, remember?). If you add five knots or so for the family, and throw in a gust correction, will you be able to get the airplane on the ground before the pavement runs out? Know your TAS on final when the density altitude is high.

Should you use short/soft field technique for takeoff at a high density altitude? Check your manual—some airplanes that use flaps to shorten the takeoff run at low altitudes restrict their use when the air is thin. Should you pull the yoke back into your lap to get the nosewheel off of the ground? You're adding the download on the horizontal stabilizer to the weight the wing has to lift, and increasing the load on the main wheels. If a field is truly soft or short, and technique is critical, go somewhere else (or take a mountain flying course).

Descent Planning

The most efficient way to descend is to maintain cruise speed while descending at a comfortable rate, and in VFR conditions you are in complete command of where and when to start down. Add 1,000 feet to the destination airport's field elevation for pattern altitude, and subtract that figure from your cruise altitude to determine how much altitude must be lost. Divide that figure by 300 and you will have the number of miles from your destination to begin your descent at 300 feet per mile.

Landing Distance

Your preflight planning must include familiarizing yourself with the runway length and condition at the destination airport. Be sure to ask the briefer what surface winds are forecast (if your destination has a weather observer) in order to anticipate which runway will be in use. Figures 8-19 and 8-20 show two different types of landing distance charts, and you will notice again that altitude and temperature (density altitude) have a definite effect on landing performance. Notice the speeds recommended by the manufacturer: they provide a safe margin above the stall and should be adhered to.

Additional airspeed means more energy that must be dissipated and more runway left behind before the wing can no longer support the aircraft and the wheels touch down. The time to go around for another landing attempt is when you are on short final and can see that you are too high or too fast, not after you have floated half the length of the runway trying to get rid of excess airspeed and altitude. Note that neither of the landing distance charts provides any guidance on how to judge your touchdown point or when to abandon the approach and go around. My personal choice is the dirty spot method. If you can't find a dirty spot on the windshield directly in front of your eyes, make one with a grease pencil. When you have turned final, set landing flaps, and have the airspeed stabilized, use the yoke to establish a pitch attitude that puts the dirty spot directly on the runway at your intended touchdown spot…that is, establish a direct line that connects your eyes with the touchdown spot and passes through the dirty spot. Trim off any pressure and watch the spot. If it moves up the runway, away from your chosen touchdown spot, you are going to overshoot and should correct with power; if it moves toward the threshold you will undershoot. Again, correct with power. The power adjustments will be small…use your ears instead of looking at the engine instruments; an adjustment that changes the sound of the engine slightly should be just about right.

What if the engine quits while on final? You know that the airplane is not going to plummet out of the sky but will continue to descend at its trim speed

Landing Distance — Flaps Lowered to 40°/Power Off/Hard Surface Runway/Zero Wind

Gross Weight Pounds	Approach Speed IAS, MPH	At Sea Level & 59° F		At 2,500 FT & 50° F		At 5,000 FT & 41° F		At 7,500 FT & 32° F	
		Ground Roll	Total to Clear 50 FT OBS	Ground Roll	Total to Clear 50 FT OBS	Ground Roll	Total to Clear 50 FT OBS	Ground Roll	Total to Clear 50 FT OBS
1600	60	445	1075	470	1135	495	1195	520	1255

Notes
1. Decrease the distances shown by 10% for each 4 knots of headwind.
2. Increase the distance by 10% for each 60°F temperature increase above standard.
3. For operation on a dry grass runway, increase distances (both "Ground Roll" and "Total to Clear 50-Foot Obstacle" by 20% of the "Total to Clear 50-Foot Obstacle" figure.

Figure 8-19. Landing distance chart

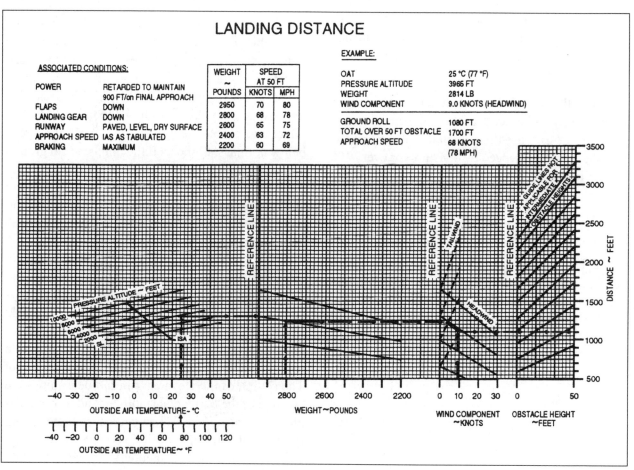

Figure 8-20. Landing distance graph

(*see* below). With no obstacles to clear, do the counterintuitive thing and lower the nose to increase airspeed and thus the kinetic energy that will carry you onto the runway surface.

Make your decision to abandon the approach while you are still 75 to 100 feet above the runway. With the airplane trimmed for approach speed, application of full power will cause the airplane to stop descending and either pitch up or fly level. Establish a positive climb rate before even thinking of flaps or landing gear. When you retract the flaps, don't dump them all at once but in increments, adjusting yoke pressure as needed. Learn how to transition into and out of a forward slip as a method of losing speed and altitude when required.

If your POH does not have a table of reduced airspeeds at weights lighter than maximum gross weight (*see* Figure 8-20), use this rule of thumb: reduce the published approach speed by one knot for every 100 pounds less than gross weight. Good landings are slow landings, and approach speed must be based on actual weight.

Use Figure 8-19:

Determine the total landing distance required to clear a 50-foot obstacle.

Pressure altitude	7,500 feet
Headwind	8 knots
Temperature	Standard
Runway surface	dry grass

Use Figure 8-20:

What is the approximate landing roll?

OAT	90°F
Pressure altitude	4,000 feet
Weight	2,800 lbs
Tailwind component	5 knots

Notice how steeply the tailwind curves in Figures 8-12 and 8-20 slope upward when compared to the downward slope of the headwind curves. A tailwind component decreases performance much more than a headwind improves it. Never land or take off with a tailwind component if you can possibly avoid it.

Ground Effect

When induced drag was discussed in Lesson 1, it was associated with low speeds and high angles of attack—typically takeoff and landing conditions. When the wing is less than one-half the wingspan above the ground, induced drag is reduced by the interaction between the ground, the wing-tip vortices, and downwash. If you can get the wing within 3 feet of the ground, induced drag is reduced by 48%. This reduction in drag is called ground effect (Figure 8-21).

All airplanes experience **ground effect** but it is more noticeable in low-wing airplanes. The reduction in induced drag causes "float" if excess airspeed is used on final; also, downwash from the wing bouncing off of the surface reduces elevator effectiveness, causing the nose to pitch down slightly. On takeoff, ground effect will enable the airplane to lift off at a speed below normal stall speed. If the pilot stays in ground effect, and accelerates before climbing, this is a useful soft-field or high-altitude technique. If the pilot attempts to climb out of ground effect before gaining at least best angle-of-climb speed (V_X), the airplane may sink back to the surface.

Trim Speed

Trim speed is a concept that belongs to both aerodynamics and performance. In Lesson 1 you were told that trim tabs provide a means of relieving control pressure, and you were warned to not use trim as a means of achieving a specific attitude or airspeed. The setting of the elevator trim tab determines the position of the horizontal stabilizer and thus the airplane's pitch attitude. When you check that the trim is in the takeoff range during your preflight runup, you ensure that the airplane will lift off and climb normally when there is sufficient airflow over the control surfaces. If you fail to perform this check, the airplane will either hug the ground and resist your efforts to make it fly, or it will pitch up into what you will recognize as an impossibly nose-high attitude and you will have to exert strong forward pressure to avoid a stall. (You can always overpower the trim, even when it is set outside of normal limits.) If you leave the elevator trim set in one position and never change it, the airplane will fly at its "trim speed." If you add power, it will climb at its trim speed (after a few oscillations up and down), and if you reduce power it will descend at trim speed. Of course, there will be an intermediate power setting where the airplane will maintain level flight at trim speed.

Try this experiment during a training flight: with the airplane trimmed for level flight, apply back pressure to the yoke and then release it, keeping the wings level with rudder pressure. The airplane will climb and descend in gradually decreasing oscillations until it is once again in level flight at its trim speed. Change the power setting, re-trim for level flight, and try again. The airplane will always return to level flight at trim speed. Now trim the elevator so that the vertical speed indicator shows a zero rate of climb or descent at the speed you use when descending from the downwind leg onto base and final, noting the power setting and where the airplane's nose is in relation to the horizon. Without touching the trim,

retard the throttle 500 rpm. With little or no effort on your part, the airplane should stabilize in a 500-foot per minute descent without changing airspeed (check the nose-down attitude). When you have lost 500 feet of altitude, return the throttle to the setting you noted earlier; the airplane should level off and maintain trim speed. Now add 500 rpm and watch what happens to the airspeed and vertical speed.

This is a very valuable tool for predictable performance: a known power setting and a known (trimmed) pitch attitude will always give you the same vertical speed and airspeed. Every time you reach for the trim wheel, you change the trim speed. Keep your airplane in trim at your desired speed. Then, when you get something in your eye or drop a chart on the floor, you know that the airplane won't immediately take off on its own.

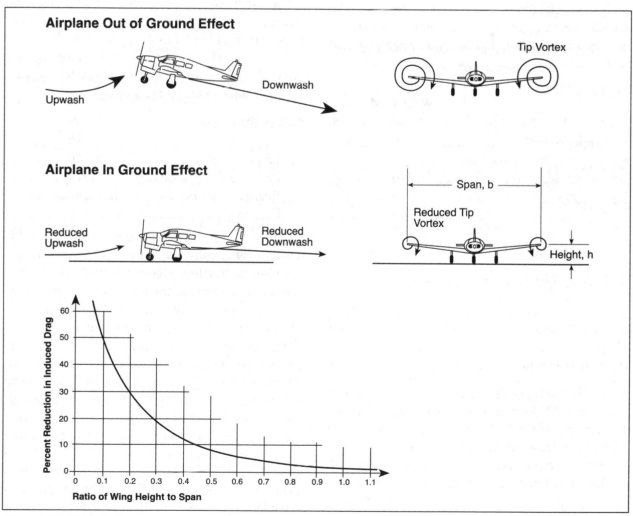

Figure 8-21. Ground effect

Lesson 8
Aircraft Performance Review Questions

Use Figure 8-7 (on Page 8–6) for review problems 1 through 4.

1. Determine the moment with the following data:

	Weight lbs	Moment/ 1,000
Empty weight	1,350	51.5
Pilot and front passenger	340	—
Fuel (std. tanks)	Capacity	—
Oil 8 qts	15	-0.2

   A— 69.9 lbs-in
   B— 74.9 lbs-in
   C— 77.0 lbs-in

2. What is the maximum amount of fuel that may be aboard the airplane on takeoff if it is loaded as follows?

	Weight lbs	Moment/ 1,000
Empty weight	1,350	51.5
Pilot and front passenger	340	—
Rear passengers	310	—
Baggage	45	—
Oil 8 qts	15	-0.2

   A— 24 gal
   B— 34 gal
   C— 40 gal

3. What is the maximum amount of baggage that may be loaded aboard the airplane for the CG to remain within the loading envelope?

	Weight lbs	Moment/ 1,000
Empty weight	1,350	51.5
Pilot and front passenger	250	—
Rear passengers	400	—
Baggage	—	—
Fuel 30 gal	—	—
Oil 8 qts	15	-0.2

   A— 120 lbs
   B— 105 lbs
   C— 90 lbs

4. Calculate the moment of the airplane and determine which category is applicable.

	Weight lbs	Moment/ 1,000
Empty weight	1,350	51.5
Pilot and front passenger	310	—
Rear passengers	96	—
Fuel 38 gal	—	—
Oil, 8 qt	—	-0.2

   A— 79.2, utility category.
   B— 80.8, utility category.
   C— 81.2, normal category.

Use Figure 8-8 and 8-9 (on Pages 8–8 and 8–9) for review problems 5, 6, and 7:

5. Determine if the airplane weight and balance are within limits.

    Front seat occupants ....340 lbs
    Rear seat occupants ....295 lbs
    Fuel..44 gal
    Baggage ....56 lbs

    A— Within limits.
    B— 20 lbs overweight, CG within limits.
    C— Weight within limits, CG out of limits forward.

6. Which action can adjust the airplane's weight to maximum gross weight and the CG within limits for takeoffs?

    Front seat occupants ....425 lbs
    Rear seat occupants ....300 lbs
    Fuel, main tanks ....44 gal

    A— Drain 12 gallons of fuel.
    B— Drain 9 gallons of fuel.
    C— Transfer 12 gallons of fuel from the main tanks to the auxiliary tanks.

7. What effect does a 35-gallon fuel burn have on the weight and balance if the airplane weighed 2,890 pounds and the moment/100 was 2,452 at takeoff?

    A— Weight is reduced by 210 lbs and the CG is unaffected
    B— Weight is reduced to 2,680 lbs and the CG moves forward.
    C— Weight is reduced by 210 lbs and the CG is aft of limits.

8. After takeoff, which airspeed would permit the pilot to gain the most altitude in a given period of time?

    A— Cruising climb speed.
    B— Best rate-of-climb speed.
    C— Best angle-of-climb speed.

9. Which combination of atmospheric conditions will reduce aircraft takeoff and climb performance?

    A— Low temperature, low relative humidity, and low density altitude.
    B— High temperature, low relative humidity, and low density altitude.
    C— High temperature, high relative humidity, and high density altitude.

10. How can pressure altitude be determined?

    A— Set the field elevation in the altimeter setting window and read the indicated altitude.
    B— Set the altimeter to zero and read the value in the altimeter setting window.
    C— Set 29.92 in the altimeter setting window and read the indicated altitude.

11. (Refer to Figure 8-18 on Page 8–17.) What fuel flow should a pilot expect at 11,000 feet on a standard day with 65 percent maximum continuous power?

    A— 10.6 gallons per hour.
    B— 11.2 gallons per hour.
    C— 11.8 gallons per hour.

12. What effect does higher density altitude have on propeller efficiency?

    A— Increased efficiency due to less friction on the propeller blades.
    B— Reduced efficiency because the propeller exerts less force than at lower density altitudes.
    C— Increased efficiency because the propeller exerts less force on the thinner air.

13. An airplane is usually affected by ground effect at what height above the surface?

    A— Between 100 and 200 feet above the surface in calm wind conditions.
    B— Less than half of the airplane's wingspan above the surface.
    C— Twice the length of the airplane's wingspan above the surface.

14. Which adverse effect must a pilot be aware of as a result of the phenomenon of ground effect during takeoff?

   A— Difficulty in getting airborne even though airspeed is sufficient for normal takeoff.

   B— Becoming airborne before reaching recommended takeoff speed.

   C— Settling back to the surface immediately after becoming airborne.

15. If you plan to land at an airport where the elevation is 7,500 feet, the indicated approach airspeed should be

   A— the same as that used at a sea level airport.

   B— lower than that used at a sea level airport.

   C— higher than that used at a sea level airport.

16. As altitude increases, the indicated airspeed at which a given airplane stalls in a particular configuration will

   A— decrease as the true airspeed decreases.

   B— decrease as the true airspeed increases.

   C— remain the same as at low altitude.

17. Of what practical value is pressure altitude?

   A— To use on all aircraft performance charts since the charts are based on pressure altitude.

   B— To use for obstacle clearance at higher altitudes where accurate altimeter settings are not available.

   C— To use for computer solutions to determine density altitude, true altitude, true airspeed, etc.

18. Determine the approximate ground roll distance for takeoff under the following conditions. *See Figure 8-12 on Page 8–12.*

OAT ....95°F
Pressure altitude .... 2,000 feet
Takeoff weight....................................2,500 lbs
Wind (headwind)...............................20 knots

   A— 650 feet

   B— 800 feet

   C— 1,000 feet

19. What effect, if any, does high humidity have on aircraft performance?

   A— It increases performance.

   B— It decreases performance.

   C— It has no effect on performance.

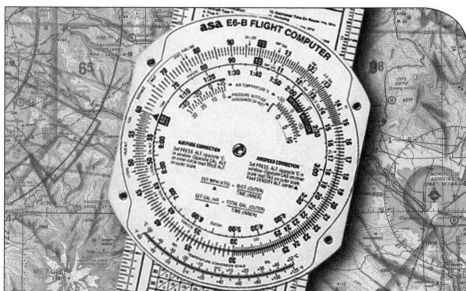

Enroute Flight

There are those who say that *real* VFR pilots navigate by a system of pilotage, ignoring the lure of electronic navigation. They lay out a course on an aeronautical chart and direct the flight of their aircraft along that course by reference to the terrain. Pilots *plan* their flights by dead reckoning. That statement deserves some explanation: in the days of sail, mariners kept track of their position as accurately as they could by estimating their speed and the effects of wind and current and having a "deduced reckoning" of where they had traveled since their last known position. They logged the result as "ded. reckoning." The airplane pilot of today lays out a course line, allows for wind and magnetic errors, derives a heading and a ground speed and estimates a time of arrival at the destination. That is dead reckoning—the planning phase. Unlike the sailor, the VFR pilot can maintain a visual track over the ground and pass over charted reference points. That is pilotage. From the early days, "pilot" has meant "navigator." Pilotage and dead reckoning are the only methods of navigation available to recreational pilots—without an instructor's endorsement, they are limited to trips of less than 50 nautical miles and cannot use electronic navigation aids. But they should read the section on the Global Positioning System in Lesson 10 (Page 10–13) anyway.

Aeronautical Charts

You will use three types of charts as a VFR pilot. The sectional chart is the one used most frequently because at roughly 8 nautical miles per inch, it affords sufficient detail for navigation by landmarks while retaining a manageable size. There are 38 sectionals covering the continental U.S., plus three Canadian provinces in the Northeast, 16 more for Alaska, and one for Hawaii. New charts are published every six months.

Sectionals show roads, freeways, railroads, power lines, lakes, rivers, terrain contours, and populated areas. Airports shown on sectional charts include public, private, military, and those to be used only in an emergency. Boundaries of controlled airspace are indicated by color tint and a variety of symbols. Before you take your checkride, become familiar with the sectional chart legend because knowing your way around a sectional will play an important role in the oral exam.

World Aeronautical Charts (WAC), at 16 nautical miles per inch, are great for really long cross-country flights because they cover more ground, but there is considerably less detail. There are 14 WAC charts that cover the U.S. and the Caribbean. Boundaries of controlled airspace are not shown. They are revised annually.

Terminal area charts are published for the busiest airports...those with Class B airspace (discussed later in this lesson). Their 4-miles-per inch scale makes them quite detailed, and properly so: you must know where you are when flying in congested airspace. For VFR pilots transiting the Class B airspace, there is a "VFR Flyways Planning Chart" on the reverse side. Revised charts are issued every six months.

The Airport/Facility Directory is issued every 56 days, and includes information not found in any other publication. In Lesson 4, I noted that the A/FD includes an Aeronautical Chart Bulletin. Now look at the chart revision frequencies noted above...the shortest is six months. What if a cell tower has been erected since the last issuance of the sectional chart you are using? What if an airport shown as uncontrolled on your chart now has an operating control tower? What if the control tower is shown on your chart but the tower frequency has changed? Unless you refer to the A/FD's Aeronautical Chart Bulletin, you will be flying blind. Every year, pilots get themselves into trouble by using out-of-date charts. Don't be one of them.

Having said that, there is no provision in Part 91 that requires you to carry any charts at all, recent or outdated. There are a number of online sources that you can refer to. Keeping in mind that web addresses come and go without notice, here are some useful URLs: www.aeronav.faa.gov is the official FAA source (from that main page go to "Free Digital Products"). Unfortunately, because sectionals are large and consumer-level printers are small, you have to print out several individual charts and tape them together. Among unofficial sources are www.flyagogo.net, www.skyvectors.com, and www.aopa.org/airports (AOPA membership not required). You can "fly" your proposed trip using Google Earth, checking out visual checkpoints along the way, and you can look at the area around your destination by using www.runwayfinder.com or www.ourairports.com; www.aopa.org/airports also includes Google map of the airport (and weather, and frequencies and just about everything else).

Geographical Coordinates

The sailor who "dead reckons" a voyage across untracked waters needs to be familiar with latitude and longitude—you do not. You will use latitude-longitude coordinates with some advanced radio navigation systems such as GPS, but lat-long coordinates do not play a large part in practical VFR flying. You will be using the lat-long lines on your WAC or sectional chart, however, so a brief explanation is in order.

Figure 9-1 shows **parallels** of latitude marching upward from the Equator (0° latitude) to the Poles (90° North or South latitude). If you slice a globe along lines of latitude, the slices get progressively smaller toward the poles, so distance measurements along latitude lines are useless.

Lines of longitude are called **meridians**, and divide the earth from pole to pole, the 0° meridian passing through Greenwich, England. Meridians are numbered eastward across Europe and Asia and westward across the Atlantic Ocean and the Americas until the 180° meridian is reached in mid-Pacific. The continental United States lies roughly between 70° and 125° West longitude and between 26° and 49° North latitude. Meridians are **Great Circles**: if you slice a globe along meridians, all of the slices will be the same size. All meridians are the same length: 10,600 nautical miles from Pole to Pole, 60 nautical miles per degree.

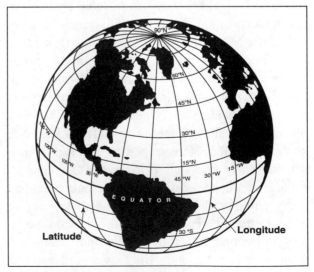

Figure 9-1. Meridians and parallels

Each degree is further divided into 60 minutes, and this makes it possible to measure distance accurately: one minute of latitude equals one **nautical mile** when measured along a line of longitude toward either pole.

As you look at your aeronautical chart, lines of longitude and latitude are at right angles. As you look at a globe, however, lines of longitude converge toward the poles. Because there is some unavoidable distortion of scale between the bottom and the top of an aeronautical chart, you should make course measurements as close as possible to the mid-latitude portion of the chart.

On the excerpt of the Seattle sectional chart, find the Easton State airport (**A**). Count up 15 minutes from the latitude line marked 47° to find the latitude of Easton State. Count left 11 minutes from the longitude line marked 121° to find the longitude of Easton State. Its geographic position is 47°15' 15" north,

121° 11' 15" west. You don't need to be any more accurate than the nearest minute in order to locate an airport using latitude and longitude. The geographic position of all airports is found in the A/FD.

Time

The measurement of time is an integral part of air navigation. Before leaving the discussion of longitude and the 0° meridian, the subject of time zones and time conversions should be covered. The only rational way to have flight times and weather information apply across the country and around the world is to have a single time reference. That reference is the time at Greenwich, England (on the 0° line of longitude). Once referred to as Greenwich Mean Time the time standard is now called Universal Coordinated Time (UTC). Each 15° of longitude east or west of Greenwich marks a one hour time difference. Figure 9-2 shows the time differences across the United States with a legend for time conversion

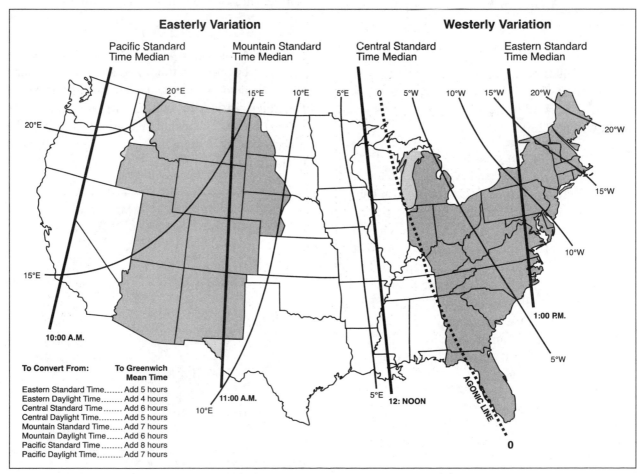

Figure 9-2. Time conversion (also showing magnetic variation)

to and from Universal Coordinated Time, or **Zulu time**. Zulu is the phonetic identifier for the letter Z; in the 24-hour clock system UTC is shown as 0800Z, 2200Z, etc. You should become familiar with time zone conversions for your area of operations. Here are two time conversion problems to illustrate:

An aircraft departs an airport in the Central Standard time zone at 0930 CST for a 2-hour flight to an airport located in the mountain standard time zone. What should the landing time be?

There are two ways of approaching this problem. First, according to the time difference chart, at the departure time of 0930 CST it is 0830 MST, and a 2 hour flight should land at 1030 MST. The second method is to add 2 hours to 0930 CST to get the CST landing time at the destination. (Forget to set your watch back?) Subtract the one hour time difference to get 1030 MST.

An aircraft departs an airport in the Pacific Standard time zone at 1030 PST for a 4-hour flight to an airport located in the Central time zone. At what ZULU time should the landing be?

What is Zulu time at departure? The chart says that to convert PST to UTC you must add 8 hours, so takeoff time is 1830Z. Arrival time after a 4-hour flight will be 2230Z.

Flight service station personnel and air traffic controllers use Zulu time, and will be reluctant to do time conversions for you. (Of course, you can buy a watch with dual time zones!) If you are planning a departure for 1800 local time and there is a forecast for thunderstorms after 2100Z at your destination, you will have to know time conversion to be able to relate that to your estimated time of arrival. As a new pilot, you will probably stay within one time zone or possibly travel between two time zones. Just remember that, for example, you live in the "plus 5" time zone (plus 4 in the summer), and conversions will come easily to you.

Statute and Nautical Mile Scale

Navigators on the sea or in the air find the use of nautical miles for distance measurement convenient, because a nautical mile is 6,000 feet (really 6,080, but that complicates things) and is also one minute of latitude. When you counted up 15 minutes to locate the latitude of Easton State airport, you counted up 15 nautical miles. You will find mileage scales for both nautical and **statute miles** on aeronautical charts and plotters (the distance between VORs in nautical miles is printed on sectional charts). The FAA uses nautical miles for all distance measurements except visibility, which is measured in statute miles. Airspeed indicators are calibrated in **knots** (nautical miles per hour) only or in knots and MPH; you will find a conversion scale on your flight computer. *Winds are always given in knots,* so you must be sure that you are dealing with like units when flight planning. The CX-2 Pathfinder electronic calculator contains conversion programs, including statute/nautical and nautical/statute miles.

Magnetic Variation

For flight planning purposes you must recognize that although the lines of latitude and longitude on charts are neatly perpendicular and relate to the **True North Pole** there is nothing in your airplane that relates to True North. The magnetic compass indicates the direction to the magnetic North Pole, which is in northern Canada (Figure 9-3).

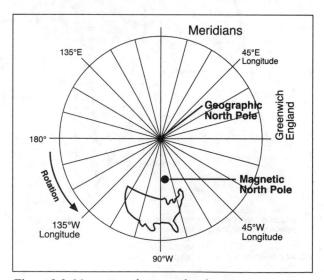

Figure 9-3. *Magnetic and true north poles*

You must take the **variation** between true north and magnetic north into account when flight planning.

Figure 9-4 shows **isogonic lines**, or lines of equal magnetic variation, across the continent. Along the line which passes through Chicago and Key West, a pilot looking toward the North Star or the True North Pole will also be looking toward the magnetic North Pole, and there will be no variation. That line of zero variation is called the **agonic line.** East or West of that line, the angle between true and magnetic north increases. A pilot in Los Angeles who measures a course line on an aeronautical chart in relation to the longitude lines (or true north) must subtract 14° from that true course to get a magnetic course (*"East is least"*), while a pilot in Philadelphia will add 10° (*"West is best"*). You will determine the true course by using your navigation plotter.

The variation on your sectional chart is almost certainly out-of-date. The isogonic lines on current sectionals were last updated in 2005 and will not be updated until 2011. Variations for navaids and airports are "assigned" and do not reflect the actual variation; variation for a VOR or airport can be up to three degrees different from actual variation. Next best source for variation is a current Airport/Facility Directory. You can get current variation information for airports along your route by going to this internet URL* (shown in footnote).

* www.ngdc.noaa.gov/geomagmodels/Declination.jsp

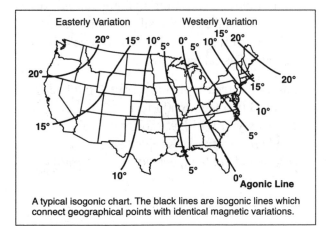

A typical isogonic chart. The black lines are isogonic lines which connect geographical points with identical magnetic variations.

Figure 9-4. *Isogonic lines*

Using the Navigation Plotter

A navigation plotter combines a protractor with mileage scales, and they are available in many forms. You use the protractor to measure the angle between a line of latitude or longitude and your course line. Refer to the Seattle sectional chart excerpt at the back of the book. Draw a line from the center of the airport symbol at Easton (**A**) to the center of the airport symbol at Wenatchee (**H**). Align the straight edge of your plotter with this course line and slide the plotter until the hole is over a vertical line of longitude; the angle should be approximately 78 degrees, indicating that the true course from Easton to Wenatchee is 078° and that the course for the return trip is 258°.

Deviation

A course, whether identified as true or magnetic, is only a line on a chart linking departure point and destination. For flight planning purposes, you must allow for magnetic influences in the airplane itself and for the effect of wind drift. Because your airplane has some iron and steel components which are affected by the earth's magnetic field, and because it contains wiring which creates a magnetic field within the airplane itself, the airplane's magnetic compass develops an error called **deviation** which varies with aircraft heading. Looking back at Figure 9-4, it is apparent that the heading of the airplane has nothing to do with magnetic variation—a pilot in Seattle must apply a 20° easterly variation regardless of the direction of flight. Because magnetic deviation is unique to each airplane and is dependent on heading, a compass correction card (Figure 9-5) must be prepared by accurately lining up the airplane on known magnetic headings, checking the magnetic compass reading, and recording the deviation error for each heading. Small adjustment magnets are provided so that the error can be minimized.

FOR (MH)	0	30	60	90	120	150	180	210	240	270	300	330
STEER (CH)	2	28	56	88	120	152	183	212	240	268	298	328

Figure 9-5. *Compass correction card*

This compass correction table is originally made at the factory but should be re-checked by a mechanic whenever cockpit equipment installations are made. When a pilot has applied variation and deviation to a measured true course, the result is the compass course:

True ± Variation = Magnetic ± Deviation = Compass

Variation is shown on navigational charts to the nearest one-half degree. You will find that rounding off to the nearest whole degree will speed up your calculations without affecting accuracy. If you make long flights over water or featureless terrain, deviation and compass course will be very important to you, and an accurate compass correction card may be a lifesaver. Pilots who fly by reference to the surface (pilotage) will make little use of compass heading except to adjust their gyroscopic heading indicators.

Any difference between an airplane's planned **course** and its **track** over the ground is caused by **wind drift**. Always compute the **wind correction angle** first, and then apply variation and deviation, as National Weather Service winds aloft forecasts are always referenced to True North.

Correcting for Wind Drift

Figure 9-6 shows the effect of wind drift on an airplane's flight path if no corrective action is taken. The wind correction angle necessary to offset the wind drift will allow the airplane's track over the ground to agree with the planned course. Determining wind correction angle with a known wind direction, wind velocity, true course and true airspeed is a trigonometry problem.

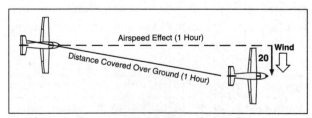

Figure 9-6. *The effect of wind*

Solving the Wind Drift Triangle

The **wind triangle** consists of four known values and two unknowns. You know the angle between true north and your course (true course), and the angle between true north and the wind direction; you also know your true airspeed and the wind velocity. With these values, you can construct a triangle to solve for the unknowns: ground speed and true heading. Refer to Figure 9-7.

Wind direction..320° true
Wind velocity..30 knots
True course...060°
True airspeed..100 knots

The vertical line represents true north. Line A-B represents the true wind, and is drawn downwind—a wind from 320° "blows" the line to 140°. The length of line A-B represents the wind velocity in convenient units. Using a protractor, draw a line of indefinite length from point A so that the angle represents the true course as measured on your chart. A line with a length representing the true airspeed (100 knots) is drawn from point B to intersect the true course line at point C. The distance from point A to point C is the ground speed, (103 knots) and the angle that line B-C makes with the true north line (043°) is the true heading. The wind correction angle (17°) is the difference between the true course and the true heading. Magnetic variation must be applied to convert true heading to magnetic heading, and deviation applied to that to get compass heading. Very few pilots draw wind triangles, because the triangle can be solved mechanically and electronically much more quickly, but it's a great way to really teach yourself the fundamentals of aerial navigation.

Winds aloft forecasts are only available for selected altitudes: 3,000 feet, 6,000 feet, 9,000 feet, etc. In most cases you will have to interpolate for your planned cruise altitude. Keep in mind that these are forecasts, and don't expect extreme accuracy.

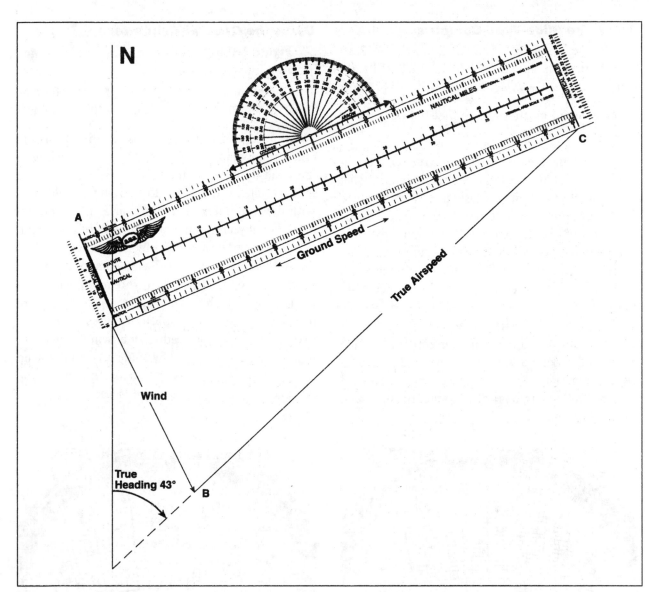

Figure 9-7. *Wind triangle*

Using The Slide-Type Computer

True course...230°
True airspeed.. 140 MPH
Wind.. 150° at 17 knots

(Convert wind or airspeed so that both are in the same units. 17 knots = 19.6 MPH)

Orient the rotatable disk so that the true wind direction (150°) is at the true index. From the center, count *up* the number of units representing wind velocity, 19.6 (Figure 9-8). Rotate the disk so that the true course (230°) is aligned with the true index; note that the wind dot is now in the correct relationship to the course. Move the slide until the wind dot falls on the speed arc representing the true airspeed 140 (Figure 9-9). You have solved the wind triangle: the ground speed (135 MPH) is read directly under the center grommet and the wind correction angle (8° left) is read under the wind dot. A left wind correction angle is subtracted from the true course and a right wind correction angle is added to the true course to get true heading.

Using the Circular Computer

See Figure 9-10:

True course...115°
True airspeed...90 knots
Wind.. 240° at 38 knots

Make a wind dot where the wind direction line crosses the wind velocity arc. Rotate the disk with the wind dot to align the true course with the true index; rotate the outer disk to align the true airspeed with the true index. The position of the wind dot now shows you the number of knots of crosswind component and headwind/tailwind component. Find the number of knots of crosswind component on the outer scale; opposite it you will read the wind correction angle. If the crosswind component is more than 10% of the true airspeed, use the larger of the two angles. Apply the headwind/tailwind component to the true airspeed to get ground speed. If the wind correction angle exceeds 5° read the "Effective True Airspeed" to the left of the true index.

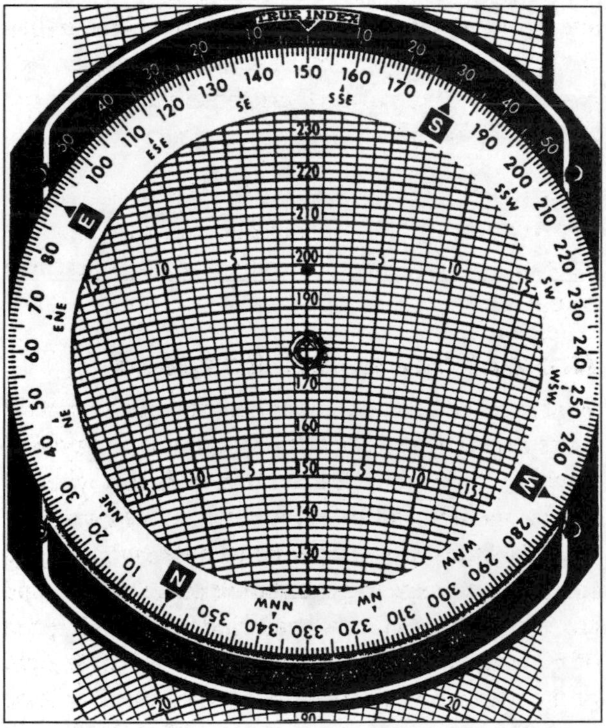

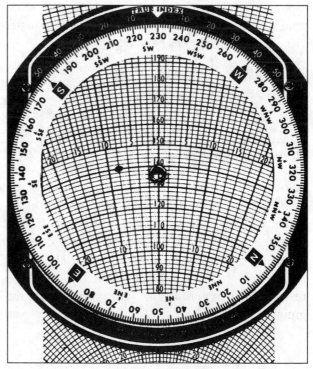

Figure 9-8

Figure 9-9

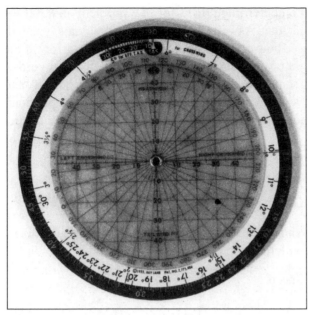

Figure 9-10. *Plotting and finding ground speed and wind correction angle*

Right crosswind component = 31 knots
Tailwind component = 21 knots
Wind correction angle is greater than 10°

Opposite 20° on "Effective True Airspeed" scale read 84.5 knots. Add 21 knot tailwind to TAS to get ground speed of 105.5.

Accuracy

Before relying too heavily on the results of wind problems, you must consider that the data you are working with is not precise. The National Weather Service wind direction forecasts are in 10° increments and can be off as much as 45° (for wind velocities forecast to be less than 25 knots) before a corrected forecast is issued. You can calculate headings to one-half of one degree but you cannot fly that accurately. Also, most pilots understand and accept deviation error in the magnetic compass but ignore it until their heading indicator fails. It is for these reasons that you must follow your progress over the ground visually.

The CX-2 Pathfinder Electronic Calculator

ASA's CX-2 Pathfinder electronic calculator offers a quick convenient means of solving wind and other navigation problems.

Time-speed-distance problems can be solved with a four-function pocket calculator, and you will learn how in this lesson. Without a table of trigonometric functions, a four-function calculator cannot do wind triangle solutions.

Personal Computers

A pilot with a computer at home or office can buy any one of a myriad of programs designed to make flight planning quick, easy, and accurate. These programs vary from the inexpensive, which read out only heading, ground speed, and time en route, to the very costly programs which not only provide flight planning information for several airplanes (so you can decide which one is most cost-efficient for the trip) but what kind of fuel and food service is available at the destination. AOPA members have access to a flight planner on the organization's website; www.aeroplanner.com is typical of free online flight planning programs. The best computer programs (regardless of cost) are those which print out a flight log for you to take along.

Subscribers to DUAT Service (*see* Lesson 7), EAA, and AOPA members also have access to flight planning and weather information through their personal computers.

Ground Speed vs. Airspeed

When you drive your automobile for one hour at 60 miles per hour, you can be fairly certain that you will travel 60 miles during that hour. In flight, whether or not one hour at 60 miles per hour will actually cover 60 miles will be determined by the wind. If you somehow manage to get airborne under control and are flying into a 60 MPH headwind with an airspeed of 60 MPH, you aren't going to make it out of sight of the airport: your speed over the ground will be zero. This is an extreme example, although pilots in the Great Plains states have a fund of stories about airplanes "flying" in strong winds that prove that it can happen. You need to develop an understanding of the airspeed/ground speed relationship on a more normal basis.

First, forget the comparison with the automobile and standardize all speed measurements in knots: the National Weather Service provides wind velocity information in knots and confusion will result if you mix units of measurement. The General Aviation Manufacturer's Association has standardized on knots for airspeed indicators. The same flight computer solution that you used to determine wind correction angle gave you a ground speed figure. You entered true airspeed and true wind direction and velocity and the computer read out ground speed. You determine true airspeed by reference to cruise performance charts (Lesson 8) or by applying the 2% per 1,000 feet rule to your indicated airspeed (Lesson 3).

No matter how you arrived at the ground speed figure, you must use it in combination with the measured distance to the destination to determine time en route.

It is important to make frequent ground speed checks while en route to ensure that your actual ground speed agrees with your planned ground speed. Remember, the winds you used in flight planning were *forecast* winds. In planning your flight you must be sure that upon arrival at your destination you have at least 30 minutes fuel left on board in the daytime and 45 minutes reserve fuel at night. Learn to think in terms of *time in your tanks* instead of distance. The Owner's Manual may say that you have a range of 450 miles, but if you are using 10 gallons per hour and have 35 gallons on board, you will only stay airborne for 3½ hours no matter how far you have managed to fly. Have in mind a clock time at which the wheels must be on the ground, and observe it—even if you must land short of your destination to refuel.

Rate Problems: Time-Speed Distance, Fuel Burn

Rate problems are solved on the slide rule side of your flight computer: the inner, rotatable disk represents time, and the outer, fixed disk represents miles or gallons. The numbers on both disks must be interpreted with common sense, because you must provide the decimal points. For instance, 30 on the

computer might be 3 for one problem and 300 for another. As you try some sample problems, you will see how common sense is applied. The arrow at the 60 on the rotatable disk is the speed or rate arrow (some instructors call it the speedometer needle), and you will use it for all calculations of miles per hour, knots, or gallons per hour: read it as "something per hour." The computer lets you mechanically solve for any single unknown in these equations:

Distance = speed x time
Gallons = fuel burn rate x time

The computer presents the information in this form, with time on the inner, rotatable disc:

$$\frac{\text{Speed}}{\text{or}} \quad = \quad \frac{\text{Distance}}{\text{or}}$$
$$\frac{\text{GPH}}{60} \quad \quad \frac{\text{Gallons}}{\text{Time}}$$

If you determine that the distance between two checkpoints is 23 nautical miles, and your elapsed time between the checkpoints is 14.3 minutes (14 minutes and 18 seconds), set 14.3 on the inner time scale opposite 23 on the outer distance scale and read 96.5 opposite the speed arrow: your ground speed is 96.5 knots. It couldn't very well be 9.65 or 965 knots, could it? Finding 14.3 and 23 in this problem isn't too difficult because numbers between 1 and 99 are read directly. *See* Figure 9-11.

In preflight planning you find that the distance to your destination is 248 NM; you learn from doing a wind problem that your predicted ground speed is 114 knots. Put the speed arrow opposite 114 (now the 10 on the outside scale is read as 100, the 11 as 110, etc.) and find 248 on the outside scale. It is between 24 and 25, now read as 240 and 250. On the inner, rotatable (time) disk opposite 248, read the estimated time en route as 132 minutes or 2:12. When elapsed time is the unknown, be careful not to confuse minutes with tenths of hours. *See* Figure 9-12.

The cruise charts tell you that your fuel consumption rate will be 8.2 gallons per hour—how much fuel will you burn on the 248 mile trip? Place the rate arrow opposite 8.2 (between 80 and 90) and find 2:12 on the inside, time scale. Across from 2:12 (or 132) you will find 18.0 on the outside scale which now represents gallons. Make sense? Just over 2 hours at 8 gallons an hour has to be just over 16 gallons. Always check computer problems "in your head" to make sure that you are in the ballpark. *See* Figure 9-13.

Time-speed-distance and fuel problems can be worked out using a typical four-function calculator by cross-multiplying and then dividing. Try the three problems above with your pocket calculator. First, remember that the speed/rate arrow represents 60 and is always at the lower left. Time is always at the lower right. See the first problem you did with the slide-rule-type computer set up for a four-function calculator in Figure 9-11. Just set the problem up on your calculator as you would on the flight computer, cross-multiply and divide. But don't throw your flight computer away—you need it for density altitude, true altitude, and true airspeed problems, plus conversions.

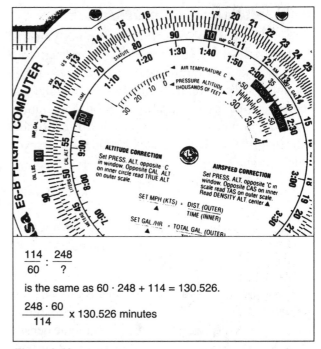

$$\frac{114}{60} : \frac{248}{?}$$

is the same as $60 \cdot 248 + 114 = 130.526$.

$$\frac{248 \cdot 60}{114} \times 130.526 \text{ minutes}$$

Figure 9-12

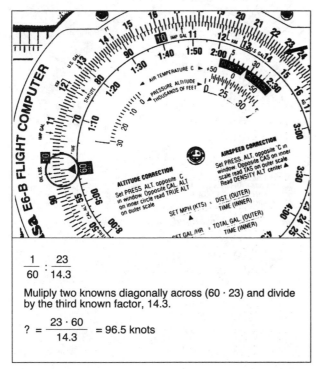

$$\frac{1}{60} : \frac{23}{14.3}$$

Muliply two knowns diagonally across ($60 \cdot 23$) and divide by the third known factor, 14.3.

$$? = \frac{23 \cdot 60}{14.3} = 96.5 \text{ knots}$$

Figure 9-11

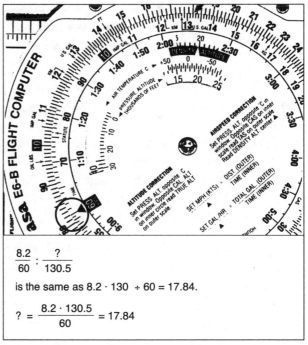

$$\frac{8.2}{60} : \frac{?}{130.5}$$

is the same as $8.2 \cdot 130 \div 60 = 17.84$.

$$? = \frac{8.2 \cdot 130.5}{60} = 17.84$$

Figure 9-13

Miscellaneous Solutions

Around the edge of your flight computer you will find arrows with NAUT and STAT for mileage conversion, and TAS for airspeed calculations. On the rotatable disk there are windows for calculations requiring input of pressure altitude and temperature. Some computers have a window for true altitude, others only provide for density altitude and airspeed calculations.

For mileage conversions, place the known value under the appropriate arrow, NAUT or STAT, and find the converted value under the other arrow. Statute miles = nautical miles x 1.15; statute mile x .87 = nautical miles (Figure 9-14).

Density altitude and airspeed problems use the same window (Figure 9-15). You need to know the air temperature and pressure altitude to compute density altitude. True airspeed calculations require air temperature, pressure altitude, and indicated airspeed. Convert temperature to Celsius (C°) if it is in Fahrenheit (F°), and place the temperature opposite the pressure altitude in the window marked for airspeed and density altitude.

The markings are very small and extreme accuracy is difficult to achieve. When you have the temperature and pressure altitude properly set you will find the density altitude in the window marked for it. Opposite the indicated airspeed on the rotatable scale, you will find true airspeed on the outside scale. Figure 9-16 shows a solution for a temperature of -10° and a pressure altitude of 7,500 feet.

The density altitude window indicates 6,300 feet. If your indicated airspeed is 120 knots and you want to know true airspeed, don't move anything—just look opposite 120 on the inner scale and read 131.5 on the outer scale.

Use common sense. Question wind correction angles of 30° to 40° or more and headwind/tailwind components that seem out of line. Use ground speed checkpoints that are 10 miles or more apart so that a small timing error will not have a major effect on your calculations, and choose checkpoints that allow accurate timing: roads, railroads, or shorelines make better checkpoints than city limits or tops of hills. Pick out a prominent landmark in your direction of

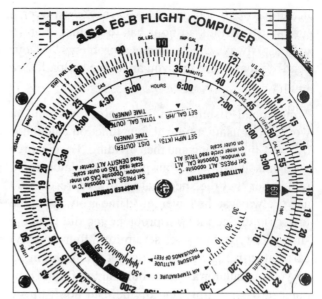

Figure 9-14. *220 Nautical = 253 Statute*

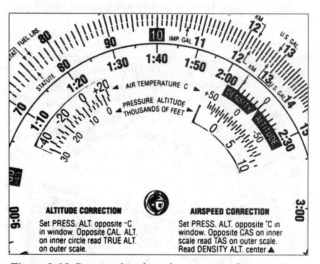

Figure 9-15. *Density altitude and true airspeed*

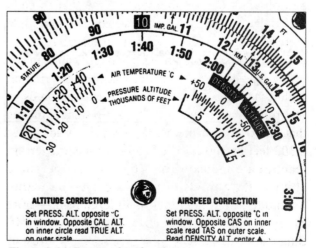

Figure 9-16. *Density altitude solution*

travel that you can see from pattern altitude, and fly toward that landmark as soon as practicable. Pilots have taken off without resetting their directional gyros to agree with their magnetic compasses (or the runway number), and have been way off course before they got out of sight of the airport. Don't rely on your flight plan information until you are over that landmark.

Always orient a chart to your direction of flight, and learn to read charts upside down, so that visual checkpoints appear in correct relationship to the nose of your airplane. Finally, if you draw a line on your chart from departure point to destination, follow the line with your finger, and fly your airplane over every visual feature (road, drive-in theater, lake, etc.) along that line, you can't possibly get lost. Above all, do not place too much reliance on GPS—you are learning to be a VFR pilot in the tradition of Lindbergh, not a slave to electronics.

Chart Reading

In other lessons you will learn how to look at your aeronautical chart to determine radio frequencies and airspace designations. To fly by pilotage you must be able to quickly and accurately identify ground reference points visually. Fold out the Seattle sectional chart excerpt at the back of the book; refer to it and its legend as you read this section. (Recreational pilots must be able to identify Class B, C, and D airspace in order to avoid it, unless this restriction has been removed by an instructor's endorsement.)

The importance of knowing the height of terrain and obstructions is obvious. Notice that in each rectangle formed by lines of latitude and longitude there is a large blue number with an adjacent smaller number. This represents the height above mean sea level of the highest terrain or man-made obstruction within that rectangle in thousands and hundreds of feet plus a safety margin. 8^3, for instance, means that you will clear the highest obstacle if you fly at 8,300 feet or higher. The heights of specific terrain features are indicated by a dot and the measured altitude; the altitude of the highest terrain within a latitude-longitude block is in large print—note Mount Rainier at the bottom of the chart and Mt. Stuart at 47°28'N 120°54'W (see letter "N" west of airport H). You will notice that the highest obstacle is at least 100 feet below the 8^3 if man-made, and

at least 300 feet below if a natural obstruction. This is for added safety. Man-made obstructions such as radio and television towers have two numbers adjacent to them. The top number (in bold italics) is the height of the top of the obstruction above mean sea level, and is the most meaningful number to you in choosing an altitude in that area—add at least 1,000 feet if you plan to fly directly over the obstruction. The number in parentheses is the actual height of the structure. Towers which are more than 1,000 feet in height (which usually require supporting guy wires that are virtually invisible) have a special symbol as shown in the chart legend. They are common in the Midwest, where they enhance television coverage in relatively flat terrain. The dot at the base of the symbol represents the exact location of the obstruction. The group obstruction symbol (two symbols close together) means that there are two *or more* towers. There are several obstruction symbols, both single and group, north and west of Seattle-Tacoma airport.

Freeways, highways, and railroads are excellent references. Notice that major freeways are identified with their route numbers—Interstate 90 crosses the chart from Seattle to the lower right corner. You can often orient yourself by noticing an interchange or an obvious jog in a road, or by the relationship between a road and some other physical feature. Because they are centered in large right-of-way areas, power lines are just as useful as roads—you can see the cleared right-of-way much further than you can see the powerlines themselves.

Drive-in theaters and racetracks make good orientation points. Be wary of lakes—in a dry year the lake you are looking for might not be the same shape as indicated on the chart—or may not exist at all!

Do not rely on the city limits depicted so clearly in yellow on sectional charts—from the air, city limits are impossible to identify.

Changes in elevation are depicted with contour lines. On the sectional chart excerpt you can see how tightly packed the contour lines are in the Cascade Mountains. Notice the interval between contour lines. The lines are every 500 feet on sectionals and every 1,000 feet on WAC charts.

Mountain passes are indicated by a pair of back-to-back parentheses—look about an inch to the left of airport **A** on the sectional chart excerpt to find Stampede Pass. These symbols do not indicate direction of flight, they simply point out that there is a pass. North of Stampede Pass, note the symbol at Snoqualmie Pass; if you fly northwest, the way the symbol is printed, you will fly into a box canyon. Always follow the natural terrain.

Always check your chart for markings that indicate parachute jumping areas (airport **G**) and low-lying cables across rivers and ravines. (Running into a skydiver or a power cable can ruin your whole day!) Where jumping is indicated, check the A/FD for details.

It is much easier to look at a prominent feature on the ground and then match it to a chart indication than it is to pick a landmark off the chart and then attempt to find that landmark on the ground. Work from the "big picture" to the chart, not the other way around.

Enroute Emergencies

When you have learned the basics of aircraft control and can fly a traffic pattern with confidence, your instructor will begin instruction in cross-country flight. Expect to hear "Where would you put it if the engine quit?" on a regular basis—this trains you to keep an eye on possible landing sites whenever you are flying. As you gain experience, your instructor will pull the throttle back to idle power and say "Engine failure—where are you going to put it?"

Engine failures due to mechanical causes are quite rare—engine stoppages are usually the result of running out of fuel (unforgivable sin) or mismanagement of the fuel system. Still, the wise pilot is always scanning the immediate area just in case. Altitude means not only a wider area from which to choose a landing spot but also more time for thinking and maneuvering, so if you fly low you are cheating yourself.

When choosing possible landing sites, remember that the airplane itself is expendable but the people inside are not. If you can reduce momentum by shedding wheels or wings against trees, bushes, or rocks, you will reduce the impact on passengers. A road should not be your first choice, because you do not see the wires, signs, and fenceposts until it is too late.

Many emergency landings would not have been necessary if the pilots had made precautionary landings when things started to unravel. There is nothing wrong with landing at an airport other than your destination airport if fuel is running low, or if the weather starts to close in. Far too many pilots have overflown airports where fuel was available, only to land in a field short of their destination. Don't let your ego write checks that your abilities can't cash.

What if you are simply disoriented? One of the best ways to run out of fuel is to fly around hoping to see something familiar or at least to see something that matches up with the chart, and realize too late that you no longer have enough fuel to reach safety. The rules are simple: if you are unsure of your location, Climb, Circle, Confess, and Comply. Climbing increases your range of action, your communications ability, and terrain clearance. Circling keeps you essentially in one location, not wandering all over the place. Confess your plight to anyone you can contact; setting 7700 on your transponder is the first step. As part of your flight planning, you should have noted the frequencies of air traffic control facilities along your route. Call "any station" on the International Distress Frequency, 121.5 MHz, and tell your story to whomever answers, then comply with any instructions you are given.

If you find yourself on top of a cloud deck and low on fuel, don't waste time looking for a hole. Call a radar facility (you should have noted the frequencies before takeoff—*see* Lesson 11), confess your situation, and ask for a radar descent through clouds. Admit that you are not instrument rated. Keep the wings level, using rudder only to make small heading changes if required, slow to flap extension speed and extend approach flaps, and reduce power to the magneto check setting (with full carb heat). This will set up a gentle descent. Concentrate on the attitude indicator and wait to break out of the clouds.

Don't expect a controller to understand your problem if you use words like "vacuum failure" or "static failure." Most controllers are not pilots, so using language that would be crystal-clear to another pilot would be useless. Instead, say something like "I can't keep the wings level" or "I can't maintain altitude."

There is an old wives' tale that a pilot who declares an emergency is inundated with a flood of paperwork when the emergency is over. Not true. The controllers who handle the situation might ask for a phone call to get the details, but the purpose of the call will not be to issue a violation. Getting lost is not a violation of FAA regulations.

Preparation for Flight Planning
(not applicable to recreational pilots)

As part of your practical test for the private pilot certificate, the examiner will ask you to plan a cross-country flight and prepare a flight log, such as Figure 11-10 (on Page 11–15), which is an FAA form. There are dozens of similar forms available from commercial sources, or you can just make up your own. Here is a checklist of items that should be included:

- The route of flight, with each leg identified by checkpoints or navigational aids.
- The magnetic course between checkpoints. Your flight log need only show the heading, but the examiner may want to see how you converted the true course to a magnetic course using variation and deviation, and how you determined the wind correction angle (Pages 9–4 to 9–9).
- The distance between checkpoints in nautical miles (Page 9–4).
- Your estimated ground speed for the leg (Pages 9–5 to 9–9). Again, do the calculations separately and put only the *answer* in the flight log, but expect to be asked how you made the calculations.
- Your estimated time between checkpoints, calculated by using the measured distance and estimated ground speed.
- Your estimate of the time you will pass over the next checkpoint. Leave this blank and update it in flight.

You will calculate "actual ground speed" when you measure the actual elapsed time between checkpoints and use the measured distance to solve the time-speed-distance problem. The only reason to write down the actual time between checkpoints is for when you and your instructor debrief after the trip is completed, but you should record the actual time over each checkpoint. I recommend that you write on the sectional chart itself rather than on the flight log—if you get disoriented you will be able to see the time at which you were over a known checkpoint. Then you can say, "Well, I was over Pine Lake ten minutes ago and I'm doing about a mile and a half a minute, so I must be within 15 miles of Pine Lake!"

Take advantage of technology and "fly" your planned route using Google Earth or the equivalent. Use www.runwayfinder.com or www.ourairports.com for a bird's-eye view of your destination and enroute airports.

Those are the "bare bones" of a flight log. Add anything else that you don't want to have to look up in a book, such as radio frequencies or runway orientation. Have available an airport diagram for both the departure and destination airports, to facilitate ground operations. Keep track of the times when you change tanks on the flight log as well.

What will you do if deteriorating weather or a passenger emergency causes you to divert to an enroute airport? (You'd be surprised how many examiners have "heart attacks" or create similar distractions just when you thought everything was going smoothly.) "You have a sick passenger. What is the direction to the nearest airport, how long will it take you to get there, and how will you contact the authorities?" Your flight log should list alternate airports and their associated frequencies, *just in case*. Learn to do an eyeball estimate of magnetic course using the compass rose around a convenient VOR symbol on the chart, and how to "guesstimate" distances at 8 miles to the inch—there won't be time to measure courses and distances accurately when the examiner is pretending to be dying.

Remember—cross-country trips are the reason you wanted to learn to fly in the first place. Make them fun, but cover all the bases.

The foregoing will apply if you are a recreational pilot undertaking the additional training required in order for an instructor to lift the 50 NM restriction.

Airspace

As you plan a cross-country flight, you know that the ability to maneuver in three dimensions makes you responsible for being aware at all times of your position, both geographic and vertical. You must ensure that you are always in compliance with the airspace regulations. These regulations are intended to keep airplanes safely separated and, in the case of VFR pilots, to provide minimum visibility and cloud clearance distances so that conflicting traffic can be seen in time for corrective action to be taken. "See and be seen" is the basis of safe operations in the **National Airspace System**.

Controlled vs. Class G (Uncontrolled) Airspace

You will encounter the terms controlled and uncontrolled airspace frequently, and you must not assume that flight in controlled airspace means that Big Brother will be watching you to detect violations, or that uncontrolled airspace is a no-man's land for flight. For your purposes as a VFR pilot, controlled and uncontrolled airspace refer to visibility and cloud clearance standards, nothing more. Controlled airspace is "controlled" to protect pilots flying under instrument flight rules from conflicts with pilots flying under visual flight rules; when a pilot operating under IFR pops out of a cloud, there should be enough visibility and cloud clearance to see and avoid a VFR flight. For this reason, you should accept the minimum visibility and cloud clearance restrictions discussed in this chapter as just that—minimums—and allow yourself a greater safety cushion whenever possible.

Controlled airspace includes Class A, B, C, D, and E airspace (Figure 9-17). Look at the sectional chart excerpt and notice the blue and magenta tints—they represent the horizontal boundaries of controlled airspace (Class A airspace begins at 18,000 feet MSL, and that is as high as a sectional chart goes). Blue is only used where it abuts Class G airspace, however.

At airports with instrument approach procedures, controlled airspace can start at the surface—each of these situations will be covered in detail later. Figure 9-17 will give you an idea of what to expect. As you can see, most controlled airspace is Class E.

On the Seattle sectional chart excerpt, follow the 072 radial of the Seattle VORTAC (**C**) eastward—it's the V-120 airway. Until you fly past TAGOR intersection and cross the magenta line, you are in Class E airspace if your airplane is at least 700 feet above the ground. The fact that the magenta tint fades in the direction of Seattle indicates that this floor applies in the entire area surrounded by the tint.

After you pass the magenta line flying eastward along the 072 degree radial, the floor of Class E airspace becomes 1,200 feet above the ground (no shading) and that situation remains until you get to the magenta dashed line around the Wenatchee VORTAC.

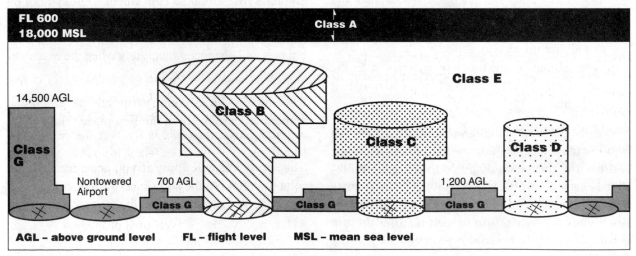

Figure 9-17. *Airspace classification*

Now look north and south of the 072 degree radial. If you turn to the north, you will cross a blue line that looks like a zipper into airspace labeled "9,500 MSL." Because the elevation of the terrain varies so rapidly in mountainous terrain, it would be impossible for you to know whether or not you were flying 1,200 feet above the surface; accordingly, the notation tells you that the floor of Class E airspace is 9,500 feet MSL, not 1,200 feet AGL, in the area bounded by the zipper lines.

You won't find any on the sectional chart excerpt, but there are places where Class G airspace extends from the surface to 14,000 feet (almost all are west of the Mississippi). Look for the solid edge of a blue vignetted line…the floor of controlled airspace on the shaded side is 1,200 feet above the surface, but the airspace on the solid-edge side is uncontrolled all the way up to 14,000 feet above sea level.

As you fly across the country, then, you will spend almost all of your time in controlled airspace; you must maintain at least 3 miles flight visibility, stay 500 feet below clouds and/or 1,000 feet above them, and maintain a horizontal distance from clouds of at least 2,000 feet. If you follow these simple rules you will not become a victim of general aviation's greatest killer, visual flight into deteriorating weather.

Three miles flight visibility sounds like more than enough, but when you are traveling over the ground at 90 knots you can see only two minutes ahead. Ask your instructor to take you up when visibility is restricted to three miles; try to go flying with your instructor when the visibility is only one mile, as it must be to fly under visual flight rules in uncontrolled airspace. Make sure that there is a qualified pilot in the other seat when you first experience restricted visibility—you may decide that your personal visibility minimum is five miles, a very wise decision. John F. Kennedy, Jr.'s fatal flight taught pilots and nonpilots alike that loss of visual reference to the horizon leads rapidly to loss of control, without the knowledge and training possessed by pilots who hold instrument ratings. Treat diminishing visibility as you would the edge of a cliff, a pit of poisonous snakes, or a river full of ravenous alligators—don't even get close.

Unless you are taking your flight training at an airport in the mountains, you will spend most of your time at altitudes below 10,000 feet MSL and the visibility and cloud clearance values above will apply. When you fly higher than 10,000 feet MSL, however, new rules apply. You will have no difficulty in remembering them if you keep in mind that there is no speed limit above that altitude. A cloud 2,000 feet away might hide a 240-knot turboprop or a 500-knot jet, so horizontal cloud clearance increases to 1 mile; these airplanes climb and descend at steep angles, so you must fly at least 1,000 feet above or below any clouds. Because of unrestricted speed, required flight visibility increases to 5 miles.

See the note on Page 5–14 about towers in Class G airspace.

Class A Airspace

Class A airspace exists from 18,000 feet MSL to Flight Level 600 (all altitudes above 18,000 feet are called Flight Levels; FL230 is 23,000 feet, more or less). To fly in Class A airspace you must be instrument rated and operating on an instrument clearance; there is no VFR flying in Class A airspace. If you have to climb higher than 18,000 feet to stay out of the clouds (got that oxygen handy?) you must call Air Traffic Control and declare an emergency to avoid getting a violation.

Class B Airspace

The most important thing for you to remember about Class B airspace is that you cannot operate within its boundaries unless you have a specific clearance from ATC to do so. Class B airspace (Figure 9-18) is shown on sectional and WAC charts by solid blue circles or arcs; each segment within the airspace is identified with what looks like a fraction. On the sectional chart excerpt the top of the fraction is 100, indicating that the top of Seattle's Class B airspace is 10,000 feet MSL; you can fly over the airspace at 10,500 feet without a clearance. If you are receiving radar flight following, don't let that fact trap you into violating Class B airspace—ask the controller "Am I cleared into the Class B?" to get the clearance on ATC's audio tape for your own protection. The use of VFR GPS waypoints (five letters, beginning with VP) will help you stay out of Class B airspace.

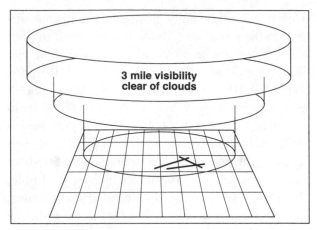

Figure 9-18. *Class B airspace*

The bottom of the fraction is the floor of the airspace in hundreds of feet; east of Bremerton National Airport (**D**) you can fly beneath the Class B airspace at 5,500 feet; west of Bremerton the Class B airspace does not exist. Note that the floor of Class B airspace over Seattle-Tacoma Airport is the surface of the airport itself.

Class B airspace is controlled airspace, of course, and you must have at least 3 miles flight visibility when flying in it. Cloud clearance is a special case, however; because a controller is keeping you away from other traffic by assigning heading and altitudes, you need not observe the cloud clearance requirements of other types of controlled airspace. "Clear of clouds" is the standard.

If you want to land at or depart from the primary airport in Class B airspace when the weather is marginal and you need a Special VFR clearance, look for the notation NO SVFR above the airport data block (*see* Seattle-Tacoma International Airport, **C**). Where you see that notation you are out of luck unless you are flying a helicopter.

Lesson 4 discusses the equipment requirements in Class B airspace, so they won't be covered here. You do need to know that the distances that define the airspace are measured horizontally on the ground, while your distance measuring equipment (DME) in the airplane reads slant range from the transmitting antenna. When your DME reads 10.0 miles, then, your horizontal distance from the antenna may be something like 9.8 miles, depending on your altitude.

Note: The distance readout from a GPS is not slant range; however, it is measured from the airport reference point, which might be near the coffee shop. Moral: Stay at least one mile outside of a charted boundary, just to be safe.

The next concern is altitude. I said earlier that you can legally fly 500 feet above the top of Class B airspace, but do you think that would be a safe thing to do when jets are climbing out at 4,000 to 6,000 feet per minute? Flight 500 feet below a shelf in the airspace, like the 5,500 feet east of Bremerton suggested earlier, might be a tad safer, but why take a chance? Unless you are going to ask for a clearance and enter Class B airspace, give it a wide berth.

As a VFR pilot, should you avoid Class B airspace entirely? What if you wanted to fly from Bremerton to an airport on the east edge of the chart excerpt. Would you fly all the way around just to keep from asking for a clearance? That doesn't make sense to me. You should have a Terminal Area Chart for the Class B airspace, and if you are a student or a sport pilot you need specific instruction and a logbook endorsement from an instructor. In the Seattle area, with those requirements met all you need to do is call the radar facility that owns the airspace (shown on the Terminal Area Chart) and say "Seattle Approach, Whizbang 2345X at 2,000 feet over Bremerton, request clearance through your airspace, destination is Ellensburg." Almost always, you will hear "Cleared to operate in the Seattle Class B airspace, maintain 2,500 feet and squawk 4566." Occasionally, however, the controller will say "unable," and you will have to fly all the way around. Student pilots are prohibited from operating to or from the following airports within Class B airspace:

Atlanta	Newark
Boston	Kennedy
Chicago	La Guardia
Dallas	San Francisco
Los Angeles	Washington National
Miami	Andrews AFB

Although all Class B airports have control towers, they do not have Class D airspace (see that section, next page).

Class C Airspace

The front portion of the Seattle sectional chart that has been excerpted for your use does not contain any Class C airspace; however, on the back of the chart you will find an excerpt of the Spokane and Whidbey Island areas, where both Spokane International (**M**) and Fairchild Air Force Base (**L**) are in Class C airspace. Figure 9-19 shows the Class C airspace at the Whidbey Island Naval Air Station (**K** on the color chart). Note how many satellite airports are located beneath the outer rings at both Spokane and Whidbey. The horizontal boundaries of Class C airspace are shown by solid magenta circles.

Many Class C areas do not operate 24 hours a day. Where operation is part-time, check the panel on the back of the sectional chart or, as advised by a chart notation near the airspace, check the A/FD for operating hours and the type of airspace the Class C reverts to when it is not in effect.

What do Spokane International and Fairchild AFB have in common? Lots of jet traffic, but not enough to qualify for designation as Class B airspace. The controllers do not need to guide your every move, as they do in Seattle, but they do need to know who you are and what you intend to do in their airspace. Note that a clearance is not required to operate in Class C airspace, just two-way communication between you and the radar controller whose airspace you want to use. Sport pilots, of course, need specific ground and flight training leading to an instructor's logbook endorsement before entering Class C airspace.

Class C airspace is shown on sectional and WAC charts by solid magenta circles or arcs; each segment within the airspace is identified with what looks like a fraction. In Figure 9-19 the top fraction is 40, indicating that the top of Whidbey Island's Class C airspace is 4,000 feet; you can fly over it at 4,500 feet without talking to anyone. The bottom of the fraction is the floor of the airspace in hundreds of feet—1,300 or 2,000. Note that the floor of Class C airspace over Whidbey Island Naval Air Station is the surface of the airport itself.

Extending a further 10 miles from the primary airport is the outer area; note that when you are at the edge of the outer area you are still 10 miles from the Class C airspace. The floor of the outer area is the lowest

altitude at which radar coverage is available, and its ceiling is the top of the radar facility's airspace. The purpose of the outer area is to give pilots an opportunity to contact ATC in plenty of time. If you do not intend to land at the primary airspace you can fly through the outer area without saying anything to anyone, although it helps other pilots if you tell the radar facility your position and intentions.

What is the official definition of "communication?" Of course, if you call ATC and get a specific response that includes your airplane's N-number, you are home free. If the radar controller replies with your N-number and says "stand by," that too constitutes two-way communication and you can continue into the Class C airspace. But what if the controller says "Aircraft calling, stand by." That is not communication because the controller might mean someone else, not you. Wait until you hear your number. Of course, if the controller says "remain clear of the Class C airspace" you must stay outside until the controller is able to handle your flight.

A special note for departures: You must be in communication with ATC while you are within the Class C airspace itself as you depart, but the controller is required to provide radar service to you until you have left the outer area, ten miles beyond the

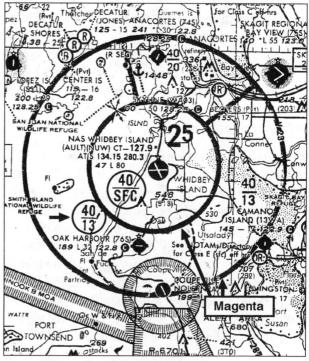

Figure 9-19. *Whidbey Island Class C airspace*

outer circle (check the A/FD for specifics...procedures vary). Give the busy controller a break and say "Terminate my radar service and thank you for your help" as soon as you are more than 10 miles from the primary airport.

A special note for arrivals: If the controller is busy and you are told to remain clear of the Class C airspace, don't despair—wait a few minutes while monitoring the frequency and try again when things slow down. If your destination airport lies within the Class C airspace boundaries, adding "Landing Podunk" to your initial call to ATC might get you priority over flights just passing through.

Aircraft equipment requirements for Class C airspace are covered in Lesson 4.

Class D Airspace

Class D airspace exists whenever a control tower is in operation, except for airports with Class B airspace (which includes tower functions). Class D airspace imposes two obligations. First, there is a communications requirement: you can't fly through Class D airspace without talking to the tower or take off/land without a clearance from the tower (although if you are taking advantage of radar traffic advisories, the radar controller will clear the way for you when passing through). Second is a weather requirement. For you to operate in Class D airspace under basic visual flight rules, the ground visibility must be at least three miles and the ceiling must be at least 1,000 feet above the ground. If the tower serves the primary airport in Class B airspace, there is no Class D airspace. Here again, sport pilots can only enter the airspace after ground and flight training with a logbook endorsement.

What are the dimensions of Class D airspace? The horizontal boundary is shown on charts with a blue dashed line (the airport symbol is blue when there is a tower at the airport); the vertical extent is from the airport elevation to 2,500 feet above the airport. Figure 9-20 shows a nice cylindrical shape for clarity, but actual dimensions will vary widely. The elevation of the top of the airspace to the next highest hundred feet is shown in a little square box near the airport symbol. (Look at any tower-controlled airport except Seattle-Tacoma to check this. Sea-Tac shows

-30 because it sits on a plateau above Puget Sound and the top of its Class D airspace is the 3,000-foot floor of the associated Class B airspace.)

The shape of Class D airspace varies with local conditions. There will be extensions to provide protected airspace for incoming instrument flights, cutouts to exempt satellite airports from the communication and weather requirements, or shelves to allow pilots to fly into and out of airports beneath the edges of the airspace (Figure 9-21). If an extension is 2 miles or less (still shown with blue dashed lines), you need tower permission to fly in that airspace; if the extension is more than 2 miles (shown with magenta dashed lines) the communication requirement does not apply to the extension. The fact that these extensions exist to protect instrument pilots is a clue that you should be alert when flying in or across them.

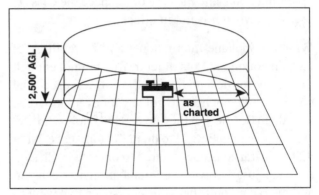

Figure 9-20. Class D airspace

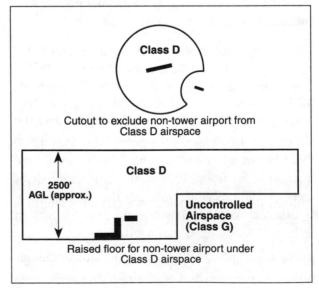

Figure 9-21. Class D, with cutouts or extensions

Look at Hoskins Airport (44T), just east of Olympia (airport **F** on the chart excerpt) inside its Class D airspace. A pilot taking off from or landing at Hoskins (44T) must communicate with Olympia Tower and advise the controller of his or her intentions. There are no examples of cutouts or shelves on the chart excerpt.

The existence of Class D airspace is dependent on an operating control tower. There are hundreds of control towers that operate part-time, and when the controller goes home the Class D airspace requirements usually go, too—the airspace then becomes Class E airspace that extends all the way to the surface (Figure 9-17 "non-towered airport").

You have to look at the A/FD to be absolutely sure which classification of airspace is left behind when the controller at a part-time tower goes home. Look at the towered airports on the sectional excerpt for the Tacoma Narrows tower (**J**). It is a part-time tower, and if you look just below the "E" you will find "See NOTAMS/Directory for Class D/E (sfc) hrs." Olympia and Paine Field are also part-time with similar notations. What "Directory" are they referring you to? The A/FD, of course. When these airports shut down, their surface areas become Class E down to 700 feet above the surface. There are part-time tower-controlled airports that go from Class D to Class G (uncontrolled) when the tower closes, but there are none on this chart. There is no substitute for the A/FD in making this determination.

Class E Airspace

This class of airspace has already been fairly well defined; it exists above the floors defined by magenta dashed lines (the surface), the blue and magenta tints (700 or 1,200 AGL), and the MSL figures in mountainous areas (or 14,500 feet MSL). It extends upward to the floor of the overlying airspace (either Class A, B, or C).

Victor airways, the blue lines identified with VOR radials, are intended to be flown on their centerlines as accurately as possible. To allow for instrument errors, the airspace is protected from obstacles/terrain for four nautical miles on either side of the centerline. Victor airways extend upward from 1,200 feet above ground level (except in mountainous

areas, where the floor of Class E airspace is designated on sectionals with a chain-link blue line) to 18,000 feet above sea level, and they do not lose their identity when passing through Class B, C, D, or E airspace.

The FAA is establishing Tango airways, to be navigated using GPS navigators. They are also blue lines, but the airway identifier is T, as in T-139. They provide an easy way to circumnavigate congested and special use airspace without giving up the accuracy of GPS. T-routes are designated for low-altitude airspace (below 18,000 feet MSL).

Move off to the right when climbing or descending; use shallow left and right turns to clear the air ahead, especially when climbing, because a nose-high attitude blocks forward visibility.

Look at the airport data block for Paine Field (**B**), Tacoma Narrows (**J**), or Olympia (**F**). See the asterisk next to the tower frequency? That means that these are part-time towers, and you can find the actual operating hours on the back of the sectional chart or in the A/FD. When the tower is not in operation the airspace reverts to Class E; the communication requirement goes away but the visibility and cloud clearance requirements of Class E airspace are the same. That is, if you want to land or take off in marginal weather you must call a flight service station for a Special VFR clearance.

Look at the Bremerton National airport (**D**) at the left edge of the chart excerpt or Wenatchee (**H**) airport at the right edge. The magenta dashed line indicates that Class E airspace extends from the floor of the overlying controlled airspace down to the surface. At Bremerton, the overlying airspace begins at either 18,000 MSL or 6,000 feet MSL if within the Seattle Class B airspace boundary. At Wenatchee (Pangborn Memorial), Class E airspace starts at the surface within the dashed, magenta line, and begins at 700 feet AGL within the magenta rectangle. In both areas, the top of Class E airspace is 18,000 feet MSL (Class A airspace).

Now look at the Ellensburg airport (**I**) at the lower right edge of the excerpt. No dashed line, but Ellensburg does have an instrument approach, although you can't tell that from the chart. An inbound instrument pilot's protection stops at 700 feet AGL at Ellensburg; below that altitude the pilot is in Class G (uncontrolled) airspace and must mix in with the VFR traffic.

Class G Airspace

An easy definition of Class G airspace is that it exists wherever other classes do not. Most of the Class G airspace lies beneath floors at 700 or 1,200 feet above the ground. In this thin sliver of airspace you can fly (in the daytime) with only 1 mile flight visibility and the ability to remain clear of clouds. Most pilots call this "scud running," because it usually means trying to stay below a ragged cloud layer in poor visibility. At night, the cloud clearance and visibility requirements in Class G airspace are the same as daytime requirements in Class E airspace—flight visibility of at least 3 miles and lots of cloud clearance. You say that you can't see the clouds at night? Then why are you scud running? (As I write this, rescue teams are removing three bodies from a Cessna 172 that hit a mountain 1,400 feet up. Low clouds, night, VFR pilot, 80 hours flight time.)

Special case: If you want to practice takeoffs and landings in Class G airspace at night with visibility less than 3 miles but more than 1 mile, you can do so if you stay within one-half mile of the runway.

There are such things as permanent, operating control towers in Class G airspace. Lake City, Florida, is one (see Page D-8 in the full-color Appendix). They have the same communications requirement as towers in Class D airspace and you would be wise to treat them the way you would treat any operating control tower.

Important note: Occasionally, the FAA establishes *temporary* control towers in Class G airspace for special functions such as fly-ins, Super Bowls, etc. As you might imagine, these towers do not show up on sectional charts (but they are announced by Notice to Airmen). Treat a temporary tower just as you would any operating control tower—mentally, draw a five-mile circle around the airport and get permission from the tower before entering its airspace.

Terminal Radar Service Area

A type of airspace that is rapidly disappearing is the Terminal Radar Service Area (TRSA, Figure 9-22). Indicated on charts by a solid black circle, a TRSA is a kind of voluntary Class C airspace. That is, radar service is available if you want it, but you don't have to use it.

Because TRSAs are usually at joint military/civil fields, though, it is to your advantage to call in and get traffic advisories. When departing from an airport in a TRSA you will be told "Call ground control for your clearance." If you don't want radar service, all you have to say is "Negative radar." You will not be surrounded by armed MPs but will be allowed to taxi out and take off just like any other kind of Class D airspace.

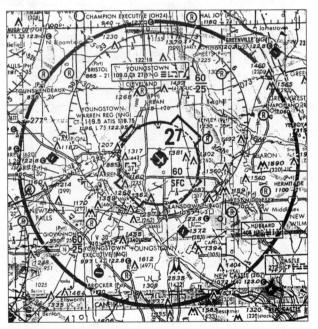

Figure 9-22. *Terminal Radar Service Area*

Special Use Airspace

There are several types of special use airspace, but they are almost all indicated on charts with blue hatching. Look just to the right of the Olympia airport at the lower left corner of the chart excerpt. The most restrictive is a **Prohibited Area**, such as that above the White House (Figure 9-23 is an example). There is no way to get permission to fly in a Prohibited Area and getting caught in one is painful for both your pocketbook and pilot certificate.

The next step down is a **Restricted Area** (Figure 9-24). They are designated and controlled by the military and usually involve firing ranges, etc. A table on each Sectional chart gives the operating hours and altitudes for each Restricted Area. The operating hours are not engraved in stone, however. During your preflight briefing, ask the FSS if a Restricted Area along your route is "hot," or give the controlling agency a call (at Navy Whidbey, the status of their Restricted Area is on the ATIS). Do not just blunder into the area, however, because the hazards you are being protected from are invisible.

Temporary Flight Restrictions. Because of the increased emphasis on security where large groups of people (or government big-wigs) are congregated, the FAA is issuing Notices to Airmen implementing Temporary Flight Restrictions (TFRs) over sporting events, political gatherings, etc. These areas do not appear on aeronautical charts, but their dimensions and locations are included in the NOTAM. It is incumbent on every pilot to make a last-minute check for such restrictions before taking off.

Check for TFRs during flight planning by going to www.aopa.org and clicking on Temporary Flight Restrictions on the right side. Check again with Flight Service by radio after takeoff to be sure that nothing new has come up.

National Security Areas. The FAA has converted some TFRs to National Security Areas, which are permanent but voluntary (pilots should avoid flying through NSAs, though). When it is deemed necessary, an NSA can be changed to prohibited airspace by NOTAM.

Warning Areas and **Alert Areas** (Figures 9-25 and 9-26) also involve the military. Warning Areas have the same kinds of hazards as Restricted Areas, but are offshore in International waters. No clearance required, but keep your eyes open. Check their status

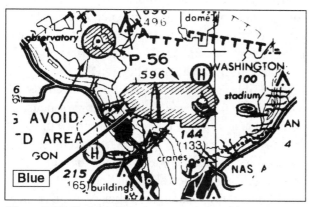

Figure 9-23. Prohibited Area

PROHIBITED, RESTRICTED, WARNING AND ALERT AREAS ON SEATTLE SECTIONAL CHART

NO.	NAME	ALTITUDE	TIME	APPROPRIATE AUTHORITY
R-6701	Admirality Inlet, Wash	to 5,000	Sunrise to sunset Mon. thru Fri. Sat. & Sun by NOTAM 24 hr. in advance	†FAA Seattle ARTC Center *Area FSS Comdr., Medium Attack Tactical Electronic Warfare Wing NAS Whidbey Island, Wash.

Figure 9-24. Restricted Area

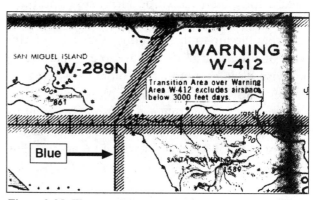

Figure 9-25. Warning Area

NO.	NAME	ALTITUDE	TIME	APPROPRIATE AUTHORITY
632	Corpus Christi, Texas	From 6,000 but not incl. 11,000	SR-2400 Mon. Fri. 1400-2400 Sun	Chief Naval Air Training

Figure 9-26. Alert Area

with the flight service station. Alert Areas involve a high volume of military training activity; again, no clearance is required but extreme vigilance (or avoidance) is.

Military Operating Areas (MOAs, Figure 9-27) are shown on charts with magenta hatching; again, look at the areas surrounding R-6703A, B, C, and D east of Olympia (that's the Army's Fort Lewis firing range, if you're curious). You do not need a clearance to fly in a MOA, but military airplanes operate in them without restriction—the regulations don't apply to them while flying in a MOA. Military pilots are not only flying at high speed, but they are not spending much time looking for traffic. Your FSS can tell you the status of a MOA, of course, but the ARTCC in whose airspace the MOA exists will be in direct contact with the military flights and can advise them of your presence. Your preflight planning should include getting Center frequencies from the A/FD. MOAs can be overflown if too big to circumnavigate; the ceiling of each MOA is given in a table on the back of the sectional.

Military Training Routes (MTRs) create the most hazard for general aviation airplanes. The good news is that they are charted: see the gray lines that run from the top to the bottom of the chart excerpt west of Ellensburg? IR and VR mean instrument and visual routes, but there is more to it than that. Routes with 4-digit numbers are flown at or below 1,500 feet AGL, while routes with 3-number identifiers are flown above 1,500 feet AGL. Nothing like flying along at 2,500 feet and seeing a flight of C-130s go under you.

"Hot" times for MTRs are available from the FSS, and you are foolish if you do not check on the status of any MTR that will cross your flight path. The military might schedule a route for several hours and only use it for a portion of that time, but you can't afford to gamble. Military jet pilots fly very fast, with their heads in their cockpits, and they are painted with camouflage colors for a reason. Never fly parallel to an MTR—the military is allowed to be as much as eight miles off the centerline. Cross military training routes at right angles to reduce your time of exposure to a minimum.

Air Defense Identification Zones

Air Defense Identification Zones exist along the Pacific, Gulf, and Atlantic coasts, and aircraft inbound to the United States from outside of the ADIZ whose place and time of arrival within the zone are unknown will be intercepted by armed military aircraft. If you will be returning to the United States (from the Bahamas, for example) and will penetrate an ADIZ you must have a DVFR (Defense Visual Flight Rules) flight plan on file giving your point of penetration and estimated time of penetration. If you are simply operating within 10 miles of the coast you are exempt from this requirement. This discussion does not include the ADIZ that surrounds Washington, DC. Special regulations apply in that area. Go to www.aopa.org and click on ADIZ procedures on the right side. Membership is not required.

Wildlife Refuge Area

Along the bottom edge of the sectional chart excerpt you will see Mount Rainier National Park. Note the line of dots that marks the boundary. Wherever you see those dots they surround a wildlife refuge area, and you are asked, not required, to stay at least 2,000 feet above the terrain to minimize the effect of aircraft noise on wildlife. If you are a seaplane pilot, check with local authorities before you fly into a state or national park; seaplane operations are severely restricted in parks.

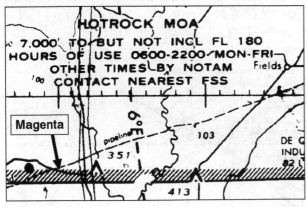

Figure 9-27. Military Operating Area

Lesson 9
Enroute Flight Review Questions

1. What is the magnetic course from Cedar Rapids (airport A in Figure Q9-1) to Fairfield (airport E)? The magnetic variation is 5°E.

   A— 013°
   B— 193°
   C— 198°

2. While flying from Cedar Rapids to Fairfield, you cross Interstate 80 at 1015, and the highway west of Wellman at 1022. What is your estimated time of arrival at Fairfield if your ground speed remains constant?

   A— 1028
   B— 1035
   C— 1040

3. Your airplane uses 8.6 gallons of fuel per hour. You plan a 250 nautical mile flight at an average ground speed of 115 knots. What is the minimum fuel required for the trip (allow a 30 minute reserve)?

   A— 18.7 gallons
   B— 23.0 gallons
   C— 15.6 gallons

4. Your ground speed between Cedar Rapids and Fairfield (52 NM) is 111 knots. At an average fuel consumption rate of 7.2 gallons per hour, how much fuel will you use en route?

   A— 3.4 gallons
   B— 2.5 gallons
   C— 4.2 gallons

5. Your true course is 270°, your true airspeed is 110 knots, the wind is from 330° at 18 knots, and the magnetic variation is 6° W. What is your ground speed and magnetic heading?

   A— 119 knots; 278°
   B— 100 knots; 264°
   C— 100 knots; 284°

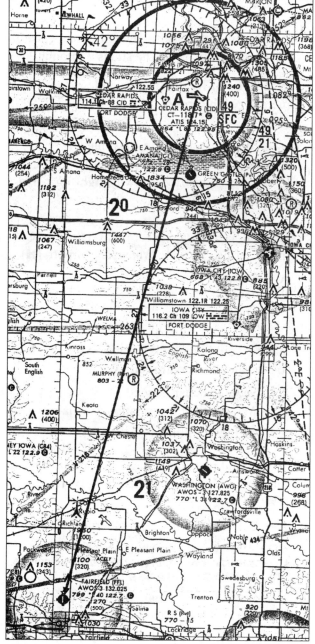

Figure Q9-1

6. Upon refueling at your destination after a 345 nautical mile flight, you take 32 gallons of fuel (tanks were full on departure). During the flight, your ground speed averaged 136 knots. What was the fuel consumption rate for this flight?

A— 11.0 gallons per hour
B— 14.0 gallons per hour
C— 12.6 gallons per hour

Refer to the full-color Seattle sectional chart excerpt at the back of this book for questions 7 through 11.

7. What kind of lighting is available at the Cashmere-Dryden airport (47° 30' 45"N, 120° 29' 15"W)?

A— No runway lighting is available.
B— Rotating beacon only.
C— Pilot-controlled runway lighting (or on request).

8. How tall is the antenna for radio station KPQ, 8 miles northwest of the Wenatchee airport, (**H**)?

A— 560 feet
B— 943 feet
C— 313 feet

9. Where would you look for information on how to activate pilot-controlled lighting?

A— Sectional chart legend.
B— Aeronautical Information Manual.
C— Airport/Facility Directory

10. How would you apply magnetic variation when planning a flight from Ellensburg (**I**) to Seattle (**C**)?

A— Subtract 47° 30' from the true course.
B— Add 18.3 degrees to the true course.
C— Subtract 18.3 degrees from the true course.

11. You are flying over Lake Kachess (near **A**) in the central Cascade Mountains. What sectional chart feature tells you the minimum safe altitude in that area?

A— Terrain with an elevation of 6,680 feet at the north end of the lake.
B— Maximum elevation number 7^9.
C— Contour lines on the mountains.

12. You are approaching an airport within Class C airspace. Which of these statements is true?

A— You must have a clearance from ATC before entering the Class C airspace.
B— You must be in two-way communication with ATC before entering the Class C airspace.
C— Your airplane must be equipped with a transponder, two-way radio, and VOR to enter Class C airspace.

13. Under what conditions, if any, may civil pilots enter a restricted area?

A— With the controlling agency's authorization.
B— On airways with ATC clearance.
C— Under no condition.

14. Under what condition may an aircraft operate from a satellite airport within Class C airspace?

A— The pilot must monitor ATC until clear of the Class C airspace.
B— The pilot must contact ATC as soon as practicable after takeoff.
C— The pilot must secure prior approval from ATC before takeoff from the satellite airport.

15. What is the upper limit of Class D airspace?

A— 18,500 MSL.
B— The base of Class A airspace.
C— Usually 2,500 feet above the surface.

16. What are the horizontal limits of Class D airspace?

A— 5 NM from the airport boundary.
B— As indicated with blue dashed lines.
C— As indicated with magenta dashed lines.

17. Class D airspace is automatically in effect when

A— its associated control tower is in operation.
B— the weather is below VFR minimums.
C— radar service is available.

18. What is the purpose of Class D airspace?

  A— To provide for the control of aircraft landing and taking off from an airport with an
  operating control tower.

  B— To provide for the control of all aircraft
  operating in the vicinity of an airport with
  an operating control tower.

  C— To restrict aircraft without radios from
  operating in the vicinity of an airport with
  an operating control tower.

19. Unless otherwise specified, Federal airways
extend from

  A— 1,200 feet above the surface upward to
  14,500 feet MSL and are 16 NM wide.

  B— 1,200 feet above the surface upward to
  18,000 feet MSL and are 8 NM wide.

  C— the surface upward to 18,000 feet MSL and
  are 4 NM wide.

20. What type airspace is associated with VOR Federal airways?

  A— Class B, C, D, or E airspace.

  B— Class E airspace.

  C— Class D airspace.

21. Class E airspace in the conterminous United
States extends to, but not including

  A— the base of Class B airspace.

  B— 3,000 feet MSL.

  C— 18,000 feet MSL.

22. What is the minimum weather condition required
for airplanes operating under Special VFR in
Class B, C, D or E airspace?

  A— 1 mile flight visibility.

  B— 1 mile flight visibility and 1,000 foot
  ceiling.

  C— 3 mile flight visibility and 1,000 foot
  ceiling.

23. For VFR flight operations above 10,000 feet MSL
and more than 1,200 feet AGL, the minimum horizontal distance from clouds required is

  A— 1,000 feet.

  B— 2,000 feet.

  C— 1 mile.

24. No person may operate an airplane within Class
B, C, D or E airspace associated with an airport
at night under special VFR unless

  A— the flight can be conducted 500 feet below
  the clouds.

  B— the airplane is equipped for instrument
  flight.

  C— the flight visibility is at least 3 miles.

25. The minimum ceiling and visibility required to
operate under basic visual flight rules in Class
C, D or E airspace are

  A— 500 feet and 1 mile.

  B— 1,000 feet and 3 mile.

  C— 1,400 feet and 2 mile.

26. In which type of airspace is VFR flight
prohibited?

  A— Class B.

  B— Class D.

  C— Class A.

27. What minimum pilot certification is required for
operating to or from the airports within the 12
restricted Class B airspaces?

  A— Student pilot certificate with appropriate
  logbook endorsements.

  B— Private pilot certificate.

  C— Private pilot certificate with an instrument
  rating.

28. What procedure is recommended when climbing
or descending VFR on an airway?

  A— Offset 4 miles or more from centerline of
  the airway before changing altitude.

  B— Advise the nearest FSS of the desired altitude change.

  C— Execute gentle banks, left and right for continuous visual scanning of the airspace.

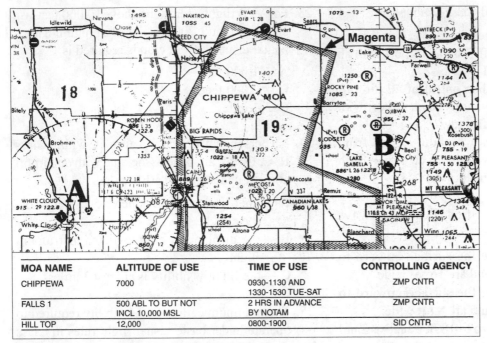

MOA NAME	ALTITUDE OF USE	TIME OF USE	CONTROLLING AGENCY
CHIPPEWA	7000	0930-1130 AND 1330-1530 TUE-SAT	ZMP CNTR
FALLS 1	500 ABL TO BUT NOT INCL 10,000 MSL	2 HRS IN ADVANCE BY NOTAM	ZMP CNTR
HILL TOP	12,000	0800-1900	SID CNTR

Figure Q9-2. Excerpt from Chicago Sectional Aeronautical Chart

Refer to Figure Q9-2 for questions 29 and 30.

29. You plan to fly under VFR from Airport A to Airport B. Regarding this flight, which of the following statements is true?

A — Flights below 7,000 feet must be operating on IFR flight plans.

B — Extreme caution should be exercised while flying through this area.

C — VFR flights are not permitted above 7,000 feet MSL.

30. Which statement is true regarding the Chippewa MOA?

A — The military services conduct low altitude navigation flights at or below 1,500 feet AGL at speeds exceeding 250 knots within this area.

B — Some training activities may necessitate acrobatic maneuvers by military aircraft within this area.

C — VFR flights between 7,000 feet and Flight Level 180 are prohibited within this area.

31. What are the visibility and cloud clearance requirements for VFR flight in Class G airspace below 10,000 feet at night?

A — One mile visibility and remain clear of clouds.

B — One mile visibility, 500 feet below, 1,000 feet above, and 2,000 horizontally from all clouds.

C — Three miles visibility, 500 feet below, 1,000 feet above, 2,000 feet horizontally from all clouds.

32. Just north of Kachess Lake your courseline crosses two Military Training Routes, VR1355 and IR313-314. From these route numbers you determine that

A — military airplanes will be flying VFR more than 1,500 feet AGL.

B — military airplanes will be flying IFR less than 1,500 feet AGL.

C — military airplanes will be flying VFR less than 1,500 feet AGL.

10 Lesson **Navigation**

If you are reading this book as a potential sport aircraft pilot you should know that training in navigation is required…however, the type of navigation is not specified. In this day and age, most airplanes with electrical systems have GPS navigators installed; if yours does not have one, I strongly recommend that you purchase a hand-held device. As you read this Lesson, pay special attention to pilotage—first, because it is what you fall back on when the batteries die or the power fails, and second, because light sport aircraft are more likely to get blown off course simply because they are more subject to the whims of the weather gods than "standard" aircraft.

There can be no in-depth discussion of "glass cockpit" navigation systems because they differ so widely in display and knob-ology. One manufacturer may include a Global Position System (GPS) navigator in his black box while another may require inputs from a separate GPS. Each system has a learning curve, some steeper than others.

As a VFR pilot, you will probably use radio aids to navigate only as a backup to pilotage, rather than as a primary method of navigation. If, however, there is a radio airway going the same way you are, many flight planning problems will be minimized (if not eliminated) by using it. As the holder of a recreation-al pilot certificate, you don't need to know anything about radio aids to navigation—but read the section on GPS anyway.

The FAA has established the **VHF Omnidirectional Range** (VOR) system as the primary means of electronic navigation in federally controlled airspace, and you will find that most airplanes have at least one VOR receiver (*see* Figure 10-1, next page). The Global Positioning System, discussed later in this lesson, is approved only when the Wide Area Augmentation System (WAAS) is included. GPS navigators without WAAS must have VOR capability. This distinction is of primary interest to pilots on instrument flight plans. Expect VOR to be around for the next decade or so. The VOR system operates in the Very High Frequency (VHF) range (108.0 MHz to 117.95 MHz), just above the FM broadcast band and below that band of frequencies designated for aircraft radio communication. VHF radio waves are subject to line-of-sight limitations (Figure 10-2) and you may find that at low altitudes you will be unable to receive a usable VOR signal.

VORs are classified as high altitude, low altitude, and terminal VORs. You should consult the Airport/Facility Directory to learn which class any VOR you propose to use falls into because the differences in

Figure 10-1. *VOR signal transmitter*

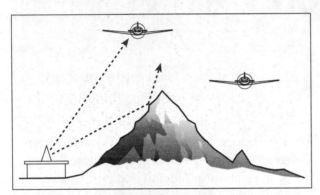

Figure 10-2. *Line-of-sight limitations*

transmitter power affect reception distance. The A/FD also lists altitudes and/or radials where the signal is unusable. *See* Figure 10-3.

Your aeronautical chart shows three symbols for VORs: VOR, VORTAC, and VOR-DME. There is no difference between these three types of stations as far as your cockpit course guidance indication is concerned. VORTAC and VOR-DME will be discussed under "Distance Measuring Equipment" in this lesson. *See* Figure 10-4.

All three types of transmitters broadcast a three-letter identifier in Morse Code, so you can be sure you have tuned the correct station and the station is transmitting a usable signal. When the transmitter is undergoing maintenance or adjustment the FAA either removes the coded identification or changes

the code to send T-E-S-T (- · ··· -). You must check the Morse code against that shown on the sectional chart to be sure the signal is usable.

The VOR ground station transmits a signal which is identifiable as 360 radials or lines of position to your airborne receiver-indicator, and these radials are oriented in relation to magnetic north. This not only eliminates consideration of magnetic variation from your flight planning calculations, but gives you a quick chart reference to magnetic directions. Selected radials are printed in blue on the navigational charts and identified as Victor (VOR) airways. Because the VOR airways are labeled with their magnetic direction, you can "eyeball" a course without precise measurement. *Note:* Do not expect VOR radials to agree with GPS…they are totally different systems.

Altitude Feet	Line of Sight Statute Miles
500	30
1,000	45
2,000	65
3,000	80
5,000	100
7,000	120
10,000	140
15,000	175

Figure 10-3. *Line-of-sight ranges*

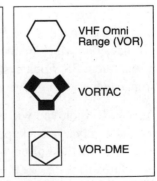

Figure 10-4. *VOR chart symbols*

Your VOR receiver has a frequency selector, an omnibearing selector (OBS), and some form of indicator/needle. You select the frequency shown on the sectional/WAC chart, identify it by listening to the Morse Code, and the VOR indicator in your cockpit provides the answers to three questions: (1) "Where is the station from my position?", (2) "Where am I in relation to the station?", and (3) "In which direction must I fly to intercept the course to my destination?"

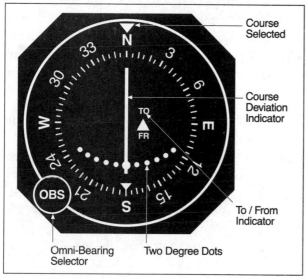

Figure 10-5. *VOR indicator*

To answer these questions, the VOR indicator uses three elements: (1) a Course Deviation Indicator (CDI) or needle, which tells you where you are in relation to a selected radial, (2) an **Omni-Bearing Selector** (OBS) which you use to select radials, and (3) a TO-FROM (or ambiguity) indicator (Figure 10-5).

When the OBS is rotated to center the CDI needle, the TO-FROM indicator will tell you where you are from the station and where the station is from you, simultaneously. In Figure 10-6 the pilot has rotated the OBS and the needle has centered with 265° selected; the TO-FROM indicator shows FROM, so the VOR is telling the pilot, "You are 265° FROM, or west of XYZ VOR, so the course TO XYZ must be 085°. Which way do you want to go?" Rotating the OBS to 085° causes the TO-FROM indicator to change to TO, although the airplane has not changed heading. *Because the VOR receiver tells the pilot the airplane's position in relation to the station, the heading of the airplane is not important.* To illustrate, in Figure 10-7 (on the next page) both cars are on North Main Street and both airplanes are located on the 360° radial—the fact that they are heading in different directions does not alter that. Changing

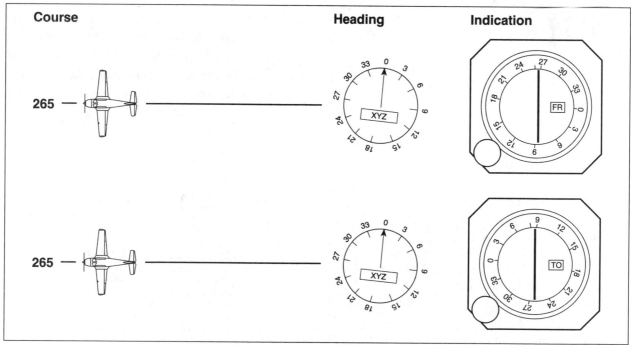

Figure 10-6. *Two indications for the same location*

the heading of the airplanes would not relocate them to the 180° radial, and turning the cars would not relocate them to South Main Street.

Figure 10-8 shows how the TO-FROM indicator is related to the VOR radial selected, and it also illustrates that heading has no effect on omni indications. All of the pilots in the illustration have selected the 010° radial with their omni-bearing selectors: airplanes A and E both have indication W, while airplanes C, F, and H have indications U, T, and

T respectively. Prove this to yourself by mentally turning all of the airplanes in the illustration to a heading of 010° to agree with the OBS—those south of the station will indicate TO, those north of the station will indicate FROM, and the CDI needle in each airplane shows the direction each must turn to intercept the 010° radial.

When you select an omni-bearing (radial), you draw an electronic dividing line between the TO and FROM areas, and you can see the result of that division in the illustration. Airplanes B, D, G, and I are neither TO nor FROM, and their VOR indicators will show a neutral or OFF flag. You will also see an OFF flag when the transmitted signal is too weak for navigational use because of distance or low altitude.

Refer to the Seattle sectional chart excerpt at the back of the book. Notice that each VOR station has a magnetic compass rose centered on it and that each has a blue box adjacent to it with the frequency and Morse Code identifier. For convenience, all VOR, VORTAC and VOR-DME stations are called VORs in this text. A pilot on a cross-country flight en route from over the Seattle VOR (**C**) to the Paine VOR (**B**) would have the VOR receiver tuned to 116.8 MHz and the CDI needle centered with the OBS set to 344°.

The TO-FROM indicator would show FROM, because the airplane is north of Seattle. Halfway to Paine VOR, the receiver is tuned to 110.6 MHz and the TO-FROM changes to TO because the airplane is south of Paine—the CDI remains centered. Passing

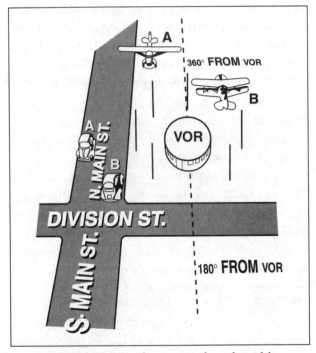

Figure 10-7. TO/FROM indication is independent of the heading

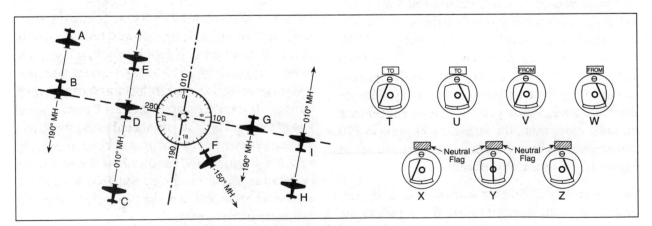

Figure 10-8. Relationship of TO/FROM indicator to selected radial

over Paine, still northbound, the indicator changes to FROM, and the pilot selects the next VOR along the way when in range. If a wind from the west drifts the airplane off course, the CDI will move off center toward the wind (left), and the pilot must select a heading into the wind which will cause the needle to move back to the center. Retain a small wind drift correction that will keep the needle centered. This is how you will navigate along VOR airways, always flying FROM the VOR behind you and then TO the VOR ahead of you, with the omni-bearing differing from your heading by only the amount of wind drift correction. As long as the radial you have selected and the heading of the aircraft agree within ±40° you will always change heading toward the needle to center it.

Orientation

If you are able to receive a good VOR signal, you can always orient yourself by simply turning the omni-bearing selector until the needle centers. Combining the indications of the omni-bearing selector and the TO-FROM flag will tell you at a glance where you are FROM the station or the direction TO the station. No math required, just read the numbers on the face of the indicator.

Occasionally, however, you will want to know your position in relation to a specific radial or airway and what heading to steer to intercept it. An easy method to accomplish this is to mentally superimpose the airplane's heading on the VOR indicator.

Let's assume that you have drawn a line from a VOR to a destination airport and determined that by following the 030 radial you will arrive over that airport. Just before takeoff, you have tuned your VOR receiver to the correct frequency and set the OBS to 030. After takeoff, departing the traffic pattern and avoiding some traffic takes you away from the desired course. When you are able to concentrate on radio navigation, the airplane's heading is 190 degrees and the omni indication is what you see in Figure 10-9A on the next page.

First, mentally divide the indicator in half, perpendicular to the selected radial; this separates the

TOs from the FROMs. In this example, we have a FROM indication; any airplane located from northwest around to southeast (300 clockwise to 120 in Figure 10-9B) would have a FROM indication. Next, imagine an arrow pointing to the station. Since we have 030 selected and are roughly north of the station, that arrow would point to the reciprocal of 030, or 210 as shown.

The CDI needle is deflected to the left, toward numbers which extend from southwest through north. This tells you that a heading selected from the left side of the omni indicator will intercept the 030 radial. Fly a heading from 211 through 299 and you will be headed back toward the VOR; fly a heading from 301 through 029 and when the needle centers you will be on your way to the destination airport.

Many VOR indicators have course deviation indicator needles that are not pivoted at the top but remain vertical as they move from one side of the indicator to the other. If your CDI needle is pivoted at the top, mentally break it loose and position it vertically. In Figure 10-9C, the dashed line represents the relocated needle. Now imagine your airplane located in the center of the VOR indicator, with its heading in agreement with the direction indicator (190, remember?). The combination of mental images allows you to visualize where your airplane is in relation to the radial. Although the needle is deflected to the left, a right turn to a heading of about 340 degrees will intercept the 030 radial so that you can proceed on course to your destination. A left turn would have been more than a 180-degree turn.

Let's now assume that as you turn north, the skies ahead are turning dark and stormy and you wisely decide to head back. A turn to any heading in the lower left quadrant (211 to 300) would take you toward your escape route. It looks as though a right turn to 250 would be a good choice. Of course, when you get around to 250, you should rotate the omni-bearing selector to 210 and re-orient your imaginary airplane. Figure 10-9D shows how the real omni indicator and your imaginary additions would look as you set up to intercept the 030 radial and return to the departure airport.

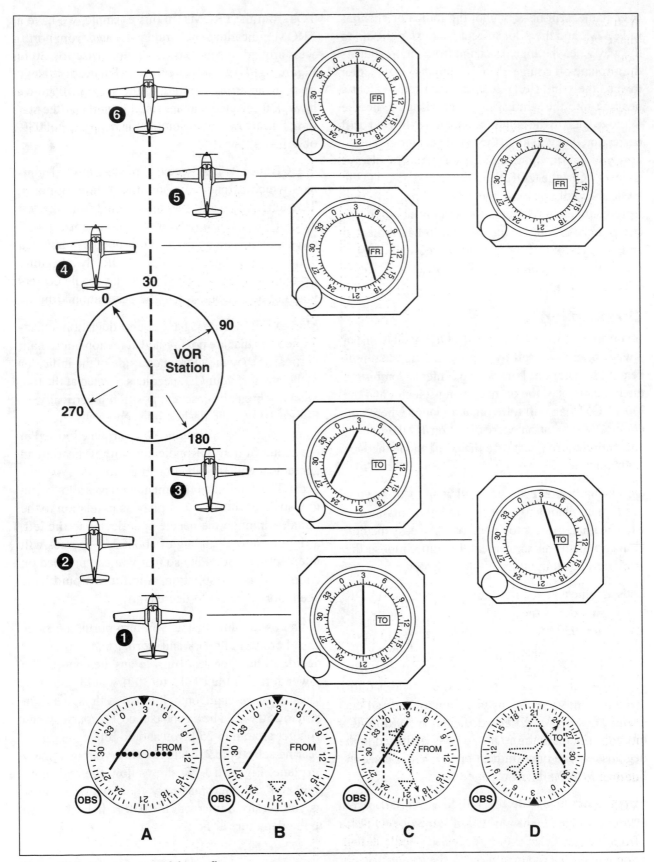

Figure 10-9. *Always fly toward the needle.*

You don't have to fly on Victor airways—you can make your own. Draw a line from the Paine VOR southwest to the Bremerton National Airport (**D**)—the bearing is about 190° from Paine to Bremerton. If you are flying north from a position over the Port Orchard airport (**E**, southeast of Bremerton National), and want to intercept the direct course between Bremerton and Paine, select 010° (the reciprocal of 190°) with your omni-bearing selector. The TO-FROM will read TO because Paine is generally north of you, and the CDI needle will deflect to the left. It is telling you, "select a heading to the left of 010° to go TO Paine." You decide to turn to 340°, 30° to the left of 010° (you "take a 30° cut"). As you intercept the radial, the needle moves into the center, and you turn to 010° plus or minus a wind correction.

Could you find the Port Orchard airport if you were a stranger to the Pacific Northwest? Draw a line from the Seattle VOR to Port Orchard (**E**) to determine which radial of the Seattle VOR the Port Orchard airport is on, and draw another line from the Paine VOR to Port Orchard to identify the radial of the Paine VOR that crosses Port Orchard. Fly outbound on the Seattle 246° radial with the #1 radio's OBS on 246°, and the #2 radio tuned to Paine with its OBS on 184°. The needle on your #2 omni head will be deflected to the right as you fly across Puget Sound, and it will center when you are over Port Orchard.

Centering the OBS needles of two VOR indicators is a good method of locating yourself if you become disoriented. Be sure both TO-FROM flags read FROM, because you want to determine your position FROM both stations. If you are not sure whether or not you have crossed a selected radial, use this rule: if the needle is on the same side as the station, you're not there yet.

In the example above, as you fly west across Puget Sound toward Port Orchard, the Paine Field VOR is to your right and the CDI needle is deflected to the right; it will center over the Port Orchard airport and deflect to the left if you go too far.

VOR needle sensitivity is a function of distance from the transmitting station. At a distance of 60 miles from the transmitter, one degree of needle deflection equals one nautical mile on the ground, or 100 feet per mile. The scale of your course deviation indicator is 20° wide (10° each side of center), so at a distance of 60 miles a half-scale needle deflection means that you are 5 miles off course. When you are 12 miles from the station, the same half-scale deflection means that you are only 1 mile off course. Figure 10-10 shows the distance represented by half-scale deflection at various distances from the VOR transmitter.

The VOR airways (the blue lines on the sectional chart) are checked regularly by the FAA for accuracy. When you fly a radial of your own choosing, there may be slight inaccuracies between your "needle centered" position on the radial and your visual position in relation to ground reference points. When the radial is considered to be totally unusable by the FAA it is listed in the A/FD. This is a good reason for you to check your position visually and to use the VOR only as a backup for VFR flight as well as listen to the Morse code station identifier before using it.

Your VOR receiver-indicator should be checked for accuracy at least every 30 days, even if you only use it as a backup to pilotage. The FAA has designated VOR checkpoints on the ground at many airports, and has also designated airborne checkpoints that can

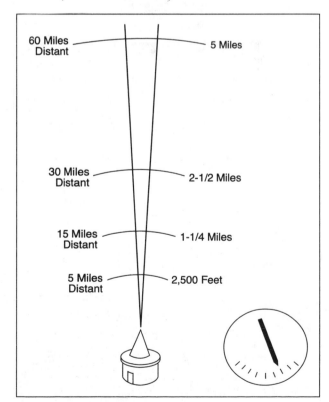

Figure 10-10. VOR signal spread vs. distance

be overflown and the VOR indication checked. The A/FD is the place to look for information on VOR checkpoints (Figure 10-11). At some large airports listed in the A/FD, a special VOR test transmitter called a VOT is installed. The VOT transmitter is designed to send a single 360° radial, so that you get a signal indicating that you are north of the station regardless of your actual location. Then, when the VOT's frequency is selected, the needle should center within ±4° of 180° TO or 360° FROM.

In many cases the transmitted VOR signal is interrupted or distorted by the terrain or similar conditions, making it inaccurate and unusable at some altitudes, or in certain directions, or both. The listing for the VOR station in the A/FD will list any such restrictions (Figure 10-12). You may also notice irregularities in the needle indication that are caused by the propeller interfering with the received signal at certain rpm settings—changing rpm will solve this problem.

For VOR practice, or to fix these concepts in your mind, go to www.fergworld.com/training/vor_training.php.

Horizontal Situation Indicator

The airplane you fly might have a Horizontal Situation Indicator (HSI), illustrated in Figure 10-13. You can see that it provides another means of displaying your airplane's position relative to a selected radial. Unlike a standard VOR display, an HSI does not have reverse sensing; whether you use the head or the tail of the arrow to point to a selected radial, the deflection will be the same and you always fly toward the needle. All glass cockpit VOR displays are HSI's… see the color Appendix (D) for examples.

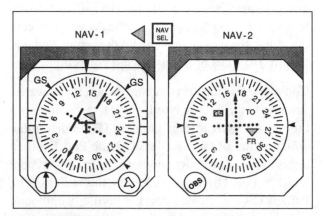

Figure 10-13. HSI

Distance Measuring Equipment

Many airplanes are equipped with distance measuring equipment (DME) which reads the distance from the transmitting station in nautical miles. Although the DME transmitter and receiver use Ultra High Frequencies (UHF), this is of no concern to the pilot; just tuning the DME to the frequency of the associated VOR does the trick. Range information from the DME is slant range from the ground up to the airplane, not horizontal range on the ground. If you are 6,000 feet above the transmitting station, the DME readout will not go below 1.0 nautical mile; accuracy suffers when close to the station because of slant range considerations (Figure 10-14).

Distance information can be received from either VORTACs or VOR-DMEs—there is no practical difference to the user. The UHF range of frequencies is even more sensitive to line-of-sight limitations than the VHF range is—you may receive an adequate VOR signal when unable to receive the associated DME because of intervening terrain. In

VOR RECEIVER CHECK
WASHINGTON

VOR RECEIVER CHECK POINTS

Facility Name (Arpt Name)	Freq/Ident	Type Check Pt. Gnd. AB/ALT	Azimuth from Fac. Mag.	Dist. from Fac. N.M.	Check Point Description
Ellensburg (Bowers Field)	117.9/ELN	A/2300	255	3.5	Over W end of rwy 07-25.
Olympia (Olympia)	113.4/OLM	G	347		On ramp in front of admin building.
Paine (Snohomish Co. (Paine Field))	114.2/PAE	G	022	0.4	On twy H east of rwy 11 threshold.
Seattle	116.8/SEA	A/2000	194	27	Over Nisqually River/I-5 bridge.
	116.8/SEA	A/1500	202	11.5	Over smelter stack.
	116.8/SEA	A/2500	307	19.5	Over NW end of bridge of state hwy 305.
Seattle (Crest Airpark)	116.8/SEA	A/200	106	10.3	Over centerline on aprch end runway 33.

VOR TEST FACILITIES (VOT)

Facility Name (Airport Name)	Frequency	Type VOT Facility	Remarks
Seattle (Boeing Field King County Intl)	108.6	G	
Spokane Intl	109.6	G	

Figure 10-11. Example from A/FD

ELLENSBURG 47°01'28"N 120°27'26"W   SEATTLE
(L) ABVORTAC 117.9   ELN   Chan 126   260° 2.5 NM to Bower Fld. 1766/21E   **L-1C, 9A**
VORTAC unusable:
  345°–005° beyond 10 NM below 8000'   005°–040° below 7000'
  040°–080° below 5000'   080°–115° beyond 18 NM below 5000'
  135°–190° beyond 25 NM below 5300'   190°–254° beyond 28 NM below 8000'
  254°–265° beyond 30 NM below 7400'   300°–325° beyond 25 NM below 10,500'
  325°–345° beyond 15 NM below 8000'
RCO 122.2   122.1R   117.9T   (SEATTLE FSS)

Figure 10-12. From A/FD: restrictions to VOR signals

addition to distance information, some DME indicators also read out ground speed and time to the station. Figure 10-15 shows a typical modern DME with its readouts. Ground speed and time readouts are correct only when you are navigating directly toward or away from the transmitting station.

As a VFR pilot, you may find that a GPS navigator is a better addition to your panel than a DME.

What Does the Future Hold for VOR?

Ground-based navigational aids such as VOR will be around for the foreseeable future—about 900 remain active as of 2011. Even the latest GPS navigators include a VOR function, and earlier (TSO 129-c) navigators require one. Expect to demonstrate your understanding of the VOR system for a good many years yet.

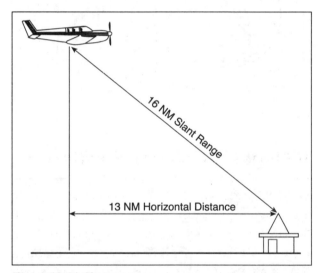

Figure 10-14. Slant range

Figure 10-15. Typical DME

Automatic Direction Finder

The automatic direction finder (ADF) receiver in your airplane (Figure 10-16) receives transmissions in the low and medium frequency ranges, generally from 190 kHz to 1750 kHz. In the range from 190 kHz to 550 kHz it is used with nondirectional beacons (NDBs) operated by the FAA or Coast Guard.

The ADF receiver will have a function switch with several positions. In the ANT or REC position it will provide no direction-finding capability, but will have good audio clarity for positive identification of the navigation station (or for listening to music, news, and sports). The TEST position will electronically deflect the ADF needle so that you can be sure that it is working, and that the signal from the navigation station is adequate for navigation.

When the switch is in the ADF position, the indicator needle will point directly to the transmitting station. In contrast to the VOR, when the airplane heading changes, the ADF needle moves. You read the angle between the needle and the nose of the airplane as a bearing *relative* to the nose. What you really want to know is the *magnetic* bearing to or from the transmit-

Figure 10-16. Automatic direction finder (ADF)

ting station, because all of your navigation is based on magnetic north. It is possible to compute **magnetic bearing** when **relative bearing** and **magnetic heading** are known. In Figure 10-17, the transmitting antenna is 90° *relative to the nose of the airplane.*

Refer to Figure 10-18.

Magnetic heading (MH): heading you are steering.

Relative bearing (RB): angle between the nose of the airplane and the ADF needle, measured *clockwise.*

Magnetic bearing to the station = MH + RB

035° + 225° = 260° to the station

Most light airplanes with ADF receivers have a rotatable card on the indicator. The card can be set to agree with the magnetic heading on the heading indicator to eliminate the mathematics.

In the illustration (Figure 10-19) the magnetic heading is 035°. Can you match the ADF indicators with the correct magnetic bearing to the station?*

305°   **045°**   **095°**

* (R = 045°, S = 305°, T = 095°)

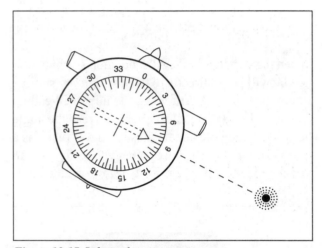

Figure 10-17. Relative bearing

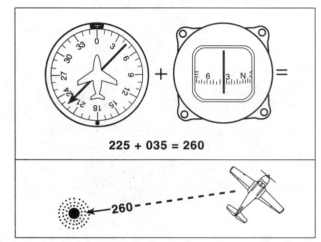

225 + 035 = 260

Figure 10-18. Bearing TO station

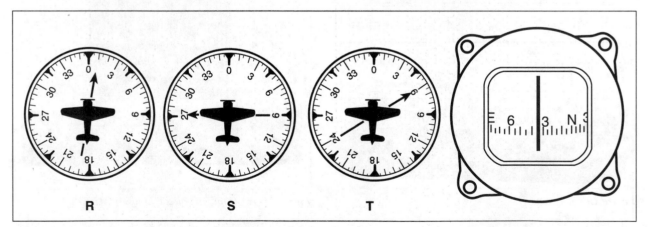

R   S   T

Figure 10-19. Magnetic compass with ADF indicators

Using Your Automatic Direction Finder

If your airplane is equipped with an automatic direction finder receiver you can use it to "home" directly to a low frequency radio station such as an FAA radio beacon or a standard broadcast station. "Homing" means that you turn your airplane so that the ADF indicator needle points directly ahead (0° relative) and continue to turn the airplane as required to keep the needle in that position. The drawback of homing is that if there is any wind, your airplane will follow a curved track arcing downwind from the straight-line track to the station. This is not only inefficient and time consuming, but you might drift close to terrain or obstacles at night (Figure 10-20).

The frequencies and antenna locations of broadcast stations are printed in blue on sectional charts. Broadcast stations are required to identify themselves only every 30 minutes, so you might be homing for quite a while on the wrong station!

To follow a straight track to a radio station using the ADF, you must establish a wind correction angle which will exactly offset wind drift. The first step in tracking is to place the needle at the 0° relative position by turning the airplane, just as in homing. As the wind blows the airplane downwind, the needle will move into the wind; when the needle has moved 5°, turn into the wind twice that amount (10°). This will make your heading 5° on the windward side of the direct course, with the ADF needle deflected 5° away from the wind. If the needle moves back toward the nose (into the wind), the wind drift correction is too small—add another 5°. If the needle moves away from the wind, the correction is too great and should be cut in half. This fine-tuning will continue until you pass over the radio antenna (Figure 10-21).

Another practical use of the ADF is establishing off-course checkpoints while on a VFR flight. If there is a low frequency station on either side of your course line, you can get an approximate position fix by noting when the ADF needle points directly off your wing tip toward the station (Figure 10-22). With a little imagination you can orient yourself in relation to a broadcast station or radio beacon using the ADF. As stated earlier, the head of the needle points to the station—so your position must be indicated by the tail of the needle. When you have the ADF receiver tuned to a station, note the position of the tail of the needle on the ADF indicator and mentally move it to the heading indicator; it will approximate your magnetic bearing from the station (Figure 10-22).

For some ADF practice, or to fix these concepts in your mind, go to www.fergworld.com/training/ adf_trainer.php.

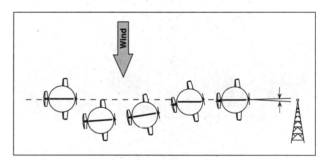

Figure 10-21. *Tracking—correcting for wind*

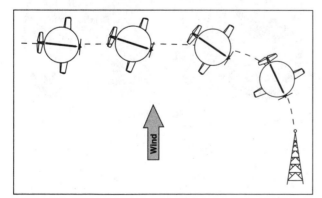

Figure 10-20. *Homing—no wind correction*

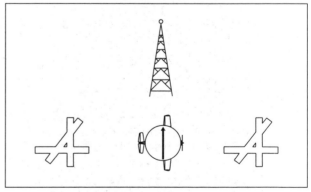

Figure 10-22. *Approximate position fix using ADF*

What Does the Future Hold for Nondirectional Beacons?

Many VFR pilots are removing ADF receivers from their panels and replacing them with GPS (later). Instrument students are no longer required to demonstrate their ability to use automatic direction finders/NDBs as of 1999. Some NDBs are owned and operated by local municipalities, however, and may remain in operation after national policy has changed. Increasingly, GPS waypoints can be used to replace NDBs. The FAA has made it clear, however, that as long as there are NDBs in the National Airspace System there will be questions about their use on knowledge exams.

Radio Magnetic Indicator

Figure 10-23 shows a type of electronic RMI (radio magnetic indicator) available in modern VOR receivers from many manufacturers. By selecting the frequency of the VOR station and TO or FROM, you get a direct digital readout of the radial on which you are located. This feature is also valuable in identifying radials which cross your course line and form intersections. Just watch the digital numbers click by until the desired radial shows up.

Figure 10-23. *Electronic RMI*

A radio magnetic indicator combines an ADF needle, one or more VOR needles, and a compass card driven by the directional gyro or similar source of magnetic information. With an RMI, the needle selected (ADF or VOR) indicates the magnetic bearing to the station continuously, without pilot input. When reading an RMI, the arrow head represents the bearing TO the station, and the tail represents bearing FROM the station. You can use the RMI to determine your bearing

from the transmitting station in the same way that you use the ADF's rotatable card, except that with an RMI the card is rotated for you by a gyro. Look at the four RMI indicators in Figure 10-24:

1. Indicator A shows that the airplane is 030° magnetic from the station, heading 330°. A left turn to 210° would take you to the station.

2. Indicator B shows the airplane crossing the 010° bearing from the station on a heading of 315°. To intercept the 180° bearing inbound to the station you would turn left to any heading between 191° and 269°.

3. Indicator C shows an airplane tracking to a station with a left crosswind from 245°. The pilot has turned left (into the wind), and the needle has moved to the right of the nose.

4. Indicator D shows an airplane tracking to a station with a right crosswind from 240°. The magnetic bearing to the station is 200°.

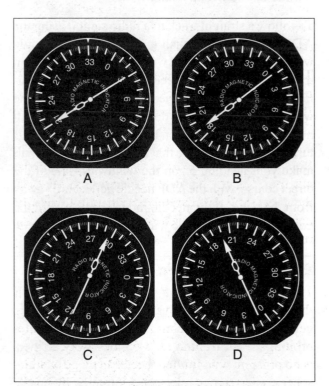

Figure 10-24. *RMI indicators*

Area Navigation

Area navigation, or RNAV, provides a means of straightline navigation using VORTACs (or VOR-DMEs) without dog-legging from station to station. The equipment allows you to establish navigational fixes called "waypoints" along the straight line course which can be identified by the DME distance and VOR radial from the VORTAC. Steering to the way-point is accomplished by the same left-right CDI needle used in VOR navigation, and distance to the waypoint is read out simultaneously. The RNAV equipment electronically "relocates" all of the enroute VORTACs so that they define the straight-line track. Several way-points can be preset, and the pilot selects them in sequence as the flight progresses.

Note: The FAA includes GPS navigation in its definition of Area Navigation; this discussion relates to non-GPS navigation—the FAA calls it "dme-dme."

An example, using the Seattle sectional chart excerpt in the back of the book, would be an RNAV route between the Olympia airport (**F**) and Harvey Field (**G**), just east of Paine Field at the top of the chart.

The first enroute waypoint would be the Seattle 273° radial at 7.3 nautical miles, and the second would be Harvey Field, using the Paine Field 064° radial at 7.8 nautical miles. These points define a straight line course between Olympia and Harvey Field. Using RNAV, you would have a continuous distance readout from Harvey Field. RNAV and GPS give you the capability of accurately navigating to airports not served by any navigational aid. RNAV is being replaced by the Global Positioning System.

Global Positioning System

The newest navigational system available to pilots is the Global Positioning System, or GPS. The system gets its input from a constellation of 24 satellites orbiting the earth about 11,000 miles away, so there is no problem with limited reception range or atmospheric interference (electronic jamming by hostile interests is a possibility). The system is designed so that at least 5 satellites are "visible" from any point on earth. Your GPS antenna must be able to "see" at least three satellites for a position fix and requires at least one more to add altitude information...but the AIM tells us that GPS altitude is not reliable,

and that we should rely on our barometric altimeters (AIM 1-1-19(a)(4)); GPS altitude is not measured above sea level, but above the "GPS spheroid," a mathematically-derived surface. Implementation of the Wide Area Augmentation System (later) will greatly increase the accuracy of altitude readouts.

GPS converts the signal from one satellite to a distance. Look at it this way: Could you determine your position by using distance measuring equipment (DME) alone? Sure you could. You would tune in one DME station and determine that your airplane is somewhere on a circle around that station with a radius equal to the DME readout. Do the same thing with three stations, and your position is where the three circles intersect.

The strength of the signal received in your airplane from a satellite is vanishingly weak...it has been compared to looking at a Christmas tree light in Los Angeles from the Empire State Building in New York. Changes in the ionosphere can introduce delays into the system. Your GPS navigator can pick up and identify the signal from each satellite, but it cannot eliminate these small errors. That is why it is only accurate to about 100 feet laterally.

GPS units are called "navigators," because unlike VOR or NDB, the pilot does not need to interpret any information...the GPS does all of the brainwork and displays the answers in digital form (courses, distances, speeds, times) and, in most cases, on a

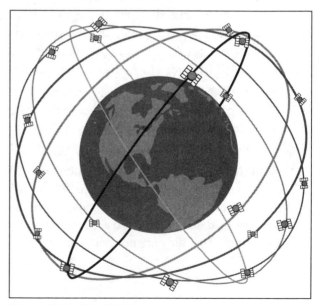

Figure 10-25. *The GPS in orbit*

"moving map," allowing the user to see the airplane's position in relation to airports, VORs, highways, rivers, cities, etc. If the GPS is turned off for a long period of time and the satellites have changed position (as they will), there is a delay on startup while the unit downloads current satellite position information.

The normal operating mode of a GPS navigator is "sequencing." This means that when you pass over a waypoint or fix the unit automatically sequences to the next waypoint or fix so you are always flying TO. All units offer non-sequencing, which is much like VOR navigation in that you can navigate FROM a waypoint or fix. This is of great value to instrument pilots, but for VFR operations I recommend using the sequencing (or "leg") mode.

The major drawback of GPS is that it is a magnet for a pilot's eyes…too much time is spent looking at the moving map and too little time is spent in scanning for traffic. Another drawback is that its ease of use can cause pilots to abandon pilotage and other means of navigation and rely solely on the GPS; if it fails, they have no idea as to where they are in relation to terrain, their destination, or nearby airports. That's why the FAA does not as yet permit the use of basic GPS, either panel-mounted or handheld, as the primary means of navigation under VFR or IFR, but tells us to use it for positional awareness only. GPS units with WAAS capability are true "sole source" navigators and require no backup.

The Global Positioning System is operated by the Department of Defense; the operating agency is the U. S. Air Force. The FAA does not have any direct control over the system; its function is limited to distributing GPS Notices to Airmen about satellite outages. Always ask your FSS briefer if there are any GPS NOTAMs when filing a flight plan in a GPS-equipped airplane.

The FAA has placed into operation the Wide Area Augmentation System (WAAS), which uses 25 Wide-area Ground Reference Stations to monitor and correct errors in the satellite signals. These stations are installed on buildings, so absent continental drift or earthquakes, they are not going anywhere…

unlike your airplane. They compare where the satellite says the building is to where the monitor knows it is, and develop correction signals. These corrections are transmitted to a low-orbit geostationary satellite (GEO) which in turn broadcasts them to aircraft receivers. Because the signal received from the GEO is much stronger than the signal received from the distant satellites, airborne receivers receive only the corrected information.

Older GPS navigators were certificated under Technical Standard Order C129a and could not be used as stand-alone units; they required the presence of a VOR receiver/indicator; newer units certificated under TSO C146a have WAAS and require no backup. See your unit's documentation to be sure what it is certificated for.

The GPS system is self-monitoring. When a satellite fails or delivers erroneous information, the navigator unit displays a Receiver Autonomous Integrity Monitoring or RAIM warning and the user must switch to another means of navigation. Handheld GPS units do not have RAIM capability and are therefore not approved by the FAA for anything other than positional awareness; your handheld could be off by 40 miles and you would never know it without looking out of the window at the terrain below.

You can check for RAIM warnings by going to www.raimprediction.net as part of your preflight planning.

The Global Positioning System is magic, compared to other means of radio navigation. Your GPS navigator lets you designate waypoints to keep your route of flight clear of Special Use Airspace and terrain (some units). It also makes your life easier by warning you when to switch tanks, provides a checklist (that you create), tells you which frequencies to use at airports along your route, and includes information on airports such as elevation, runway length, etc. Many units contain a transponder as well as transmitter-receiver controls. An excellent free interactive course on using GPS for VFR is available at the Air Safety Foundation website www.aopa.org/asf/online_courses/.

How do you know what kind of GPS you have, as a renter or prospective airplane buyer? There is only one place to find out, and that is in a required supplement to the airplane's Operating Handbook. That supplement tells you what you have, what you can do with it, and how it interfaces with other avionics. You cannot transfer what you know about one GPS in one airplane to the same GPS in another airplane, and you certainly can't apply what you know about one model of GPS to a different model.

There are some GPS functions that are fairly universal (but check the supplement!):

- A "nearest airport" function, which will list (usually) the bearing and distance to the ten nearest airports.
- A "direct" function, which supplies the bearing and distance to a selected waypoint/airport and has caused many pilots to fly into mountains or restricted airspace because they failed to keep track of where they were.
- Display of all relevant radio frequencies when an airport is selected.

The Hardware

A VOR receiver's controls consist of a frequency selector, an omnibearing selector, and some form of display; it would be hard for a ham-handed pilot to confuse their functions. Similarly, an ADF receiver has a frequency selector, a function switch, and some form of display (fixed or rotatable card); again, it is hard to imagine that a pilot would reach for the function switch when changing frequencies. A GPS navigator is totally different: If there was a switch or knob for each function, the panel would be a forest of switches and knobs. The creative minds at GPS manufacturers have harnessed the magic of microprocessors to make it possible for a single knob or switch to perform several functions, depending on how other knobs and switches are used. There is an ongoing struggle between manufacturers to come up with the latest and greatest, and that is why this book says so little about how to use a GPS navigator.

Back in the day, it was possible for an instructor to move from one airplane to another and find totally different VORs and ADFs. Not a biggie. The switches and knobs might have looked different, but their functions did not change. Today, what an instructor finds when moving from one airplane to another is that much depends on how each avionics unit interfaces with others and whether or not the owner has kept up with changes to the unit's software/firmware. Some units must be returned to the factory for changes, and the instructor may not know if a particular unit has been modified. Much more is required these days than was required in the past.

On a modern GPS navigator the function of a given button may depend on the position of a separate switch or knob, and if the pilot does not understand this, the result of pushing that button might be something totally unexpected. In some cases, simply pushing a button is not enough…you have to hold it in for two seconds. That's when *aviate-navigate-communicate* comes into play—be ready to momentarily turn the navigator or autopilot off and take over manually.

Fortunately, the avionics industry and the aviation training industry have made it possible for pilots to use either generic or unit-specific simulators on their home computers to become familiar with their installations in a non-threatening environment. Once again, it is impossible for me to provide you with useful hands-on information that applies across the board.

Multifunction Devices

Every month brings a new revelation of how a GPS can be linked to other sensors to deliver all kinds of information such as traffic alerts, weather maps, fuel burn and quantity, engine operating parameters, etc. The only limitations are panel space and money. Datalink is already available in some locations, which means that ATC communications may soon be showing up in textual form on your GPS screen rather than through your headset. When Mode S transponders are in common use, you will be able to see the location and altitude of other airplanes on your panel and they will be able to see your location and altitude. This system is in use in Alaska, along the Gulf Coast, and on the East Coast from Pennsylvania to Florida, and will soon go nationwide.

GPS for VFR Pilots

The FAA has recognized the popularity of GPS receivers, including handhelds, as supplements to visual navigation and has included some suggestions on their use in the *Aeronautical Information Manual* (AIM). Among them are the following:

Database Currency: Although a current database is required to use GPS under instrument flight rules, there is no such requirement for flights in visual conditions. However, a unit with a moving-map display might require a database in order to drive that function. If the database is not current, changes in airspace designations, special use airspace, and changed or relocated waypoints will not be available to the user. If your unit has a database, keep it current.

All handhelds lack RAIM, so the user gets no warning when the navigational solution is faulty due to poor satellite geometry, incorrect satellite data, etc. VFR pilots must back up their GPS with other means of navigation rather than follow its indications blindly.

Antenna Location: With an IFR-approved GPS, proper installation of the antenna is critical to avoid signal loss due to blanking by the aircraft structure. Users of handheld devices put the antenna wherever it is convenient. This could result in signal loss and erroneous position and navigation information. This poses a problem for renters. Pilots who own their airplanes can have an antenna permanently installed and its cable routed into the cabin.

Any permanent installation must comply with 14 CFR Part 43.

Pilots should plan a flight using GPS waypoints on the ground; trying to enter waypoints in flight diverts attention from scanning for collision hazards. The FAA is publishing GPS waypoints for use by VFR pilots on terminal area charts. Each waypoint has a five-letter designation beginning with VP— VPLOM, for example. These designations are not pronounceable and are not to be used in communication. Each waypoint has the familiar magenta flag. Use of these waypoints will aid in avoiding inadvertent entry into Class B or C airspace or other areas unfriendly to itinerant pilots. Lat-lon information for each waypoint is published in the back of the A/FD and on the legend panel of the sectional.

Until they have received additional training and an instructor's endorsement, holders of recreational pilot certificates should use GPS only to aid in positional awareness, as a backup to pilotage. After all, if you are prohibited from entering certain classes of airspace, you can use a little help in identifying their boundaries.

Common Pitfall Using GPS

The handiest function of any airborne GPS is "Direct To," and it is the function you should use least, especially if you anticipate stepping up to the instrument rating. Learn to use your unit's Flight Plan page. Take the time to enter waypoints along your desired route; learn how to add and delete waypoints. Many units will provide a warning of upcoming restricted or special use airspace but it is always possible to "Direct" yourself into a violation—or an obstruction. Face it… "Direct" is a crutch for lazy pilots.

Know what information each of the pages on your unit provides. Many pilots search around on published sources looking for radio frequencies that are available with the turn of a knob or the press of a button. Almost all manufacturers provide online user's manuals or simulators that you can practice on at home.

Handheld Devices

As I have noted, handheld GPS devices cannot be used as a primary tool for navigation purposes, only as an aid to situational awareness. However, the capability of handheld devices has exploded beyond simple navigation to include displays that warn of higher terrain in your vicinity, uplinked weather data, traffic advisories, backup flight instruments, and so forth depending on what you want to spend. I strongly recommend that pilots who do not own their own airplanes or who want a powerful backup to their panel-mounted GPS purchase a handheld. See the illustration in the color appendix on Page D-2.

Your handheld can be mounted in such a way that it can be removed without tools, and without running afoul of the regulations. Also, you can power the unit from a cigarette lighter socket but you cannot hard-wire it into the plane's electrical system. The FAA defines "portable" very strictly.

Summary

To use VOR intelligently you have to understand how it works, with radials, needles, and TO-FROM flags. To use ADF equipment intelligently you have to understand its limitations—atmospheric interference, short useful range, diurnal and shore effects—and you get involved with relative versus magnetic bearings, which brings the magnetic compass into the picture. To use GPS all you do is turn it on and you are instantly flooded with a torrent of information and you don't have to understand anything about how the system works in order to use the information.

Each manufacturer has its own way of doing things, and there is little relation between them. Some manufacturers that offer several models of GPS change the mode of operation from one model to another. Cost determines the number of features you will have available at the touch of a key or the turn of a knob. The differences are so great that it would be impossible for a book such as this to attempt to teach you how to use GPS.

Note: Because of these differences, I make no attempt to describe "how to" for GPS in the same way I treat VOR. There are excellent references available; among them are ASA's "GPS Trainer," G-1000 and Avidyne CD-ROM courses, and Max Trescott's "GPS and WAAS Instrument Flying Handbook."

Online Information

Computer users can find frequencies, geographic locations, service volumes, etc., at www.airnav.com. An interactive overview of GPS that includes lots of valuable information is available at www.asf.org/courses.

Lesson 10
Navigation Review Questions

1. Which pilot action is most likely to eliminate large fluctuations on the VOR course deviation indicator during flight?

   A— Recycle the ON-OFF switch.
   B— Disconnect the microphone.
   C— Change the engine RPM.

2. How can a pilot determine when a particular VOR is unreliable?

   A— A recorded voice stating "VOR shutdown for maintenance."
   B— A continuous series of dashes replacing the coded identification.
   C— An absence of the coded identification or T.E.S.T in Morse Code.

3. You want to track inbound on the 050° radial of a VOR station. The recommended procedure is to set the course selector to

   A— 050° and make heading corrections toward the Course Deviation Indicator (CDI needle).
   B— 050° and make heading corrections away from the Course Deviation Indicator (CDI needle).
   C— 230° and make heading corrections toward the Course Deviation Indicator (CDI needle).

4. Your magnetic heading is 300° and the ADF needle is pointing to a station bearing 085° relative to the nose of the airplane. The magnetic bearing to the station is

   A— 385°.
   B— 025°.
   C— 215°.

5. After selecting the frequency of a VOR station, you rotate the omni-bearing selector until the needle centers. The OBS reads 120° and the TO-FROM indicator shows TO. The airplane heading is 270°.

   A— You are southeast of the station.
   B— You are northwest of the station.
   C— You are west of the station.

Refer to the full-color Seattle sectional chart excerpt at the back of the book for questions 6, 7, and 8.

6. You are flying from Seattle (**C**) to Wenatchee (**H**) on the V-120 airway, with your VOR receiver tuned to 116.8 MHz and the omni-bearing selector on 072°. Directly over the north end of Kachess Lake you notice that the course deviation indicator needle is

   A— deflected to the right of center. You should change heading to the left to center the needle.
   B— deflected to the left of center. You should change heading to the left to center the needle.
   C— not centered. You should rotate the omni-bearing selector until the TO-FROM indicator changes to TO and the needle centers.

7. Approaching Wenatchee you decide to use your automatic direction finder as a backup means of radio navigation. You should tune the receiver to

   A— 1041 kHz.
   B— 111.0 MHz.
   C— 560 kHz.

8. You are over the city of Wenatchee and the airport is straight ahead. The needle on your ADF indicator (tuned in accordance with question 7) is pointing

   A — 090° relative.
   B — 180° relative.
   C — 240° relative.

9. You have become disoriented and want to use your VOR to establish your general position. You tune and identify a VOR station and rotate the OBS until the needle centers with a TO indication. The OBS reads 285°.

   A — You are northwest of the VOR and should turn to a heading of approximately 285° to fly to the station.
   B — You are southeast of the VOR and should turn to a heading of approximately 285° to fly to the station.
   C — You are southeast of the VOR and should turn to a heading of approximately 105° to fly to the station.

10. Distance Measuring Equipment (DME) is least accurate

    A — at low altitude, far from the station.
    B — at high altitude, close to the station.
    C — when heading directly toward the station.

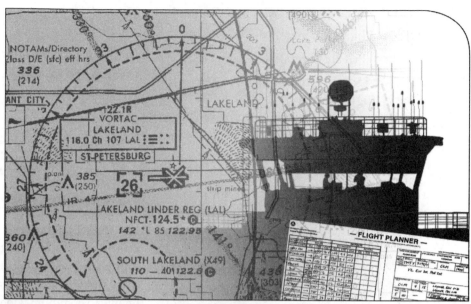

Lesson 11 Communication Procedures

When you listen to an AM radio at night, and tune down toward the lower end of the dial, you can pick up stations hundreds and even thousands of miles away. Low frequencies can be received at long distances even in the daytime, because they are not weakened or attenuated as they travel through the air and over the ground as much as are higher frequencies; however, atmospheric interference, or static, is a problem with low frequency transmissions. To avoid having critical aeronautical communications affected by static, frequencies in the Very High Frequency (VHF) range are used in aircraft radios. Radio transmissions in the VHF band are limited to line-of-sight (Figure 11-1) and that makes altitude

an important factor—as you gain altitude the range of VHF is greatly increased.

The FAA has assigned those frequencies between 118.0 MHz (megahertz—millions of cycles per second) and 136.975 MHz for radio communication.

The table below shows how they are allocated. Most modern aircraft radios are capable of transmitting and receiving on at least 720 frequencies, or channels.

The FAA spaces frequency assignments 25 kHz apart (thousands of cycles per second—126.225, 126.275). If you are assigned a frequency which your radio cannot tune, just ask for an alternate frequency.

This is an all-inclusive list of frequency assignments, emphasizing those that you will probably be using most.

Voice Communication Frequencies

118.0 to 121.4 MHz—Air Traffic Control

121.5 MHz—Emergency Frequency, ELT signals (The FAA recommends that you monitor this frequency at all times, if possible, to listen for emergency Notices to Airmen.)

Figure 11-1. *Line-of-sight radio limitations*

Continued

121.6 to 121.9 MHz—Airport Ground Control

121.95 MHz—Flight Schools

121.975 MHz—Private Aircraft Advisory (FSS)

122.0 MHz—FSS Enroute Flight Advisory Service ("Flight Watch")

122.025 to 122.075 MHz—FSS

122.1 MHz—FSS receive only

122.125 to 122.175 MHz—FSS

122.2 MHz—FSS Common Enroute Simplex

122.225 to 122.675 MHz—FSS

122.7 MHz—Unicom, uncontrolled airports

122.725 MHz—Unicom, private airports not open to public

122.75 MHz—Unicom, air-to-air, private airports not open to public

122.775 MHz—Future Unicom or Multicom

122.8 MHz—Unicom, uncontrolled airports

122.825 MHz—Future Unicom or Multicom

122.85 MHz—Multicom

122.875 MHz—Future Unicom or Multicom

122.9 MHz—Multicom, airports with no tower, FSS or Unicom

122.925 MHz—Multicom, Natural Resources

122.95 MHz—Unicom, controlled airports

122.975 MHz—Unicom, high altitude

123.0 MHz—Unicom, uncontrolled airports

123.025 MHz—Future Unicom or Multicom

123.05 and 123.075 MHz—Unicom, heliports

123.1 MHz—Search and Rescue, temporary control towers

123.15 to 123.575 MHz—Flight Test

123.6 to 123.65 MHz—FSS or Air Traffic Control (note that 123.45 is *not* available to all users)

123.675 to 128.8 MHz—Air Traffic Control

128.825 to 132.0 MHz—Aeronautical Radio, Inc. (ARINC)

132.05 to 136.975 MHz—Air Traffic Control

If you should blunder into an area where a Temporary Flight Restriction is in effect, and a couple of military jets show up off of your wing, keep in mind that not all military jets use VHF and you may be unable to communicate with them. Review the intercept procedures in Chapter 5 of the AIM.

Figure 11-2 shows a GPS/communications device with a digital display of active and standby frequencies. It's hard to find a pure communications transceiver these days.

When you select the proper communication frequency, you will transmit and receive on that frequency. Modern radios have crystal-controlled frequency selection and require no tuning. While you have the push-to-talk switch on your microphone depressed, your receiver is blocked and you cannot hear any other transmissions—each party to the communication must finish transmitting before a reply can be received. This is called **simplexing**, and most of your radio communication will be simplex. Talking on one frequency and listening on another, as you do on the telephone is called duplexing; it is used to

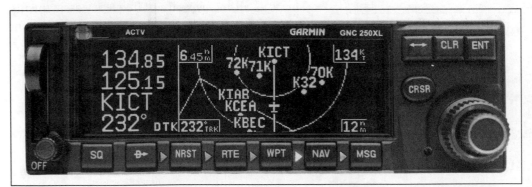

Figure 11-2. Typical GPS/communications device

communicate with flight service stations (FSS). In Figure 11-3, the St. Petersburg FSS receives on 122.1 MHz and transmits over the Lakeland VORTAC on 116.0 MHz.

The previous list gave general frequency assignments, but you need to know how to contact a specific tower, UNICOM, or flight service station. The A/FD lists all of the radio frequencies available at any airport and also includes a listing of all air route traffic control center frequencies—you will be using them for enroute radar services. Do not rely on commercial sources for frequency information; the AF/D is updated every 56 days, while most commercial directories are revised annually at best. A ready reference for most frequencies is your sectional aeronautical chart. Refer to the Seattle sectional chart and the sectional chart legend. Airports with control towers have a blue airport symbol, and very close to the symbol you will find a data block with "CT"—such as the one near the Seattle-Tacoma Airport, where "CT 119.9" is the control tower frequency. If there is an asterisk (*) following the frequency, the tower does not operate continuously. If the chart says NFCT adjacent to the airport symbol it is a non-Federal control tower, operated by a private entity.

When you listen to the **Automatic Terminal Information Service** (ATIS) frequency listed in the airport data block, you receive a continuous taped broadcast of non-control information such as ceiling and visibility, altimeter setting, wind (magnetic), runway in use, etc. If the ceiling is above 5,000 feet and the visibility is greater than 5 miles, that information might not be mentioned in the broadcast. Each time the ATIS is revised the phonetic designator is changed,

and you should include in your initial call the fact that you have listened to the ATIS: "Portland Ground Control, Cessna 1234X on the ramp with information ALFA, taxi to 10R." The UNICOM (privately operated Aeronautical Advisory Service) frequency is listed at the end of the data block. Sectional charts also include a tabulation of all control tower and ATIS frequencies in the margin (Figure 11-4).

Figure 11-5 shows how flight service station frequencies are presented on the charts. Note that some frequencies are not listed directly: the heavy line box means that 121.5 and 122.2 are available (but not shown).

CONTROL TOWER FREQUENCIES ON SEATTLE SECTIONAL CHART

Airports which have control towers are indicated on this chart by the letters CT followed by the primary VHF local control frequency. Selected transmitting frequencies for each control tower are tabulated in the adjoining spaces, the low or medium transmitting frequency is listed first followed by a VHF local control frequency and the primary VHF and UHF military frequencies, when these frequencies are available. An asterisk (*) follows the part time tower frequency remoted to the collocated full time FSS for use as Airport Advisory Service (AAS) during hours tower is closed. Receiving frequencies are shown thus: 122.5R. Hours shown are local time.

Automatic Terminal Information Service (ATIS) frequencies, shown on the face of the chart are normal arriving frequencies, all ATIS frequencies available are tabulated below.

ARS and/or PAR indicates Radar Instrument Approach available.

GRANT CO	Opr 0700-2300	118.1 124.2 247.8
GRAY AAF		126.2 248.2 ASR/PAR
LEWISTON-NEZ PERCE CO (Lewiston Twr)	Opr 0500-2200	119.4 318.8
McCHORD AFB	ATIS 109.6 270.1	124.8 259.3 ASR/PAR
McNARY (Salem Twr)	Opr 0700-2300	119.1 257.2
OLYMPIA	Opr 0800-2000	124.4 233.2
PENDLETON	Opr 0600-2200	118.7 257.8
PORTLAND HILLSBORO (Hillsboro Twr)	Opr 0700-2300	119.3* 239.3
PORTLAND INTL	ATIS 126.9 354.0	118.7 247.8 ASR

Figure 11-4. Tower and ATIS frequencies (example from sectional chart)

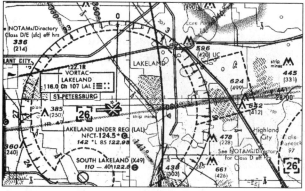

Figure 11-3. Duplex communications

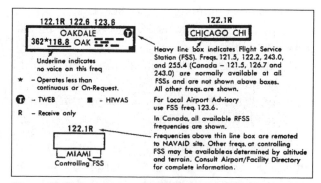

Figure 11-5. Communications boxes (from chart legend)

All other frequencies are listed above the box. If a frequency which is normally standard such as 121.5 or 122.2 is not available, it will be listed above the box with a strike-through: ~~122.2~~.

When you call a flight service station, you must advise them which remote communications outlet (RCO) you are listening to: "Prescott Radio, Ercoupe 345X, over Bisbee, listening 122.4." A thin blue-lined box indicates that the flight service station has only those frequencies that are printed outside the box. Where an FSS has a remote control capability, you will see a box with RCO, LRCO (Limited RCO), or a NAVAID frequency box with the name of the controlling FSS beneath the box (Figure 11-6). Look northwest of the Seattle-Tacoma Airport for an RCO box. Each regional A/FD includes a complete listing of flight service station remote outlets. When you use a remote outlet, be sure to include a statement of your position in your first transmission; the person on the other end is monitoring several speakers from remote outlets and needs to know where you are in order to select the correct transmitter to reply on.

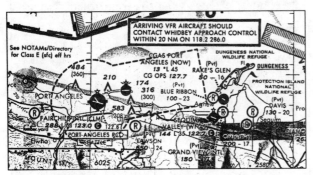

Figure 11-6. *RCO*

A new means of communication with Flight Service is the ground communication outlet (GCO). Unlike an RCO, a GCO connects a radio receiver on the ground to a telephone line; you can contact an FSS by clicking your mike button six times. GCO locations can be found only in the A/FD—they are not shown on charts. Use a GCO to close your flight plan or to get a last-minute weather briefing.

Note: Holders of recreational or sport pilot certificates cannot operate in airspace where radio communications *are required*—classes B, C, and D—without

additional training and a logbook endorsement. Students working toward these certificates can use aircraft radios under the supervision of an instructor, and the instructor can remove the limitation by a logbook endorsement when satisfied that the student is competent in the use of radio communications.

Radio Procedures

The *Aeronautical Information Manual* has a section on correct radio communications phraseology and technique, which contains a guide to the phonetic alphabet and pronunciation of numbers (this guide is also reproduced at the end of this lesson—*see* Page 11–12). The AIM also includes a Pilot/Controller Glossary of terms used in communication with air traffic controllers. You should become familiar with the contents of both. You might also want to look at www.asf.org/askatc. This site offers pilots the opportunity to ask controllers any and all questions about communications. You do not have to be a member of the Air Safety Foundation to access this site.

You will learn a lot just by listening on aircraft frequencies to hear how other pilots communicate with each other and with ground personnel. Be warned, however, that you may hear pilots use poor techniques and phraseology; just because you have heard someone say something on the radio does not mean that it is correct usage. Check with your instructor, the AIM, or my book, *Say Again, Please* for more. A visit to a flight service station, control tower, or a radar facility will convince you that everyone on the ground is prepared to help you have a safe flight and that having "mike fright" will just keep you from taking advantage of the many services available.

If you have a multimedia computer, log onto www. squawkident.com/livefeed.html and listen to communications at facilities across the nation and internationally. Don't expect to understand all of a controller's words when you first begin—it's like learning a second language.

Always listen before transmitting, so that you do not interfere with a communication in progress, and listen to what is being said—in many cases you may hear information that makes your call unnecessary. If your airplane's radio installation provides a switch so that you can transmit on either radio, be sure that you are using the correct radio before you transmit—this is a common mistake and you will hear it happen to the most grizzled old airline captains. Always begin your initial transmission with the name of the station that you are calling: "Logan Tower," "Orlando Ground," "Dallas Radio," "Podunk UNICOM," followed by your own identification (in full, if it is the initial contact): "Twin Cessna 2345X." Be sure to include your callsign, full or abbreviated, as part of every transmission.

It is not necessary to wait for an acknowledgment that communication has been established if you are reasonably certain that your transmission has been received: "Seattle Tower, Piper 2345X six miles north with BRAVO, landing." Be as brief as practicable without omitting necessary information, and always give your position when requesting a clearance from Air Traffic Control. Remember this sequence: WHO you are calling, WHO you are, WHERE you are, and WHAT your intentions are.

Be as brief as possible; every moment a controller spends listening to a long, drawn out transmission is time that cannot be devoted to other pilots. Omit unnecessary words. Compare these transmissions:

"Bigburg Ground Control, Cessna 1357X is at the south parking area with ATIS information FOXTROT. Request permission to taxi to the active runway. VFR to Littlefield."

"Ground, Cessna 1357X, south parking, Foxtrot, taxi 13, VFR Littlefield."

If you have the ATIS information, you know which runway is being used for departures; giving the ground controller your destination might result in the assignment of a more convenient runway or help the local controller direct your departure path more advantageously.

An airplane cockpit is a noisy place, and your microphone is designed to filter out engine noise if you use it properly. Hold the microphone close to your lips and speak directly into it. Holding the microphone away from your lips allows engine noise to mask your transmission.

Radio Use at Non-Tower Airports

Note: This is essential for both recreational and sport pilots. Remember that you are prohibited from entering airspace *where radio communication is required*. Radio communication is not required while en route or when landing at non-tower airports, but it sure comes in handy.

Unless an airport has an operating control tower, you do not even need to have a radio to use that airport. For safety's sake, however, you should have a radio—but do not expect all other airplanes in the area to have radios. Many airports have no radio facility. When operating in the vicinity of a non-radio airport use the **Common Traffic Advisory Frequency** (CTAF, shown as **Ⓒ** on sectional charts) listed in the Airport/Facility Directory. In most cases this will be the MULTICOM frequency 122.9 MHz, because you will be broadcasting your position and intentions in the blind (no specific addressee): "Podunk Traffic, Mooney 2345X ten miles north landing." Don't use 122.9 MHz as an airborne "party line" to talk to your friends in flight—122.75 MHz may be used for that purpose. Note also that 123.45 *is not* to be used for idle chatter; it is assigned to aircraft manufacturers and is also used by transoceanic airline flights.

At virtually every tower-controlled airport, the tower frequency becomes the CTAF when the tower is closed, so nothing changes after the controllers go home—you just don't get a reply from anyone on the ground.

At most airports with a UNICOM (Aeronautical Advisory Service), the UNICOM frequency will be the CTAF. Don't be surprised if you attempt to call UNICOM and get no reply—this is a nongovernmental service provided by the local operator, and those busy people may not hear your call. UNICOM frequencies are shared by many uncontrolled airports, and some may be so close together that pilots at different airports will interfere with one another. To avoid confusion, always begin and end your transmission with the name of the airport at which you are operating: "Podunk traffic, Grumman 2345X left downwind runway 16, touch and go, Podunk." UNICOM is used for many purposes and is quite informal, but you should not let this informality change your normal good communication habits. Be sure to use both your eyes and your radio at airports where you must taxi on the active runway to get into takeoff position, or taxi back to an exit after landing.

Some airports have installed new devices called SuperUnicoms®. They operate 24 hours a day and never take a coffee break. When you call in to an airport with a SuperUnicom, your call will be answered by a computer-generated human voice giving temperature, dew point, wind direction and velocity, altimeter setting, and favored runway (based on calls from traffic in the pattern). Pilots can also get weather information with mike clicks.

AIM paragraph 3-5-1 mentions an Airport Advisory Service at airports where there is a Flight Service Station (FSS) on the field. Since the FAA contracted FSS duties to private industry, these duties have been consolidated and chances are that you will never land at an airport with an FSS on the field. Go to www.afss.com and click on "Pilot Tips" for more details. The radio frequencies in the A/FD and on sectional charts are remoted, and the controller you talk to might be hundreds of miles from your location. However, the contractor's briefers will ensure that you can talk to someone with local knowledge, even if they can't look out the window and tell you how many planes are in the pattern.

Be sure to read the Communications section of the A/FD Legend pages in Appendix B; it makes clear how frequencies are to be used.

Communication at Airports with Operating Towers

Airspace around an airport with an operating control tower is Class D airspace (unless it is within Class B airspace); it will usually extend vertically to 2,500 feet above airport elevation and horizontally a nominal 4.4 nautical miles (the boundaries may vary, but will be charted). If you need to enter Class D airspace, you must first communicate with the tower. If you are departing, you must first receive taxi instructions (not a "taxi clearance") from the ground controller, who directs all activity on the ramps and taxiways. With few exceptions, ground control operates on 121.6, 121.7, 121.8, or 121.9

MHz. Controllers will frequently shorten this by eliminating the 121: "Contact ground point seven leaving the runway."

The ground controller will authorize you to taxi to the runway in use, but you must stop before crossing any taxiways or runways (active or not) and receive permission to cross. Think of it as a stoplight at every intersection that glows red until the controller turns it to green. Figure 11-7 illustrates a situation where a pilot taxiing from the ramp to the runup area for runway 9 would receive authorization for the whole route, but would be told to hold short of runway 27. With permission to cross, he or she would proceed to the unmarked intersection with the closed runway, stop, call for permission, and the procedure would be repeated at the hold lines for runways 36R and 36L. It is the controller's responsibility to issue precise instructions, but if you are getting close to any kind of intersection without having heard from the tower, stop and ask.

Note: Ground controllers do not use the word "cleared," because it might be misconstrued as a takeoff clearance...they say "taxi to" or "taxi across." If you are directed to "hold short" of a runway you must read that instruction back to the controller verbatim...nothing else will suffice. To avoid a runway incursion, always stop and ask for clarification of any instruction you do not understand. "What do you want me to do?" works just fine.

If you are at an unfamiliar airport, do not hesitate to ask for "progressive taxi instructions" and the controller will guide you to your destination on the field. "Student pilot" is a useful phrase to include in your transmissions.

When you are ready for takeoff, contact the tower controller for takeoff clearance. The tower (or "local") controller is responsible for all aircraft in Class D airspace and on the active runway—don't taxi onto the runway without a clearance. You must maintain communication with the tower controllers while you are in their airspace (Class D), but remember that separation from other airplanes is your responsibility; don't expect the controller to keep

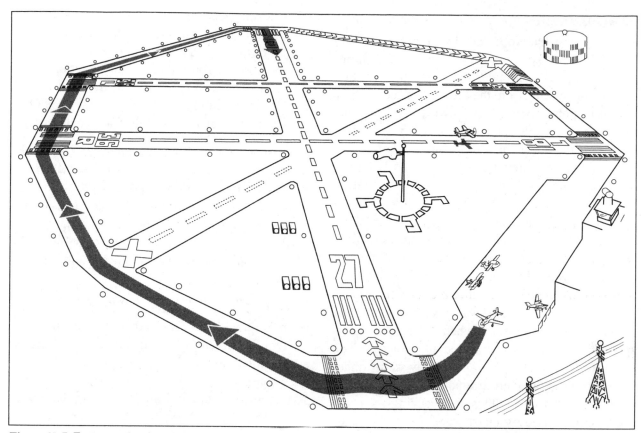

Figure 11-7. Taxiing to the active runway

you from swapping paint. When you have departed Class D airspace you are on your own (or you may request radar services). You do not have to ask the tower for permission to change frequencies after you have crossed the Class D airspace boundary.

On arrival, before you enter Class D airspace you should listen to the ATIS (if there is one) and advise the tower controller on initial contact that you have the ATIS information. Where there is no ATIS, listen on the tower frequency and note the instructions given to other pilots. Once you are sure of the runway in use, wind, and altimeter setting, you can say: "Miami Tower, Baron 2345X ten miles west with the numbers." After landing, do not change to ground control until advised to do so by the tower. Some tower-controlled airports have UNICOM, but because you will get all of your weather information and clearances from the tower, your use of UNICOM

at that tower-controlled airport will be limited to such things as calling for fuel, ordering rental cars, etc. *Note:* Towers report wind direction relative to magnetic north. In fact, any wind direction you receive by radio is referenced to magnetic north; winds in written form, such as forecasts, are referenced to true north.

If you have any questions about how your flight was handled by the tower, call as soon as practicable and talk to a quality assurance person before the tapes are erased—don't expect an answer if you wait more than 15 days.

VFR Advisory

If an airport does not have an ATIS and does not use the primary control tower frequency as the CTAF, its data block will include "VFR Advisory—125.0"; if, of course, 125.0 is the frequency to use.

Transponder

Although the **transponder** (Figure 11-8) has no microphone or speaker, it is a means of communication with ground radar facilities. Interrogation signals transmitted from the ground are received by your transponder, and it replies with a coded signal which the controller can read on the radar scope. Each time the transponder reply light flickers, it has responded to an interrogation. In congested areas the transponder will be replying to interrogation from several radars, while in remote areas it may receive only an occasional interrogation. Always set the four numbers on your transponder to 1200 when flying VFR. Otherwise, enter a specific code as directed by a radar controller while receiving radar services. *The regulations require that all transponder-equipped airplanes must have them turned on while in flight.* Be careful when setting your transponder—some codes have special meanings. Code 7700, for instance, is the emergency transponder code, used only to alert ground personnel that you are in distress. Code 7500 is the hijacking code, and code 7600 is used by instrument pilots in case of communications failure. Code 7777 belongs to the military. If a controller asks you to change codes, always acknowledge by reading the new code back to the controller.

Push your transponder's IDENT button only when told to do so by the controller. This feature causes your radar return to intensify on the controller's scope for exact identification, and when pushed it will stay activated for about 20 seconds. "Identing"

when not directed to do so might result in a mis-identification by the controller. When the transponder function switch is ON, you are in Mode A (indicating your position) only, and with the function switch in the ALT (Mode C) position, the transponder will also transmit altitude information to the ground (if an encoding altimeter is installed in the airplane).

A transponder with Mode C capability is required for operation in Class B or C airspace or when flying in controlled airspace above 10,000 feet. You can request a waiver of these requirements if you give ATC one hour's notice. Additionally, Mode C is required if you fly within 30 nautical miles of the Class B airspace's primary airport and from the surface to 10,000 feet MSL.

Almost all radar facilities require a transponder return for tracking. At those facilities with the most modern equipment, the controller does not see an actual target generated by your airplane but a computer-generated target based on your transponder. That is why you will occasionally see airplanes *visually* that have not been called to your attention by the controller; if they don't have a transponder (or if their transponder is off), they don't show up on the radar.

A newer type of transponder, Mode S, transmits your airplane's tail number in addition to position and altitude. These transponders make it possible for users to participate in the *Traffic Identification System* and *Automatic Dependent Surveillance* (ADS-B) programs. They are more expensive than Mode A/C transponders but enhance safety.

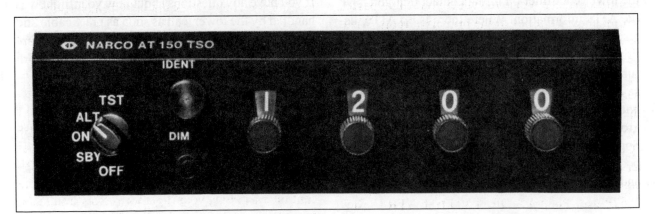

Figure 11-8. *Typical transponder*

Radar Services for VFR Pilots

There are two types of radar service available to you as a VFR pilot: radar traffic advisory service ("**flight following**") and terminal radar service. Terminal radar service, presently provided as Basic Service, includes safety alerts, traffic advisories, limited vectoring, and sequencing when available. If you tell Ground Control upon initial contact that you desire radar traffic advisories, this valuable service will be provided from the start of your flight. This service is available to recreational and sport pilots when outside of airspace in which radio communication is required, and everywhere when the restriction has been removed by an instructor.

Flight following is an under-used asset; it is free for the asking, yet many pilots fail to take advantage of it—the John F. Kennedy, Jr. accident offers a dramatic example. If you can use your aircraft radios to talk to flight service stations and control towers, you can use them to get radar service.

If you are requesting radar flight following from ground control or clearance delivery at a tower-controlled airport and receive a transponder code beginning with 01xx, 02xx, 03xx , or 04xx, understand that those codes are used only in the airspace controlled by the local radar facility; if your flight will leave terminal airspace, ask the controller for a "Center squawk."

During the flight planning process, refer to the A/FD Communications listing for airports along your route of flight. You will find frequencies for terminal radar facilities that can assist you when your flight passes within about 30 miles of the primary airport. Write down the frequencies and the names of the facilities. Then refer to the back pages of your A/FD for ARTCC frequencies and write down the facility names and frequencies along your route. Address the terminal facility as "Approach," as in Dallas Approach, and address the Center controllers as "Center"—as in Oakland Center. Tell the controller that you are a student pilot (this also works after you get your license). "Oakland Center, Teenybird 4567P over Podunk VOR, 4,500 feet, VFR to Bigtown, request flight following." The controller will ask you to change transponder codes from 1200 to a discrete code and to push the Ident button. That's

all there is to it. You remain responsible for terrain clearance and for following all regulations relating to VFR, but you will receive traffic advisories and you will have a friend with a radar scope who knows exactly where you are if you have a problem.

Note: If you have failed to write down ATC frequencies before takeoff, call the nearest FSS on 122.2, give your position, and ask "What frequency should I use to request radar flight following?"

Limited vectoring is an excellent way to fly more safely through a congested terminal area or to get to an unfamiliar airport. The radar controller will do everything possible for you, but keeping on the right side of the Federal Aviation Regulations is your responsibility. A heading which would take you into cloud or provide anything less than the required separation from clouds must be refused, and the controller advised of the reason: "Tomahawk 45X won't be able to maintain VFR on that heading." You are also required to see and avoid other aircraft. The radar is only an aid. The controller will give you traffic information using the clock in relation to your direction of movement. Each number on the clock represents 30°, and in no-wind conditions traffic at 2 o'clock would be 60° to the right of the nose. If you have established a 30° correction into a wind from the left, traffic reported at 2 o'clock would be directly off your right wing (Figure 11-9). Advisories are just that...advice. If you want vectors to avoid the traffic you must ask for them. Respond to a traffic call with either "negative contact" or "traffic in sight" if you don't ask for avoidance vectors. Saying "we're looking/searching" does not help the controller.

When you are receiving radar flight following, the controller will coordinate with control towers and other ATC facilities along the way; you need not worry about changing frequencies to get a clearance through Class B, C, or D airspace (although I would question the controller before entering Class B). *Note:* This is a trap for recreational and sport pilots who are using flight following but are prohibited from entering these classes of airspace; ask the controller handling your flight for vectors around the Class B, C, or D airspace unless this restriction has been removed by a logbook endorsement.

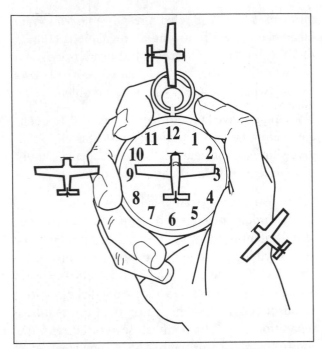

Figure 11-9. Traffic information using clock positions

The radar controller who is providing flight following is obligated to coordinate your flight through Class B, C, and D airspace with the facilities with responsibility for that airspace—you do not have to switch frequencies to negotiate clearances with ATC. The downside is that because flight following is provided on a "workload permitting" basis, a controller who is too busy to handle the coordination tasks may say "Radar service terminated; squawk VFR (1200)," dumping the task of getting clearances back in your lap. You, of course, should attempt to re-establish flight following as soon as possible after passing through the airspace in question.

The Air Traffic Control Handbook and the AIM conflict on this point; the AIM says that it is your responsibility, and the ATCH puts the onus on the controller.

TRSA service is provided in Terminal Radar Service Areas, which are outlined in black on your sectional chart (with their vertical limits), and identified in the A/FD. Participation is voluntary, but recommended. This service is *not* limited to "workload permitting," but is available at all times. You will be separated from all IFR and all participating VFR traffic, but you must remember that not all VFR pilots participate by requesting radar service and you may see airplanes that the radar controller has not called out

to you as traffic. Generally, radar only sees those airplanes with transponders, although the capability to pick up targets by radar reflection alone can be selected. Again, the responsibility to remain clear of traffic and in VFR conditions rests with you.

You will find the frequencies for terminal radar service in the A/FD, listed under the airport served by the radar facility. In some cases the ATIS advises VFR pilots to contact Approach Control and gives the frequency. This is also true upon departure from an airport with terminal radar service—the ATIS may tell you to call on a certain frequency for a clearance before calling the ground controller for taxi instructions. In a TRSA, if you do not desire radar services you need only advise the controller "Negative TRSA service," and you will be on your own—then you will be one of those non-participating aircraft that everyone else is looking out for.

Radar traffic advisory service provides only traffic advice, and that is what you will get if you "request radar flight following." If you are being provided with radar service after departure, the radar controller will "hand you off" to the next controller (with a frequency change), and that controller will in turn pass you along. If you are en route and want radar service, call the nearest FSS. They will give you the correct frequency for your present location. Radar controllers will always tell you when radar service is terminated instead of just "dropping" you. You should return the favor by always advising the radar controller when you no longer desire radar service—don't just change frequencies.

Class C airspace (*see* Pages 5–16 and 9–19) is replacing most Terminal Radar Service Areas; where they still exist, they are shown on charts with a solid black outline. At this writing there are very few TRSAs in the country.

When using radar flight following, keep in mind that most military aircraft radios operate in the UHF band, not the VHF band used in civil aviation. Military pilots do not hear any conversations between you and the radar controllers and are unaware of your position and intentions. Be aware of Military Training Routes (Lesson 9) and keep your eyes open—don't place your safety entirely in the hands of the radar controller.

ADS-B

...and now for something completely different. How do you get flight following in an area without radar service? The answer may be Automatic Dependent Surveillance–Broadcast (ADS-B). Where it is available, and if your plane is properly equipped, it fills in the blanks where radar coverage is not available due to terrain or altitude. Your GPS continuously transmits your position, track, altitude, groundspeed, and tail number to a ground based transceiver (GBT), where it is relayed to an air traffic control facility, making it possible for controllers to know all about you without using radar (this is called ADS-B out). Controllers can also see returns from other similarly equipped aircraft in your vicinity and provide separation. This is the basic ADS-B function; for a few more bucks, you can enhance it by equipping your airplane to receive the information directly from nearby airplanes and have it available in your cockpit on a multifunction display, giving you real-time traffic positions (this is called ADS-B in). The equipment also provides for datalinked weather. This is not the end of the line for radar controllers, though... providing your own separation based on ADS-B is not in the cards.

ADS-B is altitude-limited in that the transmission from your airplane to the ground is line-of-sight and may be obstructed by terrain in some areas. Still, it is good down to 2,000 feet AGL or lower wherever it is available.

ADS-B has proved its worth in Alaska, where radar coverage is limited. The service is available along the east coast and in North Dakota as well as Alaska. The FAA is installing GBTs across the continent, with completion scheduled for 2014. The FAA has proposed that "ADS-B Out" be mandatory by 2020.

Emergency Communications

The International Distress frequency for VHF is 121.5 MHz. You are required by national security policy to monitor (listen to) this frequency if possible. If you are not already in communication with some FAA facility and you become lost, disoriented or have any kind of emergency, do not hesitate to tune to 121.5 and call "MAYDAY, MAYDAY, MAYDAY STINSON 2345X calling any station!" You will get many answers—respond to the loudest one.

Do not be reluctant to call for help for fear of embarrassment—the longer you delay in confessing your predicament, the less fuel you will have to carry out the instructions of an assisting agency. In an emergency, you should also set your transponder to 7700. This sets off bells and buzzers at radar facilities and will help the controllers pinpoint your position even if you are too busy with the situation at hand to call anyone on the radio.

An "urgency" situation is supposed to be communicated by repeating the word PAN three times—to my knowledge, nobody does this. You are in an urgency situation when you are concerned about the safety of your flight and need timely but not immediate assistance; examples would be disorientation, low fuel, deteriorating weather, etc. It makes no sense to consume fuel trying to get oriented or looking for improving weather when help is available at the press of a push-to-talk button. Declaring an emergency *does not* result in a blizzard of paperwork—it might not even result in a "call this number after you land" transmission.

Ground-Controlled Approaches

If there is a military or a joint-use civil-military airport in your area, ask your instructor to take you there for a practice ground-controlled approach. This is a procedure to be used only in an emergency when unforecast weather traps you on top of clouds (after you are licensed, of course—as a student you must maintain visual contact with the ground). All you have to do during a GCA is follow instructions from the controller.

Emergency Locator Transmitter

With very limited exceptions, every airplane must carry an **Emergency Locator Transmitter** (ELT) which automatically transmits when it is turned on by a pilot in distress or by impact forces. ELTs transmit on both the VHF and UHF distress frequencies: 121.5 MHz and 243.0 MHz (used by the military). The 121.5 and 243.0 ELTs are being phased out and replaced by units that broadcast on 406 MHz. Canada will make 406 MHz ELTs mandatory in February of 2011; flight into or over Canadian airspace will be prohibited for planes without the new transmitters. The new 406 MHz ELTs broadcast the airplane's tail number, and some models broadcast a GPS-derived position. Personal locator beacons that broadcast the same information and can be carried on one's person are also available. In every case, PLBs must be registered with information identifying the owner. *Note:* There is no single approved procedure for testing personal locator beacons; check the manufacturer's instructions.

To be sure that your analog (121.5/243 Mhz) will operate in an emergency, you are allowed to turn it on *briefly* during the first five minutes of each hour (while monitoring 121.5 on your communications receiver). Because ELTs have been activated by hard landings, many pilots monitor 121.5 MHz briefly before shutting down their engines, just to be sure that no signal is being transmitted. False ELT signals must be tracked down by search and rescue forces and verified as being false; so pilots must take every precaution against error. The battery in your ELT must be replaced when one-half of its useful life has expired (or if your brief tests have accumulated one hour of transmitting time), and the service technician will mark that date on the side of the transmitter case. Find a little whisker antenna about a foot long sticking out of the aft fuselage—there will be an access door close by.

Note: Digital 406 Mhz ELTs should only be tested in accordance with the unit's manufacturer's instructions.

Radio Communication Phraseology and Technique

Always use the phonetic alphabet when identifying your aircraft and to spell out groups of letter or unusual words under difficult communications conditions. Do not make up your own phonetic equivalents; this alphabet was developed internationally to be understandable by non-English speaking pilots and ground personnel.

Phonetic Alphabet

Letter	Word (Pronunciation)
A	**ALFA** (ALFAH)
B	**BRAVO** (BRAHVOH)
C	**CHARLIE** (CHAR-LEE OR SHAR-LEE)
D	**DELTA** (DELL-TA)
E	**ECHO** (ECK-OH)
F	**FOXTROT** (FOKS-TROT)
G	**GOLF** (GOLF)
H	**HOTEL** (HOH-TEL)
I	**INDIA** (IN-DEE-AH)
J	**JULIETT** (JOO-LEE-ETT)
K	**KILO** (KEY-LOH)
L	**LIMA** (LEE-MAH)
M	**MIKE** (MIKE)
N	**NOVEMBER** (NO-VEM-BER)
O	**OSCAR** (OSS-CAH)
P	**PAPA** (PAH-PAH)
Q	**QUEBEC** (KEH-BECK)
R	**ROMEO** (ROW-ME-OH)
S	**SIERRA** (SEE-AIR-AH)
T	**TANGO** (TANG-GO)
U	**UNIFORM** (YOU-NEE-FORM)
V	**VICTOR** (VIK-TAH)
W	**WHISKEY** (WISS-KEY)
X	**XRAY** (ECKS-RAY)
Y	**YANKEE** (YANG-KEY)
Z	**ZULU** (ZOO-LOO)
1	**ONE** (WUN)
2	**TWO** (TOO)
3	**THREE** (TREE)
4	**FOUR** (FOW-ER)
5	**FIVE** (FIFE)
6	**SIX** (SIX)
7	**SEVEN** (SEVEN)
8	**EIGHT** (AIT)
9	**NINER** (NIN-ER)
0	**ZERO** (ZEE-RO)

Figures

Misunderstandings about altitude assignments can be hazardous. The examples below are taken from the *Aeronautical Information Manual* and demonstrate officially accepted techniques. However, as you monitor aviation frequencies you will hear pilots use a decimal system: TWO POINT FIVE for 2,500. The FAA has never commented on this practice and it is commonly accepted—don't try it in another country.

```
500...............................................FIVE HUNDRED
10,000......................................TEN THOUSAND
13,500...............ONE THREE THOUSAND FIVE
                                                HUNDRED
```

Pilots flying above 18,000 feet use flight levels when referring to altitude:

"CENTURION 45X LEAVING ONE SEVEN THOUSAND FOR FLIGHT LEVEL TWO THREE ZERO."

Bearings, courses, and radials are always spoken in three digits:

"CESSNA 38N TURN LEFT HEADING THREE ZERO ZERO, INTERCEPT THE DALLAS ZERO ONE FIVE RADIAL."

Address ground controllers as "SEATTLE GROUND CONTROL," control towers as "O'HARE TOWER," radar facilities as "MIAMI APPROACH," or "ATLANTA CENTER." When calling a flight service station, use *radio:* "PORTLAND RADIO, MOONEY FOUR VICTOR WHISKEY."

When making the initial contact with a controller, use your full callsign, without the initial *november:* "BOISE GROUND, PIPER THREE SIX NINER ECHO ROMEO AT THE RAMP WITH INFORMATION GOLF, TAXI FOR TAKEOFF."

Use of the last three digits is acceptable for subsequent transmissions: "ROGER, TAXI TWO EIGHT RIGHT, NINER ECHO ROMEO."

Many uncontrolled airports share UNICOM frequencies, and if you do not identify the airport at which you are operating, your transmissions may serve to confuse other pilots monitoring the frequency. Don't say, "STINSON FOUR SIX WHISKEY DOWNWIND FOR RUNWAY SIX," say "ARLINGTON TRAFFIC, STINSON FOUR SIX WHISKEY DOWNWIND FOR RUNWAY SIX, ARLINGTON." That way, pilots at other airports sharing Arlington's UNICOM frequency will not be nervously looking over their shoulders.

"Unable" and "Immediately"

The most valuable word in radio communication is "unable." It should be used whenever you are asked to do something you don't want to do or are prohibited from doing, like flying close to a cloud. An air traffic controller who hears "unable" will come up with an alternative plan. You are the pilot-in-command and the only person in position to determine the safety of a proposed action. The second most important word is "immediately." If a controller tells you to turn left immediately, or to climb immediately or to do anything else immediately, do not reach for the microphone—do it. The other side of the coin is when you need to cut corners to get on the ground in a hurry—a sick passenger, for example. When you make your initial call, tell the controller that you need to land immediately.

Online Sources

www.runwayfinder.com
www.flyagogo.net
www.ourairports.com
http://skyvector.com
www.aopa.org/airports

Note: None of these sites are official and they should be used only for planning and orientation. Aerial views are not current.

You can find the frequencies to be used at any airport at www.airnav.com.

An excellent resource for radio communication procedures is "Say It Right," produced by the Air Safety Foundation. It can be found at www.asf.org/courses.

Flight Planning

This section will give you the opportunity to put together all of the information you have learned from the rest of the book in a practical form. With your knowledge of performance charts, weather, regulations, navigational charts, publications, and the airspace system, you should be able to plan a cross-country flight that is within the capability of your airplane, while complying with the regulations at all times.

A word of caution: Statistics show that a significant number of pilots continue to fly into deteriorating weather or overfly refueling facilities with the gauges bouncing on empty because of "Plan Continuation Bias." This fancy term means that they are so fixed on making their destinations without stopping that they overlook obvious hazards. This is a form of "get-home-itis" that applies to all flights. I can't get inside of your head, I can only ask that you think clearly and realize that not getting to your destination is not the end of the world, but trying to get there in marginal weather or without a fuel stop might be the end of your world.

Filing a Flight Plan

If you took the Air Safety Foundation course on flight service stations that I recommended on Page 7–2, you know that there are only three "hubs" and ten automated flight service stations to serve the continental United States. For example, if you are in any western state, your hub is in Prescott, Arizona; the briefer you speak to has been certified to have knowledge of all of the western states. The only AFSS is in Seattle—but that is a heavy load. Be sure to tell the briefer the city and state you are departing from and the same for your destination. This will make it easier for the briefer to call up information from a national database. The days of a briefer looking out of a window or knowing what traffic is in a pattern are over.

You will file this VFR flight plan as a round-robin (or round trip), noting in the remarks section that you will be landing at Ellensburg and at Paine Field. Unless you plan to use radar flight following or make regular position reports, do not use round-robins— file separate flight plans for each leg of the flight (AIM 6-2-7). The basic purpose for filing a VFR

flight plan is to aid Search and Rescue forces if you fail to complete the flight. If you file a round-robin flight plan with a duration of five hours and run into trouble immediately after opening the flight plan with Flight Service, search efforts will not begin for five and one-half hours. That's the best argument against round-robins. On this trip, you will stay in contact with ATC. With that in mind, filling out the flight plan form should be easy. *See* Figure 11-10 and sectional chart excerpt at the back of the book.

Block 1:

You will be filing a VFR flight plan.

Block 2:

Fill in the complete registration (or "N" number) of your airplane. Be sure that friends or relatives who may be waiting for you know the registration number of your airplane.

Block 3:

Fill in the manufacturer's name and the model of the airplane (Piper PA-28) and the letter designating the equipment on board.

Here is a list of equipment designations:

/X No transponder
/T Transponder with no Mode C
/U Transponder with Mode C
/D DME but no transponder
/B DME and transponder but no Mode C
/A DME and transponder with Mode C
/M TACAN but no transponder
/N TACAN and transponder but no Mode C
/P TACAN and transponder with Mode C
/Y RNAV and LORAN, VOR/DME or INS, but no transponder
/C RNAV and LORAN, VOR/DME or INS, and transponder but no Mode C
/I RNAV and LORAN, VOR/DME or INS, and transponder with Mode C
/E Advanced RNAV and transponder with Mode C, also FMS with DME/DME and IRU position updating
/F Advanced RNAV and transponder with Mode C, also FMS with DME/DME position updating
/G Advanced RNAV and transponder with Mode C, also GNSS, including GPS or WAAS with enroute and terminal capability

US Department of Transportation
Federal Aviation Administration

— FLIGHT PLANNER —

(INFORMATION THAT YOU ENTER ON THIS FORM IS FOR PILOT'S USE ONLY.)

PREFLIGHT				EN ROUTE					
DEPARTURE PT	ROUTE			ESTIMATED			ACTUAL		
CHECK POINTS	VIA	CRS	DIST	GS	ETE	ETA	GS	ATE	ATA
GRAY RBN	→	032°	16.5	106	9.5	1110			
McCHORD AFB	→	056°	5	120	2.5	1113			
LAKE TAPPS	→	056°	13	120	6.5	1120			
PALMER	→	056°	13	120	6.5	1127			
DAM	116.8/086	095°	6	112	4.0	1131			
LESTER	117.9/088	095°	14	112	8.0	1139			
ELLENSBURG	117.9/088	095°	40	112	22.0	1201			
DE VERE	→	285°	16	86	11.0	1241			
CLE ELUM LK	→	285°	14	103	8.0	1249			
COLLIGAN LK	→	285°	28	103	16.0	1305			
PAINE FIELD	→	285°	30	103	18.0	1323			
FT. LAWTON	→	185°	17	96	11.0	1441			
SHORELINE	→	185°	9	96	6.0	1447			
OLYMPIA	→	185°	37	96	23.0	1510			

	FUEL MANAGEMENT					
	R	L	R	L		
OFF						
ON	1100					
TIME						

TIME EN ROUTE	
TOUCH-DOWN	
TAKE-OFF	1100
ATE	

FAA Form 8740-2 (10-84) SUPERSEDES PREVIOUS EDITION

FOLD ALONG THIS LINE

USE OF FAA FORM 7233-1 Approved:OMB No. 2120-0026

U.S. DEPARTMENT OF TRANSPORTATION FEDERAL AVIATION ADMINISTRATION
FLIGHT PLAN
(FAA USE ONLY) ☐ PILOT BRIEFING ☐ VNR ☐ STOPOVER — TIME STARTED — SPECIALIST INITIALS

1 TYPE	2 AIRCRAFT IDENTIFICATION	3 AIRCRAFT TYPE/ SPECIAL EQUIPMENT	4 TRUE AIRSPEED	5 DEPARTURE POINT	6 DEPARTURE TIME PROPOSED (Z)	ACTUAL (Z)	7 CRUISING ALTITUDE
☒ VFR ☐ IFR ☐ DVFR	2345 X	P.175/T	KTS	OLM	1900		VFR

8 ROUTE OF FLIGHT: V2 ELN DIR PAE DIR

9 DESTINATION (Name of airport and city)	10 EST. TIME ENROUTE HOURS	MINUTES	11 REMARKS
OLM	4	15	LAYOVER ELN 0+30 LAYOVER PAE 1+00

12 FUEL ON BOARD HOURS	MINUTES	13 ALTERNATE AIRPORT(S)	14 PILOT'S NAME, ADDRESS & TELEPHONE NUMBER & AIRCRAFT HOME BASE	15 NUMBER ABOARD
5	00	—	J. HIGGINS 555-6274 450 PARK ST. OLYMPIA, WA 17 DESTINATION CONTACT/TELEPHONE (OPTIONAL)	3

16 COLOR OF AIRCRAFT: WHITE, BLUE TRIM

CIVIL AIRCRAFT PILOTS. FAR Part 91 requires you file an IFR flight plan to operate under instrument flight rules in controlled airspace. Failure to file could result in a civil penalty not to exceed $1,000 for each violation (Section 901 of the Federal Aviation Act of 1958, as amended). Filing of a VFR flight plan is recommended as a good operating practice. See also Part 99 for requirements concerning DVFR flight plans.

FAA Form 7233-1 (8-82) CLOSE VFR FLIGHT PLAN WITH OLM FSS ON ARRIVAL

CLEARANCES/RADIO FREQUENCIES:

SEATTLE RADIO 122.2
GRAY TOWER 119.325
McCHORD TOWER 124.8
SEATTLE APPROACH 121.1
SEATTLE CENTER 132.6
ELN UNICOM 123.0
PAINE TOWER 120.2
OLM ASOS 135.725
ELN ASOS 118.375

FUEL
RIGHT LEFT
1100 1130

DEP ELN 1220
DEP PAE 1430

SPECIAL EQUIPMENT SUFFIX

A - DME, TRANSPONDER WITH ALTITUDE ENCODING
B - DME, TRANSPONDER WITH NO ALTITUDE ENCODING
C - RNAV, TRANSPONDER WITH NP ALTITUDE ENCODING
D - DME, NO TRANSPONDER
R - RNAV, TRANSPONDER WITH ALTITUDE ENCODING
T - TRANSPONDER WITH NO ALTITUDE ENCODING
U - TRANSPONDER WITH ALTITUDE ENCODING
W - RNAV, NO TRANSPONDER
X - NO TRANSPONDER

EST +5 = GMT EDT +4 = GMT
CST +6 = GMT CDT +5 = GMT
MST +7 = GMT MDT +6 = GMT
PST +8 = GMT PDT +7 = GMT

INSTRUCTIONS FOR THE USE OF THIS FORM ARE CONTAINED IN THE FAA PAMPHLET "HOW TO OBTAIN A GOOD WEATHER BRIEFING" FAA-P-8740-30A

Figure 11-10. *FAA flight planner*

/R Advanced RNAV and transponder with Mode C, plus Required Navigational Performance (meets RNP type prescribed for route segments, routes and/or area concerned)

*/J Reduced Vertical Separation Minimum (RVSM), same as /E with RVSM

*/K RVSM, same as /F with RVSM

*/L RVSM, same as /G with RVSM

*/Q RVSM, same as /R with RVSM

*/W RVSM

Block 4:

Enter your computed true airspeed at your chosen cruising altitude.

Block 5:

Enter the 3-letter identifier for the departure airport or the name of the airport if you don't know the identifier. (It's on the chart.)

Block 6:

Fill in your proposed departure time in the Coordinated Universal Time (Zulu).

Block 7:

Enter your proposed cruising altitude.

Block 8:

Define your route by navigational aids, by airways, or by freeways, but remember that if you do not arrive at your destination, searchers will rely on the information in this block to plan the initial search. If you decide to divert from your planned route *report the change to the FSS* so that searchers will not be misdirected. This information is for your benefit, not the FAA's.

* RVSM applies only above pressure altitude 29,000 feet. Do not use /W, /J, /K, /L, or /Q.

Block 9:

Enter the identifier or name of the destination airport. If it is a round-robin (as is your exercise trip) the departure airport and the destination airport will be the same—but note my caution about this kind of flight plan if flight following is not used.

Block 10:

Enter your total planned time en route including any stops along the way. It is when this total time expires that the FAA becomes concerned for your safety.

Block 11:

This block might include "sightseeing Mt. Rushmore" or "overflying Disney World" to explain planned diversions or, as in the case of your planned trip, to note that you will be on the ground at Ellensburg for 30 minutes and at Paine Field for one hour. "VFR GPS on board" might be helpful if that is all you have.

Block 12:

This block should contain the total fuel on board, not how much you expect to use. Consider the possibility that the airport you have chosen as a refueling stop might be out of gas...or its fuel truck is out of service...or the pump is electric but there has been a power failure. Carry enough fuel to reach the next potential fuel stop.

Block 13:

As a VFR pilot you are not required to file an alternate airport, but it is an excellent idea if you think you might not reach the destination airport due to weather, etc. The regulations require that you always have an alternative plan in mind if your original flight cannot be completed.

Block 14:

Fill in your complete name and address, and supply sufficient information to identify the airplane's home base and/or operator. Provide a phone number which will reach someone who is aware of your plans—possibly the airport manager or the owner of the airplane. It is this number that the FAA will call first if you have not closed your flight plan, so don't use your home phone number unless someone there could provide information on your location or plans; if you carry a cell phone, list its number here for emergency use but do not turn it on in flight.

This is a good time to think about clothing. Will you be able to walk for help from a possible forced landing in the clothes you are wearing? Survive in the fuselage overnight? Tee-shirts and sandals are comfortable, but they are not much good in an emergency.

Block 15:

Enter the total number of persons on board.

Block 16:

Enter the predominant colors of the airplane.

Almost all overdue airplane searches end with the first telephone call (the pilot has failed to close the flight plan), or with the second call (the airplane is parked at an enroute airport).

Remember to make a last-minute check for Temporary Flight Restrictions along your route, and to monitor 121.5 MHz if possible.

Preparing the Flight Log

Look up the frequencies of radar facilities that can provide flight following, and write them on your flight planning form. Refer to the A/FD and the communications panel on sectional charts.

Remember that ground speed and wind correction angle calculations require true course, true airspeed, wind direction in relation to true north, and wind velocity. Measure courses as accurately as possible using your flight plotter: this measurement is the only truly accurate element of flight planning. True airspeed figures from the airplane's performance chart were accurate when the airplane was new but its condition may no longer allow it to match the book figures. Plan conservatively—don't expect book performance.

I strongly recommend that you get your true wind direction and velocity information from a Skew-T chart (Page 7–16).

In the calculations below, the forecast wind at cruise altitude is used for figuring ground speed and heading during climb: 90 knots is used as climb true airspeed and time to cruise altitude is based on a climb rate of 500 feet per minute. During the climb, fuel consumption is 9 gallons per hour, while in cruising flight only 7 gallons per hour are consumed. When you do your own fuel burn calculations for actual cross-country trips, always overestimate by rounding off the book figure to the next highest gallons-per-hour figure. Your legal reserve for daytime VFR is 30 minutes at cruise power, so you can't touch 3.5 gallons. Accordingly, assume that only 34 gallons are available for use during this trip. Remember what I said in Lesson 9—treat wind forecasts with suspicion; assume that headwinds are stronger than forecast and tailwinds are weaker. This trip assumes that the forecasts are right on the button.

Route:

Olympia – Ellensburg – Paine Field – Olympia

1st Leg:

Pilotage to V-2, then direct.

2nd Leg:

Direct using VOR navigation.

3rd Leg:

Pilotage.

Airplane:

4 seats, fixed gear.

Gross weight 2,300 pounds, empty weight 1,364 pounds.

150 HP, fixed-pitch propeller.

Fuel capacity 38 gallons usable, 100LL.

Oil 8 quarts not included in empty weight.

2 navcomms, 360 channel comm.

200 channel nav. ADF, transponder with Mode C.

Pilot:

190 pounds.

Passengers:

185 and 110 pounds. One of the passengers shows up with a 200-pound friend who needs to get to Ellensburg to take a test tomorrow. Can you arrange the seating to stay inside the loading envelope? If the total weight exceeds the maximum allowable gross weight, will you be able to take off? If this is the case, how long will you have to fly at climb speed in order to burn off enough fuel to land safely if a return is required? If the unexpected passenger offers you $50, will this affect your decision?

The 110-pound passenger has never before flown in a light plane.

Baggage:

25 pounds. The unexpected passenger has 25 pounds of baggage. How will this affect your go/no-go decision?

Note: In addition to your Seattle Sectional Chart you should have a Seattle Terminal Area Chart on board, since you will be traversing through Class B airspace.

Weight and Balance Calculation

	Weight	Moment
Empty weight (from MFR)	1,364	51.7
Fuel (usable)	228	11.0
Baggage	25	2.0
Oil (2 gals.)	15	-0.2
Pilot and 110 lb. passenger	300	11.2
Rear passenger	185	13.5
Totals	2,117	89.2

See Figure 11-11 on the next page for the Loading Graph and Center of Gravity Moment Envelope.

Loading is within limits with most adverse weight distribution; moving the 110-pound passenger to the rear seat and the 185-pound passenger to the front seat would move the center of gravity forward. With these passengers and this fuel load you cannot mis-load the airplane.

Weather Briefing

When you call the flight service station briefer you should identify yourself as a pilot, advise the briefer of your destination and planned route of flight, and state at the outset whether you are contemplating a flight under visual or under instrument flight conditions: "I'm a VFR pilot and I'm planning a round-robin flight from Olympia to Ellensburg to Paine Field and return. I'd like a (standard, abbreviated, outlook) weather briefing."

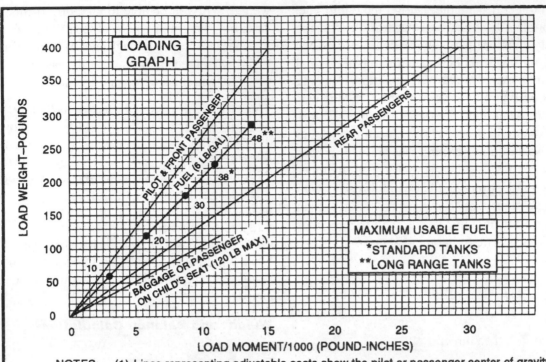

NOTES: (1) Lines representing adjustable seats show the pilot or passenger center of gravity on adjustable seats positioned for an average occupant. Refer to the Loading Arrangements diagram for forward and aft limits of occupant CG range.

(2) Engine Oil: 8 Qt. =15 Lb at –0.2 Moment/1000.

NOTE: The empty weight of this airplane does not include the weight of the oil.

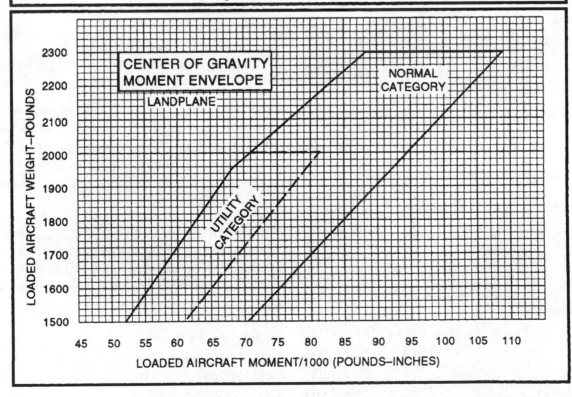

Figure 11-11

Ask for a standard briefing if you have not received a previous briefing. An abbreviated briefing should be requested if you simply want to supplement information you already have or if you want to update one or two items: "I've been watching the weather channel and listening to my NOAA weather radio and it looks good for a VFR flight over the mountains; all I need is the terminal forecast for Yakima and the winds aloft at 12,000 feet."

Ask for an outlook briefing if your departure time is more than six hours in the future: "I'm planning to depart Olympia tomorrow morning about 0700 for a VFR flight to Portland and I need an outlook briefing."

Dial 1-800-WXBRIEF (800-992-7433) for access to the Automated Flight Service Station (AFSS) system, and press 1 followed by the postal code of the state you are calling from in order to be connected to a briefer with knowledge of conditions in that state or region. For this cross-country you will enter "WA" and hear something like this:

"No hazardous weather is forecast for your route and time of flight. The synopsis is for a southwesterly flow aloft over Washington, caused by a stationary low at the surface and aloft 250 miles offshore from Vancouver Island. The airmass is somewhat unstable. At the surface, there is weak high pressure west of the Cascades. Freezing level is 8 thousand along the coast, sloping to 13 thousand at the eastern border.

"The Yakima terminal aerodrome forecast is calling for 10,000 broken until 1800Z then 7,000 scattered, wind 270° at 10 knots. Wenatchee is the same except the wind is forecast to be 320° at 10 knots. Olympia will remain essentially unchanged all day.

"The winds aloft for Seattle at 6,000 feet are forecast to be 220° at 13 knots, at 9,000 feet 210° at 21 knots.

"Restricted Area 6714 is active 13,000 feet and below. The threshold of runway 11 at Paine Field is displaced 1,100 feet eastward."

If you want to know the status of Military Operating Areas or Military Training Routes, you will have to ask the briefer; this information will not be volunteered. Be sure to ask the briefer for NOTAMs (including published NOTAMs) that affect your

flight. Be especially sure to ask about Temporary Flight Restrictions (the kind that dispatch fighter jets to make you land immediately). Also, it wouldn't hurt to check for TFRs while in-flight to avoid nasty surprises.

Planning the Flight

Your flight planning process will include fuel planning, preparing a flight log, and checking over the proposed route on your chart to be sure you haven't missed anything. In this text all of the details of planning the first leg will be examined, leaving the second and third legs for you to do.

An important part of preflight planning is reviewing your flight on the navigational chart to be sure that you are aware of any airspace restrictions, and that you know who to contact for any required clearances. You should also pick out easily identified ground speed checkpoints, and establish visual "brackets" on either side of your course and at the destination to insure that you do not wander too far off course or overfly the destination.

Planning Considerations, First Leg (Olympia to Ellensburg)

Olympia direct Gray Radio beacon to avoid R-6703A, past the northwest tip of Lake Tapps to intercept V-2 at Palmer, thence via V-2 to Ellensburg.

Overfly Nisqually Wildlife Refuge at least 2,000 feet AGL.

Use Seattle Approach/Departure Control for advisories (121.1 from Airport/Facility Directory).

Need clearance for Gray AAF and McChord AFB Class D airspace? Not if in contact with Seattle Approach Control or more than 2,800 feet MSL. (But look out for military aircraft anyway.)

May need clearance to transit Seattle Class B airspace; top of the Class B airspace is 10,000 feet MSL. You must hear "Cleared to operate in Seattle Class B airspace"; getting a radar vector is not a substitute for a clearance.

Military VFR route crosses V-2 near town of Lester (powerline also crosses beneath flightpath). Military flights will be below 1,500 feet AGL.

Hemispherical rule calls for odd 1,000 plus 500 feet eastbound when more than 3,000 feet AGL.

Highest terrain within five miles of route is 5,750 feet MSL.

Ground speed checkpoints: McChord AFB to northwest tip of Lake Tapps 13 NM; 13 NM to Palmer and V-2.

Hanson Reservoir dam to Lester, on the right, 14 NM; 40 NM to Ellensburg.

Side brackets: Puget Sound, Cascade Mountains.

End bracket: I-90 freeway.

Frequencies: Gray radiobeacon, Olympia ground control and tower, Seattle Radio (open flight plan) Seattle Approach Control (advisories), Seattle and Ellensburg VORs, Seattle Center (flight following), ELN ASOS.

Which cruise altitude would you choose for crossing the mountains eastbound?

The hemispherical rule requires that you fly eastbound at an odd-thousand-plus 500 feet. The hemispherical rule does not apply within 3,000 feet of the surface, so 6,500 feet is a possible choice, but that altitude is only 1,000 feet above the ridges, and there is a southwest wind which will create turbulence on the lee slopes. A ceiling of 6,000 feet at Stampede Pass means a cloud layer at approximately 9,800 feet, ruling out 9,500 feet as a cruise altitude. Choose 7,500 feet as your cruise altitude eastbound, and use 8,500 feet westbound. **Will you be able to see your checkpoints if the undercast does not burn off? How will you check your ground speed if this is the case? Abort or continue?**

In preparing your flight log, you should record the result of your calculations, and not the individual elements. That is, you need to know the magnetic heading, but you do not need to record the true course, the magnetic variation, or the wind for in-flight use. (*See* the FAA Flight Planner, Figure 11-10.) In addition (considering the built-in inaccuracy of the wind forecasts), computing and recording compass deviation and compass heading are unnecessary (although valuable for the FAA Knowledge Exam). If the heading indicator becomes inoperative, or of questionable accuracy, use your computed magnetic heading and the compass correction card to get compass course to steer. A compass correction card for the airplane you are using in this flight is provided here (Figure 11-12).

Flight Planning, First Leg

Begin by measuring the distance and true course for each leg, using your flight plotter. Here are the figures for the first leg, with variation and deviation applied to derive a compass course (Table 11-1). These are "no wind" courses—when wind is factored in, you have headings to follow.

Eastbound, interpolate the wind at 7,500 feet from the winds aloft given by the briefer: 220°, 13 knots at 6,000 feet and 210°, 21 knots at 9,000 feet. This is how the magnetic heading and ground speed for the first leg is calculated, rounding off fractional results (Table 11-2).

The wind will have a greater effect during the relatively slow climb than when at cruise. Only the distance, magnetic heading, and ground speed figures from these calculations will appear in your flight log.

Note: Several flight computers, both manual and electronic, were used in making the heading and ground speed calculations. Your own answer may vary slightly.

FOR	N	030	060	E	120	150	S	210	240	W	300	330
STEER	0	031	062	094	125	154	181	208	237	266	297	328

Figure 11-12. Compass correction card

	DIST	TC	VAR	MC	DEV	CC
Olympia – Gray Rbn	16.5 NM	049°	-18.5°E	030.5°	+1	031.5°
Gray Rbn – Palmer	31.0 NM	071°	-18.5°E	052.5°	+1.5	054°
Palmer – Ellensburg	58.0 NM	105.5°	-18.5°E	087.0°	+4.0	091°

Table 11-1

	TC	WIND	TAS	WCA	TH	VAR	MH	GS
Olympia – Gray Rbn	049°	215 @ 17	90	2.5°R	052°	19°	033°	106
Gray – V2 airway	071°	215 @ 17	107	5.5°R	076°	19°	057°	120
V2 – Ellensburg	106°	215 @ 17	107	79°R	115°	19°	096°	112

Table 11-2

Fuel Planning the First Leg

Using the methods for finding time, speed, distance, and fuel burn, the climb from field elevation at Olympia (206 feet MSL) to the cruising altitude of 7,500 feet should take 15 minutes and consume 3 gallons of fuel (always round fuel consumption figures off to the next highest figure). You should have 31 gallons left at the top of the climb. Using the most conservative ground speed of 90 knots, you will be 23 miles into the trip with 83 miles to go when you reach cruise altitude. If you plan to descend at cruise speed (TAS 107) maintaining a ground speed of 112 knots, you will reach Ellensburg 44 minutes after leveling off, and will consume 6 gallons during that portion of the trip. You should have 25 gallons left when you arrive at Ellensburg.

Refuel at Ellensburg? You have rented the airplane "wet," meaning that the FBO will reimburse you for any fuel you buy. But if you take the unexpected passenger and drop him off at ELN, the airplane will be 200 pounds (plus the fuel burned so far) lighter.

Flying the First Leg

Follow along on the full-color sectional chart excerpt at the back of this book.

Tune the ADF receiver to 216 kHz. After leaving the Olympia Class D airspace, climb as rapidly as possible to pass over wildlife refuge at least 2,000 feet AGL (sectional chart legend). Home (*see* Page 10–11) to Gray radiobeacon. Open VFR flight plan with Seattle Radio on 122.2 (common FSS frequency).

Contact Seattle Approach Control on 121.1 (frequency in A/FD and on back of sectional) for traffic advisories. No clearance required for Gray AAF or McChord AFB Class D airspace if above 2,800 feet MSL, but that is too close to the floor of Class B airspace—better talk to the towers. After passing the radiobeacon (start time for ground speed check), steer toward Lake Tapps; call Seattle Approach for clearance into Class B airspace before reaching 3,000 feet.

Check time at northwest tip of Lake Tapps and compute ground speed. Estimate time of arrival at Palmer. Tune #1 VOR receiver to Seattle frequency and identify. Set omni-bearing selector to 088°. Note railroad to right of V-2 passes through Palmer. As VOR course deviation needle centers, turn to predetermined magnetic heading.

The undercast has obscured all of your visual checkpoints until you get to Palmer; your fuel burn so far is an educated guess. Abort or continue? There is an emergency airfield at Easton, and Cle Elum is just on the other side of the mountains... Abort or continue?

Note that the scattered cloud layer at 10,000 feet has become a broken layer as you fly eastward. How will this affect your planned flight? Abort or continue?

Start timing opposite dam at west end of reservoir (easier to see in real life than on the chart, but you checked it with Google Earth, didn't you?). Maintain 7,500 feet MSL to comply with §91.155 (at least 500 feet below all clouds) and §91.159 (magnetic course 0° through 179° maintain odd thousand + 500 feet) noting that during part of this leg a cruising altitude of 7,500 feet will be less than 3,000 feet above the ground and the odd-even rule does not apply. Check time crossing road, powerline, and river, all of which coincide just north of the town of Lester (an abandoned airstrip will be on your right); compute ground speed and estimate time of arrival at Ellensburg. Tune VOR receiver to Ellensburg frequency and identify. Be alert for military traffic beneath you just east of Lester. Contact Ellensburg UNICOM or broadcast intentions. Note freeway crosses flight path 10 NM from airport and that airport is north of town. Report on the ground to Seattle Radio on 122.2. *See* Table 11-3 and Figure 11-13.

Planning Considerations, Second Leg (Ellensburg to Paine Field)

Ellensburg direct Paine Field via VOR.

Military training route crosses direct course just west of Kachess Lake.

Course crosses Alpine Lakes Wilderness Area (area bounded by blue dots and line).

First Leg Flight Log

Dep OLM 1100 – Cruise 7,500' MSL

CHECKPOINT	ROUTE VIA	CRS*	ESTIMATED DIST	GS	ETE	ETA	ACTUAL GS	ATE	ATA
Gray Rbn	DIR	032°	16.5	106	9.5	1110			
McChord	DIR	056°	5.0	120	2.5	1113			
Lake Tapps	DIR	056°	13.0	120	6.5	1120		8.0	
Palmer	DIR	056°	13.0	120	6.5	1127			
Dam	V-2	095°	6.0	112	4.0	1131			
Road/powerline	V-2	095°	14.0	112	8.0	1139		10.0	
Ellensburg	V-2	095°	40.0	112	22.0	1201			

The actual times en route between ground speed checkpoints have been provided; revise the ETA at Ellensburg based on the measured ground speed.

* When you have completed your wind problems, enter your computed magnetic headings in this column.

Table 11-3

Figure 11-13. *Ellensburg*

Flight will enter controlled airspace 700 feet AGL departing Ellensburg.

Flight will be in Class G airspace briefly while crossing corner of area with 9,500 feet MSL floor.

Maximum elevation figures show 9,800 feet, 7,900 feet and 8,400 feet, but highest terrain en route is 6,680 feet MSL.

Ground speed checkpoints: DeVere Airport to tip of Cle Elum Lake—14 NM; lake to Paine Field 58 NM.

Side brackets: Mt. Stuart, Mt. Daniel. End bracket: Puget Sound.

Frequencies: Seattle Radio (position report), Seattle Center (flight following), Paine VOR, Paine ATIS, Paine tower and ground control.

Call Seattle Center on 128.5 (from A/FD) for clearance into Class B airspace after crossing foothills if flight is not below 8,000 feet and 6,000 feet floors.

Flight Planning, Second Leg

Since this is a direct flight, the easiest thing to do is to measure the magnetic course from the Ellensburg VORTAC to Paine Field, using the VORTAC's compass rose—285° magnetic. For the wind problem, add 19° for magnetic variation to get the true course. The winds at 8,500 feet will not be appreciably different than those at 9,000 feet—use 220° at 21 knots for your heading and ground speed calculations.

Fuel Planning, Second Leg

The climb out of Ellensburg to 8,500 feet will take approximately 13 minutes and will consume 2 gallons of fuel. If you did not refuel at Ellensburg, you should have 23 gallons left at the top of the climb. You will reach cruising altitude 19 miles from Ellensburg with 69 miles to go at a ground speed of 103 knots (TAS 107), and during the 40 minutes between leveling off and arriving at Paine Field you will consume an additional 5 gallons, leaving 18 to burn.

Flying the Second Leg

With VOR receiver tuned to Ellensburg, set OBS on 285°. After takeoff, turn to intercept VOR radial and proceed on course. Contact Seattle Radio on 122.2 and report airborne. Keep freeway and Cle Elum airports on left until high enough to see lakes, and set course across north tips of lakes. Start timing for ground speed check opposite paved DeVere Airport. First half of this leg will be less than 3,000 feet above terrain and hemispherical rule will not apply. At north tip of Kachess Lake, be alert for military aircraft; tune VOR receiver to Paine Field and identify, make ground speed check and compute ETA at Paine Field. Note that between Snoqualmie Pass and Colligan Lake, controlled airspace floor is 9,500 feet MSL. Listen to Paine Field ATIS and make radio contact for flight into Class D airspace. (The Paine Tower record of your takeoff and landing will serve as a position report if you get lost between Paine and Olympia.) *See* Table 11-4 and Figure 11-14.

Second Leg Flight Log

Dep. ELN 1230 – Cruise altitude 8,500' MSL

CHECKPOINT	VIA	CRS*	DIST	GS	ETE	ETA	GS	ATE	ATA
DeVere Airport	DIR	285°	16.0	86	11.0	1241			
Cle Elum Lake	DIR	285°	14.0	103	8.0	1249		7.0	
Colligan Lake	DIR	285°	28.0	103	16.0	1305			
Paine Field	DIR	285°	30.0	103	18.0	1322			

Are you computing a heading and a ground speed during the climb to cruise altitude at 90 knots and 500' per minute, and also at 107 knots during cruise? This leg is flown using the ELN 285° radial and the PAE 102° radial as backup to ground reference navigation. If the wind forecast is valid, a magnetic heading of 274° should keep the VOR needle centered.

* When you have completed your wind problems, enter your computed magnetic headings in this column.

Table 11-4

Figure 11-14. *Paine Field*

Planning Considerations, Third Leg (Paine Field to Olympia)

While flying this leg, emergency landing sites are few and far between. Continually evaluate your chances of making it to Easton, Skykomish, or one of the Cle Elum airports with the wind coming out of the southwest. Will you choose a different route next time?

What if you check the weather while on the ground at ELN and learn that Stampede Pass is now reporting an overcast at 9,000 feet, putting your return trip at 8,500 feet, whether via the planned direct route to Paine Field or by simply returning along the same route you used to get to ELN, just 500 feet beneath the overcast. Which option will you select?

Paine Field direct Olympia via pilotage.

Entire flight is in controlled airspace.

Course line crosses West Point lighthouse (identified by the blue dot and the letters AI WR).

Lowest floor of Seattle Class B airspace is 3,000 feet along route.

No conflict with Bremerton National or Tacoma Narrows airports.

Use Seattle Approach for traffic advisories into Olympia.

Ground speed checkpoints: West Point lighthouse to shoreline at Port Orchard—9 miles; shoreline 37 miles to Olympia.

Side brackets: Seattle and Bremerton.

End bracket: Hills south of Olympia.

Frequencies: Paine ground and tower, Paine VOR, Seattle Center, Seattle Approach Control, Olympia VOR, Olympia tower, OLM ASOS.

Flight Planning, Third Leg

Again, since this is a direct flight, the easiest thing to do is to measure the magnetic course from the Paine VORTAC to Olympia, using the VORTAC's compass rose—183° magnetic. For the wind problem, add 19° for magnetic variation to get the true course. Use the 3,000-foot wind at 210° at 13 knots for your heading and ground speed calculations.

Fuel Planning, Third Leg

Use the winds for 3,000 feet (210° at 13 knots) and cruise at 2,500 feet MSL. The ground speed works out to 96 knots. Only 3 minutes of climb are involved, so compute the leg at a true airspeed of 107 knots. Fuel consumption for 40 minutes at 7 gallons per hour is 5 gallons, leaving 13 plus the 3.5 gallon reserve.

Flying the Third Leg

Set omni-bearing selector to 183° (Paine VORTAC) as backup to pilotage. Set course soon after taking off with West Point lighthouse straight ahead. Start timing for ground speed check over the lighthouse (the "Al RW" just off the point that shows on the sectional). Check time over shoreline east of Port Orchard and compute ground speed and ETA at Olympia. Be alert for towers left of course passing along lake and be aware of the National Security Area over the shipyards. Contact Seattle Approach Control for traffic advisories and vectoring to Olympia traffic pattern. Contact Olympia tower crossing the shoreline. *See* Table 11-5 and Figure 11-15.

Any time you refuel en route, have the line person top-off the tanks, and divide the fuel pumped into the tanks by your flying time to see what the overall fuel burn was. If you did not refuel at Ellensburg or Paine Field, you should have had 16.5 gallons in the tanks on landing, and it should take about 21.5 gallons to top the tanks. If it takes more than 21.5 gallons, adjust your fuel burn estimate upward the next time you plan a flight in this airplane. Never eat into your reserve fuel unless you are in an emergency situation and have advised ATC that you are declaring an emergency.

As your passengers deplane, what are they thinking? "This guy is a nutcase, I'll never fly in a light plane again," or "I wonder how much it costs to learn to fly?" Your actions, your decision making, and your demeanor will affect their thinking.

Third Leg Flight Log

Dep Paine 1345 – Cruise 2,500' MSL.

CHECKPOINT	VIA	CRS*	DIST	GS	ETE	ETA	GS	ATE	ATA
Fort Lawton	DIR	185°	17.0		11.0	1356			
Shoreline	DIR	185°	9.0	96	6.0	1402		9.0	
Olympia	DIR	185°	37.0	96	23.0	1426			

This leg is flown using the Paine and Olympia VORs as backups to visual navigation.

Fuel consumption for the trip is planned at 21 gallons. A 30-minute reserve (3.5 gallons) is required for day VFR, so you should have *at least* that much in the tanks upon landing at Olympia.

Did you close your flight plan with Seattle Radio?

* When you have completed your wind problems, enter your computed magnetic headings in this column.

Table 11-5

Figure 11-15. Olympia

Lesson 11
Communication Procedures Review Questions

Refer to the full-color Seattle sectional chart excerpt in the back of this book.

1. What UNICOM frequency, if any, is indicated for Seattle-Tacoma International Airport (**C**)?

   A— None is listed.
   B— 119.9 MHz.
   C— 122.95 MHz.

2. Approaching the Wenatchee Airport (**H**), which frequency would you use to obtain an airport advisory of traffic in the pattern and runway in use?

   A— 122.3 MHz
   B— 111.0 MHz
   C— 123.0 MHz

3. What is the procedure for an approach and landing at the Auburn Municipal Airport just southeast of Seattle-Tacoma Airport?

   A— Obtain a clearance from Seattle-Tacoma tower on 119.9 MHz 10 miles from Auburn.
   B— Remain below 3,000 feet MSL and receive an airport advisory on 122.8 MHz.
   C— Request a clearance from Seattle Approach Control on 122.0 MHz.

4. Operational tests of the ELT (emergency locator transmitter) should be made only

   A— during the first 5 minutes of an hour.
   B— after one-half the shelf life of the battery.
   C— upon replacing the battery.

5. When are non-rechargeable batteries of an ELT to be replaced?

   A— Every 24 months.
   B— When 50 percent of their useful life expires or they were in use for a cumulative period of one hour.
   C— At the time of each 100-hour or annual inspection.

6. To use VHF/DF facilities for assistance in locating and aircraft's position, the aircraft must have

   A— a VHF transmitter and receiver.
   B— a 4096-code transponder.
   C— a VOR receiver and DME.

7. When making routine transponder code changes, pilots should avoid inadvertent selection of which codes?

   A— 3100, 7600, 7700
   B— 7500, 7600, 7700
   C— 7000, 7600, 7700

8. When landing at an airport that does not have a tower, FSS, or UNICOM, broadcast your intentions in the blind on

   A— 123.0 MHz.
   B— 123.6 MHz.
   C— The Common Traffic Advisory Frequency.

9. Below FL180, updated enroute weather advisories should be obtained from Flight Watch on

   A— 122.1 MHz.
   B— 122.0 MHz.
   C— 122.4 MHz.

10. ATIS is the continuous broadcast of recorded information

   A— concerning nonessential information to relieve frequency congestion.
   B— concerning noncontrol information in selected high-activity terminal areas.
   C— concerning sky conditions limited to ceilings below 1,000 feet and visibilities less than 3 miles.

11. The correct method for stating 4,500 feet MSL to ATC is

   A— "FORTY-FIVE HUNDRED FEET"
   B— "FOUR POINT FIVE"
   C— "FOUR THOUSAND FIVE HUNDRED"

12. When flying HAWK N666CB, the proper phraseology for initial contact with McAlester AFSS is

   A— "McALESTER RADIO, HAWK SIX SIX SIX CHARLIE BRAVO, RECEIVING ARDMORE VORTAC, OVER."
   B— "McALESTER FLIGHT SERVICE STATION, HAWK NOVEMBER SIX CHARLIE BRAVO, RECEIVING ARDMORE VORTAC, OVER."
   C— "McALESTER STATION, HAWK SIX SIX SIX CEE BEE, RECEIVING ARDMORE VORTAC, OVER."

13. What frequency can be used to chat with a pilot in another airplane?

   A— The Common Traffic Advisory Frequency.
   B— 122.75 MHz.
   C— 122.9 MHz.

14. Refer to the sectional chart excerpt in the back of the book. Select the true statement regarding Restricted Area R-6703C near Olympia.

   A— The pilot must be instrument rated and file an IFR flight plan before penetrating this area.
   B— Flight within this Restricted Area is prohibited during hours of daylight.
   C— Before penetrating this Restricted Area, authorization must be obtained from the controlling agency.

15. While en route between Olympia and Ellensburg, updated weather information is available by contacting

   A— Ellensburg UNICOM on 123.0 MHz.
   B— Seattle Radio (flight service station) on 122.2 MHz.
   C— Seattle Flight Watch on 122.0 MHz.

16. Assume that you are over the Cle Elum Airport (47°11'00"N, 120°53'00"W) flying eastbound at 4,500 feet MSL. A westbound airplane passes at your altitude. Which statement is correct?

   A— The westbound airplane is legally at 4,500 feet MSL and you are at the wrong altitude for your direction of flight.
   B— The westbound airplane should be either 1,000 feet above or below you in controlled airspace.
   C— Both airplanes are being operated legally within 3,000 feet of the ground, where the hemispherical rule does not apply.

17. Your calls to Ellensburg UNICOM on 123.0 MHz are not answered. What action should you taken?

    A — Cancel your plans to land at Ellensburg because you cannot obtain a landing clearance.

    B — Attempt to obtain landing clearance from Seattle Radio by transmitting on 122.1 MHz and listening on 117.9 MHz.

    C — Enter the Ellensburg traffic pattern and land, announcing your position and intentions on 123.0 MHz.

18. Assume that when you contact the Paine Field tower for landing clearance you are advised that the ceiling is 900 feet and the visibility is 2 miles. Which statement is correct?

    A — You can proceed into the pattern and land, because you need only remain clear of all clouds if visibility is at least 1 mile.

    B — You must remain clear of the Paine Field Class D airspace and request a Special VFR clearance from the tower.

    C — You cannot land at Paine Field unless there is at least a 1,000 foot ceiling and 3 miles visibility.

19. On the direct route from Ellensburg to Paine Field you cross the corner of an area marked "9500 MSL". As you fly through this area at 8,500 feet MSL

    A — you must have 3 miles visibility and remain clear of all clouds.

    B — you must stay at least 1,000 feet above, 500 feet below, and 2,000 feet horizontally from all clouds and have 3 miles flight visibility.

    C — you are in uncontrolled airspace and need only 1 mile visibility and must remain clear of clouds.

20. Refer to the A/FD listings for Ellensburg and Olympia in Appendix C of this book. Which one of the following statements is true?

    A — The Ellensburg VORTAC is unusable on the 145° radial at 7,500 feet beyond 25 NM.

    B — The Olympia VORTAC is unusable on the 160° radial at 8,500 feet.

    C — The Ellensburg VORTAC is unusable on the 255° radial at 6,700 feet at a distance of 20 NM.

Answers:

1-C, 2-C, 3-B, 4-A, 5-B, 6-A, 7-B, 8-C, 9-B, 10-B, 11-C, 12-A, 13-B, 14-C, 15-C, 16-C, 17-C, 18-B, 19-C, 20-C.

Lesson 12 Putting it All Together

The preceding chapters have provided all the tools you need—you know how to make the airplane go where you want it to go, you know what makes the engine tick, you can interpret the engine and flight instruments, you know the regulations that affect your flights, you can navigate both by pilotage and electronically, and you know how your body reacts to your new-found ability to move in three dimensions. Now it is time to put it all together. Remember the 5 P's from Lesson 5?

The Plan

First and foremost is the weather. Everything else can be perfect, but if you can't fly under visual flight rules with a large margin of error, the flight just won't happen. If you read accident reports in the aviation press or look at National Transportation Safety Board website (www.ntsb.gov/ntsb/query. asp), you know that the most common cause of light plane accidents is "Continued VFR flight into IFR weather conditions." When you go to one (or several) of the websites you will find by searching for "aviation weather," you have at your fingertips graphic displays of both existing conditions and forecasts. You do not want to fly toward a destination that is reporting deteriorating weather, and you do not want to fly above anything less than scattered clouds (nor

do you want to scud run between a low cloud deck and the terrain). I recommend going to the ADDS webpage, clicking on Java Tools, and using their Flight Plan tool. This will enable you to see a cross-section of your planned flight with terrain and clouds displayed.

Weather OK, and expected to stay that way or improve? Now pin down the exact route you plan to follow. I recommend that you file a route based on airways, rather than direct, because it gives you something to fall back on if pilotage isn't working for you ("All those towns and lakes look alike!"). A GPS navigator is great for situation awareness, but pushing the "Direct to" button may find you flying through restricted airspace or seeing an F-16 close up. If you tweak your route to pass near several airports, you will have safe havens available without having to dig through a lot of publications. If you fly in the mountainous west, consider the turbulence you might encounter even on a severe-clear day, and be sure that you can give yourself a safe margin above the terrain without getting closer to the clouds than the regulations and common sense dictate.

Now it is time to prepare a flight log, listing checkpoints along the way together with the distance between checkpoints for groundspeed calculations.

Using the best forecast of winds aloft you can find (skew-T?), calculate groundspeed and heading for each leg of your flight, with the understanding that you are working with wind information that can change drastically between the time you do the flight log and the time you get airborne.

With the route and destination checked, it is time to plan for takeoff. Sound backward to you? Too many pilots have taken off in dicky-bird weather, hoping that questionable weather along the route or at the destination would get better. It's the "take a look" excuse. However, when you have flown for two hours and have only an hour to go, the psychological (and passenger) pressure to proceed is difficult to ignore. Scrap the trip and fly back for two hours? Land short and rent a car? Maybe those ceiling and visibility reports are wrong, right? Gardner's Rule: If the safe completion of your flight depends on something happening (or not happening), don't go. Your research into the weather should provide good VFR weather with a comfortable cushion for the entire duration of the flight with no "ifs."

Takeoff planning must use actual weight, as close as you can guess it, and actual density altitude at the departure airport. Figure out the distance to clear a 50-foot obstacle, and add fifty percent. If the departure route includes high terrain or obstacles, calculate the climb gradient (feet per mile) if you want to — but consider climbing to a safe clearance altitude over the departure airport. It will mess up your time-enroute calculations, but you won't hit anything on the way to the first checkpoint.

On the takeoff roll, check your airspeed; if you do not have three-quarters of planned liftoff speed at the halfway point, get on the brakes. If taking off from a high density altitude airport, have you leaned for best power? If you have, and you are still not accelerating rapidly enough, offload baggage or passengers or wait for cooler temperatures. Once airborne, use the best-rate-of-climb speed adjusted for aircraft weight and density altitude; hint: it will be slower than "book" speed.

As a VFR pilot, you have many advantages over those flying under instrument flight rules: You can change course and/or altitude at will, you don't have to talk to anyone while in Class G or E airspace, and you don't have to worry about being re-routed by ATC or maintaining a current database for your GPS navigator. Utilizing radar flight following, of course, means notifying (not asking permission from) air traffic control of heading or altitude changes, but that is a good tradeoff. During daylight hours you can see where you are going and monitor your height above the terrain. This advantage disappears at night, so this is my suggestion — at each course change, or even at each checkpoint if they are far apart, check Heading, Altitude, Airspeed, and Terrain. H-A-S-T. Have you turned to the correct heading/radial? Is your altitude appropriate for the direction of flight? Airspeed appropriate? How about altitude above the terrain? Rising terrain is sneaky, especially in the mountainous west; you can be flying along at 8,500 feet, happy as a clam, while the amount of air between your plane and the ground diminishes to zero. Controlled flight into terrain (CFIT) is an insidious killer.

Publications

The Airport/Facility Directory should be a part of your preflight planning. Note frequencies that will be used, including those for radar facilities you will use for flight following (radar services to pilots). You can find airport diagrams for many large airports online (www.aopa.org, www.landings.com, www.airnav.com, many subscription services). I hope that it goes without saying that you will have sectional and Class B (if needed) charts.

Take advantage of technology. See if there are webcams along your route that will give you a real-time look at conditions. Use Google Earth to "fly" your route. Call an FBO at your destination and any planned stops enroute to be sure that fuel is available, and ask if there are any special rules for their airport.

The Plane

Check the inspection status. Has the plane had an annual inspection and been returned to service within the past year? Any outstanding Airworthiness Directives?* Does the weight and balance fall within

* www.airweb.faa.gov/Regulatory_and_Guidance_Library/

the operating envelope, and will it stay within the envelope as fuel is burned off? Enough supplemental oxygen for everyone, if flight at oxygen altitudes is necessary? Masks for everyone? If the plane is equipped with an autopilot, have you run the pre-flight test in the flight manual supplement? If the plane is equipped with a GPS navigator, do you feel comfortable using it? A piece of equipment that you don't understand can be a distraction, and you may need to fall back on less sophisticated modes of navigation. Mastering knob-ology during visual flight will pay dividends when you begin training for the instrument rating. Is the database in the GPS navigator current?

The Pilot

How do you feel? If you could not pass a physical exam for the class of medical certificate you hold on the date of the flight, you must ground yourself. If you have a medical condition that popped up since your last visit to an FAA medical examiner, you cannot wait until your next physical is due, you must stop flying right now. But how about conditions we might consider "minor," such as a head cold? It's still a no-go decision; you might not be able to clear your ears after altitude changes.

Are you taking any medications that might be disqualifying? It is your responsibility to ensure that whatever you are taking is acceptable to the FAA; anecdotal evidence from friends does not count. Check with the AOPA, if you are a member, or go to www.faa.gov and put medication in the search box. Asking your passengers if they have any health issues is also a good idea; having someone in the back seat with excruciating ear pain when descending puts you in a quandary, because you have to descend to land.

Are you under stress? Is this trip going to make the difference between landing that big contract or losing it? Any family issues hanging over your head? No one can answer these questions but you; you can't call the AOPA or ask the FAA. You must be able to devote every brain cell to the safe completion of the planned flight.

Alcohol. Do I need to expand on this? Everyone knows that the effects of alcohol are exacerbated by altitude. Don't drink and fly; allow more than the legal minimum of eight hours from bottle to throttle.

Are you sufficiently rested? Falling asleep while enroute will not impress your passengers, and your decision making abilities will suffer if you are tired. You need your wits about you when landing, and that is when you will be most tired. Air taxi and airline pilots have prescribed rest periods dictated by the FARs; do your passengers deserve less?

Grab a doughnut and a cup of coffee and you're good to go, right? Absolutely not. Treat yourself to a decent meal before flying, and carry some energy bars or their equivalent that you can munch on enroute. You don't have to have diabetes to have an energy drop if you do not provide your body with adequate fuel. Carry a water bottle, too; soft drinks are not a good idea. Ever open a carbonated drink at 10,000 feet and have it spread over the instrument panel as a fine mist?

The Passengers

Your passengers should disembark at the destination as enthusiastic supporters of general aviation, and it is your job to ensure that nothing happens along the way to make them uncomfortable. If they are non-pilots, explain *everything*. Noises and movements that are second-nature to you are foreign to them. Before you make a power change, switch tanks, or extend the flaps/gear, tell your passengers what you are doing. This is especially important when they seem to be nervous or unusually silent. Enlist their help in looking for traffic as a means of taking their minds off of their concerns. An intercom that lets your passengers listen in will take their minds off of their concerns. This is a two-edged sword, of course…it puts them in the loop, and you should explain any transmissions that might raise red flags in their minds, but it affords them the opportunity to talk to you when you do not heed distractions. Enforce a silent cockpit as you approach the destination airport.

Use this checklist for your pre-takeoff briefing:

- Seatbelt operation and when they are required to be used (I recommend full-time use).
- Exits and their operation; what to do if you are busy (you mean "unconscious," but don't want to say so).
- When to talk and when not to talk.
- Every person is a lookout and should point out any airplanes they see.

Is this trip urgent for your passengers, or are they just along for the ride? Passengers who absolutely must arrive at a certain airport at a certain time can push you into making bad decisions; before you even start the engine(s), make sure that they understand that the flight might not go as planned, and that you might land short of your destination or even return to your starting point. Even airline pilots get diverted to alternate airports when something unexpected arises.

Programming

This is an element of single-pilot resource management that is less important to VFR pilots than it is to IFR pilots, because under visual flight rules you are not required to follow a given route or get clearances that must be flown as ATC directs. Still, if you fly an airplane with a glass cockpit and an autopilot, it is tempting to believe the machine rather than the evidence of your own eyes if an error is made in entering a flight plan into the GPS navigator. Avoid the use of a "direct to" function that might take you through restricted airspace. If your multifunction display includes terrain, make sure that your plane stays well clear; "controlled flight into terrain" accidents are often blamed on pilots who turned the navigation responsibility over to a black box.

Know what to do when your primary flight display or multifunction display goes blank, and know how to disengage the autopilot whenever you encounter a "Why is it doing that?" situations.

The Future of Flight Training

As I write this in 2011, a pilot is deemed ready for a checkride when the minimum flight experience dictated by the regulations have been logged and he or she has satisfied an instructor that the maneuvers called out in the Practical Test Standard will be performed within the tolerances allowed by the PTS. This will change in the coming years.

The goal of the FAA-Industry-Training-Standards program is to change the way pilots are evaluated toward a scenario-based method. This means that instead of flawlessly executing S-Turns Across a Road (for example), an applicant will be required to take off on a cross-country trip and demonstrate situational awareness, good decision making skills, deal with failures and unusual situations, and exhibit mastery of the technology in the cockpit. Obviously, this change in training methods reflects the growing number of sophisticated trainers that meet the definition of Technically Advanced Aircraft. There is no timetable for moving to the new methods of certification; it will be incremental.

Learner-Centered Grading

Your instructor might present you with this scenario: You work for a local television station and have been dispatched with a camera operator to get visuals from a house fire. To carry out this assignment, you must evaluate the weather, choose an appropriate route and altitude to get to the scene, and both circle the site at various altitudes and fly a rectangular course around the site while helicopters from local emergency services do their work over the scene. You can see that this is considerably different from hearing your instructor say "Today, we are going to go out and fly constant-radius turns around a point."

The purpose of grading a scenario is to track student performance, to reward the student (positive reinforcement), to warn the next instructor (if the student is instructor-shopping), and as a means of delaying recommendation for a checkride until the student is truly ready.

During the period of transition from traditional grading to learner-centered grading, your instructor should use the traditional grading scale but put you in the loop by asking you to evaluate your performance. You should articulate your own mistakes, recognize the limits of your present knowledge, and have a mental picture of what a successful outcome would look like.

At the completion of a scenario, you should be able to describe and understand the concepts, principles, and procedures involved in the scenario. You should be able to practice the scenario events with little input from your instructor, and ultimately be able to perform the scenario with no instructor input.

While carrying out the scenario, you will demonstrate your ability to gather the most important data available from within and outside of the cockpit, identify courses of action, and make appropriate decisions.

Go to www.faa.gov/education_research/training/fits for details.

This glossary includes terms from the *Aeronautical Information Manual*'s "Pilot/Controller Glossary," which is published by the FAA for the purpose of promoting a common understanding of the terms used in the Air Traffic Control system. *The Complete Private Pilot* text contains more aviation-related terms than are covered by the Pilot/Controller Glossary, and these terms have been added and marked with an asterisk (*). *Note:* Some of these additional terms repeat Pilot/Controller Glossary terms — where there are two entries for one term, the asterisked term is defined and stated more in accordance with the text of *The Complete Private Pilot*.

Terms used by the International Civil Aviation Organization (ICAO) are also defined; these are marked by the bracketed "[ICAO]" when they differ from the FAA definition of a term. The Pilot/Controller Glossary also makes many references to other government publications, such as the AIM, various regulations, and FAA Order 7110.65, a publication concerning details of the Air Traffic Control system operations. Terms most commonly used in pilot/controller communications are printed in ***bold italics***.

AAI. (*See* arrival aircraft interval).

AAR. (*See* airport arrival rate).

abbreviated IFR flight plans. An authorization by ATC requiring pilots to submit only that information needed for the purpose of ATC. It includes only a small portion of the usual IFR flight plan information. In certain instances, this may be only aircraft identification, locations, and pilot request. Other information may be requested if needed by ATC for separation/control purposes. It is frequently used by aircraft which are airborne and desire an instrument approach or by aircraft which are on the ground and desire a climb to VFR on top. (*See* VFR-On-Top) (Refer to AIM).

abeam. An aircraft is "abeam" a fix, point, or object when that fix, point, or object is approximately 90 degrees to the right or left of the aircraft track. Abeam indicates a general position rather than a precise point.

abort. To terminate a preplanned aircraft maneuver; e.g., an aborted takeoff.

ACC. [ICAO] (*See* area control center).

accelerate-stop distance available (ASDA). The runway plus stopway length declared available and suitable for the acceleration and deceleration of an airplane aborting a take-off. [ICAO] The length of the takeoff run available plus the length of the stopway if provided.

ACDO. (*See* Air Carrier District Office).

acknowledge. Let me know that you have received my message. [ICAO] Let me know that you have received and understood this message.

ACLS. (*See* Automatic Carrier Landing System).

ACLT. (*See* actual calculated landing time).

acrobatic flight. An intentional maneuver involving an abrupt change in an aircraft's attitude, an abnormal attitude, or abnormal acceleration not necessary for normal flight. (Refer to 14 CFR Part 91). [ICAO] Maneuvers intentionally performed by an aircraft involving an abrupt change in its attitude, an abnormal attitude, or an abnormal variation in speed.

active runway. (*See* runway in use/active runway/duty runway).

actual calculated landing time (ACLT). ACLT is a flight's frozen calculated landing time. An actual time determined at freeze calculated landing time (FCLT) or meter list display interval (MLDI) for the adapted vertex for each arrival aircraft based upon runway configuration, airport acceptance rate, airport arrival delay period, and other metered arrival aircraft. This time is either the vertex time of arrival (VTA) of the aircraft or the tentative calculated landing time (TCLT)/ACLT of the previous aircraft plus the arrival aircraft interval (AAI), whichever is later. This time will not be updated in response to the aircraft's progress.

actual navigation performance (ANP). (*See* required navigation performance).

additional services. Advisory information provided by ATC which includes but is not limited to the following:

1. Traffic advisories.
2. Vectors, when requested by the pilot, to assist aircraft receiving traffic advisories to avoid observed traffic.
3. Altitude deviation information of 300 feet or more from an assigned altitude as observed on a verified (reading correctly) automatic altitude readout (Mode C).
4. Advisories that traffic is no longer a factor.

Continued

5. Weather and chaff information.
6. Weather assistance.
7. Bird activity information.
8. Holding pattern surveillance.

Additional services are provided to the extent possible contingent only upon the controller's capability to fit them into the performance of higher priority duties and on the basis of limitations of the radar, volume of traffic, frequency congestions, and controller workload. The controller has complete discretion for determining if he/she is able to provide or continue to provide a service in a particular case. The controller's reason not to provide or continue to provide a service in a particular case is not subject to question by the pilot and need not be made known to him/her. (*See* traffic advisories) (Refer to AIM).

ADF. (*See* automatic direction finder).

*ADF. Automatic direction finder; a receiver with an associated indicator which points to the transmitting station.

ADIZ. (*See* Air Defense Identification Zone).

ADLY. (*See* arrival delay).

Administrator. The Federal Aviation Administrator or any person to whom he/she has delegated his/her authority in the matter concerned.

*advection. Horizontal movement of air.

advise intentions. Tell me what you plan to do.

advisory. Advice and information provided to assist pilots in the safe conduct of flight and aircraft movement. (*See* advisory service).

advisory frequency. The appropriate frequency to be used for Airport Advisory Service. (*See* Local Airport Advisory, UNICOM). (Refer to AC 90-42 and AIM).

advisory service. Advice and information provided by a facility to assist pilots in the safe conduct of flight and aircraft movement. (*See* Local Airport Advisory, traffic advisories, safety alert, additional services, radar advisory, Enroute Flight Advisory Service) (Refer to AIM).

aerial refueling. A procedure used by the military to transfer fuel from one aircraft to another during flight. (Refer to VFR/IFR wall planning charts).

aerodrome. A defined area on land or water (including any buildings, installations and equipment) intended to be used either wholly or in part for the arrival, departure, and movement of aircraft.

aerodrome beacon. [ICAO] Aeronautical beacon used to indicate the location of an aerodrome from the air.

aerodrome control service. [ICAO] Air traffic control service for aerodrome traffic.

aerodrome control tower. [ICAO] A unit established to provide air traffic control service to aerodrome traffic.

aerodrome elevation. [ICAO] The elevation of the highest point of the landing area.

aerodrome traffic circuit. [ICAO] The specified path to be flown by aircraft operating in the vicinity of an aerodrome.

*aerodynamics. The study of the forces acting on bodies moving through the air.

aeronautical beacon. A visual NAVAID displaying flashes of white and/or colored light to indicate the location of an airport, a heliport, a landmark, a certain point of a Federal airway in mountainous terrain, or an obstruction. (*See* airport rotating beacon) (Refer to AIM).

aeronautical chart. A map used in air navigation containing all or part of the following: Topographic features, hazards and obstructions, navigation aids, navigation routes, designated airspace, and airports. Commonly used aeronautical charts are:

1. *Sectional charts* (1:500,000). Designed for visual navigation of slow or medium speed aircraft. Topographic information on these charts features the portrayal of relief and a judicious selection of visual check points for VFR flight. Aeronautical information includes visual and radio aids to navigation, airports, controlled airspace, restricted areas, obstructions, and related data.

2. *VFR terminal area charts* (1:250,000). Depict Class B airspace which provides for the control or segregation of all the aircraft within Class B airspace. The chart depicts topographic information and aeronautical information which includes visual and radio aids to navigation, airports, controlled airspace, restricted areas, obstructions, and related data.

3. *World aeronautical charts* (WAC) (1:1,000,000). Provide a standard series of aeronautical charts, covering land areas of the world at a size and scale convenient for navigation by moderate speed aircraft. Topographic information includes cities and towns, principal roads, railroads, distinctive landmarks, drainage, and relief. Aeronautical information includes visual and radio aids to navigation, airports, airways, restricted areas, obstructions, and other pertinent data.

4. *Enroute low altitude charts.* Provide aeronautical information for enroute instrument navigation (IFR) in the low altitude stratum. Information includes the portrayal of airways, limits of controlled airspace, position identification and frequencies of radio aids, selected airports, minimum enroute and minimum obstruction clearance altitudes, airway distances, reporting points, restricted areas, and related data. Area charts, which are a part of this series, furnish terminal data at a larger scale in congested areas.

5. *Enroute high altitude charts.* Provide aeronautical information for enroute instrument navigation (IFR) in the high altitude stratum. Information includes the portrayal of jet routes, identification and frequencies of radio aids, selected airports, distances, time zones, Special Use airspace, and related information.

6. *Instrument approach procedures (IAP) charts.* Portray the aeronautical data which is required to execute an instrument approach to an airport. These charts depict the procedures, including all related data, and the airport diagram. Each procedure is designated for use with a specific type of electronic navigation system including NDB, TACAN, VOR, ILS/MLS, and RNAV. These charts are identified by the type of navigational aid(s) which provide final approach guidance.

7. *Instrument departure procedure (DP) charts.* Designed to expedite clearance delivery and to facilitate transition between takeoff and enroute operations. Each DP procedure is presented as a separate chart and may serve a single airport or more than one airport in a given geographical location.

8. *Standard terminal arrival (STAR) charts.* Designed to expedite air traffic control arrival procedures and to facilitate transition between enroute and instrument approach operations. Each STAR procedure is presented as a separate chart and may serve a single airport or more than one airport in a given geographical location.

9. *Airport taxi charts.* Designed to expedite the efficient and safe flow of ground traffic at an airport. These charts are identified by the official airport name; e.g., Washington National Airport.

[ICAO] A representation of a portion of the earth, its culture and relief, specifically designated to meet the requirements of air navigation.

Aeronautical Information Manual (AIM). A primary FAA publication whose purpose is to instruct airmen about operating in the National Airspace System of the U.S. It provides basic flight information, ATC Procedures and general instructional information concerning health, medical facts, factors affecting flight safety, accident and hazard reporting, and types of aeronautical charts and their use.

Aeronautical Information Publication (AIP). [ICAO] A publication issued by or with the authority of a state and containing aeronautical information of a lasting character essential to air navigation.

A/FD. (*See* Airport/Facility Directory).

affirmative. Yes.

*****AGL.** Above Ground Level.

*****agonic line.** The line of zero magnetic variation.

*****ailerons.** Movable control surfaces at the outer trailing edge of each wing. They control the airplane in rolling around the longitudinal axis of the airplane.

AIM. (*See* Aeronautical Information Manual).

AIP. [ICAO] (*See* Aeronautical Information Publication).

airborne delay. Amount of delay to be encountered in airborne holding.

Air Carrier District Office (ACDO). An FAA field office serving an assigned geographical area, staffed with Flight Standards personnel serving the aviation industry and the general public on matters related to the certification and operation of scheduled air carriers and other large aircraft operations.

aircraft. Device(s) that are used or intended to be used for flight in the air, and when used in air traffic control terminology, may include the flight crew. [ICAO] Any machine that can derive support in the atmosphere from the reactions of the air other than the reactions of the air against the earth's surface.

aircraft approach category. A grouping of aircraft based on a speed of 1.3 times the stall speed in the landing configuration at maximum gross landing weight. An aircraft shall fit in only one category. If it is necessary to maneuver at speeds in excess of the upper limit of a speed range for a category, the minimums for the next higher category should be used. For example, an aircraft which falls in Category A, but is circling to land at a speed in excess of 91 knots, should use the approach Category B minimums when circling to land. The categories are as follows:

1. *Category A.* Speed less than 91 knots.
2. *Category B.* Speed 91 knots or more but less than 121 knots.
3. *Category C.* Speed 121 knots or more but less than 141 knots.
4. *Category D.* Speed 141 knots or more but less than 166 knots.
5. *Category E.* Speed 166 knots or more.
(Refer to 14 CFR Parts 1 and 97).

aircraft classes. For the purposes of Wake Turbulence Separation Minima, ATC classifies aircraft as Heavy, Large, and Small as follows:

1. *Heavy.* Aircraft capable of takeoff weights of more than 255,000 pounds whether or not they are operating at this weight during a particular phase of flight.
2. *Large.* Aircraft of more than 41,000 pounds, maximum certificated takeoff weight, up to 255,000 pounds.
3. *Small.* Aircraft of 41,000 pounds or less maximum certificated takeoff weight.
(Refer to AIM).

aircraft conflict. Predicted conflict, within URET CCLD, of two aircraft, or between aircraft and airspace. A Red alert is used for conflicts when the predicted minimum separation is 5 nautical miles or less. A Yellow alert is used when the predicted minimum separation is between 5 and approximately 12 nautical miles. A Blue alert is used for conflicts between an aircraft and predefined airspace.

*****aircraft situation display (ASD).** ASD is a computer system that receives radar track data from all 20 CONUS ARTCCs, organizes this data into a mosaic display, and presents it on a computer screen. The display allows the traffic management coordinator multiple methods of selection and highlighting of individual aircraft or groups of aircraft. The user has the option of superimposing these aircraft positions over any number of background displays. These background options include ARTCC boundaries, any stratum of enroute sector boundaries, fixes, airways, military and other special use airspace, airports, and geopolitical boundaries. By using ASD, a coordinator can monitor any number of traffic situations or the entire systemwide traffic flows.

Aircraft Surge Launch and Recovery (ASLAR). Procedures used at USAF bases to provide increased launch and recovery rates instrument flight rules conditions. ASLAR is based on:

1. Reduced separation between aircraft which is based on time or distance. Standard arrival separation applies between participants including multiple flights until the DRAG point. The DRAG point is a published location on an ASLAR approach where aircraft landing second in a formation slows to a predetermined airspeed. The DRAG point is the reference point at which MARSA applies as expanding elements effect separation within a flight or between subsequent participating flights.

2. ASLAR procedures shall be covered in a Letter of Agreement between the responsible USAF military ATC facility and the concerned Federal Aviation Administration facility. Initial Approach Fix spacing requirements are normally addressed as a minimum.

air defense emergency. A military emergency condition declared by a designated authority. This condition exists when an attack upon the continental U.S., Alaska, Canada, or U.S. installations in Greenland by hostile aircraft or missiles is considered probable, is imminent, or is taking place. (Refer to AIM).

Air Defense Identification Zone (ADIZ). The area of airspace over land or water, extending upward from the surface, within which the ready identification, the location, and the control of aircraft are required in the interest of national security.

1. *Domestic Air Defense Identification Zone.* An ADIZ within the United States along an international boundary of the United States.

2. *Coastal Air Defense Identification Zone.* An ADIZ over the coastal waters of the United States.

3. *Distant Early Warning Identification Zone (DEWIZ).* An ADIZ over the coastal waters of the State of Alaska.

ADIZ locations and operating and flight plan requirements for civil aircraft operations are specified in 14 CFR Part 99. (Refer to AIM).

***airfoil.** A shape designed to develop lift by accelerating airflow over its surface.

Airman's Meteorological Information. (*See* AIRMET).

AIRMET. In-flight weather advisories issued only to amend the area forecast concerning weather phenomena which are of operational interest to all aircraft and potentially hazardous to aircraft having limited capability because of lack of equipment, instrumentation, or pilot qualifications. AIRMETs concern weather of less severity than that covered by SIGMETs

or Convective SIGMETs. AIRMETs cover moderate icing, moderate turbulence, sustained winds of 30 knots or more at the surface, widespread areas of ceilings less than 1,000 feet and/or visibility less than 3 miles, and extensive mountain obscurement. (*See* AWW, SIGMET, Convective SIGMET, and CWA) (Refer to AIM).

***AIRMET.** A broadcast of weather hazardous to light aircraft.

air navigation facility. Any facility used in, available for use in or designed for use in, aid of air navigation, including landing areas, lights, any apparatus or equipment for disseminating weather information, for signaling, for radio directional finding, or for radio or other electrical communication, and any other structure or mechanism having a similar purpose for guiding or controlling flight in the air or the landing and takeoff of aircraft. (*See* navigational aid).

airport. An area on land or water that is used or intended to be used for the landing and takeoff of aircraft and includes its buildings and facilities, if any.

***airport acceptance rate (AAR).** A dynamic input parameter specifying the number of arriving aircraft which an airport or airspace can accept from the ARTCC per hour. The AAR is used to calculate the desired interval between successive arrival aircraft.

airport advisory area. The area within ten miles of an airport without a control tower or where the tower is not in operation, and on which a Flight Service Station is located. (*See* Local Airport Advisory) (Refer to AIM).

***airport advisory area.** An area within 10 miles of an airport with a Flight Service Station.

airport elevation. The highest point of an airport's usable runways measured in feet from mean sea level. (*See* touchdown zone elevation, aerodrome elevation [ICAO]).

Airport/Facility Directory (A/FD). A publication designed primarily as a pilot's operational manual containing all airports, seaplane bases, and heliports open to the public including communications data, navigational facilities, and certain special notices and procedures. This publication is issued in seven volumes according to geographical area.

***Airport/Facility Directory (A/FD).** A government publication containing information on all airports including radio frequencies and navigational aids available.

airport information desk. An airport unmanned facility designed for pilot self-service briefing, flight planning, and filing of flight plans. (Refer to AIM).

airport lighting. Various lighting aids that may be installed on an airport. Types of airport lighting include:

1. *Approach Light System (ALS).* An airport lighting facility which provides visual guidance to landing aircraft by radiating light beams in a directional pattern by which the pilot aligns the aircraft with the extended centerline of the runway on his final approach for landing. Capacitor Discharge Sequential Flashing Lights/Sequenced Flashing Lights may be installed in conjunction with the ALS at some airports. Types of Approach Light Systems are:

a. *ALSF-1.* Approach Light System with Sequenced Flashing Lights in ILS Cat I configuration.

b. *ALSF-2.* Approach Light System with Sequenced Flashing Lights in ILS Cat II configuration. The ALSF-2 may operate as an SSALR when weather conditions permit.

c. *SSALF.* Simplified Short Approach Light System with Sequenced Flashing Lights.

d. *SSALR.* Simplified Short Approach Light System with Runway Alignment Indicator Lights.

e. *MALSF.* Medium Intensity Approach Light System with Sequenced Flashing Lights.

f. *MALSR.* Medium Intensity Approach Light System with Runway Alignment Indicator Lights.

g. *LDIN.* Lead In light system: Consists of one or more series of flashing lights installed at or near ground level that provides positive visual guidance along an approach path, either curving or straight, where special problems exist with hazardous terrain, obstructions, or noise abatement procedures.

h. *RAIL.* Runway Alignment Indicator Lights (Sequenced Flashing Lights which are installed only combination with other light systems).

i. *ODALS.* Omnidirectional Approach Lighting System consists of seven omnidirectional flashing lights located in approach area of a nonprecision runway. Five lights are located on the runway centerline extended with the first light located 300 feet from the threshold and extending at equal intervals up to 1,500 feet from the threshold. The other two lights are located, one on each side of the runway threshold, at a lateral distance of 40 feet from the runway edge, or 75 feet from the runway edge when installed on a runway equipped with a VASI. (Refer to Order 6850.2).

2. *Runway lights/runway edge lights.* Lights having a prescribed angle of emission used to define the lateral limits of a runway. Runway lights are uniformly spaced at intervals of approximately 200 feet, and the intensity may be controlled or preset.

3. *Touchdown zone lighting.* Two rows of transverse light bars located symmetrically about the runway centerline normally at 100-foot intervals. The basic system extends 3,000 feet along the runway.

4. *Runway centerline lighting.* Flush centerline lights spaced at 50 foot intervals beginning 75 feet from the landing threshold and extending to within 75 feet of the opposite end of the runway.

5. *Threshold Lights.* Fixed green lights arranged symmetrically left and right of the runway centerline, identifying the runway threshold.

6. *Runway End Identifier Lights (REIL).* Two synchronized flashing lights, one on each side of the runway threshold, which provide rapid and positive identification of the approach end of a particular runway.

7. *Visual Approach Slope Indicator (VASI).* An airport lighting facility providing vertical visual approach slope guidance to aircraft during approach to landing by radiating a directional pattern of high intensity read and white focused light beams which indicate to the pilot that he is "on path" if he sees red/white, "above path" if white/white, and "below path" if red/red. Some airports serving large aircraft have three bar VASIs which provide two visual glidepaths to the same runway.

8. *Precision Approach Path Indicator (PAPI).* An airport lighting facility, similar to VASI, providing vertical approach slope guidance to aircraft during approach to landing. PAPIs consist of a single row of either two or four lights, normally installed on the left side of the runway. They have an effective visual range of about 5 miles during the day and up to 20 miles at night. PAPIs radiate a directional pattern of high intensity red and white focused light beams that indicate the pilot is: "on path" if the pilot sees an equal number of white lights and red lights, with white to the left of the red; "above path" if the pilot sees more white than red lights; and "below path" if the pilot sees more red than white lights.

9. *Boundary lights.* Lights defining the perimeter of an airport or landing area. (Refer to AIM).

airport marking aids. Markings used on runway and taxiway surfaces to identify a specific runway, a runway threshold, a centerline, a hold line, etc. A runway should be marked in accordance with its present usage such as:

1. Visual.

2. Nonprecision instrument.

3. Precision instrument. (Refer to AIM).

airport reference point (ARP). The approximate geometric center of all usable runway surfaces.

Airport Reservation Office (ARO). Office responsible for monitoring the operation of the high density rule. Receives and processes requests for IFR operations at high density traffic airports.

airport rotating beacon. A visual NAVAID operated at many airports. At civil airports, alternating white and green flashes indicate the location of the airport. At military airports, the beacons flash alternately white and green, but are differentiated from civil beacons by dual peaked (two quick) white flashes between the green flashes. (*See* Special VFR operations, instrument flight rules) (Refer to AIM) (*See* aerodrome beacon [ICAO]).

airport surface detection equipment (ASDE). Radar equipment specifically designed to detect all principal features on the surface of an airport, including aircraft and vehicular traffic, and to present the entire image on a radar indicator console in the control tower. Used to augment visual observation by tower personnel of aircraft and/or vehicular movements on runways and taxiways.

airport surveillance radar (ASR). Approach control radar used to detect and display an aircraft's position in the terminal area. ASR provides range and azimuth information but does not provide elevation data. Coverage of the ASR can extend up to 60 miles.

airport taxi charts. (*See* aeronautical chart).

Airport Traffic Control Service. A service provided by a control tower for aircraft operating on the movement area and in the vicinity of an airport. (*See* movement area, tower) (*See* aerodrome control service [ICAO]).

airport traffic control tower. (*See* tower).

air route surveillance radar (ARSR). Air route traffic control center (ARTCC) radar used primarily to detect and display an aircraft's position while enroute between terminal areas. The ARSR enables controllers to provide radar air traffic control service when aircraft are within the ARSR coverage. In some instances, ARSR may enable an ARTCC to provide terminal radar services similar to but usually more limited than those provided by a radar approach control.

air route traffic control center (ARTCC). A facility established to provide air traffic control service to aircraft operating on IFR flight plans within controlled airspace and principally during the enroute phase of light. When equipment capabilities and controller workload permit, certain advisory/assistance services may be provided to VFR aircraft. (*See* NAS Stage A, enroute air traffic control service) (Refer to AIM).

airspace conflict. Predicted conflict of an aircraft and active Special Activity Airspace (SAA).

airspace hierarchy. Within the airspace classes, there is a hierarchy and, in the event of an overlap of airspace: Class A preempts Class B, Class B preempts Class C, Class C preempts Class D, Class D preempts Class E, and Class E preempts Class G.

airspeed. The speed of an aircraft relative to its surrounding air mass. The unqualified term "airspeed" means one of the following:

1. *Indicated airspeed.* The speed shown on the aircraft airspeed indicator. This is the speed used in pilot/controller communications under the general term "airspeed." (Refer to 14 CFR Part 1).
2. *True airspeed.* The airspeed of an aircraft relative to undisturbed air. Used primarily in flight planning and enroute portion of flight. When used in pilot/controller communications, it is referred to as "true airspeed" and not shortened to "airspeed."

*airspeed indicator. An instrument calibrated in speed units that measures the pressure difference between the pitot and static inputs.

airstart. The starting of an aircraft engine while the aircraft is airborne, preceded by engine shutdown during training flights or by actual engine failure.

air taxi. Used to describe a helicopter/VTOL aircraft movement conducted above the surface but normally not above 100 feet AGL. The aircraft may proceed either via hover taxi or flight at speeds more than 20 knots. The pilot is solely responsible for selecting a safe airspeed/altitude for the operation being conducted. (*See* hover taxi) (Refer to AIM).

air traffic. Aircraft operating in the air or on an airport surface, exclusive of loading ramps and parking areas. [ICAO] All aircraft in flight or operating on the maneuvering area of an aerodrome.

air traffic clearance. An authorization by air traffic control, for the purpose of preventing collision between known aircraft, for an aircraft to proceed under specified traffic conditions within controlled airspace. The pilot in command of an aircraft may not deviate from the provisions of a visual flight rules (VFR) or instrument flight rules (IFR) air traffic clearance except in an emergency or unless an amended clearance has been obtained. Additionally, the pilot may request a different clearance from that which has been issued by air traffic control (ATC) if information available to the pilot makes another course of action more practicable or if aircraft equipment limitations or company procedures forbid compliance with the clearance issued. Pilots may also request clarification or amendment, as appropriate, any time a clearance is not fully understood, or considered unacceptable because of safety of flight. Controllers should, in such instances and to the extent of operational practicality and safety, honor the pilot's request. Part 91.3(a) states: "The pilot-in-command of an aircraft is directly responsible for, and is the final authority as to, the operation of that aircraft." THE PILOT IS RESPONSIBLE TO REQUEST AN AMENDED CLEARANCE if ATC issues a clearance that would cause a pilot to deviate from a rule or regulation, or in the pilot's opinion, would place the aircraft in jeopardy. (*See* ATC instructions) (*See* air traffic control clearance [ICAO]).

air traffic control (ATC). A service operated by appropriate authority to promote the safe, orderly and expeditious flow of air traffic. (*See* air traffic control service [ICAO]).

air traffic control clearance. [ICAO] Authorization for an aircraft to proceed under conditions specified by an air traffic control unit. *Note 1:* For convenience, the term air traffic control clearance is frequently abbreviated to clearance when used in appropriate contexts. *Note 2:* The abbreviated term clearance may be prefixed by the words taxi, takeoff, departure, enroute, approach or landing to indicate the particular portion of flight to which the air traffic control clearance relates.

air traffic control service. (*See* air traffic control).

air traffic control service. [ICAO] A service provided for the purpose of:

1. Preventing collisions:
   a. Between aircraft; and
   b. On the maneuvering area between aircraft and obstructions; and
2. Expediting and maintaining an orderly flow of air traffic.

air traffic control specialist. A person authorized to provide air traffic control service. (*See* air traffic control, Flight Service Station) (*See* controller [ICAO]).

Air Traffic Control System Command Center (ATCSCC). An Air Traffic Operations Service facility consisting of four operational units.

1. *Central Flow Control Function (CFCF).* Responsible for coordination and approval of all major intercenter flow control restrictions on a system basis in order to obtain maximum utilization of the airspace. (*See* quota flow control).

2. *Central Altitude Reservation Function (CARF).* Responsible for coordinating, planning, and approving special user requirements under the Altitude Reservation (ALTRV) concept. (*See* altitude reservation).

3. *Airport Reservation Office (ARO).* Responsible for approving IFR flights at designated high density traffic airports (John F. Kennedy, LaGuardia, O'Hare, and Washington National) during specified hours. (Refer to 14 CFR Part 93 and Airport/Facility Directory).

4. *ATC Contingency Command Post.* A facility which enables the FAA to manage the ATC system when significant portions of the system's capabilities have been lost or are threatened.

air traffic service. A generic term meaning:
1. Flight Information Service,
2. Alerting Service,
3. Air Traffic Advisory Service,
4. Air Traffic Control Service,
   a. Area Control Service,
   b. Approach Control Service, or
   c. Airport Control Service.

airway. A Class E airspace area established in the form of a corridor, the centerline of which is defined by radio navigational aids. (Refer to 14 CFR Part 71, AIM) (*See* federal airways). [ICAO] A control area or portion thereof established in the form of corridor equipped with radio navigational aids.

airway beacon. Used to mark airway segments in remote mountain areas. The light flashes Morse Code to identify the beacon site. (Refer to AIM).

AIT. (*See* automated information transfer).

alerfa (alert phase). [ICAO] The code word used to designate an emergency phase wherein apprehension exists as to the safety of an aircraft and its occupants.

alert area. (*See* Special Use airspace).

alert notice (ALNOT). A request originated by a Flight Service Station (FSS) or an air route traffic control center (ARTCC) for an extensive communication search for overdue, unreported, or missing aircraft.

alerting service. A service provided to notify appropriate organizations regarding aircraft in need of search and rescue aid and assist such organizations as required.

ALNOT. (*See* alert notice).

along track distance (LTD). The distance measured from a point-in-space by systems using area navigation reference capabilities that are not subject to slant range errors.

alphanumeric display. Letters and numerals used to show identification, altitude, beacon code, and other information concerning a target on a radar display. (*See* automated radar terminal systems, NAS Stage A).

alternate aerodrome. [ICAO] An aerodrome specified in the flight plan to which a flight may proceed when it becomes inadvisable to land at the aerodrome of intended landing.

Note: The aerodrome from which a flight departs may also be an enroute or a destination alternate aerodrome for the flight.

alternate airport. An airport at which an aircraft may land if a landing at the intended airport becomes inadvisable. (*See* FAA term alternate aerodrome [ICAO]).

*altimeter. An instrument that indicates altitude by measuring changes in atmospheric pressure.

altimeter setting. The barometric pressure reading used to adjust a pressure altimeter for variations in existing atmospheric pressure or to the standard altimeter setting (29.92). (Refer to 14 CFR Part 91, AIM).

*altimeter setting. A value received from a ground station to which the altimeter setting window must be adjusted in order to correct for pressure variations.

altitude. The height of a level, point, or object measured in feet Above Ground Level (AGL) or from Mean Sea Level (MSL). (*See* flight level).

1. *MSL Altitude.* Altitude expressed in feet measured from mean sea level.

2. *AGL Altitude.* Altitude expressed in feet measured above ground level.

3. *Indicated Altitude.* The altitude as shown by an altimeter. On a pressure or barometric altimeter it is altitude as shown uncorrected for instrument error and uncompensated for variation from standard atmospheric conditions.

[ICAO] The vertical distance of a level, a point or an object considered as a point, measured from mean sea level (MSL).

altitude readout. An aircraft's altitude, transmitted via the Mode C transponder feature, that is visually displayed in 100 foot increments on a radar scope having readout capability. (*See* automated radar terminal systems, NAS Stage A, alphanumeric display) (Refer to AIM).

altitude reservation (ALTRV). Airspace utilization under prescribed conditions normally employed for the mass movement of aircraft or other special user requirements which cannot otherwise be accomplished. ALTRVs are approved by the appropriate FAA facility. (*See* Air Traffic Control System Command Center).

altitude restriction. An altitude or altitudes, stated in the order flown, which are to be maintained until reaching a specific point or time. Altitude restrictions may be issued by ATC due to traffic, terrain, or other airspace considerations.

altitude restrictions are canceled. Adherence to previously imposed altitude restrictions is no longer required during a climb or descent.

ALTRV. (*See* altitude reservation).

*****ammeter.** A meter that indicates the output of the generator or alternator in amperes, the unit of electric current.

*****amphibian.** An airplane able to land and takeoff on both land and water. Airplanes with boat hulls (and retractable wheels) and float planes (with retractable wheels) are amphibians.

AMVER. (*See* Automated Mutual Assistance Vessel Rescue System).

*****angle of attack.** The angle between the chord line and the relative wind; the pilot's best means of controlling lift development.

*****angle of incidence.** The fixed angle at which the wing is attached to the fuselage; the angle between the chord line and the longitudinal axis.

approach clearance. Authorization by ATC for a pilot to conduct an instrument approach. The type of instrument approach for which a clearance and other pertinent information is provided in the approach clearance when required. (*See* instrument approach procedure, cleared for approach) (Refer to AIM and 14 CFR Part 91).

Approach Control Facility. A terminal ATC facility that provides approach control service in a terminal area. (*See* Approach Control Service, radar approach control facility).

Approach Control Service. Air traffic control service provided by an approach control facility for arriving and departing VFR/IFR aircraft and, on occasion, enroute aircraft. At some airports not served by an approach control facility, the ARTCC provides limited approach control service. (Refer to AIM). [ICAO] Air traffic control service for arriving or departing controlled flights.

approach gate. An imaginary point used within ATC as a basis for vectoring aircraft to the final approach course. The gate will be established along the final approach course 1 mile from the outer marker (or the fix used in lieu of the outer marker) on the side away from the airport for precision approaches and 1 mile from the final approach fix on the side away from the airport for nonprecision approaches. In either case when measured along the final approach course, the gate will be no closer than 5 miles from the landing threshold.

approach light system. (*See* airport lighting).

approach sequence. The order in which aircraft are positioned while on approach or awaiting approach clearance. (*See* landing sequence). [ICAO] The order in which two or more aircraft are cleared to approach to land at the aerodrome.

approach speed. The recommended speed contained in aircraft manuals used by pilots when making an approach to landing. This speed will vary for different segments of an approach as well as for aircraft weight and configuration.

appropriate ATS authority. [ICAO] The relevant authority designated by the State responsible for providing air traffic services in the airspace concerned. In the United States, the "appropriate ATS authority" is the Program Director for Air Traffic Operations, ATO-1.

appropriate authority.

1. Regarding flight over the high seas: the relevant authority is the State of Registry.
2. Regarding flight over other than the high seas: the relevant authority is the State having sovereignty over the territory being overflown.

appropriate obstacle clearance minimum altitude. Any of the following:

(*See* minimum IFR altitude (MIA)).
(*See* minimum enroute altitude (MEA)).
(*See* minimum obstruction clearance altitude (MOCA)).
(*See* minimum vectoring altitude (MVA)).

appropriate terrain clearance minimum altitude. Any of the following:

(*See* minimum IFR altitude (MIA)).
(*See* minimum enroute altitude (MEA)).
(*See* minimum obstruction clearance altitude (MOCA)).
(*See* minimum vectoring altitude (MVA)).

apron. A defined area on an airport or heliport intended to accommodate aircraft for purposes of loading or unloading passengers or cargo, refueling, parking, or maintenance. With regard to seaplanes, a ramp is used for access to the apron from the water. [ICAO] A defined area, on a land aerodrome, intended to accommodate aircraft for purposes of loading or unloading passengers, mail or cargo, refueling, parking or maintenance.

arc. The track over the ground of an aircraft flying at a constant distance from a navigational aid by reference to distance measuring equipment (DME).

*****area aviation forecast (FA).** A forecast of general weather conditions over an area as large as several states.

area control center (ACC). [ICAO] An ICAO term for an air traffic control facility primarily responsible for ATC services being provided IFR aircraft during the enroute phase of flight. The U.S. equivalent facility is an air route traffic control center (ARTCC).

area navigation (RNAV). A method of navigation which permits aircraft operation on any desired flight path within the coverage of ground- or space-based navigation aids or within the limits of the capability of self-contained aids, or a combination of these. *Note:* Area navigation includes performance-based navigation as well as other operations that do not meet the definition of performance-based navigation.

area navigation (RNAV) approach configuration.

1. *Standard T.* An RNAV approach whose design allows direct flight to any one of three initial approach fixes (IAF) and eliminates the need for procedure turns. The standard design is to align the procedure on the extended centerline with the missed approach point (MAP) at the

runway threshold, the final approach fix (FAF), and the initial approach/intermediate fix (IAF/IF). The other two IAFs will be established perpendicular to the IF.

2. *Modified T.* An RNAV approach design for single or multiple runways where terrain or operational constraints do not allow for the standard T. The "T" may be modified by increasing or decreasing the angle from the corner IAF(s) to the IF or by eliminating one or both corner IAFs.

3. *Standard I.* An RNAV approach design for a single runway with both corner IAFs eliminated. Course reversal or radar vectoring may be required at busy terminals with multiple runways.

4. *Terminal arrival area (TAA).* The TAA is controlled airspace established in conjunction with the Standard or Modified T and I RNAV approach configurations. In the standard TAA, there are three areas: straight-in, left base, and right base. The arc boundaries of the three areas of the TAA are published portions of the approach and allow aircraft to transition from the en route structure direct to the nearest IAF. TAAs will also eliminate or reduce feeder routes, departure extensions, and procedure turns or course reversal.

   a. *Straight-in area.* A 30 NM arc centered on the IF bounded by a straight line extending through the IF perpendicular to the intermediate course.

   b. *Left base area.* A 30 NM arc centered on the right corner IAF. The area shares a boundary with the straight-in area except that it extends out for 30 NM from the IAF and is bounded on the other side by a line extending from the IF through the FAF to the arc.

   c. *Right base area.* A 30 NM arc centered on the left corner IAF. The area shares a boundary with the straight-in area except that it extends out for 30 NM from the IAF and is bounded on the other side by a line extending from the IF through the FAF to the arc.

ARINC. An acronym for Aeronautical Radio, Inc., a corporation largely owned by a group of airlines. ARINC is licensed by the FCC as an aeronautical station and contracted by the FAA to provide communications support for air traffic control and meteorological services in portions of international airspace.

*arm. The distance a weight is located from a fulcrum or datum point.

Army Aviation Flight Information Bulletin (USAFIB). A bulletin that provides air operation data covering Army, National Guard, and Army Reserve aviation activities.

ARO. (*See* Airport Reservation Office).

arresting system. A safety device consisting of two major components, namely, engaging or catching devices and energy absorption devices for the purpose of arresting both tailhook and/or nontailhook equipped aircraft. It is used to prevent aircraft from overrunning runways when the aircraft cannot be stopped after landing or during aborted takeoff. Arresting systems have various names; e.g., arresting gear, hook device, wire barrier cable. (*See* abort) (Refer to AIM).

arrival aircraft interval (AAI). An internally generated program in hundredths of minutes based upon the AAR. AAI is the desired optimum interval between successive arrival aircraft over the vertex.

arrival center. The ARTCC having jurisdiction for the impacted airport.

arrival delay (ADLY). A parameter which specifies a period of time in which no aircraft will be metered for arrival at the specified airport.

arrival sector. An operational control sector containing one or more meter fixes.

arrival sector advisory list. An ordered list of data on arrivals displayed at the PVD/MDM of the sector which controls the meter fix.

arrival sequencing program (ASP). The automated program designed to assist in sequencing aircraft destined for the same airport.

arrival time. The time an aircraft touches down on arrival.

ARSR. (*See* air route surveillance radar).

ARTCC. (*See* air route traffic control center).

ARTS. (*See* automated radar terminal system).

ASD. (*See* aircraft situation display).

ASDA. (*See* accelerate-stop distance available).

ASDA. [ICAO] (*See* accelerate-stop distance available [ICAO]).

ASDE. (*See* airport surface detection equipment).

ASLAR. (*See* Aircraft Surge Launch and Recovery).

ASP. (*See* arrival sequencing program).

ASR. (*See* airport surveillance radar).

ASR approach. (*See* surveillance approach).

*ATA. Actual time of arrival—to be filled in on your flight log and compared with your estimates to determine how the actual flight is progressing.

ATC. (*See* air traffic control).

ATCAA. (*See* ATC assigned airspace).

ATC advises. Used to prefix a message of noncontrol information when it is relayed to an aircraft by other than an air traffic controller. (*See* advisory).

ATC assigned airspace (ATCAA). Airspace of defined vertical/lateral limits, assigned by ATC, for the purpose of providing air traffic segregation between the specified activities being conducted within the assigned airspace and other IFR air traffic. (*See* Special Use airspace).

ATC clearance. (*See* air traffic clearance).

ATC clears. Used to prefix an ATC clearance when it is relayed to an aircraft by other than an air traffic controller.

ATC instructions. Directives issued by air traffic control for the purpose of requiring a pilot to take specific actions; e.g., "Turn left heading two five zero," "Go around," "Clear the runway." (Refer to 14 CFR Part 91).

ATCRBS. (*See* radar).

ATC requests. Used to prefix an ATC request when it is relayed to an aircraft by other than an air traffic controller.

ATCSCC. (*See* Air Traffic Control System Command Center).

ATCSCC delay factor. The amount of delay calculated to be assigned prior to departure.

ATCT. (*See* tower).

*ATE. Actual time enroute.

ATIS. (*See* Automatic Terminal Information Service).

*ATIS. Automatic Terminal Information Service — a recorded broadcast of noncontrol information at busy airports.

ATS Route. [ICAO] A specified route designed for the flow of traffic as necessary for the provision of air traffic services. *Note:* The term "ATS Route" is used to mean airway, advisory route, controlled or uncontrolled route, arrival or departure, etc.

*attitude. The position of the airplane's nose or wings in relation to the natural horizon.

autoland approach. An autoland approach is a precision instrument approach to touchdown and, in some cases, through the landing rollout. An autoland approach is performed by the aircraft autopilot which is receiving position information and/or steering commands from on board navigation equipment. (*See* coupled approach).

Note: Autoland and coupled approaches are flown in VFR and IFR. It is common for carriers to require their crews to fly coupled approaches and autoland approaches (if certified) when the weather conditions are less than approximately 4,000 RVR.

automated information transfer (AIT). A precoordinated process, specifically defined in facility directives, during which a transfer of altitude control and/or radar identification is accomplished without verbal coordination between controllers using information communicated in a full data block.

Automated Mutual Assistance Vessel Rescue System. A facility which can deliver, in a matter of minutes, a surface picture (SURPIC) of vessels in the area of a potential or actual search and rescue incident, including their predicted positions and their characteristics. (*See* Order 7110.65 Paragraph 10-73, In-flight contingencies).

automated radar terminal systems (ARTS). The generic term for the ultimate in functional capability afforded by several automation systems. Each differs in functional capabilities and equipment. ARTS plus a suffix roman numeral denotes a specific system. A following letter indicates a major modification to that system. In general, an ARTS displays for the terminal controller aircraft identification, flight plan data, other flight associated information; e.g., altitude, speed, and aircraft position symbols in conjunction with his radar presentation. Normal radar coexists with the alphanumeric display. In addition to enhancing visualization of the air traffic situation, ARTS facilitate intrafacility and interfacility transfer and coordination of flight information. These capabilities are enabled by specially designed computers and subsystems tailored to the radar and communications equipments and operational requirements of each automated facility. Modular design permits adoption of improvements in computer software and electronic technologies as they become available while retaining the characteristics unique to each system.

1. *ARTS II.* A programmable nontracking, computer aided display subsystem capable of modular expansion. ARTS II systems provide a level of automated air traffic control capability at terminals having low to medium activity. Flight identification and altitude may be associated with the display of secondary radar targets. The system has the capability of communicating with ARTCCs and other ARTS II, IIA, III, and IIIA facilities.

2. *ARTS IIA.* A programmable radar tracking computer subsystem capable of modular expansion. The ARTS IIA detects, tracks, and predicts secondary radar targets. The targets are displayed by means of computer generated symbols, ground speed, and flight plan data. Although it does not track primary radar targets, they are displayed coincident with the secondary radar as well as the symbols and alphanumerics. The system has the capability of communicating with ARTCCs and other ARTS II, IIA, III, and IIIA facilities.

3. *ARTS III.* The Beacon Tracking Level (BTL) of the modular programmable automated radar terminal system in use at medium to high activity terminals. ARTS III detects, tracks, and predicts secondary radar derived aircraft targets. These are displayed by means of computer generated symbols and alphanumeric characters depicting flight identification, aircraft altitude, ground speed, and flight plan data. Although it does not track primary targets, they are displayed coincident with the secondary radar as well as the symbols and alphanumerics. The system has the capability of communicating with ARTCCs and other ARTS III facilities.

4. *ARTS IIIA.* The Radar Tracking and Beacon Tracking Level (RT & BTL) of the modular, programmable automated radar terminal system. ARTS IIIA detects, tracks, and predicts primary as well as secondary radar derived aircraft targets. This more sophisticated computer driven system upgrades the existing ARTS III system by providing improved tracking, continuous data recording, and fail-soft capabilities.

automated UNICOM. Provides completely automated weather, radio check capability and airport advisory information on an Automated UNICOM system. These systems offer a variety of features, typically selectable by microphone clicks, on the UNICOM frequency. Availability will be published in the Airport/Facility Directory and approach charts.

automatic altitude report. (*See* altitude readout).

automatic altitude reporting. That function of a transponder which responds to Mode C interrogations by transmitting the aircraft's altitude in 100-foot increments.

Automatic Carrier Landing System (ACLS). U.S. Navy final approach equipment consisting of precision tracking radar coupled to a computer data link to provide continuous information to the aircraft, monitoring capability to the pilot, and a backup approach system.

automatic direction finder (ADF). An aircraft radio navigation system which senses and indicates the direction to a L/MF nondirectional radio beacon (NDB) ground transmitter. Direction is indicated to the pilot as a magnetic bearing or as a relative bearing to the longitudinal axis of the aircraft depending on the type of indicator installed in the aircraft. In certain applications, such as military, ADF operations may be based on airborne and ground transmitters in the VHF/UHF frequency spectrum. (*See* bearing, nondirectional beacon).

Automatic Terminal Information Service (ATIS). The continuous broadcast of recorded noncontrol information in selected terminal areas. Its purpose is to improve controller effectiveness and to relieve frequency congestion by automating the repetitive transmission of essential but routine information; e.g., "Los Angeles information Alfa. One three zero zero Coordinated Universal Time. Weather measured ceiling two thousand overcast, visibility three, haze, smoke, temperature seven one, dew point five seven, wind two five zero at five, altimeter two niner six. ILS Runway Two Five Left approach in use, Runway Two Five Right closed, advise you have Alfa." (Refer to AIM). [ICAO] The provision of current, routine information to arriving and departing aircraft by means of continuous and repetitive broadcasts throughout the day or a specified portion of the day.

autorotation. A rotorcraft flight condition in which the lifting rotor is driven entirely by action of the air when the rotorcraft is in motion.

1. *Autorotative Landing/Touchdown Autorotation.* Used by a pilot to indicate that he will be landing without applying power to the rotor.

2. *Low Level Autorotation.* Commences at an altitude well below the traffic pattern, usually below 100 feet AGL and is used primarily for tactical military training.

3. *180 degrees Autorotation.* Initiated from a downwind heading and is commenced well inside the normal traffic pattern. "Go around" may not be possible during the latter part of this maneuver.

Available Landing Distance (ALD). The portion of a runway available for landing and roll-out for aircraft cleared for LAHSO. This distance is measured from the landing threshold to the hold-short point.

Aviation Weather Service. A service provided by the National Weather Service (NWS) and FAA which collects and disseminates pertinent weather information for pilots, aircraft operators, and ATC. Available aviation weather reports and forecasts are displayed at each NWS office and FAA FSS. (*See* Enroute Flight Advisory Service, Transcribed Weather Broadcast, Weather Advisory, Pilots Automatic Telephone Weather Answering Service) (Refer to AIM).

AWW. (*See* severe weather forecast alerts).

*****axis of control.** An imaginary line around which the pilot controls the airplane.

azimuth (MLS). A magnetic bearing extending from an MLS navigation facility. *Note:* azimuth bearings are described as magnetic and are referred to as "azimuth" in radio telephone communications.

back-taxi. A term used by air traffic controllers to taxi an aircraft on the runway opposite to thc traffic flow. The aircraft may be instructed to back-taxi to the beginning of the runway or at some point before reaching the runway end for the purpose of departure or to exit the runway.

base leg. (*See* traffic pattern).

beacon. (*See* radar, nondirectional beacon, marker beacon, airport rotating beacon, aeronautical beacon, airway beacon).

bearing. The horizontal direction to or from any point, usually measured clockwise from true north, magnetic north, or some other reference point through 360 degrees. (*See* nondirectional beacon).

below minimums. Weather conditions below the minimums prescribed by regulation for the particular action involved; e.g., landing minimums, takeoff minimums.

blast fence. A barrier that is used to divert or dissipate jet or propeller blast.

*****bleed air.** Compressed air "bled" from the turbocharger to operate pressurization cabin heating and deicing systems.

blind speed. The rate of departure or closing of a target relative to the radar antenna at which cancellation of the primary radar target by moving target indicator (MTI) circuits in the radar equipment causes a reduction or complete loss of signal. (*See* blind velocity [ICAO]).

blind spot. An area from which radio transmissions and/or radar echoes cannot be received. The term is also used to describe portions of the airport not visible from the control tower.

blind transmission. (*See* transmitting in the blind).

blind velocity. [ICAO] The radial velocity of a moving target such that the target is not seen on primary radars fitted with certain forms of fixed echo suppression.

blind zone. (*See* blind spot).

blocked. Phraseology used to indicate that a radio transmission has been distorted or interrupted due to multiple simultaneous radio transmissions.

boundary lights. (*See* airport lighting).

braking action (good, fair, poor, or nil). A report of conditions on the airport movement area providing a pilot with a degree/quality of braking that he might expect. Braking action is reported in terms of good, fair, poor, or nil. (*See* runway condition reading).

braking action advisories. When tower controllers have received runway braking action reports which include the terms "poor" or "nil," or whenever weather conditions are conducive to deteriorating or rapidly changing runway braking conditions, the tower will include on the ATIS broadcast the statement, "BRAKING ACTION ADVISORIES ARE IN EFFECT." During the time braking action advisories are in effect, ATC will issue the latest braking action report for the runway in use to each arriving and departing aircraft. Pilots should be prepared for deteriorating braking conditions and should request current runway condition information if not volunteered by controllers. Pilots should also be prepared to provide a descriptive runway condition report to controllers after landing.

breakout. A technique to direct aircraft out of the approach stream. In the context of close parallel operations, a breakout is used to direct threatened aircraft away from a deviating aircraft.

broadcast. Transmission of information for which an acknowledgment is not expected. [ICAO] A transmission of information relating to air navigation that is not addressed to a specific station or stations.

calculated landing time (CLT). A term that may be used in place of tentative or actual calculated landing time, whichever applies.

*****calibrated airspeed.** The reading of the airspeed indicator corrected for installation or position error.

call up. Initial voice contact between a facility and an aircraft, using the identification of the unit being called and the unit initiating the call. (Refer to AIM).

call for release (CFR). Wherein the overlying ARTCC requires a terminal facility to initiate verbal coordination to secure ARTCC approval for release of a departure into the enroute environment.

*****camber.** The convexity or curvature of an airfoil from its chord.

Canadian Minimum Navigation Performance Specification (CMNPS) airspace. That portion of Canadian domestic airspace within which MNPS separation may be applied.

*****carburetor.** A device that mixes a metered amount of fuel with airflow, atomizing it for combustion.

cardinal altitudes. "Odd" or "Even" thousand foot altitudes or flight levels; e.g., 5,000, 6,000, 7,000, FL 250, FL 260, FL 270. (*See* altitude, flight level).

cardinal flight levels. (*See* cardinal altitudes).

CAT. (*See* clear air turbulence).

CDT programs. (*See* controlled departure time programs).

*****CDI.** Course Deviation Indicator—the "needle" on a VOR display that tells you if you are on the desired radial.

ceiling. The heights above the earth's surface of the lowest layer of clouds or obscuring phenomena that is reported as "broken," "overcast," or "obscuration." [ICAO] The height above the ground or water of the base of the lowest layer of cloud below 6,000 meters (20,000 feet) covering more than half the sky.

CENRAP. (*See* Center Radar ARTS Presentation/processing).

CENRAP-plus. (*See* Center Radar ARTS Presentation/processing-plus).

center. (*See* air route traffic control center).

center's area. The specified airspace within which an air route traffic control center (ARTCC) provides air traffic control and advisory service. (*See* air route traffic control center) (Refer to AIM).

*****center of gravity (CG).** That part of a body (an airplane, in this case) about which all forces are balanced.

*****center of lift.** The single point on the wing where all lifting forces are resolved (concentrated).

Center Radar ARTS Presentation/processing (CENRAP). A computer program developed to provide a backup system for airport surveillance radar in the event of a failure or malfunction. The program uses air route traffic control center radar for the processing and presentation of data on the ARTS IIA or IIIA displays.

Center Radar ARTS Presentation/processing-plus (CENRAP-plus). A computer program developed to provide a backup system for airport surveillance radar in the event of a terminal secondary radar system failure. The program uses a combination of air route traffic control center radar and terminal airport surveillance radar primary targets displayed simultaneously for the processing and presentation of data on the ARTS IIA or IIIA displays.

Center Weather Advisory (CWA). An unscheduled weather advisory issued by Center Weather Service Unit meteorologists for ATC use to alert pilots of existing or anticipated adverse weather conditions within the next 2 hours. A CWA may modify or redefine a SIGMET. (*See* AWW, SIGMET, Convective SIGMET, and AIRMET) (Refer to AIM).

Central East Pacific (CEP). An organized route system between the U.S. West Coast and Hawaii.

CEP. (*See* Central East Pacific).

CERAP. (*See* combined center—RAPCON).

*Certificate of Airworthiness. A certificate awarded at the time of manufacture and kept current by compliance with maintenance and inspection requirements.

CFR. (*See* call for release).

chaff. Thin, narrow metallic reflectors of various lengths and frequency responses, used to reflect radar energy. These reflectors when dropped from aircraft and allowed to drift downward result in large targets on the radar display.

charted VFR flyways. Charted VFR Flyways are flight paths recommended for use to bypass areas heavily traversed by large turbine powered aircraft. Pilot compliance with recommended flyways and associated altitudes is strictly voluntary. VFR Flyway Planning charts are published on the back of existing VFR Terminal Area charts.

charted visual flight procedure approach. An approach conducted while operating on an instrument flight rules (IFR) flight plan which authorizes the pilot of an aircraft to proceed visually and clear of clouds to the airport via visual landmarks and other information depicted on a charted visual flight procedure. This approach must be authorized and under the control of the appropriate air traffic control facility. Weather minimums required are depicted on the chart.

chase. An aircraft flown in proximity to another aircraft normally to observe its performance during training or testing.

chase aircraft. (*See* chase).

*chord line. An imaginary line from the leading edge to the trailing edge of an airfoil.

circle-to-land maneuver. A maneuver initiated by the pilot to align the aircraft with a runway for landing when a straight-in landing from an instrument approach is not possible or is not desirable. At tower controlled airports, this maneuver is made only after ATC authorization has been obtained and the pilot has established required visual reference to the airport. (*See* circle to runway, landing minimums) (Refer to AIM).

circle to runway (runway number). Used by ATC to inform the pilot that he must circle to land because the runway in use is other than the runway aligned with the instrument approach procedure. When the direction of the circling maneuver in relation to the airport/runway is required, the controller will state the direction (eight cardinal compass points) and specify a left or right downwind or base leg as appropriate; e.g., "Cleared VOR Runway Three Six Approach circle to Runway Two Two," or "Circle northwest of the airport for a right downwind to Runway Two Two." (*See* circle-to-land maneuver, landing minimums) (Refer to AIM).

circling approach. (*See* circle-to-land maneuver).

circling maneuver. (*See* circle-to-land maneuver).

circling minima. (*See* landing minimums).

Class A airspace. (*See* controlled airspace).

Class B airspace. (*See* controlled airspace).

*Class B airspace. Airspace division which requires a clearance from ATC for entry.

Class C airspace. (*See* controlled airspace).

*Class C airspace. A controlled airspace area where pilots must maintain two-way communication with the controlling agency, and where radar service is available to VFR pilots.

Class D airspace. (*See* controlled airspace).

Class E airspace. (*See* controlled airspace).

Class G airspace. That airspace not designated as Class A, B, C, D or E.

clear air turbulence (CAT). Turbulence encountered in air where no clouds are present. This term is commonly applied to high level turbulence associated with windshear. CAT is often encountered in the vicinity of the jet stream. (*See* windshear, jet stream).

clear of the runway.

1. A taxiing aircraft, which is approaching a runway, is clear of the runway when all parts of the aircraft are held short of the applicable holding position marking.

2. A pilot or controller may consider an aircraft, which is exiting or crossing a runway, to be clear of the runway when all parts of the aircraft are beyond the runway edge and there is no ATC restriction to its continued movement beyond the applicable holding position marking.

3. Pilots and controllers shall exercise good judgment to ensure that adequate separation exists between all aircraft on runways and taxiways at airports with inadequate runway edge lines or holding position markings.

clearance. (*See* Air Traffic Clearance).

clearance limit. The fix, point, or location to which an aircraft is cleared when issued an air traffic clearance. [ICAO] The point of which an aircraft is granted an air traffic control clearance.

Clearance void if not off by (time). Used by ATC to advise an aircraft that the departure clearance is automatically canceled if takeoff is not made prior to a specified time. The pilot must obtain a new clearance or cancel his IFR flight plan if not off by the specified time. (*See* clearance void time [ICAO]).

clearance void time. [ICAO] A time specified by an air traffic control unit at which a clearance ceases to be valid unless the aircraft concerned has already taken action to comply therewith.

Cleared as filed. Means the aircraft is cleared to proceed in accordance with the route of flight filed in the flight plan. This clearance does not include the altitude, DP, or DP Transition. (*See* request full route clearance) (Refer to AIM).

Cleared (type of) approach. ATC authorization for an aircraft to execute a specific instrument approach procedure to an airport; e.g., "Cleared for ILS Runway Three Six Approach." (*See* instrument approach procedure, approach clearance) (Refer to AIM) (Refer to 14 CFR Part 91).

cleared approach. ATC authorization for an aircraft to execute any standard or special instrument approach procedure for that airport. Normally, an aircraft will be cleared for a specific instrument approach procedure. (*See* instrument approach procedure, cleared (type of) approach) (Refer to AIM) (Refer to 14 CFR Part 91).

Cleared for takeoff. ATC authorization for an aircraft to depart. It is predicated on known traffic and known physical airport conditions.

Cleared for the option. ATC authorization for an aircraft to make a touch and go, low approach, missed approach, stop and go, or full stop landing at the discretion of the pilot. It is normally used in training so that an instructor can evaluate a student's performance under changing situations. (*See* option approach) (Refer to AIM).

Cleared through. ATC authorization for an aircraft to make intermediate stops at specified airports without refiling a flight plan while en route to the clearance limit.

Cleared to land. ATC authorization for an aircraft to land. It is predicated on known traffic and known physical airport conditions.

clearway. An area beyond the takeoff runway under the control of airport authorities within which terrain or fixed obstacles may not extend above specified limits. These areas may be required for certain turbine powered operations and the size and upward slope of the clearway will differ depending on when the aircraft was certificated. (Refer to 14 CFR Part 1).

climbout. That portion of flight operation between takeoff and the initial cruising altitude.

Climb to VFR. ATC authorization for an aircraft to climb to VFR conditions within Class B, C, D, and E surface areas when the only weather limitation is restricted visibility. The aircraft must remain clear of clouds while climbing to VFR. (*See* Special VFR) (Refer to AIM).

close parallel runways. Two parallel runways whose extended centerlines are separated by less than 4,300 feet, having a Precision Runway Monitoring (PRM) system that permits simultaneous independent ILS approaches.

closed runway. A runway that is unusable for aircraft operations. Only the airport management/military operations office can close a runway.

closed traffic. Successive operations involving takeoffs and landings or low approaches where the aircraft does not exit the traffic pattern.

cloud. A cloud is a visible accumulation of minute water droplets and/or ice particles in the atmosphere above the Earth's surface. Cloud differs from ground fog, fog, or ice fog only in that the latter are, by definition, in contact with the Earth's surface.

CLT. (*See* calculated landing time).

clutter. In radar operations, clutter refers to the reception and visual display of radar returns caused by precipitation, chaff, terrain, numerous aircraft targets, or other phenomena. Such returns may limit or preclude ATC from providing services based on radar. (*See* ground clutter, chaff, precipitation, target) (*See* radar clutter [ICAO]).

CMNPS. (*See* Canadian Minimum Navigation Performance Specification airspace).

coastal fix. A navigation aid or intersection where an aircraft transitions between the domestic route structure and the oceanic route structure.

codes. The number assigned to a particular multiple pulse reply signal transmitted by a transponder. (*See* discrete code).

***coefficient of lift.** A complex element of the lift formula which includes angle of attack as one component.

combined center—RAPCON (CERAP). An air traffic facility which combines the functions of an ARTCC and a radar approach control facility. (*See* air route traffic control center, radar approach control facility).

common point. A significant point over which two or more aircraft will report passing or have reported passing before proceeding on the same or diverging tracks. To establish/maintain longitudinal separation, a controller may determine a common point not originally in the aircraft's flight plan and then clear the aircraft to fly over the point. (*See* significant point).

common portion. (*See* common route).

common route. That segment of a North American Route between the inland navigation facility and the coastal fix.

Common Traffic Advisory Frequency (CTAF). A frequency designed for the purpose of carrying out airport advisory practices while operating to or from an airport without an operating control tower. The CTAF may be a UNICOM, MULTICOM, FSS, or tower frequency and is identified in appropriate aeronautical publications. (Refer to AC 90-42).

compass locator. A low power, low or medium frequency (L/MF) radio beacon installed at the site of the outer or middle marker of an instrument landing system (ILS). It can be used for navigation at distances of approximately 15 miles or as authorized in the approach procedure.

1. *Outer Compass Locator (LOM).* A compass locator installed at the site of the outer marker of an instrument landing system. (*See* outer marker).
2. *Middle Compass Locator (LMM).* A compass locator installed at the site of the middle marker of an instrument landing system. (*See* middle marker) (*See* locator [ICAO]).

compass rose. A circle, graduated in degrees, printed on some charts or marked on the ground at an airport. It is used as a reference to either true or magnetic direction.

composite flight plan. A flight plan which specifies VFR operation for one portion of flight and IFR for another portion. It is used primarily in military operations. (Refer to AIM).

composite route system. An organized oceanic route structure, incorporating reduced lateral spacing between routes, in which composite separation is authorized.

composite separation. A method of separating aircraft in a composite route system where, by management of route and altitude assignments, a combination of half the lateral minimum specified for the area concerned and half the vertical minimum is applied.

*compressor discharge temperature gauge. An instrument that monitors the temperature of the air being discharged from the compressor into the intake manifold of a turbocharged engine.

compulsory reporting points. Reporting points which must be reported to ATC. They are designated on aeronautical charts by solid triangles or filed in a flight plan as fixes selected to define direct routes. These points are geographical locations which are defined by navigation aids/fixes. Pilots should discontinue position reporting over compulsory reporting points when informed by ATC that their aircraft is in "radar contact."

conflict alert. A function of certain air traffic control automated systems designed to alert radar controllers to existing or pending situations between tracked targets (known IFR or VFR aircraft) that require his immediate attention/action. (*See* Mode C intruder alert).

conflict resolution. The resolution of potential conflictions between aircraft that are radar identified and in com-munication with ATC by ensuring that radar targets do not touch. Pertinent traffic advisories shall be issued when this procedure is applied. *Note:* This procedure shall not be provided utilizing mosaic radar systems.

Consolan. A low frequency, long distance NAVAID used principally for transoceanic navigation.

contact.
1. Establish communication with (followed by the name of the facility and, if appropriate, the frequency to be used).
2. A flight condition wherein the pilot ascertains the attitude of his aircraft and navigates by visual reference to the surface. (*See* contact approach, radar contact).

contact approach. An approach wherein an aircraft on an IFR flight plan, having an air traffic control authorization, operating clear of clouds with at least 1 mile flight visibility and a reasonable expectation of continuing to the destination airport in those conditions, may deviate from the instrument approach procedure and proceed to the destination airport by visual reference to the surface. This approach will only be authorized when requested by the pilot and the reported ground visibility at the destination airport is at least 1 statute mile. (Refer to AIM).

contaminated runway. A runway is considered contaminated whenever standing water, ice, snow, slush, frost in any form, heavy rubber or other substances are present. A runway is contaminated with respect to rubber deposits or other friction-degrading substances when the average friction value for any 500-foot segment of the runway within the ALD falls below the recommended minimum friction level and the average friction value in the adjacent 500-foot segments falls below the maintenance planning friction level.

conterminous U.S. The 48 adjoining States and the District of Columbia.

continental United States. The 49 States located on the continent of North America and the District of Columbia.

continue. When used as a control instruction, should be followed by another word or words clarifying what is expected of the pilot. Example: "continue taxi," "continue descent," "continue inbound" etc.

control area. [ICAO] A controlled airspace extending upwards from a specified limit above the earth.

*controllable-pitch propeller. A propeller with two (or more) blades, joined at the hub and capable of having the blade angle changed in flight by a governor to maintain a constant engine speed.

*controlled airport. An airport with an operating control tower.

controlled airspace. An airspace of defined dimensions within which air traffic control service is provided to IFR flights and to VFR flights in accordance with the airspace classification. *Note 1.* Controlled airspace is a generic term that covers Class A, Class B, Class C, Class D, and Class E airspace. *Note 2.* Controlled airspace is also that airspace within which all aircraft operators are subject to certain pilot qualifications, operating rules, and equipment requirements in 14 CFR Part 91 (for specific operating requirements, please refer to Part 91). For IFR operations in any class of controlled airspace, a pilot must file an IFR flight plan and receive an appropriate ATC clearance. Each Class B, Class C, and Class D airspace area designated for an airport contains at least one primary airport around which the airspace is designated (for specific designations and descriptions of the airspace classes, please refer to 14 CFR Part 71).

Controlled airspace in the United States is designated as follows:

1. *Class A:* Generally, that airspace from 18,000 feet MSL up to and including FL 600, including the airspace overlying the waters within 12 nautical miles of the coast of the 48 contiguous States and Alaska. Unless otherwise authorized, all persons must operate their aircraft under IFR.

2. *Class B:* Generally, that airspace from the surface to 10,000 feet MSL surrounding the nation's busiest airports in terms of airport operations or passenger enplanements. The configuration of each Class B airspace area is individually tailored and consists of a surface area and two or more layers (some Class B airspace areas resemble upside down wedding cakes), and is designed to contain

all published instrument procedures once an aircraft enters the airspace. An ATC clearance is required for all aircraft to operate in the area, and all aircraft that are so cleared receive separation services within the airspace. The cloud clearance requirement for VFR operations is "clear of clouds."

3. *Class C:* Generally, that airspace from the surface to 4,000 feet above the airport elevation (charted in MSL) surrounding those airports that have an operational control tower, are serviced by a radar approach control, and that have a certain number of IFR operations or passenger enplanements. Although the configuration of each Class C area is individually tailored, the airspace usually consists of a surface area with a 5 nautical mile (NM) radius, an outer circle with a 10 NM radius that extends from 1,200 feet to 4,000 feet above the airport elevation and an outer area. Each person must establish two-way radio communications with the ATC facility providing air traffic services prior to entering the airspace and thereafter maintain those communications while within the airspace. VFR aircraft are only separated from IFR aircraft within the airspace.

4. *Class D:* Generally, that airspace from the surface to 2,500 feet above the airport elevation (charted in MSL) surrounding those airports that have an operational control tower. The configuration of each Class D airspace area is individually tailored and when instrument procedures are published, the airspace will normally be designed to contain the procedures. Arrival extensions for instrument approach procedures may be Class D or Class E airspace. Unless otherwise authorized, each person must establish two-way radio communications with the ATC facility providing air traffic services prior to entering the airspace and thereafter maintain those communications while in the airspace. No separation services are provided to VFR aircraft.

5. *Class E:* Generally, if the airspace is not Class A, Class B, Class C, or Class D, and it is controlled airspace, it is Class E airspace. Class E airspace extends upward from either the surface or a designated altitude to the overlying or adjacent controlled airspace. When designated as a surface area, the airspace will be configured to contain all instrument procedures. Also in this class are Federal airways, airspace beginning at either 700 or 1,200 feet AGL used to transition to/from the terminal or enroute environment, enroute domestic, and offshore airspace areas designated below 18,000 feet MSL. Unless designated at a lower altitude, Class E airspace begins at 14,500 MSL over the United States, including that airspace overlying the waters within 12 nautical miles of the coast of the 48 contiguous States and Alaska, up to, but not including 18,000 feet MSL, and the airspace above FL 600.

[ICAO] An airspace of defined dimensions within which air traffic control service is provided to IFR flights and to VFR flights in accordance with the airspace classification. *Note:* Controlled airspace is a generic term which covers ATS airspace Classes A, B, C, D, and E.

controlled departure time programs. These programs are the flow control process whereby aircraft are held on the ground at the departure airport when delays are projected to occur in either the enroute system or the terminal of intended landing. The purpose of these programs is to reduce congestion in the air traffic system or to limit the duration of airborne holding in the arrival center or terminal area. A CDT is a specific departure slot shown on the flight plan as an expected departure clearance time (EDCT).

controlled time of arrival (CTA). The original estimated time of arrival adjusted by the ATCSCC ground delay factor.

controller. (*See* air traffic control specialist). [ICAO] A person authorized to provide air traffic control services.

control sector. An airspace area of defined horizontal and vertical dimensions for which a controller or group of controllers has air traffic control responsibility normally within an air route traffic control center or an approach control facility. Sectors are established based on predominant traffic flows, altitude strata, and controller workload. Pilot communications during operations within a sector are normally maintained on discrete frequencies assigned to the sector. (*See* discrete frequency).

control slash. A radar beacon slash representing the actual position of the associated aircraft. Normally, the control slash is the one closest to the interrogating radar beacon site. When ARTCC radar is operating in narrow band (digitized) mode, the control slash is converted to a target symbol.

*control yoke. The control the pilot uses to pitch and roll the airplane. Older airplanes used a "stick" and this term continues in use today.

*convection. Vertical movement of air.

Convective SIGMET. A weather advisory concerning convective weather significant to the safety of all aircraft. Convective SIGMETs are issued for tornadoes, lines of thunderstorms, embedded thunderstorms of any intensity level, areas of thunderstorms greater than or equal to VIP level 4 with an area coverage of 4/10 (40%) or more, and hail 3/4 inch or greater. (*See* AWW, SIGMET, CWA, and AIRMET) (Refer to AIM).

Convective Significant Meteorological Information. (*See* Convective SIGMET).

coordinates. The intersection of lines of reference, usually expressed in degrees/minutes/seconds of latitude and longitude, used to determine position or location.

coordination fix. The fix in relation to which facilities will handoff, transfer control of an aircraft, or coordinate flight progress data. For terminal facilities, it may also serve as a clearance for arriving aircraft.

copter. (*See* helicopter).

*Coriolis force. A force generated by the rotation of the earth that deflects the gradient wind to the right in the Northern Hemisphere.

correction. An error has been made in the transmission and the correct version follows.

coupled approach. A coupled approach is an instrument approach performed by the aircraft autopilot which is receiving position information and/or steering commands from on board navigation equipment. In general, coupled nonprecision approaches must be discontinued and flown manually at altitudes lower than 50 feet below the minimum descent altitude, and coupled precision approaches must be flown manually below 50 feet AGL. (*See* autoland approach).

Note: Coupled and autoland approaches are flown in VFR and IFR. It is common for carriers to require their crews to fly coupled approaches and autoland approaches (if certified) when the weather conditions are less than approximately 4,000 RVR.

course.

1. The intended direction of flight in the horizontal plane measured in degrees from north.
2. The ILS localizer signal pattern usually specified as the front course or the back course.
3. The intended track along a straight, curved, or segmented MLS path.
   (*See* bearing, radial, instrument landing system, Micro wave Landing System).

*course. A line connecting two points on a planned flight.

*cowling. The smooth metal or fiberglass enclosure surrounding the engine. The cowling streamlines the engine compartment and directs cooling air over the engine.

CPL. [ICAO] (*See* current flight plan).

critical engine. The engine which, upon failure, would most adversely affect the performance or handling qualities of an aircraft.

Cross (fix) at (altitude). Used by ATC when a specific altitude restriction at a specified fix is required.

Cross (fix) at or above (altitude). Used by ATC when an altitude restriction at a specified fix is required. It does not prohibit the aircraft from crossing the fix at a higher altitude than specified; however, the higher altitude may not be one that will violate a succeeding altitude restriction or altitude assignment. (*See* altitude restriction) (Refer to AIM).

Cross (fix) at or below (altitude). Used by ATC when a maximum crossing altitude at a specific fix is required. It does not prohibit the aircraft from crossing the fix at a lower altitude; however, it must be at or above the minimum IFR altitude. (*See* minimum IFR altitude, altitude restriction) (Refer to 14 CFR Part 91).

cross-country. For purposes of meeting cross-country requirements for a private or commercial certificate or the instrument rating, a flight that includes a landing at an airport more than 50 straight-line miles from the departure airport. Landings enroute are approved.

crosswind.

1. When used concerning the traffic pattern, the word means "crosswind leg." (*See* traffic pattern).
2. When used concerning wind conditions, the word means a wind not parallel to the runway or the path of an aircraft. (*See* crosswind component).

crosswind component. The wind component measured in knots at 90 degrees to the longitudinal axis of the runway.

*crosswind component. That portion of the total wind which tends to drift the airplane sideways.

cruise. Used in an ATC clearance to authorize a pilot to conduct flight at any altitude from the minimum IFR altitude up to and including the altitude specified in the clearance. The pilot may level off at any intermediate altitude within this block of airspace. Climb/descent within the block is to be made at the discretion of the pilot. However, once the pilot starts descent and verbally reports leaving an altitude in the block, he may not return to that altitude without additional ATC clearance. Further, it is approval for the pilot to proceed to and make an approach at destination airport and can be used in conjunction with:

1. An airport clearance limit at locations with a standard/special instrument approach procedure. The FARs require that if an instrument letdown to an airport is necessary, the pilot shall make the letdown in accordance with a standard/special instrument approach procedure for that airport, or
2. An airport clearance limit at locations that are within/below/outside controlled airspace and without a standard/special instrument approach procedure. Such a clearance is NOT AUTHORIZATION for the pilot to descend under IFR conditions below the applicable minimum IFR altitude nor does it imply that ATC is exercising control over aircraft in Class G airspace; however, it provides a means for the aircraft to proceed to destination airport, descend, and land in accordance with applicable FARs governing VFR flight operations. Also, this provides search and rescue protection until such time as the IFR flight plan is closed. (*See* instrument approach procedure).

cruise climb. A climb technique employed by aircraft, usually at a constant power setting, resulting in an increase of altitude as the aircraft weight decreases.

cruising altitude. An altitude or flight level maintained during enroute level flight. This is a constant altitude and should not be confused with a cruise clearance. (*See* altitude) (*See* cruising level [ICAO]).

cruising level. [ICAO] A level maintained during a significant portion of a flight.

cruising level. (*See* cruising altitude).

CT message. An EDCT time generated by the ATCSCC to regulate traffic at arrival airports. Normally, a CT message is automatically transferred from the Traffic Management System computer to the NAS enroute computer and appears as an EDCT. In the event of a communication failure between the TMS and the NAS, the CT message can be manually entered by the TMC at the enroute facility.

CTA. (*See* controlled time of arrival).

CTA. (*See* control area [ICAO]).

CTAF. (*See* Common Traffic Advisory Frequency).

***CTAF.** Common Traffic Advisory Frequency—used at uncontrolled airports by all airplanes operating at that airport. Also, a frequency to be used at a controlled airport when the tower is not in operation.

current flight plan (CPL). [ICAO] The flight plan, including changes, if any, brought about by subsequent clearances.

CVFP approach. (*See* charted visual flight procedure approach).

CWA. (*See* Center Weather Advisory) (*See* Weather Advisory).

***cylinder head temperature gauge.** An instrument which monitors the temperature of the cylinder head itself. It is a better guide to general engine overheating than is the oil temperature gauge.

DA. [ICAO] (*See* decision altitude/decision height [ICAO]).

DAIR. (*See* direct altitude and identity readout).

danger area. [ICAO] An airspace of defined dimensions within which activities dangerous to the flight of aircraft may exist at specified times. *Note:* The term "Danger Area" is not used in reference to areas within the United States or any of its possessions or territories.

data block. (*See* alphanumeric display).

dead reckoning. Dead reckoning, as applied to flying, is the navigation of an airplane solely by means of computations based on airspeed, course, heading, wind direction, and speed, ground speed, and elapsed time.

decision altitude/decision height. [ICAO] A specified altitude or height (A/H) in the precision approach at which a missed approach must be initiated if the required visual reference to continue the approach has not been established.

Note 1: Decision altitude (DA) is referenced to mean sea level (MSL) and decision height (DH) is referenced to the threshold elevation.

Note 2: The required visual reference means that section of the visual aids or of the approach area which should have been in view for sufficient time for the pilot to have made an assessment of the aircraft position and rate of change of position, in relation to the desired flight path.

decision height (DH). With respect to the operation of aircraft, means the height at which a decision must be made during an ILS, MLS, or PAR instrument approach to either continue the approach or to execute a missed approach. (*See* decision altitude/decision height [ICAO]).

decoder. The device used to decipher signals received from ATCRBS transponders to effect their display as select codes. (*See* codes, radar).

defense visual flight rules (DVFR). Rules applicable to flights within an ADIZ conducted under the visual flight rules in 14 CFR Part 91. (*See* Air Defense Identification Zone) (Refer to 14 CFR Parts 91 and 99).

Delay indefinite (reason if known) expect further clearance (time). Used by ATC to inform a pilot when an accurate estimate of the delay time and the reason for the delay cannot immediately be determined; e.g., a disabled aircraft on the runway, terminal or center area saturation, weather below landing minimums, etc. (*See* expect further clearance (time)).

delay time (DT). The amount of time that the arrival must lose to cross the meter fix at the assigned meter fix time. This is the difference between ACLT and VTA.

***density.** Weight per unit volume. A cubic foot of air that weighs two pounds is more dense than a cubic foot of air that weighs one pound.

Departure Center. The ARTCC having jurisdiction for the airspace that generates a flight to the impacted airport.

departure control. A function of an approach control facility providing air traffic control service for departing IFR and, under certain conditions, VFR aircraft. (*See* Approach Control Facility) (Refer to AIM).

Departure Sequencing Program (DSP). A program designed to assist in achieving a specified interval over a common point for departures.

departure time. The time an aircraft become airborne.

descent speed adjustments. Speed deceleration calculations made to determine an accurate VTA. These calculations start at the transition point and use arrival speed segments to the vertex.

desired course.
1. *True*—A predetermined desired course direction to be followed (measured in degrees from true north).
2. *Magnetic*—A predetermined desired course direction to be followed (measured in degrees from local magnetic north).

desired track. The planned or intended track between two waypoints. It is measured in degrees from either magnetic or true north. The instantaneous angle may change from point to point along the great circle track between waypoints.

***detonation.** The explosive burning of the fuel/air mixture in the cylinder, as opposed to smooth burning. Detonation can result in destructive forces in a matter of seconds.

detresfa (distress phase). [ICAO] The code word used to designate an emergency phase wherein there is reasonable certainty that an aircraft and its occupants are threatened by grave and imminent danger or require immediate assistance.

*deviation. A compass error caused by magnetic influences within the airplane which varies with magnetic heading.

deviations.

1. A departure from a current clearance, such as an off-course maneuver to avoid weather or turbulence.
2. Where specifically authorized in the Federal Aviation Regulations and requested by the pilot, ATC may permit pilots to deviate from certain regulations. (Refer to AIM).

*dew point. The temperature at which an air mass becomes saturated with moisture.

DF. (*See* direction finder).

DF approach procedure. Used under emergency conditions where another instrument approach procedure cannot be executed. DF guidance from an instrument approach is given by ATC facilities with DF capability. (*See* DF guidance, direction finder) (Refer to AIM).

DF fix. The geographical location of an aircraft obtained by one or more direction finders. (*See* direction finder).

DF guidance. Headings provided to aircraft by facilities equipped with direction finding equipment. These headings, if followed, will lead the aircraft to a predetermined point such as the DF station or an airport. DF guidance is given to aircraft in distress or to other aircraft which request the service. Practice DF guidance is provided when workload permits. (*See* direction finder, DF fix) (Refer to AIM).

DF steer. (*See* DF guidance).

DH. (*See* decision height).

DH. [ICAO] (*See* decision altitude/decision height [ICAO]).

direct. Straight line flight between two navigational aids, fixes, points, or any combination thereof. When used by pilots in describing off airway routes, points defining direct route segments become compulsory reporting points unless the aircraft is under radar contact.

direct altitude and identity readout (DAIR). The DAIR system is a modification to the AN/TPX-42 interrogator system. The Navy has two adaptations of the DAIR System. Carrier Air Traffic Control Direct Altitude and Identification Readout System for aircraft carriers and Radar Air Traffic Control Facility Direct Altitude and Identify Readout system for land-based terminal operations. The DAIR detects, tracks, and predicts secondary radar aircraft targets. Targets are displayed by means of computer generated symbols and alphanumeric characters depicting flight identification, altitude, ground speed, and flight plan data. The DAIR system is capable of interfacing with ARTCCs.

direction finder. A radio receiver equipped with a directional sensing antenna used to take bearings on a radio transmitter. Specialized radio direction finders are used in aircraft as air navigation aids. Others are ground based, primarily to obtain a "fix" on a pilot requesting orientation assistance or to locate downed aircraft. A location "fix" is established by the intersection of two or more bearing lines plotted on a navigational chart using either two separately located Direction Finders to obtain a fix on an aircraft or by a pilot plotting the bearing indications of his DF on two separately located ground based transmitters, both of which can be identified on his chart. UDFs receive signals in the ultra high frequency radio broadcast band; VDFs in the very high frequency band; and UVDFs in both bands. ATC provides DF service at those air traffic control towers and flight service stations listed in the Airport/Facility Directory and the DOD FLIP IFR Enroute Supplement. (*See* DF guidance, DF fix).

discrete beacon code. (*See* discrete code).

discrete code. As used in the Air Traffic Control Radar Beacon System (ATCRBS), any one of the 4096 selectable Mode 3/A aircraft transponder codes except those ending in zero zero; e.g., discrete codes: 0010, 1201, 2317, 7777; nondiscrete codes: 0100, 1200, 7700. Nondiscrete codes are normally reserved for radar facilities that are not equipped with discrete decoding capability and for other purposes such as emergencies (7700), VFR aircraft (1200), etc. (*See* radar) (Refer to AIM).

discrete frequency. A separate radio frequency for use in direct pilot/controller communications in air traffic control which reduces frequency congestion by controlling the number of aircraft operating on a particular frequency at one time. Discrete frequencies are normally designated for each control sector in enroute/terminal ATC facilities. Discrete frequencies are listed in the Airport/Facility Directory and the DOD FLIP IFR Enroute Supplement. (*See* control sector).

displaced threshold. A threshold that is located at a point on the runway other than the designated beginning of the runway. (*See* threshold) (Refer to AIM).

*displaced threshold. A threshold moved down the runway so that landing aircraft will clear obstructions in the approach path.

distance measuring equipment (DME). Equipment (airborne and ground) used to measure, in nautical miles, the slant range distance of an aircraft from the DME navigational aid. (*See* TACAN, VORTAC, Microwave Landing System).

distress. A condition of being threatened by serious and/or imminent danger and of requiring immediate assistance.

dive brakes. (*See* speed brakes).

diverse vector area (DVA). In a radar environment, that area in which a prescribed departure route is not required as the only suitable route to avoid obstacles. The area in which random radar vectors below the MVA/MIA, established in accordance with the TERPS criteria for diverse departures obstacles and terrain avoidance, may be issued to departing aircraft.

DME. (*See* distance measuring equipment).

*DME. Distance Measuring Equipment. DME operates in the UHF range and is limited to line-of-sight. It measures slant range between an airplane and a VORTAC or VOR-DME.

DME fix. A geographical position determined by reference to a navigational aid which provides distance and azimuth information. It is defined by a specific distance in nautical miles and a radial, azimuth, or course (i.e. localizer) in degrees magnetic from that aid. (*See* distance measuring equipment (DME), fix, Microwave Landing System).

DME separation. Spacing of aircraft in terms of distances (nautical miles) determined by reference to distance measuring equipment (DME). (*See* distance measuring equipment).

DOD FLIP. Department of Defense Flight Information Publications used for flight planning, en route, and terminal operations. FLIP is produced by the National Imagery and Mapping Agency (NIMA) for world wide use. United States Government Flight Information Publications (enroute charts and instrument approach procedure charts) are incorporated in DOD FLIP for use in the National Airspace System (NAS).

domestic airspace. Airspace which overlies the continental land mass of the United States plus Hawaii and U.S. possessions. Domestic airspace extends to 12 miles offshore.

downburst. A strong downdraft which induces an outburst of damaging winds on or near the ground. Damaging winds, either straight or curved, are highly divergent. The sizes of downbursts vary from 1/2 mile or less to more than 10 miles. An intense down burst often causes widespread damage. Damaging winds, lasting 5 to 30 minutes, could reach speeds as high as 120 knots.

downwind leg. (*See* traffic pattern).

DP. (*See* instrument departure procedure).

drag chute. A parachute device installed on certain aircraft which is deployed on landing roll to assist in deceleration of the aircraft.

DSP. (*See* Departure Sequencing Program).

DT. (*See* delay time).

due regard. A phase of flight wherein an aircraft commander of a State operated aircraft assumes responsibility to separate his aircraft from all other aircraft. (*See* also FAA Order 7110.65, Chapter 1, Word Meanings).

*duplex. Transmitting on one frequency while receiving on another.

duty runway. (*See* runway in use/active runway/duty runway).

DVA. (*See* diverse vector area).

DVFR. (*See* defense visual flight rules).

DVFR flight plan. A flight plan filed for a VFR aircraft which intends to operate in airspace within which the ready identification, location, and control of aircraft are required in the interest of national security.

dynamic. Continuous review, evaluation, and change to meet demands.

dynamic restrictions. Those restrictions imposed by the local facility on an "as needed" basis to manage unpredictable fluctuations in traffic demands.

EDCT. (*See* expected departure clearance time).

*EFAS. Enroute Flight Advisory Service (Flight Watch)—a weather-only position at a Flight Service Station.

EFC. (*See* expect further clearance (time)).

*elevator. A hinged surface at the rear of the horizontal stabilizer with which the pilot controls the airplane around the lateral (pitch) axis.

ELT. (*See* emergency locator transmitter).

*ELT. Emergency Locator Transmitter—a VHF/UHF transmitter designed to be turned on by impact and transmit a signal to searchers.

emergency. A distress or an urgency condition.

emergency locator transmitter (ELT). A radio transmitter attached to the aircraft structure which operates from its own power source on 121.5 MHz and 243.0 MHz. It aids in locating downed aircraft by radiating a downward sweeping audio tone, 2 to 4 times per second. It is designed to function without human action after an accident. (Refer to 14 CFR §91.3, AIM).

*empennage. The horizontal stabilizer, elevator rudder, and vertical fin or any combination thereof to control the airplane in pitch and yaw.

E-MSAW. (*See* enroute minimum safe altitude warning).

engineered performance standards (EPS). A mathematically derived runway capacity standard. EPS's are calculated for each airport on an individual basis and reflect that airport's aircraft mix, operating procedures, runway layout, and specific weather conditions. EPS's do not give consideration to staffing, experience levels, equipment outages, and in-trail restrictions as does the AAR.

enroute air traffic control services. Air traffic control service provided aircraft on IFR flight plans, generally by centers, when these aircraft are operating between departure and destination terminal areas. When equipment, capabilities, and controller workload permit, certain advisory/assistance services may be provided to VFR aircraft. (*See* NAS Stage A, air route traffic control center) (Refer to AIM).

enroute charts. (*See* aeronautical charts).

enroute descent. Descent from the enroute cruising altitude which takes place along the route of flight.

Enroute Flight Advisory Service (EFAS). A service specifically designed to provide, upon pilot request, timely weather information pertinent to his type of flight, intended route of flight, and altitude. The FSS's providing this service are listed in the Airport/Facility Directory. (*See* Flight Watch) (Refer to AIM).

enroute high altitude charts. (*See* aeronautical chart).

enroute low altitude charts. (*See* aeronautical chart).

enroute minimum safe altitude warning (E-MSAW). A function of the NAS Stage A enroute computer that aids the controller by alerting him when a tracked aircraft is below or predicted by the computer to go below a predetermined minimum IFR altitude (MIA).

Enroute Spacing Program (ESP). A program designed to assist the exit sector in achieving the required in-trail spacing.

EPS. (*See* engineered performance standards).

ESP. (*See* Enroute Spacing Program).

established. To be stable or fixed on a route, route segment, altitude, heading, etc.

estimated elapsed time. [ICAO] The estimated time required to proceed from one significant point to another. (*See* total estimated elapsed time [ICAO]).

estimated off block time. [ICAO] The estimated time at which the aircraft will commence movement associated with departure.

estimated position error. (*See* required navigation performance).

estimated time of arrival (ETA). The time the flight is estimated to arrive at the gate (scheduled operators) or the actual runway on times for nonscheduled operators.

estimated time enroute (ETE). The estimated flying time from departure point to destination (liftoff to touchdown).

ETA. (*See* estimated time of arrival).

ETE. (*See* estimated time enroute).

execute missed approach. Instructions issued to a pilot making an instrument approach which means continue inbound to the missed approach point and execute the missed approach procedure as described on the Instrument Approach Procedure Chart or as previously assigned by ATC. The pilot may climb immediately to the altitude specified in the missed approach procedure upon making a missed approach. No turns should be initiated prior to reaching the missed approach point. When conducting an ASR or PAR approach, execute the assigned missed approach procedure immediately upon receiving instructions to "execute missed approach." (Refer to AIM).

*exhaust gas temperature gauge. An instrument used for proper leaning of the mixture. If the mixture contains too much fuel or too much air, the exhaust gas temperature will be lower than peak (use the manufacturer's recommended EGT setting).

Expect (altitude) at (time) or (fix). Used under certain conditions to provide a pilot with an altitude to be used in the event of two-way communications failure. It also provides altitude information to assist the pilot in planning. (Refer to AIM).

expected departure clearance time (EDCT). The runway release time assigned to an aircraft in controlled departure time programs and shown on the flight progress strip as an EDCT.

Expect further clearance (time) (EFC). The time a pilot can expect to receive clearance beyond a clearance limit.

Expect further clearance via (airways, routes or fixes). Used to inform a pilot of the routing he can expect if any part of the route beyond a short range clearance limit differs from that filed.

expedite. Used by ATC when prompt compliance is required to avoid the development of an imminent situation.

FAF. (*See* final approach fix).

*FAR. Federal Aviation Regulations.

fast file. A system whereby a pilot files a flight plan via telephone that is tape recorded and then transcribed for transmission to the appropriate air traffic facility. Locations having a fast file capability are contained in the Airport/Facility Directory. (Refer to AIM).

FAWP. Final approach waypoint.

FCLT. (*See* freeze calculated landing time).

*FB. A winds and temperatures aloft forecast.

feathered propeller. A propeller whose blades have been rotated so that the leading and trailing edges are nearly parallel with the aircraft flight path to stop or minimize drag and engine rotation. Normally used to indicate shutdown of a reciprocating or turboprop engine due to malfunction.

federal airways. (*See* low altitude airway structure).

feeder fix. The fix depicted on Instrument Approach Procedure Charts which establishes the staring point of the feeder route.

feeder route. A route depicted on instrument approach procedure charts to designate routes for aircraft to proceed from the enroute structure to the initial approach fix (IAF). (*See* instrument approach procedure).

ferry flight. A flight for the purpose of:

1. Returning an aircraft to base.
2. Delivering an aircraft from one location to another.
3. Moving an aircraft to and from a maintenance base.

Ferry flights, under certain conditions, may be conducted under terms of a special flight permit.

field elevation. (*See* airport elevation).

filed. Normally used in conjunction with flight plans, meaning a flight plan has been submitted to ATC.

filed enroute delay. Any of the following preplanned delays at points/areas along the route of flight which require special flight plan filing and handling techniques.

1. *Terminal Area Delay.* A delay within a terminal area for touch and go, low approach, or other terminal area activity.
2. *Special Use Airspace Delay.* A delay within a Military Operating Area, Restricted Area, Warning Area, or ATC Assigned Airspace.
3. *Aerial Refueling Delay.* A delay within an Aerial Refueling Track or Anchor.

filed flight plan. The flight plan as filed with an ATS unit by the pilot or his designated representative without any subsequent changes or clearances.

final. Commonly used to mean that an aircraft is on the final approach course or is aligned with a landing area. (*See* final approach course, final approach—IFR, traffic pattern, segments of an instrument approach procedure).

final approach. [ICAO] The part of an instrument approach procedure which commences at the specified final approach fix, or point, or where such a fix or point is not specified.

1. At the end of the last procedure turn, base turn, or inbound turn of a racetrack procedure, if specified; or
2. At the point of interception of the last track specified in the approach procedure; and ends at a point in the vicinity of an aerodrome from which:
   a. A landing can be made; or
   b. A missed approach procedure is initiated.

final approach course. A bearing/radial/track of an instrument approach landing to a runway or an extended runway centerline all without regard to distance.

final approach fix (FAF). The fix from which the final approach (IFR) to an airport is executed and which identifies the beginning of the final approach segment. It is designated on Government charts by the Maltese Cross symbol for nonprecision approaches and the lightning bolt symbol for precision approaches; or when ATC directs a lower than published Glideslope/Path Intercept Altitude, it is the resultant actual point of the glideslope/path intercept. (*See* final approach point, glideslope intercept altitude, segments of an instrument approach procedure).

final approach—IFR. The flight path of an aircraft which is inbound to an airport on a final instrument approach course, beginning at the final approach fix or point and extending to the airport or the point where a circle-to-land maneuver or a missed approach is executed. (*See* segments of an instrument approach procedure, final approach fix, final approach course, final approach point) (*See* final approach [ICAO]).

final approach point (FAP). The point, applicable only to a nonprecision approach with no depicted FAF (such as an on-airport VOR), where the aircraft is established inbound on the final approach course from the procedure turn and where the final approach descent may be commenced. The FAP serves as the FAF and identifies the beginning of the final approach segment. (*See* final approach fix, segments of an instrument approach procedure).

final approach segment. (*See* segments of an instrument approach procedure). [ICAO] That segment of an instrument approach procedure in which alignment and descent for landing are accomplished.

final controller. The controller providing information and final approach guidance during PAR and ASR approaches utilizing radar equipment. (*See* radar approach).

final monitor aid (FMA). A high resolution color display that is equipped with the controller alert system hardware/software which is used in the precision runway monitor (PRM) system. The display includes alert algorithms providing the target predictors, a color change alert when a target penetrates or is predicted to penetrate the no transgression zone (NTZ), a color change alert if the aircraft transponder becomes inoperative, synthesized voice alerts, digital mapping, and like features contained in the PRM system. (*See* radar approach).

final monitor controller. Air traffic control specialist assigned to radar monitor the flight path of aircraft during simultaneous parallel and simultaneous close parallel ILS approach operations. Each runway is assigned a final monitor controller during simultaneous parallel and simultaneous close parallel ILS approaches. Final monitor controllers shall utilize the precision runway monitor (PRM) system during simultaneous close parallel ILS approaches.

FIR. (*See* flight information region).

first tier center. The ARTCC immediately adjacent to the impacted center.

fix. A geographical position determined by visual reference to the surface, by reference to one or more radio NAVAIDs, by celestial plotting, or by another navigational device.

fix balancing. A process whereby aircraft are evenly distributed over several available arrival fixes reducing delays and controller workload.

*fixed-pitch propeller. A propeller, forged from one solid piece of metal or laminated from several plies of wood, with a fixed pitch or blade angle.

flag. A warning device incorporated in certain airborne navigation and flight instruments indicating that:

1. Instruments are inoperative or otherwise not operating satisfactorily, or
2. Signal strength or quality of the received signal falls below acceptable values.

flag alarm. (*See* flag).

flameout. An emergency condition caused by a loss of engine power.

flameout pattern. An approach normally conducted by a single-engine military aircraft experiencing loss or anticipating loss of engine power or control. The standard overhead approach starts at a relatively high altitude over a runway ("high key") followed by a continuous 180 degree turn to a high, wide position ("low key") followed by a continuous

180 degree turn final. The standard straight-in pattern starts at a point that results in a straight-in approach with a high rate of descent to the runway. Flameout approaches terminate in the type approach requested by the pilot (normally fullstop).

*flaps. Hinged surfaces at the trailing edge of the wing which are deflected symmetrically to lower the stalling speed and allow for a steeper angle of descent while on a landing approach.

flight check. A call sign prefix used by FAA aircraft engaged in flight inspection/certification of navigational aids and flight procedures. The word "recorded" may be added as a suffix; e.g., "Flight Check 320 recorded" to indicate that an automated flight inspection is in progress in terminal areas. (*See* flight inspection) (Refer to AIM).

flight following. (*See* traffic advisories).

*flight following. A workload-permitting service which ATC radar facilities provide to VFR pilots.

flight information region (FIR). An airspace of defined dimensions within which Flight Information Service and Alerting Service are provided.

1. *Flight Information Service.* A service provided for the purpose of giving advice and information useful for the safe and efficient conduct of flights.

2. *Alerting Service.* A service provided to notify appropriate organizations regarding aircraft in need of search and rescue aid and to assist such organizations as required.

Flight Information Service. A service provided for the purpose of giving advice and information useful for the safe and efficient conduct of flights.

flight inspection. In-flight investigation and evaluation of a navigational aid to determine whether it meets established tolerances. (*See* navigational aid, flight check).

flight level. A level of constant atmospheric pressure related to a reference datum of 29.92 inches of mercury. Each is stated in three digits that represent hundreds of feet. For example, flight level 250 represents a barometric altimeter indication of 25,000 feet; flight level 255, an indication of 25,500 feet.

[ICAO] A surface of constant atmospheric pressure which is related to a specific pressure datum, 1013.2 hPa (1013.2 mb), and is separated from other such surfaces by specific pressure intervals.

Note 1: A pressure type altimeter calibrated in accordance with the standard atmosphere:

1. When set to a QNH altimeter setting, will indicate altitude;

2. When set to a QFE altimeter setting, will indicate height above the QFE reference datum; and

3. When set to a pressure of 1013.2 hPa (1013.2 mb), may be used to indicate flight levels.

Note 2: The terms height and altitude, used in Note 1 above, indicate altimetric rather than geometric heights and altitudes.

flight line. A term used to describe the precise movement of a civil photogrammetric aircraft along a predetermined course(s) at a predetermined altitude during the actual photographic run.

flight management systems (FMS). A computer system that uses a large data base to allow routes to be preprogrammed and fed into the system by means of a data loader. The system is constantly updated with respect to position accuracy by reference to conventional navigation aids. The sophisticated program and its associated data base ensures that the most appropriate aids are automatically selected during the information update cycle.

flight management system procedure (FMSP). An arrival, departure, or approach procedure developed for use by aircraft with a slant (/) E or slant (/) F equipment suffix.

flight path. A line, course, or track along which an aircraft is flying or intended to be flown. (*See* track, course).

flight plan. Specified information relating to the intended flight of an aircraft that is filed orally or in writing with an FSS or an ATC facility. (*See* fast file, filed) (Refer to AIM).

flight plan area. The geographical area assigned by regional air traffic divisions to a flight service station for the purpose of search and rescue for VFR aircraft, issuance of NOTAMs, pilot briefing, in-flight services, broadcast, emergency services, flight data processing, international operations, and aviation weather services. Three letter identifiers are assigned to every flight service station and are annotated in AFDs and Order 7350.5 as tie-in facilities. (*See* fast file, filed) (Refer to AIM).

flight recorder. A general term applied to any instrument or device that records information about the performance of an aircraft in flight or about conditions encountered in flight. Flight recorders may make records of airspeed, outside air temperature, vertical acceleration, engine RPM, manifold pressure, and other pertinent variables for a given flight. [ICAO] Any type of recorder installed in the aircraft for the purpose of complementing accident/incident investigation. *Note: See* Annex 6, Part I, for specifications relating to flight recorders.

Flight Service Station (FSS). Air traffic facilities which provide pilot briefing, enroute communications and VFR search and rescue services, assist lost aircraft and aircraft in emergency situations, relay ATC clearances, originate Notices to Airmen, broadcast aviation weather and NAS information, receive and process IFR flight plans, and monitor NAVAIDs. In addition, at selected locations, FSS's provide Enroute Flight Advisory Service (Flight Watch), take weather observations, issue airport advisories, and advise Customs and Immigration of transborder flights. (Refer to AIM).

*Flight Service Station (FSS). Air traffic facilities which provide pilot briefings, enroute communications, and many other services to pilots.

Flight Standards District Office (FSDO). An FAA field office serving an assigned geographical area and staffed with Flight Standards personnel who serve the aviation industry and the general public on matters relating to the certification and operation of air carrier and general aviation aircraft. Activities include general surveillance of operational safety, certification of airmen and aircraft, accident prevention, investigation, enforcement, etc.

flight test. A flight for the purpose of:

1. Investigating the operation/flight characteristics of an aircraft or aircraft component.
2. Evaluating an applicant for a pilot certificate or rating.

flight visibility. (*See* visibility).

Flight Watch. A shortened term for use in air/ground contacts to identify the flight service station providing Enroute Flight Advisory Service; e.g., "Oakland Flight Watch." (*See* Enroute Flight Advisory Service).

***Flight Watch.** Another name for Enroute Flight Advisory Service, a weather-information-only service of the Flight Service Station.

FLIP. (*See* DOD FLIP).

flow control. Measures designed to adjust the flow of traffic into a given airspace, along a given route, or bound for a given aerodrome (airport) so as to ensure the most effective utilization of the airspace. (*See* quota flow control) (Refer to Airport/Facility Directory).

fly-by waypoint. A fly-by waypoint requires the use of turn anticipation to avoid overshoot of the next flight segment.

fly heading (degrees). Informs the pilot of the heading he should fly. The pilot may have to turn to, or continue on, a specific compass direction in order to comply with the instructions. The pilot is expected to turn in the shorter direction to the heading unless otherwise instructed by ATC.

fly-over waypoint. A fly-over waypoint precludes any turn until the waypoint is overflown and is followed by an intercept maneuver of the next flight segment.

FMA. (*See* final monitor aid).

FMS. (*See* flight management system).

FMSP. (*See* flight management system procedure).

formation flight. More than one aircraft which, by prior arrangement between the pilots, operate as a single aircraft with regard to navigation and position reporting. Separation between aircraft within the formation is the responsibility of the flight leader and the pilots of the other aircraft in the flight. This includes transition periods when aircraft within the formation are maneuvering to attain separation from each other to effect individual control and during join-up and breakaway.

1. A standard formation is one in which a proximity of no more than 1 mile laterally or longitudinally and within 100 feet vertically from the flight leader is maintained by each wingman.

2. Nonstandard formations are those operating under any of the following conditions:
   a. When the flight leader has requested and ATC has approved other than standard formation dimensions.
   b. When operating within an authorized altitude reservation (ALTRV) or under the provisions of a letter of agreement.
   c. When the operations are conducted in airspace specifically designed for a special activity.

(*See* Altitude Reservation) (Refer to 14 CFR Part 91).

FRC. (*See* request full route clearance).

freeze/frozen. Terms used in referring to arrivals which have been assigned ACLTs and to the lists in which they are displayed.

freeze calculated landing time (FCLT). A dynamic parameter number of minutes prior to the meter fix calculated time of arrival for each aircraft when the TCLT is frozen and becomes an ACLT (i.e., the VTA is updated and consequently the TCLT is modified as appropriate until FCLT minutes prior to meter fix calculated time of arrival, at which time updating is suspended and an ACLT and a frozen meter fix crossing time (MFT) is assigned).

freeze speed parameter (FSPD). A speed adapted for each aircraft to determine fast and slow aircraft. Fast aircraft freeze on parameter FCLT and slow aircraft freeze on parameter MLDI.

friction measurement. A measurement of the friction characteristics of the runway pavement surface using continuous self-watering friction measurement equipment in accordance with the specifications, procedures and schedules contained in AC 150/5320-12, *Measurement, Construction, and Maintenance of Skid-Resistant Airport Pavement Surfaces.*

***front.** Where two air masses with different properties meet.

FSDO. (*See* Flight Standards District Office).

FSPD. (*See* freeze speed parameter).

FSS. (*See* Flight Service Station).

fuel dumping. Airborne release of usable fuel. This does not include the dropping of fuel tanks. (*See* jettisoning of external stores).

***fuel injection.** An induction system which delivers a metered amount of fuel to each cylinder.

fuel remaining. A phrase used by either pilots or controllers when relating to the fuel remaining on board until actual fuel exhaustion. When transmitting such information in response to either a controller question or pilot initiated cautionary advisory to air traffic control, pilots will state the APPROXIMATE NUMBER OF MINUTES the flight can continue with the fuel remaining. All reserve fuel SHOULD BE INCLUDED in the time stated, as should an allowance for established fuel gauge system error.

fuel siphoning. Unintentional release of fuel caused by overflow, puncture, loose cap, etc.

fuel venting. (*See* fuel siphoning).

*fuselage. The main body of the airplane to which the wings and empennage are attached. Passenger and crew seating is in the fuselage.

*G. The force of gravity: one times the weight of an object.

gate hold procedures. Procedures at selected airports to hold aircraft at the gate or other ground location whenever departure delays exceed or are anticipated to exceed 15 minutes. The sequence for departure will be maintained in accordance with initial call up unless modified by flow control restrictions. Pilots should monitor the ground control/clearance delivery frequency for engine start/taxi advisories or new proposed start/taxi time if the delay changes. (*See* flow control).

GCA. (*See* ground controlled approach).

general aviation. That portion of civil aviation which encompasses all facets of aviation except air carriers holding a certificate of public convenience and necessity from the Civil Aeronautics Board and large aircraft commercial operators. [ICAO] All civil aviation operations other than scheduled air services and nonscheduled air transport operations for renumeration or hire.

geo map. The digitized map markings associated with the ASR-9 Radar System.

glide path. (*See* glide slope).

glidepath intercept altitude. (*See* glideslope intercept altitude).

glide slope. Provides vertical guidance for aircraft during approach and landing. The glideslope/glidepath is based on the following:

1. Electronic components emitting signals which provide vertical guidance by reference to airborne instruments during instrument approaches such as ILS/MLS, or
2. Visual ground aids, such as VASI, which provide vertical guidance for a VFR approach or for the visual portion of an instrument approach and landing.
3. PAR. Used by ATC to inform an aircraft making a PAR approach of its vertical position (elevation) relative to the descent profile.

   (*See* glide path [ICAO]).

glide path. [ICAO] A descent profile determined for vertical guidance during a final approach.

glideslope intercept altitude. The minimum altitude to intercept the glide slope/path on a precision approach. The intersection of the published intercept altitude with the glide slope/path, designated on Government charts by the lightning bolt symbol, is the precision FAF; however, when ATC directs a lower altitude, the resultant lower intercept position is then the FAF. (*See* final approach fix, segments of an instrument approach procedure).

global positioning system (GPS). A space-base radio positioning, navigation, and time-transfer system. The system provides highly accurate position and velocity information, and precise time, on a continuous global basis, to an unlimited number of properly equipped users. The system is unaffected by weather, and provides a worldwide common grid reference system. The GPS concept is predicated upon accurate and continuous knowledge of the spatial position of each satellite in the system with respect to time and distance from a transmitting satellite to the user. The GPS receiver automatically selects appropriate signals from the satellites in view and translates these into three-dimensional position, velocity, and time. System accuracy for civil users is normally 100 meters horizontally.

go ahead. Proceed with your message. Not to be used for any other purpose.

go around. Instructions for a pilot to abandon his approach to landing. Additional instructions may follow. Unless otherwise advised by ATC, a VFR aircraft or an aircraft conducting visual approach should overfly the runway while climbing to traffic pattern altitude and enter the traffic pattern via the crosswind leg. A pilot on an IFR flight plan making an instrument approach should execute the published missed approach procedure or proceed as instructed by ATC; e.g., "Go around" (additional instructions if required). (*See* low approach, missed approach).

*GPO. Government Printing Office.

GPS. (*See* global positioning system).

*gradient wind, gradient force. The wind (and the force that drives it) caused solely by pressure differences.

*great circle. An imaginary circle on the face of the earth cut by a plane which passes through the center of the earth. All meridians are Great Circles, and the equator is a Great Circle.

ground clutter. A pattern produced on the radar scope by ground returns which may degrade other radar returns in the affected area. The effect of ground clutter is minimized by the use of moving target indicator (MTI) circuits in the radar equipment resulting in a radar presentation which displays only targets which are in motion. (*See* clutter).

ground communication outlet (GCO). An unstaffed, remotely controlled, ground/ground communications facility. Pilots at uncontrolled airports may contact ATC and FSS via VHF to a telephone connection to obtain an instrument clearance or close a VFR or IFR flight plan. They may also get an updated weather briefing prior to takeoff. Pilots will use four "key clicks" on the VHF radio to contact the appropriate ATC facility or six "key clicks" to contact the FSS. The GCO system is intended to be used only on the ground.

ground controlled approach (GCA). A radar approach system operated from the ground by air traffic control personnel transmitting instructions to the pilot by radio. The approach may be conducted with surveillance radar (ASR) only or with both surveillance and precision approach radar (PAR). Usage of the term "GCA" by pilots is discouraged except when referring to a GCA facility. Pilots should specifically request a "PAR" approach when a precision radar approach is desired or request an "ASR" or "surveillance" approach when a nonprecision radar approach is desired. (*See* radar approach).

*ground controller. An air traffic control specialist in a control tower who controls operations on the ramps and taxiways of a controlled airport.

ground delay. The amount of delay attributed to ATC, encountered prior to departure, usually associated with a CDT program.

*ground effect. A reduction in induced drag experienced when the wing is within one-half wing span of the ground.

ground speed. The speed of an aircraft relative to the surface of the earth.

ground stop. Normally, the last initiative to be utilized; this method mandates that the terminal facility will not allow any departures to enter the ARTCC airspace until further notified.

ground visibility. (*See* visibility).

*gyroscopic precession. A slow movement of the axis of a spinning body, noticeable in gyroscopic heading indicators as a drift away from agreement with the magnetic compass.

HAA. (*See* height above airport).

HAL. (*See* height above landing).

handoff. An action taken to transfer the radar identification of an aircraft from one controller to another if the aircraft will enter the receiving controller's airspace and radio communications with the aircraft will be transferred.

HAT. (*See* height above touchdown).

have numbers. Used by pilots to inform ATC that they have received runway, wind, and altimeter information only.

Hazardous In-Flight Weather Advisory Service (HIWAS). Continuous recorded hazardous in-flight weather forecasts broadcasted to airborne pilots over selected VOR outlets defined as a HIWAS broadcast area.

hazardous weather information. Summary of Significant Meteorological Information (SIGMET/WS), Convective Significant Meteorological Information (Convective SIGMET/WST), urgent pilot weather reports (urgent PIREP/UUA), Center Weather Advisories (CWA), Airmen's Meteorological Information (AIRMET/WA) and any other weather such as isolated thunderstorms that are rapidly developing and increasing in intensity, or low ceilings and visibilities that are becoming widespread which is considered significant and are not included in a current hazardous weather advisory.

*heading. The direction in which the airplane is pointing. When correcting for wind drift, the heading will differ from the course by several degrees.

*headwind component. That portion of the reported wind which opposes the forward motion of the airplane.

heavy (aircraft). (*See* aircraft classes).

height above airport (HAA). The height of the minimum descent altitude above the published airport elevation. This is published in conjunction with circling minimums. (*See* minimum descent altitude).

height above landing (HAL). The height above a designated helicopter landing area used for helicopter instrument approach procedures. (Refer to 14 CFR Part 97).

height above touchdown (HAT). The height of the decision height or minimum descent altitude above the highest runway elevation in the touchdown zone (first 3,000 feet of the runway). HAT is published on instrument approach charts in conjunction with all straight-in minimums. (*See* decision height, minimum descent altitude).

helicopter. Rotorcraft that, for its horizontal motion, depends principally on its engine driven rotors. [ICAO] A heavier than air aircraft supported in flight chiefly by the reactions of the air on one or more power driven rotors on substantially vertical axes.

helipad. A small, designated area, usually with a prepared surface, on a heliport, airport, landing/takeoff area, apron/ramp, or movement area used for takeoff, landing, or parking of helicopters.

heliport. An area of land, water, or structure used or intended to be used for the landing and takeoff of helicopters and includes its buildings and facilities if any.

heliport reference point (HRP). The geographic center of a heliport.

hertz (Hz). The standard radio equivalent of frequency in cycles per second of an electromagnetic wave. Kilohertz (kHz) is a frequency of one thousand cycles per second. Megahertz (MHz) is a frequency of one million cycles per second.

HF. (*See* high frequency).

HF communications. (*See* high frequency communications).

high frequency (HF). The frequency band between 3 and 30 MHz. (*See* high frequency communications).

high frequency communications. High radio frequencies (HF) between 3 and 30 MHz used for air-to-ground voice communication in overseas operations.

high speed exit. (*See* high speed taxiway).

high speed taxiway. A long radius taxiway designed and provided with lighting or marking to define the path of aircraft, traveling at high speed (up to 60 knots), from the runway center to a point on the center of a taxiway. Also referred to as long radius exit or turnoff taxiway. The high speed taxiway is designed to expedite aircraft turning off the runway after landing, thus reducing runway occupancy time.

high speed turnoff. (*See* high speed taxiway).

HIWAS. (*See* Hazardous In-flight Weather Advisory Service).

HIWAS area. (*See* Hazardous In-flight Weather Advisory Service).

HIWAS broadcast area. A geographical area of responsibility including one or more HIWAS outlet areas assigned to an AFSS/FSS for hazardous weather advisory broadcasting.

HIWAS outlet area. An area defined as a 150 NM radius of a HIWAS outlet, expanded as necessary to provide coverage.

holding procedure. (*See* hold procedure).

hold procedure. A predetermined maneuver which keeps aircraft within a specified airspace while awaiting further clearance from air traffic control. Also used during ground operations to keep aircraft within a specified area or at a specified point while awaiting further clearance from air traffic control. (*See* holding fix) (Refer to AIM).

holding fix. A specified fix identifiable to a pilot by NAVAIDs or visual reference to the ground used as a reference point in establishing and maintaining the position of an aircraft while holding. (*See* fix, visual holding) (Refer to AIM).

holding point. [ICAO] A specified location, identified by visual or other means, in the vicinity of which the position of an aircraft in flight is maintained in accordance with air traffic control clearances.

hold for release. Used by ATC to delay an aircraft for traffic management reasons; i.e., weather, traffic volume, etc. Hold for release instructions (including departure delay information) are used to inform a pilot or a controller (either directly or through an authorized relay) that an IFR departure clearance is not valid until a release time or additional instructions have been received. (*See* holding point [ICAO]).

hold-short point. A point on the runway beyond which a landing aircraft with a LAHSO clearance is not authorized to proceed. This point may be located prior to an intersecting runway, taxiway, predetermined point, or approach/departure flight path.

hold-short position marking. The painted runway marking located at the hold-short point on all LAHSO runways.

hold-short position lights. Flashing in-pavement white lights located at specified hold-short points.

hold-short position signs. Red and white holding signs located alongside the hold-short point.

homing. Flight toward a NAVAID, without correcting for wind, by adjusting the aircraft heading to maintain a relative bearing of zero degrees. (*See* bearing). [ICAO] The procedure of using the direction finding equipment of one radio station with the emission of another radio station, where at least one of the stations is mobile, and whereby the mobile station proceeds continuously towards the other station.

*homing. Navigating to a nondirectional beacon by simply keeping the ADF needle pointed directly to the nose of the airplane.

*horizontal situation indicator (HSI). An instrument that incorporates a heading indicator and an omni-indicator to show the pilot the airplane's position in relation to a VOR radial as seen from a point above the airplane.

*horizontal stabilizer. An airfoil-shaped surface at the rear of the airplane that develops a negative lift force to balance (stabilize) the airplane's pitch attitude.

hover check. Used to describe when a helicopter/VTOL aircraft requires a stabilized hover to conduct a performance/power check prior to hover taxi, air taxi, or takeoff. Altitude of the hover will vary based on the purpose of the check.

hover taxi. Used to describe a helicopter/VTOL aircraft movement conducted above the surface and in ground effect at airspeeds less than approximately 20 knots. The actual height may vary, and some helicopters may require hover taxi above 25 feet AGL to reduce ground effect turbulence or provide clearance for cargo sling loads. (*See* air taxi, hover check) (Refer to AIM).

How do you hear me? A question relating to the quality of the transmission or to determine how well the transmission is being received.

Hz. (*See* hertz).

IAF. (*See* initial approach fix).

IAP. (*See* instrument approach procedure).

IAWP. Initial approach waypoint.

ICAO. [ICAO] (*See* International Civil Aviation Organization [ICAO]).

icing. The accumulation of airframe ice. Types of icing are:
1. *Rime Ice.* Rough, milky, opaque ice formed by the instantaneous freezing of small supercooled water droplets.
2. *Clear Ice.* A glossy, clear, or translucent ice formed by the relatively slow freezing of large supercooled water droplets.
3. *Mixed.* A mixture of clear ice and rime ice.
   Intensity of icing:
4. *Trace.* Ice becomes perceptible. Rate of accumulation is slightly greater than the rate of sublimation. Deicing/anti-icing equipment is not utilized unless encountered for an extended period of time (over 1 hour).
5. *Light.* The rate of accumulation may create a problem if flight is prolonged in this environment (over 1 hour). Occasional use of deicing/anti-icing equipment removes/prevents accumulation. It does not present a problem if the deicing/anti-icing equipment is used.
6. *Moderate.* The rate of accumulation is such that even short encounters become potentially hazardous and use of deicing/anti-icing or flight diversion is necessary.
7. *Severe.* The rate of accumulation is such that deicing/anti-icing equipment fails to reduce or control the hazard. Immediate flight diversion is necessary.

ident. A request for a pilot to activate the aircraft transponder identification feature. This will help the controller to confirm an aircraft identity or to identify an aircraft. (Refer to AIM).

ident feature. The special feature in the Air Traffic Control Radar Beacon System (ATCRBS) equipment. It is used to immediately distinguish one displayed beacon target from other beacon targets. (*See* ident).

IF. (*See* intermediate fix).

IFIM. (*See* International Flight Information Manual).

If no transmission received for (time). Used by ATC in radar approaches to prefix procedures which should be followed by the pilot in event of lost communications. (*See* lost communications).

IFR. (*See* instrument flight rules).

IFR aircraft. An aircraft conducting flight in accordance with instrument flight rules.

IFR conditions. Weather conditions below the minimum for flight under visual flight rules. (*See* instrument meteorological conditions).

IFR departure procedure. (*See* IFR takeoff minimums and departure procedures) (Refer to AIM).

IFR flight. (*See* IFR aircraft).

IFR landing minimums. (*See* landing minimums).

IFR military training routes (IR). Routes used by the Department of Defense and associated Reserve and Air Guard units for the purpose of conducting low altitude navigation and tactical training in both IFR and VFR weather conditions below 10,000 feet MLS at airspeeds in excess of 250 knots IAS.

IFR takeoff minimums and departure procedures. 14 CFR Part 91, prescribes standard takeoff rules for certain civil users. At some airports, obstructions or other factors require the establishment of nonstandard takeoff minimums, departure procedures, or both to assist pilots in avoiding obstacles during climb to the minimum enroute altitude. Those airports are listed in NOS/DOD Instrument Approach Charts (IAPs) under a section entitled "IFR Takeoff Minimums and Departure Procedures." The NOS/DOD IAP chart legend illustrates the symbol used to alert the pilot to nonstandard takeoff minimums and departure procedures. When departing IFR from such airports or from any airport where there are no departure procedures, DPs, or ATC facilities available, pilots should advise ATC of any departure limitations. Controllers may query a pilot to determine acceptable departure directions, turns, or headings after takeoff. Pilots should be familiar with the departure procedures and must assure that their aircraft can meet or exceed any specified climb gradients.

IFWP. Intermediate Fix Waypoint.

IF/IAWP. Intermediate fix/initial approach waypoint. The waypoint where the final approach course of a T approach meets the crossbar of the T. When designated (in conjunction with a TAA) this waypoint will be used as an IAWP when approaching the airport from certain directions, and as an IFWP when beginning the approach from another IAWP.

ILS. (*See* instrument landing system).

ILS categories.
1. *ILS Category I.* An ILS approach procedure which provides for approach to a height above touchdown of not less than 200 feet and with runway visual range of not less than 1,800 feet.
2. *ILS Category II.* An ILS approach procedure which provides for approach to a height above touchdown of not less than 100 feet and with runway visual range of not less than 1,200 feet.
3. *ILS Category III.*
   a. *IIIA.* An ILS approach procedure which provides for approach without a decision height minimum and with runway visual range of not less than 700 feet.
   b. *IIIB.* An ILS approach procedure which provides for approach without a decision height minimum and with runway visual range of not less than 150 feet.
   c. *IIIC.* An ILS approach procedure which provides for approach without a decision height minimum and without runway visual range minimum.

ILS PRM Approach. An instrument landing system (ILS) approach conducted to parallel runways whose extended centerlines are separated by less than 4,300 feet and the parallel runways have a Precision Runway Monitoring (PRM) system that permits simultaneous independent ILS approaches.

IM. (*See* inner marker).

IMC. (*See* instrument meteorological conditions).

immediately. Used by ATC when such action compliance is required to avoid an imminent situation.

INCERFA (uncertainty phase). [ICAO] The code word used to designate an emergency phase wherein there is concern about the safety of an aircraft or its occupants. In most cases this phase involves an aircraft which is overdue or unreported.

Increase speed to (speed). (*See* speed adjustment).

***indicated airspeed.** What the airspeed indicator reads, uncorrected for position and installation error. See calibrated airspeed.

***induced drag.** Drag which is the inevitable result of lift generation. Induced drag increases with increased angle of attack and is greatest at low speeds that require large angles of attack.

inertial navigation system (INS). An RNAV system which is a form of self-contained navigation. (*See* area navigation/RNAV).

in-flight refueling. (*See* aerial refueling).

in-flight weather advisory. (*See* Weather Advisory).

information request (INREQ). A request originated by an FSS for information concerning an overdue VFR aircraft.

initial approach fix (IAF). The fixes depicted on instrument approach procedure charts that identify the beginning of the initial approach segment(s). (*See* fix, segments of an instrument approach procedure).

initial approach segment. (*See* segments of an instrument approach procedure). [ICAO] That segment of an instrument approach procedure between the initial approach fix and the intermediate approach fix or, where applicable, the final approach fix or point.

inland navigation facility. A navigation aid on a North American Route at which the common route and/or the non-common route begins or ends.

inner marker (IM). A marker beacon used with an ILS (CAT II) precision approach located between the middle marker and the end of the ILS runway, transmitting a radiation pattern keyed at six dots per second and indicating to the pilot, both aurally and visually, that he is at the designated decision height (DH), normally 100 feet above the touchdown zone elevation, on the ILS CAT II approach. It also marks progress during a CAT III approach. (*See* instrument landing system) (Refer to AIM).

inner marker beacon. (*See* inner marker).

INREQ. (*See* information request).

INS. (*See* inertial navigation system).

instrument approach. (*See* instrument approach procedure).

instrument approach procedure (IAP). A series of predetermined maneuvers for the orderly transfer of an aircraft under instrument flight conditions from the beginning of the initial approach to a landing or to a point from which a landing may be made visually. It is prescribed and approved for a specific airport by competent authority. (*See* segments of an instrument approach procedure) (Refer to 14 CFR Part 91, AIM).

1. U.S. civil standard instrument approach procedures are approved by the FAA as prescribed under 14 CFR Part 97 and are available for public use.

2. U.S. military standard instrument approach procedures are approved and published by the Department of Defense.

3. Special instrument approach procedures are approved by the FAA for individual operators but are not published in 14 CFR Part 97 for public use.

[ICAO] A series of predetermined maneuvers by reference to flight instruments with specified protection from obstacles from the initial approach fix, or where applicable, from the beginning of a defined arrival route to a point from which a landing can be completed and thereafter, if a landing is not completed, to a position at which holding or enroute obstacle clearance criteria apply.

instrument approach procedures charts. (*See* aeronautical chart).

instrument departure procedure (DP). A preplanned instrument flight rule (IFR) air traffic control departure procedure printed for pilot use in graphic and/or textual form. DPs provide transition from the terminal to the appropriate enroute structure. (*See* IFR takeoff minimums and departure procedures.) (Refer to AIM.)

instrument departure procedure (DP) charts. (*See* aeronautical chart.)

instrument flight rules (IFR). Rules governing the procedures for conducting instrument flight. Also a term used by pilots and controllers to indicate type of flight plan. (*See* visual flight rules, instrument meteorological conditions, visual meteorological conditions) (Refer to AIM). [ICAO] A set of rules governing the conduct of flight under instrument meteorological conditions.

instrument landing system (ILS). A precision instrument approach system which normally consists of the following electronic components and visual aids:

1. *Localizer.* (*See* localizer).

2. *Glideslope.* (*See* glideslope).

3. *Outer Marker.* (*See* outer marker).

4. *Middle Marker.* (*See* middle marker).

5. *Approach Lights.* (*See* airport lighting).
   (Refer to 14 CFR Part 91, AIM).

instrument meteorological conditions (IMC). Meteorological conditions expressed in terms of visibility, distance from cloud, and ceiling less than the minima specified for visual meteorological conditions. (*See* visual meteorological conditions, instrument flight rules, visual flight rules).

instrument runway. A runway equipped with electronic and visual navigation aids for which a precision or nonprecision approach procedure having straight-in landing minimums has been approved. [ICAO] One of the following types of runways intended for the operation of aircraft using instrument approach procedures:

1. *Nonprecision Approach Runway.* An instrument runway served by visual aids and nonvisual aid providing at least directional guidance adequate for a straight-in approach.

2. *Precision Approach Runway, Category I.* An instrument runway served by ILS and visual aids intended for operations down to 60 m (200 feet) decision height and down to an RVR of the order to 800 m.

3. *Precision Approach Runway, Category II.* An instrument runway served by ILS and visual aids intended for operations down to 30 m (100 feet) decision height and down to an RVR of the order of 400 m.

4. *Precision Approach Runway, Category III.* An instrument runway served by ILS to and along the surface of the runway and:

   a. Intended for operations down to an RVR of the order of 200 m (no decision height being applicable) using visual aids during the final phase of landing;

Continued

b. Intended for operations down to an RVR of the order of 50 m (no decision height being applicable) using visual aids for taxiing;

c. Intended for operations without reliance on visual reference for landing or taxiing.

Note 1: See Annex 10, Volume I, Part I Chapter 3, for related ILS specifications.

Note 2: Visual aids need not necessarily be matched to the scale of nonvisual aids provided. The criterion for the selection of visual aids is the conditions in which operations are intended to be conducted.

integrity. The ability of a system to provide timely warnings to users when the system should not be used for navigation.

intermediate approach segment. (*See* segments of an instrument approach procedure). [ICAO] That segment of an instrument approach procedure between either the intermediate approach fix and the final approach fix or point, or between the end of a reversal, race track or dead reckoning track procedure and the final approach fix or point, as appropriate.

intermediate fix (IF). The fix that identifies the beginning of the intermediate approach segment of an instrument approach procedure. The fix is not normally identified on the instrument approach chart as an intermediate fix (IF). (*See* segments of an instrument approach procedure).

intermediate landing. On the rare occasion that this option is requested, it should be approved. The departure center, however, must advise the ATCSCC so that the appropriate delay is carried over and assigned at the intermediate airport. An intermediate landing airport within the arrival center will not be accepted without coordination with and the approval of the ATCSCC.

international airport. Relating to international flight, it means:

1. An airport of entry which has been designated by the Secretary of Treasury or Commissioner of Customs as an international airport for customs service.

2. A landing rights airport at which specific permission to land must be obtained from customs authorities in advance of contemplated use.

3. Airports designated under the Convention on International Civil Aviation as an airport for use by international commercial air transport and/or international general aviation.

(Refer to Airport/Facility Directory and IFIM). [ICAO] Any airport designated by the Contracting State in whose territory it is situated as an airport of entry and departure for international air traffic, where the formalities incident to customs, immigration, public health, animal and plant quarantine and similar procedures are carried out.

International Civil Aviation Organization. [ICAO] A specialized agency of the United Nations whose objective is to develop the principles and techniques of international air navigation and to foster planning and development of international civil air transport. ICAO Regions include:

AFI. African-Indian Ocean Region

CAR. Caribbean Region

EUR. European Region

MID/ASIA. Middle East/Asia Region

NAM. North American Region

NAT. North Atlantic Region

PAC. Pacific Region

SAM. South American Region

International Flight Information Manual (IFIM). A publication designed primarily as a pilot's preflight planning guide for flights into foreign airspace and for flights returning to the U.S. from foreign locations.

***international standard atmosphere (ISA).** See standard day.

interrogator. The ground based surveillance radar beacon transmitter/receiver, which normally scans in synchronism with a primary radar, transmitting discrete radio signals which repetitiously request all transponders on the mode being used to reply. The replies received are mixed with the primary radar returns and displayed on the same plan position indicator (radar scope). Also, applied to the airborne element of the TACAN/DME system. (*See* transponder) (Refer to AIM).

intersecting runways. Two or more runways which cross or meet within their lengths. (*See* intersection).

intersection.

1. A point defined by any combination of courses, radials, or bearings of two or more navigational aids.

2. Used to describe the point where two runways, a runway and a taxiway, or two taxiways cross or meet.

intersection departure. A departure from any runway intersection except the end of the runway. (*See* Intersection).

intersection takeoff. (*See* intersection departure).

***inversion.** When warm air overlies cold air; the reverse of a stable condition.

IR. (*See* IFR military training routes).

I say again. The message will be repeated.

***isobars.** Lines of equal barometric pressure on a weather map.

***isogonic lines.** Lines of equal magnetic variation.

jamming. Electronic or mechanical interference which may disrupt the display of aircraft on radar or the transmission/reception of radio communications/navigation.

jet blast. Jet engine exhaust (thrust stream turbulence). (*See* wake turbulence).

jet route. A route designed to serve aircraft operations from 18,000 feet MSL up to and including flight level 450. The routes are referred to as "J" routes with numbering to identify the designated route; e.g., J105. (*See* Class A airspace) (Refer to 14 CFR Part 71).

jet stream. A migrating stream of high speed winds present at high altitudes.

jettisoning of external stores. Airborne release of external stores; e.g., tiptanks, ordnance. (*See* fuel dumping) (Refer to 14 CFR Part 91).

joint use restricted area. (*See* Restricted Area).

*kHz. Kilohertz (thousands of cycles per second); a measure of radio frequency.

*knot. One nautical mile per hour. (It is redundant to say "90 knots per hour.")

known traffic. With respect to ATC clearances, means aircraft whose altitude, position, and intentions are known to ATC.

*Kollsman window. The altimeter setting window.

LAA. (*See* Local Airport Advisory).

LAAS. (*See* Low Altitude Alert System).

LAHSO. An acronym for "Land and Hold Short Operation." These operations include landing and holding short of an intersecting runway, a taxiway, a predetermined point, or an approach/departure flightpath.

LAHSO. Dry. Land and hold short operation on runways that are dry.

LAHSO. Wet. Land and hold short operations on runways that are wet (but not contaminated).

land and hold short operations (LAHSO). Operations which include simultaneous takeoffs and landings and/or simultaneous landings when a landing aircraft is able and is instructed by the controller to hold-short of the intersecting runway/taxiway or designated hold-short point. Pilots are expected to promptly inform the controller if the hold short clearance cannot be accepted. (*See* parallel runways). (Refer to AIM).

landing area. Any locality either on land, water, or structures, including airports/heliports and intermediate landing fields which is used, or intended to be used, for the landing and takeoff of aircraft whether or not facilities are provided for the shelter, servicing, or for receiving or discharging passengers or cargo. [ICAO] That part of a movement area intended for the landing or takeoff of aircraft.

landing direction indicator. A device which visually indicates the direction in which landings and takeoffs should be made. (*See* tetrahedron) (Refer to AIM).

landing distance available (LDA). [ICAO] The length of runway which is declared available and suitable for the ground run of an aeroplane landing.

*landing gear. The two main wheels and the nosewheel (or tailwheel).

landing minimums. The minimum visibility prescribed for landing a civil aircraft while using an instrument approach procedure. The minimum applies with other limitations set forth in 14 CFR Part 91 with respect to the Minimum Descent Altitude (MDA) or Decision Height (DH) prescribed in the instrument approach procedures as follows:

1. Straight-in landing minimums. A statement of MDA and visibility, or DH and visibility, required for a straight-in landing on a specified runway, or

2. Circling minimums. A statement of MDA and visibility required for the circle-to-land maneuver.

Descent below the established MDA or DH is not authorized during an approach unless the aircraft is in a position from which a normal approach to the runway of intended landing can be made and adequate visual reference to required visual cues is maintained. (*See* straight-in landing, circle-to-land maneuver, decision height, minimum descent altitude, visibility, instrument approach procedure) (Refer to 14 CFR Part 91).

landing roll. The distance from the point of touchdown to the point where the aircraft can be brought to a stop or exit the runway.

landing sequence. The order in which aircraft are positioned for landing (*See* approach sequence).

last assigned altitude. The last altitude/flight level assigned by ATC and acknowledged by the pilot. (*See* maintain) (Refer to 14 CFR Part 91).

*lateral axis. A line drawn from wing tip to wing tip.

lateral separation. The lateral spacing of aircraft at the same altitude by requiring operation on different routes or in different geographical locations. (*See* separation).

LDA. (*See* localizer-type directional aid).

LDA. [ICAO] (*See* landing distance available [ICAO]).

LF. (*See* low frequency).

lighted airport. An airport where runway and obstruction lighting is available. (*See* airport lighting) (Refer to AIM).

light gun. A hand held directional light signaling device which emits a brilliant narrow beam of white, green, or red light as selected by the tower controller. The color and type of light transmitted can be used to approve or disapprove anticipated pilot actions where radio communication is not available. The light gun is used for controlling traffic operating in the vicinity of the airport and on the airport movement area. (Refer to AIM).

line up and wait (LUAW). Used by ATC to inform a pilot to taxi onto the departure runway to "line up and wait." It is not authorization for takeoff. It is used when takeoff clearance cannot be issued immediately, due to traffic or other reasons.

*loadmeter. An ammeter which is calibrated to indicate the electrical load on the alternator in amperes.

Local Airport Advisory (LAA). A service provided by flight service stations or the military at airports not serviced by an operating control tower. This service consists of providing information to arriving and departing aircraft concerning wind direction and speed, favored runway, altimeter setting, pertinent known traffic, pertinent known field conditions, airport taxi routes and traffic patterns, and authorized instrument approach procedures. This information is advisory in nature and does not constitute an ATC clearance (*See* airport advisory area).

localizer. The component of an ILS which provides course guidance to the runway. (*See* Instrument Landing System) (Refer to AIM) (*See* localizer course [ICAO]).

localizer course (ILS). [ICAO] The locus of points, in any given horizontal plane, at which the DDM (difference in depth of modulation) is zero.

localizer offset. An angular offset of the localizer from the runway extended centerline in a direction away from the no transgression zone (NTZ) that increases the normal operating zone (NOZ) width. An offset requires a 50 foot increase in DH and is not authorized for CAT II and CAT III approaches.

localizer-type directional aid (LDA). A NAVAID used for nonprecision instrument approaches with utility and accuracy comparable to a localizer but which is not a part of a complete ILS and is not aligned with the runway. (Refer to AIM).

localizer usable distance. The maximum distance from the localizer transmitter at a specified altitude, as verified by flight inspection, at which reliable course information is continuously received. (Refer to AIM).

local traffic. Aircraft operating in the traffic pattern or within sight of the tower, or aircraft known to be departing or arriving from flight in local practice areas, or aircraft executing practice instrument approaches at the airport. (*See* traffic pattern).

locator. [ICAO] An LM/MF NDB used as an aid to final approach. *Note:* A locator usually has an average radius of rated coverage of between 18.5 and 46.3 km (10 and 25 NM).

*longitudinal axis. An imaginary line from the nose to the tail of the airplane.

longitudinal separation. The longitudinal spacing of aircraft at the same altitude by a minimum distance expressed in units of time or miles. (*See* separation) (Refer to AIM).

lost communications. Loss of the ability to communicate by radio. Aircraft are sometimes referred to as NORDO (No Radio). Standard pilot procedures are specified in 14 CFR Part 91. Radar controllers issue procedures for pilots to follow in the event of lost communications during a radar approach when weather reports indicate that an aircraft will likely encounter IFR weather conditions during the approach. (Refer to 14 CFR Part 91, AIM).

low altitude airway structure. The network of airways serving aircraft operations up to but not including 18,000 feet MSL. (*See* airway) (Refer to AIM).

Low altitude alert, check your altitude immediately. (*See* safety alert).

Low Altitude Alert System (LAAS). An automated function of the TPX-42 that alerts the controller when a Mode C transponder equipped aircraft on an IFR flight plan is below a predetermined minimum safe altitude. If requested by the pilot, LAAS monitoring is also available to VFR Mode C transponder equipped aircraft.

low approach. An approach over an airport or runway following an instrument approach or a VFR approach including the go around maneuver where the pilot intentionally does not make contact with the runway. (Refer to AIM).

low frequency (LF). The frequency band between 30 and 300 kHz. (Refer to AIM).

MAA. (*See* maximum authorized altitude).

Mach number. The ratio of true airspeed to the speed of sound; e.g., Mach 0.82, Mach 1.6. (*See* airspeed).

Mach technique. [ICAO] Describes a control technique used by air traffic control whereby turbojet aircraft operating successively along suitable routes are cleared to maintain appropriate Mach numbers for a relevant portion of the enroute phase of flight. The principle objective is to achieve improved utilization of the airspace and to ensure that separation between successive aircraft does not decrease below the established minima.

*magnetic bearing. The direction to or from a transmitting station measured in relation to magnetic north.

*magnetic compass. A direction-indicating device that reacts to the earth's magnetic field.

*magnetic north. The direction to the magnetic North Pole, located in Northern Canada.

*magneto. A self-powered source of ignition using fixed magnets.

MAHWP. Missed approach holding waypoint.

maintain.

1. Concerning altitude/flight level, the term means to remain at the altitude/flight level specified. The phrase "climb and" or "descend and" normally precedes "maintain" and the altitude assignment; e.g., "descend and maintain 5,000."
2. Concerning other ATC instructions, the term is used in its literal sense; e.g., maintain VFR.

maintenance planning friction level. The friction level specified in AC 150/5320-12, *Measurement, Construction, and Maintenance of Skid Resistant Airport Pavement Surfaces,* which represents the friction value below which the runway pavement surface remains acceptable for any category or class of aircraft operations but which is beginning to show signs of deterioration. This value will vary depending on the particular friction measurement equipment used.

Make short approach. Used by ATC to inform a pilot to alter his traffic pattern so as to make a short final approach. (*See* traffic pattern).

mandatory altitude. An altitude depicted on an instrument Approach Procedure Chart requiring the aircraft to maintain altitude at the depicted value.

*manifold. A pipe with several lateral outlets. In an airplane, the intake manifold delivers the fuel/air mixture to the cylinders; the exhaust manifold collects the exhaust from the cylinders, and pipes it overboard or through a turbocharger.

*manifold pressure. An indirect measure of power output obtained by measuring the pressure of the air in the intake manifold. The higher the pressure, the greater the power output of the engine.

MAP. (*See* missed approach point).

marker beacon. An electronic navigation facility transmitting a 75 MHz vertical fan or boneshaped radiation pattern. Marker beacons are identified by their modulation frequency and keying code, and when received by compatible airborne equipment, indicate to the pilot, both aurally and visually, that he is passing over the facility. (*See* outer marker, middle marker, inner marker) (Refer to AIM).

MARSA. (*See* military authority assumes responsibility for separation of aircraft).

MAWP. Missed approach waypoint.

maximum authorized altitude (MAA). A published altitude representing the maximum usable altitude or flight level for an airspace structure or route segment. It is the highest altitude on a Federal airway, jet route, area navigation low or high route, or other direct route for which an MEA is designated in 14 CFR Part 95 at which adequate reception of navigation aid signals is assured.

*mayday. The international radio telephony distress signal. When repeated three times, it indicates imminent and grave danger and that immediate assistance is requested. (*See* pan-pan) (Refer to AIM).

*mayday. The voice equivalent of SOS; used to declare an emergency.

MCA. (*See* minimum crossing altitude).

MDA. (*See* minimum descent altitude).

MEA. (*See* minimum enroute IFR altitude).

*meridians. Lines of longitude—running from pole to pole and all the same length. Each degree of latitude measured along a line of longitude equals 60 nautical miles.

*METAR. An hourly weather observation from an accredited observer.

meteorological impact statement (MIS). An unscheduled planning forecast describing conditions expected to begin within 4 to 12 hours which may impact the flow of air traffic in a specific center's (ARTCC) area.

meter fix time (MFT)/slot time. A calculated time to depart the meter fix in order to cross the vertex at the ACLT. This time reflects descent speed adjustment and any applicable time that must be absorbed prior to crossing the meter fix.

meter list display interval (MLDI). A dynamic parameter which controls the number of minutes prior to the flight plan calculated time of arrival at the meter fix for each aircraft, at which time the TCLT is frozen and becomes an ACLT; i.e., the VTA is updated and consequently the TCLT modified as appropriate until frozen at which time updating is suspended and an ACLT is assigned. When frozen, the flight entry is inserted into the arrival sector's meter list for display on the sector PVD/MDM. MLDI is used if filed true airspeed is less than or equal to freeze speed parameters (FSPD).

metering. A method of time regulating arrival traffic flow into a terminal area so as not to exceed a predetermined terminal acceptance rate.

metering airports. Airports adapted for metering and for which optimum flight paths are defined. A maximum of 15 airports may be adapted.

metering fix. A fix along an established route from over which aircraft will be metered prior to entering terminal airspace. Normally, this fix should be established at a distance from the airport which will facilitate a profile descent 10,000 feet above airport elevation (AAE) or above.

metering position(s). Adapted PVDs/MDMs and associated "D" positions eligible for display of a metering position list. A maximum of four PVDs/MDMs may be adapted.

metering position list. An ordered list of data on arrivals for a selected metering airport displayed on a metering position PVD/MDM.

MFT. (*See* meter fix time/slot time).

MHA. (*See* minimum holding altitude).

*MHz. Megahertz (millions of cycles per second); a measure of radio frequency.

MIA. (*See* minimum IFR altitudes).

microburst. A small downburst with outbursts of damaging winds extending 2.5 miles or less. In spite of its small horizontal scale, an intense microburst could induce wind speeds as high as 150 knots. (Refer to AIM).

Microwave Landing System (MLS). A precision instrument approach system operating in the microwave spectrum which normally consists of the following components:

1. Azimuth station.
2. Elevation station.
3. Precision distance measuring equipment.
   (*See* MLS categories).

middle compass locator. (*See* compass locator).

middle marker (MM). A marker beacon that defines a point along the glideslope of an ILS normally located at or near the point of decision height (ILS Category I). It is keyed to transmit alternate dots and dashes, with the alternate dots and dashes keyed at the rate of 95 dot/dash combinations per minute on a 1300 Hz tone, which is received aurally and visually by compatible airborne equipment. (*See* marker beacon, instrument landing system) (Refer to AIM).

mid RVR. (*See* visibility).

miles in trail. A specified distance between aircraft, normally, in the same stratum associated with the same destination or route of flight.

military authority assumes responsibility for separation of aircraft (MARSA). A condition whereby the military services involved assume responsibility for separation between participating military aircraft in the ATC system. It is used only for required IFR operations which are specified in letters of agreement or other appropriate FAA or military documents.

Military Operations Area (MOA). (*See* Special Use airspace).

military training routes (MTR). Airspace of defined vertical and lateral dimensions established for the conduct of military flight training at airspeeds in excess of 250 knots IAS. (*See* IFR military training routes and VFR military training routes).

minima. (*See* minimums).

minimum crossing altitude (MCA). The lowest altitude at certain fixes at which an aircraft must cross when proceeding in the direction of a higher minimum enroute IFR altitude (MEA). (*See* minimum enroute IFR altitude).

minimum descent altitude (MDA). The lowest altitude, expressed in feet above mean sea level, to which descent is authorized on final approach or during circle-to-land maneuvering in execution of a standard instrument approach procedure where no electronic glideslope is provided. (*See* nonprecision approach procedure).

minimum enroute IFR altitude (MEA). The lowest published altitude between radio fixes which assures acceptable navigational signal coverage and meets obstacle clearance requirements between those fixes. The MEA prescribed for a Federal airway or segment thereof, area navigation low or high route or other direct route applies to the entire width of the airway, segment, or route between the radio fixes defining the airway, segment, or route. (Refer to 14 CFR Parts 91 and 95; AIM).

minimum friction level. The friction level specified in AC 150/5320-12, *Measurement, Construction, and Maintenance of Skid Resistant Airport Pavement Surfaces,* that represents the minimum recommended wet pavement surface friction value for any turbojet aircraft engaged in LAHSO. This value will vary with the particular friction measurement equipment used.

minimum fuel. Indicates that an aircraft's fuel supply has reached a state where, upon reaching the destination, it can accept little or no delay. This is not an emergency situation but merely indicates an emergency situation is possible should any undue delay occur. (Refer to AIM).

minimum holding altitude (MHA). The lowest altitude prescribed for a holding pattern which assures navigational signal coverage, communications, and meets obstacle clearance requirements.

minimum IFR altitudes (MIA). Minimum altitudes for IFR operations as prescribed in 14 CFR Part 91. These altitudes are published on aeronautical charts and prescribed in Part 95 for airways and routes, and in Part 97 for standard instrument approach procedures. If no applicable minimum altitude is prescribed in Part 95 or Part 97, the following minimum IFR altitude applies:

1. In designated mountainous areas, 2,000 feet above the highest obstacle within a horizontal distance of 4 nautical miles from the course to be flown; or

2. Other than mountainous areas, 1,000 feet above the highest obstacle within a horizontal distance of 4 nautical miles from the course to be flown; or

3. As otherwise authorized by the Administrator or assigned by ATC.

(*See* minimum enroute IFR altitude, minimum obstruction clearance altitude, minimum crossing altitude, minimum safe altitude, minimum vectoring altitude) (Refer to 14 CFR Part 91).

Minimum Navigation Performance Specification (MNPS). A set of standards which require aircraft to have a minimum navigation performance capability in order to operate in MNPS designated airspace. In addition, aircraft must be certified by their State of Registry for MNPS operation.

Minimum Navigation Performance Specifications Airspace (MNPSA). Designated airspace in which MNPS procedures are applied between MNPS certified and equipped aircraft. Under certain conditions, non-MNPS aircraft can operate in MNPSA. However, standard oceanic separation minima is provided between the non-MNPS aircraft and other traffic. Currently, the only designated MNPSA is described as follows:

1. Between FL 285 and FL 420;

2. Between latitudes 27° N and the North Pole;

3. In the east, the eastern boundaries of the CTA's Santa Maria Oceanic, Shanwick Oceanic, and Reykjavik;

4. In the west, the western boundaries of CTA's Reykjavik and Gander Oceanic and New York Oceanic excluding the area west of 60° W and south of 38°30' N.

minimum obstruction clearance altitude (MOCA). The lowest published altitude in effect between radio fixes on VOR airways, off airway routes, or route segments which meets obstacle clearance requirements for the entire route segment and which assures acceptable navigational signal coverage only within 25 statute (22 nautical) miles of a VOR. (Refer to 14 CFR Parts 91 and 95).

minimum reception altitude (MRA). The lowest altitude at which an intersection can be determined. (Refer to 14 CFR Part 95).

minimum safe altitude (MSA).

1. The minimum altitude specified in 14 CFR Part 91 for various aircraft operations.

2. Altitudes depicted on approach charts which provide at least 1,000 feet of obstacle clearance for emergency use within a specified distance from the navigation facility upon which a procedure is predicated. These altitudes will be identified as Minimum sector altitudes or emergency safe altitudes and are established as follows:

   a. *Minimum sector altitudes.* Altitudes depicted on approach charts which provide at least 1,000 feet of obstacle clearance within a 25 mile radius of the navigation facility upon which the procedure is predicated. Sectors depicted on approach charts must be at least 90 degrees in scope. These altitudes are for emergency use only and do not necessarily assure acceptable navigational signal coverage. (*See* minimum sector altitude [ICAO]).

   b. *Emergency safe altitudes.* Altitudes depicted on approach charts which provide at least 1,000 feet of obstacle clearance in nonmountainous areas and 2,000 feet of obstacle clearance in designated mountainous areas within a 100 mile radius of the navigation facility upon which the procedure is predicated and normally used only in military procedures. These altitudes are identified on published procedures as "emergency safe altitudes."

minimum safe altitude warning (MSAW). A function of the ARTS III computer that aids the controller by alerting him when a tracked Mode C equipped aircraft is below or is predicted by the computer to go below a predetermined minimum safe altitude. (Refer to AIM).

minimum sector altitude. [ICAO] The lowest altitude which may be used under emergency conditions which will provide a minimum clearance of 300 m (1,000 feet) above all obstacles located in an area contained within a sector of a circle of 46 km (25 NM) radius centered on a radio aid to navigation.

minimums. Weather condition requirements established for a particular operation or type of operation; e.g., IFR take-off or landing, alternate airport for IFR flight plans, VFR flight, etc. (*See* landing minimums, IFR takeoff minimums, VFR conditions, IFR conditions) (Refer to 14 CFR Part 91, AIM).

minimum vectoring altitude (MVA). The lowest MSL altitude at which an IFR aircraft will be vectored by a radar controller, except as otherwise authorized for radar approaches, departures, and missed approaches. The altitude meets IFR obstacle clearance criteria. It may be lower than the published MEA along an airway or J-route segment. It may be utilized for radar vectoring only upon the controller's determination that an adequate radar return is being received from the aircraft being controlled. Charts depicting minimum vectoring altitudes are normally available only to the controllers and not to pilots. (Refer to AIM).

minutes in trail. A specified interval between aircraft expressed in time. This method would more likely be utilized regardless of altitude.

MIS. (*See* meteorological impact statement).

missed approach.

1. A maneuver conducted by a pilot when an instrument approach cannot be completed to a landing. The route of flight and altitude are shown on instrument approach procedure charts. A pilot executing a missed approach prior to the Missed Approach Point (MAP) must continue along the final approach to the MAP. The pilot may climb immediately to the altitude specified in the missed approach procedure.

2. A term used by the pilot to inform ATC that he is executing the missed approach.

3. At locations where ATC radar service is provided, the pilot should conform to radar vectors when provided by ATC in lieu of the published missed approach procedure.

(*See* missed approach point) (Refer to AIM).

missed approach point (MAP). A point prescribed in each instrument approach procedure at which a missed approach procedure shall be executed if the required visual reference does not exist. (*See* missed approach, segments of an instrument approach procedure).

missed approach procedure. [ICAO] The procedure to be followed if the approach cannot be continued.

missed approach segment. (*See* segments of an instrument approach procedure).

MLDI. (*See* meter list display interval).

MLS. (*See* Microwave Landing System).

MLS categories.

1. *MLS Category I.* An MLS approach procedure which provides for an approach to a height above touchdown of not less than 200 feet and a runway visual range of not less than 1,800 feet.

2. *MLS Category II.* Undefined until data gathering/analysis completion.

3. *MLS Category III.* Undefined until data gathering/analysis completion.

MM. (*See* middle marker).

MNPS. (*See* Minimum Navigation Performance Specification).

MNPSA. (*See* Minimum Navigation Performance Specifications airspace).

MOA. (*See* Military Operations Area).

MOCA. (*See* minimum obstruction clearance altitude).

mode. The letter or number assigned to a specific pulse spacing of radio signals transmitted or received by ground interrogator or airborne transponder components of the Air Traffic Control Radar Beacon System (ATCRBS). Mode A (military Mode 3) and Mode C (altitude reporting) are used in air traffic control. (*See* transponder, interrogator, radar) (Refer to AIM) (*See* mode [ICAO]).

*Mode A. The "location only" mode of a transponder.

*Mode C. The "ALT" position on the transponder function switch. If an encoding altimeter is installed, Mode C will transmit your altitude to the ground radar facility.

mode (SSR Mode). [ICAO] The letter or number assigned to a specific pulse spacing of the interrogation signals transmitted by an interrogator. There are 4 modes, A, B, C and D specified in Annex 10, corresponding to four different interrogation pulse spacings.

Mode C intruder alert. A function of certain air traffic control automated systems designed to alert radar controllers to existing or pending situations between a tracked target (known IFR or VFR aircraft) and an untracked target (unknown IFR or VFR aircraft) that requires immediate attention/action. (*See* conflict alert).

*moment. The product of a distance multiplied by a weight; used in loading calculations.

monitor. (When used with communication transfer) listen on a specific frequency and stand by for instructions. Under normal circumstances do not establish communications.

monitor alert (MA). A function of the ETMS that provides traffic management personnel with a tool for predicting potential capacity problems in individual operational sectors. The MA is an indication that traffic management personnel need to analyze a particular sector for actual activity and to determine the required action(s), if any, needed to control the demand.

monitor alert parameter (MAP). The number designated for use in monitor alert processing by the ETMS. The MAP is designated for each operational sector for increments of 15 minutes.

movement area. The runways, taxiways, and other areas an of airport/heliport which are utilized for taxiing/hover taxiing, air taxiing, takeoff, and landing of aircraft, exclusive of loading ramps and parking areas. At those airport/heliports with a tower, specific approval for entry onto the movement area must be obtained from ATC. [ICAO] That part of an aerodrome to be used for the takeoff, landing and taxiing of aircraft, consisting of the maneuvering area and the apron(s).

moving target indicator (MTI). An electronic device which will permit radar scope presentation only from targets which are in motion. A partial remedy for ground clutter.

MRA. (*See* minimum reception altitude).

MSA. (*See* minimum safe altitude).

MSAW. (*See* minimum safe altitude warning).

MTI. (*See* moving target indicator).

MTR. (*See* military training routes).

MULTICOM. A mobile service not open to public correspondence used to provide communications essential to conduct the activities being performed by or directed from private aircraft.

multiple runways. The utilization of a dedicated arrival runway(s) for departures and a dedicated departure runway(s) for arrivals when feasible to reduce delays and enhance capacity.

MVA. (*See* minimum vectoring altitude).

NAS. (*See* National Airspace System).

NAS Stage A. The enroute ATC system's radar, computers and computer programs, controller plan view displays (PVDs/Radar Scopes), input/output devices, and the related communications equipment which are integrated to form the heart of the automated IFR air traffic control system. This equipment performs Flight Data Processing (FDP) and Radar Data Processing (RDP). It interfaces with automated terminal systems and is used in the control of enroute IFR aircraft. (Refer to AIM).

National Airspace System (NAS). The common network of U.S. airspace; air navigation facilities, equipment and services, airports or landing areas; aeronautical charts, information and services; rules, regulations and procedures, technical information, and manpower and material. Included are system components shared jointly with the military.

National Beacon Code Allocation Plan airspace. Airspace over United States territory located within the North American continent between Canada and Mexico, including adjacent territorial waters outward to about boundaries of oceanic control areas (CTA)/Flight Information Regions (FIR). (*See* flight information region).

National Flight Data Center (NFDC). A facility in Washington D.C., established by FAA to operate a central aeronautical information service for the collection, validation, and dissemination of aeronautical data in support of the activities of government, industry, and the aviation community. The information is published in the National Flight Data Digest. (*See* National Flight Data Digest).

National Flight Data Digest (NFDD). A daily (except weekends and Federal holidays) publication of flight information appropriate to aeronautical charts, aeronautical publications, Notices to Airmen, or other media serving the purpose of providing operational flight data essential to safe and efficient aircraft operations.

National Route Program (NRP). The NRP is a set of rules and procedures which are designed to increase the flexibility of user flight planning within published guidelines.

National Search and Rescue Plan. An interagency agreement which provides for the effective utilization of all available facilities in all types of search and rescue missions.

*nautical mile. One minute of latitude; 6,080 feet (rounded off to 6,000 feet for convenience).

NAVAID. (*See* navigational aid).

NAVAID classes. VOR, VORTAC, AND TACAN aids are classed according to their operational use. The three classes of NAVAIDs are:

T — Terminal.

L — Low altitude.

H — High altitude.

The normal service range for T, L, and H class aids is found in the FAAAIMTOC. Certain operational requirements make it necessary to use some of these aids at greater service ranges than specified. Extended range is made possible through flight inspection determinations. Some aids also have lesser service range due to location, terrain, frequency protection, etc. Restrictions to service range are listed in Airport/Facility Directory.

navigable airspace. Airspace at and above the minimum flight altitudes prescribed in the FARs including airspace needed for safe takeoff and landing. (Refer to 14 CFR Part 91).

navigational aid (NAVAID). Any visual or electronic device airborne or on the surface which provides point-to-point guidance information or position data to aircraft in flight. (*See* air navigation facility).

NBCAP airspace. (*See* National Beacon Code Allocation Plan airspace).

NDB. (*See* nondirectional beacon).

*NDB. Nondirectional beacon — used for navigation with an automatic direction finder.

negative. "No," or "permission not granted," or "that is not correct."

negative contact. Used by pilots to inform ATC that:

1. Previously issued traffic is not in sight. It may be followed by the pilot's request for the controller to provide assistance in avoiding the traffic.

2. They were unable to contact ATC on a particular frequency.

NFDC. (*See* National Flight Data Center).

NFDD. (*See* National Flight Data Digest).

night. The time between the end of evening civil twilight and the beginning of morning civil twilight, as published in the American Air Almanac, converted to local time. [ICAO] The hours between the end of evening civil twilight and the beginning of morning civil twilight or such other period between sunset and sunrise as may be specified by the appropriate authority. *Note:* Civil twilight ends in the evening when the center of the sun's disk is 6 degrees below the horizon and begins in the morning when the center of the sun's disk is 6 degrees below the horizon.

no gyro approach. A radar approach/vector provided in case of a malfunctioning gyro compass or directional gyro. Instead of providing the pilot with headings to be flown, the controller observes the radar track and issues control instructions "turn right/left" or "stop turn" as appropriate. (Refer to AIM).

no gyro vector. (*See* no gyro approach).

no transgression zone (NTZ). The NTZ is a 2,000-foot-wide zone, located equidistant between parallel runway final approach courses in which flight is not allowed.

nonapproach control tower. Authorizes aircraft to land or takeoff at the airport controlled by the tower or to transit the Class D airspace. The primary function of a nonapproach control tower is the sequencing of aircraft in the traffic pattern and on the landing area. Nonapproach control towers also separate aircraft operating under instrument flight rules clearances from approach controls and centers. They provide ground control services to aircraft, vehicles, personnel and equipment on the airport movement area.

noncommon route/portion. That segment of a North American Route between the inland navigation facility and a designated North American terminal.

noncomposite separation. Separation in accordance with minima other than the composite separation minimum specified for the area concerned.

nondirectional beacon (NDB). An L/MF or UHF radio beacon transmitting nondirectional signals whereby the pilot of an aircraft equipped with direction finding equipment can determine his bearing to or from the radio beacon and "home" on or track to or from the station. When the radio beacon is installed in conjunction with the Instrument Landing System marker, it is normally called a Compass Locator. (*See* compass locator, automatic direction finder).

nonmovement areas. Taxiways and apron (ramp) areas not under the control of air traffic.

nonprecision approach. (*See* nonprecision approach procedure).

nonprecision approach procedure. A standard instrument approach procedure in which no electronic glide slope is provided; e.g., VOR, TACAN, NDB, LOC, ASR, LDA, or SDF approaches.

nonradar. Precedes other terms and generally means without the use of radar, such as:

1. *Nonradar approach.* Used to describe instrument approaches for which course guidance on final approach is not provided by ground based precision or surveillance radar. Radar vectors to the final approach course may or may not be provided by ATC. Examples of nonradar approaches are VOR, NDB, TACAN, and ILS/MLS approaches. (*See* final approach, IFR, final approach course, radar approach, instrument approach procedure).

2. *Nonradar Approach Control.* An ATC facility providing approach control service without the use of radar. (*See* approach control facility, approach control service).

Continued

3. *Nonradar arrival.* An aircraft arriving at an airport without radar service or at an airport served by a radar facility and radar contact has not been established or has been terminated due to a lack of radar service to the airport. (*See* radar arrival, radar service).

4. *Nonradar route.* A flight path or route over which the pilot is performing his own navigation. The pilot may be receiving radar separation, radar monitoring, or other ATC services while on a nonradar route. (*See* radar route).

5. *Nonradar separation.* The spacing of aircraft in accordance with established minima without the use of radar; e.g., vertical, lateral, or longitudinal separation. (*See* radar separation) (*See* nonradar separation [ICAO]).

nonradar separation. [ICAO] The separation used when aircraft position information is derived from sources other than radar.

NOPAC. (*See* North Pacific).

NORDO. (*See* lost communications).

normal operating zone (NOZ). The NOZ is the operating zone within which aircraft flight remains during normal independent simultaneous parallel ILS approaches.

North American route. A numerically coded route preplanned over existing airway and route systems to and from specific coastal fixes serving the North Atlantic. North American Routes consist of the following:

1. *Common route/portion.* That segment of a North American Route between the inland navigation facility and the coastal fix.

2. *Noncommon route/portion.* That segment of a North American Route between the inland navigation facility and a designated North American terminal.

3. *Inland Navigation Facility.* A navigation aid on a North American Route at which the common route and/or the noncommon route begins or ends.

4. *Coastal fix.* A navigation aid or intersection where an aircraft transitions between the domestic route structure and oceanic route structure.

North Mark. A beacon data block sent by the host computer to be displayed by the ARTS on a 360 degree bearing at a locally selected radar azimuth and distance. The North Mark is used to ensure correct range/azimuth orientation during periods of CENRAP.

North Pacific (NOPAC). An organized route system between the Alaskan west coast and Japan.

***northerly turning error.** An error in the magnetic compass induced by the vertical component of the earth's magnetic field.

NOTAM. (*See* Notice To Airmen).

Notice To Airmen (NOTAM). A notice containing information (not known sufficiently in advance to publicize by other means) concerning the establishment, condition, or change in any component (facility, service, or procedure of, or hazard in the National Airspace System) the timely knowledge of which is essential to personnel concerned with flight operations.

1. *NOTAM(D).* A NOTAM given (in addition to local dissemination) distant dissemination beyond the area of responsibility of the Flight Service Station. These NOTAMs will be stored and available until canceled.

2. *NOTAM(L).* A NOTAM given local dissemination by voice and other means, such as telautograph and telephone, to satisfy local user requirements.

3. *FDC NOTAM.* A NOTAM regulatory in nature, transmitted by USNOF and given system wide dissemination. (*See* NOTAM [ICAO]).

NOTAM. [ICAO] A notice containing information concerning the establishment, condition or change in any aeronautical facility, service procedure or hazard, the timely knowledge of which is essential to personnel concerned with flight operations.

Class I Distribution. Distribution by means of telecommunication.

Class II Distribution. Distribution by means other than telecommunications.

Notices To Airmen Publication. A publication issued every 28 days, designed primarily for the pilot, which contains current NOTAM information considered essential to the safety of flight as well as supplemental data to other aeronautical publications. The contraction NTAP is used in NOTAM text. (*See* Notice To Airmen).

NTAP. (*See* Notices To Airmen Publication).

***NTSB.** National Transportation Safety Board.

Numerous targets vicinity (location). A traffic advisory issued by ATC to advise pilots that targets on the radar scope are too numerous to issue individually. (*See* Traffic Advisories).

***NWS.** National Weather Service, the source of all government weather information.

***OBS.** Omni-bearing selector—used in VOR navigation to select radials.

obstacle. An existing object, object of natural growth, or terrain at a fixed geographical location or which may be expected at a fixed location within a prescribed area with reference to which vertical clearance is or must be provided during flight operation.

obstacle free zone (OFZ). The OFZ is a three dimensional volume of airspace which protects for the transition of aircraft to and from the runway. The OFZ clearing standard precludes taxiing and parked airplanes and object penetrations, except for frangible NAVAID locations that are fixed by function. Additionally, vehicles, equipment, and personnel may be authorized by air traffic control to enter the area using the provisions of FAAO 7110.65, Para. 3-1-5, VEHICLES/EQUIPMENT/PERSONNEL ON RUNWAYS. The runway OFZ and when applicable, the inner-approach OFZ, and the inner-transitional OFZ, comprise the OFZ.

1. *Runway OFZ.* The runway OFZ is a defined volume of airspace centered above the runway. The runway OFZ is the airspace above a surface whose elevation at any point is the same as the elevation of the nearest point on the runway centerline. The runway OFZ extends 200 feet beyond each end of the runway. The width is as follows:

   a. For runways serving large airplanes, the greater of:
      (1) 400 feet, or
      (2) 180 feet, plus the wingspan of the most demanding airplane, plus 20 feet per 1,000 feet of airport elevation.

   b. For runways serving only small airplanes:
      (1) 300 feet for precision instrument runways.
      (2) 250 feet for other runways serving small airplanes with approach speeds of 50 knots, or more.
      (3) 120 feet for other runways serving small airplanes with approach speeds of less than 50 knots.

2. *Inner-approach OFZ.* The inner-approach OFZ is a defined volume of airspace centered on the approach area. The inner-approach OFZ applies only to runways with an approach lighting system. The inner-approach OFZ begins 200 feet from the runway threshold at the same elevation as the runway threshold and extends 200 feet beyond the last light unit in the approach lighting system. The width of the inner-approach OFZ is the same as the runway OFZ and rises at a slope of 50 (horizontal) to 1 (vertical) from the beginning.

3. *Inner-transitional OFZ.* The inner transitional surface OFZ is a defined volume of airspace along the sides of the runway and inner-approach OFZ and applies only to precision instrument runways. The inner-transitional surface OFZ slopes 3 (horizontal) to 1 (vertical) out from the edges of the runway OFZ and inner-approach OFZ to a height of 150 feet above the established airport elevation.

(Refer to AC 150/5300-13, Chap. 3 and FAAO 7110.65, Para. 3-1-5, VEHICLES/EQUIPMENT/PERSONNEL ON RUNWAYS).

obstruction. Any object/obstacle exceeding the obstruction standards specified by 14 CFR Part 77, Subpart C.

obstruction light. A light or one of a group of lights, usually red or white, frequently mounted on a surface structure or natural terrain to warn pilots of the presence of an obstruction.

*occlusion. A type of weather front formed when a cold front overtakes a warm front.

oceanic airspace. Airspace over the oceans of the world, considered international airspace, where oceanic separation and procedures per the International Civil Aviation Organization are applied. Responsibility for the provisions of air traffic control service in this airspace is delegated to various countries, based generally upon geographic proximity and the availability of the required resources.

Oceanic Display And Planning System (ODAPS). An automated digital display system which provides flight data processing, conflict probe, and situation display for oceanic air traffic control.

oceanic navigational error report (ONER). A report filed when an aircraft exiting oceanic airspace has been observed by radar to be off course. ONER reporting parameters and procedures are contained on Order 7110.82, Monitoring of Navigational Performance In Oceanic Areas.

Oceanic Published Route. A route established in international airspace and charted or described in flight information publications, such as route charts, DOD Enroute Charts, chart supplements, NOTAMs and track messages.

oceanic transition route (OTR). An ATS Route established for the purpose of transitioning aircraft to/from an organized track system.

ODAPS. (*See* Oceanic Display and Planning System).

off course. A term used to describe a situation where an aircraft has reported a position fix or is observed on radar at a point not on the ATC approved route of flight.

offshore control airspace area. That portion of airspace between the U.S. 12 NM limit and the oceanic CTA/FIR boundary within which air traffic control is exercised. These areas are established to provide air traffic control services. Offshore/Control Airspace Areas may be classified as either Class A airspace or Class E airspace.

off route vector. A vector by ATC which takes an aircraft off a previously assigned route. Altitudes assigned by ATC during such vectors provide required obstacle clearance.

offset parallel runways. Staggered runways having centerlines which are parallel.

OFT. (*See* outer fix time).

OFZ. (*See* obstacle free zone).

OM. (*See* outer marker).

Omega. An RNAV system designed for long range navigation based upon ground based electronic navigational aid signals.

*omnidirectional. Visible or usable in all directions.

one-minute weather. The most recent one minute updated weather broadcast received by a pilot from an uncontrolled airport ASOS/AWOS.

ONER. (*See* oceanic navigational error report).

operational. (*See* due regard).

on course.

1. Used to indicate that an aircraft is established on the route centerline.
2. Used by ATC to advise a pilot making a radar approach that his aircraft is lined up on the final approach course.

   (*See* on course indication).

on course indication. An indication on an instrument, which provides the pilot a visual means of determining that the aircraft is located on the centerline of a given navigational track, or an indication on a radar scope that an aircraft is on a given track.

opposite direction aircraft. Aircraft are operating in opposite directions when:

1. They are following the same track in reciprocal directions; or
2. Their tracks are parallel and the aircraft are flying in reciprocal directions; or
3. Their tracks intersect at an angle of more than 135 degrees.

option approach. An approach requested and conducted by a pilot which will result in either a touch and go, missed approach, low approach, stop and go, or full stop landing. (*See* cleared for the option) (Refer to AIM).

organized track system (OTS). A moveable system of oceanic tracks that traverses the North Atlantic between Europe and North America the physical position of which is determined twice daily taking the best advantage of the winds aloft. *Also:* A series of ATS routes which are fixed and charted; i.e., CEP, NOPAC, or flexible and described by NOTAM; i.e., NAT track message.

OROCA. An off-route altitude which provides obstruction clearance with a 1,000-foot buffer in nonmountainous terrain areas and a 2,000 foot buffer in designated mountainous areas within the United States. This altitude may not provide signal coverage from ground-based navigational aids, air traffic control radar, or communications coverage.

***orographic.** Induced by the presence of mountains.

OTR. (*See* oceanic transition route).

OTS. (*See* organized track system).

out. The conversation is ended and no response is expected.

outer area (associated with Class C airspace). Non-regulatory airspace surrounding designated Class C airspace airports wherein ATC provides radar vectoring and sequencing on a full-time basis for all IFR and participating VFR aircraft. The service provided in the outer area is called Class C service which includes: IFR/IFR. standard IFR separation; IFR/VFR. traffic advisories and conflict resolution; and VFR/VFR. traffic advisories and, as appropriate, safety alerts. The normal radius will be 20 nautical miles with some variations based on site specific requirements. The outer area extends outward from the primary Class C airspace airport and extends from the lower limits of radar/radio coverage up to the ceiling of the approach control's delegated airspace excluding the Class C charted area and other airspace as appropriate. (*See* controlled airspace, conflict resolution).

outer compass locator. (*See* compass locator).

outer fix. A general term used within ATC to describe fixes in the terminal area, other than the final approach fix. Aircraft are normally cleared to these fixes by an Air Route Traffic Control Center or an Approach Control Facility. Aircraft are normally cleared from these fixes to the final approach fix or final approach course. *Also:* An adapted fix along the converted route of flight, prior to the meter fix, for which crossing times are calculated and displayed in the metering position list.

outer fix time (OFT). A calculated time to depart the outer fix in order to cross the vertex at the ACLT. The time reflects descent speed adjustments and any applicable delay time that must be absorbed prior to crossing the meter fix.

outer marker (OM). A marker beacon at or near the glideslope intercept altitude of an ILS approach. It is keyed to transmit two dashes per second on a 400 Hz tone, which is received aurally and visually by compatible airborne equipment. The OM is normally located four to seven miles from the runway threshold on the extended centerline of the runway. (*See* marker beacon, instrument landing system) (Refer to AIM).

over. My transmission is ended; I expect a response.

overhead maneuver. A series of predetermined maneuvers prescribed for aircraft (often in formation) for entry into the visual flight rules (VFR) traffic pattern and to proceed to a landing. An overhead maneuver is not an instrument flight rules (IFR) approach procedure. An aircraft executing an overhead maneuver is considered VFR and the IFR flight plan is canceled when the aircraft reaches the "initial point" on the initial approach portion of the maneuver. The pattern usually specifies the following:

1. The radio contact required of the pilot.
2. The speed to be maintained.
3. An initial approach 3 to 5 miles in length.
4. An elliptical pattern consisting of two 180 degree turns.
5. A break point at which the first 180 degree turn is started.
6. The direction of turns.
7. Altitude (at least 500 feet above the conventional pattern).
8. A "Roll-out" on final approach not less than 1/4 mile from the landing threshold and not less than 300 feet above the ground.

overlying center. The ARTCC facility that is responsible for arrival/departure operations at a specific terminal.

***overrun.** A stabilized area of pavement not used for normal operations at the end of a runway.

***P-factor.** A force which causes a left-turning tendency at low speed and high power in airplanes with propellers that turn clockwise.

P time. (*See* proposed departure time).

pan-pan. The international radio telephony urgency signal. When repeated three times, indicates uncertainty or alert followed by the nature of the urgency. (*See* mayday) (Refer to AIM).

PAR. (*See* precision approach radar).

parallel ILS approaches. Approaches to parallel runways by IFR aircraft which, when established inbound toward the airport on the adjacent final approach courses, are radar separated by at least 2 miles. (*See* final approach course, simultaneous ILS approaches).

parallel MLS approaches. (*See* parallel ILS approaches).

parallel offset route. A parallel track to the left or right of the designated or established airway/route. Normally associated with Area Navigation (RNAV) operations. (*See* area navigation).

parallel runways. Two or more runways at the same airport whose centerlines are parallel. In addition to runway number, parallel runways are designated as L (left) and R (right) or, if three parallel runways exist, L (left), C (center), or R (right).

parallels. Lines of latitude, which are parallel from the equator to the poles.

parasite drag. Drag that does not contribute to lift generation; drag caused by landing gear struts, cooling intakes, antennas, rivet heads, etc.

PATWAS. (*See* Pilots Automatic Telephone Weather Answering Service).

PBCT. (*See* proposed boundary crossing time).

permanent echo. Radar signals reflected from fixed objects on the earth's surface; e.g., buildings, towers, terrain. Permanent echoes are distinguished from "ground clutter" by being definable locations rather than large areas. Under certain conditions they may be used to check radar alignment.

photo reconnaissance (PR). Military activity that requires locating individual photo targets and navigating to the targets at a preplanned angle and altitude. The activity normally requires a lateral route width of 16 NM and altitude range of 1,500 feet to 10,000 feet AGL.

PIDP. (*See* programmable indicator data processor).

pilotage. Navigation from point to point by ground reference.

pilot briefing. A service provided by the FSS to assist pilots in flight planning. Briefing items may include weather information, NOTAMs, military activities, flow control information, and other items as requested. (Refer to AIM).

pilot in command. The pilot responsible for the operation and safety of an aircraft during flight time. (Refer to 14 CFR Part 91).

Pilots Automatic Telephone Weather Answering Service (PATWAS). A continuous telephone recording containing current and forecast weather information for the pilots. (*See* Flight Service Station) (Refer to AIM).

pilot's discretion. When used in conjunction with altitude assignments, means that ATC has offered the pilot the option of starting climb or descent whenever he wishes and conducting the climb or descent at any rate he wishes. He may temporarily level off at any intermediate altitude. However, once he has vacated an altitude, he may not return to that altitude.

pilot weather report (PIREP). A report of meteorological phenomena encountered by aircraft in flight. (Refer to AIM).

PIREP. (*See* pilot weather report).

PIREPs. Pilot reports of inflight weather.

pitch axis. An imaginary line drawn from wing tip to wing tip; also called lateral axis.

pitot-static system. A pressure-measuring system that provides input to the airspeed indicator, altimeter, and vertical speed indicator.

pitot tube. A forward-facing tube or aperture that measures ram air pressure, then delivers that pressure to the airspeed indicator.

point out. (*See* radar point out).

polar track structure (PTS). A system of organized routes between Iceland and Alaska which overlie Canadian MNPS Airspace.

position lights. The red, green, and white lights required for night flight.

position report. A report over a known location as transmitted by an aircraft to ATC. (Refer to AIM).

position symbol. A computer generated indication shown on a radar display to indicate the mode of tracking.

practice instrument approach. An instrument approach procedure conducted by a VFR or an IFR aircraft for the purpose of pilot training or proficiency demonstrations.

prearranged coordination. A standardized procedure which permits an air traffic controller to enter the airspace assigned to another air traffic controller without verbal coordination. The procedures are defined in a facility directive which ensures standard separation between aircraft.

precipitation. Any or all forms of water particles (rain, sleet, hail, or snow) that fall from the atmosphere and reach the surface.

precision approach. (*See* precision approach procedure).

precision approach procedure. A standard instrument approach procedure in which an electronic glide slope/glide path is provided; e.g., ILS/MLS and PAR. (*See* instrument landing system, Microwave Landing System, precision approach radar).

precision approach radar (PAR). Radar equipment in some ATC facilities operated by the FAA and/or the military services at joint use civil/military locations and separate military installations to detect and display azimuth, elevations, and range of aircraft on the final approach course to a runway. This equipment may be used to monitor certain nonradar approaches, but is primarily used to conduct a precision instrument approach (PAR) wherein the controller issues guidance instructions to the pilot based on the aircraft's position in relation to the final approach course (azimuth), the glide path (elevation), and the distance (range) from the touchdown point on the runway as displayed on the radar scope. (*See* glide path, PAR) (Refer to AIM).

The abbreviation "PAR" is also used to denote preferential arrival routes in ARTCC computers. (*See* preferential routes). [ICAO] Primary radar equipment used to determine the position of an aircraft during final approach, in terms of lateral and vertical deviations relative to a nominal approach path, and in range relative to touchdown. *Note:* Precision approach radars are designed to enable pilots of aircraft to be given guidance by radio communications during the final stages of the approach to land.

precision runway monitor (PRM). Provides air traffic controllers with high precision secondary surveillance data for aircraft on final approach to parallel runways that have centerlines separated by less than 4,300 feet. High resolution color monitoring displays (FMA) are required to present surveillance track data to controllers along with detailed maps depicting approaches and no transgression zone.

preferential routes. Preferential routes (PDRs, PARs, and PDARs) are adapted in ARTCC computers to accomplish inter/intrafacility controller coordination and to assure that flight data is posted at the proper control positions. Locations having a need for these specific inbound and out bound routes normally publish such routes in local facility bulletins, and their use by pilots minimizes flight plan route amendments. When the workload or traffic situation permits, controllers normally provide radar vectors or assign requested routes to minimize circuitous routing. Preferential routes are usually confined to one ARTCC's area and are referred to by the following names or acronyms:

1. *Preferential departure route (PDR).* A specific departure route from an airport or terminal area to an enroute point where there is no further need for flow control. It may be included in a standard instrument departure (DP) or preferred IFR route.
2. *Preferential arrival route (PAR).* A specific arrival route from an appropriate enroute point to an airport or terminal area. It may be included in a standard terminal arrival (STAR) or preferred IFR route. The abbreviation "PAR" is used primarily within the ARTCC and should not be confused with the abbreviation for Precision Approach Radar.
3. *Preferential departure and arrival route (PDAR).* A route between two terminals which are within or immediately adjacent to one ARTCC's area. PDARs are not synonymous with preferred IFR routes but may be listed as such as they do accomplish essentially the same purpose. (*See* preferred IFR routes, NAS Stage A).

preferred IFR routes. Routes established between busier airports to increase system efficiency and capacity. They normally extend through one or more ARTCC areas and are designed to achieve balanced traffic flows among high density terminals. IFR clearances are issued on the basis of these routes except when severe weather avoidance procedures or other factors dictate otherwise. Preferred IFR routes are listed in the Airport/Facility Directory. If a flight is planned to or from an area having such routes but the departure or arrival point is not listed in the Airport/Facility Directory, pilots may use that part of a preferred IFR route which is appropriate for the departure or arrival point that is listed. Preferred IFR routes are correlated with DPs and STARs and may be defined by airways, jet routes, direct routes between NAVAIDs, waypoints, NAVAID radials/DME, or any combinations thereof. (*See* instrument departure procedure, standard terminal arrival, preferential routes, Center's area) (Refer to Airport/Facility Directory and Notices to Airmen Publication).

preflight pilot briefing. (*See* pilot briefing).

prevailing visibility. (*See* visibility).

PRM. (*See* ILS PRM approach and precision runway monitor).

procedure turn (PT). The maneuver prescribed when it is necessary to reverse direction to establish an aircraft on the intermediate approach segment or final approach course. The outbound course, direction of turn, distance within which the turn must be completed, and minimum altitude are specified in the procedure. However, unless otherwise restricted, the point at which the turn may be commenced and the type and rate of turn are left to the discretion of the pilot. [ICAO] A maneuver in which a turn is made away from a designated track followed by a turn in the opposite direction to permit the aircraft to intercept and proceed along the reciprocal of the designated track. *Note 1:* Procedure turns are designated "left" or "right" according to the direction of the initial turn. *Note 2:* Procedure turns may be designated as being made either in level flight or while descending, according to the circumstances of each individual approach procedure.

procedure turn inbound. That point of a procedure turn maneuver where course reversal has been completed and an aircraft is established inbound on the intermediate approach segment or final approach course. A report of "procedure turn inbound" is normally used by ATC as a position report for separation purposes. (*See* final approach course, procedure turn, segments of an instrument approach procedure).

profile descent. An uninterrupted descent (except where level flight is required for speed adjustment; e.g., 250 knots at 10,000 feet MSL) from cruising altitude/level to interception of a glideslope or to a minimum altitude specified for the initial or intermediate approach segment of a nonprecision instrument approach. The profile descent normally terminates at the approach gate or where the glideslope or other appropriate minimum altitude is intercepted.

programmable indicator data processor (PIDP). The PIDP is a modification to the AN/TPX-42 interrogator system currently installed in fixed RAPCONs. The PIDP detects, tracks, and predicts secondary radar aircraft targets. These are displayed by means of computer generated symbols and alphanumeric characters depicting flight identification, aircraft altitude, ground speed, and flight plan data. Although primary radar targets are not tracked, they are displayed coincident with the secondary radar targets as well as with the other symbols and alphanumerics. The system has the capability of interfacing with ARTCCs.

progress report. (*See* position report).

progressive taxi. Precise taxi instructions given to a pilot unfamiliar with the airport or issued in stages as the aircraft proceeds along the taxi route.

Prohibited Area. (*See* Special Use airspace). [ICAO] An airspace of defined dimensions, above the land areas or territorial waters of a State, within which the flight of aircraft is prohibited.

proposed boundary crossing time (PBCT). Each center has a PBCT parameter for each internal airport. Proposed internal flight plans are transmitted to the adjacent center if the flight time along the proposed route from the departure airport to the center boundary is less than or equal to the value of PBCT or if airport adaptation specifies transmission regardless of PBCT.

proposed departure time (P time). The time a scheduled flight will depart the gate (scheduled operators) or the actual runway off time for nonscheduled operators. For EDCT purposes, the ATCSCC adjusts the "P" time for scheduled operators to reflect the runway off times.

protected airspace. The airspace on either side of an oceanic route/track that is equal to one-half the lateral separation minimum except where reduction of protected airspace has been authorized.

PT. (*See* procedure turn).

PTS. (*See* polar track structure).

published route. A route for which an IFR altitude has been established and published; e.g., Federal Airways, Jet Routes, Area Navigation Routes, Specified Direct Routes.

queuing. (*See* staging/queuing).

QNE. The barometric pressure used for the standard altimeter setting (29.92 inches Hg).

QNH. The barometric pressure as reported by a particular station.

quadrant. A quarter part of a circle, centered on a NAVAID, oriented clockwise from magnetic north as follows: NE quadrant 000 to 089, SE quadrant 090 to 179, SW quadrant 180 to 269, NW quadrant 270 to 359.

quick look. A feature of NAS Stage A and ARTS which provides the controller the capability to display full data blocks of tracked aircraft from other control positions.

quota flow control (QFLOW). A flow control procedure by which the Central Flow Control Function (CFCF) restricts traffic to the ARTC Center area having an impacted airport, thereby avoiding sector/area saturation. (*See* Air Traffic Control System Command Center) (Refer to Airport/Facility Directory).

radar. A device which, by measuring the time interval between transmission and reception of radio pulses and correlating the angular orientation of the radiated antenna beam or beams in azimuth and/or elevation, provides information on range, azimuth, and/or elevation of objects in the path of the transmitted pulses.

1. *Primary Radar.* A radar system in which in a minute portion of a radio pulse transmitted from a site is reflected by an object and then received back at that site for processing and display at an air traffic control facility.

2. *Secondary Radar/Radar Beacon (ATCRBS).* A radar system in which the object to be detected is fitted with cooperative equipment in the form of a radio receiver/transmitter (transponder). Radar pulses transmitted from the searching transmitter/receiver (interrogator) site are received in the cooperative equipment and used to trigger a distinctive transmission from the transponder. This reply transmission rather than a reflected signal, is then received back at the transmitter/receiver site for processing and display at an air traffic control facility.

(*See* transponder, interrogator) (Refer to AIM). [ICAO] A radio detection device which provides information on range, azimuth and/or elevation objects.

Primary Radar. [ICAO] A radar system which uses reflected radio signals.

Secondary Radar. [ICAO] A radar system wherein a radio signal transmitted from a radar station initiates the transmission of a radio signal from another station.

radar advisory. The provision of advice and information based on radar observations. (*See* advisory service).

radar altimeter. (*See* radio altimeter).

radar approach. An instrument approach procedure which utilizes Precision Approach Radar (PAR) or Airport Surveillance Radar (ASR). (*See* surveillance approach, airport surveillance radar, precision approach radar, instrument approach procedure) (Refer to AIM). [ICAO] An approach, executed by an aircraft, under the direction of a radar controller.

radar approach control facility. A terminal ATC facility that uses radar and nonradar capabilities to provide approach control services to aircraft arriving, departing, or transiting airspace controlled by the facility. (*See* Approach Control Service).

Provides radar ATC services to aircraft operating in the vicinity of one or more civil and/or military airports in a terminal area. The facility may provide services of a ground controlled approach (GCA); i.e., ASR and PAR approaches. A radar approach control facility may be operated by FAA, USAF, US Army, USN, USMC, or jointly by FAA and a military service. Specific facility nomenclatures are used for administrative purposes only and are related to the physical location of the facility and the operating service generally as follows:

Army Radar Approach Control (ARAC) (Army).
Radar Air Traffic Control Facility (RATCF) (Navy/FAA).
Radar Approach Control (RAPCON) (Air Force/FAA).
Terminal Radar Approach Control (TRACON) (FAA).
Tower/Airport Traffic Control Tower (ATCT) (FAA). (Only those towers delegated approach control authority.).

radar arrival. An aircraft arriving at an airport served by a radar facility and in radar contact with the facility. (*See* nonradar).

radar beacon. (*See* radar).

radar clutter. [ICAO] The visual indication on a radar display of unwanted signals.

radar contact.

1. Used by ATC to inform an aircraft that it is identified on the radar display and radar flight following will be provided until radar identification is terminated. Radar service may also be provided within the limits of necessity and capability. When a pilot is informed of "radar contact," he automatically discontinues reporting over compulsory reporting points. (*See* radar flight following, radar contact lost, radar service, radar service terminated) (Refer to AIM).
2. The term used to inform the controller that the aircraft is identified and approval is granted for the aircraft to enter the receiving controllers airspace.

[ICAO] The situation which exists when the radar blip or radar position symbols of a particular aircraft is seen and identified on a radar display.

Radar contact lost. Used by ATC to inform a pilot that radar data used to determine the aircraft's position is no longer being received, or is no longer reliable and radar service is no longer being provided. The loss may be attributed to several factors including the aircraft merging with weather or ground clutter, the aircraft operating below radar line of sight coverage, the aircraft entering an area of poor radar return, failure of the aircraft transponder, or failure of the ground radar equipment. (*See* clutter, radar contact).

radar environment. An area in which radar service may be provided. (*See* radar contact, radar service, additional services, traffic advisories).

radar flight following. The observation of the progress of radar identified aircraft, whose primary navigation is being provided by the pilot, wherein the controller retains and correlates the aircraft identity with the appropriate target or target symbol, displayed on the radar scope. (*See* radar contact, radar service) (Refer to AIM).

radar identification. The process of ascertaining that an observed radar target is the radar return from a particular aircraft. (*See* radar contact, radar service). [ICAO] The process of correlating a particular radar blip or radar position symbol with a specific aircraft.

radar identified aircraft. An aircraft, the position of which has been correlated with an observed target or symbol on the radar display. (*See* radar contact, radar contact lost).

radar monitoring. (*See* radar service).

radar navigational guidance. (*See* radar service).

radar point out. An action taken by a controller to transfer the radar identification of an aircraft to another controller if the aircraft will or may enter the airspace or protected airspace of another controller and radio communications will not be transferred.

radar required. A term displayed on charts and approach plates and included in FDC NOTAMs to alert pilots that segments of either an instrument approach procedure or a route are not navigable because of either the absence or unusability of a NAVAID. The pilot can expect to be provided radar navigational guidance while transiting segments labeled with this term. (*See* radar route, radar service).

radar route. A flight path or route over which an aircraft is vectored. Navigational guidance and altitude assignments are provided by ATC. (*See* flight path, route).

radar separation. (*See* radar service).

radar service. A term which encompasses one or more of the following services based on the use of radar which can be provided by a controller to a pilot of a radar identified aircraft.

1. *Radar monitoring.* The radar flight following of aircraft, whose primary navigation is being performed by the pilot, to observe and note deviations from its authorized flight path, airway, or route. When being applied specifically to radar monitoring of instrument approaches; i.e., with precision approach radar (PAR) or radar monitoring of simultaneous ILS/MLS approaches, it includes advice and instructions whenever an aircraft nears or exceeds the prescribed PAR safety limit or simultaneous ILS/MLS no transgression zone. (*See* additional services, traffic advisories).
2. *Radar navigational guidance.* Vectoring aircraft to provide course guidance.
3. *Radar separation.* Radar spacing of aircraft in accordance with established minima.

[ICAO] Term used to indicate a service provided directly by means of radar.

Radar monitoring. [ICAO] The use of radar for the purpose of providing aircraft with information and advice relative to significant deviations from nominal flight path.

Radar separation. [ICAO] The separation used when aircraft position information is derived from radar sources.

Radar service terminated. Used by ATC to inform a pilot that he will no longer be provided any of the services that could be received while in radar contact. Radar service is automatically terminated, and the pilot is not advised in the following cases:

1. An aircraft cancels its IFR flight plan, except within Class B airspace, Class C airspace, a TRSA, or where Basic Radar service is provided.

2. An aircraft conducting an instrument, visual, or contact approach has landed or has been instructed to change to advisory frequency.

3. An arriving VFR aircraft, receiving radar service to a tower controlled airport within Class B airspace, Class C airspace, a TRSA, or where sequencing service is provided, has landed; or to all other airports, is instructed to change to tower or advisory frequency.

4. An aircraft completes a radar approach.

radar surveillance. The radar observation of a given geographical area for the purpose of performing some radar function.

radar traffic advisories. Advisories issued to alert pilots to known or observed radar traffic which may affect the intended route of flight of their aircraft. (*See* traffic advisories).

radar traffic information service. (*See* traffic advisories).

radar vectoring. [ICAO] Provision of navigational guidance to aircraft in the form of specific headings, based on the use of radar.

radar weather echo intensity levels. Existing radar systems cannot detect turbulence. However, there is a direct correlation between the degree of turbulence and other weather features associated with thunderstorms and the radar weather echo intensity. The National Weather Service has categorized radar weather echo intensity for precipitation into six levels. These levels are sometimes expressed during communications as "VIP LEVEL" 1 through 6 (derived from the component of the radar that produces the information—Video Integrator and Processor). The following list gives the "VIP LEVELS" in relation to the precipitation intensity within a thunderstorm:

Level 1. WEAK
Level 2. MODERATE
Level 3. STRONG
Level 4. VERY STRONG
Level 5. INTENSE
Level 6. EXTREME

(*See* AC 00-45, *Aviation Weather Services*).

radial. A magnetic bearing extending from a VOR/VOR-TAC/TACAN navigation facility.

***radial.** A line FROM a VOR station. Radials used as airways are printed in blue on sectional charts.

radio.
1. A device used for communication.
2. Used to refer to a Flight Service Station; e.g., "Seattle Radio" is used to call Seattle FSS.

radio altimeter. Aircraft equipment which makes use of the reflection of radio waves from the ground to determine the height of the aircraft above the surface.

radio beacon. (*See* nondirectional beacon).

radio detection and ranging. (*See* radar).

radio magnetic indicator (RMI). An aircraft navigational instrument coupled with a gyro compass or similar compass that indicates the direction of a selected NAVAID and indicates bearing with respect to the heading of the aircraft.

ramp. (*See* apron).

random altitude. An altitude inappropriate for direction of flight and/or not in accordance with FAA Order 7110.65, paragraph 4-5-1.

random route. Any route not established or charted/published or not otherwise available to all users.

RC. (*See* road reconnaissance).

RCAG. (*See* remote communication air/ground facility).

RCC. (*See* Rescue Coordination Center).

RCO. (*See* Remote Communications Outlet).

RCR. (*See* runway condition reading).

***read back.** Repeat my message back to me.

receiver autonomous integrity monitoring (RAIM). A technique whereby a civil GNSS receiver/processor determines the integrity of the GNSS navigation signals without reference to sensors or non-DoD integrity systems other than the receiver itself. This determination is achieved by a consistency check among redundant pseudorange measurements.

receiving controller. A controller/facility receiving control of an aircraft from another controller/facility.

receiving facility. (*See* receiving controller).

***Reduce speed to (speed).** (*See* speed adjustment).

***region of reversed command.** That area in the power/airspeed relationship where it takes more power to go more slowly, and less power to increase speed.

REIL (Runway End Identifier Lights). (*See* airport lighting).

***relative bearing.** The direction to a transmitting station measured clockwise from the nose of the airplane.

***relative wind.** Wind caused by motion. A moving body experiences relative wind in calm air.

release time. A departure time restriction issued to a pilot by ATC (either directly or through an authorized relay) when necessary to separate a departing aircraft from other traffic. [ICAO] Time prior to which an aircraft should be given further clearance or prior to which it should not proceed in case of radio failure.

remote communications air/ground facility (RCAG). An unmanned VHF/UHF transmitter/receiver facility which is used to expand ARTCC air/ground communications coverage and to facilitate direct contact between pilots and controllers. RCAG facilities are sometimes not equipped with emergency frequencies 121.5 MHz and 243.0 MHz. (Refer to AIM).

Remote Communications Outlet (RCO). An unmanned communications facility remotely controlled by air traffic personnel. RCOs serve FSS's. RTRs serve terminal ATC facilities. An RCO or RTR may be UHF or VHF and will extend the communication range of the air traffic facility. There are several classes of RCOs and RTRs. The class is determined by the number of transmitters or receivers. Class A through G are used primarily for air/ground purposes. RCO and RTR class O facilities are nonprotected outlets subject to undetected and prolonged outages. RCO (O's) and RTR (O's) where established for the express purpose of providing ground to ground communications between air traffic control specialists and pilots located at a satellite airport for delivering enroute clearances, issuing departure authorizations, and acknowledging instrument flight rules cancellations or departure/landing times. As a secondary function, they may be used for advisory purposes whenever the aircraft is below the coverage of the primary air/ground frequency.

remote transmitter/receiver (RTR). (*See* Remote Communications Outlet).

report. Used to instruct pilots to advise ATC of specified information; e.g., "Report passing Hamilton VOR."

reporting point. A geographical location in relation to which the position of an aircraft is reported. (*See* compulsory reporting points) (Refer to AIM). [ICAO] A specified geographical location in relation to which the position of an aircraft can be reported.

Request full route clearance. Used by pilots to request that the entire route of flight be read verbatim in an ATC clearance. Such request should be made to preclude receiving an ATC clearance based on the original filed flight plan when a filed IFR flight plan has been revised by the pilot, company, or operations prior to departure.

required navigation performance (RNP). A statement of the navigational performance necessary for operation within a defined airspace. The following terms are commonly associated with RNP:

1. *Required Navigation Performance Level or Type (RNP-X).* A value, in nautical miles (NM), from the intended horizontal position within which an aircraft would be at least 95 percent of the total flying time.

2. *Required Navigation Performance (RNP) Airspace.* A generic term designating airspace, route(s), leg(s), operation(s), or procedure(s) where minimum required navigational performance (RNP) have been established.

3. *Actual Navigation Performance (ANP).* A measure of the current estimated navigational performance. Also referred to as Estimated Position Error (EPE).

4. *Estimated Position Error (EPE).* A measure of the current estimated navigational performance. Also referred to as Actual Navigation Performance (ANP).

5. *Lateral Navigation (LNAV).* A function of area navigation (RNAV) equipment which calculates, displays, and provides lateral guidance to a profile or path.

6. *Vertical Navigation (VNAV).* A function of area navigation (RNAV) equipment which calculates, displays, and provides vertical guidance to a profile or path.

Rescue Coordination Center (RCC). A Search and Rescue (SAR) facility equipped and manned to coordinate and control SAR operations in an area designated by the SAR plan. The U.S. Coast Guard and the U.S. Air Force have responsibility for the operation of RCCs. (*See* Rescue Coordination Centre [ICAO]).

Rescue Coordination Centre. [ICAO] A unit responsible for promoting efficient organization of search and rescue service and for coordinating the conduct of search and rescue operations within a search and rescue region.

resolution advisory. A display indication given to the pilot by the Traffic Alert And Collision Avoidance Systems (TCAS II) recommending a maneuver to increase vertical separation relative to an intruding aircraft. Positive, negative, and vertical speed limit (VSL) advisories constitute the resolution advisories. A resolution advisory is also classified as corrective or preventive.

Restricted Area. (*See* Special Use airspace). [ICAO] An airspace of defined dimensions, above the land areas or territorial waters of a State, within which the flight of aircraft is restricted in accordance with certain specified conditions.

Resume own navigation. Used by ATC to advise a pilot to resume his own navigational responsibility. It is issued after completion of a radar vector or when radar contact is lost while the aircraft is being radar vectored. (*See* radar contact lost, radar service terminated).

Resume normal speed. Used by ATC to advise that previously issued speed control restrictions are deleted. An instruction to "resume normal speed" does not delete speed restrictions that are applicable to published procedures of upcoming segments of flight, unless specifically stated by ATC. This does not relieve the pilot of those speed restrictions which are applicable to 14 CFR §91.117.

***rich mixture.** A fuel mixture with more than one part of fuel to fifteen of air.

RMI. (*See* radio magnetic indicator).

***RMI.** Radio magnetic indicator—a combination heading indicator, VOR indicator and ADF indicator.

RNAV. (*See* area navigation).

***RNAV.** Area navigation. A random-route method of navigation using VORTACs and VOR-DMEs.

RNAV approach. An instrument approach procedure which relies on aircraft area navigation equipment for navigational guidance. (*See* instrument approach procedure, area navigation).

road reconnaissance (RC). Military activity requiring navigation along roads, railroads, and rivers. Reconnaissance route/route segments are seldom along a straight line and normally require a lateral route width of 10 NM to 30 NM and an altitude range of 500 feet to 10,000 feet AGL.

roger. I have received all of your last transmission. It should not be used to answer a question requiring a yes or a no answer. (*See* affirmative, negative).

*roll axis. An imaginary line from nose to tail, also called longitudinal axis.

rollout RVR. (*See* visibility).

route. A defined path, consisting of one or more courses in a horizontal plane, which aircraft traverse over the surface of the earth. (*See* airway, jet route, published route, unpublished route).

route segment. As used in Air Traffic Control, a part of a route that can be defined by two navigational fixes, two NAVAIDs or a fix and a NAVAID. (*See* fix, route). [ICAO] A portion of a route to be flown, as defined by two consecutive significant points specified in a flight plan.

RSA. (*See* runway safety area).

RTR. (*See* remote transmitter/receiver).

*rudder. A hinged surface at the rear of the vertical fin with which the pilot controls the airplane around the yaw axis.

runway. A defined rectangular area on a land airport prepared for the landing and takeoff run of aircraft along its length. Runways are normally numbered in relation to their magnetic direction rounded off to the nearest 10 degrees; e.g., Runway 01, Runway 25. (*See* parallel runways). [ICAO] A defined rectangular area on a land aerodrome prepared for the landing and takeoff of aircraft.

runway centerline lighting. (*See* airport lighting).

runway condition reading (RCR). Numerical decelerometer readings relayed by air traffic controllers at USAF and certain civil bases for use by the pilot in determining runway braking action. These readings are routinely relayed only to USAF and Air National Guard Aircraft. (*See* braking action).

Runway End Identifier Lights (REIL). (*See* airport lighting).

runway gradient. The average slope, measured in percent, between two ends or points on a runway. Runway gradient is depicted on government aerodrome sketches when total runway gradient exceeds 0.3%.

runway heading. The magnetic direction that corresponds with the runway centerline extended, not the painted runway number. When cleared to "fly or maintain runway heading," pilots are expected to fly or maintain the heading that corresponds with the extended centerline of the departure runway. Drift correction shall not be applied; e.g., Runway 4, actual magnetic heading of the runway centerline 044, fly 044.

runway in use/active runway/duty runway. Any runway or runways currently being used for takeoff or landing. When multiple runways are used, they are all considered active runways. In the metering sense, a selectable adapted item which specifies the landing runway configuration or direction of traffic flow. The adapted optimum flight plan from each transition fix to the vertex is determined by the runway configuration for arrival metering processing purposes.

runway lights. (*See* airport lighting).

runway markings. (*See* airport marking aids).

runway overrun. In military aviation exclusively, a stabilized or paved area beyond the end of a runway, of the same width as the runway plus shoulders, centered on the extended runway centerline.

runway profile descent. An instrument flight rules (IFR) air traffic control arrival procedure to a runway published for pilot use in graphic and/or textual form and may be associated with a STAR. Runway profile descents provide routing and may depict crossing altitudes, speed restrictions, and headings to be flown from the enroute structure to the point where the pilot will receive clearance for and execute an instrument approach procedure. A runway profile descent may apply to more than one runway if so stated on the chart. (Refer to AIM).

runway safety area (RSA). A defined surface surrounding the runway prepared, or suitable, for reducing the risk of damage to airplanes in the event of an undershoot, overshoot, or excursion from the runway. The dimensions of the RSA vary and can be determined by using the criteria contained within Advisory Circular 150/5300-13, Chapter 3. Figure 3-1 in Advisory Circular 150/5300-13 depicts the RSA. The design standards dictate that the RSA shall be:

1. Cleared, graded, and have no potentially hazardous ruts, humps, depressions, or other surface variations;

2. Drained by grading or storm sewers to prevent water accumulation;

3. Capable, under dry conditions, of supporting snow removal equipment, aircraft rescue and firefighting equipment, and the occasional passage of aircraft without causing structural damage to the aircraft; and,

4. Free of objects, except for objects that need to be located in the runway safety area because of their function. These objects shall be constructed on low impact resistant supports (frangible mounted structures) to the lowest practical height with the frangible point to higher than 3 inches above grade.

(Refer to AC 150/5300-13, Chapter 3.).

Runway Use Program. A noise abatement runway selection plan designed to enhance noise abatement efforts with regard to airport communities for arriving and departing aircraft. These plans are developed into runway use programs and apply to all turbojet aircraft 12,500 pounds or heavier; turbojet aircraft less than 12,500 pounds are included only if the airport proprietor determines that the aircraft creates a noise problem. Runway use programs are coordinated with FAA offices, and safety criteria used in these programs are developed by the Office of Flight Operations. Runway use programs are administered by the Air Traffic Service as "Formal" or "Informal" programs.

1. *Formal Runway Use Program.* An approved noise abatement program which is defined and acknowledged in a Letter of Understanding between Flight Operations, Air Traffic Service, the airport proprietor, and the users. Once

Continued

established, participation in the program is mandatory for aircraft operators and pilots as provided for in FAR 91.87.

2. *Informal Runway Use Program.* An approved noise abatement program which does not require a Letter of Understanding, and participation in the program is voluntary for aircraft operators/pilots.

runway visibility value. (*See* visibility).

runway visual range. (*See* visibility).

SAA. (*See* special activity airspace).

safety alert. A safety alert issued by ATC to aircraft under their control if ATC is aware the aircraft is at an altitude which, in the controller's judgment, places the aircraft in unsafe proximity to terrain, obstructions, or other aircraft. The controller may discontinue the issuance of further alerts if the pilot advises he is taking action to correct the situation or has the other aircraft in sight.

1. *Terrain/Obstruction Alert.* A safety alert issued by ATC to aircraft under their control if ATC is aware the aircraft is at an altitude which, in the controller's judgment, places the aircraft in unsafe proximity to terrain/obstructions, e.g., "Low Altitude Alert, check your altitude immediately."

2. *Aircraft Conflict Alert.* A safety alert is issued by ATC to aircraft under their control if ATC is aware of an aircraft that is not under their control at an altitude which, in the controller's judgment, places both aircraft in unsafe proximity to each other. With the alert, ATC will offer the pilot an alternate course of action when feasible; e.g., "Traffic Alert, advise you turn right heading zero niner zero or climb to eight thousand immediately."

The issuance of a safety alert is contingent upon the capability of the controller to have an awareness of an unsafe condition. The course of action provided will be predicated on other traffic under ATC control. Once the alert is issued, it is solely the pilot's prerogative to determine what course of action, if any, he will take.

sail back. A maneuver during high wind conditions (usually with power off) where float plane movement is controlled by water rudders or opening and closing cabin doors.

same direction aircraft. Aircraft are operating in the same direction when:

1. They are following the same track in the same direction; or

2. Their tracks are parallel and the aircraft are flying in the same direction; or

3. Their tracks intersect at an angle of less than 45 degrees.

SAR. (*See* search and rescue).

Say again. Used to request a repeat of the last transmission. Usually specifies transmission or portion thereof not understood or received; e.g., "Say again all after ABRAM VOR."

Say altitude. Used by ATC to ascertain an aircraft's specific altitude/flight level. When the aircraft is climbing or descending, the pilot should state the indicated altitude rounded to the nearest 100 feet.

Say heading. Used by ATC to request an aircraft heading. The pilot should state the actual heading of the aircraft.

SDF. (*See* simplified directional facility).

sea lane. A designated portion of water outlined by visual surface markers for and intended to be used by aircraft designed to operate on water.

Search and Rescue (SAR). A service which seeks missing aircraft and assists those found to be in need of assistance. It is a cooperative effort using the facilities and services of available Federal, state and local agencies. The U.S. Coast Guard is responsible for coordination of search and rescue for the Maritime Region, and the U.S. Air Force is responsible for search and rescue for the Inland Region. Information pertinent to search and rescue should be passed through any air traffic facility or be transmitted directly to the Rescue Coordination Center by telephone. (*See* Flight Service Station, Rescue Coordination Center) (Refer to AIM).

Search and Rescue Facility. A facility responsible for maintaining and operating a search and rescue (SAR) service to render aid to persons and property in distress. It is any SAR unit, station, NET, or other operational activity which can be usefully employed during an SAR Mission; e.g., a Civil Air Patrol Wing, or a Coast Guard Station. (*See* Search and Rescue).

sectional aeronautical charts. (*See* aeronautical chart).

sector list drop interval (SLDI). A parameter number of minutes after the meter fix time when arrival aircraft will be deleted from the arrival sector list.

see and avoid. When weather conditions permit, pilots operating IFR or VFR are required to observe and maneuver to avoid other aircraft. Right-of-way rules are contained in 14 CFR Part 91. *Also:* A visual procedure where in pilots of aircraft flying in visual meteorological conditions (VMC), regardless of type of flight plan, are charged with the responsibility to observe the presence of other aircraft and to maneuver their aircraft as required to avoid the other aircraft. Right of way rules are contained in Part 91. (*See* instrument flight rules, visual flight rules, visual meteorological conditions, instrument meteorological conditions).

segmented circle. A system of visual indicators designed to provide traffic pattern information at airports without operating control towers. (Refer to AIM).

segments of an instrument approach procedure. An instrument approach procedure may have as many as four separate segments depending on how the approach procedure is structured.

1. *Initial approach.* The segment between the initial approach fix and the intermediate fix or the point where the aircraft is established on the intermediate course or final approach course. (*See* initial approach segment [ICAO]).

2. *Intermediate approach.* The segment between the intermediate fix or point and the final approach fix. (*See* intermediate approach segment [ICAO]).

3. *Final approach.* The segment between the final approach fix or point and the runway, airport, or missed approach point. (*See* final approach segment [ICAO]).

4. *Missed approach.* The segment between the missed approach point or the point of arrival at decision height and the missed approach fix at the prescribed altitude. (Refer to 14 CFR Part 97) (*See* missed approach procedure [ICAO]).

selected ground delays. A traffic management procedure whereby selected flights are issued ground delays to better regulate traffic flows over a particular fix or area.

separation. In air traffic control, the spacing of aircraft to achieve their safe and orderly movement in flight and while landing and taking off. (*See* separation minima). [ICAO] Spacing between aircraft, levels or tracks.

separation minima. The minimum longitudinal, lateral, or vertical distances by which aircraft are spaced through the application of air traffic control procedures. (*See* separation).

service. A generic term that designates functions or assistance available from or rendered by air traffic control. For example, Class C service would denote the ATC services provided within a Class C airspace area.

severe weather avoidance plan (SWAP). An approved plan to minimize the affect of severe weather on traffic flows in impacted terminal and/or ARTCC areas. SWAP is normally implemented to provide the least disruption to the ATC system when flight through portions of airspace is difficult or impossible due to severe weather.

severe weather forecast alerts (AWW). Preliminary messages issued in order to alert users that a Severe Weather Watch Bulletin (WW) is being issued. These messages define areas of possible severe thunderstorms or tornado activity. The messages are unscheduled and issued as required by the National Severe Storm Forecast Center at Kansas City, Missouri. (*See* SIGMET, Convective SIGMET, CWA, AIRMET).

SFA. (*See* single frequency approach).

SFO. (*See* simulated flame out).

SHF. (*See* super high frequency).

short range clearance. A clearance issued to a departing IFR flight which authorizes IFR flight to a specific fix short of the destination while air traffic control facilities are coordinating and obtaining the complete clearance.

short takeoff and landing aircraft (STOL). An aircraft which, at some weight within its approved operating weight, is capable of operating from a STOL runway in compliance with the applicable STOL characteristics, airworthiness, operations, noise, and pollution standards. (*See* Vertical Takeoff and Landing Aircraft).

SIAP (standard instrument approach procedure). (*See* instrument approach procedure).

sidestep maneuver. A visual maneuver accomplished by a pilot at the completion of an instrument approach to permit a straight-in landing on a parallel runway not more than 1,200 feet to either side of the runway to which the instrument approach was conducted. (Refer to AIM).

SIGMET. A weather advisory issued concerning weather significant to the safety of all aircraft. SIGMET advisories cover severe and extreme turbulence, severe icing, and widespread dust or sandstorms that reduce visibility to less than 3 miles. (*See* AWW, Convective SIGMET, CWA, and AIRMET) (Refer to AIM) (*See* SIGMET information [ICAO]).

SIGMET information. [ICAO] Information issued by a meteorological watch office concerning the occurrence or expected occurrence of specified enroute weather phenomena which may affect the safety of aircraft operations.

significant meteorological information. (*See* SIGMET).

significant point. A point, whether a named intersection, a NAVAID, a fix derived from a NAVAID(s), or geographical coordinate expressed in degrees of latitude and longitude, which is established for the purpose of providing separation, as a reporting point, or to delineate a route of flight.

*simplexing. Communication where one person must complete a transmission before the other person can begin; transmitting and receiving on the same frequency.

simplified directional facility (SDF). A NAVAID used for nonprecision instrument approaches. The final approach course is similar to that of an ILS localizer except that the SDF course may be offset from the runway, generally not more than 3 degrees, and the course may be wider than the localizer, resulting in a lower degree of accuracy. (Refer to AIM).

simulated flameout. A practice approach by a jet aircraft (normally military) at idle thrust to a runway. The approach may start at a runway (high key) and may continue on a relatively high and wide down wind leg with a continuous turn to final. It terminates in landing or low approach. The purpose of this approach is to simulate a flameout. (*See* flameout).

simultaneous ILS approaches. An approach system permitting simultaneous ILS/MLS approaches to airports having parallel runways separated by at least 4,300 feet between centerlines. Integral parts of a total system are ILS/MLS, radar, communications. ATC procedures, and appropriate airborne equipment. (*See* parallel runways) (Refer to AIM).

simultaneous MLS approaches. (*See* simultaneous ILS approaches).

simultaneous operations on intersecting runways. Operations which include simultaneous takeoffs and landings and/or simultaneous landings when a landing aircraft is able and is instructed by the controller to hold short of the intersecting runway or designated hold short point. Pilots are expected to promptly inform the controller if the hold short clearance cannot be accepted. (*See* parallel runways) (Refer to AIM).

single direction routes. Preferred IFR Routes which are sometimes depicted on high altitude enroute charts and which are normally flown in one direction only. (*See* preferred IFR routes) (Refer to Airport/Facility Directory).

single frequency approach (SFA). A service provided under a letter of agreement to military single piloted turbojet aircraft which permits use of a single UHF frequency during approach for landing. Pilots will not normally be required to change frequency from the beginning of the approach to touchdown except that pilots conducting an enroute descent are required to change frequency when control is transferred from the air route traffic control center to the terminal facility. The abbreviation "SFA" in the DOD FLIP IFR Supplement under "Communications" indicates this service is available at an aerodrome.

single piloted aircraft. A military turbojet aircraft possessing one set of flight controls, tandem cockpits, or two sets of flight controls but operated by one pilot is considered single piloted by ATC when determining the appropriate air traffic service to be applied. (*See* single frequency approach).

slash. A radar beacon reply displayed as an elongated target.

SLDI. (*See* sector list drop interval).

slot time. (*See* meter fix time/slot time).

slow taxi. To taxi a float plane at low power or low RPM.

SN. (*See* system strategic navigation).

Speak slower. Used in verbal communications as a request to reduce speech rate.

special activity airspace (SAA). Any airspace with defined dimensions within the National Airspace System wherein limitations may be imposed upon aircraft operations. This airspace may be restricted areas, prohibited areas, military operations areas, air ATC assigned airspace, and any other designated airspace areas. The dimensions of this airspace are programmed into URET CCLD and can be designated as either active or inactive by screen entry. Aircraft trajectories are constantly tested against the dimensions of active areas and alerts issued to the applicable sectors when violations are predicted.

special emergency. A condition of air piracy or other hostile act by a person(s) aboard an aircraft which threatens the safety of the aircraft or its passengers.

special instrument approach procedure. (*See* instrument approach procedure).

Special Use airspace. Airspace of defined dimensions identified by an area on the surface of the earth wherein activities must be confined because of their nature and/or wherein limitations may be imposed upon aircraft operations that are not a part of those activities. Types of Special Use airspace are:

1. *Alert Area.* Airspace which may contain a high volume of pilot training activities or an unusual type of aerial activity, neither of which is hazardous to aircraft. Alert Areas are depicted on aeronautical charts for the information of nonparticipating pilots. All activities within an Alert Area are conducted in accordance with Federal Aviation

Regulations, and pilots of participating aircraft as well as pilots transiting the area are equally responsible for collision avoidance.

2. *Controlled Firing Area.* Airspace wherein activities are conducted under conditions so controlled as to eliminate hazards to nonparticipating aircraft and to ensure the safety of persons and property on the ground.

3. *Military Operations Area (MOA).* An MOA is airspace established outside of Class A airspace area to separate or segregate certain nonhazardous military activities from IFR traffic and to identify for VFR traffic where these activities are conducted. (Refer to AIM).

4. *Prohibited Area.* Airspace designated under 14 CFR Part 73 within which no person may operate an aircraft without the permission of the using agency. (Refer to enroute charts, AIM).

5. *Restricted Area.* Airspace designated under 14 CFR Part 73, within which the flight of aircraft, while not wholly prohibited, is subject to restriction. Most restricted areas are designated joint use and IFR/VFR operations in the area may be authorized by the controlling ATC facility when it is not being utilized by the using agency. Restricted areas are depicted on enroute charts. Where joint use is authorized, the name of the ATC controlling facility is also shown. (Refer to 14 CFR Part 73 and AIM).

6. *Warning Area.* A warning area is airspace of defined dimensions extending from 3 nautical miles outward from the coast of the United States, that contains activity that may be hazardous to nonparticipating aircraft. The purpose of such warning area is to warn nonparticipating pilots of the potential danger. A warning area may be located over domestic or international waters or both.

Special VFR conditions. Meteorological conditions that are less than those required for basic VFR flight in Class B, C, D, or E surface areas and in which some aircraft are permitted flight under visual flight rules. (*See* Special VFR operations) (Refer to 14 CFR Part 91).

Special VFR flight. [ICAO] A VFR flight cleared by air traffic control to operate within Class B, C, D, and E surface areas in meteorological conditions below VMC.

Special VFR operations. Aircraft operating in accordance with clearances within Class B, C, D, and E surface areas in weather conditions less than the basic VFR weather minima. Such operations must be requested by the pilot and approved by ATC. (*See* Special VFR conditions) (*See* Special VFR flight [ICAO]).

speed. (*See* airspeed, ground speed).

speed adjustment. An ATC procedure used to request pilots to adjust aircraft speed to a specific value for the purpose of providing desired spacing. Pilots are expected to maintain a speed of plus or minus 10 knots or 0.02 mach number of the specified speed.

Examples of speed adjustments are:

1. "Increase/reduce speed to mach point (number)."

2. "Increase/reduce speed to (speed in knots)" or "Increase/reduce speed (number of knots) knots."

speed brakes. Moveable aerodynamic devices on aircraft that reduce airspeed during descent and landing.

speed segments. Portions of the arrival route between the transition point and the vertex along the optimum flight path for which speeds and altitudes are specified. There is one set of arrival speed segments adapted from each transition point to each vertex. Each set may contain up to six segments.

squawk (mode, code, function). Activate specific modes/codes/functions on the aircraft transponder, e.g., "Squawk three/alfa, two one zero five, low." (*See* transponder).

staging/queuing. The placement, integration, and segregation of departure aircraft in designated movement areas of an airport by departure fix, EDCT, and/or restriction.

stall. Loss of lift caused by exceeding the critical angle of attack and destroying the smooth flow of air over an airfoil.

standard datum plane. A standard of atmospheric pressure measurement that assumes the sea level pressure to be 29.92 inches Hg.

standard day. Sea level altitude, a temperature of 15°C or 59°F and a barometric pressure of 29.92" Hg (1013.2 mb).

standard instrument approach procedure. (*See* instrument approach procedure).

standard rate turn. A turn of three degrees per second.

standard terminal arrival (STAR). A preplanned instrument flight rule (IFR) air traffic control arrival procedure published for pilot use in graphic and/or textual form. STARs provide transition from the enroute structure to an outer fix or an instrument approach fix/arrival waypoint in the terminal area.

standard terminal arrival charts. (*See* aeronautical chart).

stand by. Means the controller or pilot must pause for a few seconds, usually to attend to other duties of a higher priority. Also means to wait as in "stand by for clearance." The caller should reestablish contact if a delay is lengthy. "Stand by" is not an approval or denial.

STAR. (*See* standard terminal arrival).

state aircraft. Aircraft used in military, customs and police service, in the exclusive service of any government, or of any political subdivision, thereof including the government of any state, territory, or possession of the United States or the District of Columbia, but not including any government-owned aircraft engaged in carrying persons or property for commercial purposes.

static. At rest or in equilibrium; not dynamic or moving.

static restrictions. Those restrictions that are usually not subject to change, fixed, in place, and/or published.

static source. A point on the airplane where no air pressure is exerted as a result of movement through the air; a reference input for the airspeed indicator; the source of air pressure change information for the altimeter and vertical speed indicator.

stationary reservations. Altitude reservations which encompass activities in a fixed area. Stationary reservations may include activities, such as special tests of weapons systems or equipment, certain U.S. Navy carrier, fleet, and antisubmarine operations, rocket, missile and drone operations, and certain aerial refueling or similar operations.

statute mile. A 5,280-foot mile.

stepdown fix. A fix permitting additional descent within a segment of an instrument approach procedure by identifying a point at which a controlling obstacle has been safely overflown.

step taxi. To taxi a float plane at full power or high RPM.

step turn. A maneuver used to put a float plane in a planing configuration prior to entering an active sea lane for takeoff. The STEP TURN maneuver should only be used upon pilot request.

stereo route. A routinely used route of flight established by users and ARTCCs identified by a coded name; e.g., ALPHA 2. These routes minimize flight plan handling and communications.

STOL aircraft. (*See* short takeoff and landing aircraft).

stop altitude squawk. Used by ATC to inform an aircraft to turn off the automatic altitude reporting feature of its transponder. It is issued when the verbally reported altitude varies 300 feet or more from the automatic altitude report. (*See* altitude readout, transponder).

stop-and-go. A procedure wherein an aircraft will land, make a complete stop on the runway, and then commence a takeoff from that point. (*See* low approach, option approach).

stop burst. (*See* stop stream).

stop buzzer. (*See* stop stream).

stopover flight plan. A flight plan format which permits in a single submission the filing of a sequence of flight plans through interim full stop destinations to a final destination.

stop squawk (mode or code). Used by ATC to tell the pilot to turn specified functions of the aircraft transponder off. (*See* stop altitude squawk, transponder).

stop stream. Used by ATC to request a pilot to suspend electronic countermeasure activity. (*See* jamming).

stopway. An area beyond the takeoff runway no less wide than the runway and centered upon the extended centerline of the runway, able to support the airplane during an aborted takeoff, without causing structural damage to the airplane, and designated by the airport authorities for use in decelerating the airplane during an aborted takeoff.

straight-in approach—IFR. An instrument approach wherein final approach is begun without first having executed a procedure turn, not necessarily completed with a straight-in landing or made to straight-in landing minimums. (*See* landing minimums, straight-in approach—VFR, straight-in landing).

straight-in approach—VFR. Entry into the traffic pattern by interception of the extended runway centerline (final approach course) without executing any other portion of the traffic pattern. (*See* traffic pattern).

straight-in landing. A landing made on a runway aligned within 30 degrees of the final approach course following completion of an instrument approach. (*See* straight-in approach—IFR).

straight-in landing minimums. (*See* landing minimums).

straight-in minimums. (*See* straight-in landing minimums).

strategic planning. Planning whereby solutions are sought to resolve potential conflicts.

*struts, supports. The main landing gear and nose wheel have struts to absorb the shock of landing. Wing sets are braced to the fuselage to support the wing and help absorb any wing movement in relation to the fuselage when landing or in turbulence. Low-wing airplanes and some high-wing airplanes have no external bracing.

substitutions. Users are permitted to exchange CTAs. Normally, the airline dispatcher will contact the ATCSCC with this request. The ATCSCC shall forward approved substitutions to the TMUs who will notify the appropriate terminals. Permissible swapping must not change the traffic load for any given hour of an EQF program.

substitute route. A route assigned to pilots when any part of an airway or route is unusable because of NAVAID status. These routes consist of:

1. Substitute routes which are shown on U.S. Government charts.
2. Routes defined by ATC as specific NAVAID radials or courses.
3. Routes defined by ATC as direct to or between NAVAIDs.

sunset and sunrise. The mean solar times of sunset and sunrise as published in the Nautical Almanac, converted to local standard time for the locality concerned. Within Alaska, the end of evening civil twilight and the beginning of morning civil twilight, as defined for each locality.

super high frequency (SHF). The frequency band between 3 and 30 gigahertz (GHz). The elevation and azimuth stations of the Microwave Landing System operate from 5031 MHz to 5091 MHz in this spectrum.

supplemental weather service location. Airport facilities staffed with contract personnel who take weather observations and provide current local weather to pilots via telephone or radio. (All other services are provided by the parent FSS).

SUPPS. Refers to ICAO Document 7030 Regional Supplementary Procedures. SUPPS contain procedures for each ICAO Region which are unique to that Region and are not covered in the worldwide provisions identified in the ICAO Air Navigation Plan. Procedures contained in chapter 8 are based in part on those published in SUPPS.

surface area. The airspace contained by the lateral boundary of the Class B, C, D, or E airspace designated for an airport that begins at the surface and extends upward.

SURPIC (surface picture). A description of surface vessels in the area of a Search and Rescue incident including their predicted positions and their characteristics. (*See* Order 7110.65, Paragraph 10-7-4, In-flight Contingencies).

surveillance approach. An instrument approach wherein the air traffic controller issues instructions, for pilot compliance, based on aircraft position in relation to the final approach course (azimuth), and the distance (range) from the end of the runway as displayed on the controller's radar scope. The controller will provide recommended altitudes on final approach if requested by the pilot. (Refer to AIM).

SWAP. (*See* severe weather avoidance plan).

SWSL. (*See* supplemental weather service location).

system strategic navigation (SN). Military activity accomplished by navigating along a preplanned route using internal aircraft systems to maintain a desired track. This activity normally requires a lateral route width of 10 NM and altitude range of 1,000 feet to 6,000 feet AGL with some route segments that permit terrain following.

TACAN. (*See* tactical air navigation).

TACAN-only aircraft. An aircraft, normally military, possessing TACAN with DME but no VOR navigational system capability. Clearances must specify TACAN or VORTAC fixes and approaches.

*tachometer. An instrument which reads revolutions per minute. Used on bicycles and automobiles as well as airplanes.

tactical air navigation (TACAN). An ultra high frequency electronic rho-theta air navigation aid which provides suitably equipped aircraft a continuous indication of bearing and distance to the TACAN station. (*See* VORTAC) (Refer to AIM).

*TAF. (*See* terminal aerodrome forecast).

tailwind. Any wind more than 90 degrees to the longitudinal axis of the runway. The magnetic direction of the runway shall be used as the basis for determining the longitudinal axis.

takeoff area. (*See* landing area).

takeoff distance available (TODA). [ICAO] The length of the takeoff run available plus the length of the clearway, if provided.

takeoff run available (TORA). [ICAO] The length of runway declared available and suitable for the ground run of an aeroplane takeoff.

target. The indication shown on a radar display resulting from a primary radar return or a radar beacon reply. (*See* radar, target symbol). [ICAO] In radar:

1. Generally, any discrete object which reflects or retransmits energy back to the radar equipment.
2. Specifically, an object of radar search or surveillance.

target resolution. A process to insure that correlated radar targets do not touch. Target resolution shall be applied as follows:

1. Between the edges of two primary targets or the edges of the ASR-9 primary target symbol.
2. Between the end of the beacon control slash and the edge of a primary target.
3. Between the ends of two beacon control slashes.

MANDATORY TRAFFIC ADVISORIES AND SAFETY ALERTS SHALL BE ISSUED WHEN THIS PROCEDURE IS USED.

Note: This procedure shall not be provided utilizing mosaic radar systems.

target symbol. A computer generated indication shown on a radar display resulting from a primary radar return or a radar beacon reply.

taxi. The movement of an airplane under its own power on the surface of an airport. Also, it describes the surface movement of helicopters equipped with wheels. (*See* air taxi, hover taxi) (Refer to AIM).

taxi patterns. Patterns established to illustrate the desired flow of ground traffic for the different runways or airport areas available for use.

TCAS. (*See* Traffic Alert and Collision Avoidance System).

TCH. (*See* threshold crossing height).

TCLT. (*See* tentative calculated landing time).

TDZE. (*See* touchdown zone elevation).

Telephone Information Briefing Service (TIBS). A continuous telephone recording of meteorological and/or aeronautical information. (Refer to AIM).

tentative calculated landing time (TCLT). A projected time calculated for adapted vertex for each arrival aircraft based upon runway configuration, airport acceptance rate, airport arrival delay period, and other metered arrival aircraft. This time is either the VTA of the aircraft or the TCLT/ACLT of the previous aircraft plus the AAI, whichever is later. This time will be updated in response to an aircraft's progress and its current relationship to other arrivals.

*Terminal Aerodrome Forecast (TAF). A forecast of weather conditions at a specific airport.

terminal area. A general term used to describe airspace in which approach control service or airport traffic control service is provided.

terminal area facility. A facility providing air traffic control service for arriving and departing IFR, VFR, Special VFR, and on occasion enroute aircraft. (*See* Approach Control Facility, tower).

terminal VFR radar service. A national program instituted to extend the terminal radar services provided instrument flight rules (IFR) aircraft to visual flight rules (VFR) aircraft. The program is divided into four types of service referred to as basic radar service, Terminal Radar Service Area (TRSA) service, Class B service and Class C service. The type of service provided at a particular location is contained in the Airport/Facility Directory.

1. *Basic Radar Service:* These services are provided for VFR aircraft by all commissioned terminal radar facilities. Basic radar service includes safety alerts, traffic advisories, limited radar vectoring when requested by the pilot, and sequencing at locations where procedures have been established for this purpose and/or when covered by a letter of agreement. The purpose of this service is to adjust the flow of arriving IFR and VFR aircraft into the traffic pattern in a safe and orderly manner and to provide traffic advisories to departing VFR aircraft.
2. *TRSA Service:* This service provides, in addition to basic radar service, sequencing of all IFR and participating VFR aircraft to the primary airport and separation between all participating VFR aircraft. The purpose of this service is to provide separation between all participating VFR aircraft and all IFR aircraft operating within the area defined as a TRSA.
3. *Class C Service:* This service provides, in addition to basic radar service, approved separation between IFR and VFR aircraft, and sequencing of VFR aircraft, and sequencing of VFR arrivals to the primary airport.
4. *Class B Service:* This service provides, in addition to basic radar service, approved separation of aircraft based on IFR, VFR, and/or weight, and sequencing of VFR arrivals to the primary airport(s).

(*See* controlled airspace, Terminal Radar Service Area) (Refer to AIM, Airport/Facility Directory).

Terminal Radar Service Area (TRSA). Airspace surrounding designated airports wherein ATC provides radar vectoring, sequencing, and separation on a full-time basis for all IFR and participating VFR aircraft. Service provided in a TRSA is called Stage III Service. The AIM contains an explanation of TRSA. TRSAs are depicted on VFR aeronautical charts. Pilot participation is urged but is not mandatory. (*See* terminal radar program) (Refer to AIM, Airport/Facility Directory).

terminal—very high frequency omnidirectional range station (TVOR). A very high frequency terminal omnirange station located on or near an airport and used as an approach aid. (*See* navigational aid, VOR).

terrain following (TF). The flight of a military aircraft maintaining a constant AGL altitude above the terrain or the highest obstruction. The altitude of the aircraft will constantly change with the varying terrain and/or obstruction.

tetrahedron. A device normally located on uncontrolled airports and used as a landing direction indicator. The small end of a tetrahedron points in the direction of landing. At controlled airports, the tetrahedron, if installed, should be disregarded because tower instructions supersede the indicator. (*See* segmented circle) (Refer to AIM).

TF. (*See* terrain following).

That is correct. The understanding you have is right.

360 overhead. (*See* overhead approach).

threshold. The beginning of that portion of the runway usable for landing. (*See* airport lighting, displaced threshold).

***threshold.** The beginning of the landing surface at the approach end of a runway.

threshold crossing height (TCH). The theoretical height above the runway threshold at which the aircraft's glideslope antenna would be if the aircraft maintains the trajectory established by the mean ILS glideslope or MLS glidepath. (*See* glideslope, threshold).

threshold lights. (*See* airport lighting).

TIBS. (*See* Telephone Information Briefing Service).

time group. Four digits representing the hour and minutes from the Coordinated Universal Time (UTC) clock. FAA uses UTC for all operations. The term "Zulu" may be used to denote UTC. The word "local" or the time zone equivalent shall be used to denote local when local time is given during radio and telephone communications. When written, a time zone designator is used to indicate local time; e.g. "0205M" (Mountain). The local time may be based on the 24-hour clock system. The day begins at 0000 and ends at 2359.

TMPA. (*See* traffic management program alert).

TMU. (*See* traffic management unit).

TODA. [ICAO] (*See* takeoff distance available).

***TO-FROM indicator.** Used in VOR navigation to tell the pilot whether the selected radial is the direction TO or FROM the transmitter; also called ambiguity indicator.

TORA. [ICAO] (*See* takeoff run available).

torching. The burning of fuel at the end of an exhaust pipe or stack of a reciprocating aircraft engine, the result of an excessive richness in the fuel air mixture.

***torque.** A twisting force; used as a term of convenience in flight instruction to describe several forces which combine to create a left-turning tendency.

total estimated elapsed time. [ICAO] For IFR flights, the estimated time required from takeoff to arrive over the designated point, defined by reference to navigation aids, from which it is intended that an instrument approach procedure will be commenced, or, if no navigation aid is associated with the destination aerodrome, to arrive over the destination aerodrome. For VFR flights, the estimated time required from takeoff to arrive over the destination aerodrome. (*See* estimated elapsed time).

touch-and-go. An operation by an aircraft that lands and departs on a runway without stopping or exiting the runway.

touch-and-go landing. (*See* touch-and-go).

touchdown.

1. The point at which an aircraft first makes contact with the landing surface.
2. Concerning a precision radar approach (PAR), it is the point where the glidepath intercepts the landing surface.

[ICAO] The point where the nominal glidepath intercepts the runway. *Note:* Touchdown as defined above is only a datum and is not necessarily the actual point at which the aircraft will touch the runway.

touchdown RVR. (*See* visibility).

touchdown zone. The first 3,000 feet of the runway beginning at the threshold. The area is used for determination of touchdown zone elevation in the development of straight-in landing minimums for instrument approaches. [ICAO] The portion of a runway, beyond the threshold, where it is intended landing aircraft first contact the runway.

touchdown zone elevation (TDZE). The highest elevation in the first 3,000 feet of the landing surface, TDZE is indicated on the instrument approach procedure chart when straight-in landing minimums are authorized. (*See* touchdown zone).

touchdown zone lighting. (*See* airport lighting).

tower. A terminal facility that uses air/ground communications, visual signaling, and other devices to provide ATC services to aircraft operating in the vicinity of an airport or on the movement area. Authorizes aircraft to land or takeoff at the airport controlled by the tower or to transit the Class D airspace area regardless of flight plan or weather conditions (IFR or VFR). A tower may also provide approach control services (radar or nonradar). (*See* Airport Traffic Control Service, Approach Control Facility, Approach Control Service, movement area, Tower Enroute Control Service) (Refer to AIM) (*See* aerodrome control tower [ICAO]).

***tower controller.** An air traffic control specialist in a control tower who controls operations on the active runway and in the airport traffic area. (Also "local controller.")

Tower Enroute Control Service (TECS). The control of IFR enroute traffic within delegated airspace between two or more adjacent approach control facilities. This service is designed to expedite traffic and reduce control and pilot communication requirements.

tower to tower. (*See* Tower Enroute Control Service).

TPX-42. A numeric beacon decoder equipment/system. It is designed to be added to terminal radar systems for beacon decoding. It provides rapid target identification, reinforcement of the primary radar target, and altitude information from Mode C. (*See* automated radar terminal systems, transponder).

track. The actual flight path of an aircraft over the surface of the earth. (*See* course, route, flight path). [ICAO] The projection on the earth's surface of the path of an aircraft, the direction of which path at any point is usually expressed in degrees from North (True, Magnetic, or Grid).

*track. The actual path over the ground followed by an airplane.

traffic.

1. A term used by a controller to transfer radar identification of an aircraft to another controller for the purpose of coordinating separation action. Traffic is normally issued:

   a. in response to a handoff or point out,

   b. in anticipation of a handoff or point out, or

   c. in conjunction with a request for control of an aircraft.

2. A term used by ATC to refer to one or more aircraft.

traffic advisories. Advisories issued to alert pilots to other known or observed air traffic which may be in such proximity to the position or intended route of flight of their aircraft to warrant their attention. Such advisories may be based on:

1. Visual observation.

2. Observation of radar identified and nonidentified aircraft targets on an ATC radar display, or

3. Verbal reports from pilots or other facilities.

The word "traffic" followed by additional information, if known, is used to provide such advisories; e.g., "Traffic, 2 o'clock, one zero miles, southbound, eight thousand."

Traffic advisory service will be provided to the extent possible depending on higher priority duties of the controller or other limitations; e.g., radar limitations, volume of traffic, frequency congestion, or controller workload. Radar/nonradar traffic advisories do not relieve the pilot of his responsibility to see and avoid other aircraft. Pilots are cautioned that there are many times when the controller is not able to give traffic advisories concerning all traffic in the aircraft's proximity; in other words, when a pilot requests or is receiving traffic advisories, he should not assume that all traffic will be issued. (Refer to AIM).

Traffic alert (aircraft call sign), turn (left/right) immediately, (climb/descend) and maintain (altitude). (*See* safety alert).

Traffic Alert and Collision Avoidance System (TCAS). An airborne collision avoidance system based on radar beacon signals which operates independent of ground based equipment. TCAS-I generates traffic advisories only. TCAS-II generates traffic advisories, and resolution (collision avoidance) advisories in the vertical plane.

traffic information. (*See* traffic advisories).

traffic in sight. Used by pilots to inform a controller that previously issued traffic is in sight. (*See* negative contact, traffic advisories).

traffic management program alert (TMPA). A term used in a Notice to Airmen (NOTAM) issued in conjunction with a special traffic management program to alert pilots to the existence of the program and to refer them to either the Notices to Airmen publication or a special traffic management program advisory message for program details. The contraction TMPA is used in NOTAM text.

traffic management unit (TMU). The entity in ARTCCs and designated terminals responsible for direct involvement in the active management of facility traffic. Usually under the direct supervision of an assistant manager for traffic management.

Traffic no factor. Indicates that the traffic described in a previously issued traffic advisory is no factor.

Traffic no longer observed. Indicates that the traffic described in a previously issued traffic advisory is no longer depicted on radar, but may still be a factor.

traffic pattern. The traffic flow that is prescribed for aircraft landing at, taxiing on, or taking off from an airport. The components of a typical traffic pattern are upwind leg, crosswind leg, downwind leg, base leg, and final approach.

1. *Upwind leg.* A flight path parallel to the landing runway in the direction of landing.

2. *Crosswind leg.* A flight path at right angles to the landing runway off its upwind end.

3. *Downwind leg.* A flight path parallel to the landing runway in the direction opposite to landing. The downwind leg normally extends between the crosswind leg and the base leg.

4. *Base leg.* A flight path at right angles to the landing runway off its approach end. The base leg normally extends from the downwind leg to the intersection of the extended runway centerline.

5. *Final approach.* A flight path in the direction of landing along the extended runway centerline. The final approach normally extends from the base leg to the runway. An aircraft making a straight-in approach VFR is also considered to be on final approach.

(*See* straight-in approach — VFR, taxi patterns) (Refer to AIM, 14 CFR Part 91) (*See* aerodrome traffic circuit [ICAO]).

*trailing edge. The sharp edge of the wing; flaps and ailerons are hinged at the trailing edge of the wing.

Transcribed Weather Broadcast (TWEB). In Alaska only: a continuous recording of meteorological and aeronautical information that is broadcast on L/MF and VOR facilities for pilots. (Refer to AIM).

transfer of control. That action whereby the responsibility for the separation of an aircraft is transferred from one controller to another. [ICAO] Transfer of responsibility for providing air traffic control service.

transferring controller. A controller/facility transferring control of an aircraft to another controller/facility. (*See* transferring unit/controller [ICAO]).

transferring facility. (*See* transferring controller).

transferring unit/controller. [ICAO] Air traffic control unit/ air traffic controller in the process of transferring the responsibility for providing air traffic control service to an aircraft to the next air traffic control unit/air traffic controller along the route of flight.

Note: See definition of accepting unit/controller.

transition.

1. The general term that describes the change from one phase of flight or flight condition to another; e.g., transition from enroute flight to the approach or transition from instrument flight to visual flight.

2. A published procedure (SID Transition) used to connect the basic SID to one of several enroute airways/jet routes, or published procedure (STAR Transition) used to connect one of several enroute airways/jet routes to the basic STAR. (Refer to SID/STAR Charts).

transitional airspace. That portion of controlled airspace wherein aircraft change from one phase of flight or flight condition to another.

transition point. A point at an adapted number of miles from the vertex at which an arrival aircraft would normally commence descent from its enroute altitude. This is the first fix adapted on the arrival speed segments.

transmissiometer. An apparatus used to determine visibility by measuring the transmission of light through the atmosphere. It is the measurement source of determining runway visual range (RVR) and runway visibility valve (RVV). (*See* visibility).

transmitting in the blind. A transmission from one station to other stations in circumstances where two-way communication cannot be established, but where it is believed that the called stations may be able to receive the transmission.

transponder. The airborne radar beacon receiver/transmitter portion of the Air Traffic Control Radar Beacon System (ATCRBS) which automatically receives radio signals from interrogators on the ground, and selectively replies with a specific reply pulse or pulse group only to those interrogations being received on the mode to which it is set to respond. (*See* interrogator) (Refer to AIM). [ICAO] A receiver/transmitter which will generate a reply signal upon proper interrogation; the interrogation and reply being on different frequencies.

*****transponder.** A UHF transmitter which replies to coded inquiries from ground radar stations, giving your position and possibly your altitude for identification and traffic separation purposes.

transponder codes. (*See* codes).

*****trim tabs.** Small adjustable tabs on control surfaces (elevator, rudder and ailerons) used by the pilot to relieve control forces. Typically, the tab moves opposite to desired control surface movement deflecting the elevator trim tab downward causes the elevator to move upward.

TRSA. (*See* Terminal Radar Service Area).

*****TRSA.** Terminal Radar Service Area—an area where radar service is available to VFR pilots on a voluntary basis; outlined in black on sectional charts.

*****true airspeed.** Indicated airspeed corrected for temperature and pressure altitude.

*****true airspeed indicator.** An airspeed indicator which allows the pilot to set temperature and altitude values and read true airspeed directly.

*****true North Pole.** The northern extremity of the earth's axis; where all of the lines of longitude meet.

*****true wind.** The actual movement of air over the earth's surface.

*****turbocharged.** An engine with intake air compressed by a turbine-driven compressor.

turbojet aircraft. An aircraft having a jet engine in which the energy of the jet operates a turbine which in turn operates the air compressor.

turboprop aircraft. An aircraft having a jet engine in which the energy of the jet operates a turbine which drives the propeller.

turn anticipation. Maneuver anticipation.

TWEB. (*See* Transcribed Weather Broadcast).

TVOR. (*See* terminal—very high frequency omnidirectional range station).

two-way radio communications failure. (*See* lost communications).

UDF. (*See* direction finder).

UHF. (*See* ultrahigh frequency).

*****UHF.** Ultrahigh Frequency range, 300 MHz to 3,000 MHz. Used for DME and some radar equipment.

ultrahigh frequency (UHF). The frequency band between 300 and 3,000 MHz. The bank of radio frequencies used for military air/ground voice communications. In some instances this may go as low as 225 MHz and still be referred to as UHF.

ultralight vehicle. An aeronautical vehicle operated for sport or recreational purposes which does not require FAA registration, an airworthiness certificate, nor pilot certification. They are primarily single occupant vehicles, although some two place vehicles are authorized for training purposes. Operation of an ultralight vehicle in certain airspace requires authorization from ATC. (*See* 14 CFR Part 103).

unable. Indicates inability to comply with a specific instruction, request, or clearance.

*****uncontrolled airport.** An airport without a control tower or an airport with a tower outside of the tower's hours of operation.

under the hood. Indicates that the pilot is using a hood to restrict visibility outside the cockpit while simulating instrument flight. An appropriately rated pilot is required in the other control seat while this operation is being conducted. (Refer to 14 CFR Part 91).

UNICOM. A nongovernment communication facility which may provide airport information at certain airports. Locations and frequencies of UNICOMs are shown on aeronautical charts and publications. (Refer to AIM, Airport/Facility Directory).

*UNICOM. An acronym for Universal Communications. Also called Aeronautical Advisory Service, a radio service operated by individuals at airports to provide services to pilots. Not used for air traffic control purposes.

unpublished route. A route for which no minimum altitude is published or charted for pilot use. It may include a direct route between NAVAIDs, a radial, a radar vector, or a final approach course beyond the segments of an instrument approach procedure. (*See* published route, route).

upwind leg. (*See* traffic pattern).

urgency. A condition of being concerned about safety and of requiring timely but not immediate assistance; a potential distress condition. [ICAO] A condition concerning the safety of an aircraft or other vehicle, or of person on board or in sight, but which does not require immediate assistance.

USAFIB. (*See* Army Aviation Flight Information Bulletin).

UVDF. (*See* direction finder).

*variation. The angular difference between measurements in relation to true north and magnetic north. Variation is independent of aircraft heading.

VASI. (*See* Visual Approach Slope Indicator).

*VASI. Visual Approach Slope Indicator—a means of providing approach slope guidance to VFR pilots.

VDF. (*See* direction finder).

VDP. (*See* visual descent point).

vector. A heading issued to an aircraft to provide navigational guidance by radar. (*See* radar vectoring [ICAO]).

*vector. A heading to steer, received from a controller.

*venturi. A tube with a restriction which accelerates air and reduces pressure. Venturis are used in carburetors and on older airplanes to provide vacuum to power flight instruments.

verify. Request confirmation of information; e.g., "verify assigned altitude."

verify specific direction of takeoff (or turns after takeoff). Used by ATC to ascertain an aircraft's direction of takeoff and/or direction of turn after takeoff. It is normally used for IFR departures from an airport not having a control tower. When direct communication with the pilot is not possible, the request and information may be relayed through an FSS, dispatcher, or by other means. (*See* IFR takeoff minimums and departure procedures).

vertex. The last fix adapted on the arrival speed segments. Normally, it will be the outer marker of the runway in use. However, it may be the actual threshold or other suitable common point on the approach path for the particular runway configuration.

vertex time of arrival (VTA). A calculated time of aircraft arrival over the adapted vertex for the runway configuration in use. The time is calculated via the optimum flight path using adapted speed segments.

*vertical axis. An imaginary line through the center of gravity which intersects the lateral and longitudinal axes; also called yaw axis.

*vertical fin. A fixed vertical airfoil at the rear of the airplane which stabilizes the airplane in the vertical axis.

vertical navigation (VNAV). A function of area navigation (RNAV) equipment which calculates, displays, and provides vertical guidance to a profile or path.

vertical separation. Separation established by assignment of different altitudes or flight levels. (*See* separation). [ICAO] Separation between aircraft expressed in units of vertical distance.

*vertical speed indicator. An instrument which indicates rate of change in altitude by measuring rate of change of air pressure.

vertical takeoff and landing aircraft (VTOL). Aircraft capable of vertical climbs and/or descents and of using very short runways or small areas for takeoff and landings. These aircraft include, but are not limited to, helicopters. (*See* short takeoff and landing aircraft).

very high frequency (VHF). The frequency band between 30 and 300 MHz. Portions of this band, 108 to 118 MHz, are used for certain NAVAIDs; 118 to 136 MHz are used for civil air/ground voice communications. Other frequencies in this band are used for purposes not related to air traffic control.

very high frequency omnidirectional range station. (*See* VOR).

very low frequency (VLF). The frequency band between 3 and 30 kHz.

VFR. (*See* visual flight rules).

VFR aircraft. An aircraft conducting flight in accordance with visual flight rules. (*See* visual flight rules).

VFR conditions. Weather conditions equal to or better than the minimum for flight under visual flight rules. The term may be used as an ATC clearance/instruction only when:

1. An IFR aircraft requests a climb/descent in VFR conditions.

2. The clearance will result in noise abatement benefits where part of the IFR departure route does not conform to an FAA approved noise abatement route or altitude.

3. A pilot has requested a practice instrument approach and is not on an IFR flight plan.

Continued

All pilots receiving this authorization must comply with the VFR visibility and distance from cloud criteria in 14 CFR Part 91. Use of the term does not relieve controllers of their responsibility to separate aircraft in Class B and Class C airspace or TRSAs as required by FAA Order 7110.65. When used as an ATC clearance/instruction the term may be abbreviated "VFR;" e.g., "MAINTAIN VFR," "CLIMB/ DESCEND VFR," etc.

VFR flight. (*See* VFR aircraft).

VFR military training routes. Routes used by the Department of Defense and associated Reserve and Air Guard units for the purpose of conducting low altitude navigation and tactical training under VFR below 10,000 feet MSL at airspeeds in excess of 250 knots IAS.

VFR not recommended. An advisory provided by a flight service station to a pilot during a preflight or in-flight weather briefing that flight under visual flight rules is not recommended. To be given when the current and/or forecast weather conditions are at or below VFR minimums. It does not abrogate the pilot's authority to make his own decision.

VFR-On-Top. ATC authorization for an IFR aircraft to operate in VFR conditions at any appropriate VFR altitude (as specified in Federal Aviation Regulations and as restricted by ATC). A pilot receiving this authorization must comply with the VFR visibility, distance from cloud criteria, and the minimum IFR altitudes specified in 14 CFR Part 91. The use of this term does not relieve controllers of their responsibility to separate aircraft in Class B and Class C airspace or TRSAs as required by FAA Order 7110.65.

VFR terminal area charts. (*See* aeronautical chart).

VHF. (*See* very high frequency).

*VHF. Very High Frequency range. 30 MHz to 300 MHz range, limited to line-of-sight.

*VHF/DF. Very High Frequency Direction Finding—a service available at some Flight Service Stations to orient lost pilots. No equipment other than a transmitter and a receiver is required in order to use this service.

VHF omnidirectional range/tactical air navigation. (*See* VORTAC).

video map. An electronically displayed map on the radar display that may depict data such as airports, heliports, runway centerline extensions, hospital emergency landing areas, NAVAIDs and fixes, reporting points, airway/route centerlines, boundaries, handoff points, special use tracks, obstructions, prominent geographic features, map alignment indicators, range accuracy marks, minimum vectoring altitudes.

visibility. The ability, as determined by atmospheric conditions and expressed in units of distance, to see and identify prominent unlighted objects by day and prominent lighted objects by night. Visibility is reported as statute miles, hundreds of feet or meters. (Refer to 14 CFR Part 91, AIM).

1. *Flight visibility.* The average forward horizontal distance from the cockpit of an aircraft in flight, at which prominent unlighted objects may be seen and identified by day and prominent lighted objects may be seen and identified by night.

2. *Ground visibility.* Prevailing horizontal visibility near the earth's surface as reported by the United States National Weather Service or an accredited observer.

3. *Prevailing visibility.* The greatest horizontal visibility equaled or exceeded throughout at least half the horizon circle which need not necessarily be continuous.

4. *Runway visibility value (RVV).* The visibility determined for a particular runway by a transmissometer. A meter provides a continuous indication of the visibility (reported in miles or fractions of miles) for the runway. RVV is used in lieu of prevailing visibility in determining minimums for a particular runway.

5. *Runway visual range (RVR).* An instrumentally derived value, based on standard calibrations, that represents the horizontal distance a pilot will see down the runway from the approach end. It is based on the sighting of either high intensity runway lights or on the visual contrast of other targets whichever yields the greater visual range. RVR, in contrast to prevailing or runway visibility, is based on what a pilot in a moving aircraft should see looking down the runway. RVR is horizontal visual range, not slant visual range. It is based on the measurement of a transmissometer made near the touchdown point of the instrument runway and is reported in hundreds of feet. RVR is used in lieu of RVV and/or prevailing visibility in determining minimums for a particular runway.

   a. *Touchdown RVR.* The RVR visibility readout values obtained from RVR equipment serving the runway touchdown zone.

   b. *Mid-RVR.* The RVR readout values obtained from RVR equipment located midfield of the runway.

   c. *Rollout RVR.* The RVR readout values obtained from RVR equipment located nearest the rollout end of the runway.

[ICAO] The ability, as determined by atmospheric conditions and expressed in units of distance, to see and identify prominent unlighted objects by day and prominent lighted objects by night.

Flight visibility. [ICAO] The visibility forward from the cockpit of an aircraft in flight.

Ground visibility. [ICAO] The visibility at an aerodrome as reported by an accredited observer.

Runway visual range (RVR). [ICAO] The range over which the pilot of an aircraft on the centerline of a runway can see the runway surface markings or the lights delineating the runway or identifying its centerline.

visual approach. An approach conducted on an instrument flight rules (IFR) flight plan which authorizes the pilot to proceed visually and clear of clouds to the airport. The pilot must, at all times, have either the airport or the preceding aircraft in sight. This approach must be authorized and under the control of the appropriate air traffic control facility. Reported weather at the airport must be ceiling at or above 1,000 feet and visibility of 3 miles or greater. [ICAO] An approach by an IFR flight when either part or all of an instrument approach procedure is not completed and the approach is executed in visual reference to terrain.

Visual Approach Slope Indicator (VASI). (*See* airport lighting).

visual descent point (VDP). A defined point on the final approach course of a nonprecision straight-in approach procedure from which normal descent from the MDA to the runway touchdown point may be commenced, provided the approach threshold of that runway, or approach lights, or other markings identifiable with the approach end of that runway are clearly visible to the pilot.

visual flight rules (VFR). Rules that govern the procedures for conducting flight under visual conditions. The term "VFR" is also used in the United States to indicate weather conditions that are equal to or greater than minimum VFR requirements. In addition, it is used by pilots and controllers to indicate type of flight plan. (*See* instrument flight rules, instrument meteorological conditions, visual meteorological conditions) (Refer to 14 CFR Part 91 and AIM).

visual holding. The holding of aircraft at selected, prominent geographical fixes which can be easily recognized from the air. (*See* holding fix).

visual meteorological conditions (VMC). Meteorological conditions expressed in terms of visibility, distance from cloud, and ceiling equal to or better than specified minima. (*See* instrument flight rules, instrument meteorological conditions, visual flight rules).

visual separation. A means employed by ATC to separate aircraft in terminal areas and en route airspace in the NAS. There are two ways to effect this separation:

1. The tower controller sees the aircraft involved and issues instructions, as necessary, to ensure that the aircraft avoid each other.

2. A pilot sees the other aircraft involved and upon instructions from the controller provides his own separation by maneuvering his aircraft as necessary to avoid it. This may involve following another aircraft or keeping it in sight until it is no longer a factor. (*See*: see and avoid) (Refer to 14 CFR Part 91).

VLF. (*See* very low frequency).

VMC. (*See* visual meteorological conditions).

VNAV. (*See* vertical navigation).

voice switching and control system (VSCS). The VSCS is a computer controlled switching system that provides air traffic controllers with all voice circuits (air to ground and ground to ground) necessary for air traffic control.

VOR. A ground based electronic navigation aid transmitting very high frequency navigation signals, 360 degrees in azimuth, oriented from magnetic north. Used as the basis for navigation in the National Airspace System. The VOR periodically identifies itself by Morse Code and may have an additional voice identification feature. Voice features may be used by ATC or FSS for transmitting instructions/information to pilots. (*See* navigational aid) (Refer to AIM).

*VOR. VHF Omnidirectional Range. The basis for the airways system.

*VOR-DME. The civilian equivalent of a VORTAC, with both navigation and distance measuring signals, under the control of the FAA.

VORTAC. A navigation aid providing VOR azimuth, TACAN azimuth, and TACAN distance measuring equipment (DME) at one site. (*See* distance measuring equipment, navigational aid, TACAN, VOR) (Refer to AIM).

*VORTAC. A VOR colocated with a military TACAN (tactical aid to navigations) station. Civilians use the navigational signal from the VOR and the distance information from the TACAN.

VOR test signal. (*See* VOT).

*vortex. A mass of air having a whirling or circular motion. *plural*: vortices.

vortices. Circular patterns of air created by the movement of an airfoil through the air when generating lift. As an airfoil moves through the atmosphere in sustained flight, an area of low pressure is created above it. The air flowing from the high pressure area to the low pressure area around and about the tips of the airfoil tends to roll up into two rapidly rotating vortices, cylindrical in shape. These vortices are the most predominant parts of aircraft wake turbulence and their rotational force is dependent upon the wing loading, gross weight, and speed of the generating aircraft. The vortices from medium to heavy aircraft can be of extremely high velocity and hazardous to smaller aircraft. (*See* aircraft classes, wake turbulence) (Refer to AIM).

VOT. A ground facility which emits a test signal to check VOR receiver accuracy. Some VOTs are available to the user while airborne, and others are limited to ground use only. (Refer to 14 CFR Part 91, AIM, Airport/Facility Directory).

*VOT. A special transmitter located at major airports to test VOR receivers for accuracy.

VR. (*See* VFR military training route).

VSCS. (*See* voice switching and control system).

VTA. (*See* vertex time of arrival).

VTOL aircraft. (*See* vertical takeoff and landing aircraft).

WA. (*See* AIRMET, Weather Advisory).

WAAS. (*See* wide-area augmentation system).

wake turbulence. Phenomena resulting from the passage of an aircraft through the atmosphere. The term includes vortices, thrust stream turbulence, jet blast, jet wash, propeller wash, and rotor wash both on the ground and in the air. (*See* aircraft classes, jet blast, vortices) (Refer to AIM).

Warning Area. (*See* Special Use airspace).

waypoint. A predetermined geographical position used for route/instrument approach definition, or progress reporting purposes, that is defined relative to a VORTAC station or in terms of latitude/longitude coordinates.

Weather Advisory (WS) (WST) (WA) (CWA). In aviation weather forecast practice, an expression of hazardous weather conditions not predicted in the area forecast, as they affect the operation of air traffic and as prepared by the NWS. (*See* SIGMET, AIRMET).

when able. When used in conjunction with ATC instructions, gives the pilot the latitude to delay compliance until a condition or even has been reconciled. Unlike "pilot discretion," when instructions are prefaced "when able," the pilot is expected to seek the first opportunity to comply. Once a maneuver has been initiated, the pilot is expected to continue until the specifications of the instructions have been met. "When able," should not be used when expeditious compliance is required.

wide-area augmentation system (WAAS). The WAAS is a satellite navigation system consisting of the equipment and software which augments the GPS Standard Positioning Service (SPS). The WAAS provides enhanced integrity, accuracy, availability, and continuity over and above GPS SPS. The differential correction function provides improved accuracy required for precision approach.

wilco. I have received your message, understand it, and will comply with it.

wind correction angle. The angular difference between course and heading.

wind drift. The sideways motion over the ground caused by a crosswind.

wind shear. A change in wind speed and/or wind direction in a short distance resulting in a tearing or shearing effect. It can exist in a horizontal or vertical direction and occasionally in both.

wind triangle. A graphic means of computing wind correction angle and ground speed.

wing-tip vortices. (*See* vortices).

words twice.

1. As a request: "Communication is difficult. Please say every phrase twice."
2. As information: "Since communications are difficult, every phrase in this message will be spoken twice."

world aeronautical charts. (*See* aeronautical chart).

WS. (*See* SIGMET, Weather Advisory).

WST. (*See* Convective SIGMET, Weather Advisory).

yaw axis. A vertical line through the center of gravity that intersects the longitudinal and lateral axes. The pilot uses rudder to control the airplane around the yaw axis.

Zulu time (Z). Time in relation to the time at Greenwich, England; also called Greenwich Mean Time.

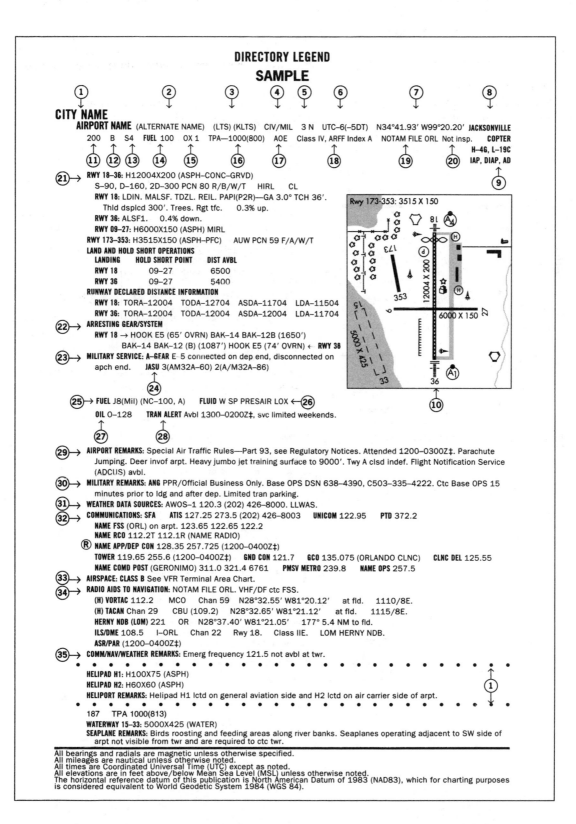

DIRECTORY LEGEND
SAMPLE

① ② ③ ④ ⑤ ⑥ ⑦ ⑧

CITY NAME
AIRPORT NAME (ALTERNATE NAME) (LTS) (KLTS) CIV/MIL 3 N UTC–6(–5DT) N34°41.93' W99°20.20' JACKSONVILLE
200 B S4 **FUEL** 100 OX 1 TPA—1000(800) AOE Class IV, ARFF Index A NOTAM FILE ORL Not insp. **COPTER**
⑪ ⑫ ⑬ ⑭ ⑮ ⑯ ⑰ ⑱ ⑲ ⑳ H–4G, L–19C
IAP, DIAP, AD
⑨

㉑→ **RWY 18–36:** H12004X200 (ASPH–CONC–GRVD)
S–90, D–160, 2D–300 PCN 80 R/B/W/T HIRL CL
RWY 18: LDIN. MALSF. TDZL. REIL. PAPI(P2R)—GA 3.0° TCH 36'.
Thld dsplcd 300'. Trees. Rgt tfc. 0.3% up.
RWY 36: ALSF1. 0.4% down.
RWY 09–27: H6000X150 (ASPH) MIRL
RWY 173–353: H3515X150 (ASPH–PFC) AUW PCN 59 F/A/W/T
LAND AND HOLD SHORT OPERATIONS

LANDING	HOLD SHORT POINT	DIST AVBL
RWY 18	09–27	6500
RWY 36	09–27	5400

RUNWAY DECLARED DISTANCE INFORMATION
RWY 18: TORA–12004 TODA–12704 ASDA–11704 LDA–11504
RWY 36: TORA–12004 TODA–12004 ASDA–12004 LDA–11704
㉒→ **ARRESTING GEAR/SYSTEM**
RWY 18 → HOOK E5 (65' OVRN) BAK–14 BAK–12B (1650')
BAK–14 BAK–12 (B) (1087') HOOK E5 (74' OVRN) ← **RWY 36**
㉓→ **MILITARY SERVICE: A–GEAR** E–5 connected on dep end, disconnected on
apch end. **JASU** 3(AM32A–60) 2(A/M32A–86)
㉔

㉕→ **FUEL** J8(Mil) (NC–100, A) **FLUID** W SP PRESAIR LOX ←㉖
OIL O–128 **TRAN ALERT** Avbl 1300–0200Z‡, svc limited weekends.
㉗ ㉘

Rwy 173-353: 3515 X 150

㉙→ **AIRPORT REMARKS:** Special Air Traffic Rules—Part 93, see Regulatory Notices. Attended 1200–0300Z‡. Parachute
Jumping. Deer invof arpt. Heavy jumbo jet training surface to 9000'. Twy A clsd indef. Flight Notification Service
(ADCUS) avbl.
㉚→ **MILITARY REMARKS:** ANG PPR/Official Business Only. Base OPS DSN 638–4390, C503–335–4222. Ctc Base OPS 15
minutes prior to ldg and after dep. Limited tran parking.
㉛→ **WEATHER DATA SOURCES:** AWOS–1 120.3 (202) 426–8000. LLWAS.
㉜→ **COMMUNICATIONS: SFA** **ATIS** 127.25 273.5 (202) 426–8003 **UNICOM** 122.95 **PTD** 372.2
NAME FSS (ORL) on arpt. 123.65 122.65 122.2
NAME RCO 112.2T 112.1R (NAME RADIO)
Ⓡ **NAME APP/DEP CON** 128.35 257.725 (1200–0400Z‡)
TOWER 119.65 255.6 (1200–0400Z‡) **GND CON** 121.7 **GCO** 135.075 (ORLANDO CLNC) **CLNC DEL** 125.55
NAME COMD POST (GERONIMO) 311.0 321.4 6761 **PMSV METRO** 239.8 **NAME OPS** 257.5
㉝→ **AIRSPACE: CLASS B** See VFR Terminal Area Chart.
㉞→ **RADIO AIDS TO NAVIGATION:** NOTAM FILE ORL. VHF/DF ctc FSS.
(H) VORTAC 112.2 MCO Chan 59 N28°32.55' W81°20.12' at fld. 1110/8E.
(H) TACAN Chan 29 CBU (109.2) N28°32.65' W81°21.12' at fld. 1115/8E.
HERNY NDB (LOM) 221 OR N28°37.40' W81°21.05' 177° 5.4 NM to fld.
ILS/DME 108.5 I–ORL Chan 22 Rwy 18. Class IIE. LOM HERNY NDB.
ASR/PAR (1200–0400Z‡)
㉟→ **COMM/NAV/WEATHER REMARKS:** Emerg frequency 121.5 not avbl at twr.

• •
HELIPAD H1: H100X75 (ASPH)
HELIPAD H2: H60X60 (ASPH) ①
HELIPORT REMARKS: Helipad H1 lctd on general aviation side and H2 lctd on air carrier side of arpt.
• •
187 TPA 1000(813)
WATERWAY 15–33: 5000X425 (WATER)
SEAPLANE REMARKS: Birds roosting and feeding areas along river banks. Seaplanes operating adjacent to SW side of
arpt not visible from twr and are required to ctc twr.

All bearings and radials are magnetic unless otherwise specified.
All mileages are nautical unless otherwise noted.
All times are Coordinated Universal Time (UTC) except as noted.
All elevations are in feet above/below Mean Sea Level (MSL) unless otherwise noted.
The horizontal reference datum of this publication is North American Datum of 1983 (NAD83), which for charting purposes
is considered equivalent to World Geodetic System 1984 (WGS 84).

⑩ SKETCH LEGEND

RUNWAYS/LANDING AREAS

Hard Surfaced . . . .

Metal Surface . . . .

Sod, Gravel, etc. . . . .

Light Plane, ...
Ski Landing Area or Water

Under Construction . . . . .

Closed . . . .

Helicopter Landings Area . . . . Ⓗ

Displaced Threshold . . . .

Taxiway, Apron and Stopways . .

MISCELLANEOUS BASE AND CULTURAL FEATURES

Buildings . . . .

Power Lines . . . . —T——T—

Fence . . . . ×××××

Towers . . . .

Tanks . . . .

Oil Well . . . .

Smoke Stack . . . .

Obstruction   5812   Λ

Controlling Obstruction . . . .   +5812

Trees . . . .

Populated Places . . . .

Cuts and Fills . . . . . .   Cut   Fill

Cliffs and Depressions . .

Ditch . . . .

Hill . . . .

RADIO AIDS TO NAVIGATION

VORTAC . . . ⬡   VOR . . . . ⬡

VOR/DME . . ⌑   NDB . . . . . . ⊙

TACAN . . . . ⬠   NDB/DME . . . . ⊡

MISCELLANEOUS AERONAUTICAL FEATURES

Airport Beacon . . . .   ☆

Wind Cone . . . .

Landing Tee . . . .   ⊢

Tetrahedron . . . .   ►

Control Tower . . . .

APPROACH LIGHTING SYSTEMS

A dot '●' portrayed with approach lighting letter identifier indicates sequenced flashing lights (F) installed with the approach lighting system e.g. Ⓐ Negative symbology, e.g., Ⓐ Ⓥ indicates Pilot Controlled Lighting (PCL).

Runway Centerline Lighting . . . . .

Ⓐ Approach Lighting System ALSF-2 . .

Ⓐ₁ Approach Lighting System ALSF-1 . .

Ⓐ₂ Short Approach Lighting System SALS/SALSF . . . .

Ⓐ₃ Simplified Short Approach Lighting System (SSALR) with RAIL . . . . .

Ⓐ₄ Medium Intensity Approach Lighting System (MALS and MALSF)/(SSALS and SSALF) . . . .

Ⓐ₅ Medium Intensity Approach Lighting System (MALSR) and RAIL . . . . . .

Ⓞ Omnidirectional Approach Lighting System (ODALS) . . . .

Ⓓ Navy Parallel Row and Cross Bar . . .

⊕ Air Force Overrun . . . .

Ⓥ Visual Approach Slope Indicator with Standard Threshold Clearance provided

Ⓥ₂ Pulsating Visual Approach Slope Indicator (PVASI)

Ⓥ₃ Visual Approach Slope Indicator with a threshold crossing height to accomodate long bodied or jumbo aircraft

Ⓥ₄ Tri-color Visual Approach Slope Indicator (TRCV)

Ⓥ₅ Approach Path Alignment Panel (APAP)

Ⓟ Precision Approach Path Indicator (PAPI)

DIRECTORY LEGEND
LEGEND

This directory is a listing of data on record with the FAA on all open to the public airports, military facilities and selected private use facilities specifically requested by the Department of Defense (DoD) for which a DoD Instrument Approach Procedure has been published in the U.S. Terminal Procedures Publication. Additionally this listing contains data for associated terminal control facilities, air route traffic control centers, and radio aids to navigation within the conterminous United States, Puerto Rico and the Virgin Islands. Joint civil/military and civil airports are listed alphabetically by state, associated city and airport name and cross-referenced by airport name. Military facilities are listed alphabetically by state and official airport name and cross-referenced by associated city name. Navaids, flight service stations and remote communication outlets that are associated with an airport, but with a different name, are listed alphabetically under their own name, as well as under the airport with which they are associated.

The listing of an open to the public airport in this directory merely indicates the airport operator's willingness to accommodate transient aircraft, and does not represent that the facility conforms with any Federal or local standards, or that it has been approved for use on the part of the general public. Military and private use facilities published in this directory are open to civil pilots only in an emergency or with prior permission. See Special Notice Section, Civil Use of Military Fields.

The information on obstructions is taken from reports submitted to the FAA. Obstruction data has not been verified in all cases. Pilots are cautioned that objects not indicated in this tabulation (or on the airports sketches and/or charts) may exist which can create a hazard to flight operation. Detailed specifics concerning services and facilities tabulated within this directory are contained in the Aeronautical Information Manual, Basic Flight Information and ATC Procedures.

The legend items that follow explain in detail the contents of this Directory and are keyed to the circled numbers on the sample on the preceding pages.

① CITY/AIRPORT NAME

Civil and joint civil/military airports and facilities in this directory are listed alphabetically by state and associated city. Where the city name is different from the airport name the city name will appear on the line above the airport name. Airports with the same associated city name will be listed alphabetically by airport name and will be separated by a dashed rule line. A solid rule line will separate all others. FAA approved helipads and seaplane landing areas associated with a land airport will be separated by a dotted line. Military airports are listed alphabetically by state and official airport name.

② ALTERNATE NAME

Alternate names, if any, will be shown in parentheses.

③ LOCATION IDENTIFIER

The location identifier is a three or four character FAA code followed by a four-character ICAO code assigned to airports. ICAO codes will only be published at joint civil/military, and military facilities. If two different military codes are assigned, both codes will be shown with the primary operating agency's code listed first. These identifiers are used by ATC in lieu of the airport name in flight plans, flight strips and other written records and computer operations. Zeros will appear with a slash to differentiate them from the letter "O".

④ OPERATING AGENCY

Airports within this directory are classified into two categories, Military/Federal Government and Civil airports open to the general public, plus selected private use airports. The operating agency is shown for military, private use and joint civil/military airports. The operating agency is shown by an abbreviation as listed below. When an organization is a tenant, the abbreviation is enclosed in parenthesis. No classification indicates the airport is open to the general public with no military tenant.

A	US Army	MC	Marine Corps
AFRC	Air Force Reserve Command	N	Navy
AF	US Air Force	NAF	Naval Air Facility
ANG	Air National Guard	NAS	Naval Air Station
AR	US Army Reserve	NASA	National Air and Space Administration
ARNG	US Army National Guard	P	US Civil Airport Wherein Permit Covers
CG	US Coast Guard		Use by Transient Military Aircraft
CIV/MIL	Joint Use Civil/Military	PVT	Private Use Only (Closed to the Public)
DND	Department of National Defense Canada		

⑤ AIRPORT LOCATION

Airport location is expressed as distance and direction from the center of the associated city in nautical miles and cardinal points, e.g., 4 NE.

⑥ TIME CONVERSION

Hours of operation of all facilities are expressed in Coordinated Universal Time (UTC) and shown as "Z" time. The directory indicates the number of hours to be subtracted from UTC to obtain local standard time and local daylight saving time UTC–5(–4DT). The symbol ‡ indicates that during periods of Daylight Saving Time effective hours will be one hour earlier than shown. In those areas where daylight saving time is not observed the (–4DT) and ‡ will not be shown. Daylight saving time is in effect from 0200 local time the second Sunday in March to 0200 local time the first Sunday in November. Canada and all U.S. Conterminous States observe daylight saving time except Arizona and Puerto Rico, and the Virgin Islands. If the state observes daylight saving time and the operating times are other than daylight saving times, the operating hours will include the dates, times and no ‡ symbol will be shown, i.e., April 15–Aug 31 0630–1700Z, Sep 1–Apr 14 0600–1700Z.

DIRECTORY LEGEND

⑦ GEOGRAPHIC POSITION OF AIRPORT—AIRPORT REFERENCE POINT (ARP)

Positions are shown as hemisphere, degrees, minutes and hundredths of a minute and represent the approximate geometric center of all usable runway surfaces.

⑧ CHARTS

Charts refer to the Sectional Chart and Low and High Altitude Enroute Chart and panel on which the airport or facility is located. Helicopter Chart locations will be indicated as COPTER. IFR Gulf of Mexico West and IFR Gulf of Mexico Central will be depicted as GOMW and GOMC.

⑨ INSTRUMENT APPROACH PROCEDURES, AIRPORT DIAGRAMS

IAP indicates an airport for which a prescribed (Public Use) FAA Instrument Approach Procedure has been published. DIAP indicates an airport for which a prescribed DoD Instrument Approach Procedure has been published in the U.S. Terminal Procedures. See the Special Notice Section of this directory, Civil Use of Military Fields and the Aeronautical Information Manual 5–4–5 Instrument Approach Procedure Charts for additional information. AD indicates an airport for which an airport diagram has been published. Airport diagrams are located in the back of each A/FD volume alphabetically by associated city and airport name.

⑩ AIRPORT SKETCH

The airport sketch, when provided, depicts the airport and related topographical information as seen from the air and should be used in conjunction with the text. It is intended as a guide for pilots in VFR conditions. Symbology that is not self-explanatory will be reflected in the sketch legend. The airport sketch will be oriented with True North at the top. Airport sketches will be added incrementally.

⑪ ELEVATION

The highest point of an airport's usable runways measured in feet from mean sea level. When elevation is sea level it will be indicated as "00". When elevation is below sea level a minus "−" sign will precede the figure.

⑫ ROTATING LIGHT BEACON

B indicates rotating beacon is available. Rotating beacons operate sunset to sunrise unless otherwise indicated in the AIRPORT REMARKS or MILITARY REMARKS segment of the airport entry.

⑬ SERVICING—CIVIL

S1: Minor airframe repairs.	S5: Major airframe repairs.
S2: Minor airframe and minor powerplant repairs.	S6: Minor airframe and major powerplant repairs.
S3: Major airframe and minor powerplant repairs.	S7: Major powerplant repairs.
S4: Major airframe and major powerplant repairs.	S8: Minor powerplant repairs.

⑭ FUEL

CODE	FUEL	CODE	FUEL
80	Grade 80 gasoline (Red)	B+	Jet B, Wide-cut, turbine fuel with FS–II*, FP** minus 50° C.
100	Grade 100 gasoline (Green)		
100LL	100LL gasoline (low lead) (Blue)	J4 (JP4)	(JP–4 military specification) FP** minus 58° C.
115	Grade 115 gasoline (115/145 military specification) (Purple)		
A	Jet A, Kerosene, without FS–II*, FP** minus 40° C.	J5 (JP5)	(JP–5 military specification) Kerosene with FS–11, FP** minus 46°C.
A+	Jet A, Kerosene, with FS–II*, FP** minus 40°C.	J8 (JP8)	(JP–8 military specification) Jet A–1, Kerosene with FS–II*, FP** minus 47°C.
A1	Jet A–1, Kerosene, without FS–II*, FP** minus 47°C.	J8+100	(JP–8 military specification) Jet A–1, Kerosene with FS–II*, FP** minus 47°C, with-fuel additive package that improves thermo stability characteristics of JP–8.
A1+	Jet A–1, Kerosene with FS–II*, FP** minus 47° C.		
		J	(Jet Fuel Type Unknown)
B	Jet B, Wide-cut, turbine fuel without FS–II*, FP** minus 50° C.	MOGAS	Automobile gasoline which is to be used as aircraft fuel.

*(Fuel System Icing Inhibitor)
**(Freeze Point)

<u>NOTE:</u> Certain automobile gasoline may be used in specific aircraft engines if a FAA supplemental type certificate has been obtained. Automobile gasoline, which is to be used in aircraft engines, will be identified as "MOGAS", however, the grade/type and other octane rating will not be published.

Data shown on fuel availability represents the most recent information the publisher has been able to acquire. Because of a variety of factors, the fuel listed may not always be obtainable by transient civil pilots. Confirmation of availability of fuel should be made directly with fuel suppliers at locations where refueling is planned.

⑮ OXYGEN—CIVIL

OX 1 High Pressure	OX 3 High Pressure—Replacement Bottles
OX 2 Low Pressure	OX 4 Low Pressure—Replacement Bottles

⑯ TRAFFIC PATTERN ALTITUDE

Traffic Pattern Altitude (TPA)—The first figure shown is TPA above mean sea level. The second figure in parentheses is TPA above airport elevation. Multiple TPA shall be shown as "TPA—See Remarks" and detailed information shall be shown in the Airport or Military Remarks Section. Traffic pattern data for USAF bases, USN facilities, and U.S. Army airports (including those on which ACC or U.S. Army is a tenant) that deviate from standard pattern altitudes shall be shown in Military Remarks.

DIRECTORY LEGEND

(17) AIRPORT OF ENTRY, LANDING RIGHTS, AND CUSTOMS USER FEE AIRPORTS

U.S. CUSTOMS USER FEE AIRPORT—Private Aircraft operators are frequently required to pay the costs associated with customs processing.

AOE—Airport of Entry. A customs Airport of Entry where permission from U.S. Customs is not required to land. However, at least one hour advance notice of arrival is required.

LRA—Landing Rights Airport. Application for permission to land must be submitted in advance to U.S. Customs. At least one hour advance notice of arrival is required.

NOTE: Advance notice of arrival at both an AOE and LRA airport may be included in the flight plan when filed in Canada or Mexico. Where Flight Notification Service (ADCUS) is available the airport remark will indicate this service. This notice will also be treated as an application for permission to land in the case of an LRA. Although advance notice of arrival may be relayed to Customs through Mexico, Canada, and U.S. Communications facilities by flight plan, the aircraft operator is solely responsible for ensuring that Customs receives the notification. (See Customs, Immigration and Naturalization, Public Health and Agriculture Department requirements in the International Flight Information Manual for further details.)

US Customs Air and Sea Ports, Inspectors and Agents

Northeast Sector (New England and Atlantic States—ME to MD)	407–975–1740
Southeast Sector (Atlantic States—DC, WV, VA to FL)	407–975–1780
Central Sector (Interior of the US, including Gulf states—MS, AL, LA)	407–975–1760
Southwest East Sector (OK and eastern TX)	407–975–1840
Southwest West Sector (Western TX, NM and AZ)	407–975–1820
Pacific Sector (WA, OR, CA, HI and AK)	407–975–1800

(18) CERTIFICATED AIRPORT (14 CFR PART 139)

Airports serving Department of Transportation certified carriers and certified under 14 CFR part 139 are indicated by the Class and the ARFF Index; e.g. Class I, ARFF Index A, which relates to the availability of crash, fire, rescue equipment. Class I airports can have an ARFF Index A through E, depending on the aircraft length and scheduled departures. Class II, III, and IV will always carry an Index A.

14 CFR PART 139 CERTIFICATED AIRPORTS
AIRPORT CLASSIFICATIONS

Type of Air Carrier Operation	Class I	Class II	Class III	Class IV
Scheduled Air Carrier Aircraft with 31 or more passenger seats	X			
Unscheduled Air Carrier Aircraft with 31 or more passengers seats	X	X		X
Scheduled Air Carrier Aircraft with 10 to 30 passenger seats	X	X	X	

14 CFR–PART 139 CERTIFICATED AIRPORTS
INDICES AND AIRCRAFT RESCUE AND FIRE FIGHTING EQUIPMENT REQUIREMENTS

Airport Index	Required No. Vehicles	Aircraft Length	Scheduled Departures	Agent + Water for Foam
A	1	<90'	≥1	500#DC or HALON 1211 or 450#DC + 100 gal H$_2$O
B	1 or 2	≥90', <126'	≥5	Index A + 1500 gal H$_2$O
		≥126', <159'	<5	
C	2 or 3	≥126', <159'	≥5	Index A + 3000 gal H$_2$O
		≥159', <200'	<5	
D	3	≥159', <200'		Index A + 4000 gal H$_2$O
		>200'	<5	
E	3	≥200'	≥5	Index A + 6000 gal H$_2$O

> Greater Than; < Less Than; ≥ Equal or Greater Than; ≤ Equal or Less Than; H$_2$O–Water; DC–Dry Chemical.

NOTE: The listing of ARFF index does not necessarily assure coverage for non-air carrier operations or at other than prescribed times for air carrier. ARFF Index Ltd.—indicates ARFF coverage may or may not be available, for information contact airport manager prior to flight.

(19) NOTAM SERVICE

All public use landing areas are provided NOTAM "D" (distant dissemination) and NOTAM "L" (local dissemination) service. Airport NOTAM file identifier is shown for individual airports, e.g. "NOTAM FILE IAD". See AIM, Basic Flight Information and

DIRECTORY LEGEND

ATC Procedures for detailed description of NOTAM's. Current NOTAMs are available from Flight Service Stations at 1–800–WX–BRIEF. Real time Military NOTAMs are available using the DoD Internet NOTAM Distribution System (DINS) www.notams.jcs.mil.

⑳ FAA INSPECTION

All airports not inspected by FAA will be identified by the note: Not insp. This indicates that the airport information has been provided by the owner or operator of the field.

㉑ RUNWAY DATA

Runway information is shown on two lines. That information common to the entire runway is shown on the first line while information concerning the runway ends is shown on the second or following line. Runway direction, surface, length, width, weight bearing capacity, lighting, and slope, when available are shown for each runway. Multiple runways are shown with the longest runway first. Direction, length, width, and lighting are shown for sea-lanes. The full dimensions of helipads are shown, e.g., 50X150. Runway data that requires clarification will be placed in the remarks section.

RUNWAY DESIGNATION

Runways are normally numbered in relation to their magnetic orientation rounded off to the nearest 10 degrees. Parallel runways can be designated L (left)/R (right)/C (center). Runways may be designated as Ultralight or assault strips. Assault strips are shown by magnetic bearing.

RUNWAY DIMENSIONS

Runway length and width are shown in feet. Length shown is runway end to end including displaced thresholds, but excluding those areas designed as overruns.

RUNWAY SURFACE AND LENGTH

Runway lengths prefixed by the letter ''H'' indicate that the runways are hard surfaced (concrete, asphalt, or part asphalt–concrete). If the runway length is not prefixed, the surface is sod, clay, etc. The runway surface composition is indicated in parentheses after runway length as follows:

(AFSC)—Aggregate friction seal coat	(GRVL)—Gravel, or cinders	(PSP)—Pierced steel plank
(ASPH)—Asphalt	(MATS)—Pierced steel planking,	(RFSC)—Rubberized friction seal coat
(CONC)—Concrete	landing mats, membranes	(TURF)—Turf
(DIRT)—Dirt	(PEM)—Part concrete, part asphalt	(TRTD)—Treated
(GRVD)—Grooved	(PFC)—Porous friction courses	(WC)—Wire combed

RUNWAY WEIGHT BEARING CAPACITY

Runway strength data shown in this publication is derived from available information and is a realistic estimate of capability at an average level of activity. It is not intended as a maximum allowable weight or as an operating limitation. Many airport pavements are capable of supporting limited operations with gross weights in excess of the published figures. Permissible operating weights, insofar as runway strengths are concerned, are a matter of agreement between the owner and user. When desiring to operate into any airport at weights in excess of those published in the publication, users should contact the airport management for permission. Runway strength figures are shown in thousand of pounds, with the last three figures being omitted. Add 000 to figure following S, D, 2S, 2T, AUW, SWL, etc., for gross weight capacity. A blank space following the letter designator is used to indicate the runway can sustain aircraft with this type landing gear, although definite runway weight bearing capacity figures are not available, e.g., S, D. Applicable codes for typical gear configurations with S=Single, D=Dual, T=Triple and Q=Quadruple:

CURRENT	NEW	NEW DESCRIPTION
S	S	Single wheel type landing gear (DC3), (C47), (F15), etc.
D	D	Dual wheel type landing gear (BE1900), (B737), (A319), etc.
T	D	Dual wheel type landing gear (P3, C9).
ST	2S	Two single wheels in tandem type landing gear (C130).
TRT	2T	Two triple wheels in tandem type landing gear (C17), etc.
DT	2D	Two dual wheels in tandem type landing gear (B707), etc.
TT	2D	Two dual wheels in tandem type landing gear (B757, KC135).
SBTT	2D/D1	Two dual wheels in tandem/dual wheel body gear type landing gear (KC10).
None	2D/2D1	Two dual wheels in tandem/two dual wheels in tandem body gear type landing gear (A340–600).
DDT	2D/2D2	Two dual wheels in tandem/two dual wheels in double tandem body gear type landing gear (B747, E4).
TTT	3D	Three dual wheels in tandem type landing gear (B777), etc.
TT	D2	Dual wheel gear two struts per side main gear type landing gear (B52).
TDT	C5	Complex dual wheel and quadruple wheel combination landing gear (C5).

DIRECTORY LEGEND

AUW—All up weight. Maximum weight bearing capacity for any aircraft irrespective of landing gear configuration.

SWL—Single Wheel Loading. (This includes information submitted in terms of Equivalent Single Wheel Loading (ESWL) and Single Isolated Wheel Loading).

PSI—Pounds per square inch. PSI is the actual figure expressing maximum pounds per square inch runway will support, e.g., (SWL 000/PSI 535).

Omission of weight bearing capacity indicates information unknown.

The ACN/PCN System is the ICAO standard method of reporting pavement strength for pavements with bearing strengths greater than 12,500 pounds. The Pavement Classification Number (PCN) is established by an engineering assessment of the runway. The PCN is for use in conjunction with an Aircraft Classification Number (ACN). Consult the Aircraft Flight Manual, Flight Information Handbook, or other appropriate source for ACN tables or charts. Currently, ACN data may not be available for all aircraft. If an ACN table or chart is available, the ACN can be calculated by taking into account the aircraft weight, the pavement type, and the subgrade category. For runways that have been evaluated under the ACN/PCN system, the PCN will be shown as a five-part code (e.g. PCN 80 R/B/W/T). Details of the coded format are as follows:

(1) The PCN NUMBER—The reported PCN indicates that an aircraft with an ACN equal or less than the reported PCN can operate on the pavement subject to any limitation on the tire pressure.

(2) The type of pavement:
R — Rigid
F — Flexible

(3) The pavement subgrade category:
A — High
B — Medium
C — Low
D — Ultra-low

(4) The maximum tire pressure authorized for the pavement:
W — High, no limit
X — Medium, limited to 217 psi
Y — Low, limited to 145 psi
Z — Very low, limited to 73 psi

(5) Pavement evaluation method:
T — Technical evaluation
U — By experience of aircraft using the pavement

NOTE: Prior permission from the airport controlling authority is required when the ACN of the aircraft exceeds the published PCN or aircraft tire pressure exceeds the published limits.

RUNWAY LIGHTING

Lights are in operation sunset to sunrise. Lighting available by prior arrangement only or operating part of the night and/or pilot controlled lighting with specific operating hours are indicated under airport or military remarks. At USN/USMC facilities lights are available only during airport hours of operation. Since obstructions are usually lighted, obstruction lighting is not included in this code. Unlighted obstructions on or surrounding an airport will be noted in airport or military remarks. Runway lights nonstandard (NSTD) are systems for which the light fixtures are not FAA approved L-800 series: color, intensity, or spacing does not meet FAA standards. Nonstandard runway lights, VASI, or any other system not listed below will be shown in airport remarks or military service. Temporary, emergency or limited runway edge lighting such as flares, smudge pots, lanterns or portable runway lights will also be shown in airport remarks or military service. Types of lighting are shown with the runway or runway end they serve.

NSTD—Light system fails to meet FAA standards.
LIRL—Low Intensity Runway Lights.
MIRL—Medium Intensity Runway Lights.
HIRL—High Intensity Runway Lights.
RAIL—Runway Alignment Indicator Lights.
REIL—Runway End Identifier Lights.
CL—Centerline Lights.
TDZL—Touchdown Zone Lights.
ODALS—Omni Directional Approach Lighting System.
AF OVRN—Air Force Overrun 1000′ Standard Approach Lighting System.
LDIN—Lead-In Lighting System.
MALS—Medium Intensity Approach Lighting System.
MALSF—Medium Intensity Approach Lighting System with Sequenced Flashing Lights.
MALSR—Medium Intensity Approach Lighting System with Runway Alignment Indicator Lights.

SALS—Short Approach Lighting System.
SALSF—Short Approach Lighting System with Sequenced Flashing Lights.
SSALS—Simplified Short Approach Lighting System.
SSALF—Simplified Short Approach Lighting System with Sequenced Flashing Lights.
SSALR—Simplified Short Approach Lighting System with Runway Alignment Indicator Lights.
ALSAF—High Intensity Approach Lighting System with Sequenced Flashing Lights.
ALSF1—High Intensity Approach Lighting System with Sequenced Flashing Lights, Category I, Configuration.
ALSF2—High Intensity Approach Lighting System with Sequenced Flashing Lights, Category II, Configuration.
SF—Sequenced Flashing Lights.
OLS—Optical Landing System.
WAVE-OFF.

NOTE: Civil ALSF2 may be operated as SSALR during favorable weather conditions. When runway edge lights are positioned more than 10 feet from the edge of the usable runway surface a remark will be added in the "Remarks" portion of the airport entry. This is applicable to Air Force, Air National Guard and Air Force Reserve Bases, and those joint civil/military airfields on which they are tenants.

DIRECTORY LEGEND

VISUAL GLIDESLOPE INDICATORS

APAP—A system of panels, which may or may not be lighted, used for alignment of approach path.

| PNIL | APAP on left side of runway | PNIR | APAP on right side of runway |

PAPI—Precision Approach Path Indicator

| P2L | 2-identical light units placed on left side of runway | P4L | 4-identical light units placed on left side of runway |
| P2R | 2-identical light units placed on right side of runway | P4R | 4-identical light units placed on right side of runway |

PVASI—Pulsating/steady burning visual approach slope indicator, normally a single light unit projecting two colors.

| PSIL | PVASI on left side of runway | PSIR | PVASI on right side of runway |

SAVASI—Simplified Abbreviated Visual Approach Slope Indicator

| S2L | 2-box SAVASI on left side of runway | S2R | 2-box SAVASI on right side of runway |

TRCV—Tri-color visual approach slope indicator, normally a single light unit projecting three colors.

| TRIL | TRCV on left side of runway | TRIR | TRCV on right side of runway |

VASI—Visual Approach Slope Indicator

V2L	2-box VASI on left side of runway	V6L	6-box VASI on left side of runway
V2R	2-box VASI on right side of runway	V6R	6-box VASI on right side of runway
V4L	4-box VASI on left side of runway	V12	12-box VASI on both sides of runway
V4R	4-box VASI on right side of runway	V16	16-box VASI on both sides of runway

NOTE: Approach slope angle and threshold crossing height will be shown when available; i.e., –GA 3.5° TCH 37'.

PILOT CONTROL OF AIRPORT LIGHTING

Key Mike	Function
7 times within 5 seconds	Highest intensity available
5 times within 5 seconds	Medium or lower intensity (Lower REIL or REIL-Off)
3 times within 5 seconds	Lowest intensity available (Lower REIL or REIL-Off)

Available systems will be indicated in the airport or military remarks, e.g., ACTIVATE HIRL Rwy 07–25, MALSR Rwy 07, and VASI Rwy 07—122.8.

Where the airport is not served by an instrument approach procedure and/or has an independent type system of different specification installed by the airport sponsor, descriptions of the type lights, method of control, and operating frequency will be explained in clear text. See AIM, "Basic Flight Information and ATC Procedures," for detailed description of pilot control of airport lighting.

RUNWAY SLOPE

When available, runway slope data will only be provided for those airports with an approved FAA instrument approach procedure. Runway slope will be shown only when it is 0.3 percent or greater. On runways less than 8000 feet, the direction of the slope up will be indicated, e.g., 0.3% up NW. On runways 8000 feet or greater, the slope will be shown (up or down) on the runway end line, e.g., RWY 13: 0.3% up., RWY 21: Pole. Rgt tfc. 0.4% down.

RUNWAY END DATA

Information pertaining to the runway approach end such as approach lights, touchdown zone lights, runway end identification lights, visual glideslope indicators, displaced thresholds, controlling obstruction, and right hand traffic pattern, will be shown on the specific runway end. "Rgt tfc"—Right traffic indicates right turns should be made on landing and takeoff for specified runway end.

LAND AND HOLD SHORT OPERATIONS (LAHSO)

LAHSO is an acronym for "Land and Hold Short Operations." These operations include landing and holding short of an intersection runway, an intersecting taxiway, or other predetermined points on the runway other than a runway or taxiway. Measured distance represents the available landing distance on the landing runway, in feet.

Specific questions regarding these distances should be referred to the air traffic manager of the facility concerned. The Aeronautical Information Manual contains specific details on hold–short operations and markings.

RUNWAY DECLARED DISTANCE INFORMATION

TORA—Take-off Run Available. The length of runway declared available and suitable for the ground run of an aeroplane take–off.

TODA—Take-off Distance Available. The length of the take–off run available plus the length of the clearway, if provided.

ASDA—Accelerate-Stop Distance Available. The length of the take–off run available plus the length of the stopway, if provided.

LDA—Landing Distance Available. The length of runway which is declared available and suitable for the ground run of an aeroplane landing.

㉒ ARRESTING GEAR/SYSTEMS

Arresting gear is shown as it is located on the runway. The a–gear distance from the end of the appropriate runway (or into the overrun) is indicated in parentheses. A–Gear which has a bi–direction capability and can be utilized for emergency approach end engagement is indicated by a (B). The direction of engaging device is indicated by an arrow. Up to 15 minutes advance notice may be required for rigging A–Gear for approach and engagement. Airport listing may show availability of other than US Systems. This information is provided for emergency requirements only. Refer to current aircraft operating manuals for specific engagement weight and speed criteria based on aircraft structural restrictions and arresting system limitations.

Following is a list of current systems referenced in this publication identified by both Air Force and Navy terminology:

DIRECTORY LEGEND

BI–DIRECTIONAL CABLE (B)

TYPE	DESCRIPTION
BAK–9	Rotary friction brake.
BAK–12A	Standard BAK–12 with 950 foot run out, 1–inch cable and 40,000 pound weight setting. Rotary friction brake.
BAK–12B	Extended BAK–12 with 1200 foot run, 1¼ inch Cable and 50,000 pounds weight setting. Rotary friction brake.
E28	Rotary Hydraulic (Water Brake).
M21	Rotary Hydraulic (Water Brake) Mobile.

The following device is used in conjunction with some aircraft arresting systems:

BAK–14	A device that raises a hook cable out of a slot in the runway surface and is remotely positioned for engagement by the tower on request. (In addition to personnel reaction time, the system requires up to five seconds to fully raise the cable.)
H	A device that raises a hook cable out of a slot in the runway surface and is remotely positioned for engagement by the tower on request. (In addition to personnel reaction time, the system requires up to one and one–half seconds to fully raise the cable.)

UNI–DIRECTIONAL CABLE

TYPE	DESCRIPTION
MB60	Textile brake—an emergency one–time use, modular braking system employing the tearing of specially woven textile straps to absorb the kinetic energy.
E5/E5–1/E5–3	Chain Type. At USN/USMC stations E–5 A–GEAR systems are rated, e.g., E–5 RATING–13R–1100 HW (DRY), 31L/R–1200 STD (WET). This rating is a function of the A–GEAR chain weight and length and is used to determine the maximum aircraft engaging speed. A dry rating applies to a stabilized surface (dry or wet) while a wet rating takes into account the amount (if any) of wet overrun that is not capable of withstanding the aircraft weight. These ratings are published under Military Service.

FOREIGN CABLE

TYPE	DESCRIPTION	US EQUIVALENT
44B–3H	Rotary Hydraulic) (Water Brake)	
CHAG	Chain	E–5

UNI–DIRECTIONAL BARRIER

TYPE	DESCRIPTION
MA–1A	Web barrier between stanchions attached to a chain energy absorber.
BAK–15	Web barrier between stanchions attached to an energy absorber (water squeezer, rotary friction, chain). Designed for wing engagement.

NOTE: Landing short of the runway threshold on a runway with a BAK–15 in the underrun is a significant hazard. The barrier in the down position still protrudes several inches above the underrun. Aircraft contact with the barrier short of the runway threshold can cause damage to the barrier and substantial damage to the aircraft.

OTHER

TYPE	DESCRIPTION
EMAS	Engineered Material Arresting System, located beyond the departure end of the runway, consisting of high energy absorbing materials which will crush under the weight of an aircraft.

㉓ MILITARY SERVICE

Specific military services available at the airport are listed under this general heading. Remarks applicable to any military service are shown in the individual service listing.

㉔ JET AIRCRAFT STARTING UNITS (JASU)

The numeral preceding the type of unit indicates the number of units available. The absence of the numeral indicates ten or more units available. If the number of units is unknown, the number one will be shown. Absence of JASU designation indicates non–availability.

The following is a list of current JASU systems referenced in this publication:

USAF JASU (For variations in technical data, refer to T.O. 35–1–7.)

ELECTRICAL STARTING UNITS:

A/M32A–86	AC: 115/200v, 3 phase, 90 kva, 0.8 pf, 4 wire
	DC: 28v, 1500 amp, 72 kw (with TR pack)
MC–1A	AC: 115/208v, 400 cycle, 3 phase, 37.5 kva, 0.8 pf, 108 amp, 4 wire
	DC: 28v, 500 amp, 14 kw
MD–3	AC: 115/208v, 400 cycle, 3 phase, 60 kva, 0.75 pf, 4 wire
	DC: 28v, 1500 amp, 45 kw, split bus
MD–3A	AC: 115/208v, 400 cycle, 3 phase, 60 kva, 0.75 pf, 4 wire
	DC: 28v, 1500 amp, 45 kw, split bus
MD–3M	AC: 115/208v, 400 cycle, 3 phase, 60 kva, 0.75 pf, 4 wire
	DC: 28v, 500 amp, 15 kw

DIRECTORY LEGEND

MD–4	AC: 120/208v, 400 cycle, 3 phase, 62.5 kva, 0.8 pf, 175 amp, "WYE" neutral ground, 4 wire, 120v, 400 cycle, 3 phase, 62.5 kva, 0.8 pf, 303 amp, "DELTA" 3 wire, 120v, 400 cycle, 1 phase, 62.5 kva, 0.8 pf, 520 amp, 2 wire

AIR STARTING UNITS

AM32–95	150 +/– 5 lb/min (2055 +/– 68 cfm) at 51 +/– 2 psia
AM32A–95	150 +/– 5 lb/min @ 49 +/– 2 psia (35 +/– 2 psig)
LASS	150 +/– 5 lb/min @ 49 +/– 2 psia
MA–1A	82 lb/min (1123 cfm) at 130° air inlet temp, 45 psia (min) air outlet press
MC–1	15 cfm, 3500 psia
MC–1A	15 cfm, 3500 psia
MC–2A	15 cfm, 200 psia
MC–11	8,000 cu in cap, 4000 psig, 15 cfm

COMBINED AIR AND ELECTRICAL STARTING UNITS:

AGPU	AC: 115/200v, 400 cycle, 3 phase, 30 kw gen
	DC: 28v, 700 amp
	AIR: 60 lb/min @ 40 psig @ sea level
AM32A–60*	AIR: 120 +/– 4 lb/min (1644 +/– 55 cfm) at 49 +/– 2 psia
	AC: 120/208v, 400 cycle, 3 phase, 75 kva, 0.75 pf, 4 wire, 120v, 1 phase, 25 kva
	DC: 28v, 500 amp, 15 kw
AM32A–60A	AIR: 150 +/– 5 lb/min (2055 +/– 68 cfm at 51 +/– psia
	AC: 120/208v, 400 cycle, 3 phase, 75 kva, 0.75 pf, 4 wire
	DC: 28v, 200 amp, 5.6 kw
AM32A–60B*	AIR: 130 lb/min, 50 psia
	AC: 120/208v, 400 cycle, 3 phase, 75 kva, 0.75 pf, 4 wire
	DC: 28v, 200 amp, 5.6 kw

*NOTE: During combined air and electrical loads, the pneumatic circuitry takes preference and will limit the amount of electrical power available.

USN JASU

ELECTRICAL STARTING UNITS:

NC–8A/A1	DC: 500 amp constant, 750 amp intermittent, 28v;
	AC: 60 kva @ .8 pf, 115/200v, 3 phase, 400 Hz.
NC–10A/A1/B/C	DC: 750 amp constant, 1000 amp intermittent, 28v;
	AC: 90 kva, 115/200v, 3 phase, 400 Hz.

AIR STARTING UNITS:

GTC–85/GTE–85	120 lbs/min @ 45 psi.
MSU–200NAV/A/U47A–5	204 lbs/min @ 56 psia.
WELLS AIR START SYSTEM	180 lbs/min @ 75 psi or 120 lbs/min @ 45 psi. Simultaneous multiple start capability.

COMBINED AIR AND ELECTRICAL STARTING UNITS:

NCPP–105/RCPT	180 lbs/min @ 75 psi or 120 lbs/min @ 45 psi. 700 amp, 28v DC. 120/208v, 400 Hz AC, 30 kva.

JASU (ARMY)

59B2–1B	28v, 7.5 kw, 280 amp.

OTHER JASU

ELECTRICAL STARTING UNITS (DND):

CE12	AC 115/200v, 140 kva, 400 Hz, 3 phase
CE13	AC 115/200v, 60 kva, 400 Hz, 3 phase
CE14	AC/DC 115/200v, 140 kva, 400 Hz, 3 phase, 28vDC, 1500 amp
CE15	DC 22–35v, 500 amp continuous 1100 amp intermittent
CE16	DC 22–35v, 500 amp continuous 1100 amp intermittent soft start

AIR STARTING UNITS (DND):

CA2	ASA 45.5 psig, 116.4 lb/min

COMBINED AIR AND ELECTRICAL STARTING UNITS (DND)

CEA1	AC 120/208v, 60 kva, 400 Hz, 3 phase DC 28v, 75 amp
	AIR 112.5 lb/min, 47 psig

ELECTRICAL STARTING UNITS (OTHER)

C–26	28v 45kw 115–200v 15kw 380–800 Hz 1 phase 2 wire
C–26–B, C–26–C	28v 45kw: Split Bus: 115–200v 15kw 380–800 Hz 1 phase 2 wire
E3	DC 28v/10kw

AIR STARTING UNITS (OTHER):

A4	40 psi/2 lb/sec (LPAS Mk12, Mk12L, Mk12A, Mk1, Mk2B)
MA–1	150 Air HP, 115 lb/min 50 psia
MA–2	250 Air HP, 150 lb/min 75 psia

CARTRIDGE:

MXU–4A	USAF

DIRECTORY LEGEND

25 FUEL—MILITARY

Fuel available through US Military Base supply, DESC Into–Plane Contracts and/or reciprocal agreement is listed first and is followed by (Mil). At commercial airports where Into–Plane contracts are in place, the name of the refueling agent is shown. Military fuel should be used first if it is available. When military fuel cannot be obtained but Into–Plane contract fuel is available, Government aircraft must refuel with the contract fuel and applicable refueling agent to avoid any breach in contract terms and conditions. Fuel not available through the above is shown preceded by NC (no contract). When fuel is obtained from NC sources, local purchase procedures must be followed. The US Military Aircraft Identaplates DD Form 1896 (Jet Fuel), DD Form 1897 (Avgas) and AF Form 1245 (Avgas) are used at military installations only. The US Government Aviation Into–Plane Reimbursement (AIR) Card (currently issued by AVCARD) is the instrument to be used to obtain fuel under a DESC Into–Plane Contract and for NC purchases if the refueling agent at the commercial airport accepts the AVCARD. A current list of contract fuel locations is available online at www.desc.dla.mil/Static/ProductsAndServices.asp; click on the Commercial Airports button.

See legend item 14 for fuel code and description.

26 SUPPORTING FLUIDS AND SYSTEMS—MILITARY

CODE

ADI	Anti–Detonation Injection Fluid—Reciprocating Engine Aircraft.
W	Water Thrust Augmentation—Jet Aircraft.
WAI	Water–Alcohol Injection Type, Thrust Augmentation—Jet Aircraft.
SP	Single Point Refueling.
PRESAIR	Air Compressors rated 3,000 PSI or more.
De–Ice	Anti–icing/De–icing/Defrosting Fluid (MIL–A–8243).

OXYGEN:

LPOX	Low pressure oxygen servicing.
HPOX	High pressure oxygen servicing.
LHOX	Low and high pressure oxygen servicing.
LOX	Liquid oxygen servicing.
OXRB	Oxygen replacement bottles. (Maintained primarily at Naval stations for use in acft where oxygen can be replenished only by replacement of cylinders.)
OX	Indicates oxygen servicing when type of servicing is unknown.

NOTE: Combinations of above items is used to indicate complete oxygen servicing available;

LHOXRB	Low and high pressure oxygen servicing and replacement bottles;
LPOXRB	Low pressure oxygen replacement bottles only, etc.

NOTE: Aircraft will be serviced with oxygen procured under military specifications only. Aircraft will not be serviced with medical oxygen.

NITROGEN:

LPNIT — Low pressure nitrogen servicing.
HPNIT — High pressure nitrogen servicing.
LHNIT — Low and high pressure nitrogen servicing.

27 OIL—MILITARY

US AVIATION OILS (MIL SPECS):

CODE	GRADE, TYPE
O–113	1065, Reciprocating Engine Oil (MIL–L–6082)
O–117	1100, Reciprocating Engine Oil (MIL–L–6082)
O–117+	1100, O–117 plus cyclohexanone (MIL–L–6082)
O–123	1065, (Dispersant), Reciprocating Engine Oil (MIL–L–22851 Type III)
O–128	1100, (Dispersant), Reciprocating Engine Oil (MIL–L–22851 Type II)
O–132	1005, Jet Engine Oil (MIL–L–6081)
O–133	1010, Jet Engine Oil (MIL–L–6081)
O–147	None, MIL–L–6085A Lubricating Oil, Instrument, Synthetic
O–148	None, MIL–L–7808 (Synthetic Base) Turbine Engine Oil
O–149	None, Aircraft Turbine Engine Synthetic, 7.5c St
O–155	None, MIL–L–6086C, Aircraft, Medium Grade
O–156	None, MIL–L–23699 (Synthetic Base), Turboprop and Turboshaft Engines
JOAP/SOAP	Joint Oil Analysis Program. JOAP support is furnished during normal duty hours, other times on request. (JOAP and SOAP programs provide essentially the same service, JOAP is now the standard joint service supported program.)

28 TRANSIENT ALERT (TRAN ALERT)—MILITARY

Tran Alert service is considered to include all services required for normal aircraft turn–around, e.g., servicing (fuel, oil, oxygen, etc.), debriefing to determine requirements for maintenance, minor maintenance, inspection and parking assistance of transient aircraft. Drag chute repack, specialized maintenance, or extensive repairs will be provided within the capabilities and priorities of the base. Delays can be anticipated after normal duty hours/holidays/weekends regardless of the hours of transient maintenance operation. Pilots should not expect aircraft to be serviced for TURN–AROUNDS during time periods when servicing or maintenance manpower is not available. In the case of airports not operated exclusively by US military, the servicing indicated by the remarks will not always be available for US military

DIRECTORY LEGEND

aircraft. When transient alert services are not shown, facilities are unknown. NO PRIORITY BASIS—means that transient alert services will be provided only after all the requirements for mission/tactical assigned aircraft have been accomplished.

29 AIRPORT REMARKS

The Attendance Schedule is the months, days and hours the airport is actually attended. Airport attendance does not mean watchman duties or telephone accessibility, but rather an attendant or operator on duty to provide at least minimum services (e.g., repairs, fuel, transportation).

Airport Remarks have been grouped in order of applicability. Airport remarks are limited to those items of information that are determined essential for operational use, i.e., conditions of a permanent or indefinite nature and conditions that will remain in effect for more than 30 days concerning aeronautical facilities, services, maintenance available, procedures or hazards, knowledge of which is essential for safe and efficient operation of aircraft. Information concerning permanent closing of a runway or taxiway will not be shown. A note "See Special Notices" shall be applied within this remarks section when a special notice applicable to the entry is contained in the Special Notices section of this publication.

Parachute Jumping indicates parachute jumping areas associated with the airport. See Parachute Jumping Area section of this publication for additional Information.

Landing Fee indicates landing charges for private or non-revenue producing aircraft. In addition, fees may be charged for planes that remain over a couple of hours and buy no services, or at major airline terminals for all aircraft.

Note: Unless otherwise stated, remarks including runway ends refer to the runway's approach end.

30 MILITARY REMARKS

Military Remarks published at a joint Civil/Military facility are remarks that are applicable to the Military. At Military Facilities all remarks will be published under the heading Military Remarks. Remarks contained in this section may not be applicable to civil users. The first group of remarks is applicable to the primary operator of the airport. Remarks applicable to a tenant on the airport are shown preceded by the tenant organization, i.e., (A) (AF) (N) (ANG), etc. Military airports operate 24 hours unless otherwise specified. Airport operating hours are listed first (airport operating hours will only be listed if they are different than the airport attended hours or if the attended hours are unavailable) followed by pertinent remarks in order of applicability. Remarks will include information on restrictions, hazards, traffic pattern, noise abatement, customs/agriculture/immigration, and miscellaneous information applicable to the Military.

Type of restrictions:

CLOSED: When designated closed, the airport is restricted from use by all aircraft unless stated otherwise. Any closure applying to specific type of aircraft or operation will be so stated. USN/USMC/USAF airports are considered closed during non–operating hours. Closed airports may be utilized during an emergency provided there is a safe landing area.

OFFICIAL BUSINESS ONLY: The airfield is closed to all transient military aircraft for obtaining routine services such as fueling, passenger drop off or pickup, practice approaches, parking, etc. The airfield may be used by aircrews and aircraft if official government business (including civilian) must be conducted on or near the airfield and prior permission is received from the airfield manager.

AF OFFICIAL BUSINESS ONLY OR NAVY OFFICIAL BUSINESS ONLY: Indicates that the restriction applies only to service indicated.

PRIOR PERMISSION REQUIRED (PPR): Airport is closed to transient aircraft unless approval for operation is obtained from the appropriate commander through Chief, Airfield Management or Airfield Operations Officer. Official Business or PPR does not preclude the use of US Military airports as an alternate for IFR flights. If a non–US military airport is used as a weather alternate and requires a PPR, the PPR must be requested and confirmed before the flight departs. The purpose of PPR is to control volume and flow of traffic rather than to prohibit it. Prior permission is required for all aircraft requiring transient alert service outside the published transient alert duty hours. All aircraft carrying hazardous materials must obtain prior permission as outlined in AFJI 11–204, AR 95–27, OPNAVINST 3710.7.

Note: OFFICIAL BUSINESS ONLY AND PPR restrictions are not applicable to Special Air Mission (SAM) or Special Air Resource (SPAR) aircraft providing person or persons on aboard are designated Code 6 or higher as explained in AFJMAN 11–213, AR 95–11, OPNAVINST 3722–8J. Official Business Only or PPR do not preclude the use of the airport as an alternate for IFR flights.

31 WEATHER DATA SOURCES

Weather data sources will be listed alphabetically followed by their assigned frequencies and/or telephone number and hours of operation.

ASOS—Automated Surface Observing System. Reports the same as an AWOS–3 plus precipitation identification and intensity, and freezing rain occurrence;

AWOS—Automated Weather Observing System

  AWOS–A—reports altimeter setting (all other information is advisory only).

  AWOS–1—reports altimeter setting, wind data and usually temperature, dew point and density altitude.

  AWOS–2—reports the same as AWOS–1 plus visibility.

  AWOS–3—reports the same as AWOS–1 plus visibility and cloud/ceiling data.

  AWOS–3P reports the same as the AWOS–3 system, plus a precipitation identification sensor.

  AWOS–3PT reports the same as the AWOS–3 system, plus precipitation identification sensor and a thunderstorm/lightning reporting capability.

  AWOS–3T reports the same as AWOS–3 system and includes a thunderstorm/lightning reporting capability.

  See AIM, Basic Flight Information and ATC Procedures for detailed description of Weather Data Sources.

DIRECTORY LEGEND

HIWAS—See RADIO AIDS TO NAVIGATION

LAWRS—Limited Aviation Weather Reporting Station where observers report cloud height, weather, obstructions to vision, temperature and dewpoint (in most cases), surface wind, altimeter and pertinent remarks.

LLWAS—indicates a Low Level Wind Shear Alert System consisting of a center field and several field perimeter anemometers.

SAWRS—identifies airports that have a Supplemental Aviation Weather Reporting Station available to pilots for current weather information.

SWSL—Supplemental Weather Service Location providing current local weather information via radio and telephone.

TDWR—indicates airports that have Terminal Doppler Weather Radar.

WSP—indicates airports that have Weather System Processor.

When the automated weather source is broadcast over an associated airport NAVAID frequency (see NAVAID line), it shall be indicated by a bold ASOS, AWOS, or HIWAS followed by the frequency, identifier and phone number, if available.

㉜ COMMUNICATIONS

Airport terminal control facilities and radio communications associated with the airport shall be shown. When the call sign is not the same as the airport name the call sign will be shown. Frequencies shall normally be shown in descending order with the primary frequency listed first. Frequencies will be listed, together with sectorization indicated by outbound radials, and hours of operation. Communications will be listed in sequence as follows:

Single Frequency Approach (SFA), Common Traffic Advisory Frequency (CTAF), Automatic Terminal Information Service (ATIS) and Aeronautical Advisory Stations (UNICOM) or (AUNICOM) along with their frequency is shown, where available, on the line following the heading "COMMUNICATIONS." When the CTAF and UNICOM frequencies are the same, the frequency will be shown as CTAF/UNICOM 122.8.

The FSS telephone nationwide is toll free 1–800–WX–BRIEF (1–800–992–7433). When the FSS is located on the field it will be indicated as "on arpt". Frequencies available at the FSS will follow in descending order. Remote Communications Outlet (RCO) providing service to the airport followed by the frequency and FSS RADIO name will be shown when available.

FSS's provide information on airport conditions, radio aids and other facilities, and process flight plans. Airport Advisory Service (AAS) is provided on the CTAF by FSS's for select non-tower airports or airports where the tower is not in operation.

(See AIM, Para 4–1–9 Traffic Advisory Practices at Airports Without Operating Control Towers or AC 90–42C.)

Aviation weather briefing service is provided by FSS specialists. Flight and weather briefing services are also available by calling the telephone numbers listed.

Remote Communications Outlet (RCO)—An unmanned air/ground communications facility that is remotely controlled and provides UHF or VHF communications capability to extend the service range of an FSS.

Civil Communications Frequencies-Civil communications frequencies used in the FSS air/ground system are operated on 122.0, 122.2, 123.6; emergency 121.5; plus receive-only on 122.1.

    a. 122.0 is assigned as the Enroute Flight Advisory Service frequency at selected FSS RADIO outlets.

    b. 122.2 is assigned as a common enroute frequency.

    c. 123.6 is assigned as the airport advisory frequency at select non-tower locations. At airports with a tower, FSS may provide airport advisories on the tower frequency when tower is closed.

    d. 122.1 is the primary receive-only frequency at VOR's.

    e. Some FSS's are assigned 50 kHz frequencies in the 122–126 MHz band (eg. 122.45). Pilots using the FSS A/G system should refer to this directory or appropriate charts to determine frequencies available at the FSS or remoted facility through which they wish to communicate.

Emergency frequency 121.5 and 243.0 are available at all Flight Service Stations, most Towers, Approach Control and RADAR facilities.

Frequencies published followed by the letter "T" or "R", indicate that the facility will only transmit or receive respectively on that frequency. All radio aids to navigation (NAVAID) frequencies are transmit only.

TERMINAL SERVICES

SFA—Single Frequency Approach.

CTAF—A program designed to get all vehicles and aircraft at airports without an operating control tower on a common frequency.

ATIS—A continuous broadcast of recorded non-control information in selected terminal areas.

D–ATIS—Digital ATIS provides ATIS information in text form outside the standard reception range of conventional ATIS via landline & data link communications and voice message within range of existing transmitters.

AUNICOM—Automated UNICOM is a computerized, command response system that provides automated weather, radio check capability and airport advisory information selected from an automated menu by microphone clicks.

UNICOM—A non-government air/ground radio communications facility which may provide airport information.

PTD—Pilot to Dispatcher.

APP CON—Approach Control. The symbol ® indicates radar approach control.

TOWER—Control tower.

GCA—Ground Control Approach System.

GND CON—Ground Control.

GCO—Ground Communication Outlet—An unstaffed, remotely controlled, ground/ground communications facility. Pilots at uncontrolled airports may contact ATC and FSS via VHF to a telephone connection to obtain an instrument clearance or close a VFR or IFR flight plan. They may also get an updated weather briefing prior to takeoff. Pilots will use four "key clicks" on the

DIRECTORY LEGEND

VHF radio to contact the appropriate ATC facility or six "key clicks" to contact the FSS. The GCO system is intended to be used only on the ground.
DEP CON—Departure Control. The symbol Ⓡ indicates radar departure control.
CLNC DEL—Clearance Delivery.
PRE TAXI CLNC—Pre taxi clearance.

VFR ADVSY SVC—VFR Advisory Service. Service provided by Non-Radar Approach Control.
Advisory Service for VFR aircraft (upon a workload basis) ctc APP CON.
COMD POST—Command Post followed by the operator call sign in parenthesis.
PMSV—Pilot-to-Metro Service call sign, frequency and hours of operation, when full service is other than continuous. PMSV installations at which weather observation service is available shall be indicated, following the frequency and/or hours of operation as "Wx obsn svc 1900–0000Z‡" or "other times" may be used when no specific time is given. PMSV facilities manned by forecasters are considered "Full Service". PMSV facilities manned by weather observers are listed as "Limited Service".
OPS—Operations followed by the operator call sign in parenthesis.
CON
RANGE
FLT FLW—Flight Following
MEDIVAC
NOTE: Communication frequencies followed by the letter "X" indicate frequency available on request.

㉝ AIRSPACE

Information concerning Class B, C, and part-time D and E surface area airspace shall be published with effective times. Class D and E surface area airspace that is continuous as established by Rulemaking Docket will not be shown.
CLASS B—Radar Sequencing and Separation Service for all aircraft in CLASS B airspace.
CLASS C—Separation between IFR and VFR aircraft and sequencing of VFR arrivals to the primary airport.
TRSA—Radar Sequencing and Separation Service for participating VFR Aircraft within a Terminal Radar Service Area.
Class C, D, and E airspace described in this publication is that airspace usually consisting of a 5 NM radius core surface area that begins at the surface and extends upward to an altitude above the airport elevation (charted in MSL for Class C and Class D). Class E surface airspace normally extends from the surface up to but not including the overlying controlled airspace.
When part-time Class C or Class D airspace defaults to Class E, the core surface area becomes Class E. This will be formatted as:
AIRSPACE: CLASS C svc "times" ctc **APP CON** other times CLASS E:
or
AIRSPACE: CLASS D svc "times" other times CLASS E.
When a part-time Class C, Class D or Class E surface area defaults to Class G, the core surface area becomes Class G up to, but not including, the overlying controlled airspace. Normally, the overlying controlled airspace is Class E airspace beginning at either 700′ or 1200′ AGL and may be determined by consulting the relevant VFR Sectional or Terminal Area Charts. This will be formatted as:
AIRSPACE: CLASS C svc "times" ctc **APP CON** other times CLASS G, with CLASS E 700′ (or 1200′) AGL & abv:
or
AIRSPACE: CLASS D svc "times" other times CLASS G with CLASS E 700′ (or 1200′) AGL & abv:
or
AIRSPACE: CLASS E svc "times" other times CLASS G with CLASS E 700′ (or 1200′) AGL & abv.
NOTE: AIRSPACE SVC "TIMES" INCLUDE ALL ASSOCIATED ARRIVAL EXTENSIONS. Surface area arrival extensions for instrument approach procedures become part of the primary core surface area. These extensions may be either Class D or Class E airspace and are effective concurrent with the times of the primary core surface area. For example, when a part-time Class C, Class D or Class E surface area defaults to Class G, the associated arrival extensions will default to Class G at the same time. When a part-time Class C or Class D surface area defaults to Class E, the arrival extensions will remain in effect as Class E airspace.
NOTE: CLASS E AIRSPACE EXTENDING UPWARD FROM 700 FEET OR MORE ABOVE THE SURFACE, DESIGNATED IN CONJUNCTION WITH AN AIRPORT WITH AN APPROVED INSTRUMENT PROCEDURE.
Class E 700′ AGL (shown as magenta vignette on sectional charts) and 1200′ AGL (blue vignette) areas are designated when necessary to provide controlled airspace for transitioning to/from the terminal and enroute environments. Unless otherwise specified, these 700′/1200′ AGL Class E airspace areas remain in effect continuously, regardless of airport operating hours or surface area status. These transition areas should not be confused with surface areas or arrival extensions.
(See Chapter 3, AIRSPACE, in the Aeronautical Information Manual for further details)

DIRECTORY LEGEND

㉞ RADIO AIDS TO NAVIGATION

The Airport/Facility Directory lists, by facility name, all Radio Aids to Navigation that appear on FAA, AeroNav Products Visual or IFR Aeronautical Charts and those upon which the FAA has approved an Instrument Approach Procedure, with exception of selected TACANs. Military TACAN information will be published for Military facilities contained in this publication. All VOR, VORTAC, TACAN, ILS and MLS equipment in the National Airspace System has an automatic monitoring and shutdown feature in the event of malfunction. Unmonitored, as used in this publication, for any navigational aid, means that monitoring personnel cannot observe the malfunction or shutdown signal. The NAVAID NOTAM file identifier will be shown as ''NOTAM FILE IAD'' and will be listed on the Radio Aids to Navigation line. When two or more NAVAIDS are listed and the NOTAM file identifier is different from that shown on the Radio Aids to Navigation line, it will be shown with the NAVAID listing. NOTAM file identifiers for ILSs and its components (e.g., NDB (LOM)) are the same as the associated airports and are not repeated. Automated Surface Observing System (ASOS), Automated Weather Observing System (AWOS), and Hazardous Inflight Weather Advisory Service (HIWAS) will be shown when this service is broadcast over selected NAVAIDs.

NAVAID information is tabulated as indicated in the following sample:

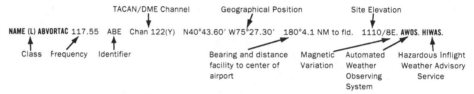

VOR unusable 020°–060° byd 26 NM blo 3,500'

Restriction within the normal altitude/range of the navigational aid (See primary alphabetical listing for restrictions on VORTAC and VOR/DME).

Note: Those DME channel numbers with a (Y) suffix require TACAN to be placed in the ''Y'' mode to receive distance information.

HIWAS—Hazardous Inflight Weather Advisory Service is a continuous broadcast of inflight weather advisories including summarized SIGMETs, convective SIGMETs, AIRMETs and urgent PIREPs. HIWAS is presently broadcast over selected VOR's throughout the U.S.

ASR/PAR—Indicates that Surveillance (ASR) or Precision (PAR) radar instrument approach minimums are published in the U.S. Terminal Procedures. Only part-time hours of operation will be shown.

RADIO CLASS DESIGNATIONS

VOR/DME/TACAN Standard Service Volume (SSV) Classifications

SSV Class	Altitudes	Distance (NM)
(T) Terminal	1000' to 12,000'	25
(L) Low Altitude	1000' to 18,000'	40
(H) High Altitude	1000' to 14,500'	40
	14,500' to 18,000'	100
	18,000' to 45,000'	130
	45,000' to 60,000'	100

NOTE: Additionally, (H) facilities provide (L) and (T) service volume and (L) facilities provide (T) service. Altitudes are with respect to the station's site elevation. Coverage is not available in a cone of airspace directly above the facility.

CONTINUED ON NEXT PAGE

DIRECTORY LEGEND
CONTINUED FROM PRECEDING PAGE

The term VOR is, operationally, a general term covering the VHF omnidirectional bearing type of facility without regard to the fact that the power, the frequency protected service volume, the equipment configuration, and operational requirements may vary between facilities at different locations.

AB	Automatic Weather Broadcast.
DF	Direction Finding Service.
DME	UHF standard (TACAN compatible) distance measuring equipment.
DME(Y)	UHF standard (TACAN compatible) distance measuring equipment that require TACAN to be placed in the ''Y'' mode to receive DME.
GS	Glide slope.
H	Non-directional radio beacon (homing), power 50 watts to less than 2,000 watts (50 NM at all altitudes).
HH	Non-directional radio beacon (homing), power 2,000 watts or more (75 NM at all altitudes).
H-SAB	Non-directional radio beacons providing automatic transcribed weather service.
ILS	Instrument Landing System (voice, where available, on localizer channel).
IM	Inner marker.
ISMLS	Interim Standard Microwave Landing System.
LDA	Localizer Directional Aid.
LMM	Compass locator station when installed at middle marker site (15 NM at all altitudes).
LOM	Compass locator station when installed at outer marker site (15 NM at all altitudes).
MH	Non-directional radio beacon (homing) power less than 50 watts (25 NM at all altitudes).
MLS	Microwave Landing System.
MM	Middle marker.
OM	Outer marker.
S	Simultaneous range homing signal and/or voice.
SABH	Non-directional radio beacon not authorized for IFR or ATC. Provides automatic weather broadcasts.
SDF	Simplified Direction Facility.
TACAN	UHF navigational facility-omnidirectional course and distance information.
VOR	VHF navigational facility-omnidirectional course only.
VOR/DME	Collocated VOR navigational facility and UHF standard distance measuring equipment.
VORTAC	Collocated VOR and TACAN navigational facilities.
W	Without voice on radio facility frequency.
Z	VHF station location marker at a LF radio facility.

DIRECTORY LEGEND
ILS FACILITY PEFORMANCE CLASSIFICATION CODES

Codes define the ability of an ILS to support autoland operations. The two portions of the code represent Official Category and farthest point along a Category I, II, or III approach that the Localizer meets Category III structure tolerances.

Official Category: I, II, or III; the lowest minima on published or unpublished procedures supported by the ILS.

Farthest point of satisfactory Category III Localizer performance for Category I, II, or III approaches: A – 4 NM prior to runway threshold, B – 3500 ft prior to runway threshold, C – glide angle dependent but generally 750–1000 ft prior to threshold, T – runway threshold, D – 3000 ft after runway threshold, and E – 2000 ft prior to stop end of runway.

ILS information is tabulated as indicated in the following sample:

ILS/DME 108.5 I–ORL Chan 22 Rwy 18. Class IIE. LOM HERNY NDB.

ILS Facility Performance
Classification Code

FREQUENCY PAIRING PLAN AND MLS CHANNELING

MLS CHANNEL	VHF FREQUENCY	TACAN CHANNEL	MLS CHANNEL	VHF FREQUENCY	TACAN CHANNEL	MLS CHANNEL	VHF FREQUENCY	TACAN CHANNEL
500	108.10	18X	568	109.45	31Y	636	114.15	88Y
502	108.30	20X	570	109.55	32Y	638	114.25	89Y
504	108.50	22X	572	109.65	33Y	640	114.35	90Y
506	108.70	24X	574	109.75	34Y	642	114.45	91Y
508	108.90	26X	576	109.85	35Y	644	114.55	92Y
510	109.10	28X	578	109.95	36Y	646	114.65	93Y
512	109.30	30X	580	110.05	37Y	648	114.75	94Y
514	109.50	32X	582	110.15	38Y	650	114.85	95Y
516	109.70	34X	584	110.25	39Y	652	114.95	96Y
518	109.90	36X	586	110.35	40Y	654	115.05	97Y
520	110.10	38X	588	110.45	41Y	656	115.15	98Y
522	110.30	40X	590	110.55	42Y	658	115.25	99Y
524	110.50	42X	592	110.65	43Y	660	115.35	100Y
526	110.70	44X	594	110.75	44Y	662	115.45	101Y
528	110.90	46X	596	110.85	45Y	664	115.55	102Y
530	111.10	48X	598	110.95	46Y	666	115.65	103Y
532	111.30	50X	600	111.05	47Y	668	115.75	104Y
534	111.50	52X	602	111.15	48Y	670	115.85	105Y
536	111.70	54X	604	111.25	49Y	672	115.95	106Y
538	111.90	56X	606	111.35	50Y	674	116.05	107Y
540	108.05	17Y	608	111.45	51Y	676	116.15	108Y
542	108.15	18Y	610	111.55	52Y	678	116.25	109Y
544	108.25	19Y	612	111.65	53Y	680	116.35	110Y
546	108.35	20Y	614	111.75	54Y	682	116.45	111Y
548	108.45	21Y	616	111.85	55Y	684	116.55	112Y
550	108.55	22Y	618	111.95	56Y	686	116.65	113Y
552	108.65	23Y	620	113.35	80Y	688	116.75	114Y
554	108.75	24Y	622	113.45	81Y	690	116.85	115Y
556	108.85	25Y	624	113.55	82Y	692	116.95	116Y
558	108.95	26Y	626	113.65	83Y	694	117.05	117Y
560	109.05	27Y	628	113.75	84Y	696	117.15	118Y
562	109.15	28Y	630	113.85	85Y	698	117.25	119Y
564	109.25	29Y	632	113.95	86Y			
566	109.35	30Y	634	114.05	87Y			

FREQUENCY PAIRING PLAN AND MLS CHANNELING

The following is a list of paired VOR/ILS VHF frequencies with TACAN channels and MLS channels.

TACAN CHANNEL	VHF FREQUENCY	MLS CHANNEL	TACAN CHANNEL	VHF FREQUENCY	MLS CHANNEL	TACAN CHANNEL	VHF FREQUENCY	MLS CHANNEL
2X	134.5	-	19Y	108.25	544	25X	108.80	-
2Y	134.55	-	20X	108.30	502	25Y	108.85	556
11X	135.4	-	20Y	108.35	546	26X	108.90	508
11Y	135.45	-	21X	108.40	-	26Y	108.95	558
12X	135.5	-	21Y	108.45	548	27X	109.00	-
12Y	135.55	-	22X	108.50	504	27Y	109.05	560
17X	108.00	-	22Y	108.55	550	28X	109.10	510
17Y	108.05	540	23X	108.60	-	28Y	109.15	562
18X	108.10	500	23Y	108.65	552	29X	109.20	-
18Y	108.15	542	24X	108.70	506	29Y	109.25	564
19X	108.20	-	24Y	108.75	554	30X	109.30	512

DIRECTORY LEGEND

TACAN CHANNEL	VHF FREQUENCY	MLS CHANNEL	TACAN CHANNEL	VHF FREQUENCY	MLS CHANNEL	TACAN CHANNEL	VHF FREQUENCY	MLS CHANNEL
30Y	109.35	566	63X	133.60	-	95Y	114.85	650
31X	109.40	-	63Y	133.65	-	96X	114.90	-
31Y	109.45	568	64X	133.70	-	96Y	114.95	652
32X	109.50	514	64Y	133.75	-	97X	115.00	-
32Y	109.55	570	65X	133.80	-	97Y	115.05	654
33X	109.60	-	65Y	133.85	-	98X	115.10	-
33Y	109.65	572	66X	133.90	-	98Y	115.15	656
34X	109.70	516	66Y	133.95	-	99X	115.20	-
34Y	109.75	574	67X	134.00	-	99Y	115.25	658
35X	109.80	-	67Y	134.05	-	100X	115.30	-
35Y	109.85	576	68X	134.10	-	100Y	115.35	660
36X	109.90	518	68Y	134.15	-	101X	115.40	-
36Y	109.95	578	69X	134.20	-	101Y	115.45	662
37X	110.00	-	69Y	134.25	-	102X	115.50	-
37Y	110.05	580	70X	112.30	-	102Y	115.55	664
38X	110.10	520	70Y	112.35	-	103X	115.60	-
38Y	110.15	582	71X	112.40	-	103Y	115.65	666
39X	110.20	-	71Y	112.45	-	104X	115.70	-
39Y	110.25	584	72X	112.50	-	104Y	115.75	668
40X	110.30	522	72Y	112.55	-	105X	115.80	-
40Y	110.35	586	73X	112.60	-	105Y	115.85	670
41X	110.40	-	73Y	112.65	-	106X	115.90	-
41Y	110.45	588	74X	112.70	-	106Y	115.95	672
42X	110.50	524	74Y	112.75	-	107X	116.00	-
42Y	110.55	590	75X	112.80	-	107Y	116.05	674
43X	110.60	-	75Y	112.85	-	108X	116.10	-
43Y	110.65	592	76X	112.90	-	108Y	116.15	676
44X	110.70	526	76Y	112.95	-	109X	116.20	-
44Y	110.75	594	77X	113.00	-	109Y	116.25	678
45X	110.80	-	77Y	113.05	-	110X	116.30	-
45Y	110.85	596	78X	113.10	-	110Y	116.35	680
46X	110.90	528	78Y	113.15	-	111X	116.40	-
46Y	110.95	598	79X	113.20	-	111Y	116.45	682
47X	111.00	-	79Y	113.25	-	112X	116.50	-
47Y	111.05	600	80X	113.30	-	112Y	116.55	684
48X	111.10	530	80Y	113.35	620	113X	116.60	-
48Y	111.15	602	81X	113.40	-	113Y	116.65	686
49X	111.20	-	81Y	113.45	622	114X	116.70	-
49Y	111.25	604	82X	113.50	-	114Y	116.75	688
50X	111.30	532	82Y	113.55	624	115X	116.80	-
50Y	111.35	606	83X	113.60	-	115Y	116.85	690
51X	111.40	-	83Y	113.65	626	116X	116.90	-
51Y	111.45	608	84X	113.70	-	116Y	116.95	692
52X	111.50	534	84Y	113.75	628	117X	117.00	-
52Y	111.55	610	85X	113.80	-	117Y	117.05	694
53X	111.60	-	85Y	113.85	630	118X	117.10	-
53Y	111.65	612	86X	113.90	-	118Y	117.15	696
54X	111.70	536	86Y	113.95	632	119X	117.20	-
54Y	111.75	614	87X	114.00	-	119Y	117.25	698
55X	111.80	-	87Y	114.05	634	120X	117.30	-
55Y	111.85	616	88X	114.10	-	120Y	117.35	-
56X	111.90	538	88Y	114.15	636	121X	117.40	-
56Y	111.95	618	89X	114.20	-	121Y	117.45	-
57X	112.00	-	89Y	114.25	638	122X	117.50	-
57Y	112.05	-	90X	114.30	-	122Y	117.55	-
58X	112.10	-	90Y	114.35	640	123X	117.60	-
58Y	112.15	-	91X	114.40	-	123Y	117.65	-
59X	112.20	-	91Y	114.45	642	124X	117.70	-
59Y	112.25	-	92X	114.50	-	124Y	117.75	-
60X	133.30	-	92Y	114.55	644	125X	117.80	-
60Y	133.35	-	93X	114.60	-	125Y	117.85	-
61X	133.40	-	93Y	114.65	646	126X	117.90	-
61Y	133.45	-	94X	114.70	-	126Y	117.95	-
62X	133.50	-	94Y	114.75	648			
62Y	133.55	-	95X	114.80	-			

(35) **COMM/NAV/WEATHER REMARKS:**
These remarks consist of pertinent information affecting the current status of communications, NAVAIDs and weather.

Use these A/FD excerpts and the back of the sectional chart legend along with the foldout Seattle sectional excerpt with the many interactive exercises throughout the text. You'll find all the airport and navigation details referenced in the book within this appendix. Follow along as Bob Gardner takes you on a cross-country flight from Olympia to Ellensburg, Paine Field and back to Olympia in Lesson 11.

ELLENSBURG   N47°01.46′ W120°27.50′   NOTAM FILE ELN.   **SEATTLE**
  (H) VORTACW 117.9   ELN   Chan 126   259° 3.0 NM to Bowers Fld. 1770/21E.   **HIWAS.**   **H–1C, L–13A**
  VORTAC unusable:
    090°–158° byd 10 NM   163°–268° byd 33 NM
    158°–163° byd 27 NM
  VOR portion unusable:
    300°–040° byd 25 NM   040°–080° byd 34 NM
  DME unusable:
    055°–070° byd 21 NM   163°–268° byd 33 NM
    070°–090° byd 34 NM   300°–055° byd 21 NM
    090°–158° byd 10 NM   350°–025° byd 15 NM
    158°–163° byd 27 NM
  RCO 122.2 (SEATTLE RADIO)

ELLENSBURG
  BOWERS FLD   (ELN)   2 N   UTC–8(–7DT)   N47°01.98′ W120°31.84′   **SEATTLE**
    1764   B   S4   **FUEL** 100LL, JET A   TPA—2598(834)   NOTAM FILE ELN   **H–1C, L–13A**
    RWY 07–25: H5590X150 (ASPH)   S–28   0.8% up E   **IAP**
      RWY 07: Tree.   RWY 25: P–line.
    RWY 11–29: H4301X150 (CONC)   S–35, D–57, 2D–100
      MIRL   0.4% up NW
      RWY 29: REIL. PAPI(P2R)—GA 3.0° TCH 40′.
    AIRPORT REMARKS: Attended Mon–Fri 1500–0300Z‡, Sat–Sun
      1500–0200Z‡. Rwy 07–25 CLOSED Dec 15–Feb 28, no
      maintenance avail. Rwy 07–25 has weeds growing through cracks
      in pavement first 2000′. ACTIVATE MIRL Rwy 11–29—123.0.
    WEATHER DATA SOURCES: ASOS 118.375 (509) 925–2040. HIWAS 117.9
      ELN.
    COMMUNICATIONS: CTAF/UNICOM: 123.0
      ELLENSBURG RCO 122.2 (SEATTLE RADIO)
      SEATTLE CENTER APP/DEP CON 132.6
    RADIO AIDS TO NAVIGATION: NOTAM FILE ELN.
      ELLENSBURG (H) VORTACW 117.9   ELN   Chan 126   N47°01.46′
      W120°27.50′   259° 3.0 NM to fld. 1770/21E. HIWAS.

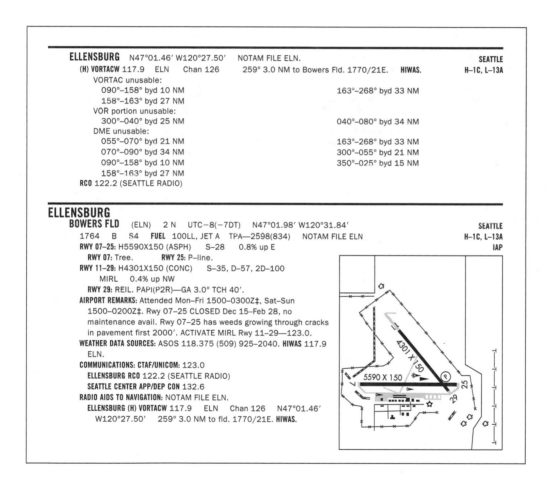

EVERETT

SNOHOMISH CO (PAINE FLD) (PAE) 6 SW UTC–8(–7DT) N47°54.42′ W122°16.89′

606 B S4 **FUEL** 100LL, JET A OX 1, 3 TPA–See Remarks LRA

ARFF Index—See Remarks NOTAM FILE PAE

Rwy 16L-34R: 3000 X 75

RWY 16R–34L: H9010X150 (ASPH–CONC–GRVD) S–100, D–200, 2S–175, 2D–350, 2D/2D2–830 HIRL CL
  RWY 16R: MALSR. PAPI(P4R)—GA 2.8°. Rgt tfc.
  RWY 34L: MALSF. PAPI(P4L) GA 3.0° TCH 75′. Trees.
RWY 11–29: H4514X75 (ASPH) S–30 MIRL 0.9% up SE
  RWY 11: VASI(V2L)—GA 3.25° TCH 60′. Thld dsplcd 799′. Trees.
  RWY 29: VASI(V2R)—GA 4.0° TCH 57′. Trees.
RWY 16L–34R: H3000X75 (ASPH) S–12.5 MIRL
  RWY 16L: REIL. PAPI(P2L)—GA 3.0°. Pole.
  RWY 34R: REIL. PAPI(P2R)—GA 3.0°. Pole. Rgt tfc.
AIRPORT REMARKS: Attended 1500–0500Z‡. For jet and helicopter fuel after hrs call 425–355–6600. Helicopters prohibited at fueling islands. Flocks of large and small birds in vicinity of arpt. Class I, ARFF Index B. Arpt CLOSED to air carrier ops with more than 30 passenger seats 0500–1500Z‡ except PPR ctc arpt ops 425–388–5110/5480. For additional ARFF capability ctc arpt ops 425–388–5110. Rwy 11–29 and Rwy 16L–34R CLOSED between 0500–1500Z‡. First 1000′ of Rwy 16R is concrete. Large acft fly W pattern over water, small acft fly E pattern over arpt. Be alert for converging tfc on base to final legs Rwys 16R–34L 0500–1500Z‡. Training flights discouraged after 0600Z‡. Rwy 16R–34L touch-and-go ldgs prohibited Mon–Fri 1500–1700Z‡. Rwy 16L–34R and Rwy 11–29 limited to helicopters 8,000 lbs or less. Twy A–2 restricted to 30,000 lbs. Avoid overflight of Boeing ramp NE corner of arpt due to JET blast. Rwy 34L departures discouraged in calm wind conditions. Avoid intersection departures from Rwy 16L–34R and Rwy 29. Avoid intersection departures from Rwy 11 except from Twy Delta 1 intersection. Twy E lgts OTS indef. Areas not visible from twr include E edge of S 1200′ of Twy A, Twy E from SE corner of west hangars to Twy A, mid section of outer terminal ramp, Twy H from NW edge of west hangars to Twy E, NE edge of inner terminal ramp. Twy C clsd between Twy D1 and Twy A. Noise sensitive arpt, for noise abatement procedures and tfc procedures call arpt ops 425–388–5125. It is requested that pilots adhere to the following noise abatement procedures unless otherwise instructed by twr, itinerant arrival and low apch of small acft over 250 horsepower authorized on Rwy 29, Rwy 16L and Rwy 34R. Itinerant departure of small acft over 250 horsepower on Rwy 11 and Rwy 34R. If access to Boeing ramp required ctc Boeing Flight Dispatch 206–655–3421 for approval during normal duty hours. TPA–1606 (1000) for light acft, 2006 (1400) for heavy acft. When twr clsd ACTIVATE HIRL Rwy 16R–34L, MALSR Rwy 16R and PAPI Rwy 34L—CTAF. Landing fee for acft over 30,000 lbs GWT.
WEATHER DATA SOURCES: ASOS (425) 355–6192. LAWRS.
COMMUNICATIONS: CTAF 132.95 **ATIS** 128.65 (425)355–9797. **UNICOM:** 122.95
  PAINE RCO 122.55 (SEATTLE RADIO)
Ⓡ **SEATTLE CENTER APP/DEP CON** 128.5
  PAINE TOWER 132.95 (acft arrival W of centerline or departure Rwy 16R–34L) 120.2 (acft arrival E of centerline or departure Rwy 16L–34R) (1500–0500Z‡) **GND CON** 121.8 **CLNC DEL** 126.75
AIRSPACE: CLASS D svc 1500–0500Z‡ other times CLASS E.
RADIO AIDS TO NAVIGATION: NOTAM FILE PAE.
  PAINE (L) VORW/DME 110.6 PAE Chan 43 N47°55.19′ W122°16.67′ at fld. 670/20E.
  RITTS NDB (LOM) 396 PA N48°03.17′ W122°17.33′ 158° 8.8 NM to fld.
  ILS 109.3 I–PAE Rwy 16R Class IE. LOM RITTS NDB. LOC unusable byd 15° left of course. LOC/GS unmonitored (0500–1500Z‡)
COMM/NAV/WEATHER REMARKS: Emerg frequency 121.5 not avbl at twr.

OLYMPIA

HOSKINS FLD (44T) 5 SE UTC−8(−7DT) N46°59.54′ W122°49.67′ SEATTLE

213 NOTAM FILE SEA

RWY 07–25: 2015X116 (TURF) 0.5% up E.

    RWY 07: Trees.   RWY 25: Trees.

AIRPORT REMARKS: Unattended. No helicopters. No ultralights. Noise abatement procedures in effect; call arpt manager 360–491–6723. Geese and ducks on and invof arpt. Mole hills west end. Recommend land Rwy 07, depart 25 when wind condition permits. Rwy 07–25 no line of sight between rwy ends.

COMMUNICATIONS: CTAF 122.9

- -

OLYMPIA RGNL (OLM) 4 S UTC−8(−7DT) N46°58.16′ W122°54.15′ SEATTLE

209 B S4 FUEL 100, 100LL, JET A OX 1, 3, 4 LRA NOTAM FILE OLM H–1B, L–1D

RWY 17–35: H5501X150 (ASPH–GRVD) S–75, D–94, 2S–87, 2D–142 HIRL IAP, AD

    RWY 17: MALSR. PAPI(P4L)—GA 3.0° TCH 54′.

    RWY 35: REIL. PAPI(P4L)—GA 3.0° TCH 54′. Rgt tfc.

RWY 08–26: H4157X150 (ASPH) S–30

    RWY 08: Rgt tfc.   RWY 26: Tree.

AIRPORT REMARKS: Attended 1600–0200Z‡. Twy lgts on Twy W, Twy A, Twy G, Twy L and Twy B. When twr clsd ACTIVATE HIRL Rwy 17–35, MALSR Rwy 17, PAPI Rwy 17 and Rwy 35, REIL Rwy 35, twy lgts and directional signage—CTAF. Landing fee.

WEATHER DATA SOURCES: ASOS 135.725 (360) 943–1278. HIWAS 113.4 OLM.

COMMUNICATIONS: CTAF 124.4   ATIS 135.725   UNICOM 122.95

Ⓡ SEATTLE APP/DEP CON 121.1

    TOWER 124.4 (1600–0400Z‡)   GND CON 121.6

AIRSPACE: CLASS D svc 1600–0400Z‡ other times CLASS E.

RADIO AIDS TO NAVIGATION: NOTAM FILE OLM.

    (H) VORTACW 113.4   OLM   Chan 81   N46°58.30′

    W122°54.11′   at fld. 200/19E. HIWAS.

    DME unusable:

        223°–258° byd 20 NM blo 4,100′

        258°–283° byd 30 NM blo 4,100′

        358°–043° byd 10 NM blo 6,000′

        358°–043° byd 20 NM blo 7,000′

  ILS 111.9   I–OLM   Rwy 17.   Unmonitored during hours twr closed. LOC unusable byd 25° right of course.

COMM/NAV/WEATHER REMARKS: Emerg frequency 121.5 not avbl at twr.

Ⓡ **SEATTLE CENTER** H–1–3, L–1–2–11–13

(KZSE)

  Antelope Mountain – 124.85

  Arcata – **124.85**

  Badger Mountain – **127.05** 127.05 **134.95** 134.95

  Beacon Hill – **127.05** 127.05 **120.3** 120.3

  Cottonwood – 123.95 **118.55**

  Dallesport – **126.6** 126.6

  Fort Lawton – **127.05** 127.05

  Hoquiam – **128.3**

  Horton – **132.075** 125.8 121.4

  Kimberly – **135.45**

  Klamath Falls – **134.9** 127.6

  Lakeside – 123.95

  Lakeview – **135.35** 127.6

  Larch Mountain – **128.3** 128.3 **126.6** 126.6

  Marlin – 126.1

  Medford – **135.15** 124.85 121.4

  Mohler – **128.45**

  Mullan Pass – **128.45**

  Nassel – 124.2

  Neah Bay – **125.1** 125.1

  Redmond – **121.35 134.9 135.35** 128.15

  Rex-Parrett – **121.35**

  Scappoose – 124.2 128.15

  Spokane – 123.95 119.225

  Stampede Pass – **134.95** 134.95

  The Dalles – **135.45** 119.65

  Wallula – 132.6

  Wenatchee – 126.1

  Whidbey Island – **134.95** 134.95 128.5 **125.1** 125.1

  Yakima – **135.525** 135.525 132.6 **120.3** 120.3 **118.55**

CONTROL TOWER FREQUENCIES ON SEATTLE SECTIONAL CHART

Airports with control towers are indicated on the face of the chart by the letters CT followed by the primary VHF local control frequency (ies). Information for each tower is listed in the table below. Operational hours are local time. The primary VHF and UHF local control frequencies are listed. An asterisk (*) indicates the part-time tower frequency is remoted to a collocated full-time FSS for use as Airport Advisory Service (AAS) during hours the tower is closed. The primary VHF and UHF ground control frequencies are listed.

Automatic Terminal Information Service (ATIS) frequencies shown on the face of the chart are primary arrival VHF/UHF frequencies. All ATIS frequencies are listed in the table below. ATIS operational hours may differ from tower operational hours.

ASR and/or PAR indicate Radar Instrument Approach available.

"MON-FRI" indicates Monday through Friday.

CONTROL TOWER	OPERATES	TWR FREQ	GND CON	ATIS	ASR/PAR
ABBOTSFORD	0700-2300	119.4 (INNER) 121.0 (OUTER) 295.0	121.8	119.8	
BELLINGHAM INTL	0700-2230	124.9 379.3	127.4 379.3	134.45	
BOEING/KING CO INTL	CONTINUOUS	118.3 (309°-127° & DEP RWY 13L/31R) 120.6 (128°-308° & DEP RWY 13R/31L) 257.8	121.9	127.75	
EASTERN OREGON RGNL	0600-2000	119.7 257.8	121.9 257.8		
FAIRCHILD AFB	CONTINUOUS	120.35 233.7	123.6 275.8	257.625	
FELTS	0600-2000	132.5 239.025	121.7	120.55	
GRANT CO INTL	0600-2200	118.25 (E) 128.0 (W) 257.8	121.9	119.05	
GRAY AAF (JB LEWIS-MCCHORD)	CONTINUOUS EXC HOL	119.325 256.8	121.9 290.2	124.65 306.2	PAR
LEWISTON-NEZ PERCE CO	0600-2200	119.4 318.8	121.9		
MCCHORD (JB LEWIS-MCCHORD)	CONTINUOUS	124.8 259.3	118.175 279.65	109.6 270.1	
MCNARY	0700-2100	119.1 257.2	121.9	124.55	
OLYMPIA RGNL	0800-2000	124.4 254.25	121.6	135.725	
PORTLAND-HILLSBORO	0600-2200	119.3 239.3	121.7	127.65	
PORTLAND INTL	CONTINUOUS	118.7 257.8 (RWY 10L/28R) 123.775 251.125 (RWYS 3/21 & 10R/28L)	121.9 348.6	128.35 269.9	
PORTLAND-TROUTDALE	0700-2200	120.9 254.3	121.8	135.625	
RENTON	0700-2000 OCT-APR 0700-2100 MAY-SEP	124.7 256.9	121.6 256.9	126.95	
SEATTLE-TACOMA INTL	CONTINUOUS	119.9 239.3 (RWYS 16L/34R, 16C/34C) 120.95 239.3 (RWY 16R/34L)	121.7	118.0	
SNOHOMISH CO (PAINE)	0700-2100	120.2 (ARR E OF CNTRLN OR DEP RWY 16L/34R) 132.95 (ARR W OF CNTRLN OR DEP RWY 16R/34L) 256.7	121.8 339.8	128.65	
SPOKANE INTL	CONTINUOUS	118.3 278.3	121.9 348.6	124.325 254.375	
TACOMA NARROWS	0800-2000	118.5 253.5	121.8	124.05	
TRI-CITIES	0600-2200	135.3 323.3	121.8	125.65	
VICTORIA INTL	0600-2400	119.1 (OUTER) 119.7 (INNER) 239.6	121.9 361.4	118.8	
WALLA WALLA RGNL	0630-1900	118.5 289.4	121.6 289.4		
WHIDBEY ISLAND NAS/AULT	CONTINUOUS	127.9 340.2	121.75 336.4	134.15 281.5	ASR/PAR
YAKIMA/MCALLISTER	0600-2200	133.25 257.8	121.9	125.25	

CLASS B, CLASS C, TRSA AND SELECTED APPROACH CONTROL FREQUENCIES

FACILITY	FREQUENCIES	SERVICE AVAILABILITY
SEATTLE CLASS B	119.2 284.7 (341°-075°) 120.1 290.9 (199°-300°) 126.5 377.15 (161°-198°) 119.2 284.7 (RWYS 16 076°-160°) 125.9 290.9 (RWYS 16 301°-340°) 120.4 269.125 (RWYS 34 301°-340°) 125.9 290.9 (RWYS 34 076°-160°)	CONTINUOUS
FAIRCHILD AFB/ SPOKANE CLASS C	123.75 282.25 (205°-025°) 133.35 263.0 (026°-204°)	CONTINUOUS
PORTLAND CLASS C	118.1 284.6 (100°-279°) 124.35 299.2 (280°-099°)	CONTINUOUS
WHIDBEY ISLAND CLASS C	118.2 285.65 (W) 120.7 270.8 (E)	CONTINUOUS

PFD/MFD

Garmin G1000

*Both images above are referenced
on Pages 3-1 and 3-2.*

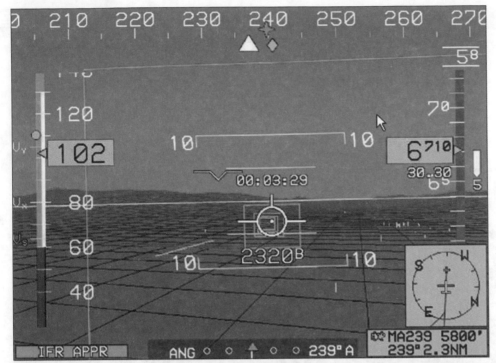

Chelton "Highway in the Sky"

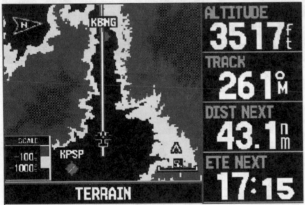

The terrain display is available on handheld devices as well as panel installations.

Garmin handheld

Another popular flight display, by Avidyne

Images on this page are referenced on Pages 3-12, 10-7, and 10-17.

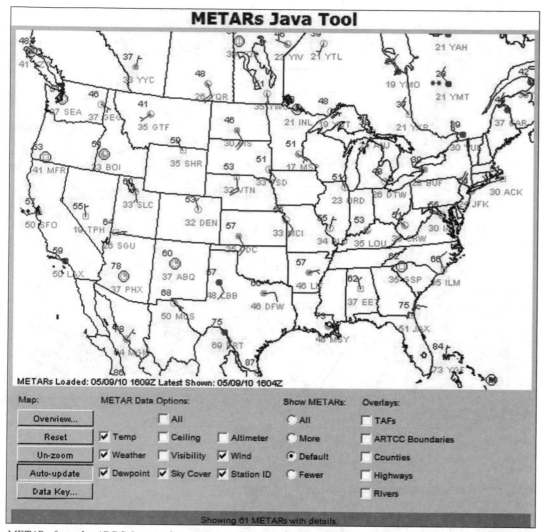

METARs from the ADDS Java tools page

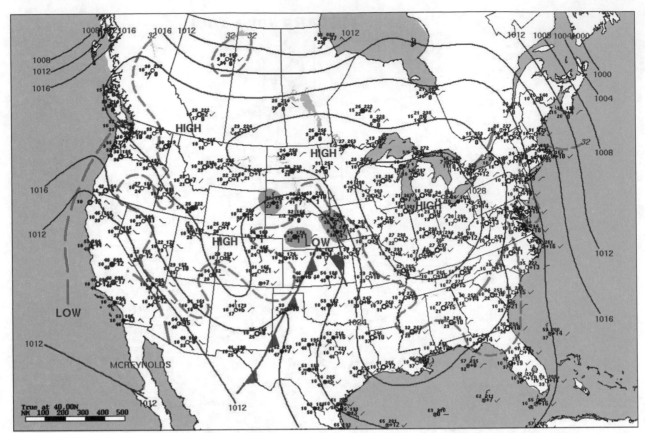

Surface analysis from ADDS page

(Pages 6-2, 7-11)

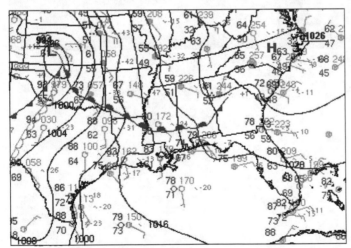

Excerpt of surface analysis, showing station models

(Page 6-2)

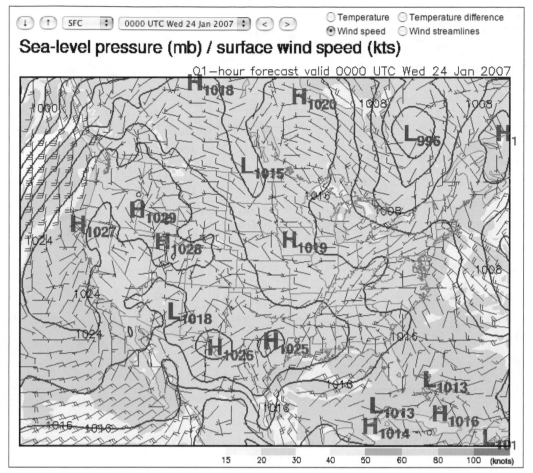

Winds aloft from ADDS page. Note the choices available at top of the screen. (Page 7-15)

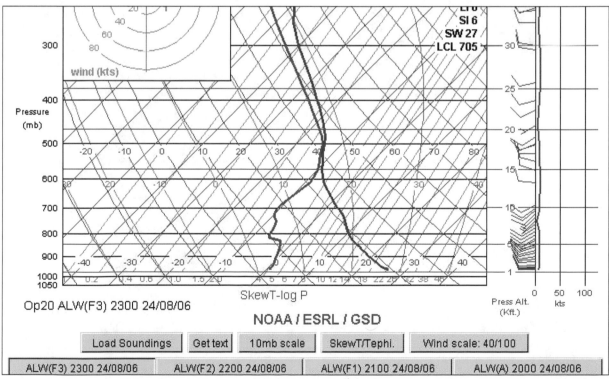

Skew-T (Page 7-16)

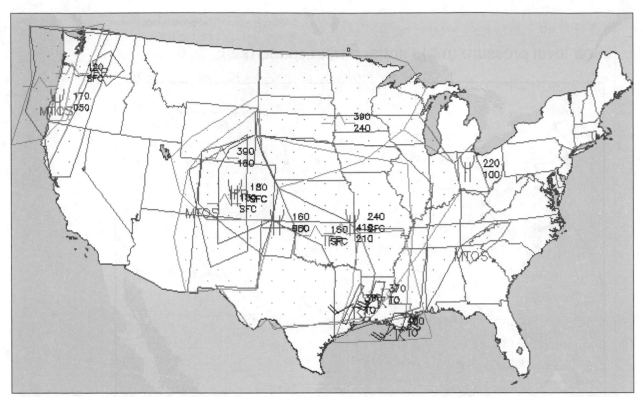

SIGMETs and AIRMETs

(Page 7-12)

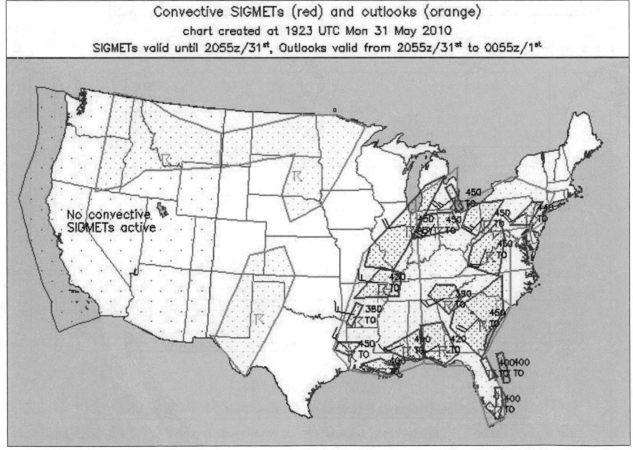

Convective SIGMET

(Page 7-12)

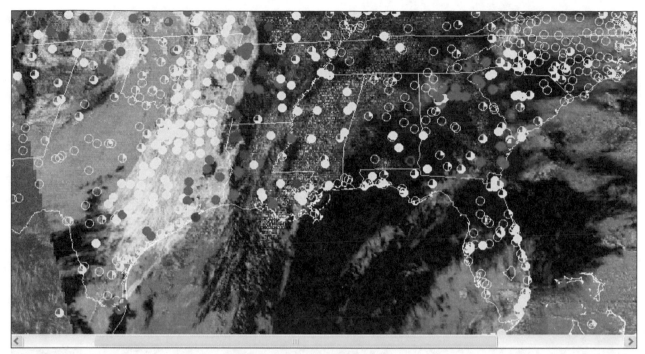

ADDS satellite image—"Eastern U.S. with flight conditions."   *(Page 7-7, 7-18)*

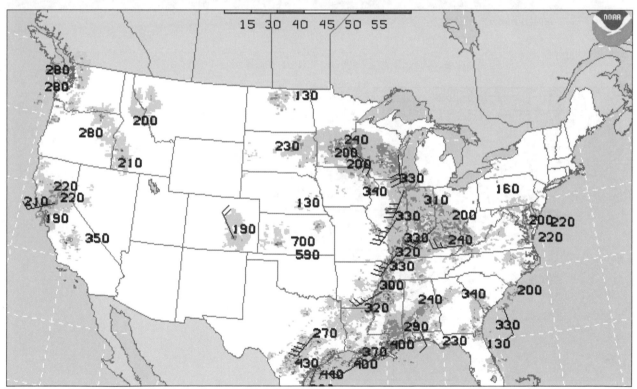

Radar summary   *(Page 7-11)*

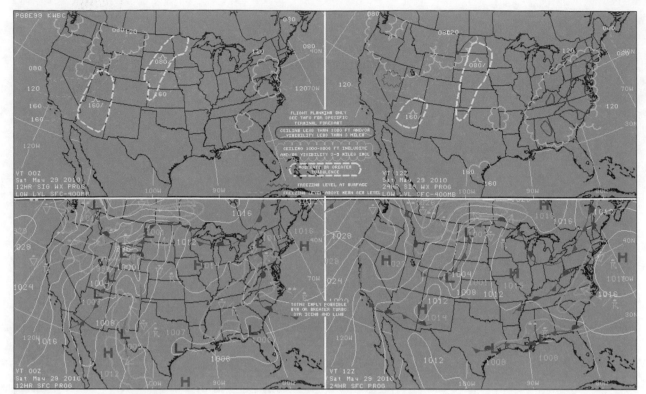

Four-panel low-level prognostic charts (Page 7-20)

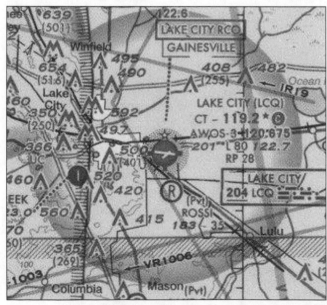

Lake City, FL Class G with tower,
excerpt from Jacksonville sectional chart (Page 5-14, 9-22)

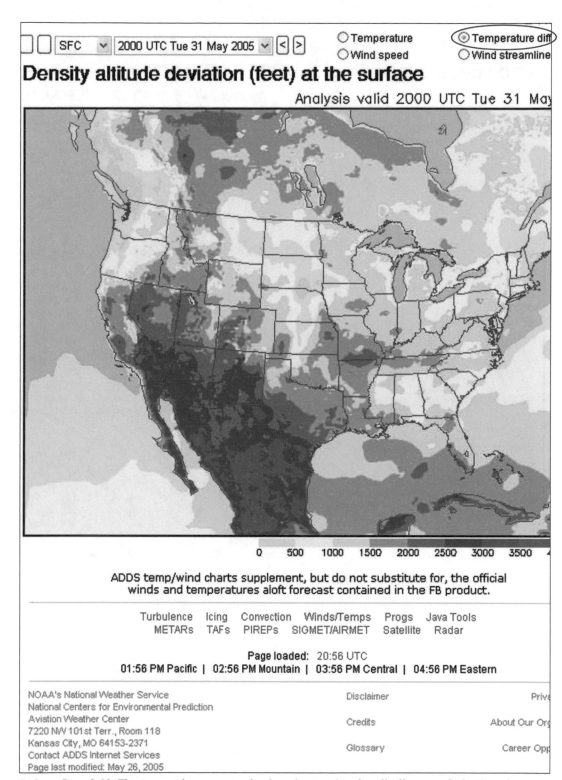

Refer to Page 8-10. This is a quick way to visualize how density altitude will affect your flight. Note the choices at the top of the screen (circled).

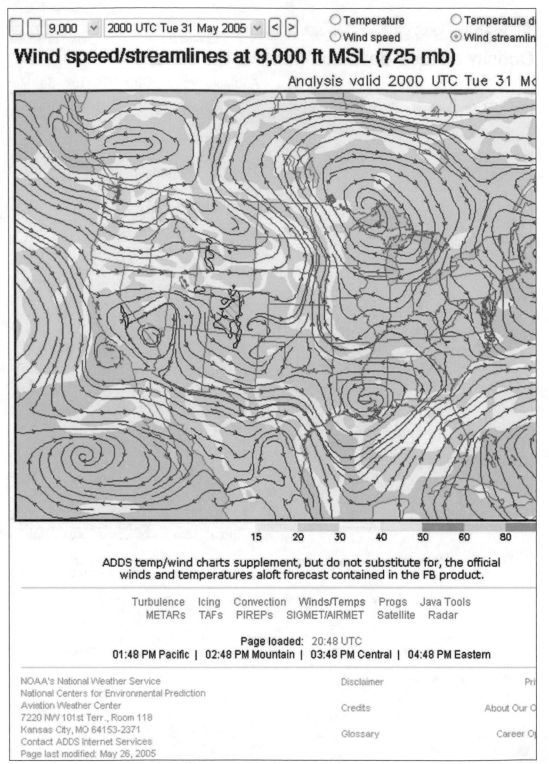

The "big picture" on winds aloft. Note choices at top.

(Page 7-15)

Airport Signs
from Aeronautical Information Manual (AIM)

Figure A. *Runway Holding Position Sign*

Figure B. *Holding Position Sign at beginning of takeoff runway*

Figure C. *Holding Position Sign for a Taxiway that intersects the intersection of two runways*

Figure D. *Holding Position Sign for ILS Critical Area*

Figure E. *Holding Position Sign for a runway approach area*

Figure F. *Sign Prohibiting Aircraft Entry into an area*

Figure G. *Runway Location Sign*

Figure H. *Direction Sign for runway exit*

Figure I. *Destination Sign for common taxiing route to two runways*

Figure J. *Destination Sign for different taxiing routes to two runways*

Figure K. *Runway Distance Remaining Sign indicating 3,000 feet of runway remaining*

Index

Italic page numbers refer to figures.

Notes

Notes

Notes